MARY CAMPBELL'S dBASE IV HANDBOOK

MARY CAMPBELL'S dBASE IV HANDBOOK

Mary Campbell

BANTAM BOOKS
TORONTO • NEW YORK • LONDON • SYDNEY • AUCKLAND

MARY CAMPBELL'S dBASE™ IV HANDBOOK
A Bantam Book / July 1989

ISBN 0-553-34776-4

Published simultaneously in the United States and Canada

Bantam Books are published by Bantam Books, Inc. Its trademark, consisting of the words "Bantam Books" and the portrayal of a rooster, is Registered in U.S. Patent and Trademark Office and in other countries. Marca Registrada, Bantam Books, Inc., 666 Fifth Avenue, New York, New York 10103.

PRINTED IN THE UNITED STATES OF AMERICA

0 9 8 7 6 5 4 3 2 1

Acknowledgments

I would like to thank the following people who contributed so much to the quality of the final product:

Gabrielle Lawrence for her work on all phases of the project.

Novell, Inc. for all of their assistance, with special thanks to Mike, Susan, and Sharon.

Kenzi Sugihara, Steve Guty, and Terry Nasta of Bantam Books for handling all the in-house tasks necessary for book production.

Malcolm Rubel and Bruce Wendel who took time from their busy schedules to handle the technical review.

May Chapman who did the copy editing.

Matt Chenelle for checking the Getting Started sections to ensure a perfect set of keystrokes.

Contents

CHAPTER 6

CHAPTER 7

PART III

CHAPTER 8

CHAPTER 9

PART IV

CHAPTER 10

CHAPTER 11

CHAPTER 15

Functions and Expressions 541

CHAPTER 16

Conditions, Branches, and Loops 597

CHAPTER 17

Writing Programs to Handle Input and Output 623

CHAPTER 18

Using Professional Programming Techniques 663

PART VI

PART VII

Introduction

dBASE IV is a greatly enhanced and expanded version of Ashton-Tate's popular dBASE III+ package. It builds on the feature set of prior releases and provides a user interface that is oriented toward the objects you want to create, such as databases, reports, or labels.

Although dBASE IV brings a new user interface and many new features, such as a template language, you will find that some tasks follow the same basic process that you used for earlier releases. Designing a new database is one example. Although a new field type for floating-point numeric entries has been added, the basic design screen is identical with the old one.

From the Control Center dBASE IV is much more intuitive than dBASE III+ in the ASSIST mode. Features like query building by entering examples provide an easy way to locate the data that you need. A sophisticated report-building tool makes it easy to create custom reports. Building views of multiple databases and indexing are also tasks that have become easier. dBASE IV's new macro language feature provides a quick and time-efficient way to handle repetitive programming tasks.

Conventions

A set of conventions were developed for this book to offer consistency throughout the chapters. Since dBASE offers so many options, a set of standards used throughout the book will help you learn more about dBASE IV as quickly as possible.

Capital letters are used throughout the book for field names, database names, dBASE commands, dBASE functions, and DOS commands. You can expect to see filenames that look like ORDERS, STUDENTS, and ACCT. The use of capital letters will help to differentiate these entries from the rest of the text.

You do not need to use the capitalization used in this book for your entries. Either upper or lower case can be used for all entries except data fields and text on design screens. Although these screens also accept any capitalization, esthetics may indicate a specific approach. Also, once you enter data with a specific capitalization, it will be important to maintain the capitalization style when you use options like the query-by-example feature that allows you to provide an example of what the records you are looking for contain.

dBASE IV menu options can be selected by activating menus with F10 and highlighting the menu choice you want to use. You can also make menu selections by pressing the ALT key and the first letter of the menu option desired. Although you can use either method, the second method is used throughout this book. The options in dBASE IV's pull-down menus can be selected by typing the first letter of the selection or by highlighting the first letter of each selection. Although menu selections are specified in full, the first letter of each menu selection is listed separately and highlighted as a reminder of the quick entry method.

Special keys like ESC, BACKSPACE, and ENTER are shown in small capital letters. When several of these keys are used in combination, they are joined with a hyphen as in ALT-L.

Examples in the book that require you to make entries to duplicate them will show your responses in boldface. An instruction for an entry might read "Type an **L**, then type **Wilson Lighting Company**."

Release Notes

Appendix A is especially designed for dBASE III+ users who are upgrading to dBASE IV. This appendix provides a quick overview of all the new features in dBASE IV.

Although dBASE IV includes all the basic features in dBASE III+, this book is designed specifically for the dBASE IV user. It covers the new features of the package with an emphasis on how to use all the features most effectively. Throughout the book you will find tip boxes that help you get the most from dBASE IV's features. A special Getting Started section at the end of most chapters will give you hands-on practice with the concepts presented in the chapter.

If you are still using dBASE III+, you can contact Ashton-Tate directly for information on upgrading to the new release. The cost of the upgrade is dependent on which release of the product you are currently using. Regardless of the release, an upgrade is significantly less expensive than purchasing a new copy of the product. Contact Ashton Tate at (213) 329-9989 for more information on the upgrade.

Organization of This Book

This book consists of twenty-two chapters and four appendixes. The chapters are organized into six different parts. Part I provides the commands you will need for designing databases and entering records; it is designed to take advantage of the easy-to-use menu structure provided by the Control Center. Part I consists of the first three chapters in this book.

This introduction provides a look at the organizational structure and the conventions followed throughout the book. This section can help you maximize your learning with the rest of the book by enabling you to focus your energies on chapters that offer you the greatest payback.

Chapter 1 provides information on installing dBASE IV on your system for the first time. It proceeds to starting a dBASE session and making menu selections. After completing this chapter you will be familiar with options like menu selections, the help system, and special keyboard keys used by dBASE IV.

Chapter 2 provides you the essentials for designing your database systems. After discussing design concepts, you will be introduced to the design work surface that dBASE IV provides for your definitions. You will learn when to use each of the field types. You will also learn how and when to make modifications to the structure of your databases.

Chapter 3 provides the tools for entering and maintaining database records. You will learn how to add records to an existing database and delete and change existing record entries. You will learn how to copy and move data. You will also learn how to use the search and replace options that dBASE IV offers.

Part II focuses on tools for accessing data in your database. The chapters in this section also focus on the use of the Control Center to accomplish these tasks.

Chapter 4 introduces you to techniques for organizing your database. dBASE IV's greatly expanded indexing capability allows you to index your files many different ways. The new .MDX files allow you to assign Tag names to as many as 47 indexes in one large index file rather than having to create a new file for each new index as you did with dBASE III+. You will also learn how to create a second database with the records physically arranged in a different sequence. The packing features covered in this chapter will enable you to free up the space occupied by deleted records in the database.

Chapter 5 covers the many facets of dBASE IV's new query features. You can use menu selections to build temporary views of the database that meet your exact requirements. Queries also allow you to update records based on a set of specifications. Linking records in two files is also a task that can be accomplished with the query design screen.

Chapter 6 shows you how to produce formal presentation quality reports. You can choose to use the label feature to place your data on label stock. You will learn how to customize both reports and labels in this chapter.

Chapter 7 teaches you to design custom screens. These screens allow you to enter or display your data in any format. You can enhance your custom screens with color options or validity checking to prevent inappropriate entries.

Part III covers the use of the dBASE IV utilities for accessing files. In addition, the creation and use of dBASE IV catalogs are covered.

Chapter 8 covers all the options on the dBASE IV Tools menu with the exception of macros. You will learn how to use the Tools options for changing the default setting for the current session. You will also learn about the import and export features. The DOS utilities covered in this chapter provide a shortcut approach to entering DOS file commands through menu selections.

Chapter 9 covers the features of dBASE IV catalogs. It also explains the distinction between catalogs and directories. You will learn how to use catalogs to organize your data better.

Part IV covers advanced dBASE IV features that are beyond the Control Center but not to the detail level of program coding. In this section you will learn about making entries at the dot prompt, creating macros, and using the template language that is part of the Developer's Edition of dBASE IV and the application generator.

Everything you can do from the Control Center can be accomplished from the dot prompt. Chapter 10 introduces the syntax rules for dot prompt. In addition memory variables are introduced as a means for storing variable information. This chapter also tells you how to obtain help and make corrections from the dot prompt.

Chapter 11 discusses the new dBASE IV macro features. You will learn the techniques for recording, naming, and executing macros. You can create your own macros with the tools in this chapter or try some of the ready-to-run macros that are included.

The Applications Generator covered in Chapter 12 allows a user to develop an application without programming. You can observe the easy-to-use procedure for developing a simple application.

Chapter 13 covers dBASE IV's template language. The template language is new to the dBASE IV Developer's Edition and allows you to create patterns for reports, forms, labels, or the applications generator. Templates allow you to make many different versions of a report or form from their object files.

Part V focuses on the tools needed for dBASE IV programming. You will be introduced to programming concepts as well as dBASE IV's programming building blocks. Functions, variables, and programming commands are all covered in this part of the book.

Chapter 14 is designed for the dBASE IV programming novice. It introduces techniques that can help insure success in programming. You will learn how to follow dBASE IV's syntax rules in this chapter as well as how to design, code, and test a program.

Chapter 15 focuses on dBASE IV's expanded list of functions. Functions are keywords that cause dBASE IV to perform a special operation for you. Functions can perform computations, check a system variable, or convert data. They are frequently used in expressions and are a necessity in dBASE IV programming. You will also be introduced to the concept of a user-defined function in this chapter.

Chapter 16 covers the basic dBASE IV commands for handling input and output. You will see examples of program routines for entering data and displaying data.

Chapter 17 covers the commands needed to add sophistication to your programming. Condition checking, iteration, and multiple option processing are all topics that are covered in this chapter.

Chapter 18 adds techniques that can help you create dBASE IV programs the way professionals do. You will learn to use modular programs, pass data from module to module, improve both the code readability and the documentation from the examples in this chapter.

Part VI provides the information you are looking for if you are running dBASE IV in a networked environment. It provides information on installing the networked version and designing network application. A chapter on SQL (structured query language) concepts is also included in this section.

Chapter 19 covers the information you will need to install and administer the operation of dBASE IV on a network. The security measures available through dBASE IV and the network software are both discussed. Novell Netware 286 is the focus of this chapter, with specific instructions for using dBASE IV with this network software. Much of the information is easily adaptable to other supported networks.

Although network applications use many of the same building blocks as single-user systems, there are a number of special considerations in the design and implementation of network programs. Chapter 20 focuses on these issues. You will see some of the options available to you from the examples in this chapter.

Chapter 21 contains a complete network application with all of the steps required for its development from start to finish. Although it is a simple system, it can serve as a working example to explore the various network features.

Chapter 22 provides an introduction to dBASE IV SQL concepts. It explains the SQL interface currently available in dBASE IV.

The five appendixes in this book provide important summaries for dBASE IV. Appendix A contains a concise history of the upgrade differences for a user migrating from dBASE III+ to dBASE IV. Appendix B contains a summary of all the special dBASE IV keys. Appendix C provides a command reference. Appendix D contains a summary of the dBASE IV functions, and Appendix E covers SQL commands.

How to Get the Most from This Book

Getting the most benefit from this book requires you to access your current level of knowledge with dBASE III+. If you are an experienced dBASE III+ user, you will want to start with Chapter 1 to obtain information on installing the package and a quick overview of the Control Center. You can then proceed to Appendix A to review the differences in the two products. After that you can determine which topics you want to review more closely and use the references in Appendix A to determine which topics you want to review in greater detail.

If you are a new or moderately experienced dBASE IV user you will want to proceed from start to finish through at least the first two parts of the book. This information will provide a perspective of all the features that dBASE IV offers through the Control Center menus. You can then determine your readiness for exploring some of the advanced topics like macros, the application generator, programming, and networks.

PART I

Designing and Creating Databases with dBASE IV

CHAPTER 1

Getting Started with dBASE IV

Now that you have a copy of dBASE IV, you are no doubt anxious to begin using the program. You will need to spend a little time installing your software before you can get to work. You will also want to familiarize yourself with some of the basic terminology and the new user interface that is a part of dBASE IV.

If you are a new dBASE IV user, take your time and go over the material in this chapter carefully. The basic skills that you will learn for using the menu system are used for everything you do with dBASE IV. If you are already using dBASE IV, you will want to skim through this chapter quickly and focus your attention on Chapter 2.

System Requirements

To run dBASE IV you need an IBM XT, an IBM AT, an IBM Personal System/2 models 30, 50, 60, 70, and 80, a Compaq Deskpro 286, or a Compaq Deskpro 386. You can also use a computer that is 100 percent compatible with one of these systems.

Like other new software offerings, dBASE IV requires more computer power than its predecessor, dBASE III+. The current version of dBASE IV requires a hard disk with 3.8M of free space for the program files. dBASE IV requires a minimum of 512K RAM just to run the program. Although dBASE IV 1.1 can run in a system with only conventional memory, it is designed to utilize both extended and expanded memory. Each time you load dBASE IV it searches for a LIM 4.0 expanded memory driver. It utilizes expanded memory if it finds this driver. In lieu of the expanded memory driver, dBASE IV looks for an XMS version 2 driver for extended memory. If neither extended nor expanded memory options are available, dBASE IV uses the VDISK standard for the management of overlay caching, large text files, and screen saves. Although dBASE IV appears to be compatible with some memory-resident TSRs (such as INSET, Side Kick, and Lotus Metro) certain dBASE IV features that require a large amount of memory, such as reporting, do not have sufficient memory to operate when these TSR programs are in memory.

dBASE IV supports most of the popular printer models. dBASE IV also supports both monochrome or color display monitors, allowing you to use the computer with most system configurations as long as you have a hard disk and sufficient memory. Support is available for both 25- and 43-line display.

dBASE IV requires PC-DOS version 2.0 or greater. If you are using Compaq DOS you must have version 3.31 or greater.

Installing dBASE IV

This section covers the steps necessary to install dBASE IV on a single-user system. If you are using dBASE IV on a network, you will want to consult Chapter 19 for installation instructions. Although the entire installation process is automated, the various steps are described here briefly so you will know what to expect before beginning. dBASE IV needs a minimum of 3.8M of hard disk space for installation. If your hard disk does not have enough space, you must remove some of the hard disk's contents before you can install dBASE IV. To begin installation, you need to insert the installation disk in drive A, type **INSTALL**, and press ENTER. Other than requiring you to answer a few questions, dBASE IV does all the work.

Registering Your Software

Since Ashton-Tate has removed copy protection from the package, they have introduced a copy discouragement technique that requires you to register your copy of the software before installing it on your hard disk. You will be asked to provide information like your name and the name of your company. This information will become a permanent part of the copy that you install and will be displayed every time you load dBASE.

dBASE IV allows you to verify the registration entries before finalizing them. Once you confirm these entries they will become a permanent part of your introductory screen with no provision for making changes.

Setting Up Your Hardware

dBASE IV needs to know what type of hardware you are using to tailor the copy you place on your hard disk to your exact system configuration. Your first task is to tell dBASE IV that you are not installing a multiuser system.

The next step requires you to describe your monitor to dBASE IV. You must select from a variety of options that describe whether your monitor supports color and the type of graphics adaptor that you are using. You can also eliminate the white snow flecks that appear on a some monitors, if you have this problem.

Your printer is the only other hardware that you need to describe to dBASE IV. You first select the manufacturer of your printer and then select the particular model. You must also specify the DOS device address that will be used for directing the printer output, normally LPT1. You can select up to four printers to use with dBASE IV.

dBASE IV permits you to verify hardware selections before updating your disk. Once you are satisfied that you have selected the proper equipment, the next step is copying the necessary file from the original disks to your hard drive. If you decide that you want to change these settings later, you can change them once dBASE IV is installed using the DBSETUP program that accompanies dBASE IV.

❑ **Tip: Select Multiple Printers during installation.**

If you have more than one printer attached to your computer you will want to select more than one printer option during installation. You can elect to use any of the selected printers without having to redo installation.

Installing dBASE IV Files on Your Hard Disk

dBASE IV guides the copying of the disks to your hard drive. It suggests dBASE as the default directory and drive C as the default drive but accepts changes to the default drive and/or the directory. If you plan to use both a single-user and a multiuser version of dBASE IV, you must use separate directories for the single-user version and the multiuser version.

dBASE IV checks your hard disk to insure that there is sufficient space for the files that install copies to the hard disk. If adequate space is unavailable, installation ends at this point. If your hard disk has adequate space, the install program checks for an existing copy of dBASE IV and allows you to overwrite it if one exists. When the copy process begins, dBASE IV will ask you to insert the disks in order by the numbers printed on the disks.

Updating AUTOEXEC.BAT and CONFIG.SYS

Once the installation program has copied the necessary dBASE IV files to your hard disk, the install program has the option to modify the AUTOEXEC.BAT and CONFIG.SYS files. Your computer executes the AUTOEXEC.BAT file when you turn the computer on. dBASE IV changes the AUTOEXEC.BAT file so you can use dBASE IV from any directory.

The second file sets DOS parameters to configure the computer for your needs. With dBASE IV, you will need to expand the number of files that can be open at one time beyond the default of three, and you will also want to increase the number of buffers available, to improve performance. The installation program changes the setting for the number of files open to 40 and the buffers setting to 15.

If your computer has more than one operating system, such as DOS and O/S 2, you must modify the AUTOEXEC.BAT and CONFIG.SYS files that the DOS version uses. Usually, this means instructing the installation program not to modify the two files and modifying them at a later point using DBSETUP or a file editor.

dBASE IV also gives you the opportunity to copy nonessential files. These include sample files and tutorial files. If hard-disk space is limited, you may want to skip this option.

Using Uninstall

dBASE IV provides a Uninstall routine that allows you to quickly remove all the dBASE IV program files from your hard disk. Any data files that you created with dBASE are unaffected by this procedure, making it a better option than DEL *.* or deleting files individually. Uninstall automatically removes empty subdirectories as well.

You can run the Uninstall procedure by typing DBSETUP at the DOS prompt. Uninstall dBASE IV is an option from the menu that is presented. You can also use the DBSETUP program to make changes to the initial install parameters if you add another printer or change the type of monitor that you are using.

Creating a Backup Copy

Although dBASE IV requires you to register your software by entering your name before installing it, you are no longer prevented from making a backup copy. You will want to copy each disk in the package with the DOS DISKCOPY command. Once the copy is complete, you will want to store the original disks in a safe off-site location for complete protection against the loss of the program. As you begin to create database files you can begin to store the data file backups in the same location.

Beginning and Ending dBASE IV

Once you have installed dBASE IV you can start the program by turning on your computer and typing **DBASE**. A batch file, DBASE.BAT, is placed in the root directory of your hard disk during

❑

Tip: A quick start alternative.

You can bypass the license agreement screen that normally displays when you start dBASE IV. If you type **DBASE /T** at the DOS prompt, dBASE IV starts much quicker. You bypass the need for pressing ENTER that is required when you enter only DBASE.

installation. This file contains the required DOS instructions to activate the proper subdirectory and start dBASE.

For version 1.0, dBASE IV supports a quick test entry feature. You can start dBASE IV by typing **DBASE /T** and pressing ENTER. You will not need to acknowledge the license agreement screen if you use this approach.

If you type DBASE or DBASE /T and you see the message "Bad command or file name", change to the subdirectory containing the dBASE IV program files. If you used the installation defaults or the instructions in this chapter, the program will be in the subdirectory C:\DBASE. To activate this subdirectory, type **CD \DBASE**. Next, you can type **DBASE** or **DBASE /T** to start dBASE IV. If dBASE starts, change the PATH statement in your AUTOEXEC.BAT file to include the dBASE subdirectory. If dBASE does not start, check that you have installed dBASE correctly.

When you are working with the menu system there are two ways to end dBASE IV. You can press ALT-E and type a Q. You can activate

❑

Tip: Use the Speed keys for menu selections.

If you use the F10 key to activate the menu, you must move the highlight to the menu option you want to use. Pressing the ALT key in combination with the first letter in the menu option activates the menu and displays the pull-down menu for that option. For example, pressing ALT-C in the Control Panel activates the Catalog selections.

the menu by pressing F10 then highlighting Exit and typing a **Q**. If you are working at the dot prompt, you can type **quit** to end dBASE IV.

If you use any of these methods for exiting, dBASE IV will close any open files and allow you to exit from the program in an orderly fashion. If you turn your system off to end the program, you run the risk of losing data.

An Overview of the dBASE IV Components

dBASE IV offers all of the capabilities of dBASE III+ in addition to many new features. The package now provides a Control Center screen that is the first step in accessing any other activities. The Control Center provides access to the entire set of dBASE IV menus as well as to the work surfaces used to design dBASE IV objects like reports, labels, and custom screens. The term object is used here to maintain consistency with Ashton-Tate's terminology, which refers to the ability to create objects from the Control Center and other locations. You will find many new options in these menus, including macro features to capture the keystrokes for a task so you can reuse them.

In addition to all the Control Center options, dBASE IV still provides for entries at the dot prompt. From the Control Center all that is required is pressing ESC and typing a **Y** to move to the dot prompt mode. The screen in Figure 1-1 shows where the dot prompt name comes from, since all that is visible on the screen before typing your request is a dot. The format of the dot commands exactly matches the syntax of commands used in dBASE IV's programming language. The option to use the dot prompt entry gives you the full power of the programming language with the knowledge that the Control Center menu commands can be restored with just a few keystrokes. You can return to the Control Center at any time by typing **ASSIST** or pressing F2 and pressing ENTER.

dBASE IV provides access to an applications generator program. This special tool allows you to create custom applications with dBASE IV without the need for programming. A template language is part of the dBASE IV developer's edition or can be purchased separately from Ashton-Tate. It allows you to create patterns for creating dBASE IV objects like reports and custom screens.

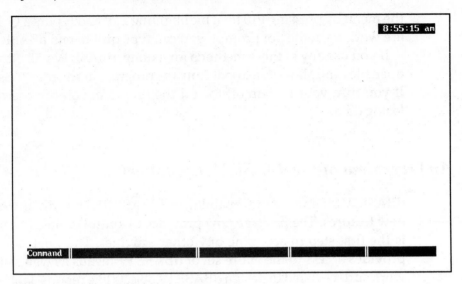

Figure 1-1 Dot Prompt screen

If you decide to code your application, dBASE IV provides a full-featured language that allows you to perform any task. The dBASE IV language offers the ultimate in customization and flexibility but requires a greater time investment than the other options.

dBASE IV Control Center

dBASE IV provides a totally revamped assisted-user interface. The screen that is initially presented upon loading the package is the Control Center. From this launching pad you can access any dBASE IV object such as a database, a report, a label design, or a custom screen. These objects are created with the work surfaces that can be accessed through Control Center menu options. You can also use the Control Center menu to work with an assortment of utility programs.

The Control Center Screen Figure 1-2 shows a sample Control Center screen. There are six different parts to this screen. A *menu bar* at the top provides access to tools for handling files and catalogs. Several lines down the screen, the name of the active *catalog* is displayed. A catalog is a special file used by dBASE IV to relate all the files pertaining to an application. The catalog organizes the interface to dBASE IV and controls the filenames that show on the Control Center screen. Every

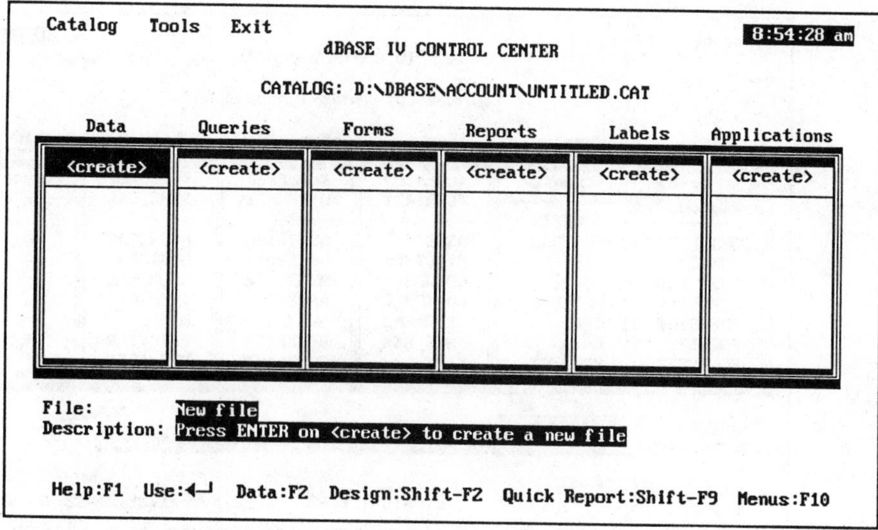

Figure 1-2 Control Center screen

directory has a catalog, since dBASE IV creates a file named UNTITLED.CAT if there is no other file with a .CAT extension on the disk.

The catalog name displayed on the Control Center screen is a file that dBASE IV reads to determine which files it makes available for your selection in the *panels* on this screen. Any files that you create are automatically added to the current catalog. dBASE IV is able to remember the catalog you were using in your last dBASE IV session. Unless you change the CONFIG.DB file to specify a specific catalog at the start of a dBASE IV session, dBASE will automatically open the catalog that was open at the end of your last dBASE IV session.

The panels on the Control Center screen are labeled with the type of files that they contain. They allow you to access reports, labels, application programs, forms, and queries in addition to databases. Each of the panels presents a create option that allows you to create a new file of the specified type. The horizontal lines in the control panel separate active or open files from inactive files. If a file is active, the name of the file will appear above the line with the <create> alternative.

As you look at the sample screen in Figure 1-3, you will see that the Data panel displays the database file EMPLOYEE as active along with the forms file NEWHIRE1, the report file HIRENAME and the labels file PERS_LBL.

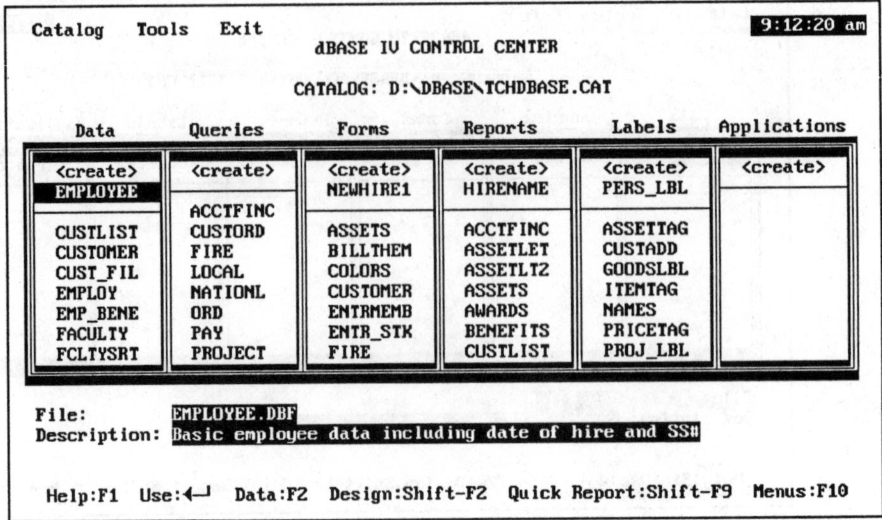

Figure 1-3 Control Center screen with files active

The maximum number of entries in any panel is 200. Once this limit is reached, you will need to delete some catalog entries before creating new ones. You can delete files from the disk and from the catalog by pressing the delete key and responding to dBASE IV's prompt messages or by making a menu selection. A file must be closed before it can be deleted.

Beneath the panels is an area reserved for *file information*. This location displays the name of the file where the cursor or highlight is positioned. If you have added a description for this filename, dBASE IV displays the description on the line beneath the filename.

Like other dBASE IV screens, the Control Center displays a navigation line and a message line. The *navigation line* is used to provide information on keys that allow you to access data and design screens quickly. The *message line* is blank unless dBASE IV is displaying information about options that are available at a particular point in time.

Working with Control Center Files To work with any of the control center files, the file must be open. For database files, this means that the name of the file must appear above the horizontal line in the control panel. To open any database file that is below the line, move to the filename and press ENTER. This causes dBASE IV to place a menu box

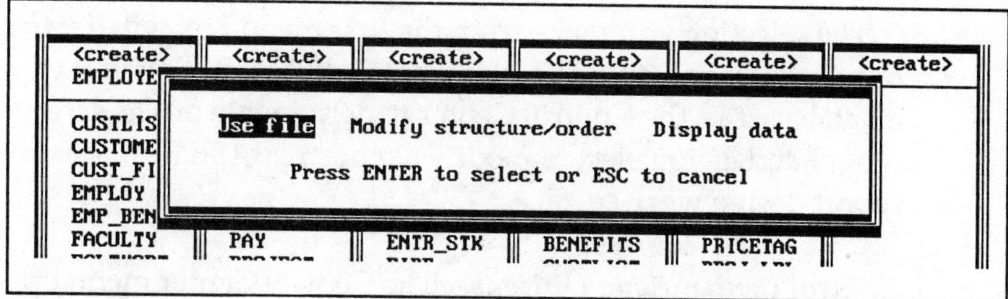

Figure 1-4 Initial screen when selecting a database file

on the screen that allows you to select from several options. The Use option opens the database without taking any other action.

Once a database is opened, files in the other panels that are related to the database will appear above the line in their panel. These files are not opened unless you specifically decide to use one of them to display data or perform some other activity. If you highlight one of these files and press ENTER, another box will be displayed for you to select the desired action as long as the default SET INSTRUCT ON is still in effect. The boxes all differ depending on the type of file that you highlight.

Figure 1-4 provides a look at the menu box when a database is selected. The first choice is the one used most frequently, since its job is to activate the database in order to use it for other tasks. Figure 1-5 displays the box that appears when a report file is selected. Although the boxes differ, dBASE IV has attempted to present the selections so that the option selected most often is the highlighted selection. You can select this option by pressing ENTER. To select one of the other options, you can move to the desired option and press ENTER or type the first letter of the option.

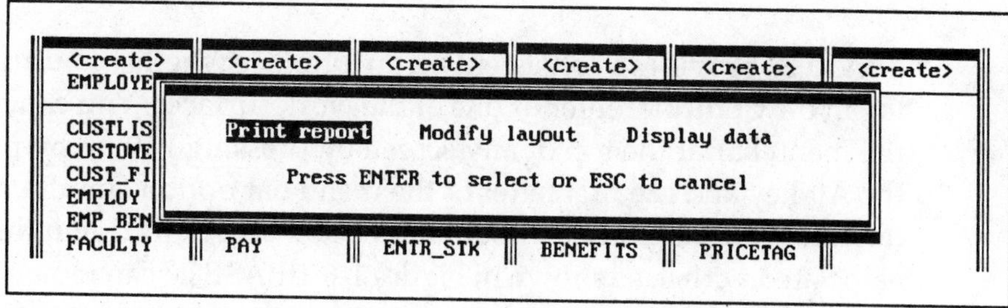

Figure 1-5 Initial menu screen when selecting a report file

The selection you make from the first menu box will determine the screen that is presented next. If you tell dBASE IV that you want to use a database file, the Control Center panels remain on the screen. On the other hand, if you elect to modify a report, dBASE IV places you in the report design work surface.

Control Center Menu Options The Control Center menu options are somewhat limited, since they do not work with design objects like reports and labels. These commands provide the tools for working with catalogs, directories, and files.

After invoking the menu, you can change either the catalog or the DOS directory with options available in the submenu choices for Tools. You can add or remove individual file entries from the catalog. You can use menu options to add or remove files from the current directory.

With other menu selections, you can access a screen to enter DOS commands directly or use a set of DOS utilities that allow you to handle common DOS tasks like copying, deleting, and renaming files. Sorting the list of file names and marking files to work with them as a group are other options. All of these options are covered in detail in Chapter 8, which covers file commands.

The Control Center menu options provide access to import and export utilities. You can use these to import data from programs like Lotus 1-2-3, PFS:FILE, dBASE II, Framework II, or RapidFile. You can export data to any of these formats as well as SYLK, fixed-length text field format, blank, and character delimited files. The many options offered make it easy to use data from another program in dBASE IV or to export portions of you dBASE IV data to other programs.

dBASE IV Menu Options

dBASE IV provides a consistent menu interface whether you are working in the Control Center or one of the work surfaces. You can activate the menu bar at the top of any screen by pressing F10, or by pressing the Alt key and the first letter of the menu bar option simultaneously. dBASE IV highlights the first menu option and pulls down the menu associated with it, as shown in Figure 1-6. dBASE IV can remember the last selection that you made from a pull-down menu in the current session and will highlight this choice for you. The exception to this rule is when you exit the design for any dBASE IV object and reenter it.

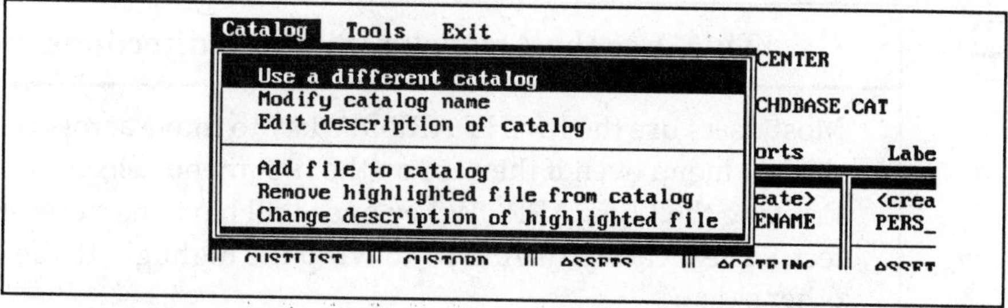

Figure 1-6 Pull-down menu for the Catalog option in the Control Center menu

Upon reentry dBASE IV does not remember the selection made at the end of the last session.

Once a pull-down menu displays, you can use the LEFT and RIGHT ARROW keys to move to a menu to the right or left of the current menu and that menu will pull down in place of the current menu. You can select any item in the current menu by typing the first letter of the selection. Selections that are dimmed are not selectable at the current time. Selections that have a symbol similar to a triangle on its side next to them indicate that you will be presented a fill-in menu box for these items. Other key options include ESC to back out of the selection, END to move to the last menu choice, and HOME to move to the first item in the pull-down menu. Some screens require selections that are supported by TAB, ENTER, and SHIFT-TAB to move between lists of choices, and PageUp and PageDown to move up and down in the list of choices.

Tip: Do not use the first letter to activate menu bars.

Many programs allow you to select an option from a menu bar by typing the first letter of the menu option. dBASE IV does not support this approach and will attempt to select an option in the current pull-down menu if you type a letter. To select a menu-bar option, use the ALT key in combination with the first letter of the menu to activate the menu you need quickly. Next, type the first letter of the pull-down menu choice that you want.

Tip: Use the Arrow keys in both directions.

Most users use the RIGHT ARROW key to move across to the last menu even if they are on the first menu selection. Pressing the LEFT ARROW key once will have the same effect, since it causes dBASE IV to wrap the highlight to the other side.

The UP ARROW key works the same way in a pull-down menu. Although you can use the DOWN ARROW key to move from the top to the bottom of the menu, pressing the UP ARROW key when you are positioned on the top selection will place the highlight on the last option.

dBASE IV Work Surfaces

dBASE IV provides a different work surface for every object accessible from the Control Center. These work surfaces are tailored to the design and data entry tasks that form the nucleus of dBASE IV. Special key assignments make it easy for you to switch from one task to another as you alternate between design and entry tasks.

Each of these work surfaces has a different appearance, since it is tailored to the object you are working with. The work surface for the database design is shown in Figure 1-7. It is designed to make the task of entering database definitions easier by its columnar type layout.

The work surface for looking at database records once they have been entered is completely different. In fact, you have a choice of two ways to see it. You can work with the data one record at a time on an Edit work surface like the one shown in Figure 1-8. You can choose to look at many records at once by pressing F2 once you have added some records to a database. Pressing F2 toggles between the Browse and Edit mode displays. The Browse work surface is shown in Figure 1-9.

Creating reports and labels are again very different tasks from the database activities discussed. The work surfaces for these tasks are very different. Figure 1-10 shows the report design work surface with some of the report bands that can be defined to shape your report. Designing a label means providing the layout for one label. dBASE IV provides a

Layout Organize Append Go To Exit 9:18:03 am

Bytes remaining: 4000

Num	Field Name	Field Type	Width	Dec	Index
1		Character			N

Database D:\dbase\<NEW> Field 1/1

Enter the field name. Insert/Delete field:Ctrl-N/Ctrl-U

Field names begin with a letter and may contain letters, digits and underscores

Figure 1-7 Database design screen

blank label format where you can add fields that will display on the label. Figure 1-11 provides a look at the label design work surface.

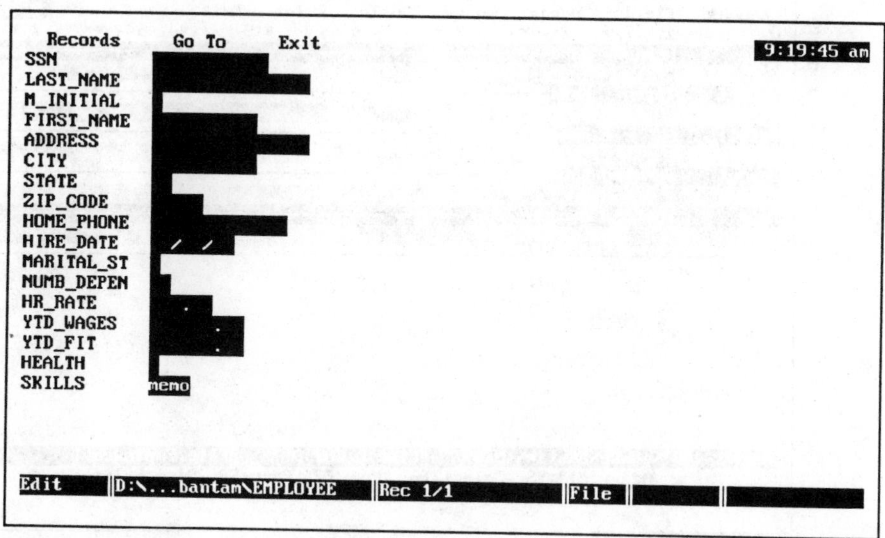

Figure 1-8 Edit screen

Records Fields Go To Exit 9:41:32 am

SSN	LAST_NAME	M_INITIAL	FIRST_NAME	ADDRESS	CITY	ST
215-98-7765	Harris	H	Henry	1711 Weaver Ave	Towson	MD
543-78-9090	Roberts	G	George	32 Albert Dr	Cleveland	OH

Browse D:\...bantam\EMPLOYEE Rec 2/2 File

View and edit fields

Figure 1-9 Browse screen

dBASE IV provides two basic modes for editing text on work surfaces. These are the layout mode and the word-wrap modes. When the

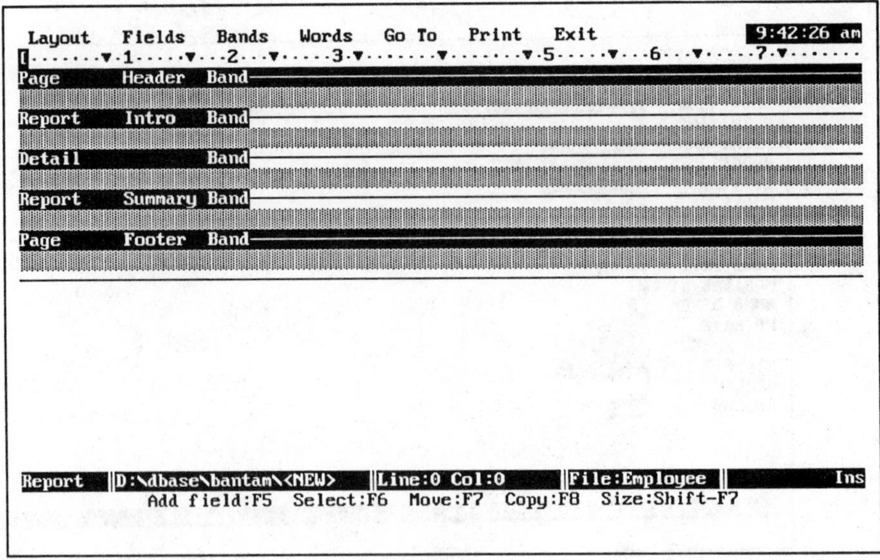

Figure 1-10 Report design work surface

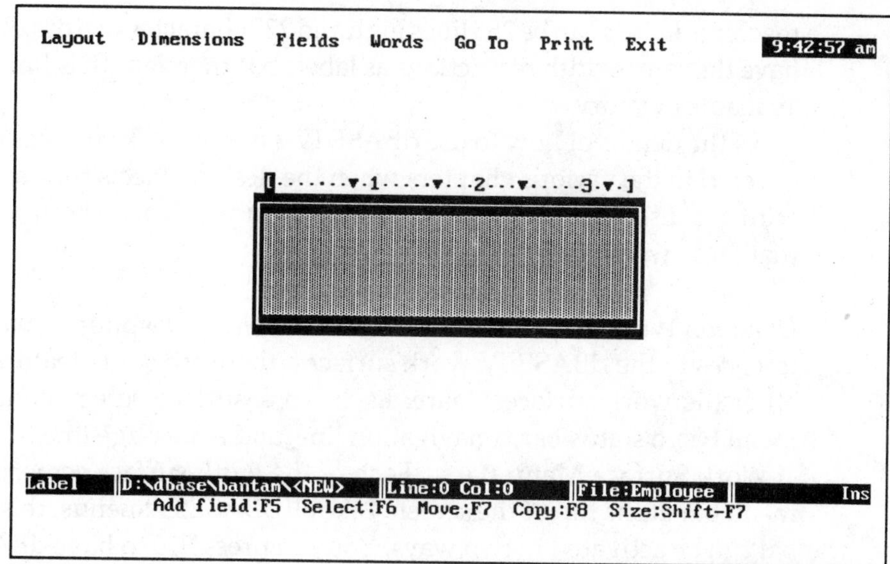

Figure 1-11 Label design work surface

work surface you are working on supports word wrap, you can expect dBASE IV to treat your entries similar to the way that a word processing package would. This means that dBASE IV will automatically wrap long words at the ends of lines and make adjustments as you edit the text on the work surface. The command line edit window that you will use from dot prompt mode in Chapter 10 for macros, memo fields, programs, and text files always operate in word-wrap mode. Word wrap is also used at times in designing reports if you specify a word-wrap band. The width used for word-wrap mode varies depending on your task. The default is 65 characters for memo fields, 255 characters for reports, and 1,024 characters for programs and text files. The background of the work surface when you are in word wrap is a solid color versus the shaded pattern used for layout mode.

Layout mode is used for forms, labels, and sometimes in reports. It offers advantages for the drawing of lines and boxes and allows the exact placement of text. Layout mode makes it easy to copy design elements from one location to another in a design. Layout work surfaces have both width and length limitations, which are again determined by the work surface you are using. The Form work surface has a width restriction of 80 and a total length restriction controlling the number of forms for a single record determined by the memory on your machine. Labels can be 255 lines high and 237 characters across. Reports have the same width restrictions as labels but their length is limited by available memory.

All the details of how to use dBASE IV's many work surfaces will be covered in the various chapters when the design objects they are used with are discussed. In the next section, you will learn about features that these work surfaces have in common.

Common Work Surface Screen Characteristics Despite the many differences in the dBASE IV work surfaces, there are some features that all of the work surfaces share. Each work surface screen contains a menu bar, a status bar, a navigation line, and a message line.

Work Surface Menu Bars Each of the work surface screens has a menu bar at the top of the screen. Like all dBASE IV menus, this menu bar can be activated in two ways. You can press F10 to have dBASE IV activate the menu bar and pull down the menu for the first item in the menu bar. You can also select the pull-down menu that you want to use by pressing the ALT key in combination with the first letter in the menu bar option. In other words, if the menu bar offers the option Exit, you can select it by pressing ALT-E.

The right side of the menu bar displays the time of day. dBASE IV obtains the current time from the DOS time stored in the memory of your computer. If this number is incorrect, either you responded incorrectly to the DOS time prompt or you need to reset your computer's internal battery-operated clock.

Status Bars Most of the work surfaces also have a status bar at the bottom of the screen. For most work surfaces this bar is divided into five sections. The first section of the status bar displays the work surface screen that you are currently using. It might contain the word Report, Browse, Edit, or Query.

The next section of the status bar displays the current file with which you are working. It contains the pathname for the file. This includes the drive and any subdirectories needed to specify the path.

The next section of the status bar indicates the location of the cursor. The type of work surface you are in affects how dBASE IV displays this information. If you are in the Edit work surface, dBASE IV tells you which record the cursor is in. If you are in the Report work surface, dBASE IV displays the line and column numbers.

The next section of the status bar displays the source of the data displayed on the screen. This section may contain the name of a database file or a view created with a Query.

dBASE IV uses the remaining area on the status line to display indicators. You might see an indicator telling you that the record is locked, if you are working on a multiuser system. If the record is marked to be deleted, Del appears in this area. Ins indicates that Insert mode is On, causing dBASE to add the characters you type to the ones that are already on the screen. The Caps and Num indicators tell you that these options are on. If you choose, you can disable the display of the status line. If you elect to do this, dBASE IV uses the top right corner of the screen to display the indicators and refers to it as the Scoreboard. You can use the SET STATUS command to change the status line display. You can use the SET SCOREBOARD command to change the display of the Scoreboard. Both commands are discussed in more detail in Chapter 8.

The Work Surface Navigation Line A navigation line appears beneath the status line on the work surface screen. Although it is blank on a few of the screens, in most cases it provides information about accomplishing the tasks that the work surface supports. As an example, in the Report Design work surface, this line tells you how to add a field, select an object, move, copy, or size a field. On the Query Design work surface, this line tells you how to move to another field or file skeleton, how to activate a pick list, and how to display the data for the query. In short, this line eliminates the need to remember the key assignments for all of these tasks, since a quick glance at this line will tell you what to do. While you will soon remember the keys to use for the features you use all the time, you can continue to rely on the navigation line as a crutch for those options that you use infrequently.

The Work Surface Message Line The work surface message line is the bottom line on your screen. When you activate the menu bar at the top of the screen, this line tells you what the highlighted menu selection does. This line can also provide you directions or tell you about the current item on the work surface.

Moving Around on the Work Surfaces A cursor marks you current location on a work surface. If the cursor marks the location for a single character, it is the width of one character. Sometimes the cursor is wider because it marks the location of an entire field or group of characters. The term highlight is often used to refer to the wider cursor.

The keys used to move the cursor may differ depending on the work surface you are using. The functions of the various keys are summarized in the next section and discussed in more detail in the chapters where the work surfaces are introduced.

Keyboard Options

Many people are familiar with a typewriter's keyboard; however, a computer keyboard contains several keys that do not have an equivalent on the typewriter. dBASE IV supports the use of many of the special keys on your keyboard. Although dBASE IV uses the special keys in a similar fashion across all work surfaces, many keys have special meanings in the various dBASE IV work surfaces. There are still a subset of keys that have the same meaning regardless of the environment that you are in when you use them. Table 1-1 presents a summary of these keys.

The keys that have distinctive meaning in the various dBASE IV environments are listed in Table 1-2. You must look at the second column of this table to ascertain the environment for the action presented is in the last column of the table.

dBASE IV utilizes the function keys to provide additional functionality and as a shortcut for selections that can be made with navigation keys and menu selections. Again, the assignments for these keys are tailored to specific work surfaces. All of the function key assignments are not available on a given work surface. Table 1-3 summarizes the function key assignments used for dBASE IV.

The dBASE Help System

dBASE IV's help system is easy to access and is much more comprehensive than in earlier versions of the package. Some help information is automatically displayed on the screen in the message and navigation lines. You can invoke other help information when you need assistance.

Table 1-1 Summary of Key Assignments for All Work Surfaces

Key	*Action*
BACKSPACE	Deletes the previous character.
CTRL-END	Saves the current entries and ends the task.
DEL	Deletes the current selection.
ESC	Abandons changes and leaves. Also abandons current selection.
INS	Toggles between insert mode for entries and typeover or overstrike.
→	Moves to the right one position.
←	Moves to the left one position.
↑	Moves up one row.
↓	Moves down one row.
CTRL →	Magnifies the effect of the right arrow key, moving to the beginning of the next word or field.
CTRL ←	Magnifies the effect of the left arrow key, moving to the beginning of the previous word or field.

Table 1-2 Special Key Assignments by Mode

Key	*Work Surface*	*Effect*
↓	Edit	Moves to the next field.
↑	Edit	Moves to the previous field.
Ctrl-Backspace	Layout, Word wrap	Deletes the previous word.
Ctrl-End	Memo field	Moves out of a memo field.
Ctrl-Enter	Design work surfaces	Save work and continues with design.
Ctrl-Home	Memo field	Moves into a memo field.
Ctrl-Page Down	Browse, Edit	Moves to the current field in the last record.
	Layout	Moves to the bottom of the layout surface.
	Word wrap	Moves to the end of the text.
Ctrl-Page Up	Browse, Edit	Moves to the current field in the first record.

(continued)

Table 1-2 Special Key Assignments by Mode ***(continued)***

Key	*Work Surface*	*Effect*
Ctrl-Page Up *(continued)*	Layout	Moves to the top of the work surface.
	Word wrap	Moves to the beginning of text.
End	Browse	Moves to the last field.
	Edit	Moves to the end of the field.
	Layout	Moves to the last field on the line.
	Queries	Move to the last skeleton column.
	Word wrap	Moves to the last text.
Enter	Browse, Edit	Moves to the next field.
	Layout (Insert on),	Ends the line.
	Word wrap	Moves to the next line.
Home	Browse	Moves to the beginning of a record.
	Edit	Moves to the beginning of a field.
	Queries	Moves to the first skeleton column.
	Word wrap	Indents.
Page Down	Browse, Edit, Layout, Word wrap	Displays the next screen.
Page Up	Browse, Edit, Layout, Word wrap	Displays the previous screen.
Shift Tab	Browse, Edit	Moves to the previous field.
	Layout, Word wrap	Moves to the previous Tab stop.
Tab	Browse, Edit	Moves to the next field.
	Layout, Word wrap (Insert Off)	Moves to the next Tab stop.
	Queries	Moves to the next column.
	Word wrap (Insert On)	Inserts a Tab.

You can access dBASE IV's help information in several ways. The method you will use depends on whether you are working from Assist

Table 1-3 Function Key Assignments

Key	*Effect*
F1 (Help)	Activates help information.
Shift-F1 (Pick)	Displays a list of selections for the current field.
F2 (Data)	Switches between Browse and Edit mode formats for reviewing data.
Shift-F2 (Design)	Activates the design screen.
F3 (Previous)	Moves to review previous information.
Shift-F3 (Find Previous)	Locates the previous occurrence of a search string.
F4 (Next)	Moves to the next information.
Shift-F4 (Find Next)	Locates the next occurrence of a search string.
F5 (Field)	Adds or modifies fields on the layout screen. Adds or removes fields for queries.
Shift-F5 (Find)	Finds a search string.
F6 (Extend Select)	Allows you to select a contiguous group of fields or text.
Shift-F6 (Replace)	Replaces a search string with another string.
F7 (Move)	Moves text and fields.
Shift-F7 (Size)	Changes a column width or the size of a design element.
F8 (Copy)	Copies fields and text.
Shift-F8 (Ditto)	Copies data from the same field in the previous record.
F9 (Zoom)	Enlarges and shrinks the display of information.
Shift-F9 (Quick Report)	Produces a Quick Report.
F10 (Menu)	Activates the menu bar.
Shift-F10 (Macros)	Activates the macro box.

mode at the dot prompt or with the menu system. The three possibilities for invoking help are

1. Press the F1 (Help) key.
2. Select Help from the bottom options at the bottom of an error box.

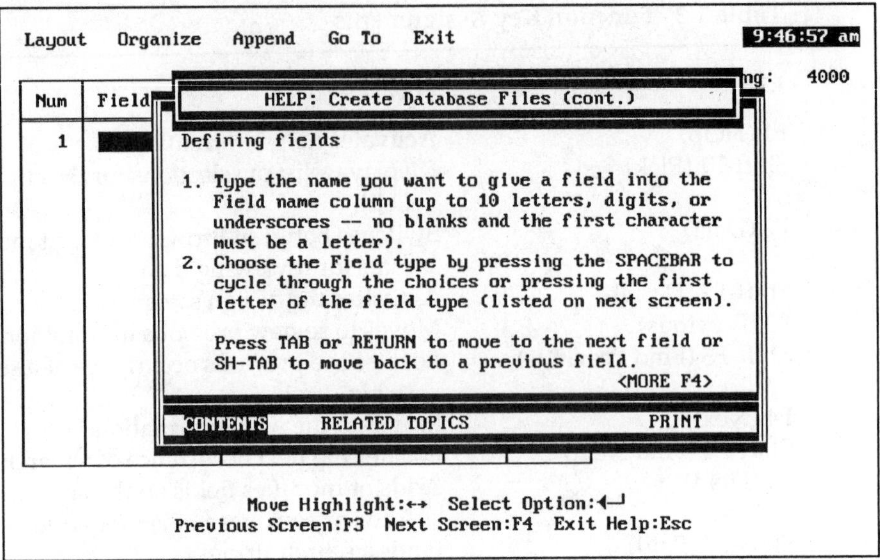

Figure 1-12 Help screen for creating a database

3. Type **help** at the dot prompt. You can follow the word help with the name of the command for which you need help as in **help display**.

The help provided for the menu system commands focuses on these options. dBASE IV attempts to determine the topic for which you need help by your location in the program. The help box that is displayed looks something like Figure 1-12. In this example, the title at the top of the help box indicates that it is for Create Database Files. The text that follows provides details on the topic. You can continue to view help screens by pressing F3 for the previous help screen in the sequence or F4 if you want to move forward through the screens.

The buttons at the bottom of the help screens provide additional options. You can choose Contents, Related Topics, or Print. The Contents option allows you to move through the hierarchical arrangement of help topics. Figure 1-13 displays the first contents box that appears. Once you have invoked contents, you can reach a higher overview level by pressing F3 (Previous)to see a screen like the one in Figure 1-14. To move from a higher level back to more detailed information, press the F4 (Next) key. Related Topics allows you to choose from a list of related

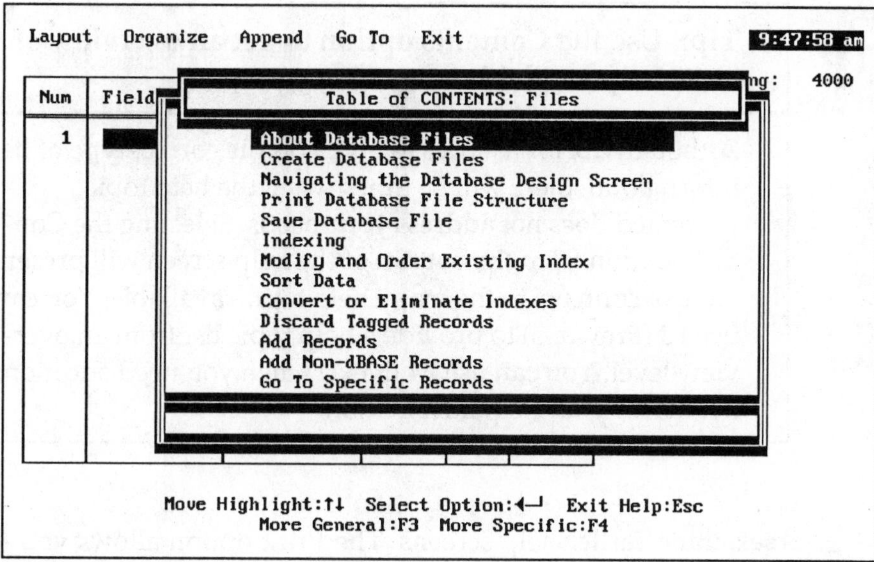

Figure 1-13 Contents screen

topics that dBASE IV displays. The BACKUP button only appears if you have moved forward from previous help screens. It allows you to

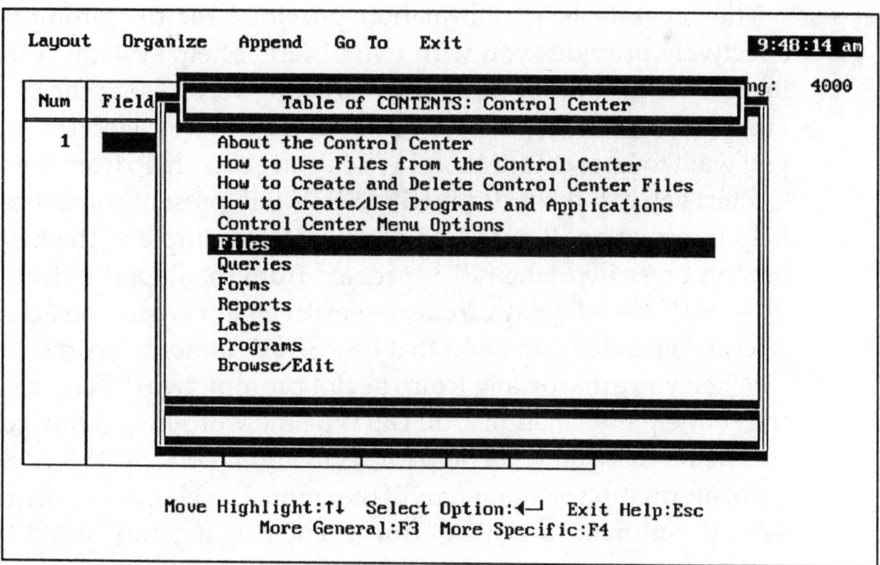

Figure 1-14 Higher-level Contents options

❑

Tip: Use the Contents option to get an overview of the help available.

Although dBASE IV tries to give you the correct type of help information, there will be times when the help topic presented does not address your needs. Selecting the Contents option from the bottom of the help screen will present a table of contents to the many help topics available. You can use F3 (Previous) to provide a help topic list from an overview level. You can use F4 (Next) when you need additional details for your help information.

reexamine earlier help screens. The Print option allows you to print only the contents of the help box on the screen.

You can select from the various help button options by pressing the RIGHT ARROW key or the SPACEBAR to move to the right. You can move to the left with the LEFT ARROW key or the BACKSPACE key. Once a button is highlighted, ENTER completes the selection. To select a button without moving the highlight or selection bar, type the first letter of the option.

The separate help information provided for dot prompt entries effectively provides you with two different help systems. When you invoke help from dot prompt by pressing F1 or using the command HELP, dBASE IV displays menus that allow you to select the topic that you want to know more about. When you access help from the Control Center, you can press F1 and dBASE IV will present context-sensitive help information. Figure 1-15 provides an example of the help information presented when F1 is pressed from the Report design screen. dBASE IV also displays context-sensitive help when you select Help after trying a dot command that dBASE IV cannot interpret.

When you are working from the dot prompt, two different activities trigger help information. You can type the word help followed by the command that you want help for, as in HELP USE. dBASE IV displays help information on the syntax of the command Use, as shown in Figure 1-16. If you make a syntax error in entering a command, dBASE IV offers you a menu that offers help as one of the options.

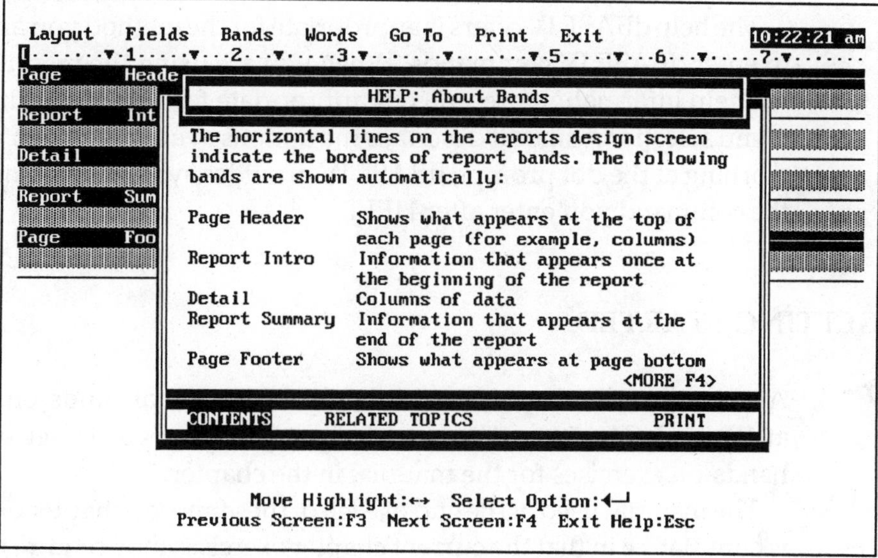

Figure 1-15 Report help screen

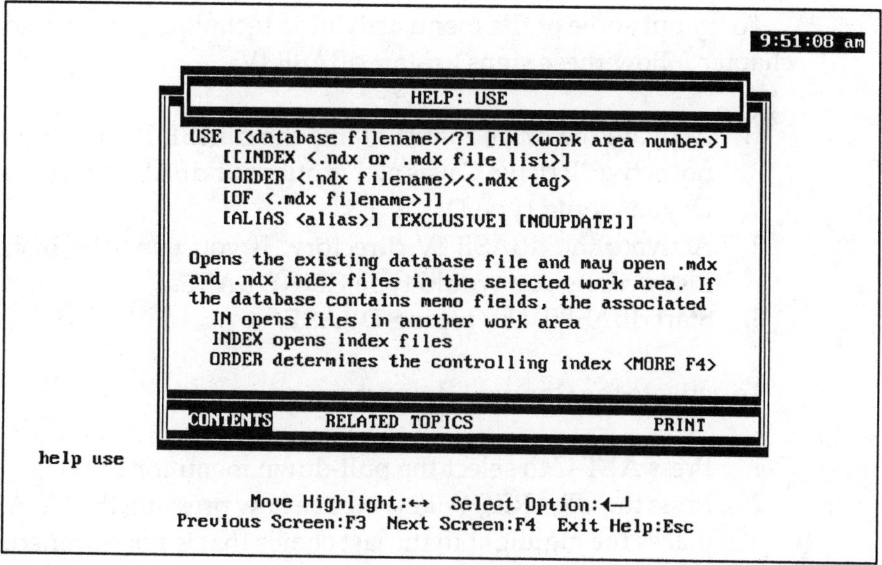

Figure 1-16 Help screen from the dot prompt

The help dBASE IV offers is appropriate for the method you are using to enter dBASE IV commands. When you are using the menu system the help information presented is appropriate for a user working with menu selections, since it describes the options available. When you are working at the dot prompt, dBASE IV provides syntax information for the command you enter after HELP.

GETTING STARTED

➤ Almost all of the chapters in this book have a special hands-on section at the end. These sections are designed to give you a set of short hands-on exercises for the material in the chapter.

The material used at the end of each of these end-of-chapter exercises is cumulative in that the current chapter exercises may require the files created in earlier exercises. Since each of these sections have been designed to be as short as possible without missing any key concepts, you will find that they will enable you to build your dBASE IV skills set quickly. To expedite the completion of examples in later chapters, you will want to keep each of the files that you create in these end-of-chapter exercises.

To try out some of the menu activation techniques presented in this chapter follow these steps to start dBASE IV:

1. Activate the drive that contains the dBASE IV directory if it is not active. If drive C was active but your dBASE drive was drive D, you would type **D:**.
2. Activate the dBASE IV directory. If you used the installation instructions you would type **CD \DBASE**.
3. Start dBASE IV by typing **DBASE**.

To activate the Control Center menu options:

1. Press ALT-C to select the pull-down menu for Catalog.
2. Press the UP ARROW key. Notice how pressing the UP ARROW places the highlight in the last choice that is not dimmed. This is because it is already at top of the menu.

3. Press the LEFT ARROW key. Notice how the menu for the last menu option Exit is highlighted, since there were no additional options to the left.
4. Press the LEFT ARROW key a second time. This time the highlight does move to the left, since a menu option is available.
5. Type an **E** to select Export from the Tools menu.
6. When the new fill-in menu displays, press ESC to go back to the previous menu. Press Esc a second time to leave the Control Center menu.

To look at the create screen:

1. Move to the Data panel of the Control Center and highlight <create>.
2. Press ENTER to move to the design screen.
3. Press ALT-L to invoke the Layout menu.
4. Press the RIGHT ARROW key to the Organize menu.
5. Press the RIGHT ARROW key to move to the Append menu.
6. Press the RIGHT ARROW key to move to the Go To menu. Note that all of these options as well as the ones in previous menus are dimmed, since the database design has not yet been started.
7. Press ALT_E and type an **A** for Abandon changes and exit.
8. Press ALT-E again since you are now in the Control Center and want to exit from dBASE IV. Type a **Q** to select Quit to DOS.

CHAPTER 2

Designing and Creating dBASE IV Systems

Defining information requirements and designing database files are the first tasks in creating a new dBASE IV application. It is important that you complete the definition phase before you begin entering the file structure on the database design screen. Beginning the design before adequately addressing your needs will result in an inefficient design that is likely to require many modifications.

Once you have decided on a file structure, you will be ready to define your database design to dBASE IV. The interface for the Control Center and design work surface make the task easy. Each field in the database design is entered on a line on the design work surface. Other information like the field type, width, number of decimal places and whether or not to create an index with entries from the field are entered on the same line. dBASE IV makes your job as easy as possible, filling in some of the entries for certain field types. With all the information for the fields and their attributes stored in a tabular arrangement it is easy to locate and change any of the information. You will also find that many of the techniques used on the database design screen for making entries and selecting menu options are usable in other dBASE IV tasks.

Once you have completed your initial design, dBASE IV is flexible enough to support changes. Before you enter records, any change can be made. After data is stored in the database, a few limitations apply but you will still find that it is easy to modify your database file to meet your changing needs.

With the design complete, you will be ready to approach the next step of adding data. Appending records from other files is addressed in this chapter. Adding data from the keyboard is covered in Chapter 3.

Defining Your Information Requirements

Database management systems are an important part of many business operations like payroll, inventory control, accounts receivable processing, patient care, and personnel. These systems are composed of information databases and the necessary programs, reports, screen designs, and other components to provide a complete solution for handling input, processing, and output connected with each application. dBASE IV provides the framework with which to build any of these systems. It allows you to create the necessary database for information storage and also allows you to handle the necessary computations and other processing requirements for the data stored in the system. dBASE IV also supports the design of custom screens, labels, and reports with menu-driven selection.

Building one or more databases is the first step to building your database system. A good database design will need to meet both current and projected future requirements. This means that the database will need to store all the information required to meet current and projected needs. Each element of data stored in the database is referred to as a field. You can think of a field as the smallest usable unit of information. As an example, an individual's name might be James E. Smith. The smallest unit is each character in the name but a character is neither usable nor meaningful by itself. The name shown can be broken down into three fields containing first name, last name, and middle initial. Although in some instances you might elect to create a field containing all the components of the name, usually you will want to break data like this down into its individual components. A good starting place for defining the fields that you need is to examine all of the system's inputs and outputs.

Identifying Individual Data Fields

Identifying the individual fields of information is easiest if you have an established system. Regardless of whether the system is a paper system or an automated system, your task will be made easier by having a defined starting point. You can make a list of all of the fields on the source documents for the system. As you examine the output of the system, you can add data fields that are not currently in the input list. If you find that you cannot calculate these fields from other data fields, you will need to add them to the database if you expect to include them in system outputs.

If you do not have an existing system, your task is much more difficult. You must define the output you expect from the system and identify the source of each individual field. When you are working from scratch you will increase your chances of successfully designing an efficient system if you plan for iteration in this process. You can add enhancements and continue to supplement the list of fields as you review the current list.

Whether you are starting from scratch or using an existing system, you will want to supplement the information in the list of fields that you are creating with input from the various users of the system to determine if additions, deletions, or changes are appropriate. The best way to obtain this information is to schedule a brief interview to discuss each individual user's requirements. If system inputs and outputs are available, they will serve as a good starting point for these discussions.

One Field or Two

As you identify each new piece of information, you will need to ask yourself if you have defined it as the smallest possible meaningful element. Rather than assign one field to hold several related pieces of information, you will have more flexibility with other dBASE IV design features if you split the information into multiple fields.

Defining a name field is a good example of this concept. First name, middle initial, last name, and perhaps title could all be stored in a field called NAME. You could record either first name or last name first in the field, but either choice would restrict you. Placing the first name at the beginning of the field would eliminate the ability to sort the records unless you wanted them in first-name sequence. Placing the last name first would not allow you to create mailing labels. A solution to these potential problems is four separate fields. This will allow you to use one field or all the fields in custom reports, screens, or labels. You can also use them in any sequence that you desire.

Defining and Organizing the Fields

As you identify each new field, you will want to record it on a sheet of paper. Since dBASE IV will require you to assign a field name later, you may as well record names that dBASE IV will accept. dBASE IV supports field names as long as ten characters. They can be composed of characters, numeric digits, and the underscore symbol. Field names cannot include spaces and must begin with a character.

Next to each field you will want to record the type of data that the field contains. dBASE IV supports each of the field type entries shown in Table 2-1. If you plan to enter characters like A–Z, you will want to choose a Character type field. This field type is also appropriate for fields containing alphanumeric entries (both letters and numbers). The Character type will support the inclusion of special symbols and must be selected for entries that are basically numeric but contain editing characters for clarity, such as social security numbers like 213-56-7865. The Character type can also be appropriate for numeric entries that can begin with a zero where you do not want this leading zero dropped. Zip codes are a good example since you do not want a zip code of 07865 to appear 7865.

Numeric data that you plan to use in computations can be stored in either a Numeric or a Float field. Numeric fields should be used where you need to be able to use the exact number you stored. A selection of a Numeric type would be appropriate for financial calculations. The

❑

Tip: Use standard file names for common information across files.

If you use standard names for common information like name and address, one report and one label design can be used for any of your database files.

Table 2-1 Field Types

Field Type	*Type of Entry Supported*	*Typical Usage*
Character	Any ASCII character	Name, address, numbers like part numbers, social security numbers, and other numbers containing dashes or slashes
Numeric	Any fixed number with or without decimal places	Salary, number of dependents
Float	A very large or very small number where quick multiplication or division is needed	Scientific
Date	A month, day, and year	Date of hire, date of birth, order date
Logical	Y, N, T, or F in upper or lower case	Results from a survey or any field where a true/false value is needed
Memo	Free-form text entry of any length	Abstracts, contracts, descriptive information

Float type field is used more in scientific calculations where an approximation is appropriate.

Logical fields can store entries representing true or false. You can have logical fields that will accept entries of T or F or you may expand the allowable entries to also include Y or N. Logical fields always have a field width of one.

Date type fields are designed to store dates in one of dBASE IV's acceptable formats. Date fields are automatically assigned a field width of eight.

The last type of field is the memo field. It is ideal for free-form text entry or documents. It is not limited to the 254 characters allowed in a Character type field.

The field type that you select will dictate the entries that are valid for the field. Although you can change field types by revising the structure, this can have an effect on existing field entries. You will want to invest the time during the design phase evaluating the field types appropriate for your data rather than attempting to change them later.

The maximum length you wish to allow for each field is another important consideration. dBASE IV will limit your entry for a field to the number of characters that you specify. For numeric fields, you will need to allow for a decimal point when you calculate the field width. If you plan to enter negative numbers in the field, you will also want to allow one position for the entry of a minus sign.

One Database or Two

With the definition complete, you need to decide how to organize the data. The first decision is whether to use one database for all the data elements that you have defined or to use several. One consideration that affects your decision is whether it is logical to group all the elements in one database. As an example, an individual deciding to create an accounting system may record data elements that pertain to accounts receivable and accounts payable. Since the data elements needed for accounts receivable pertain to customers and the data elements for accounts payable pertain to suppliers, multiple databases are needed.

The other important factor in determining the number of databases needed is the duplication or redundancy that results from putting all the fields in one database. Looking a little more closely at the needs for managing accounts receivable data, you might find that you needed to record a customer name, address, city, state, zip, phone, date, item ordered, quantity, unit price, and total amount. Putting all these elements in one database would result in a significant level of redundancy if the same customer orders more than once. A new record would be required for each order and the customer name and address information would need to be duplicated in each record. A better solution might be to have separate order and customer databases. If you add a customer identification number to each of these files, dBASE IV will allow you to link the information in the two files when necessary.

Field Order

Key fields that control access to a file should be the first fields in the database. This means that the customer ID number would be likely to be the first field in both the order and customer files discussed in the previous section. Placing this information at the front of the record will make it visible immediately in the Browse and Edit screens.

The remaining fields should be entered in logical groups by placing like information in adjacent fields. You would want to enter the address fields for street address, city, state, and zip code in sequence.

An Application Example

Figure 2-1 shows a subset of a potential list of fields for a payroll/personnel system. These fields were identified by examining the company's manual payroll system and interviewing individuals in their human resources department. The initial list of fields identified from examining the employment application, payroll register, checks, check stubs, and management reports were provided to each individual interviewed to ensure that the new system would meet the future needs of each of these individuals.

Fields for the employee's name and address are shown as Character type fields. The salary, current gross and net pay, year-to-date gross and net pay, and deductions are shown as Numeric type fields since they provide an exact number. The date of hire and current payroll date are shown as Date type fields. Fields indicating whether or not the individual participates in specific benefit plans are an ideal match with the Logical field type supported by dBASE IV as long as you only need to record participation and nonparticipation. The employee skills field is an ideal match with the Memo field type.

❑

Tip: Place key fields near the beginning of the record.

Place key fields near the beginning of your record. If you tend to use fields like last name and social security number to access the data in an employee file, you should place these fields as the first fields in the design. Having them at the beginning allows dBASE IV to access the information more efficiently. It also ensures that when you are browsing through the data or displaying a Quick Report on the screen, these key fields will be visible.

Field	Type
(1) Social security number	Character
(2) Last name	Character
(3) First name	Character
(4) Middle initial	Character
Payroll date	Date
Hourly rate	Number
Regular hours	
Pay date	
Overtime hours	
(5) Street address	
Phone number	
Skills	
(8) Zip code	
(6) City	
(7) State	
Date of hire	
Gross pay	
Net pay	
YTD gross pay	
YTD FIT	
Marital status	
Number of deductions	
YTD net pay	

Figure 2-1 Subset of fields for a payroll/personnel system

To avoid duplication, more than one database is needed. Otherwise, the record created for each payroll period must contain an employee's name, address, and skills among other fields. Figure 2-2 provides one example of the final structure, given that employee data and weekly

Tip: Selecting the correct numeric field type.

Evaluate the options for fields that contain numeric digits. dBASE IV supports both Numeric and Float for field types. Use Numeric when you need exact numeric entries. Use fixed when a close approximation will be sufficient. Float is much more efficient for operations involving multiplication and division.

Employee Master File

Field Name	Type	Width
SSN	Character	11
LAST_NAME	Character	15
M_INITIAL	Character	1
FIRST_NAME	Character	10
ADDRESS	Character	15
CITY	Character	10
STATE	Character	2
ZIP_CODE	Numeric	5
HOME_PHONE	Character	13
HIRE_DATE	Date	8
MARITAL_ST	Character	1
NUMB_DEPEN	Numeric	2
HR_RATE	Numeric	6
YTD_WAGES	Numeric	9
YTD_FIT	Numeric	9
HEALTH	Logical	1
SKILLS	Memo	10

Weekly Payroll File

Field Name	Type	Width
SSN	Character	11
WEEK_END	Date	8
REG_HOURS	Numeric	5
OVT_HOURS	Numeric	5

Figure 2-2 One possible database structure for the payroll/personnel data: employee master file (a) and weekly payroll file (b)

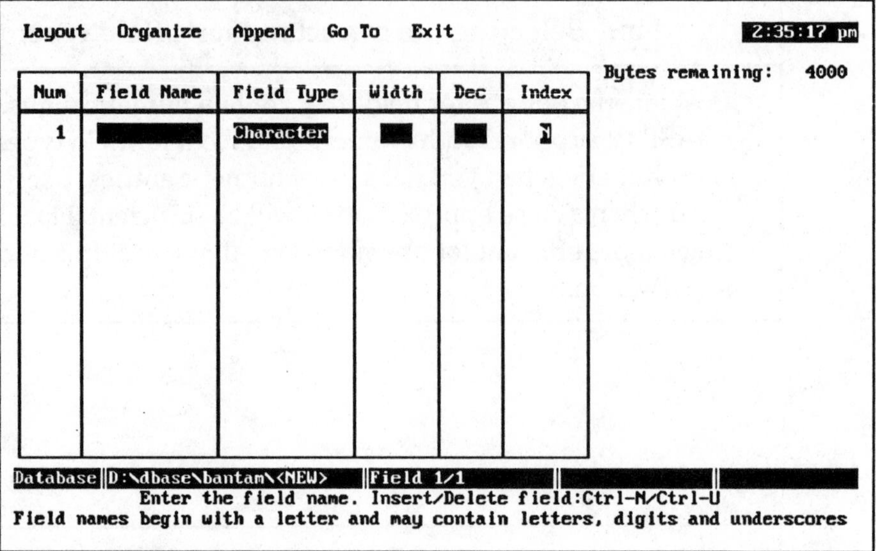

Figure 2-3 dBASE IV design screen

payroll data are needed. An employee ID number or social security number can be the link between the two files.

Another design possibility is expanding the number of files used to store information to include a third file. A separate database may be established for personnel information, with the basic employee information required for payroll stored in a payroll master file. The three files would then be the payroll master file, the weekly payroll transactions file, and the personnel master file. All three files could be linked on employee identification numbers or social security numbers.

Using the Design Work Surface

The database design work surface is easy to access from the Control Center. All you need to do is highlight <create> in the Data panel and press ENTER. dBASE IV immediately positions you in a design screen that looks like Figure 2-3. If you needed to modify an existing database structure, you would highlight the database that you want to modify in the Data panel and press SHIFT-F2, or press ENTER and select Modify layout/order. You can begin entering field specifications immediately, or you can invoke any of the menu options by pressing the

ALT key and the first letter of the menu bar selection that you want. The menu selections offer options for printing the database structure, organizing the data in a database, moving to fields within the structure, and saving the design.

Many of the size and length specifications that existed in earlier dBASE releases have been expanded to the point where they are unlikely to be a limiting factor as you attempt to implement your design. A dBASE IV file can now have a maximum of one billion records with as many as two billion bytes of information in the file. Each record within a dBASE IV file can have a maximum of 4,000 bytes split between as many as 256 fields. Given adequate memory and a CONFIG.SYS file that has been modified appropriately, you can have as many as 10 database files open at one time. Open files of all types including the database files can be 99.

Completing Design Column Entries

When you are ready to complete the columns on the design screen, you will begin by entering the field name of the first field. dBASE IV handles assignment of field numbers in the leftmost column labeled Num. When you begin designing a file, the Num column will automatically contain a 1 since that is the first field in the database. You will be able to move from column to column by either filling a column completely with your entry or by pressing ENTER. The UP and DOWN ARROW keys will allow you to move between fields, and the LEFT and RIGHT ARROW keys will allow you to move within a field. You can save your changes by pressing ENTER with the highlight on the line after the last set of completed field entries. You can also press CTRL-END, CTRL-W, or ALT-E followed by pressing ENTER. Pressing ESC before saving your changes will cause dBASE IV to prompt you to see if you are willing to lose all your changes. After saving your changes you can press F2 to move to the Browse/Edit screen. Pressing SHIFT-F2 will cause dBASE IV to display the queries design screen if your structure is already saved.

Making Modifications as You Design

Until you add records, you can make changes without any detrimental effect on the database. You can insert or remove fields at any location

Layout Organize Append Go To Exit 2:37:02 pm

Bytes remaining: 3883

Num	Field Name	Field Type	Width	Dec	Index
1	LAST_NAME	Character	15		N
2	M_INITIAL	Character	1		N
3	FIRST_NAME	Character	10		N
4	ADDRESS	Character	15		N
5	CITY	Character	10		N
6	STATE	Character	2		N
7	ZIP_CODE	Numeric	5	0	N
8	HOME_PHONE	Character	13		N
9	HIRE_DATE	Date	8		N
10	MARITAL_ST	Character	1		N
11	NUMB_DEPEN	Numeric	2	0	N
12	HR_RATE	Numeric	6	2	N
13	YTD_WAGES	Numeric	9	2	N
14	YTD_FIT	Numeric	9	2	N
15	HEALTH	Logical	1		N
16	SKILLS	Memo	10		N

Database D:\...bantam\EMPLOYEE Field 1/16

Enter the field name. Insert/Delete field:Ctrl-N/Ctrl-U

Field names begin with a letter and may contain letters, digits and underscores

Figure 2-4 Database requiring a new field

in the database structure. You can use the Go To menu option if you wish to position yourself in the proper location, or you can use the UP and DOWN ARROW key to position the cursor at the proper location. When you insert a field by pressing CTRL-N, it is inserted above the cursor location. Deleting a field requires that you place the cursor in the line containing the field that you wish to delete and press CTRL-U.

Given the database in Figure 2-4, you may want to add SSN as the first field in the record. The first step in inserting a new field is to position the cursor on the LAST_NAME field and then press CTRL-U and enter the definitions for the field in the proper columns.

After reviewing the menu options briefly, you can explore the design specifications entries more closely. Each of the columns and options are explained in detail.

The Database Design Menu Bar

The menu bar at the top of the database design screen offers five selections: Layout, Organize, Append, Go To, and Exit. The last option allows you to exit the design screen and provides the option of exiting with and without saving. The other selections each offer a variety of selections that either assist with the database design process or offer

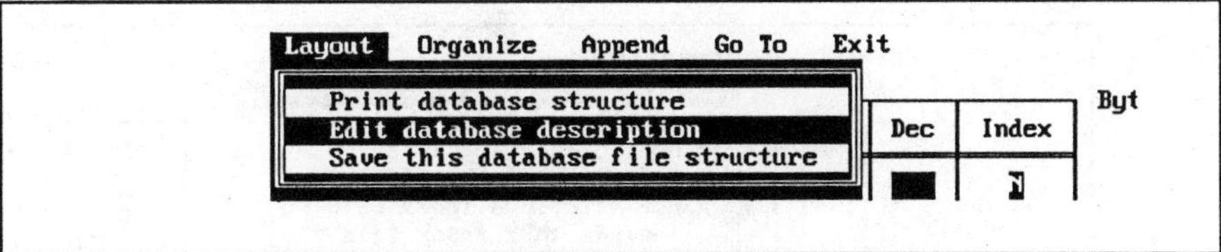

Figure 2-5 Layout menu options

additional functionality, such as changing the order of records in an existing database. Each option is explored in detail later in this chapter or a subsequent chapter. For now, you will want to have at least a general idea of the features offered by the menu bar selections.

The Layout menu provides the three options shown in Figure 2-5. One option allows you to create a printed copy of the database structure. This is useful for documentation purposes; a current copy of the structure should always be maintained. The layout menu provides a selection that permits you to add or change the file descriptions stored in dBASE IV catalogs. The last option provides a quick-save feature that saves the current structure and allows you to proceed with additions and changes. You can use this option when you want to save the database design using a different filename than you used when saving the original structure. You can also use this last option to save the database design as you change the design. The first time you use this option, dBASE IV expects you to supply a filename for the database that consists of from one to eight characters with no spaces. Subsequent saves only require you to press ENTER to accept the name that you used the last time.

Tip: Save the structure as you go.

Don't wait to finish the database design before saving. Save the structure as you proceed through the design. Only a few seconds are required and you avoid the risk of losing what you have completed. The best way to save is to press CTRL-ENTER. Since dBASE IV returns you to the design screen when you use this option, little time is lost.

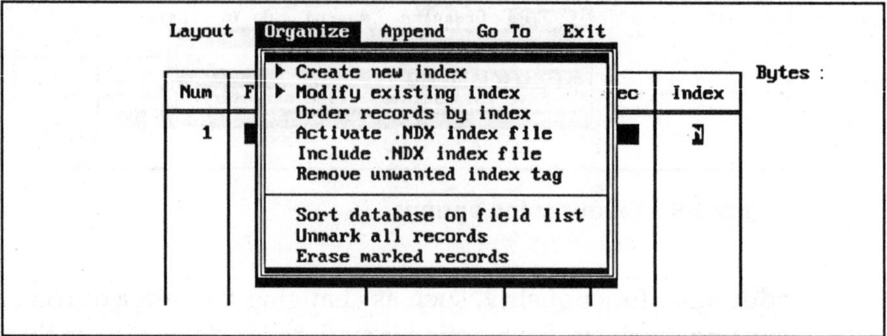

Figure 2-6 Organize menu

The Organize menu shown in Figure 2-6 provides a variety of options for changing the order of the records in your database. Most of these options will not be explored until Chapter 4 since it is necessary to enter records in the database to see the impact of changing the record order.

The Append menu shown in Figure 2-7 provides a number of ways to add records to the end of your database. It can be used for a new database or one that already contains records. The menu selections allow you to add records from the keyboard or an existing file.

In a lengthy design, the options shown in the Go To menu in Figure 2-8 speed up moving through the structure of the database. The number shown in the Num column is the one to use for the Field Number choice. The other selections move you to the top or bottom field in the design.

Field Names

Every field in a database must have a unique field name. You will use this name to reference the data within the field. Later as you design

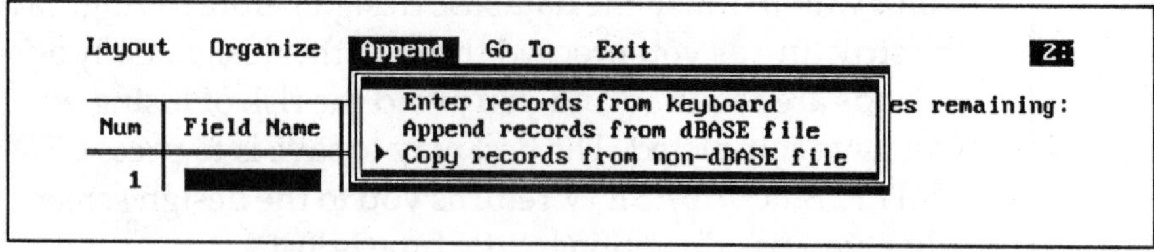

Figure 2-7 Append menu

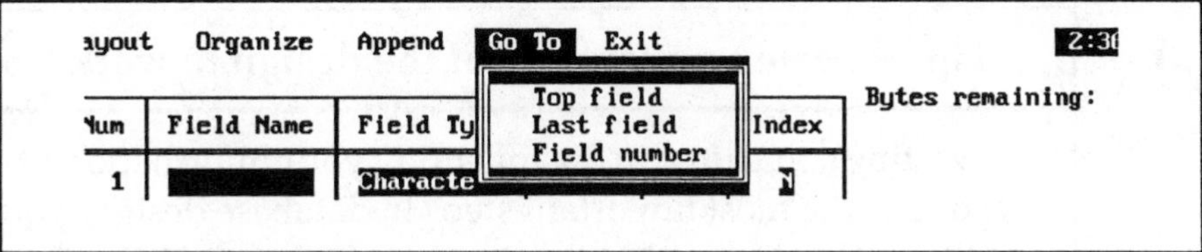

Figure 2-8 Go To menu

reports, screens or other dBASE IV objects, you will include a field by placing its field name on the design work surface for the object you are creating. Following a few simple rules ensures that dBASE IV accepts each of your names. It can also help to establish consistency from database to database.

dBASE IV Limitations

dBASE IV places a length limitation of 10 characters on any field name. The first character must be alphabetic but the other positions can contain numbers or the underscore symbol (_). Spaces cannot be used in the field name.

dBASE IV will accept your entry in upper or lower case. As you enter the field name, dBASE converts all characters to their uppercase equivalent character.

Setting Your Own Standards

You must follow the rules that dBASE IV has established for field names, but you may want to establish some standards of your own. Using standard names for similar fields allows you to use reports and labels with more than one database. As an example, a client file containing name and address information could use the same field names as a vendor file with the same type of information. A custom label format referencing fields called NAME, ADDRESS, CITY, STATE, and ZIP_CODE can be used with both databases. If you ever needed to bring data from both files together, the query designed for this purpose will show the origin of each field to enable you to distinguish the

❏ **Tip: Create a paper copy of the design to work from.**

Investing some time in documenting your information needs is one of the most important steps in database design. You will want to ensure that you have created a rough paper copy of the design before entering the design into dBASE IV. Although the paper copy adds a little time at the beginning of the process, the improved planning that it fosters will save you a significant amount of time at the conclusion of the design process.

NAME field in the CLIENT database from the NAME field from the VENDOR database.

Field Types and Attributes

You can customize your database design with more than your own field names. dBASE IV allows you to establish field types and length attributes for each field in the database. Selecting appropriate options will help ensure an efficient design. It will also put dBASE IV's features to work to help ensure that the data is edited as it is entered.

Field Types

Selecting the correct field type is an important step. dBASE IV provides six field types: Character, Numeric, Float, Date, Logical, and Memo. Your selection controls the type of data that you can enter into each of your database fields. dBASE IV can perform calculations with numeric, float, and date type fields directly. If you want a field to contain values other than dates that you can use in calculations, you must select Numeric or Float. The type Numeric supports the entry of fixed numbers. The Float field type is useful when you want to store floating-point numbers for speedy multiplication and division calculations. Choosing a data type other than Numeric or Float will not allow you to perform calculations directly. When you create custom edit screens (see Chapter 7), you will find that your choice of field type also affects the custom pictures and templates that you can use to further restrict field entries.

dBASE IV makes it easy for you to select the correct field type. Although Character is initially suggested for every field, you can change to any of the other field types by moving to the Type column and pressing the SPACEBAR to cycle through the various type options. You can also select a field type by typing the first letter of the field type, such as typing M for Memo or L for Logical.

Character Fields Character fields are alphanumeric fields that accept any ASCII character. dBASE IV places a length limit of 254 characters on each Character type field.

You will want to select a Character field type for data like name, address, city, and state. Anytime you want to include specialized edit characters in fields like social security numbers or telephone numbers you will want to use a Character field type. dBASE IV will allow you to enter dashes (-) or parentheses and can also be instructed to automatically enter these characters for you. Also, with fields containing numeric data like zip codes, you may want to use a Character field type to prevent initial zeros from being dropped. With Numeric and Float fields, if the first digit is a zero dBASE IV will remove zeros at the beginning of numbers. A zip code of 05789 would be incorrectly shown as 5789.

Number Fields Numeric fields can have a length of up to 20 digits including the decimal point. If you choose to define the number as having zero decimal places, you can use all 20 digits for whole numbers. The largest number that can be represented in either of the numeric

Tip: Group related information.

When you enter the fields in a new database design, group related field items together. Grouping related field entries makes it easy to spot missing fields and will also be helpful when designing advanced dBASE IV objects like queries and forms.

field types is 0.9E+308 (or 0.9 times 10 raised to the 308th power) and the smallest number is 0.1E-307 (or 0.1×10^{-307}).

Numeric Field Type Numeric type fields are the type used most frequently for numbers in dBASE IV and should be selected anytime that you want to use an exact number in your calculations. This field type is extremely efficient when many additions and subtractions are required, although it does not achieve the same performance with multiplication and division as the Float field type. These numeric fields can have from 10 to 20 digits depending on the current precision setting.

A Numeric field type must be used whenever you need exact numeric representations like age, number of dependents, loan amounts, salaries, or budget figures. The number that you enter for these fields will appear on all reports that show the field and will be used in all calculations involving the field. You will use this field type more than the numeric Float type option in most dBASE IV applications.

Float Field Type The Float field type is used when you wish to have dBASE IV treat an entry as a floating-point number. This field type is appropriate for the storage of very large or very small numbers, especially when an approximation is appropriate. The limit on the length of a Float field is 20. If you use decimal fractions, the decimal point will use one of the twenty positions in the field.

Float field types are very efficient for operations involving multiplication and division. When you are entering scientific research findings, measuring minor production deviations, or measuring long or short distances, the Float field type is the best solution. Although a Float type field can have 20 digits, it is only accurate for the first 15.9 digits. The remaining digits are approximations.

Date Fields dBASE IV has a special field type for the entry of dates. A field formatted as a date can be displayed in several ways using one of the dBASE IV date formats.

dBASE IV automatically sets date fields to a length of eight, which reflects how it stores the dates in the database. Internally, it stores your dates as YYYYMMDD with January 9, 1989 stored as 19890109.

dBASE IV allows eight positions for a date entry as the default setting. This displays January 9, 1989 as 01/09/89. You can change dBASE IV to display the full year for dates by changing the century setting. With SET CENTURY ON, January 9, 1989 appears as 01/09/1989. You will want to store all dates in a Date type field. This allows dBASE IV to handle setting range limits and other formatting options. Fields like date of hire, birth date, order date, and date received should all be defined as a Date type field.

Logical Fields Logical fields are specialized and allow for limited entry of a single character. You can use Y or N or T or F. These letters represent Yes, No, True, and False, respectively. dBASE IV displays Y and N entries as T and F for some screens, such as the Browse screen. dBASE accepts either upper- or lowercase entries for these entries.

You could define a Character field with a length of one for these same entries but would lose the automatic validity-checking made possible by the restricted entries that a Logical type field accepts. With a Character type field you could erroneously enter an "M" rather than an "N" but this data entry mistake is not possible with a Logical field type.

Logical fields are appropriate when you need to record whether or not an employee is a member of a specific health plan. It can also be used to record survey responses where users responded with Yes or No answers.

Memo Fields dBASE IV's memo fields allow you to store lengthy text entries in a separate file and recall them as needed. When you enter data in a field defined as a memo field, the data is not stored as part of the database. dBASE IV stores the data in a separate file. The file containing the memo data has the same name of the database file but a different filename extension. The database file has a filename extension of .DBF and the memo file has a filename extension of .DBT. The memo field in the database file stores a pointer to the location where the actual data is stored. As soon as you tell dBASE IV that the field type is Memo, dBASE automatically sets the width of the field to 10, since this is the length that it requires to store the pointer to the data that you will enter into the field later.

The length of the data that you enter into a Memo field is limited only by the amount of RAM memory on your system. This makes Memo fields ideal for storing an abstract, a contract, a legal brief, a description of employee skills, or any other document that you want associated with a particular record in a database.

dBASE IV opens the file containing the Memo field data when you open its associated database. Danger exists when you elect to copy a file with a Memo field to another disk or directory. If you do not copy both files to the new disk or directory, when you access the database, dBASE IV will not find the file containing the Memo data. dBASE IV will prompt you, asking if you want it to create a blank memo file. You should respond N since a Y response will ensure that you can never again use the original Memo field entries with the database.

Attributes

Selecting a field type is an essential part of creating a new field. For such fields as memo fields or logical fields, no further action is required. Other field types require that you enter a field width. In addition numeric field types require you to specify the number of decimal digits. These additional items are referred to as field attributes.

Width You can define the width for a Character field to be from 1 to 254 characters. Numeric and Float fields can have as many as 20 digits. The field widths for the other field types are automatically set by dBASE IV. Date fields are 8, logical fields are 1, and memo fields are 10 positions to allow for the pointer.

Decimal Places When you enter a length for a Numeric or Float field type, the highlight is positioned in the Dec column. dBASE IV wants you to accept the 0 decimal place indicator or change it to an appropriate number. You can define a number to have as many as 18 decimal digits if the number has a length of 20. You must ensure that the number of decimal digits defined is at least two less than the width of the field. These extra two positions allow for a decimal point and an optional minus sign.

You will need to define decimal digits when you plan to enter unit cost figures. An hourly wage rate, a unit cost figure and the cost of a taxi ride are all fields where you will want to use decimal digits.

Creating an Index for a Field

Indexing a database by a field allows you to display the records in the database by the order of the index values for the field, if you choose. Rather than arranging the records in order by the values in the index field, dBASE IV creates a table of index field values and the corresponding record numbers. dBASE IV then stores these entries in a special index file. dBASE IV can read the entries in the index file and retrieve the records indicated by the record numbers in the table. Indexes provide a fast way to look at data in a variety of sequences without the need for physically changing the order of the records in the database file.

Although you will explore indexes in more detail in Chapter 4, you will want to explore setting a field as an index while you are creating a data structure. This allows you to set up the index before you enter data.

Index Files

dBASE IV greatly expands the indexing capability of the package. dBASE III+ was limited to 7 indexes for a database. Now indexes are stored in a file that can hold multiple indexes. These .MDX files can store up to 47 indexes for a database, unlike the single index capability found in dBASE III+'s .NDX files. dBASE IV also supports multiple .MDX files, allowing as many as 10 .NDX and .MDX index files open for a database.

dBASE IV has other index enhancements. You can create an index by a field while you are designing the file structure simply by typing a Y in the Index column for the field. Since dBASE IV automatically assigns a Tag name to keep track of each index, it automatically assigns the field name as the tag name for the index. You can control the sequence in which the records display by deciding which of these Tags you want to use to control the record sequence. To establish record order by a specific Tag sequence, you select Order records by index from the Organize menu and specify the Tag name.

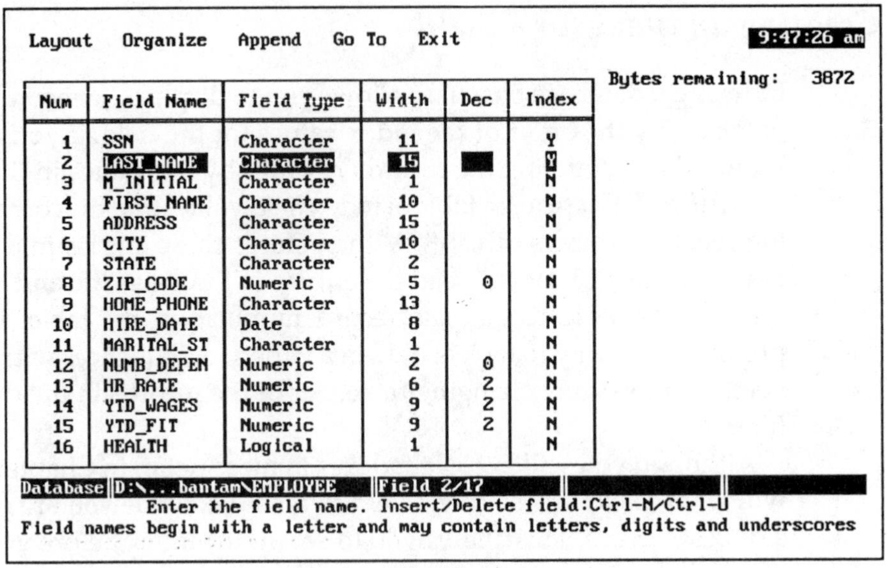

Layout Organize Append Go To Exit 9:47:26 am

Bytes remaining: 3872

Num	Field Name	Field Type	Width	Dec	Index
1	SSN	Character	11		Y
2	LAST_NAME	Character	15		Y
3	M_INITIAL	Character	1		N
4	FIRST_NAME	Character	10		N
5	ADDRESS	Character	15		N
6	CITY	Character	10		N
7	STATE	Character	2		N
8	ZIP_CODE	Numeric	5	0	N
9	HOME_PHONE	Character	13		N
10	HIRE_DATE	Date	8		N
11	MARITAL_ST	Character	1		N
12	NUMB_DEPEN	Numeric	2	0	N
13	HR_RATE	Numeric	6	2	N
14	YTD_WAGES	Numeric	9	2	N
15	YTD_FIT	Numeric	9	2	N
16	HEALTH	Logical	1		N

Database D:\...bantam\EMPLOYEE Field 2/17

Enter the field name. Insert/Delete field:Ctrl-N/Ctrl-U

Field names begin with a letter and may contain letters, digits and underscores

Figure 2-9 Creating two index fields during design

Index Tags

Every index must be assigned an Index Tag. Index Tags follow the same rules as field names in terms of length and allowable characters. In fact, when you create an index from the design screen, dBASE IV uses the field name as the Index Tag name. Figure 2-9 shows a structure where two fields will be used to create an index. The Tag Names for the two indexes will be SSN and LAST_NAME.

In Chapter 4, you will learn a method for creating an index after a file is designed. The same naming rules apply to the new index options, although more sophisticated indexes can be developed by using several fields. In these cases you will probably want to create a Tag Name representative of the multiple fields included in the index.

Using an Index

dBASE IV automatically maintains all indexes in an MDX file. As you add, delete, or modify the field values for which there are index tags, dBASE IV will update the index records in the .MDX file. After you add records to your database (see Chapter 3), you will learn how to select a master index to control the order in which database records display.

Removing Index Tags

Maintaining indexes that you do not need is a wasteful use of your system resources. Removing unneeded indexes from the .MDX file will improve the processing time as you add records, create reports, and browse through the records in your database.

To remove Index Tags from an .MDX file:

1. Press ALT-O to select the Organize menu.
2. Type an **R** to select Remove unwanted index tag.
3. Highlight the Index Tag that you want to remove and press ENTER.
4. Repeat the procedure to remove additional Index Tags.

Finalizing the Design

There are almost too many options for finalizing the design. CTRL-END is one option. Another is to invoke the Exit option in the menu bar by pressing ALT-E and typing an **S** to select Save changes and exit. Pressing ENTER with the cursor in the empty field name column after the last field or pressing Ctrl-W also works. If the design has never been saved, dBASE IV prompts you for a filename. Once you press ENTER, dBASE IV saves the file to disk. dBASE appends .DBF to the name that you enter, since all dBASE IV database files have this filename extension.

dBASE IV prompts to see if you want to add records immediately. Typing a **Y** indicates that you do and will cause dBASE to display the data entry screen in either Browse or Edit screen, as discussed in the next chapter.

Typing an **N** indicates that you do not want to add records at the present time and causes dBASE to return you to the Control Center. You can use this later approach when you want to save the design when it is not completed. To continue working with the structure you can press ENTER with the database name highlighted to cause dBASE IV to display the menu shown in Figure 2-10. If you select Modify structure/order, you will be returned to the design work surface to continue your design task with the knowledge that the design on the screen is on disk in the event of a power failure. A timesaving approach is to use

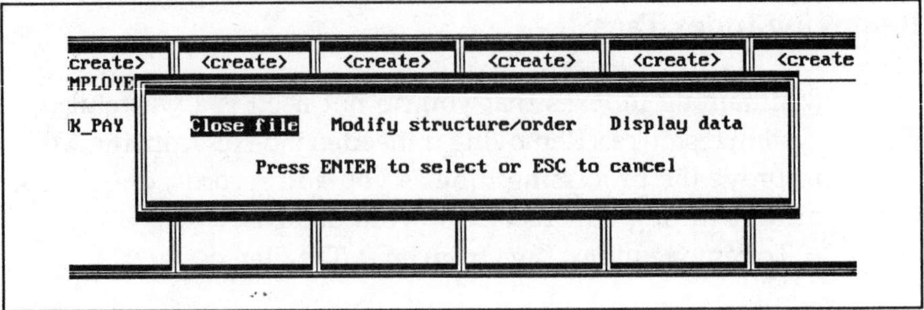

Figure 2-10 Menu presented when an open database is selected from the Control Center

the Layout menu command Save this database file structure. This command returns you to the design screen immediately after saving the structure to allow you to continue with additions and changes.

Appending Records

dBASE IV allows you to add records from the keyboard or other files. Adding records from the keyboard is covered in Chapter 3. Adding records from another dBASE file or another file type such as 1-2-3 is covered in this chapter. This feature is particularly advantageous if you need to create a file that contains a subset of the fields in an existing file. When you are appending information from another dBASE file you will want to use the same field names as are in the existing dBASE file for the fields that you wish to copy. When you append records from a non-dBASE file, you must check that the order of the data matches the field order in the database to which you are appending records. You will also want to check to ensure that the field widths in your database are adequate to hold the data that you will be adding. If the fields are not wide enough, entries will be truncated.

Appending Data from Another dBASE File

You can append data from an existing dBASE file if the field names in the two files are the same. You will also want to look at the field widths, since a longer field width in the file you are appending from will result

Layout Organize Append Go To Exit 9:55:04 am

Bytes remaining: 3963

Num	Field Name	Field Type	Width	Dec	Index
1	STUDENT_ID	Character	6		Y
2	LAST_NAME	Character	15		N
3	MIDDLE_INT	Character	1		N
4	FIRST_NAME	Character	10		N
5	GPA	Numeric	5	3	N
6	CREDITS	Numeric	3	0	N

Figure 2-11 Existing dBASE IV file

in the truncation of character data and the conversion of larger numeric data to asterisks in the new file. After entering the field definition on the design work surface for the new file, you must save the structure before attempting to append records. You can save the design by pressing ALT-L and typing an **S** for Save this database file structure. Since this method of saving returns you to the design screen, you can press ALT-A to activate the Append pull-down menu. Type an **A** to select Append records from dBASE file. Given an existing file that looks like Figure 2-11 and a new file design that looks like Figure 2-12, the Append operation adds the data shown in Figure 2-13 to the new file.

Adding Records from Another File Type

dBASE IV supports the direct addition of data from many file types into a dBASE IV file. If you select Copy records from non-dBASE IV file from the Append menu, dBASE is able to add data from any of the file types shown in Figure 2-14.

Layout Organize Append Go To Exit 10:06:38 am

Bytes remaining: 3971

Num	Field Name	Field Type	Width	Dec	Index
1	STUDENT_ID	Character	6		Y
2	LAST_NAME	Character	15		N
3	CREDITS	Numeric	3	0	N
4	GPA	Numeric	5	3	N

Figure 2-12 New dBASE IV design

Records Fields Go To Exit 10:07:14 am

STUDENT_ID	LAST_NAME	CREDITS	GPA
012390	Larson	115	3.998
098732	Patterson	110	3.564
564321	Myers	93	2.987
786543	Calvert	21	1.995
897654	York	35	3.992

Figure 2-13 New dBASE IV file after Append

❑

Tip: Database settings can affect the result of an Append operation.

If the records in the database file that you are appending from are marked for deletion, their presence in the new file is affected by the deleted records setting. If SET DELETED is OFF, these records are appended to the new file and are not marked for deletion in the new database. If SET DELETED is ON, records marked for deletion are not appended.

If SET AUTOSAVE is OFF, the file directory that you are appending to is not fully updated until the file is closed. With SET AUTOSAVE as ON, the file directory is updated after each record is appended.

❑

Tip: An index file must be open to be updated by Append.

If you have defined indexes for the file that you are appending to, you will want to be sure that they are open if you want them updated by Append. MDX files are automatically opened when you select Use from the menu. NDX files must be specifically opened if you want them updated.

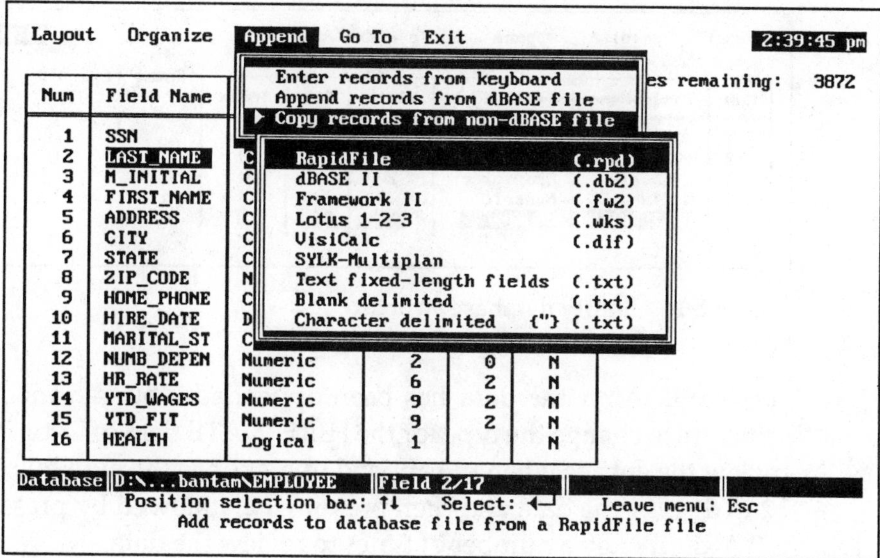

Figure 2-14 Selecting a file type for Append

Given the Lotus 1-2-3 Release 1A work sheet shown in Figure 2-15, you can convert the data to dBASE IV easily. Although dBASE IV does not match the 1-2-3 column headings with the database field names, it is important that you keep them. If the 1-2-3 work sheet does not have column headings, the first record is lost.

Since dBASE IV does not match on field types, the sequence of the fields in the Lotus 1-2-3 file must exactly match the dBASE IV file to which you are appending. After appending to the empty database structure shown in Figure 2-16, the records look like the ones in Figure 2-17. The dates in both the 1-2-3 file and the initial dBASE IV design were shown as characters. Attempts to use a 1-2-3 date entry were not

E4: [W11] 325.99 READY

	A	B	C	D	E	F
1	PO_NUMB	PURCH_DATE	ITEM	UNITS	UNIT_PRICE	
2	897653	04/15/89	Chair	30	125.95	
3	786543	05/22/89	Desk	10	567.75	
4	876540	06/30/89	Credenza	100	325.99	

Figure 2-15 Lotus 1-2-3 work sheet data

Layout Organize Append Go To Exit 10:10:57 am

Bytes remaining: 3955

Num	Field Name	Field Type	Width	Dec	Index
1	PO_NUMBER	Character	6		Y
2	PURCH_DATE	Character	8		N
3	ITEM	Character	20		N
4	UNITS	Numeric	4	0	N
5	UNIT_PRICE	Numeric	7	2	N

Figure 2-16 Empty database structure

successful. After the data has been appended, you can modify the structure to change the type for the HIRE_DATE field to Date. You can review the entries when the append operation is through by pressing F2 to display the data and then pressing F2, followed by pressing the UP ARROW key a number of times to review the data.

Since dBASE IV does not directly support Lotus 1-2-3 Release 2 or 2.01 with Append, another approach may be preferable. Rather than using the 1-2-3 Translate program to create Release 1A versions of Release 2 spreadsheets, you can use this same program to convert Release 2 models directly into a dBASE III+ file. With this method, 1-2-3 date entries are converted properly. You can then append these records to your dBASE IV file.

Editing the File Description

When you highlight a filename in one of the Control Center panels, the file description for the file displays in the line beneath the filename. This information can assist you in determining whether or not you have

Records Fields Go To Exit 10:21:35 am

PO_NUMBER	PURCH_DATE	ITEM	UNITS	UNIT_PRICE
397653	04/15/89	Chair	30	125.95
786543	05/22/89	Desk	10	567.75
876540	06/30/89	Credenza	100	325.99

Figure 2-17 Database after appending Lotus 1-2-3 data

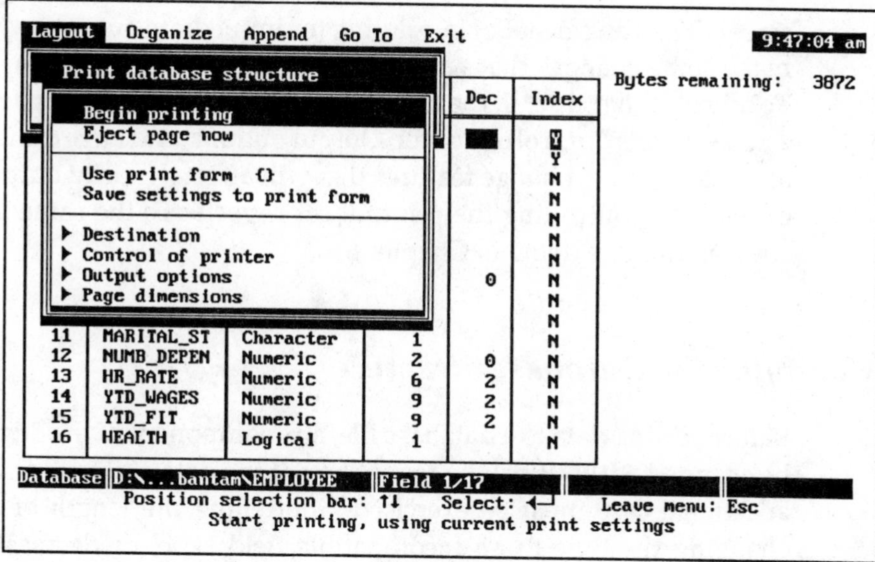

Figure 2-18 Print menu

the correct file. Despite the benefit of viewing file descriptions, dBASE IV does not automatically ask you to supply a file description when you create a new file. Entering or modifying a description will require an action on your part. To add or modify a file description from the database design screen, first press ALT-L to invoke the Layout menu. The next step is typing an E and entering the description before finalizing with CTRL-END. To add or modify a file description from the Control Center, press ALT-C to invoke the Catalog menu. The next step is typing a **C** for Change description of highlighted file. Finally, type the file description and press ENTER.

If a description already exists, the procedure is still the same. The only difference is that you must edit the description that currently exists or remove it by pressing HOME and CTRL-Y.

Printing the Database Structure

You can print a copy of the database structure with a selection from the layout menu at the top of the screen. First, you need to press ALT-L and type a **P**. The Print menu shown in Figure 2-18 will appear on the screen. You can select Begin printing for immediate output or you can make some changes that will affect the output before printing starts. To advance the paper to the top of the next form, select Eject page now. The selections Control of printer, Output options, and Page dimensions also allow you to change features that will affect the print output. The options for controlling the printout for reports are the same and are covered in more detail in Chapter 6.

Modifying the Database Structure

Before adding data to a database file, any component of the design can be changed without risking loss of any of the data. After adding data, additional care must be exercised. Shortening the length of a field, changing the type to an incompatible field type, or decreasing the number of decimal digits, and combining field name changes with positional changes are all alterations that can cause you to lose data once you have entered data in your database. When you want to make several modifications to your database, make one modification at a time and view the data in the database. If the changes are what you want, back up the database to another filename and make the next modification. If the changes are not what you want, copy the backup to the original filename so you can use the database as it existed before the changes.

Creating a backup copy of your data with a different name is a good precaution to beginning the design revision, since the loss of data can require significant reentry time. If your database is named EMPLOY, you can create a copy called BKEMPLOY with these actions:

1. Press ALT-T then type a **D** to select Dos utilities.
2. Move the highlight to the filename EMPLOY.DBF in the current directory.
3. Press ALT-O and type a **C** to select Copy.
4. Type an **S** to select Single copy. Press ENTER to accept the current drive and directory or type new entries and press ENTER.
5. Type **BKEMPLOY.DBF** and press CTRL-END to complete the copy.
6. Press ALT-E and ENTER to return to the Control Center.

If you are backing up a database that contains a memo field, you must perform steps 2 through 5 again, replacing .DBT with .DBF.

Changing Field Names

You can change the names that you originally assigned to your database fields. You will want to limit your activities to this one type of change and save the database. If additional types of changes are required, you can start the modification process again and make the remaining changes.

To change a field name, all you need to do is move to the line and column containing the field name that you wish to change and make the editing changes.

Changing Field Types

When data is entered into a database, dBASE IV checks for compatibility with the field type. This check ensures that any data in the file is compatible with your definitions. If you attempt to change the field type, the new field type may be incompatible with your data. dBASE IV does not warn you about this possibility. It makes the change that you requested but may destroy your data in the process. For

❑

Tip: Do not combine field name changes with other structure changes.

Save the database structure after making field name changes. Even if you have other modifications to make, the field name changes should not be combined with other actions. dBASE IV creates a new database when you make field name changes and copies the data from the old structure. It then deletes the old structure and renames the new structure. When you change field names, dBASE IV relies on the position of each of the fields to determine where to copy the data. Making position changes at the same time as field name changes does not allow dBASE IV to copy the data to the correct fields.

❑ **Tip: Create a backup copy before modifying field types.**

Accidentally changing a field to an incompatible field type results in lost data. A change from a Memo type field to a Character field results in destruction of all the Memo field data. If you make a copy of your database file before making these changes, you can always use the copy if the original file is destroyed. If the database contains a Memo field remember to copy both the .DBF and .DBT file when creating your backup copy.

example, if you change a character field to a Numeric field, your character data is lost forever unless you have a backup copy of the database file that you can use. On the other hand, changing a Numeric field to a Character field will not result in the destruction of any data.

Table 2-2 presents a summary of the effects of the field type changes that are supported for each of the data types. You will want to review this carefully before making any changes to a field type in your database.

Changing Field Attributes

After adding data to the file you must also evaluate attribute changes before making them. You can always extend the width of a field. Shortening it will cause a problem if you have fields that utilize the full field width. Character field entries are truncated and numeric field entries are replaced by asterisks with the additional or converted characters lost forever, even if you subsequently expand the width again.

Increasing the number of decimal digits without a corresponding increase in the field width can also cause data loss. You will want to remember that the decimal point and minus sign count when you compute the required width for a field.

Table 2-2 Effects of Field Type Modifications

Field Type	*Proposed Change*	*Effect*
Character	Numeric or Float	Alpha data is destroyed; Numeric digits to first non-numeric is converted.
Character	Date	Data in the format MM/DD/YY is converted.
Character	Logical	Data is converted to T if first character is a T or a Y, otherwise, converted to an F.
Character	Memo	Data is lost.
Numeric/Float	Character	Converted.
Numeric/Float	Float/Numeric	Converted.
Numeric/Float	Any other change	Data is lost.
Date	Character	Converted.
	Any other change	Data is lost.
Logical	Character	No effect on existing data; entries in fields will no longer be restricted to T, F, Y, or N.
	Any other change	Data is destroyed.
Memo	Any other field type	Data in the memo fields is destroyed.

GETTING STARTED

➤ To apply some of the concepts introduced in this chapter, you can create the EMPLOYEE and WK_PAY database introduced earlier in the chapter. Follow these steps to create the EMPLOYEE file:

1. Use the arrow keys to highlight <create> in the Data panel of the Control Center and press ENTER.
2. Type **SSN** and press ENTER. Press ENTER to accept Character for the type. Type **11** for the width and press ENTER. Type a Y to create an index for this field (the Tag name will be SSN).

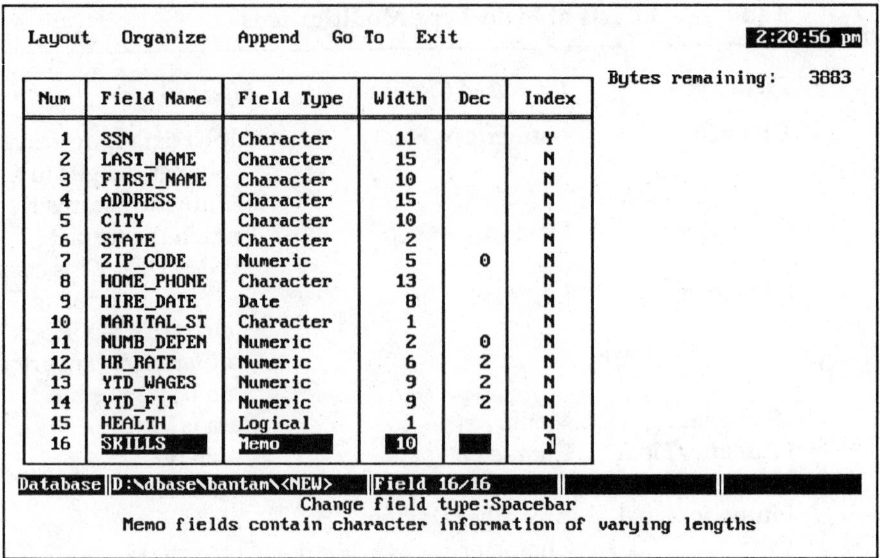

Layout Organize Append Go To Exit 2:20:56 pm

Bytes remaining: 3883

Num	Field Name	Field Type	Width	Dec	Index
1	SSN	Character	11		Y
2	LAST_NAME	Character	15		N
3	FIRST_NAME	Character	10		N
4	ADDRESS	Character	15		N
5	CITY	Character	10		N
6	STATE	Character	2		N
7	ZIP_CODE	Numeric	5	0	N
8	HOME_PHONE	Character	13		N
9	HIRE_DATE	Date	8		N
10	MARITAL_ST	Character	1		N
11	NUMB_DEPEN	Numeric	2	0	N
12	HR_RATE	Numeric	6	2	N
13	YTD_WAGES	Numeric	9	2	N
14	YTD_FIT	Numeric	9	2	N
15	HEALTH	Logical	1		N
16	SKILLS	Memo	10		N

Database D:\dbase\bantam\<NEW> Field 16/16

Change field type:Spacebar

Memo fields contain character information of varying lengths

Figure 2-19 The completed file structure for the EMPLOYEE file

3. Complete the entries for the remaining fields as shown in Figure 2-19.
4. Review the fields to ensure correctness and determine if any fields are missing.

To insert the middle name field that you left out of the database:

1. Move the highlight to the FIRST_NAME field.
2. Press CTRL-N to insert a field.
3. Type **M_INITIAL** and press ENTER. Press ENTER to accept the Character type field. Type a **1** and press ENTER. Press ENTER to finalize the field entry.
4. Press CTRL-END to save the database design. Type **EMPLOYEE** and press ENTER. Respond by typing an **N** when dBASE IV prompts about adding records.

To create the payroll database for weekly payroll transactions:

1. Highlight <create> in the Data panel of the Control Center and press ENTER. dBASE IV will close the EMPLOYEE file and place you on the design work surface for the new file.

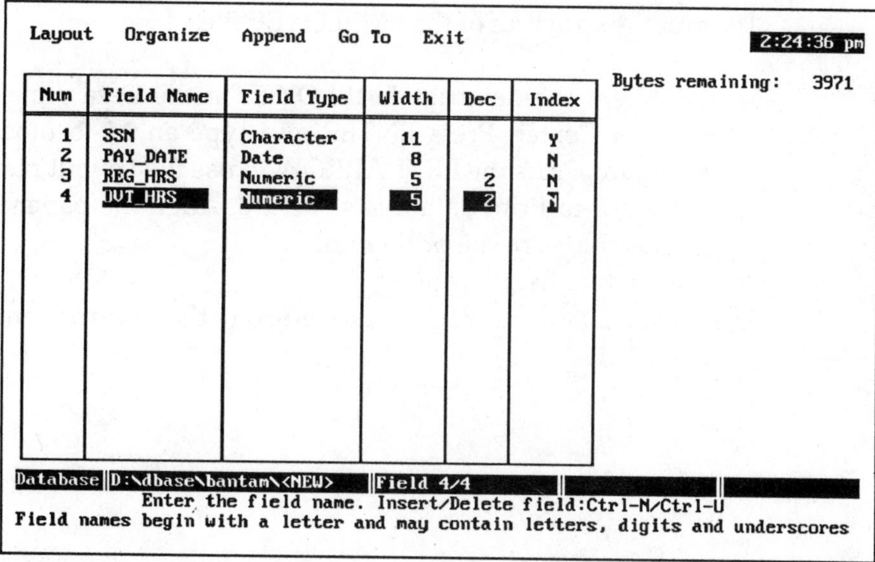

Figure 2-20 The completed file structure for WK_PAY

2. Type **SSN** and press ENTER. Press ENTER to accept the field type. Type **11** and press ENTER. Type a **Y** to index by this field.
3. Complete the entries for the remaining fields using the information in Figure 2-20.
4. Press CTRL-END to save the file design. Type **WEEK_PAY** for the filename and press ENTER. Type an **N** to return to the Control Center.

To modify a field definition after the design is saved to disk:

1. Highlight the filename WEEK_PAY in the Data panel of the Control Center. Press ENTER.
2. Type an **M** to select Modify structure/order to have dBASE IV place you on the design work surface for the file. Press ESC.
3. Move to the field you wish to change. To change the field name for OVT_HRS, move to this field and type **OVTME_HRS**. Press CTRL-END to resave the design. Press ENTER to confirm the filename and type an **N**. A change to a field name should not be combined with other types of file structure changes.

To print the structure of the EMPLOYEE file:

1. Highlight the database EMPLOYEE in the Data panel of the Control Center. Press ENTER and type an **M** to modify the structure. Press the LEFT ARROW to use the Layout menu.
2. Type a **P** to Print database structure. Align the paper in your printer and turn the printer on.
3. Type a **B** to Begin printing.
4. Press ALT-E and type an **A** to return to the Control Center.

CHAPTER 3

Data Entry and Editing

Once you build a database structure you are ready to enter data into the database. In the last chapter you looked at adding records to your completed file from another dBASE IV file or a different file format. Normally you will not be fortunate enough to have the data in machine readable format and will have to enter the data directly from the keyboard.

dBASE IV allows you to make your entries from an Edit screen that shows only the fields in the current record or a Browse screen that displays fields from a number of records. The techniques that you master for adding records in either of these formats can be applied to editing field entries in existing records.

In addition to the basic options for entering and editing records, this chapter also covers some of the changes that you can make to fields to make your data entry job easier. You will learn how to use the search feature as a timesaving option to locate a specific record in the database that you want to edit.

Appending Records

dBASE IV automatically presents an Edit screen for the entry of data after you create a database. You can use this screen to enter new records or modify existing data. This screen appears after you save the new database structure and respond with a **Y** when dBASE IV prompts

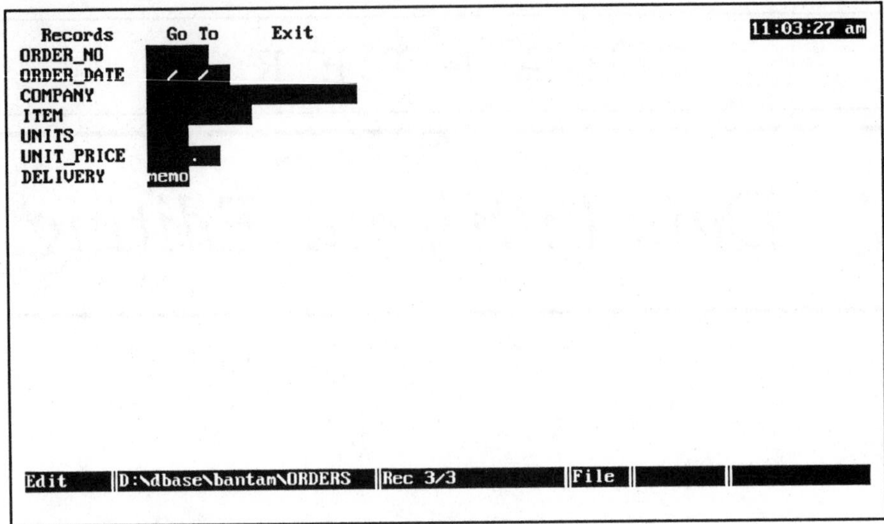

Figure 3-1 Typical Edit screen format

about adding records. Figure 3-1 provides an example of a typical Edit screen format.

dBASE IV supports a second format for the entry of data called a Browse screen. Figure 3-2 presents a Browse format for the same file shown in Figure 3-1. You can toggle between the two formats by pressing the F2 key, as long as your file contains database records. With either format, dBASE IV saves your changes whenever it has enough information to fill a buffer that it can write to the disk. If you want dBASE IV to save after each record you can SET AUTOSAVE ON. With AUTOSAVE ON, every time you switch to a new record, switch between Browse and Edit mode, or press ALT-E followed by selecting Exit to return to the Control Center, dBASE IV will save your changes.

dBASE IV always remembers the mode that you were in the last time that you worked with database records and presents data in this format even if you are looking at a different database or working in a new dBASE IV session. The only exception is that a newly created database always displays in the Edit format. In fact, you cannot use the Browse mode for a new database until you have entered at least one character in a field of the database or appended a blank record.

Despite the appearance difference in the Edit and Browse screens, both formats present the same data. These formats also share a common

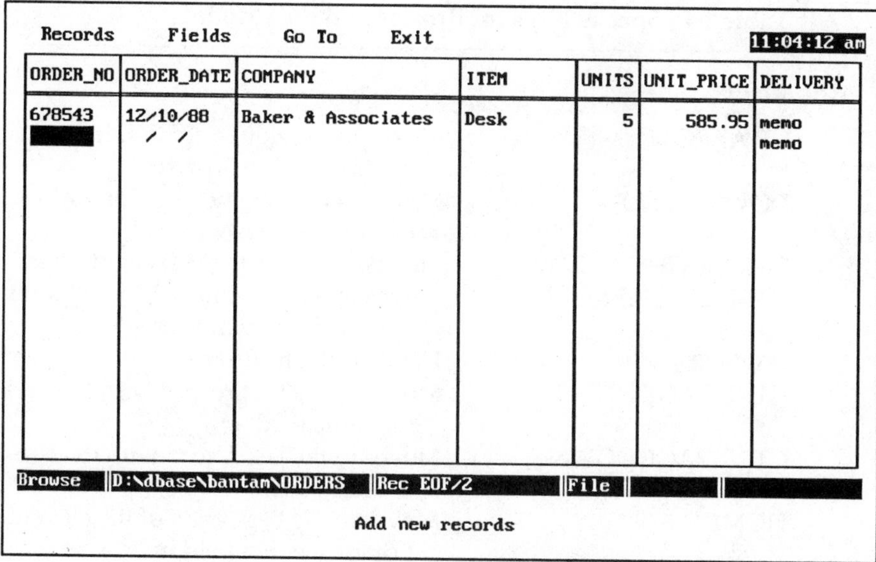

Figure 3-2 Browse format for the same database as Figure 3-1

set of keystrokes that can be used for completing tasks in either environment. These keystrokes are summarized in Table 3-1.

If you save a database without entering records, the database will still be active, as evidenced by its location above the line in the Data panel. You can move to the database name in the Data panel and press F2 to activate the Edit screen for entering records. If the database already has a custom report, form, or labels, you can move to the filename in the respective panels and press F2 to invoke the same display. As long as SET INSTRUCT is ON, you can also highlight the database name in the Data panel and press ENTER to invoke the menu shown in Figure 3-3. By typing a **D** or highlighting Display data and pressing ENTER you will be in the same screen. The Use file option allows you to open a database file without taking any other action and the Modify structure/order selection takes you to the database design screen that you worked with in Chapter 2.

Using the Edit Screen

dBASE IV automatically creates an Edit form for any database by listing each of the field names down the left side of the screen. The Edit format is the format commonly used for the entry of new records since it

Table 3-1 Special Keys for Browse and Edit Mode

Key	*Meaning*
UP ARROW	Moves to previous field in Edit or the previous record in Browse.
DOWN ARROW	Moves to the next field in Edit or the next record in Browse.
CTRL-RIGHT ARROW	Moves to the next word (beginning).
CTRL-LEFT ARROW	Moves to the previous word (beginning).
PAGE UP	Displays the previous screen.
PAGE DOWN	Displays the next screen.
CTRL-PAGE UP	Moves to the first record with the cursor on the same field.
CTRL-PAGE DOWN	Moves to the last record with the cursor on the same field.
HOME	Moves to the beginning of the current field in Edit or the first field in Browse.
END	Moves to the end of the field in Edit or the last field in Browse.
CTRL-HOME	Opens a Memo field for entry or edit.
CTRL-END	Closes a Memo field if one is open. Saves changes to Browse or Edit screens.
TAB	Moves to the next field.
SHIFT-TAB	Moves to the previous field.
ENTER	Moves to the next field.
ESC	Cancels changes and does not save.
CTRL-T	Deletes from the cursor to the end of the current word.
CTRL-Y	Deletes from the cursor to the end of the field.
F2	Switches to the opposite display format.
F3	Moves to the next field. If the field is a Memo field, dBASE opens the field.
F4	Moves to the previous field. If the field is a Memo field, dBASE opens it.
F6	Used to extend the selection of text in Memo fields.
F7	Used to move selected Memo field text.
F8	Used to copy selected Memo field data.
F9	Enlarges and shrinks Memo fields to full screen display.
F10	Activates the menu at the top of the Edit, Browse, and Memo field screens.

(continued)

Table 3-1 Special Keys for Browse and Edit Mode *(continued)*

Key	*Meaning*
SHIFT-F3	Finds the previous occurrence of the current Search string setting.
SHIFT-F4	Finds the next occurrence of the current Search string setting.
SHIFT-F6	Requests the Search and Replace operation in a Memo field.
SHIFT-F7	Changes the size of a column in Browse mode.
SHIFT-F8	Copies data from the previous record using the corresponding field for the entry.

restricts the display to a single record and can display more fields from a record at one time than the Browse format.

If there are more fields than will fit on one Edit screen, dBASE IV creates additional screens as needed. The size of the highlighted area following each field is dictated by the width that you select for the field in the design screen. Later, in Chapter 7, you will learn how to create your own custom screen designs.

To enter a record using this Edit form, you type the entries for each field beginning with the top field. If a field entry completely fills the field, dBASE IV automatically positions the cursor in the following field as long as the default value for SET CONFIRM is maintained as OFF. If the entry does not fill the field, pressing ENTER causes dBASE IV to move to the next field. As shown in Table 3-1, you can also use

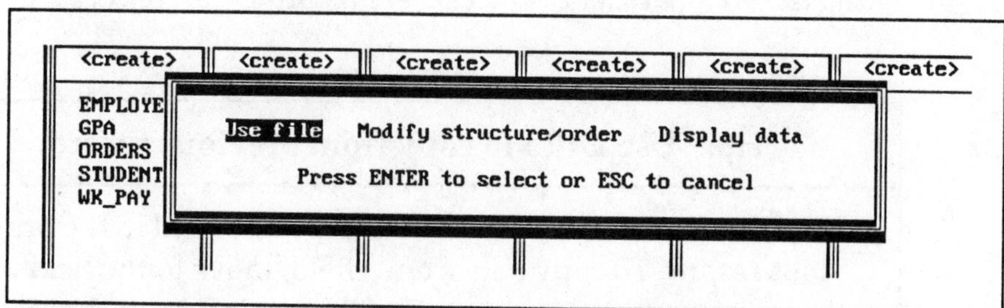

Figure 3-3 Instruct menu for a file in the Data panel

❑ **Tip: Switching between design and entry quickly.**

Hopefully you will not need to change the design structure frequently, but you may have occasion to make frequent changes to the order of records. To facilitate changing between design and edit, you will want to enter Edit or Browse mode by pressing F2 from the database design screen. This allows you to switch back to design with SHIFT-F2 at any time and will also allow you to return to Edit or Browse by pressing F2.

the TAB and SHIFT-TAB keys to move from field to field. Finalizing the entry of the last field in a record causes dBASE IV to automatically display a new record entry form or line.

Entry Restrictions The field types that you established during the design process will control your entries in each field of a record. Data that does not match the field type selected will be rejected and dBASE IV will beep to notify you of the entry problem as long as SET BELL option has not been changed to OFF. Data beyond the width chosen will not be stored within the field. Depending on your setting for Confirm, this data may be entered in the next field if it is the correct data type. You can consult Chapter 8 for instructions on changing the Confirm setting.

If you attempt to enter numeric data in a Character field, dBASE IV will store the numeric digits as characters and will not be able to use the numbers in calculations. Attempting to enter character data in a Numeric or Float field will cause dBASE IV to reject your entry.

❑ **Tip: Use Ditto to copy from previous record.**

The Ditto option copies data from the same field in the previous record. To copy data from a field, move to the field in the new record that you want to fill with data from the same field in the previous record and press SHIFT-F8.

Layout Organize Append Go To Exit 1:53:54 am

Bytes remaining: 3935

Num	Field Name	Field Type	Width	Dec	Index
1	ORDER_NO	Character	6		Y
2	ORDER_DATE	Date	8		N
3	COMPANY	Character	20		N
4	ITEM	Character	10		N
5	UNITS	Numeric	4	0	N
6	UNIT_PRICE	Numeric	7	2	N
7	DELIVERY	Memo	10		N

Figure 3-4 Database design

Likewise, entering anything other than T, F, Y, or N for a Logical field will cause dBASE IV to reject the entry. Date fields are also restricted to what dBASE IV considers to be valid date entries and must be in the format MM/DD/YY with the default date format setting. If you change the date default format setting, you must enter the date information in the same format that dBASE IV displays the date.

Entering a Sample Record After creating the database design in Figure 3-4, you can enter records immediately by responding with a Y to the prompt at the bottom of the screen. To enter the first record shown in Figure 3-5, a number of steps are required:

1. Type **453216** for the ORDER_NO. Note that you do not need to press ENTER since the data fills the field.
2. Type **120988** for the ORDER_DATE. The /'s are generated by dBASE IV and do not need to be entered. Again, the field is filled making ENTER unnecessary.

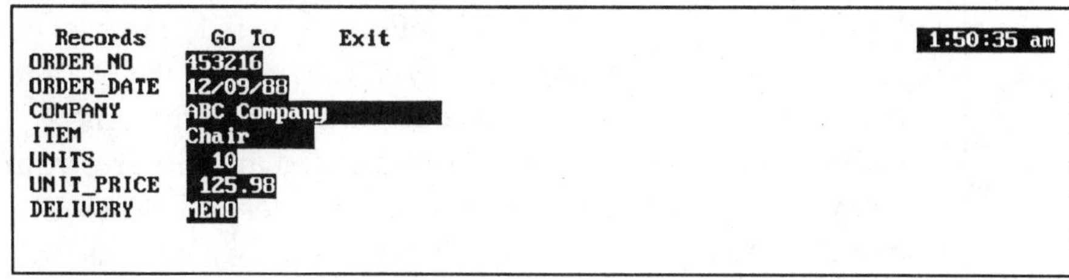

Records Go To Exit 1:50:35 am
ORDER_NO 453216
ORDER_DATE 12/09/88
COMPANY ABC Company
ITEM Chair
UNITS 10
UNIT_PRICE 125.98
DELIVERY MEMO

Figure 3-5 Entering the first record

3. Type **ABC Company**. Press ENTER to finalize the field and move to the next field since the data does not fill the field width.
4. Type **Chair** and press ENTER.
5. Type **10** and press ENTER.
6. Type **125.98** and press ENTER. The cursor is on the Memo field. To bypass entry for this field, press ENTER. Note that a new form is displayed. dBASE IV saved the first record. Use Page Up to display the completed record again.

Although the record entries are finalized, you can continue to modify the data as often as you wish. If you decide to change an existing entry and move back to an earlier record with PgUp when you make your change, the new entries will replace the old. When you are finished adding records, press CTRL-END or press ALT-E and type an **E** to select Exit to end data entry. Either of these actions will ensure that all of your data is saved to disk.

Using the Browse Screen

The Browse screen provides another way to view the information in your database. The Browse format displays data in a tabular arrangement with each record across a single line of the screen. The UP and DOWN ARROW keys will move you from record to record. If you prefer to move more quickly, the options in the Go To menu discussed later in this chapter will be of assistance.

The TAB key moves the cursor one field to the right. SHIFT-TAB moves to the previous field, one to the left of the current field. The END

❑ **Tip: Use Carry to enter many similar records.**

If you have records with many of the same field entries, you can change the settings for Carry. If Carry is set to ON, a new record will appear as the exact duplicate of a previous record. You can edit the record as needed and finalize your entry. When a completely new record is needed, you will need to replace every field. When you create a new record, it will be an exact duplicate of this new record.

Records	Fields	Go To	Exit			1:51:09 am
ORDER_NO	ORDER_DATE	COMPANY	ITEM	UNITS	UNIT_PRICE	DELIVERY
453216	12/09/88	ABC Company	Chair	10	125.98	MEMO

Figure 3-6 Browse display for the first record

key has a different effect than in Edit mode since it moves you to the last field. The HOME key moves the cursor to the first field.

Switching to Browse screen after entering the first database record in Figure 3-5 produces the display shown in Figure 3-6. If Control Center is on the screen, you can highlight the database name and press F2 to display the Edit screen again. To switch to Browse screen, press F2 a second time. If you switch display modes without saving the data first, the switching process itself will cause dBASE IV to save the current record even if the record is incomplete. You can continue making changes and save again by moving to the next record or pressing CTRL-END when you are through.

To enter a record in the Browse format requires the same basic steps as Edit. First, use the DOWN ARROW key to move to the row beneath the existing record and respond by typing a **Y** when dBASE IV asks if you want to add a record. Next, follow these steps to add the second record:

1. Type **678543** for the ORDER_NO. Note that you do not need to press ENTER, since the data fills the field.
2. Type **121088** for the ORDER_DATE. The /'s are generated by dBASE IV and do not need to be entered. Again, the field is filled, making ENTER unnecessary.
3. Type **Baker & Associates**. Press ENTER to finalize the field and move to the next field since the data does not fill the field width.
4. Type **Desk** and press ENTER.
5. Type **5** and press ENTER.
6. Type **585.95** and press ENTER. dBASE IV positions the cursor on the Memo field. Press ENTER to bypass this field. Note that the cursor moves down to the next row for the addition of a new record, producing the display shown in Figure 3-7. Use the UP ARROW key to move to the existing record and use the TAB and

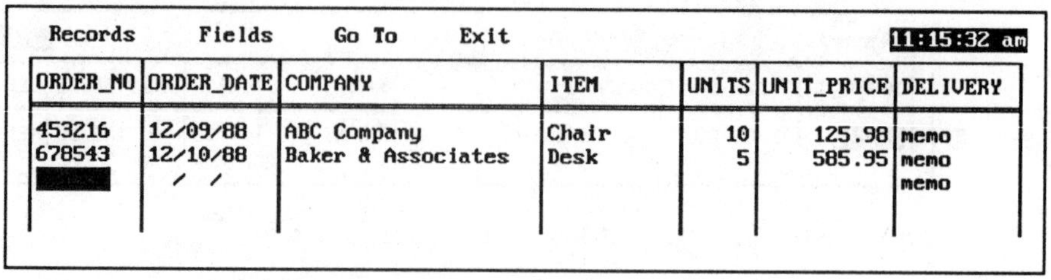

Records Fields Go To Exit 11:15:32 am

ORDER_NO	ORDER_DATE	COMPANY	ITEM	UNITS	UNIT_PRICE	DELIVERY
453216	12/09/88	ABC Company	Chair	10	125.98	memo
678543	12/10/88	Baker & Associates	Desk	5	585.95	memo
	/ /					memo

Figure 3-7 Ready for the addition of the next record

SHIFT-TAB key to move from field to field. Press CTRL-END to finalize the entry and return to the Control Center.

Using Memo Fields

The procedure for entering Memo field data is different than for any of the other field types. Although you can display memo data from the Browse and Edit screen with a few extra keystrokes, this data is not stored as part of the database file. A special file with the same name as the database file but a different filename extension is used to store all the Memo field data for a database.

The only entry that appears on the Edit or Browse screens is the word memo or MEMO. The lowercase entry is displayed for Memo fields that do not contain an entry. The word memo is capitalized as soon as an entry is added to the field.

The data entered in a Memo field is displayed within dBASE IV but is actually stored in a separate file. The file has the same name as the dBASE IV file but uses a .DBT filename extension.

❑ **Tip: Check the location of the cursor carefully when you switch between Edit and Browse mode.**

Although the same record is always active, dBASE IV sometimes moves the cursor to a different field. Typing without looking at the cursor location may not produce the results that you expect.

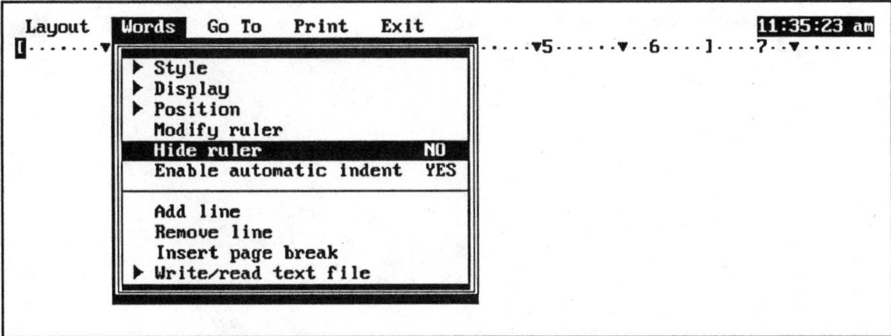

Figure 3-8 Memo field menu

The menu shown in Figure 3-8 provides a variety of features to assist you with Memo fields. Like other dBASE IV menus you can activate this menu with F10 once the Edit screen for the Memo field displays, or you can use the ALT key in combination with a letter key as with the ALT-W combination used to pull down the Words menu shown in the example. You can use the menu options to affect your entries, position you within the Memo field, save the portion of the field that you have entered, or print the Memo field entry.

Making the Entry

To make an entry in a Memo field, you can move the cursor to the Memo field and press CTRL-HOME or F9. To add entries for the Memo fields in the Orders file, you might prefer to use the Browse screen since you can make the entry in one record, finalize it, and use the DOWN ARROW key to move immediately to the Memo field in the next record.

dBASE IV displays its word-wrap edit mode screen as shown in Figure 3-9. This screen supports text entries in a fashion similar to the popular word processors. The techniques used for making Memo field entries will apply to tasks relating to the entry of custom report designs and dBASE IV programs. Although some of the menu options at the top of the word-wrap screen change for the other two tasks, you will find that many features use identical menu selections.

The default width of the word-wrap lines for Memo fields are 65 positions. dBASE IV allows you to type free-form onto this surface and wraps the words that do not fit on a line to the next line. A blinking

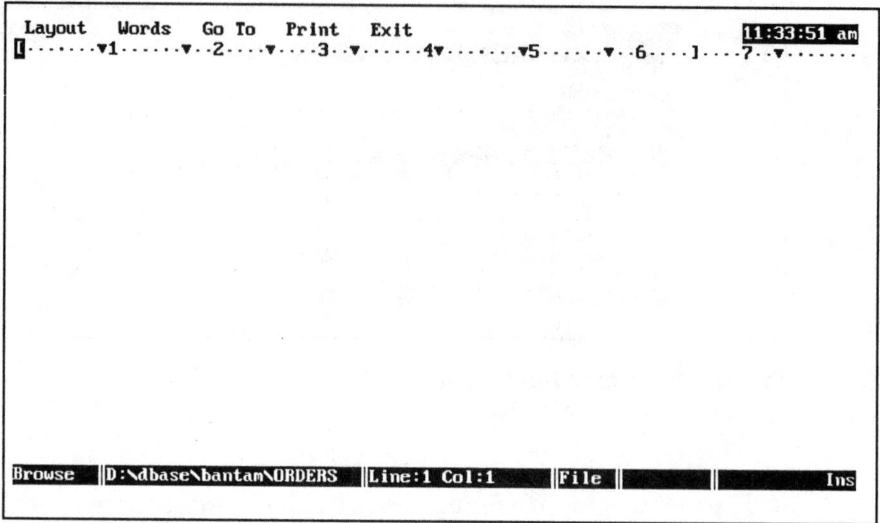

Figure 3-9 Word-wrap edit mode screen

cursor marks your position in the entry. The size of this cursor changes as you toggle between Insert and Overstrike mode for entries. With the default setting of On for Insert, the cursor is taller and the bottom of the screen displays an Insert indicator. Text that you type is inserted in front of the cursor in Insert mode rather than replacing the entries on the screen.

The ENTER key is used to end a short line in word-wrap mode. This key can also indicate the end of a paragraph. Figure 3-10 shows a Memo field that contains three short line entries.

To save the current memo field you can press CTRL-END. dBASE IV will return you to the Edit or Browse display with the cursor on the

Tip: You can move to a Memo field and begin your entries with one easy step if you are on the field preceding or following the Memo field.

Pressing F3 to move to the previous field automatically opens the word-wrap screen for the Memo field if you are on the field following the Memo field. Use F4 if the Memo field is the next field.

```
Layout   Words   Go To   Print   Exit                                        11:40:07 am
[·······▼1······▼··2····▼····3··▼······4▼·······▼5█·····▼··6····]····7··▼·······
Deluxe blue leather upholstery
Antique brass trim
Delivery needed by May 15 for Technology Week Tour
```

Figure 3-10 Memo field with three short lines

memo field that you just entered. You can press the TAB key, ENTER, or F4 to move to the next field. To save the memo field and continue working in the field, press ALT-L and ENTER to select Save this memo field.

Adding and Removing Lines

You can insert data in a Memo field by typing the new text with the Insert mode on. You can delete text with either the DELETE key or the BACKSPACE key.

If you want to add or delete text without affecting the word wrap of the lines that precede or follow the line, a different approach is needed. You can press CTRL-Y to delete the data in the current line. You can also use ALT-W to invoke the Words pull-down menu and type an **R** to remove a line. In both cases, the data and the blank line are deleted from the Memo field.

To add a line press ALT-W then type an **A** to add a line. The line is added below the line containing the cursor. To add a few lines to separate the delivery date information from the color selections for the order, the cursor was moved to the line beginning with an A and ALT-W was pressed followed by typing an **A**. This procedure was repeated to add another line before the delivery information, as shown in Figure 3-11.

Modifying the Contents of a Memo Field

dBASE IV allows you to make modifications to the contents of a Memo field just as you can make modifications to any other field in the database. After reactivating the Memo field you can insert text, delete

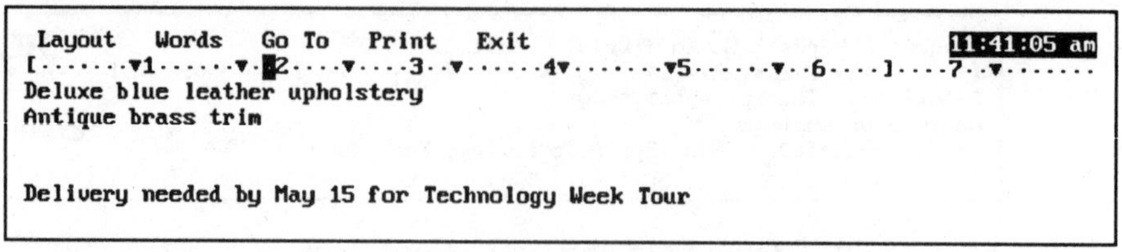

```
Layout   Words   Go To   Print   Exit                                    11:41:05 am
[·······▼1······▼·2····▼····3··▼·······4▼········▼5······▼··6····]····7··▼·······
Deluxe blue leather upholstery
Antique brass trim

Delivery needed by May 15 for Technology Week Tour
```

Figure 3-11 Adding a line before the delivery information

text, or make any other changes you feel are appropriate. Pressing CTRL-END at the end of your changes causes dBASE IV to save the updated copy to disk. Pressing ESC allows you to abort the changes.

Using Another Editor

Although the default is to use dBASE IV's own editor for Memo fields, you can configure the program to use one of the popular word processors that supports ASCII files. The ASCII mode will ensure that word processing control characters are not added to the basic Memo field entries.

You must use the DBSETUP program to modify the CONFIG.DB file to change the editor for Memo fields. Once you type **DBSETUP** and press ENTER, DBSETUP displays an initial menu. Press ALT-C and type an **M** to modify the CONFIG.DB file. Type a new drive and pathname where DBSETUP will find CONFIG.DB if the drive specification is not correct. Press ENTER. DBSETUP displays the different categories into which DBSETUP has divided the settings.

Press the RIGHT ARROW to move to the General settings. Type a **W**, which moves the highlight to the WP setting and selects it since it is the only one that starts with a W. When DBSETUP prompts you for the name of the editor, type the name that you would type to activate the editor from the DOS prompt and press ENTER. You do not have to include the extension if it is .BAT, EXE, or .COM. You should precede the editor name with the drive and directory where the program is stored. After you enter the setting, save the CONFIG.DB file by pressing ALT-E once and ENTER several times to return to the original DBSETUP menus. Then press ALT-E and ENTER to exit the DBSETUP program.

Using a different editor requires more memory when you edit a Memo field. When you edit the Memo field, dBASE IV loads

COMMAND.COM and the editor into memory. If the editor is too big to fit into available memory, dBASE IV displays the message "Program too big to fit into memory" when you try to edit a Memo field. When you edit a Memo field with an alternate editor, you must exit from the editor to leave the Memo field.

Copying, Moving, and Deleting Memo Field Entries

You can select a word, a line, or several paragraphs of Memo field data. First move the cursor to the first character that you wish to select. Press F6 to begin the select process. Move the cursor to the last character that you wish to select with the arrows keys, to move a line or a character at a time. If you use the CTRL key in combination with the arrow keys, dBASE IV will move the cursor a word or page at a time. Once you have selected the data, it will be highlighted. To complete the selection process, you need to press ENTER.

The text highlighted in Figure 3-12 was selected by positioning the cursor in the line above Delivery and using the ARROW keys to highlight the desired text. You can proceed to copy, move, or delete text once you select it.

Moving and Copying Selected Memo Field Data

Once you select data in a Memo field, you can copy or move it to a new location. After selecting the Memo field data that you want to work with, you will want to move the cursor to the blank line where you wish to place the data. If you press F8, dBASE IV will leave the original data

❑ **Tip: If you are using another editor to edit Memo fields, you may want to include the pathname in the AUTOEXEC.BAT file.**

This way you will not need to remember to supply it when you make the entry in DBSETUP. For example, if you want to use WordStar as the Memo field editor, include the line PATH C:\WS in your AUTOEXEC.BAT file if you are storing WordStar in the WS subdirectory on drive C.

```
Layout   Words   Go To   Print   Exit                                  11:42:11 am
[·······▼1······▼··2····▼····3··▼·······4▼·······▼5······▼··6····]····7··▼·······
Deluxe blue leather upholstery
Antique brass trim

Delivery needed by May 15 for Technology Week Tour
```

Figure 3-12 Selected text highlighted

at its current location and place it in the new location as well. If you press F7, dBASE IV moves the data from its original location to the current line. The line containing the original entry is not automatically removed from the Memo field. When you copy or move data, dBASE IV reformats the Memo field.

The data selected in Figure 3-12 was moved to the top of the screen by adding a few lines at the top of the screen with the Words menu then pressing F7. The result looks like Figure 3-13.

Printing Memo Fields

Since Memo fields can contain complete documents like leases, legal briefs, and contracts, you may want to print a copy of the field. You can use the print options available from the menu at the top of the Memo field. To look at these options, press ALT-P. The menu shown in Figure 3-14 appears. You will quickly gain familiarity with this menu and the submenus for options marked with a triangle, since these same features will be used to print reports and labels.

Basic Print Operation If you just need a quick printout of the Memo field data, the Begin printing option will provide what you need. After invoking the print menu all you need to do is type a **B** to use it.

Tip: You can use F6 repeatedly to extend the selection process to a word or a line.

The first time you press F6, dBASE IV begins selecting data. Press it again and dBASE IV will highlight the word. Press it again and the entire line is highlighted.

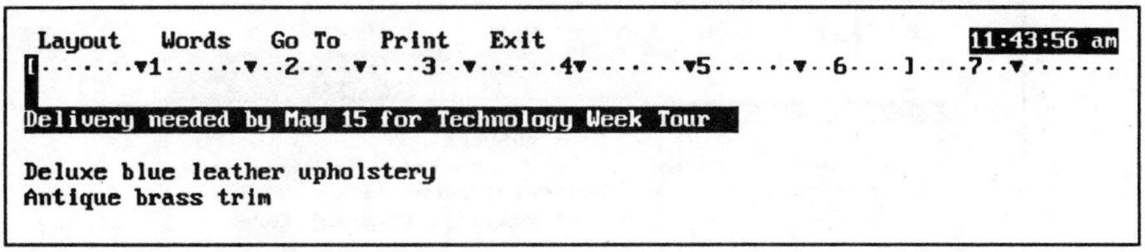

```
 Layout   Words   Go To   Print   Exit                                  11:43:56 am
[.......▼1......▼..2....▼....3..▼.......4▼.......▼5......▼..6....]....7..▼.......

Delivery needed by May 15 for Technology Week Tour

Deluxe blue leather upholstery
Antique brass trim
```

Figure 3-13 Revised memo screen

If you don't get the form-feed options that you expect, you might want to make a change to the default settings that cause dBASE IV to form-feed before printing but not after printing. You can choose Eject page now by typing an E after invoking the Print menu to solve you immediate problem. dBASE IV will eject the page currently in the printer. You can change the setting that affects form feeding with the Control of Printer submenu. The New Page option can be set to generate a new page before printing, after printing, or both before and after printing.

You can choose to show the line numbers when your Memo field is printed by selecting Line Numbers from the Print menu. This selection operates on a toggle switch basis and reverses the current setting each time it is selected. Figure 3-15 shows the line numbering that dBASE IV adds when this setting is changed to Yes.

Controlling the Printer The options available when you select Control of printer affect several aspects of printing. From the menu shown in Figure 3-16 you can choose options that affect the size and quality of print, page advancement options, and the transmission of control codes to the printer at the beginning and end of printing the Memo field. Once you have made your selections in this menu, press ESC to return to the Print menu.

Affecting Print Size and Quality The Text pitch option is selected by typing a T once you have used ALT-P to invoke the Print menu and

❑ **Tip: After moving a line of a Memo field to a new location you will need to use ALT-W followed by an R to remove the blank line in the original location.**

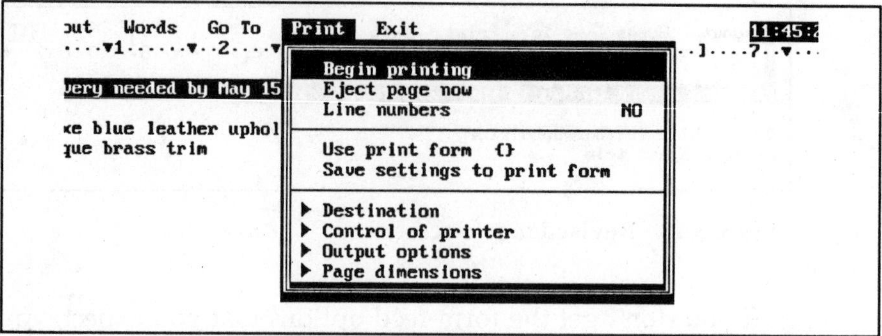

Figure 3-14 Print options for Memo fields

have selected Control of printer by typing a **C**. dBASE IV offers four selections for this option: Default, Pica, Elite, and Condensed. Default uses your current printer pitch setting. Pica characters are printed 10 to the inch. This choice is the largest size characters available. Elite is 12 characters to the inch. Condensed is smaller with the exact number of characters printed determined by the printer brand and model used. You can press the SPACEBAR to cycle through the available selections.

The Quality print option allows you to determine whether to use a draft print quality or the best that is available on a dot matrix printer. The setting Default accepts the printer's current setting without change. A setting of Yes uses the best quality available and No uses draft mode. You can change the setting by highlighting Quality print and pressing the SPACEBAR until the option you want displays.

Controlling Paper Feeding The next three options in the Control of printer menu affect paper feeding. When you select the New page option, you can choose to eject a page before printing, after printing,

```
1
2 Delivery needed by May 15 for Technology Week Tour
3
4 Deluxe blue leather upholstery
5 Antique brass trim
6
```

Figure 3-15 Line numbers added to memo entries

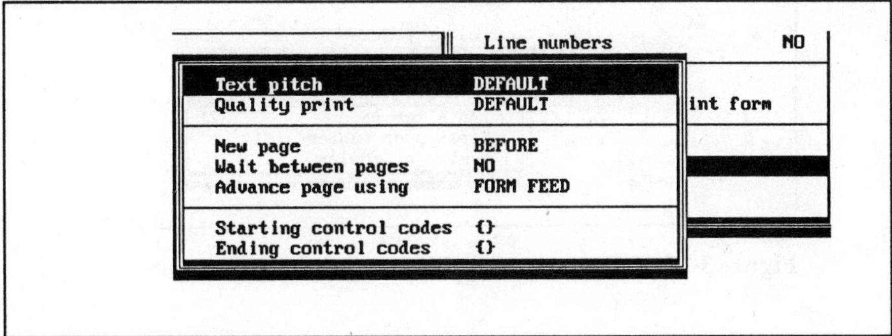

Figure 3-16 Control of Printer menu options

both before and after printing, or not at all. After selecting the option, press the SPACEBAR to cycle through the options, stopping when the selection you want is displayed.

If you are using a printer that requires you to manually feed sheets of paper into it, you will want to select Wait between pages to toggle the setting to Yes. The default is No and can be reestablished by selecting the option again.

The method of advancing the paper to the top of the next form is selected with the Advance page using option. The default setting is to use Form feed to move to the top of the next page. If you are using nonstandard-size forms, the Line feed option for this setting allows you to advance the paper the specific number of lines needed to reach the top of the next form.

Sending Printer Control Codes The third set of options on the Control of printer menu allow you to utilize all the special features of your printer that are not directly supported with dBASE IV menu selections. This means that you can select Landscape or Portrait mode for a laser printer, select a different size or style characters, or any other feature that your printer supports.

The features supported by your printer are listed in your printer manual. Normally printer manuals list the features in a tabular format with the ASCII code sequence needed to invoke each feature. Since the codes assigned to each feature vary by printer make and model, it is important that you identify the codes for your printer.

If you select Starting Control codes and enter a set of printer control characters, dBASE IV will transmit these characters to your printer before transmitting any text from the Memo field. ASCII codes less than

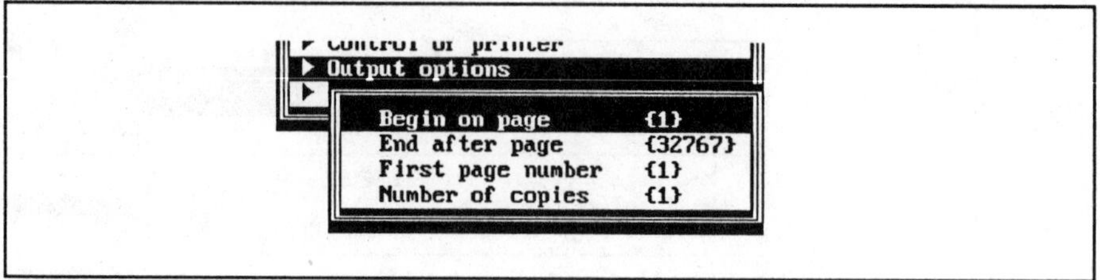

Figure 3-17 Print output options

32 must be enclosed on brackets {} to enter them from the keyboard. The ESC code is an ASCII code 27 and is used as a part of many special print codes. To transmit an ESC code sequence to the printer you would enter {027}. Since this code is used frequently, dBASE IV also supports the entry of {esc} or {escape}. If your printer manual indicates that you needed an ASCII code of 18 to invoke the feature you want, the entry you would need is {018}.

The Ending control codes option allows you to transmit codes to your printer when the Memo field has stopped printing. Since many printer codes are used in pairs with one code starting an option and another stopping it, this option allows you to enter a code to stop a feature invoked at the beginning of printing. For many of the codes, not turning them off means they remain in effect until your printer is turned off, even though you do not transmit the codes again on subsequent print requests.

Selecting Output Options The output options determine the pages printed for a Memo field that spans multiple pages. They also control page numbering and allow for multiple copies from one print request. Typing an **O** to select Output options from the print menu produces the menu of options shown in Figure 3-17. Pressing ESC returns you to the initial Print menu.

The default settings for the beginning and ending pages are 1 and 32,767 respectively. With no changes, these settings will print all the pages in the Memo field. You can change either setting if you do not need a complete printout of the report.

The First page number option assigns the page number you specify to the first page printed. This setting allows you to print the first page of a Memo field but to assign it number 30 as a page number. This

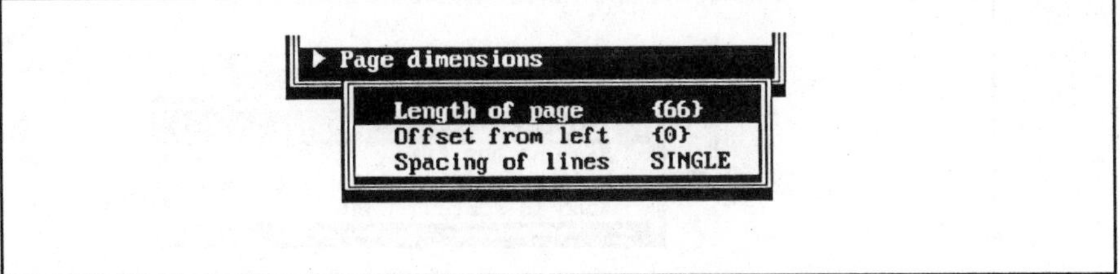

Figure 3-18 Page dimensions menu

allows you to integrate the printout into another document. The default setting for this option is 1.

The default setting for the number of copies is 1. You can change this setting to any number up to 32,767.

Changing Page Dimensions The Page dimensions menu shown in Figure 3-18 allows you to control the size of the page and the placement of text on the paper. The Length of page selection can be set at any number up to 32,767. Normally it is set at 66 since you can print 66 lines on a sheet of 11-inch paper if your printer prints six lines to the inch. If you change to double spacing you do not have to change this setting, since you are only telling dBASE IV how many lines of single-spaced text will fit on the page, not the actual number that will print.

The Offset from left option allows you to shift print output to the right if information is printing too close to the left edge of the paper. The default setting for this option is zero. The maximum setting is 32,767 meaning that 32,767 columns would be skipped before printing would begin. A more representative number is something like an offset of 3 or 5 columns.

The last option in the Page dimension menu is the spacing. dBASE IV supports single, double or triple spacing. You can change the default setting of single by selecting the Spacing of lines option and pressing the SPACEBAR to cycle through the selections. Once you have made your selections in this menu, press ESC to return to the Print menu.

Controlling the Destination You can choose to send your print output to a printer or a file with the selections in the Destination menu shown in Figure 3-19. To change the location move the highlight to Write to and press the SPACEBAR to alter the default of PRINTER to DOS FILE.

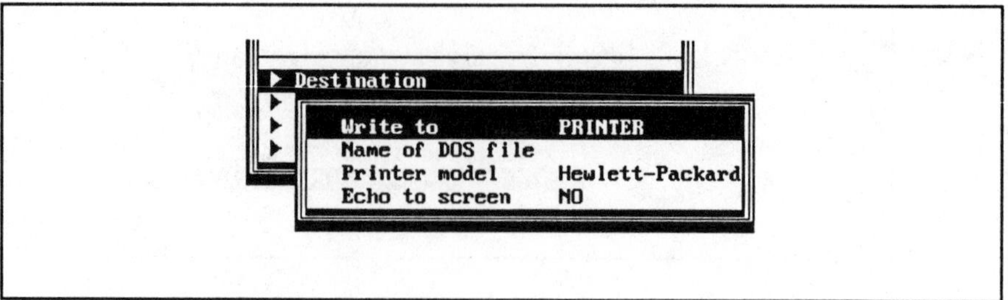

Figure 3-19 Print destination menu

If you choose to write the output to a file for later printing or incorporation into another program, dBASE IV provides a default name for the file that is the same as the database with a filename extension of .PRT. You can select Name of file option and specify the filename to which the output should be written. If you want to use a directory other than the current directory, you need to enter the complete pathname.

If you choose to write the output to a printer, select Printer model and choose any of the printers selected during installation. After selecting Printer model, you can press the SPACEBAR to cycle between the options. If you have added a new printer to your system after installation, you will need to use DBSETUP to add the driver for the new printer.

The Echo to screen option is more appropriate for the output of reports or labels than for Memo fields. If you change this setting to Yes, data is displayed on the monitor as it is being printed. Once you have finished using this menu, press ESC to return to the Print menu.

Saving Print Settings After making all your specifications for printing, you can save these options to a print form with the selection Save Settings to print form from the main Print menu. You specify a name of from one to eight characters and dBASE IV creates a file with this name, adding the filename extension .PRF. The name that you enter cannot include spaces and should be restricted to letters, numeric digits, and the underscore symbol.

The availability of this option can save significant time if you frequently need to create multiple copies or change the length of the page setting or any of the other options. Once saved, you can recall the print settings by selecting Use print form from the main print menu. When you type the name that you supplied for the print form or highlight it from the list, and press ENTER, your settings will be available for the current print request.

Memo Words Menu

You have already seen the Words menu options for adding and removing lines from a Memo field. Some of the other Words menu options are not available in the Memo field editor and are reserved for more sophisticated output options like reports and labels. These options are dimmed and are not selectable. Other options allow you to add page breaks, change the effect of the TAB and SHIFT-TAB keys, and to read and write ASCII files.

The first menu option that is selectable allows you to hide the ruler that appears under the menu. This option is a toggle setting that changes each time you select Hide ruler.

Automatic Indentation The Enable automatic indent option allows you to use the TAB and SHIFT-TAB keys to change the left margin setting at the beginning of a paragraph. If you Change Enable automatic indent to ON, you can use the TAB and SHIFT-TAB keys to change the left margin to the next or previous tab stop.

If Enable automatic indent is OFF, pressing the TAB and SHIFT-TAB keys do not change the left margin. Pressing TAB and SHIFT-TAB revert to changing the position of the cursor.

Page Breaks You can force a page break at any location in a Memo field with the Words menu selection Insert page break. The position of the cursor at the time you invoke this command will dictate the page break location when the document prints.

Reading and Writing ASCII Files ASCII files provide an option for sharing data between dBASE IV and other programs. dBASE IV supports the direct transfer of data for Memo fields to and from ASCII files.

Given the nature of data used in Memo fields, the support for the ASCII format can save significant data entry time. If you have contracts, legal briefs, leases, or other documents stored in an ASCII format and wish to add them as a Memo field, a simple command supports this use. All you need to do is activate the Memo field by pressing F9, move to where you want the text in the ASCII file placed, press ALT-W for the Words pull-down menu, and type a **W** for Write/Read text file. Typing an **R** will select Read text from file. Once you type the name of the ASCII file and press ENTER, dBASE IV enters the contents of the text file at the cursor location.

If you need a copy of the information in a Memo field to use with another program, the solution is easy if the other program will read ASCII data. You can use the Write selection to file option to write the contents of a Memo field to an ASCII file. Once you type the filename and press ENTER, the current Memo field is written to the file. If you only want to write a portion of the Memo field to the text file, select the portion of the Memo field that you want written before you write the text to the file. This feature allows you to transfer a copy of a lease or other document to a word processing or desktop publishing package.

Modifying Records

You can make changes to records that are already in the database by activating the record you wish to change, moving to the field that you want to alter, and typing the new information. If the new entry is shorter than the existing entry, you will need to press DEL for each of the remaining characters you want to remove or use the CTRL-Y key to delete from the cursor position to the end of the field.

A number of special features are available through the Records menu shown in Figure 3-20 that will make the modification process easier. You can use these features to provide a shortcut approach to clearing data from a record or to undo changes to the current record. Other options in the Fields menu in the Browse mode provides a more limited

❑

Tip: Use quick editing keys to delete text.

The CTRL-T keys will delete from the cursor location to the beginning of the next word. The CTRL-Y key sequence will delete from the cursor to the end of the field. Both options are faster than the BACKSPACE or DELETE keys.

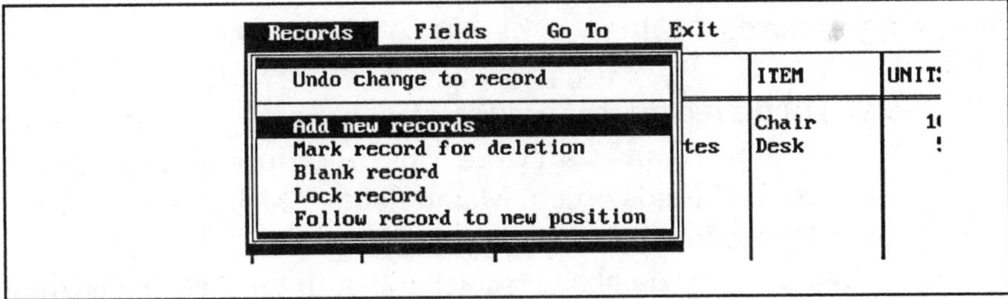

Figure 3-20 Records menu

clearing action by blanking the current field. The Go To menu provides options that are similar to the Go To features used with the database design screen.

Undoing Changes

You can undo any of the changes you make to a record as long as the record is still active. If you change a record, move to another record and come back to the record again, dBASE IV has already saved the changes that you made even if it has not physically written them to the disk. To undo current record changes press ALT-R to select the Records menu and type a **U** to choose Undo change to record. dBASE IV undoes every change made to the record and does not restrict the undo operation to the current field.

When you move to another record in the database, the changes made to the previous record are saved in dBASE IV's buffer. They will also be saved to disk immediately if SET AUTOSAVE is ON. If you press F2 to toggle between Edit and Browse, changes to the current record are also saved. Once the changes are saved to disk, you will no longer be able to undo record changes to the previous record. dBASE IV dims the section in the menu to show that the selection is no longer available.

Adding New Records

When you want to add new records to the database, you can use the Add new records option in the Records menu. This menu option moves the cursor to the end of the database. This is equivalent to pressing CTRL-PGDN and typing a **Y**.

Blanking Records

If you find a record that needs major changes, you may find it easier to blank the record and start over. This procedure removes the data from all the record fields except Memo fields. The blank record remains in the database for you to modify as you choose.

To blank any database record, make the record the current record then press ALT-R to activate the Records menu. Type a **B** to select Blank record. Although it remains in the database, the original records entries will not interfere with the new entries. If you decide not to use this record, you should mark it for deletion and remove it from the database. You can mark a record by highlighting the record that you want to remove and selecting Mark record for deletion from the Records menu. You can also use CTRL-U to mark the records. Then, switch to the database design screen and select Erase marked records from the Organize menu. After you confirm your menu selection, dBASE IV compresses the records and physically removes the ones marked for deletion. The Organize menu in the database design screen also has the Unmark marked records to unmark any marked records in the database. You can unmark individual records that have been marked for deletion by moving to the record in the Edit or Browse mode and selecting the Clear deletion mark menu option from the Records menu or pressing CTRL-U. You will look more closely at the options for deleted records in Chapter 4.

Following a Record to a New Position

When you create the design for a database, you can enter a Y in the index column to have dBASE IV create an index for the file. This means that dBASE IV will create a TAG entry in an index file that will keep track of the values in the index field in order to provide them to you in sequential order. Each record in the index points to the next record that you will want to see, if you are allowing the index to control the order in which your records display. If you are altering a field that the database currently uses to order the records, a change to the indexed field may change the location of the record in the index since the index is controlling the order of the records. When the record is relocated in the database, the next record will depend on the setting for Follow record to new position in the Records menu. With the option set to No, you will continue to display the records that surrounded the record before the change to the index field. If the setting is Yes, the records displayed will be those that surround the changed record in its new location, since dBASE IV will update the location of the index record pointer. If an index is not active, this option will not be selectable from the Records menu.

Adding Fields

If you decide that you need a new field while entering data, you can switch to the database design work surface, add the new field and continue entering data. The steps required depend on whether you reached Edit or Browse through the design screen. If you entered from the design screen, SHIFT-F2 will return you to the design screen to make your change. You can then make your change, use the Layout option to save the design, and switch back to the entry mode you left by pressing F2. If you did not enter from the design screen, you will need to save the current record by pressing CTRL-END, press ENTER when you return to the Control Center, and type an **M** to Modify the structure/order of the database. Once you have finished making the change you can proceed in the same fashion as with the other approach.

If you need to enter the data for this new field in a number of existing records, you will find it easier to do the additions from Browse mode. You use the freeze option to make the new field the only field that can be edited. Freezing a field is one of several options available from the Fields menu.

Altering Fields

dBASE IV supports changes to features that affect the appearance of individual fields and the actions that you can take to edit them. You can make these changes through the Fields menu options shown in Figure 3-21 available in the Browse screen. Although these changes are unavailable in the default Edit screen, you will learn how you can create custom edit screens, called forms, that use these options in Chapter 7.

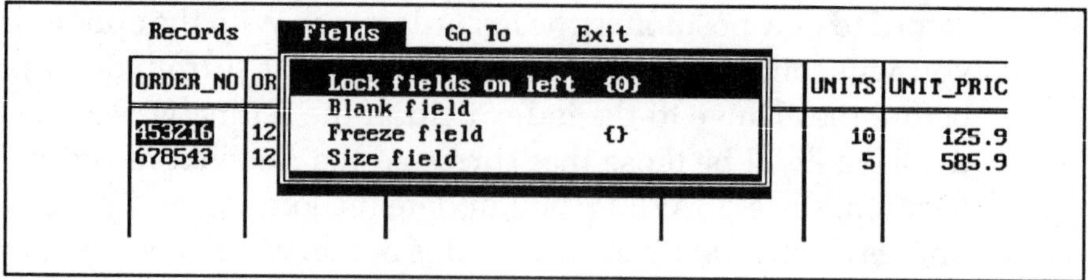

Figure 3-21 Fields menu options

Locking

You can change the Browse screen so the display always includes one or more fields on the left side of the screen. For example, if you are entering data into a database that has 15 fields, you may want to lock the first two in place so you will still remember which record you are using as you enter data in the last few fields. Figure 3-22 displays the beginning of a database that contains more fields than appear on the screen. As dBASE IV scrolls the fields that it displays to the right so you can enter data into the last fields, you become unable to see the identifying information in the first two columns. You can lock the first two fields by pressing HOME to move to the first field, pressing ALT-F for the Fields menu, typing an **L** for Lock fields on left, typing a **2** as the number of fields that you want locked onto the screen, and pressing ENTER.

Once you press END, dBASE IV changes the Browse screen to look like Figure 3-23. When you lock fields on the left, dBASE IV locks the fields that are on the screen when you lock fields. Therefore, it is not

Records   Fields   Go To   Exit   10:36:03 pm

SSN	LAST_NAME	M_INITIAL	FIRST_NAME	ADDRESS	CITY	ST
215-90-8761	Jenkins	M	Mary	11 North St.	Cleveland	OH
675-98-1239	Foster	G	Charles	67 Green Rd.	Chicago	IL
654-11-9087	Garrison	H	Henry	56 Chesaco Lane	Baltimore	MD
888-99-7654	Larson	J	Karen	45 York Rd.	Cleveland	OH
555-66-7777	Walker	P	Paula	123 Lucy Lane	Chicago	IL

Figure 3-22 Beginning fields in a database

Records   Fields   Go To   Exit   10:36:50 pm

SSN	LAST_NAME	NUMB_DEPEN	HR_RATE	YTD_WAGES	YTD_FIT	HEALTH	SKIL
215-90-8761	Jenkins	1	9.75	3450.00	431.50	T	MEMO
675-98-1239	Foster	1	8.50	7890.00	890.00	F	MEMO
654-11-9087	Garrison	3	12.50	9875.00	1200.00	T	MEMO
888-99-7654	Larson	0	15.75	12800.00	1575.50	T	MEMO
555-66-7777	Walker	6	13.75	13575.00	1100.00	T	MEMO

Figure 3-23 Moving to the end of the database after locking fields

necessarily the first fields of a database that are locked. If you have locked fields that are not at the beginning of the database, dBASE IV will not let you access the data in the fields to the left of the locked fields. To unlock fields, press ALT-F, type an **L**, type a **0** (zero) as the number of fields that you want locked, and press ENTER.

Freezing

If you want to access only one field of data from the Browse screen, you may want to freeze it. A frozen field only allows you to move from one record to another while you stay in the same field. You can freeze a field by pressing ALT-F for the Fields menu, typing an F for Freeze field, typing the field name that you want frozen, and pressing ENTER. To unfreeze a field, press ALT-F, type an **F**, press HOME and CTRL-T, and press ENTER. You can combine locked and frozen fields, although

❑ **Tip: Freeze or lock files for editing.**

When you freeze a field, it is the only field that can be edited. This is a good solution when you add a new field to a database and want to edit all the records to add an entry for the new field. When you lock fields at the left of the screen in place, it allows you to edit fields on the far right side of the database in Browse mode and still have the benefit of seeing critical identifying information displaying on the left side of the screen.

you will want to lock the fields that you want on the left side of the screen before you freeze the field that you want to use.

Deleting Entries

dBASE IV allows you to eliminate the entry in the current field that contains the cursor. To move an entry for an individual field in a record in the Browse screen, press ALT-F to activate the Fields menu. Next, type a **B** to select Blank field. If you do not want to blank the entire field, position the cursor on the last character that you want to keep and press CTRL-Y. This menu option is the same as pressing CTRL-Y at the beginning of the field.

Sizing

You can change the display width for fields in the Browse screen without affecting the amount of space reserved for a field in the database. This means that a field with a width of 10 will always use 10 characters of storage space in the database regardless of whether you change the field display width to 5 or 20. dBASE IV will not let you change the display field width for Memo fields. To change the field display size, press ALT-F to invoke the Fields menu and type an **S** for size. Press the LEFT and RIGHT ARROWS to expand or contract the field widths. When the column is the size that you want, press ENTER. You can also change the size by pressing SHIFT-F7 instead of pressing ALT-F and typing an **S**.

The limitations on change are that a field can be no wider than 78 characters and no narrower than 4. The column width dBASE IV uses to display the data is always as wide as the field name even if dBASE IV uses a narrower width to display the field data. For Numeric, Floating, and Date fields, the column cannot be narrower than the field width.

Making the display width wider than the actual field width has no effect on the data that you can enter in the field, since dBASE IV highlights the portion of the display field width it uses when you are on the field. Making the display width narrower causes dBASE IV to scroll the data for the field within the width provided as you enter or edit the field entry.

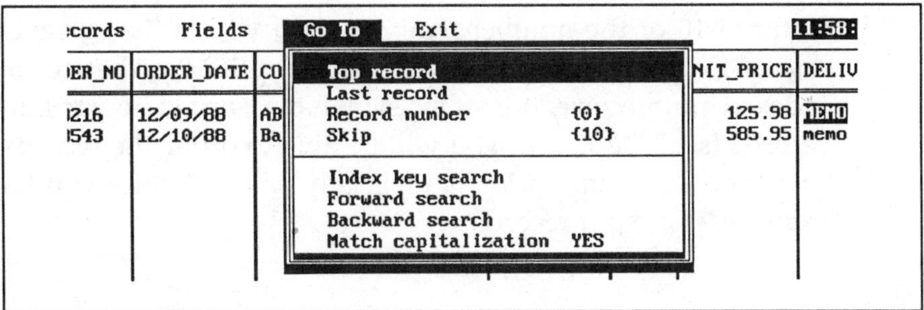

Figure 3-24 Go To menu options

Positioning on the Correct Record with Go To

The first step to modifying a record is positioning the cursor on the record that you wish to change. Many options exist to move the cursor, with the choice of the correct option dictated by the screen mode in which you are working, the number of records in the database, and the distance of the desired record from the current record. If you are working in Browse mode and need to move only a few records, the UP and DOWN ARROW keys will provide the quickest solution. If you are working in Edit mode, Page Up and Page Down provide similar capabilities.

For either mode, you can use the Go To menu shown in Figure 3-24 when the distance that you need to travel is greater than a few records. Selecting Top record or Last record places you on the first and last database records, respectively. If you happen to know the record number, using the Record number option is the quickest option. The Skip option allows you to enter the number of records that you would like to skip. Typing an S and pressing ENTER uses the default skip

❑ **Tip: Move backward by using a negative skip number.**

You can move toward the top of the database with the skip option. Rather than enter a positive number to move you toward the end of the database, enter a negative number to move you toward the beginning of the database.

factor of 10 or the number that you used within the current editing session for this menu option. Any of these options can be used on either indexed or unindexed files. Once you have learned how to index your records (see Chapter 4), you will be able to order the records in any sequence. The Skip option is especially valuable once you know the exact order of your records.

Using the Index Key for Searching

If your database is indexed, you can quickly locate a record you want using an index search. If you know the value of the index field for a record that you wish to modify, this is the quickest way to modify it. In an index search, dBASE IV uses the current index to quickly find the record with the value in the index field equal to the Search string that you provide. To perform an index search, the database must be indexed on the field(s) that you want to use to find a record. If you have indexed a database by more than one field, you will need to return to the database design screen and select Order records by index from the Organize menu. You can supply the field name as the Tag name for the index that you created by typing a **Y** in the Index column when you created the database. In the next chapter you will learn that you can also create new indexes after a file structure is finalized. When you master this new procedure you will be able to activate any of these indexes as well.

To locate a record with the index feature from the Edit or Browse mode, press ALT-G for the Go To menu and type an **I** for an index search. dBASE IV displays the index expression for the current index tag and prompts you for the search value that you want to use to find a particular record. Since all the index expressions that you have created have consisted of simple field names, enter the data associated with the field name shown and press ENTER. If dBASE IV finds a record that contains your entry, it makes the record current. If dBASE IV cannot find the record, it displays the message Not Found and waits for you to press a key before displaying the Go To menu again.

The results just described are achieved if the Near setting is set to the default of OFF. If the Near setting is at ON, dBASE IV activates the

> **Tip: Changing the Match capitalization option in the Go To menu will not affect the operation of an Index key search.**

ord that would appear after a matching record with the desired field value, if it existed.

When you provide a search string, you must keep these search string rules in mind:

- The capitalization of the Search string must match the index entries. For example, if you are looking for Jones, you must enter Jones not JONES or jones. If you have indexed the database using a conversion function such as UPPER or LOWER, you must enter a Search string that matches the converted entries dBASE IV creates when indexing the database. For example, if you are looking for JONES and the database was indexed using the LOWER function, you must enter jones.
- There is no wildcard option (see below) for an index key search. All characters are taken literally, including asterisks and question marks.
- You do not have to provide the entire entry if the database is indexed using a character field. For example, if you are looking for Hatterfield, you can enter Hat. Since dBASE IV locates the first record that matches the Search string, you must enter a search string that provides enough information so dBASE IV can find the one that you want. For example, if you enter Hat, dBASE IV will find Hatley before it finds Hatterfield. This assumes that the Exact setting is at its default of OFF. If the Exact setting is set to ON, you must provide the entire entry; otherwise, dBASE IV will only find entries of Hat.
- If you are using an index based on Numeric, Floating, and Date fields, you must provide the entire entry in the Search string.
- dBASE IV determines what the type of data for a Search string should be by the field that you indexed on. Therefore, you do not need to include quotes with Character strings or braces with dates.

Searching for Character Strings

The forward and backward search feature allows you to look for entries in a particular field of the database. Although you do not have to have an index to perform this type of search, it is slower than an index key search since dBASE IV must read more data. The Memo field editing screen also contains a Go To menu that operates similar to the Go To menu in the Browse and Edit screens.

Conducting a Forward Search When you perform an index key search, the cursor can be on any field in the database. Since dBASE IV can use any field in the database in an attempt to match a string that you enter, your cursor must be on the field that you want dBASE IV to check.

Once you have positioned the cursor on the field that you want to check, press ALT-G for Go To, type an **F** for Forward search. Next enter your Search string in the prompt box and press ENTER. dBASE IV starts from the current database record when performing the search and, if you did not start from the beginning of the database, starts at the beginning after searching from the current location to the end of the database. dBASE IV displays the next matching record if one exists. You can select Forward Search again to find the next matching record, or you can press the SHIFT-F4 key to find the next matching record. Pressing SHIFT-F3 will find the previous matching record. If there is no match, a message will inform you that no matches exist. When you perform a search again, dBASE IV will display the Search string from

❑

Tip: You do not need to reposition the cursor to search the entire database.

dBASE IV starts at the current cursor location and moves toward the end of the database. When dBASE IV reaches the end of the database, it starts searching from the beginning of the database to the location where you started the search. Regardless of the starting position, all the records will also be checked with a backward search.

the last search that you performed. By typing any letter, dBASE IV will remove the prior entry so you can enter the new one.

dBASE IV supports the use of the wildcard characters * and ? and uses these characters to substitute for other characters in your data. A question mark (?) represents a single character and an asterisk (*) represents one or more characters. Unlike some other programs that only support the use of an asterisk at the end of an entry, dBASE IV supports it at the beginning or the end of the entry. Search strings of **ABC Company, ABC *, A?? Company, *Company,** and **??? Company** would all match with ABC Company. Although the wildcard characters offer the potential to save typing time, overuse of these characters will result in a waste of time, since you will look at many records that do not meet your needs.

Conducting a Backward Search A Backward search starts at the current record in the database and searches toward the beginning of the database. Once reaching the beginning, it moves to the end of the database and continues searching until it reaches the current record.

Other than choosing Backward search rather than Forward search from the menu, the procedure for using this command is the same as Forward search. You will want to choose this command when you know that the record you want precedes the current record, or if you feel that the odds are better that dBASE IV will find the record that you want before the current record.

Capitalization for Text Searches You can use the Match capitalization option to control whether or not dBASE IV uses a case-sensitive search. When Match capitalization is set to Yes, a Search string of Smith will only match with Smith. If Match capitalization is set to NO, a search string of Smith will match with smith, Smith, SMITH, and SmItH.

The setting No is useful when you do not want to search for all possibilities of capitalization. It also helps to locate entries with capitalization errors as in Theodore Smith, where the capitalization was maintained for the H accidentally. The capitalization option will also provide assistance with replacement options available on design screen for reports, forms, and labels.

Tip: Use Search and Replace to avoid long entries.

If you need to enter long or technical terms a number of places in a Memo field entry, you can use a short abbreviation that is unlikely to be a part of your other entries. When you are finished making your entries, use Search and Replace to make the proper substitution for you.

Memo Field Searching You can invoke the Search option from the Go To menu in the Memo field screen or you can use the SHIFT-F5 key sequence. The same rules that apply to database fields apply to Memo field searches. You can also move the cursor to a specific line number by selecting Go to Line Number from the Go To menu, entering the line number that you want to move to and pressing ENTER.

Using the Search and Replace Option for Memo Fields

You cannot change the contents of a database field with a Search and Replace operation. To change the contents of a database field you can find the record and type a new value or use the Update Query option introduced in Chapter 5. To change some of the text in a Memo field, dBASE IV offers a Search and Replace option.

You can invoke this feature by selecting Replace from the Go To menu or by pressing SHIFT-F6. Type the text you wish to find and press ENTER. Next, type the replacement text and press ENTER. When the first occurrence is found, dBASE IV displays the message Replace/Skip/All/Quit (R/S/A/Esc) at the bottom of the screen. You can type **R** to replace the occurrence currently highlighted, type **A** to replace all occurrences of the Search string, type an **S** to skip the occurrence currently highlighted, or press ESC to stop the Search and Replace operation. If you select R or S, dBASE IV continues searching for additional occurrences of the Search string. dBASE IV displays the message "Occurrences Replaced:" followed by the number of occurrences replaced when you have completed the replace menu option.

GETTING STARTED

➤ You will want to try out the new skills presented in this chapter by entering a few records into the employee database that you designed in Chapter 2. You will enter five records in this database, including entries in the Memo fields. You will want to follow these steps for entering the records:

1. Activate the EMPLOYEE database by highlighting the filename in the Data panel of the Control Center, pressing ENTER, and typing a D.
2. When the Edit screen appears, type **215-90-8761** for the SSN. You do not need to press ENTER since the entry fills the field.
3. Type **Jenkins** for the LAST_NAME and press ENTER.
4. Type **M** for M_INITIAL. You do not need to press ENTER since the entry fills the field.
5. Type **Mary** for the FIRST_NAME and press ENTER.
6. Type **11 North St.** and press ENTER.
7. Type **Cleveland** and press ENTER.
8. Type **OH**.
9. Type **44124**.
10. Type **(216)999-9999**.
11. Type **122088**.
12. Type **M**.
13. Type **1** and press ENTER.
14. Type **9.75**.
15. Type **3450** and press ENTER.
16. Type **431.5** and press ENTER.
17. Type **T**.
18. Press CTRL-HOME to activate the word-wrap screen for entering the Memo field. Type **Typing, Switchboard operator** and press ENTER. Type **Some Spanish** and press CTRL-END.
19. Press ENTER to finalize the entry of the first record.

Add four additional records to the database by making the entries shown for the four records below. You can follow the same procedure you used for the first record.

EMPLOYEE RECORD	2
SSN	675-98-1239
LAST_NAME	Foster
M_INITIAL	G
FIRST_NAME	Charles
ADDRESS	67 Green Rd.
CITY	Chicago
STATE	IL
ZIP_CODE	30912
HOME_PHONE	(312)777-9999
HIRE_DATE	012489
MARITAL_ST	S
NUMB_DEPEN	1
HR_RATE	8.5
YTD_WAGES	7890
YTD_FIT	890
HEALTH	F
SKILLS	

Machine lathe operator, drill press operator, fork lift operator, microwave tower repair

EMPLOYEE RECORD	3
SSN	654-11-9087
LAST_NAME	Garrison
M_INITIAL	H
FIRST_NAME	Henry
ADDRESS	56 Chesaco Lane
CITY	Baltimore
STATE	MD
ZIP_CODE	21237
HOME_PHONE	(301)222-2222
HIRE_DATE	020587
MARITAL_ST	M
NUMB_DEPEN	3
HR_RATE	12.5
YTD_WAGES	9875
YTD_FIT	1200
HEALTH	T

SKILLS
Computer operator
BASIC, FORTRAN, COBOL, C, and PASCAL programming classes completed

EMPLOYEE RECORD	4
SSN	888-99-7654
LAST_NAME	Larson
M_INITIAL	J
FIRST_NAME	Karen
ADDRESS	45 York Rd.
CITY	Cleveland
STATE	OH
ZIP_CODE	44132
HOME_PHONE	(216)779-0000
HIRE_DATE	070782
MARITAL_ST	M
NUMB_DEPEN	0
HR_RATE	15.75
YTD_WAGES	12800
YTD_FIT	1575.5
HEALTH	T

SKILLS
Computer programming in the following languages: C, SNOBOL, ALGOL, PASCAL, PL/1, COBOL, BASIC, and FORTRAN

EMPLOYEE RECORD	5
SSN	555-66-7777
LAST_NAME	Walker
M_INITIAL	P
FIRST_NAME	Paula
ADDRESS	123 Lucy Lane
CITY	Chicago
STATE	IL
ZIP_CODE	31245
HOME_PHONE	(312)888-7777
HIRE_DATE	031584
MARITAL_ST	M
NUMB_DEPEN	6

HR_RATE	13.75
YTD_WAGES	13575
YTD_FIT	1100
HEALTH	T
SKILLS	

Master craftsman, wood working, plastering, mason

Now that you have entered the first five records in the EMPLOYEE file, you can try out some of the editing options that Lotus 1-2-3 allows. First use the Page Up key to move to the record for Henry Garrison. Press the TAB key twice to move to the M_INITIAL field. Type a **G** to change the entry for M_INITIAL.

Press F2 to switch to the Browse mode. Press ALT-G to activate the Go To menu and type a **T** to move to the top. Use the TAB key to move to the LAST_NAME field. Press ALT-G and type an **F** for Forward search. Type **Larson** and press ENTER. Notice how dBASE IV positions the cursor in the Larson record.

Use the END key to move to the SKILLS field. Press CTRL-HOME to edit the Memo field. Press ALT-G to activate the Go To menu. Type an **R** to select Replace. Type **FORTRAN** and press ENTER for the Search string. Type **RPG** and press ENTER for the Replace string. When dBASE IV highlights FORTRAN, type an **R** to replace the entry. Press CTRL-END to save the changed Memo field. Press HOME and PAGE UP to move to the SSN field in the first record.

Press ALT-F to activate the Fields menu. Type an **L** to select Lock fields, type a **2** to lock the two leftmost fields on the screen and press ENTER. Press the TAB key to move to the Memo field. Notice how the two fields are frozen on the screen.

Open the current Memo field by pressing CTRL-HOME. Position the paper in your printer at the top of a form and turn the printer on. Press ALT-P and type a **B** to begin printing. Press CTRL-END to return to the Browse screen. Press Alt-E to select Exit and ENTER to return to the Control Center.

PART II

Accessing Database Information

CHAPTER 4

Organizing the Database

When you create a database without indexes, the data is always in the order in which the database records were entered. A different sequence for the database records may make it easier to find the records that you need. dBASE IV provides two techniques for controlling the sequence of the data in the database. Both achieve the same results by allowing you to view the data in a different sequence, but the techniques are very different.

One method changes the physical sequence of the records, rearranging them into the order you define in a process known as sorting. dBASE compares the records sort key on the field(s) that you specify and rearranges the records according to the values in the sort field(s). Although sorting is discussed in this chapter for completeness of coverage, in most cases you will want to use the more efficient indexing method of resequencing records.

The second method for organizing the records in a database is called indexing. Indexing does not alter the physical sequence of the records in the database, only the order in which they are presented. When you index a file, dBASE builds a set of index file entries containing each of the values in the field that you are indexing on. The index entries are arranged in sequence according to the field values and contain a reference to the record number in the database containing the specific index value. dBASE can then read the index to determine which records have the particular entry. Since the index entries are maintained in logical sequence, dBASE can present the records in that order.

Part of the organization you might want to do for a database is to purge data that is no longer required. The Organize menu on the database design screen provides an option that allows you to remove records marked for deletion. You have already seen in Chapter 3 that the default is to continue to show these records in Edit and Browse screens as well as output like reports and labels. You can change the default setting to allow these records to remain in the database but no longer display. Another option is packing the database to remove these records from the database permanently. Once the database is packed, the only way that you can restore the records is to reenter them, since the Unmark option in the Organize menu will no longer work.

Sorting a Database

When you sort a database, dBASE creates a second copy of the original database. The records in the new database are sequenced according to the entries in the field or fields that you specify as the sort fields. The second copy of the database is stored as a permanent file on your disk. If you decided to sort a large database a number of times, a significant amount of disk space is used. You might want to delete each sorted database before producing another version of the database in a different sequence.

The sort feature is available through the database design screen. If you are in the process of entering data, you will need to save the current record and return to this screen. The procedure that you use will depend on whether you moved to the data entry screen from the Control Center or from design. If you moved to Edit or Browse from design, you can press SHIFT-F2 to return to the design screen. If you started data entry from the Control Center, you will need to use ALT-E

❑

Tip: Index the database rather than sort it if disk space is limited.

Sorting requires double file space at least temporarily. The original database is retained, and a second database in the new sequence is created.

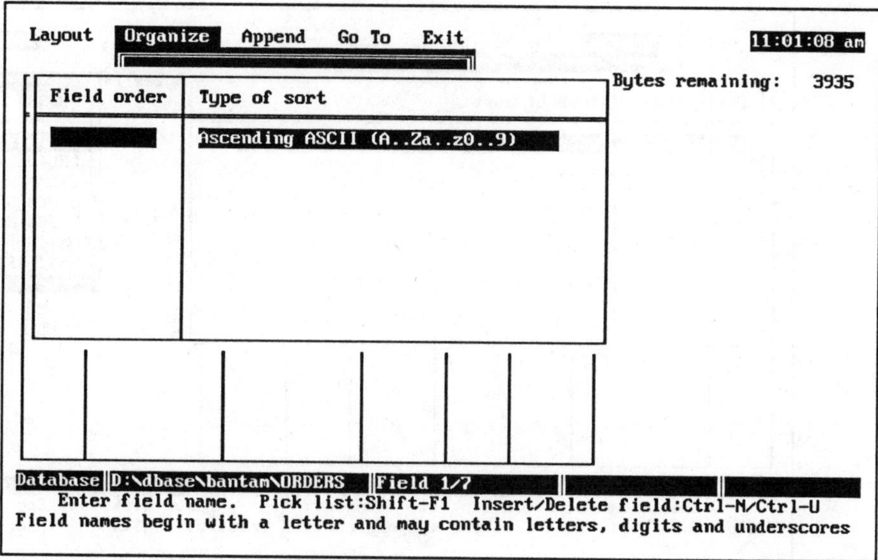

Figure 4-1 Box for entering sort fields

followed by pressing ENTER to select Exit and return to the Control Panel. With the database that you wish to sort highlighted, you can press SHIFT-F2 or ENTER followed by typing an **M**. From the design screen, press ALT-O to select the Organize menu. Type an **S** to select sort on field list. A box for entering sort fields like the one in Figure 4-1 is displayed.

Specifying Sort Keys

dBASE allows you to enter as many as 10 fields to control the sort from the database design screen. Each sort field is entered on one line of the sort field box. Fields at the top of the list are higher in priority than those lower down in the list. In fact, dBASE does not look at the fields lower in the list unless more than one record contains the same field entries in the fields above it. If all the records have unique entries in the first field that you specify, dBASE will ignore the other fields in the sort list.

To select the first field, press SHIFT-F1 to activate the pick list. Figure 4-2 shows the fields for the ORDERS file. Although the intensity of the field names is not obvious in the figure, you will find that fields that are not available as a sort field are dimmer than the other entries. These

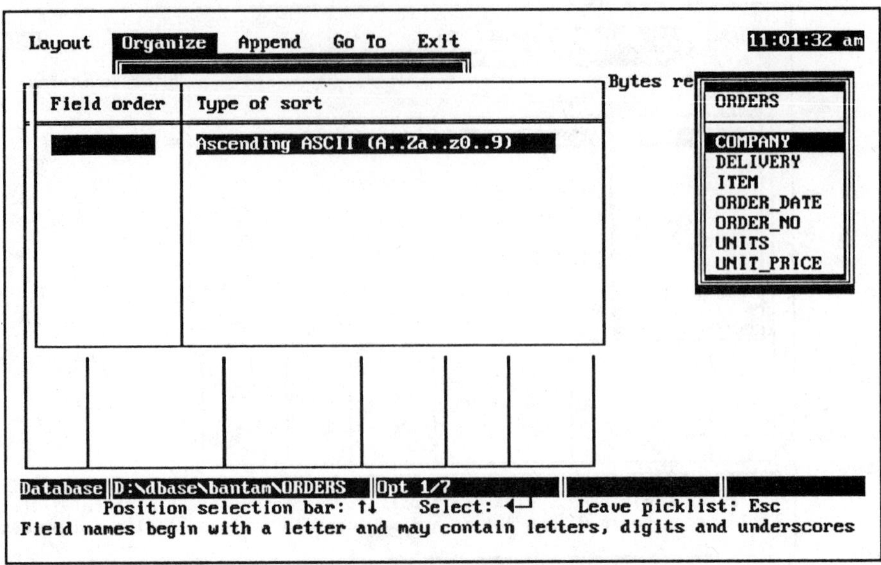

Figure 4-2 Using the Pick list to select the fields in the ORDERS file

dimmed entries would include Logical fields and Memo fields. The first field that you select functions as the primary key, which controls the sequence of the sort.

The second column of the sort key table can be used to control the sort sequence. The four options available are ascending, descending, ascending dictionary, and descending dictionary. The major difference between the options is whether the entries are arranged from highest to lowest and whether the sort is case sensitive. Table 4-1 shows the effect of specific field entries when the various sort sequences are selected. Figure 4-3 shows the change made to this column by pressing the SPACEBAR once.

When you choose one of the ascending sort sequences, dBASE sorts numbers in the field ahead of any entries that begin with letters. In a field that contains entries like street addresses, the field entries with numeric entries at the beginning of the street address will precede all the entries that do not have numbers at the front of the entry. If you want numeric entries to fall at the end of the list, you will need to choose one of the descending sort options.

Since the ASCII sort sequences place upper- and lowercase entries in different positions, you will want to use a dictionary sort anytime your

Table 4-1 Effect of sort sequence selections on a Selection of Part Numbers

Sort Sequence	*Data order*
Ascending	098765 .. 998765
	A23412 .. Z34215
	a45678 .. z21345
Descending	998765 .. 098765
	z21345 .. a45678
	Z34216 .. A23412
Ascending dictionary	098765 .. 998765
	A23412 .. a45678
	Z34216 .. z21345
Descending dictionary	998765 .. 098765
	z21345 .. Z34216
	a45678 .. A23412

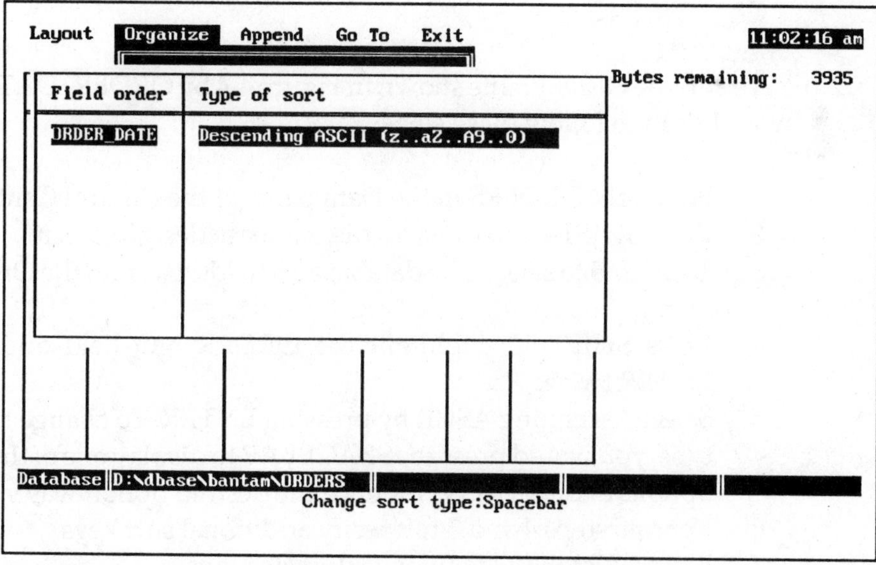

Figure 4-3 Changing the type of sort with the spacebar

Records Fields Go To Exit 2:12:28 pm

ORDER_NO	ORDER_DATE	COMPANY	ITEM	UNITS	UNIT_PRICE	DELIVERY
453216	12/09/88	ABC Company	Chair	10	125.98	MEMO
678543	12/10/88	Baker & Associates	Desk	5	585.95	memo
789654	12/15/88	ABC Company	Cabinet	3	129.95	memo
986541	12/16/88	Carlston & Sons	Mailers	100	1.35	memo
001254	01/03/89	Lewis Brothers	Chair	5	89.95	memo
001298	01/10/89	Baker & Associates	Desk	5	585.95	memo
001325	01/15/89	Able Bakery	Cabinet	2	129.95	memo
001359	01/17/89	BBB Bakery	Cabinet	3	129.95	memo

Figure 4-4 ORDERS file records before sorting

sort field contains inconsistent capitalization. Otherwise, you will need to check two different alphabetical lists to find the data that you need. Entries like abbott construction, ABC COMPANY, CALVIN INC., and carson's repair would create two separate alphabetical lists, as they would be shown like this when sorted in ascending sequence:

abbott construction
carson's repair
ABC COMPANY
CALVIN, INC.

To sort the ORDERS file shown in Figure 4-4 by ORDER_DATE, you would need to follow these steps:

1. Highlight ORDERS in the Data panel of the Control Center.
2. Press SHIFT-F2 to move to the database design screen.
3. Type an **S** to select Sort database on fields list from the Organize menu.
4. Press SHIFT-F1, highlight the ORDER_NO field and press ENTER twice.
5. Select Ascending ASCII by pressing ENTER. To change the sort type, you would press the SPACEBAR to display one of the other options and press ENTER once the desired option was visible.
6. Repeats steps 4 and 5 to specify additional sort keys.
7. Press CTRL-END to finalize the selections.
8. Type a valid filename in response to the prompt. For the ORDERS file you can type **ORDERNO** and press ENTER.

ORDER_NO	ORDER_DATE	COMPANY	ITEM	UNITS	UNIT_PRICE	DELIVERY
001254	01/03/89	Lewis Brothers	Chair	5	89.95	memo
001298	01/10/89	Baker & Associates	Desk	5	585.95	memo
001325	01/15/89	Able Bakery	Cabinet	2	129.95	memo
001359	01/17/89	BBB Bakery	Cabinet	3	129.95	memo
453216	12/09/88	ABC Company	Chair	10	125.98	MEMO
678543	12/10/88	Baker & Associates	Desk	5	585.95	memo
789654	12/15/88	ABC Company	Cabinet	3	129.95	memo
986541	12/16/88	Carlston & Sons	Mailers	100	1.35	memo

Records Fields Go To Exit 1:57:18 pm

Figure 4-5 Sorted records in the file created from the ORDER records

9. After the sort completes, move to the Data panel of the Control Center and activate the database ORDERNO to display the sorted records. Figure 4-5 provides a look at the sequence in which the records in the new file would appear.

Changing Sort Key Specifications

dBASE retains the sorted database on your disk until you delete it. To eliminate one of these files from disk you can use the Tools menu available from the Control Center. Press ALT-T to activate the Tools menu then type a D to select DOS utilities. Next press ALT-O to select

❑

Tip: Delete unnecessary sorted databases.

Sorted copies of your database are not automatically updated as you add records to your database. Keeping extra copies of sorted databases not only wastes disk space but also adds to the risk that you will use a noncurrent file. Since these copies quickly become out of sync with the original database, you would normally retain only one of the two databases. You will need to close the open database before deleting it by highlighting the database name in the Control Center, pressing Enter, and typing a C.

the Operations option from the Utilities menu and type a **D** to tell dBASE that you want to delete a file. Type the name of the sorted file and press ENTER. Confirm the deletion by typing a **Y**. This will allow you to reuse this space and create a database sorted in a different sequence. A shortcut approach that achieves the same result is to highlight the name of the file that you wish to delete in the Control Center and press the DEL key. Type a Y to confirm that you wish to remove the file from the current catalog, then type another Y to confirm that you wish to delete the file.

When you invoke the sort feature a second time, dBASE does not display the sort information from the previous sort. If you want to reuse the space allocated to a sorted file created earlier without deleting the earlier sorted file first, you can specify the name of the existing file when dBASE asks for a name for the sorted file. You will need to respond to dBASE's Overwrite/Cancel prompt by typing an **O** to have dBASE reuse the space.

You can make changes to the sort key specifications before finalizing them. If you need to add a field at a location other than at the bottom of the list, you can use CTRL-N to insert a line above the cursor location and enter the specifications for another sort key on this line. You can delete a field from the list by placing the cursor in the line for the field that you no longer need and pressing CTRL-U. dBASE does not save this list for your modification once you have executed the sort request by pressing CTRL-END. The next set of sort specifications that you enter must be entered from the beginning even if they are similar to the last sort specifications used.

❑ **Tip: Effect of copying the sorted file over the original file.**

If you want to use a file in the new sequence on an ongoing basis, the best approach is to copy the sorted file over the original file. This will allow you to use any reports, labels, and custom forms that were designed for the original file. If you delete the original file and begin to use the sorted file, dBASE will not automatically activate the reports, labels, and forms. Once you complete the copy, you can delete the sorted file.

Indexing a Database

Indexes provide a quick and efficient way to see the records in your database in a variety of different sequences. The index feature allows you to order the database records in either ascending or descending sequence by the entries in any field in the database. You can also create expressions involving multiple fields and sequence the database records by the resulting expression value generated from each record. In addition to allowing you to display records as if they were sorted, an index provides a quick-search capability on the index field. This feature was discussed in Chapter 3 with the options for the Go To menu.

Indexing a database produces the same result as an ascending or descending ASCII sort. Unlike the sort procedure, indexing a database does not require you to create a separate copy of the database. The index entries are arranged according to the sequence you specify. Each of these entries points to the database record used to create this index entry. When the index is the master or controlling index for a database, dBASE IV reads the index entries to determine the order in which it should display the records. If your database contained these three records, they would appear in the order shown unless they were indexed:

REC NO	*Location*	*Amount*
1	Texas	56750
2	Alabama	45000
3	Montana	35000

If you were to index the records by Location, the index entries would be in order as Alabama, Montana, and Texas. The records would display in the sequence 2, 3, and 1. If you index the same records by Amount and let this new index control the sequence in which the records are presented, it would be 3, 2, and 1.

Once indexed, dBASE maintains the index for the database with the addition, deletion, and modification of index field entries as long as the index is open. If a database has multiple indexes, only one can function as the master or controlling index.

dBASE IV supports the indexing methods of earlier versions of the package and also offers an enhanced index method that gives you the opportunity to greatly increase the number of indexes for each database file. Earlier releases of dBASE required the creation of an .NDX file for each index that you created. Once created, you needed to remember to open the NDX files every time you used the database or additions and changes to the database would cause the indexes to be out of sync with the database records and require recreation.

dBASE IV's New .MDX Files

dBASE IV no longer requires a separate file for each index. When you create a database, a .DBF file is created to contain the structure design and your data. When you create the first index for a new .DBF file, dBASE creates an .MDX file for this database. The .MDX file is automatically opened when the database is opened making it impossible to forget to update an index if database records change.

An .MDX file can hold 47 separate indexes. Each index is identified by assigning a tag of from 1 to 10 characters that uniquely identify the index. These tag names follow the same rules as field names in that they must start with a letter and cannot contain spaces or special symbols other than the underline symbol (_).

There are two ways to create index entries in an .MDX file. You have already learned one way when you created a database structure and added a Y to the Index column. The SSN and LAST_NAME fields in the EMPLOYEE database shown in Figure 4-6 indicates that an indexes for these fields were established during the design process. Each field containing a Y in the Index column created a tag entry in the MDX file for the database. These Tag entries are the same as the field names. You can modify the database structure to add Y's to the Index column for other fields and dBASE will create a new index file as you save the design.

A second approach that will build an index for existing records and begin updating the index for new entries is to press ALT-O to select Organize then type a **C** to select Create new index. The menu in Figure 4-7 appears and allows you to specify the index.

The first entry you will want to make is to assign a Tag name. With the highlight on Name of index in the new menu, press ENTER. Next type a Tag name of up to 10 characters and press ENTER. The cursor

Layout Organize Append Go To Exit 2:08:23 pm

Bytes remaining: 3872

Num	Field Name	Field Type	Width	Dec	Index
1	SSN	Character	11		Y
2	LAST_NAME	Character	15		Y
3	M_INITIAL	Character	1		N
4	FIRST_NAME	Character	10		N
5	ADDRESS	Character	15		N
6	CITY	Character	10		N
7	STATE	Character	2		N
8	ZIP_CODE	Numeric	5	0	N
9	HOME_PHONE	Character	13		N
10	HIRE_DATE	Date	8		N
11	MARITAL_ST	Character	1		N
12	NUMB_DEPEN	Numeric	2	0	N
13	HR_RATE	Numeric	6	2	N
14	YTD_WAGES	Numeric	9	2	N
15	YTD_FIT	Numeric	9	2	N
16	HEALTH	Logical	1		N

Database ‖D:\...bantam\EMPLOYEE ‖Field 1/17

Enter the field name. Insert/Delete field:Ctrl-N/Ctrl-U

Field names begin with a letter and may contain letters, digits and underscores

Figure 4-6 Index indicators for SSN and LAST_NAME

moves to Index expression. You can press ENTER to begin entering an index expression. Next, enter a field name or build an expression

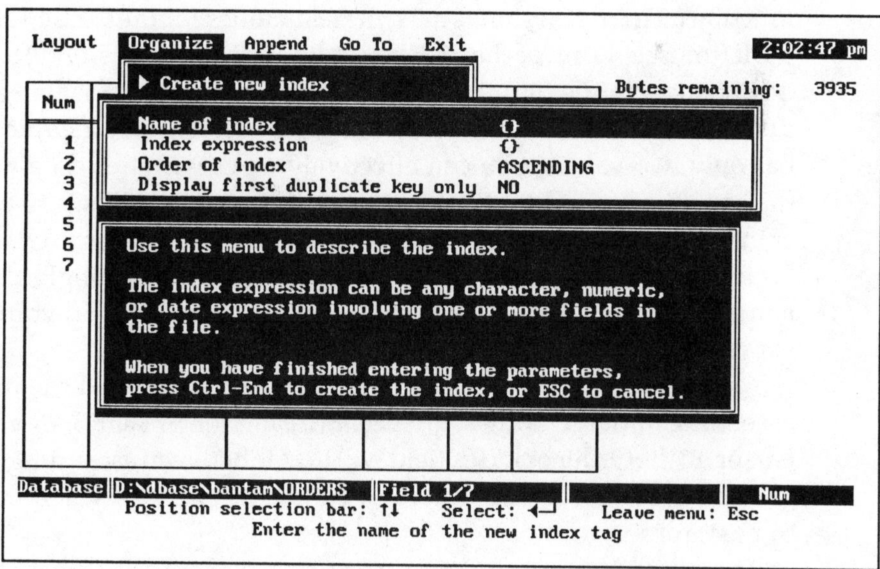

Figure 4-7 Defining a new index

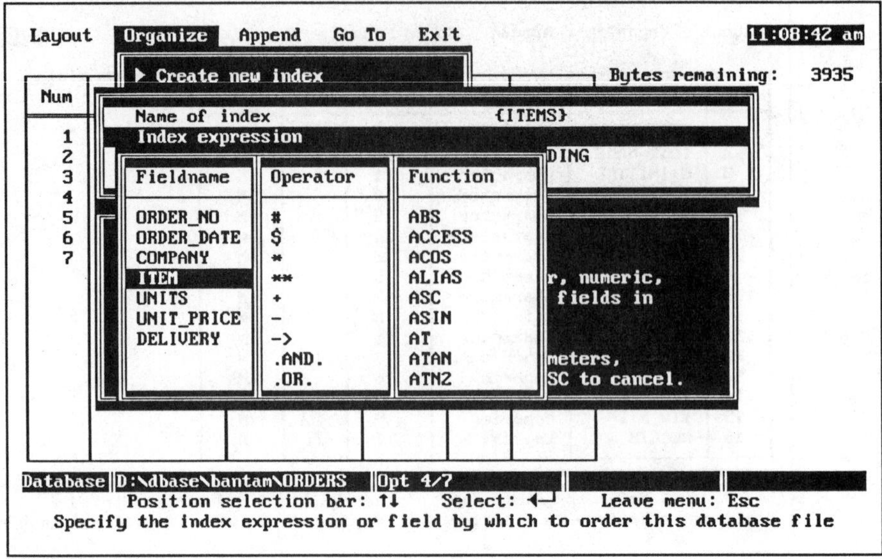

Figure 4-8 Selecting fields from the left column

consisting of multiple field names, functions, and operators. For now, you can focus on a simple index consisting of a field name, and in the next section you can tackle more complex examples. Pressing SHIFT-F1 causes dBASE to present a pick list of field names, operators, and functions. Figure 4-8 shows a list of field names for the ORDERS file in the leftmost column of the pick box. Although the intensity differences do not show in the figure, Memo fields and Logical fields will appear dimmer and will not be selectable as index fields. Since a Logical field has only two values, you can effectively work with this data without the benefit of an index. Another option for Logical fields is to use one of the dBASE functions to convert the Logical field entries to characters for index entries. To index this file by COMPANY, highlight the field name and press ENTER twice. dBASE adds braces around your index expression.

Your next option is whether you want dBASE to build the index in ascending or descending sequence. Pressing the SPACEBAR with the cursor on the Order of index field will toggle between ascending, which goes from lowest to highest value, and descending, which uses the opposite order.

If there are duplicate index entries you can show only the first entry, if you prefer. You can make this change with the option Display first

Records	Fields	Go To	Exit			2:15:32 pm
ORDER_NO	ORDER_DATE	COMPANY	ITEM	UNITS	UNIT_PRICE	DELIVERY
453216	12/09/88	ABC Company	Chair	10	125.98	MEMO
789654	12/15/88	ABC Company	Cabinet	3	129.95	memo
001325	01/15/89	Able Bakery	Cabinet	2	129.95	memo
001359	01/17/89	BBB Bakery	Cabinet	3	129.95	memo
678543	12/10/88	Baker & Associates	Desk	5	585.95	memo
001298	01/10/89	Baker & Associates	Desk	5	585.95	memo
986541	12/16/88	Carlston & Sons	Mailers	100	1.35	memo
001254	01/03/89	Lewis Brothers	Chair	5	89.95	memo

Figure 4-9 Records in COMPANY order with index in effect

duplicate key only. Like the last setting, this is a toggle option that can be changed by highlighting the option and pressing the SPACEBAR.

To create the index, press CTRL-END. The delay that occurs allows dBASE to build the index. This can range from seconds to minutes depending on the size of the file and the complexity of calculations required. When you build a new index, this index becomes the master index that controls the order of the records until you select another index to control the order of the records or create another new index. To see the data in Company sequence, press F2. As shown in Figure 4-9, the records are presented in COMPANY order. BBB Bakery precedes Baker and Associates due to the difference in capitalization of the two entries. To present the COMPANY entries in dictionary sequence you will need to use the UPPER function presented later in this chapter.

Building More Complex Index Expressions

You can combine several fields into a dBASE expression and index the database based on the result of these expressions. dBASE expressions can include arithmetic operators to perform a computation before building an index. You may need to use functions to transform some of the data that you use in expressions.

Using Multiple Fields in an Index You can combine multiple Character fields to build an index with the values from these fields. Indexing a file like the EMPLOYEE file is a good example of where this can be useful. If you index the EMPLOYEE file by LAST_NAME there may be several employees with the same last name. You could have multiple records with last names like Campbell, Harris, Smith, Jones, or any other common name. If you had a record for Keith Campbell, David Campbell, and Catherine Campbell, the order of the Campbell records would be determined by the original order of these records in the database. If you wanted to use the FIRST_NAME field as part of the index sequence, you can build an index expression like LAST_NAME+FIRST_NAME. This will cause dBASE to combine the Character strings for the two fields into a longer string and index by the entire expression. The order of the index entries are:

Camp	John
Campbell	Catherine
Campbell	David
Campbell	Keith
Deaver	Jim

You cannot combine other field types with Character fields in building an index expression. If you need to combine other field types, you will need to convert the data they contain to character data before combining them. The functions covered in a later section will allow you to make the necessary data conversions. You can combine up to 16 fields for the index expression, although dBASE limits the length of the combined data values to 100 characters.

Building an Index with the Result of a Computation Since index expressions support the use of arithmetic operators, you can index a database on the result of a computation. You could use this capability to index on the net purchase amount after a discount is applied to the purchase amount. Depending on the field names, the expression might be PURCHASE- (PURCHASE*DISCOUNT). Another option is indexing on a price extension, if only the unit price and number of units are stored in the database. This expression might look like UNITS*UNIT_PRICE. You can enter these index expressions by typing them from the keyboard or by using the SHIFT-F1 pick option to select operators and fields.

Tip: Be careful not to combine two Numeric fields for a two-field index.

If you write an index expression as LAST_NAME+FIRST_NAME for two Character fields, dBASE uses LAST_NAME as the first index field and combines it with the values in FIRST_NAME. If you attempted to take two Numeric fields like COURSE_NO and BUILDING and wanted to build an index to sequence with both fields, you could not use COURSE_NO+BUILDING. With a course number of 1204 and a building of 82, you would expect an index value of 120482; but dBASE interprets the + as addition and indexes based on 1286. Numeric data must be converted to characters before you can use the + operator to index on two Numeric fields.

Using Functions in an Index Expression You can use some of the dBASE functions covered in Chapter 15 to combine incompatible data types or to transform the data in some other fashion. Normally, functions are used to transform the numeric or date data into a character format that can be combined with other character entries. Another option is transforming the data into upper case to allow the creation of a dictionary-type index for a field that contains upper- and lowercase entries. The data in the database is not altered, only the copy of the data that is used in the construction of the index entries.

Transforming Character Entries to Upper Case The index that you created for the ORDERS file by COMPANY resulted in the entry BBB Bakery appearing before Baker & Associates. Since dBASE uses an ASCII sequence for the index, case differences will always result in a

Tip: The F9 key is convenient when entering complex expressions. Pressing F9 will display the index expression across a fill line at the bottom of the screen.

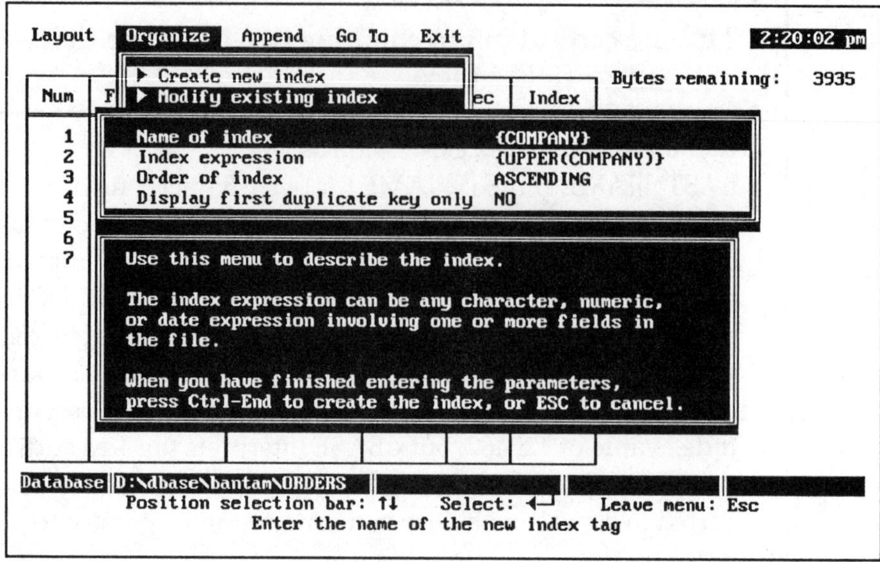

Figure 4-10 Using the UPPER function in an index

list that is not the same as a dictionary sort. To overcome this difficulty for fields with inconsistent capitalization, you can use the UPPER function when building the index.

dBASE functions are available in the pick box that you can activate with SHIFT-F1. All are shown in the rightmost column of the box and when selected add both the keyword and the required parentheses to your index expression. You need to move to the left one position after the addition and supply the required arguments for the selected functions. You may also need to press INS to switch to the Insert mode so the function arguments do not overwrite the right parentheses. For the UPPER function, all that is required is supplying the name of the field that you want converted as the index is built. Arguments that must be supplied for other functions are discussed separately.

Figure 4-10 shows the entry UPPER(COMPANY). If you prefer you can type the entire entry from the keyboard rather than using SHIFT-F1 to select the various components. The records in Figure 4-11 show the order achieved with this index. Note that BBB Bakery follows Baker and Associates achieving the alphabetical sequence without regard to the case of the record entries although you will notice that dBASE did not alter the entries in the records.

Records Fields Go To Exit 2:19:01 pm

ORDER_NO	ORDER_DATE	COMPANY	ITEM	UNITS	UNIT_PRICE	DELIVERY
453216	12/09/88	ABC Company	Chair	10	125.98	MEMO
789654	12/15/88	ABC Company	Cabinet	3	129.95	memo
001325	01/15/89	Able Bakery	Cabinet	2	129.95	memo
678543	12/10/88	Baker & Associates	Desk	5	585.95	memo
001298	01/10/89	Baker & Associates	Desk	5	585.95	memo
001359	01/17/89	BBB Bakery	Cabinet	3	129.95	memo
986541	12/16/88	Carlston & Sons	Mailers	100	1.35	memo
001254	01/03/89	Lewis Brothers	Chair	5	89.95	memo

Figure 4-11 Change in order of records when COMPANY is converted to uppercase

Combining Two Numeric Fields If you use a + in an index expression between two numeric fields, dBASE performs an addition operation for the values in the two fields and builds the index with the result of the addition. In many cases, this is not the result that you want to achieve. Attempting to index on UNIT-PRICE within UNITS would not be achieved by entering UNITS+UNIT_PRICE. Rather, dBASE would add units of 2 to UNIT-PRICE of 129.95 and use 131.95 as the value of the index expression.

The STR function can solve this problem. This function expects a numeric value as its first argument and converts it to a string. The next argument allows you to specify the length of the string including a decimal point, minus sign, and both whole number and decimal digits. If this optional argument is not supplied, dBASE uses a length of 10. Specifying a number less than the number of digits to the left of the decimal point in the number creates a string consisting of asterisks.

The second optional argument allows you to specify the number of decimal digits. A whole number is created if you do not supply this argument. If the number has more decimal digits than are used in the string, the number is rounded to create the string.

To index the ORDERS database by UNITS and UNIT-PRICE, the expression STR(UNITS,3)+STR(UNIT_PRICE,6,2) is used as shown at the bottom of Figure 4-12. The F9 Zoom option was used to display the expression on this line. Figure 4-13 shows the result of the index operation. The entries for the records with five units will demonstrate how the index entries are constructed:

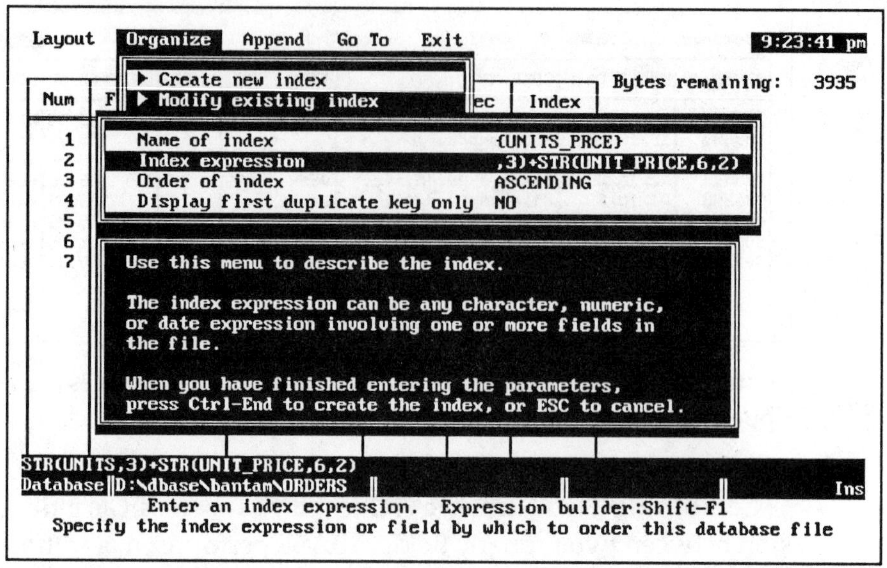

Figure 4-12 Converting numeric entries to strings to build an index

005089.95
005585.95
005585.95

Combining Dates with Characters Indexing cannot be created by combining Date and Character fields unless the Date field is converted to a Character string first. To complete the conversion the DTOC function is used. Its only argument is the Date field that you wish to

Records Fields Go To Exit 9:24:37 pm

ORDER_NO	ORDER_DATE	COMPANY	ITEM	UNITS	UNIT_PRICE	DELIVERY
001325	01/15/89	Able Bakery	Cabinet	2	129.95	memo
789654	12/15/88	ABC Company	Cabinet	3	129.95	memo
001359	01/17/89	BBB Bakery	Cabinet	3	129.95	memo
001254	01/03/89	Lewis Brothers	Chair	5	89.95	memo
678543	12/10/88	Baker & Associates	Desk	5	585.95	memo
001298	01/10/89	Baker & Associates	Desk	5	585.95	memo
453216	12/09/88	ABC Company	Chair	10	125.98	MEMO
986541	12/16/88	Carlston & Sons	Mailers	100	1.35	memo

Figure 4-13 Result of the index operation

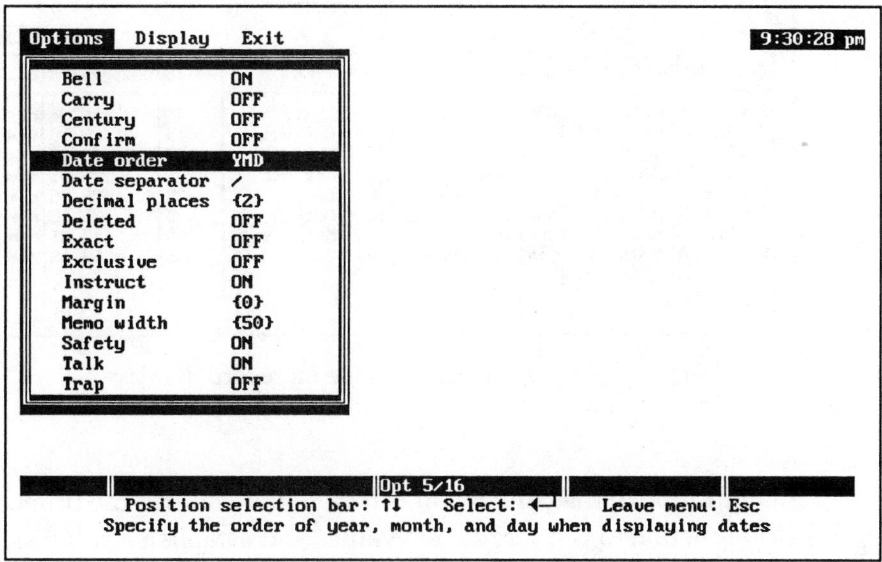

Figure 4-14 Using the Settings options to change the date order

convert. You can build an index with the expression COMPANY+DTOC(ORDER_DATE). The only problem with this approach is that the month lists first in the date and will result in a Character string that shows the month in the first position. This lists the records so that an order for 1/10/89 displays before an order for 12/10/88.

To cause the 1988 records to display before the 1989 records, you need to change the default display format for dBASE dates. You can make this change from the Tools menu in the Control Center. Activate Tools by pressing ALT-T from the Control Center. Type an **S** to select Settings. The menu will be active when the Settings screen shown in Figure 4-14 appears. Type a **D** to move to Date order. Press the SPACEBAR to select the YMD order. Use the RIGHT ARROW key to move to the Exit menu and press ENTER. Reindex the file with the same expression and note that the index is built so that all of the 1988 records for a company display before their 1989 transactions. The records for Baker & Associates in Figure 4-15 show the change made by this index.

Building an Index with Logical Field Entries dBASE does not allow you to select a Logical field in an index expression. You can use the T and F entries in logical fields to build index expressions if you convert the entries to Character strings. Although there is not a com-

ORDER_NO	ORDER_DATE	COMPANY	ITEM	UNITS	UNIT_PRICE	DELIVERY
453216	88/12/09	ABC Company	Chair	10	125.98	MEMO
789654	88/12/15	ABC Company	Cabinet	3	129.95	memo
001325	89/01/15	Able Bakery	Cabinet	2	129.95	memo
001359	89/01/17	BBB Bakery	Cabinet	3	129.95	memo
678543	88/12/10	Baker & Associates	Desk	5	585.95	memo
001298	89/01/10	Baker & Associates	Desk	5	585.95	memo
986541	88/12/16	Carlston & Sons	Mailers	100	1.35	memo
001254	89/01/03	Lewis Brothers	Chair	5	89.95	memo

Records Fields Go To Exit 9:29:43 pm

Figure 4-15 Effect of date order change on record display

mand to make the conversion directly, you can use the immediate if (IIF) function to test for the two values and establish a valid Character string for either of the possibilities.

If you want to build an index with the entries from a Logical field called INS, you can use the following for the index expression:

```
IIF(INS,"T","F")
```

The index entries for records with a true value in their Logical field INS will contain a T and the index entries for records with a false value in the INS field will contain an F. Since these entries are Character strings, you can use them in combination with other Character fields when constructing your index expression.

Continuing to Use .NDX Files

NDX files were the only option for indexing databases prior to dBASE IV. You may still have NDX files for databases created earlier and wish to maintain them. This is a little more work than the MDX file option because they are not handled automatically like MDX files. First, since these files were not created from within dBASE IV, they will not be in the catalog. Second, you will need to take a specific action to open these files.

To add an NDX file to the current catalog, you can use a command on the Organize menu. Press ALT-O to activate the Organize pull-

Tip: Make sure you return to the Control Center before activating the database design screen to include the file in the catalog if you are working from the dot prompt.

Proceeding from the Control Center will ensure that there is a catalog open. This will cause only .NDX files for the current database to appear in the list of options to activate a .NDX file.

down menu from the database design screen. Type an **I** to select Include .NDX file and highlight the name of the .NDX file that you wish to add to the current catalog. dBASE automatically activates the .NDX file at the time it adds it to the current catalog.

Since .NDX files are not updated automatically you must activate these files to have them updated for additions and changes. To activate an .NDX file you must be in the database design screen. Press ALT-O and type an **A** to select Activate .NDX file. dBASE displays the names of all the .NDX files in the current catalog for your selection.

You can still create .NDX files for dBASE IV databases but must now do so from the dot prompt with the INDEX ON command. Since .NDX files are not updated unless they are opened each time you use a database, it is essential that you activate the index file for appending records or editing fields used to build the .NDX file entries.

Deleting Index Tags

Keeping indexes that are no longer needed is a waste of system resources, since dBASE will maintain the index for all changes and additions in the index field. To delete an index tag that you no longer need, select the Organize menu on the design screen by pressing ALT-O and typing an **R** for Remove unwanted index tag. dBASE displays a list of the tags and their associated expressions. You can highlight the one you no longer need and press ENTER to remove it.

Removing Deleted Records

You can mark records for deletion in several ways. You have already seen how you can use the CTRL-U option or the Records menu option to Remove a record from the database. These actions mark a record as deleted but do not purge the record from the database.

dBASE IV's approach of retaining deleted records offers both an advantage and a disadvantage. Keeping the record in the database offers an advantage since it allows you to unmark the record if you later decide that you need it. The disadvantage is that the default settings for dBASE allow a record marked for deletion to appear on the screen and in reports and labels.

Unmarking Deleted Records

You can restore records marked for deletion one by one from the Edit or Browse screens by highlighting a deleted record and pressing CTRL-U. This can be a slow process with a large database and many records to unmark. A shortcut is to restore all deleted records. To restore the records, you must be in the database design screen. Press ALT-O and type a **U** to select Unmark all records. After confirming your request, dBASE removes the delete marks from all the deleted records in the database.

❑ **Tip: Rather than pack a database every time you delete a record, set Deleted Off.**

When you delete a record you normally do not want to see it in a report; yet dBASE will continue to display the record with its default setting. Change the DELETED setting to OFF, and it will appear that an immediate pack operation is being performed without the delay experienced by packing a large database.

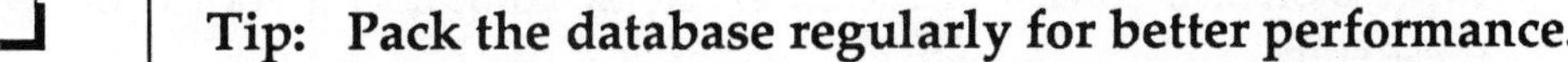

Tip: Pack the database regularly for better performance.

An excess of deleted records will slow down access to the records that are not deleted. Extra data that needs to be read as you browse or edit the database, as well as index file entries that require maintenance, use system resources unnecessarily.

Changing Settings to Stop Displaying Deleted Records

If you are uncertain about removing deleted records from the database and have the disk space to allow the records to remain, you can remove these records from view in edit screens and reports and labels. To make this change you will change the DELETED setting to OFF with the Tools Settings selection available from the Control Center.

Packing the Database

Packing your database eliminates the records that are marked for deletion. Even if you have Deleted set to Off so you do not see deleted records, you will want to pack the database occasionally. Packing the database deletes these records and compresses the space required for data storage, making your system run much more effectively.

To remove records marked for deletion from the database, move to the database design screen from the Control Center by highlighting the database name, pressing ENTER, and typing an **M**. Type an **E** to select Erase-marked records from the Organize menu.

GETTING STARTED

➤ You can try out your newly acquired skills for organizing the records in your databases with the EMPLOYEE file. As a first step you can create several new indexes for this file. The first index will organize the records in zip code sequence. Since only one field is required, the index expression will consist of the single field. To build the index follow these steps:

1. Highlight EMPLOYEE in the Data panel of the Control Center. Press SHIFT-F2 to move to the design screen.
2. Since the Organize menu is already on the screen, you can type a **C** to select Create a new index.
3. Press ENTER to select Index name. Type ZIP_CODE and press ENTER.
4. Press ENTER to select Index expression. Press SHIFT-F1 to list the field names. Highlight ZIP_CODE in the list of field names and press ENTER twice.
5. Press CTRL-END to finalize your entries and build the index.
6. Press F2 to view the data records. Since the last index created is the master index, the records will appear in zip code sequence.

You can create a more complex index for the EMPLOYEE file by indexing on the Logical field HEALTH. You will probably want to use a second index field to organize the records that have the same logical value. LAST_NAME will be used as the second field in the index. Follow these steps:

1. Press SHIFT-F2 to return to the design screen.
2. Type a **C** to select Create a new index from the Organize menu.
3. Press ENTER to select Index name. Type HLTH_LNME and press ENTER.
4. Press ENTER to select Index expression. Press SHIFT-F1 then use the RIGHT ARROW key to move to the third column. Highlight IIF in the list of functions and press ENTER.
5. Press INS to switch to the Insert mode and move to the left one position. Type **HEALTH,"T","F"**.
6. Press F9 to display the index expression at the bottom of the screen and continue with your entry by typing a **+**, pressing SHIFT-F1, using the LEFT ARROW to move to the list of field names, highlighting LAST_NAME, and pressing ENTER.
7. Press ENTER to complete the index expression.
8. Press CTRL-END to finalize your entries and build the index.
9. Press F2 to view the data records.

Although indexing is more efficient than sorting, you will want to try the sort features. You can use the second database created with the sort operation to practice record deletion without losing the employee records that you will need in later chapters. To sort the database in order by STATE and within STATE by CITY follow these steps:

1. Press SHIFT-F2 to return to the design screen.
2. Type an **S** to sort the records.
3. Press SHIFT-F1, highlight STATE, and press ENTER three times.
4. Press SHIFT-F1, highlight CITY, and press ENTER twice.
5. Press CTRL-END.
6. Type **EMPSTCTY** and press ENTER.
7. dBASE IV will display a message indicating that it is sorting the records. When it finishes, press ALT-E and type an **A** to Abandon changes and exit.
8. Highlight EMPSTCTY in the Data panel of the Control Center and press ENTER. Type a **D** to display the records.

To practice deleting records with the EMPSTCTY database follow these steps:

1. With the cursor on the first record, press CTRL-U to mark the record for deletion.
2. Press the DOWN ARROW key twice to move to the third record. Press ALT-R and type an **M** to mark the third record.
3. Press the DOWN ARROW key to move to the fifth record. Press CTRL-U to mark it for deletion.
4. Press the UP ARROW key twice and press CTRL-U to unmark the third record.

The two records marked for deletion are still in the database. You can pack the database to eliminate these records with these steps:

1. Press CTRL-END to return to the Control Center.
2. Press SHIFT-F2 to return to the database design screen.
3. Type an **E** to erase the records marked for deletion.
4. Type a **Y** to confirm the deletion.
5. Press F2 to view the remaining records when dBASE finishes packing the file.

To delete the EMPSTCTY database follow these steps:

1. Return to the Control Center by pressing ALT-E and typing an **E** for Exit.
2. Press ENTER with EMPSTCTY highlighted and type a **C** to close the file since you cannot delete an open file.
3. Highlight the EMPSTCTY file in the Data panel.
4. Press the DEL key and type a **Y** twice to remove the file from the catalog and delete it from the disk.

CHAPTER 5

Queries

The Query features of dBASE IV allow you to define a group of records that you wish to work with. Unlike the features in the Edit and Browse Go To menus, which searched for a particular record, Query features allow you to isolate an entire group of records that meet your specifications. You can display Query results on the screen or use the Query in combination with features like reports and labels.

dBASE IV provides a two-faceted query capability. The first type of query, a View query, allows you to work with a subset of your database records. You can display this subset of records on the screen or use them to create a report or a set of labels. dBASE IV builds a special view of the database in memory that provides access to the records meeting your needs. Although a permanent copy of the view records is only maintained in the original database from which the view was built, the Query can be saved and reused to display the view again.

When you build View queries you are not limited to the contents of one database. If your databases contain fields allowing you to link their records, you can access data from as many as eight databases at once. This allows you to design a database system with more than one database, a feature that can prevent duplication of data.

The second type of query is an Update query. This type of query allows you to make changes to each record that meets your specifications.

dBASE IV has provided expanded features for queries. Even tasks supported by Queries in earlier releases of the product have been enhanced with features like the Query-By-Example (QBE) option that allows you to define an example of the type of record you wish to locate.

Designing Queries

dBASE IV provides a new approach to the creation of queries. A graphic interface allows you to create a query by supplying examples of the records you wish to select. dBASE IV's fill-in-the-blank approach is called Query-By-Example and provides a quick way to create simple queries.

Accessing the Query Design Work Surface

You can access the Query design work surface in many ways. If you are in the Control Center, you can move to the <create> option in the Queries panel and press ENTER or SHIFT-F2. To open an existing Query, you can highlight the Query name in the Control Center and press SHIFT-F2. If the default setting for INSTRUCT has been left at ON, highlighting the Query name and pressing ENTER displays a menu similar to the database menu. You can select Modify query from this menu by typing an **M**.

If you are already working in a database file, you can access the Query design screen by pressing SHIFT-F2 from the Edit, Browse, database design, reports, labels, or forms screens.

Components of the Query Design Screen

The components of the Query design screen depends on whether you are creating a View or an Update query. Although the screen is the same, different components are used for each type of query. You can examine the Update query screen in more detail in the section on Update queries.

A completed View query contains at least two sections. The first section is known as the File skeleton and is shown at the top of Figure 5-1. If a database is open at the time you create a query, dBASE IV automatically adds the File skeleton for this database to the top of the screen. If there is no database open, you need to add a File skeleton by

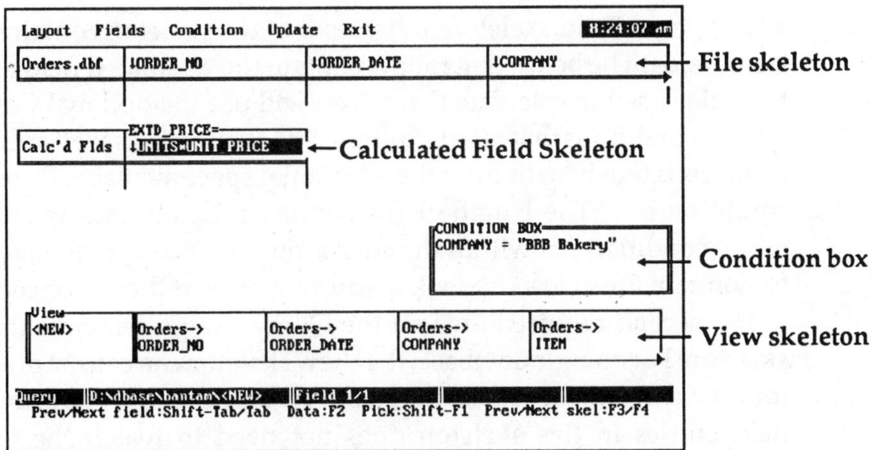

Figure 5-1 Sample Query design screen

pressing ALT-L to invoke the layout menu shown in Figure 5-2. Typing an **A** for Add file to query allows you to select from a list of the database files in the current catalog. You can combine up to eight different File skeletons in a View query.

The first box in the File skeleton contains the name of the database. Subsequent boxes contain the field names in the database.

Two optional areas of the queries screen are Calculated Fields skeleton and a Condition box. The Calculated Fields skeleton is used when you want to compute a result based on the contents of one or more database fields. When dBASE IV executes the query, the calculated field is computed for each record in the database. The first box in

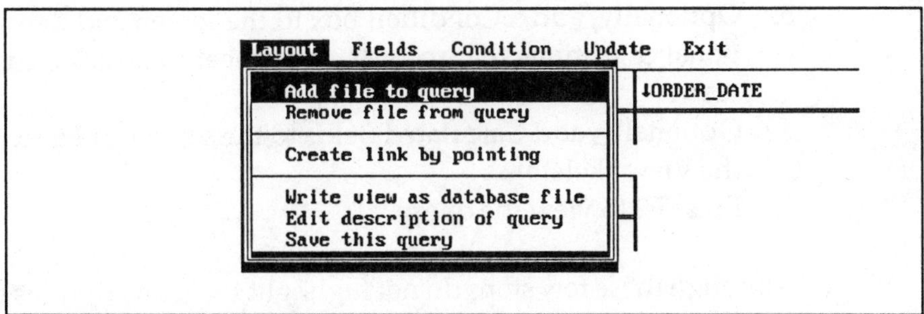

Figure 5-2 Layout menu

a Calculated Field skeleton indicates that the skeleton contains calculated fields. The boxes that follow contain the calculated fields and the formulas used to calculate them. You will use the optional Condition box for conditions that affect multiple File skeletons, as well as complex conditions that benefit from the additional space available through the condition box. The length of the condition determines whether the entire condition fits within the condition box. You can always use F9 to Zoom in for a close-up look if you cannot read the entire condition.

The second required area on the Query design screen is the View skeleton. For a single database, the View skeleton can consist of an entry for each of the database fields or a subset of the fields. The order of the field entries in this skeleton does not need to match the order of the fields in the database. When you use multiple databases in a query, the View skeleton can consist of some or all of the fields from the files included in the query. If you have saved the query previously, the name that you assigned to the query displays in the first box of the View skeleton. dBASE IV shows both the file and field name in each of the remaining boxes of the View skeleton.

At a minimum you will make entries in at least the File skeleton to create a View query. The steps that you might follow are

1. Activate a database file and select <create> from the Query panel to move to the Query design screen.
2. Place examples in the File skeleton to define the records you want to place in the view. Optionally, add summary or sort operators.
3. Optionally, add additional files to the File skeleton area and establish links.
4. Add or remove fields from the View skeleton.
5. Optionally, add a Condition box to the screen and define additional conditions that records must meet to be selected for the view.
6. Optionally, add Calculated fields to the screen and add them to the View skeleton.
7. Press F2 to view the query.

Although these few steps do not highlight the many options that are available, reading through each of the sections that follow will introduce you to the full set of options for View queries.

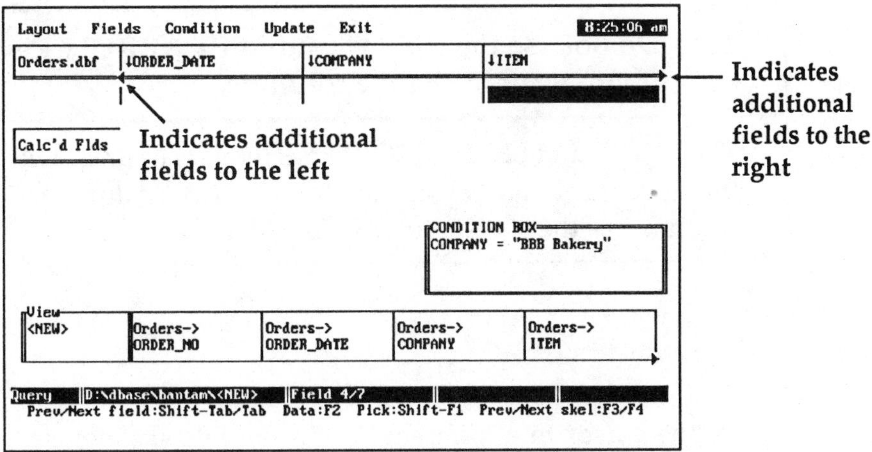

Figure 5-3 File skeleton with arrows indicating additional fields

Moving Around on the Query Design Screen

You can move between the various design elements with the F3 Previous and F4 Next keys. If the only design elements on the screen are a File and a View skeleton, these keys will toggle from one to the other. You can also use them to move to the Calculated Field skeleton and the Condition box.

To move from column to column in the skeletons, use the TAB and SHIFT-TAB keys. TAB moves you one column to the right and SHIFT-TAB moves you one column to the left. You can press the HOME key to move to the first column and the END key to move to the last column. If there are additional fields on the right or left sides of the File skeleton, dBASE IV adds arrow heads to the line under the fields names as shown in Figure 5-3.

If you have multiple File skeletons on the screen you can move from one to the other with the F3 and F4 keys. A small arrow like the one shown in Figure 5-4 appears on the left side of the screen to let you know if there are additional skeletons above or below the skeleton currently on the screen. With more File skeletons than can fit on one screen, use the PgUp and PgDn keys to move between screens. CTRL-PgUp and CTRL-PgDn can be used to move to the first and last File skeletons, respectively. Pressing the UP ARROW and DOWN ARROW keys

Tip: Do not use the RIGHT and LEFT ARROW keys if you want to change columns.

The RIGHT and LEFT ARROW keys move the cursor within the current column. If you want to move from column to column, use the SHIFT and SHIFT-TAB keys.

moves the cursor to a different line in the File skeleton so you can include multiple examples in a field.

Adding, Removing, and Moving Skeleton Entries

The options for working with File skeletons and View skeletons are different. The capabilities included focus on the features that each of these skeletons offer.

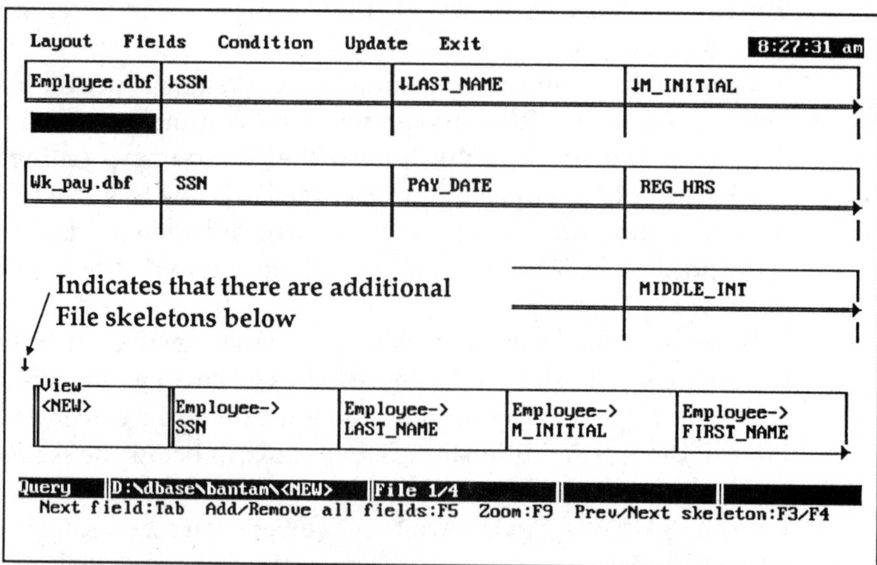

Figure 5-4 Query design screen with multiple File skeletons

File Skeleton Options When you are working with the File skeleton, you can add or remove an entire skeleton at once. Since the skeleton represents the complete structure of a file, you cannot select specific fields. You must either use the entire File skeleton or none of it.

To add a File skeleton to the design screen, press ALT-L and type an **A**. Select from the list of filenames presented or select a directory to select a database in another directory. To remove a skeleton from the design screen, press ALT-L for the Layout menu, move the cursor to the skeleton that you wish to remove. Press ALT-L and type an **R** to remove the skeleton from the view.

View Skeleton Options If you have a database open at the time you create a Query, dBASE IV automatically adds the field names from this database to the View skeleton. If you want only a few fields from the database in the View skeleton, you might prefer to close the open database before you create a Query. In this fashion, you can add each field that you need to the view in any sequence you choose without moving and deleting fields. If you want to add all of the fields to the View skeleton, move to below the database name in the File skeleton and press F5. If the View skeleton already has some of the fields included, pressing F5 below the database names adds the remaining ones. If you press F5 when all of the fields are in the View skeleton, dBASE IV removes them from the View skeleton.

To add a field to a View skeleton from the File skeleton, press ALT-F to invoke the Fields menu shown in Figure 5-5 and type an A to Add a field to the view. dBASE IV adds the current field name in the File or Calculated Fields skeleton to the View skeleton. Pressing the F5 Field key provides a shortcut approach to achieve the same result. If you are adding a Calculated field that does not have a name, dBASE IV prompts you to supply one.

❑ **Tip: Open a database file after entering query.**

If you wait to open a file until after you have told dBASE IV that you want to create a query, you can add a file for the File skeleton and select fields for the View skeleton one by one in any order you desire.

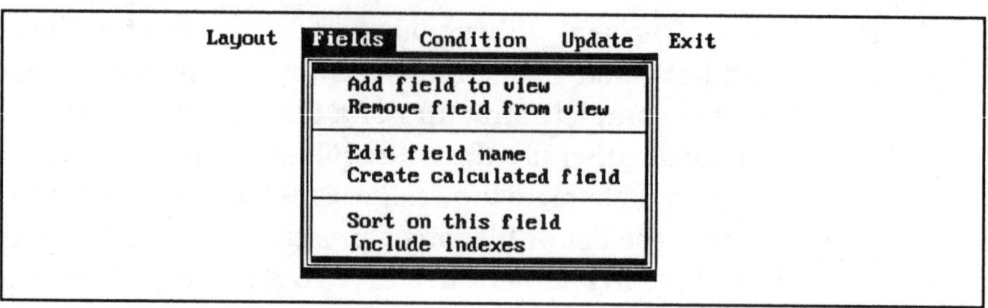

Figure 5-5 Fields menu

To remove a field from a View skeleton, move to the field, press ALT-F for the Fields menu and type an **R** for Remove field from view. dBASE IV removes the current field from the View skeleton. Like adding fields, you can press the F5 Field key, which achieves the same result. You can remove multiple fields by moving to a field in the View or File skeleton, pressing F6, highlighting the adjacent fields that you want to remove, and pressing F5.

You can add all the fields from a File skeleton to a View skeleton by moving to the box for the file name in the skeleton and pressing F5. If the fields from this file are already in the skeleton, pressing F5 removes all the fields from the View skeleton.

You can also change the field names that dBASE IV displays as the field names. To change the field names, move to the field in the View skeleton that you want to rename, press ALT-F and type an **E** for Edit field name. When dBASE IV prompts for a field name, type any field name and press ENTER. dBASE IV displays the new field name above the old one in the View skeleton. Changing the field name only changes the text that appears in place of the field name. It does not change the

Tip: Use both the Add and Remove options to add most of the fields.

The quickest way to add most of the fields in a File skeleton to a View skeleton is to add all the fields by moving to the filename in the skeleton and pressing F5, followed by using the Remove command to eliminate the fields that are no longer required.

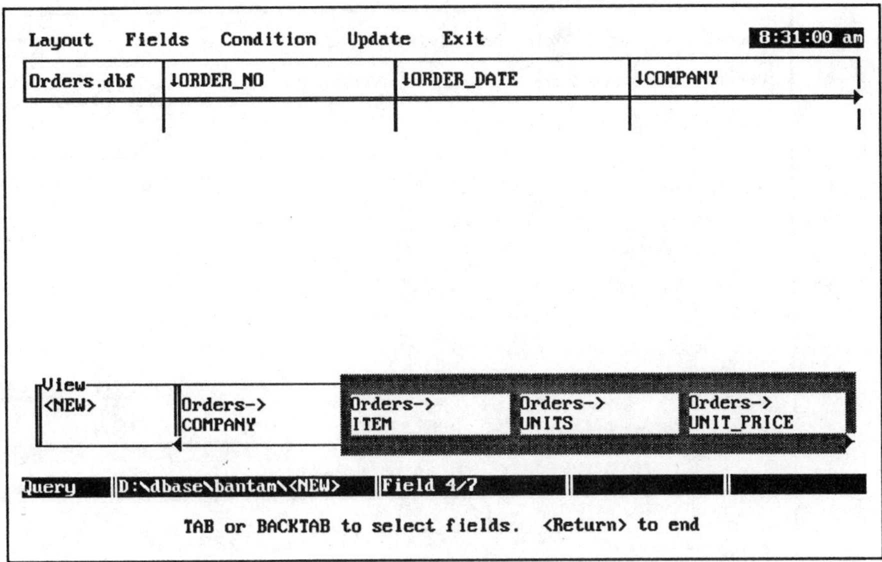

Figure 5-6 Selecting multiple fields

original database, nor does it change the information that appears in the field. If you change field names in a Query and then write the view as a database file, the database file will use the new field name you have given.

To remove fields from a View skeleton, move to the field in the View skeleton that you no longer need and press ALT-F and type an **R** to select Remove field from view or press the F5 Fields key. You also want to remember the shortcut mentioned earlier to remove all of a file's fields from a View skeleton by positioning on the filename in the File skeleton and press F5.

Since a View skeleton defines how dBASE IV displays the data meeting your specifications, you want to ensure that the order of the fields listed in the view matches your needs. The normal order is to add each new field at the end of the View skeleton. To move one or more fields, move to the first field that you wish to move. Press F6 Extend Select, then use the TAB and SHIFT-TAB keys to extend the selection to additional fields. TAB stretches the selection to the right and SHIFT-TAB extends it to the left. Figure 5-6 shows the ITEM, UNITS, and UNIT_PRICE fields selected with this method. When all the fields that you wish to select are highlighted, press ENTER. Next, press F7 Move and move the cursor to the location where you want the selected

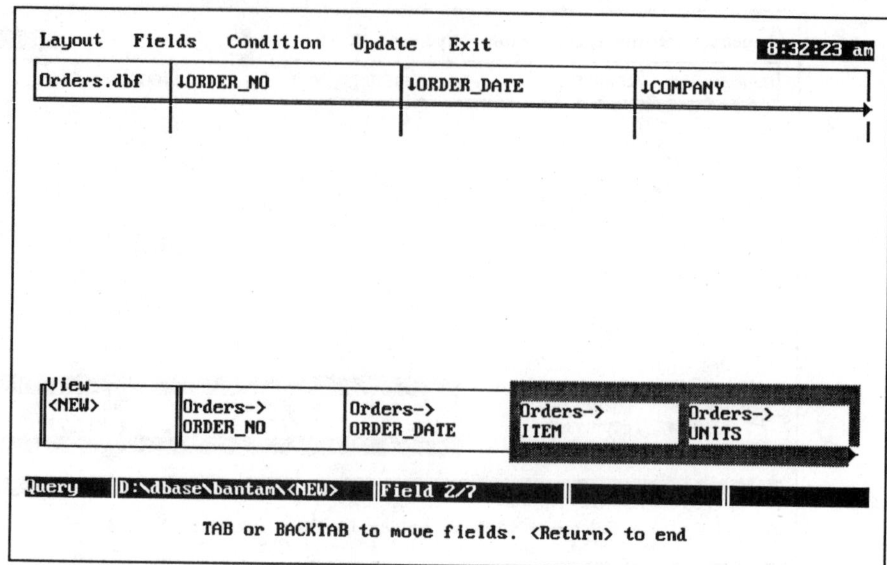

Figure 5-7 Fields after repositioning

fields. Figure 5-7 shows the three fields selected earlier being repositioned in the View skeleton. When you press ENTER the fields are placed immediately following the current location.

Entering Simple Conditions

Entering conditions requires you to supply an example of the records that you want to isolate with the query. You can enter an example for any type of field except a Memo field by entering the example directly under the field name in the File skeleton. For Memo fields, you can only enter your specifications through a Condition box.

❑ **Tip: Use the F9 Zoom key to enlarge your view.**

You can use the Zoom key to enlarge the current column in a skeleton or a Condition box. Press it a second time to return to normal size. The enlarged size makes it much easier to enter examples and expressions in these boxes.

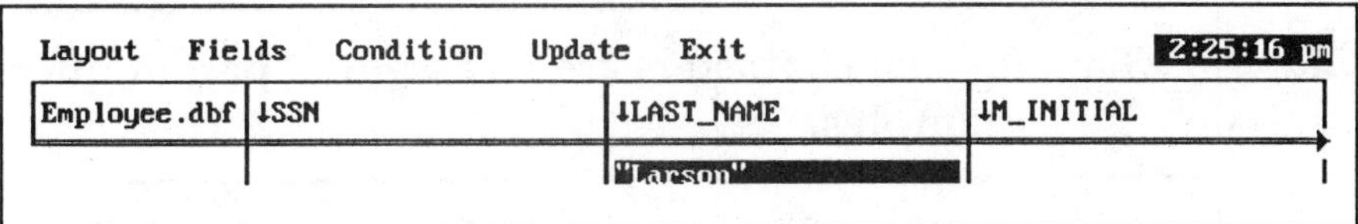

Figure 5-8 Query design with a character type example

Examples in the File skeleton boxes are assumed to look for records that contain an entry equal to the example that you supply unless you use an operator specifying another condition. To isolate records with a LAST_NAME of Larson in a view, you would enter **"Larson"** in the box under LAST_NAME as shown in Figure 5-8. The quotation marks are necessary and as much a part of the entry as Larson since the field contains character data. When you press F2 after making this entry, dBASE IV displays a view that contains only the records with Larson in the LAST_NAME field.

Numeric and Float field data are entered just as you entered it in the database. Logical fields require a small change. Data in these fields was entered as T, F, t, f, Y, or N; to isolate records with these entries you must surround the entries with decimal points, as in .T. and .F. To isolate records for a specific date, you must enter the date inside curly braces like **{03/15/84}** as shown in Figure 5-9.

Isolating the Data Records

Once you have entered an example in the File skeleton, you can have dBASE IV apply this specification to the database records by pressing F2. dBASE IV displays the subset of the database records that match your example as shown in Figure 5-10, where records were isolated with the entry **"Chicago"** under the CITY box.

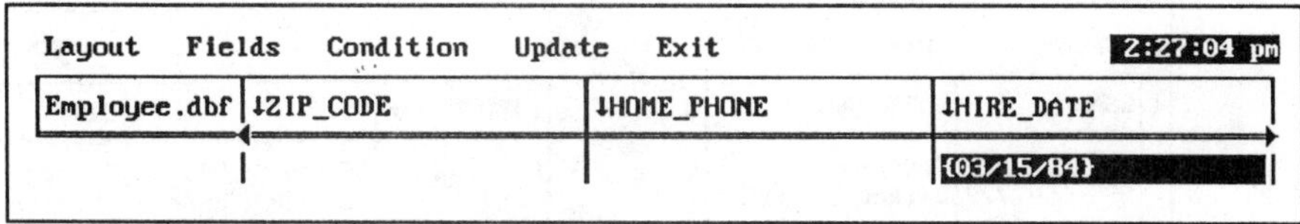

Figure 5-9 Query design with a date type example

Tip: Special characters are an essential part of query examples.

Remember to use quotation marks around character data and braces around dates. Without these characters, dBASE IV cannot process your query requests properly.

You can return to the Query design screen by pressing SHIFT-F2 or by pressing ALT-E and typing a **T** to Transfer to query design. To enter another Query you need to clear the existing Query. You can move back to the Query design and clear the existing entries by deleting examples with DEL, BACKSPACE, or CTRL-Y. You can activate the Exit menu and type an **E** to select the Exit option from this menu. Once you are back at the Control Center you can select <create> to develop a new query.

Using Operators Other than Equal

dBASE IV supports a variety of operators as you build your queries. You can use any of the operators listed in Table 5-1. These operators allow you to test for conditions like less than and greater than as well as a Soundex and pattern match, which match records based on their sound or their letter pattern. In addition dBASE IV supports the use of the arithmetic operators in your conditions allowing you to perform calculations before checking a condition.

Using Operators The examples you have entered thus far have not used operators. Whenever an operator is not entered, dBASE IV uses

Records Fields Go To Exit 2:28:48 pm

SSN	LAST_NAME	M_INITIAL	FIRST_NAME	ADDRESS	CITY	ST
375-98-1239	Foster	G	Charles	67 Green Rd.	Chicago	IL
555-66-7777	Walker	P	Paula	123 Lucy Lane	Chicago	IL

Figure 5-10 View of records with CITY equaling Chicago

Tip: Delete existing entries before starting a new query

Completing new query entries does not erase the existing examples. You can clear the contents of any of the Query example boxes or the Condition box by positioning the cursor on the first character and pressing CTRL-Y.

an implied equal to. You can use the less than and greater than operators for all types of fields except Memo fields. You enter an example in the same manner as with the equal condition except that you precede the entry with one of the logical operators. To isolate employee records with an hourly rate greater than 10, you would enter **>10** in the File skeleton under HR_RATE. To isolate records that also include those with an hourly rate of 10, you would enter **>=10** in the same location.

You can combine the less than and greater than operators with other field types. If you create a View query with the entry **>"A"** in the LAST_NAME field, you will find all the records that begin with any letter including A's, like Able, Abbott, and Anderson, as each of these entries is greater than A. On the other hand looking for records with **<"Z"** under the LAST_NAME field includes all the records in the database except for the ones that started with the letter Z.

Table 5-1 Condition Operators

#	Not equal to
<>	Not equal to
=	Equal to
>	Greater than
<	Less than
>=	Greater than or equal to
<=	Less than or equal to
$	Contains
Like	Matches a pattern
Sounds like	Has a sound similar to the entry although spelling may differ

Tip: Set DELETED ON.

If you do not want deleted records to appear in the result of your View queries, use Tools Settings to set DELETED ON. Deleted records are not purged from the database, but they no longer appear in queries.

You can combine either < or > with an equal to condition by combining the < or the > with an = symbol. The entry **>10** excludes 10 whereas **>=10** includes 10.

The not equal condition can use either <> or #. Entering **#10** looks for all records with any entry other than 10 for the field.

Using the Contains Operator The $ is used to represent contains. This operator allows you to look for all records that contain the Character string shown. Entering **$"& Son"** as shown in Figure 5-11 looks for this sequence of characters anywhere in the COMPANY entries. Given the database in Figure 5-12, dBASE IV would create a view displaying the record for Carlston & Sons.

Pattern Matching The Like operator allows you to use the wildcard characters * and ? as part of the example you specify. The asterisk (*) represents one or more characters and matches with any entry regardless of case. The question mark (?) represents any single character and

Tip: Use the contains operator rather than wildcard characters when you are uncertain of the position of text.

You can create a pattern when searching for an entry, but you must have some awareness of the placement of the characters you are looking for. The Contains ($) option allows you to search for text without regard for its placement within the text.

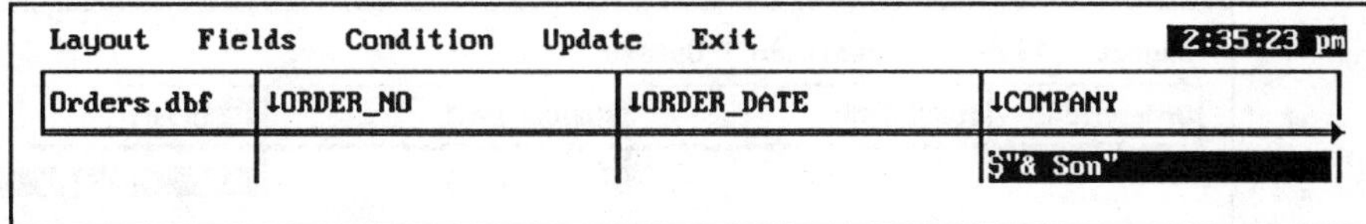

Figure 5-11 Query design with contains operator

does not consider case in the matching process. Other parts of the example entered are matched on a case-sensitive basis. Entering **Like "A?am*"** matches with Adams, Adamski, Arams, and many other entries as long as the first letter is a capital A followed by any character, a lowercase letter combination **am**, and any Character string.

In addition to using the * and ? in any location within a string, you can use them repeatedly. Entries of Like "*aba*" and Like "?at??th?" are acceptable.

Figure 5-13 shows the entry **Like "*Bakery"**. This entry is designed to isolate those records that contain an entry followed by the word Bakery. Pressing F2 after this entry results in the display of two records from the ORDERS file as shown in Figure 5-14.

Soundex Matches Soundex matches attempt to match entries by sounds rather than spelling. A mathematical computation is performed to compute the way an example word or phrase sounds. These same mathematical computations are performed on words in the database. A four-character code is developed for your entry in the following manner:

Records Fields Go To Exit 2:35:43 pm

ORDER_NO	ORDER_DATE	COMPANY	ITEM	UNITS	UNIT_PRICE	DELIVERY
453216	12/09/88	ABC Company	Chair	10	125.98	MEMO
678543	12/10/88	Baker & Associates	Desk	5	585.95	memo
789654	12/15/88	ABC Company	Cabinet	3	129.95	memo
986541	12/16/88	Carlston & Sons	Mailers	100	1.35	memo
001254	01/03/89	Lewis Brothers	Chair	5	89.95	memo
001298	01/10/89	Baker & Associates	Desk	5	585.95	memo
001325	01/15/89	Able Bakery	Cabinet	2	129.95	memo
001359	01/17/89	BBB Bakery	Cabinet	3	129.95	memo

Figure 5-12 ORDERS database used in the query examples

```
Layout   Fields   Condition   Update   Exit                          2:37:44 pm
Orders.dbf | ↓ORDER_NO        | ↓ORDER_DATE        | ↓COMPANY
           |                  |                    | Like "*Bakery"
```

Figure 5-13 Query design with like operator and asterisk

- All occurrences of the following letters are dropped unless they are in the first position of the entry: a, e, h, i, o, u, w, y.
- The first letter is retained.
- The following digits are substituted for the next three letters that are not dropped:

1	b f p v
2	c g j k q s x z
3	d t
4	l
5	m n
6	r

- Double occurrences of a letter are replaced with a single digit.
- Substitutions stop after the third digit is added to the first letter. If a non-alpha character other than leading blanks is encountered first before three digits are added, the code substitutions stop at this point.
- 0000 returned in the first nonblank code is nonalphabetic.

The entry of **Sounds like "Smith"** in Figure 5-15 generates a code of S53 since the i and the h are dropped. This would match with Smith, Smythe, and Smyth. You do not need to be concerned with the Soundex

```
Records    Fields    Go To    Exit                                   2:37:30 pm
```

ORDER_NO	ORDER_DATE	COMPANY	ITEM	UNITS	UNIT_PRICE	DELIVERY
001325	01/15/89	Able Bakery	Cabinet	2	129.95	memo
001359	01/17/89	BBB Bakery	Cabinet	3	129.95	memo

Figure 5-14 View query of design in Figure 5-13

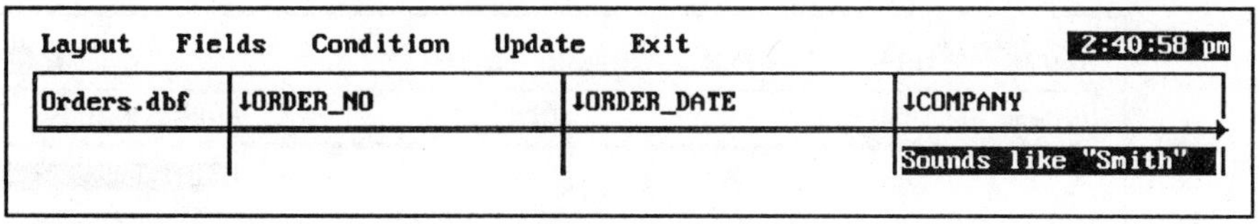

Layout	Fields	Condition	Update	Exit	2:40:58 pm
Orders.dbf	↓ORDER_NO	↓ORDER_DATE	↓COMPANY		
			Sounds like "Smith"		

Figure 5-15 Query design with Sounds like operator

code generated; these entries would never be supplied. The code is shown only to provide insight into the manner in which dBASE IV handles the Soundex entries.

Combining Conditions

There are several ways to combine conditions depending on whether you want to combine conditions for a single field of the database or different fields. You can use the example entries to enter all combination conditions except those that use multiple File skeletons. These must be entered through Condition boxes.

You can place more than one condition in a field separated by a comma as a way of joining two conditions with an implied AND that means a record must match each of the entries to be eligible to be placed in the view. Entering **>100,<500** in the UNIT_PRICE field as shown in Figure 5-16 identifies records where the UNIT_PRICE is greater than 100 **and** less than 500. Both conditions must be met for a record to display. Figure 5-17 shows the records in the view for the ORDERS file when F2 is pressed.

You can enter several examples in one File skeleton. These examples are automatically joined by an implied "AND" as long as they are placed in the same row of the skeleton. Figure 5-18 shows entries in the ITEM and UNIT_PRICE fields and isolates the records where the ITEM

Tip: Check the logic of compound conditions carefully.

It is difficult to record conditions that use AND and OR. Read through the conditions slowly and carefully and test the results with a group of records to verify that it is working correctly.

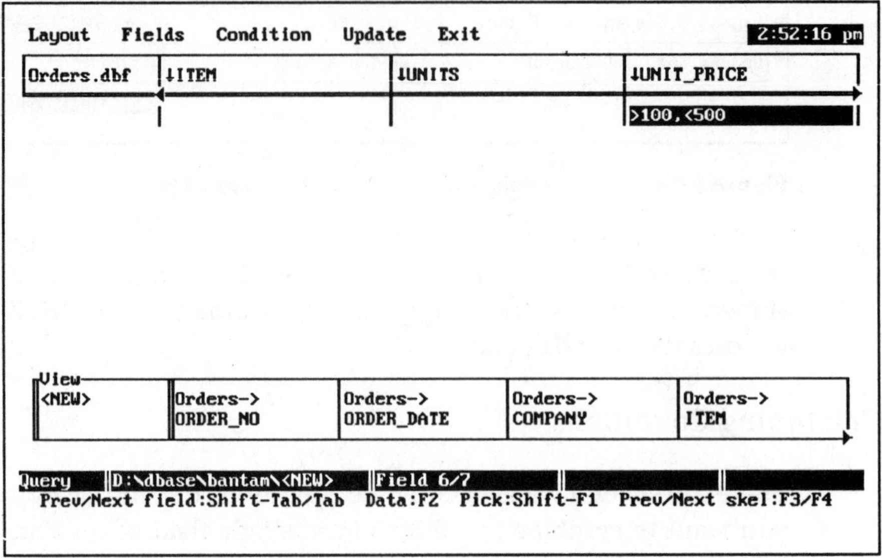

Figure 5-16 Query design with two examples joined by AND

in the record is Cabinet **and** the UNIT_PRICE is greater than 100 and less than 500. Additional entries on this row would add conditions that records must meet before displaying in the resulting view.

You can create queries that use an implied **or** to join queries by using multiple lines in the same File skeleton. Entries placed on one row are automatically joined with an implied **or** to entries placed in another row of the skeleton. You can use this technique to accept multiple entries for one field, as in Figure 5-19, where the ITEM field contains Cabinet in one row and Desk in another. If a record contains either of

Records Fields Go To Exit 2:52:00 pm

ORDER_NO	ORDER_DATE	COMPANY	ITEM	UNITS	UNIT_PRICE	DELIVERY
453216	12/09/88	ABC Company	Chair	10	125.98	MEMO
789654	12/15/88	ABC Company	Cabinet	3	129.95	memo
001325	01/15/89	Able Bakery	Cabinet	2	129.95	memo
001359	01/17/89	BBB Bakery	Cabinet	3	129.95	memo
001546	01/18/89	Smythe Company	Desk	4	495.00	memo

Figure 5-17 View query of design in Figure 5-16

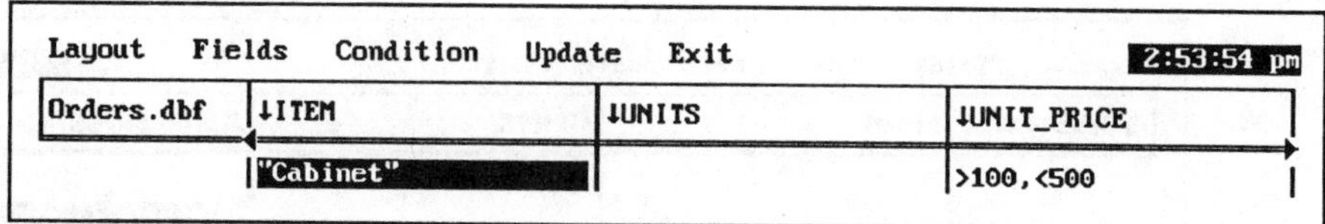

Figure 5-18 Query design with examples in ITEM and UNIT_PRICE

these entries in its ITEM field, the record displays in the view. Moving with the DOWN ARROW key to add additional rows allows you to accept additional entries for a field.

Joining conditions in different fields with an or condition works the same way. Placing the entries on different lines changes the implied joiner to an or. Figure 5-20 displays the entry >50 for the UNITS field and >500 for the UNIT_PRICE field. Since the entries are placed on different rows in the File skeleton, a record that meets either of the conditions will display. The resulting ORDERS records in Figure 5-21 show that the first record was placed in the view because its UNIT_PRICE exceeded 500 even though the UNITS field contained only a 5. The same is true for the selection of the third record. The second record was added to the view based on the condition for UNITS since it is for more than 50 units although its UNIT_PRICE is substantially less than 500.

Using both condition joiners can be a little more difficult. Figure 5-22 shows a Query design screen where the conditions ITEM equal Cabinet **and** UNIT_PRICE greater than 100 and less than 500 were joined with the condition ITEM equal Desk with an implied **or** condition. Since the price condition is only joined with Cabinet, there is no price limitation on desks. The Query produces the results in Figure 5-23 that include a desk for 585.95. If you want the price limitation on both items you need to repeat it on both lines of the query form, as shown in Figure 5-24.

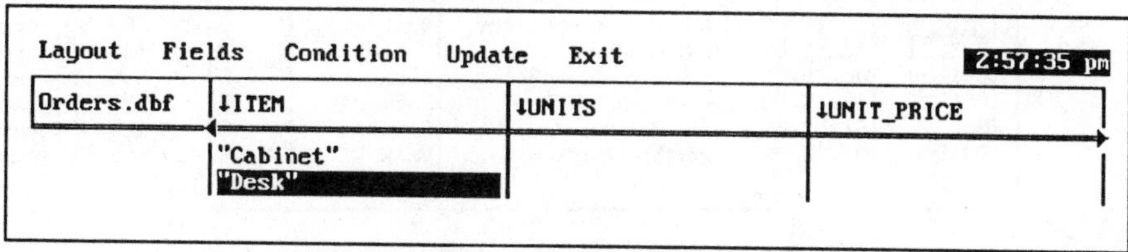

Figure 5-19 Query design with two examples joined by OR

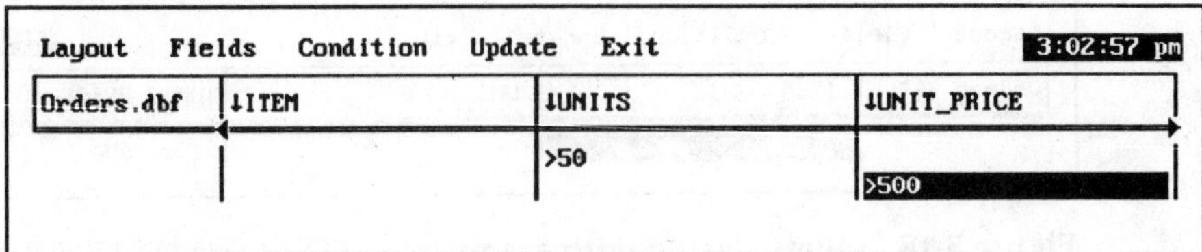

Figure 5-20 Query design with two examples joined by OR

Records Fields Go To Exit 3:02:44 pm

ORDER_NO	ORDER_DATE	COMPANY	ITEM	UNITS	UNIT_PRICE	DELIVERY
678543	12/10/88	Baker & Associates	Desk	5	585.95	memo
986541	12/16/88	Carlston & Sons	Mailers	100	1.35	memo
001298	01/10/89	Baker & Associates	Desk	5	585.95	memo

Figure 5-21 View query of design in Figure 5-20

Layout Fields Condition Update Exit 2:58:46 pm

Orders.dbf	↓ITEM	↓UNITS	↓UNIT_PRICE
	"Cabinet"		>100,<500
	"Desk"		

Figure 5-22 Query design with examples joined by OR and AND

Records Fields Go To Exit 2:59:11 pm

ORDER_NO	ORDER_DATE	COMPANY	ITEM	UNITS	UNIT_PRICE	DELIVERY
678543	12/10/88	Baker & Associates	Desk	5	585.95	memo
789654	12/15/88	ABC Company	Cabinet	3	129.95	memo
001298	01/10/89	Baker & Associates	Desk	5	585.95	memo
001325	01/15/89	Able Bakery	Cabinet	2	129.95	memo
001359	01/17/89	BBB Bakery	Cabinet	3	129.95	memo
001546	01/18/89	Smythe Company	Desk	4	495.00	memo

Figure 5-23 View query of design in Figure 5-22

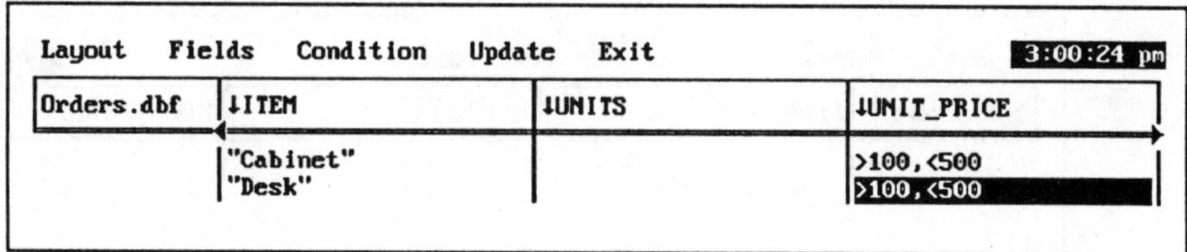

Figure 5-24 Query design with examples joined by OR and AND

Condition Boxes

Condition boxes are ideal for specifications that span fields and databases. You do not have to enter your specifications in individual boxes, since the field names that you specify as part of the condition allow dBASE IV to process the condition against an entire record.

You can also use Condition boxes for simple queries. They take a little more time than building examples on the File skeleton since you must always include the field name and an operator, even if the equal operator is being implied. The special operators Like and Sounds like require the use of functions when used within the Condition box.

To enter a simple condition like a date comparison in a box, you must either move to the Condition box with F3 or F4 if it exists, or add one if it is not there. To display a Condition box on the screen, press ALT-C to activate the Condition menu. Type an **A** to add a Condition box to the screen. You can type your condition in the box or use the SHIFT-F1 Pick box option to select each component of the condition. Press SHIFT-F1 and select ORDER_DATE by highlighting the field name and pressing ENTER. Although you could pick the operator by activating the Pick box again, typing a > requires fewer keystrokes. Next, since dates must be in braces, {01/10/89} is typed to complete the Condition

❑ **Tip: Use the F9 Zoom key for lengthy condition entries.**

You can zoom in on one column in a File skeleton by pressing F9. Pressing F9 a second time returns the normal column size.

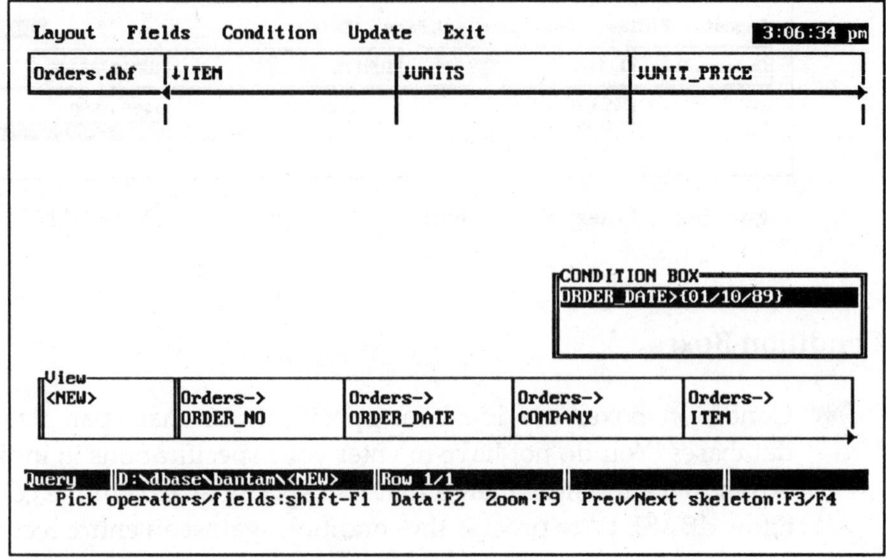

Figure 5-25 Query design with Condition box

box entry shown in Figure 5-25. Pressing F2 to display the View data shows the records in Figure 5-26.

You can combine the current condition with a second that only isolates records where the COMPANY matches BBB*. First press SHIFT-F2 to return to the Query design screen. Press SHIFT-F1 to pick and highlight .AND. in the middle column and press ENTER. Press SHIFT-F1 again and highlight LIKE in the third column. dBASE IV inserts LIKE() in the expression. Use the LEFT ARROW key to move one position to the left since functions require you to enter arguments within the parentheses. The LIKE function requires two arguments. The first argument is the pattern you want to look for and the second

Records Fields Go To Exit 3:06:02 pm

ORDER_NO	ORDER_DATE	COMPANY	ITEM	UNITS	UNIT_PRICE	DELIVERY
001325	01/15/89	Able Bakery	Cabinet	2	129.95	memo
001359	01/17/89	BBB Bakery	Cabinet	3	129.95	memo
001546	01/18/89	Smythe Company	Desk	4	495.00	memo

Figure 5-26 View query of design in Figure 5-25

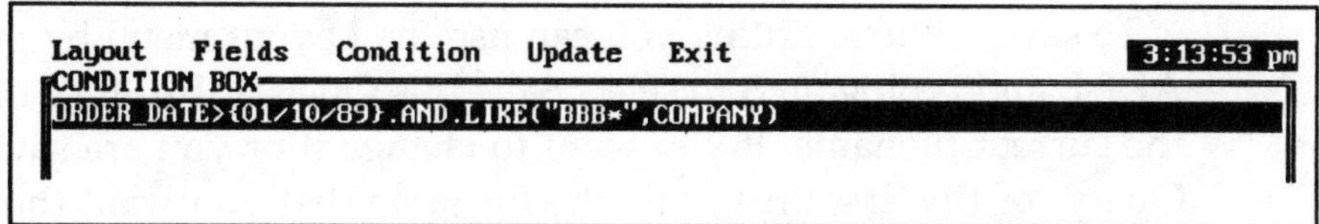

Figure 5-27 Expanded Condition box with multiple conditions

is the name of the field that you want to search for this pattern. Type **"BBB*",COMPANY** for the two function arguments, as shown in Figure 5-27. In the Query-By-Example option, the same results could have been achieved by typing **Like "BBB*"** beneath the COMPANY field.

Condition boxes can create a view containing nothing but records marked for deletion. The entry DELETED() in a Condition box will place deleted records in the view. You can use this capability along with the feature introduced later in this chapter to create a new database from a view and write all the deleted records to a database before packing the database.

In addition to using the Condition menu option to add a Condition box when none exists, you can also select the Delete condition box option to remove a box currently on the screen. When you delete a box, the box and the condition it contains is removed from the screen. If you add the box back at a later time you will need to reenter the condition, since dBASE IV forgets the condition when you delete the condition box. The Show condition box option allows you to toggle between always showing the Condition box on the screen and showing only the words CONDITION BOX when the Condition box is not active. If you elect to show only the word CONDITION, when you move to the Condition box it resumes its normal size and can still be expanded to full screen size with the F9 (Zoom) option.

Saving the Query

You can save a Query when you are finished and ready to exit. With a more complex Query, requiring a greater investment of time, you may elect to save several times while creating the Query. If you choose you can save it as a different name each time, allowing you to capture a copy as you test each portion of the Query.

To save without exiting you can use the Layout menu by pressing ALT-L and typing an **S** to select Save this Query. dBASE IV displays the current filename. If you want to change it or you are saving the Query for the first time, type the filename that you want the Query saved as and press ENTER. To save a query again without providing the same filename, press CTRL-ENTER. dBASE IV appends a .QBE filename extension for View queries and a .UPD extension for Update files. When you exit using the Exit menu, dBASE IV does not display the filename.

dBASE IV checks the syntax of the Query before saving it and prompts you to make corrections by placing the cursor at the location of the error and displaying the message Syntax error. After making corrections you can attempt the save operation again.

The Layout menu option Edit description of query allows you to add a description of the Query to the current catalog. This description displays when the filename is highlighted in the Query panel of the Control Center.

Algebraic Conditions

Although most queries can be created with a series of examples within File skeleton fields, sometimes you will want to compare one field with another. To do this you must place an example variable in the field that you wish to use in the comparison. In the File skeleton for the field you are comparing with this field, you will need to create an algebraic expression that references this example variable.

In a monthly expense record you may have a field for the current month's expenses and the annual budget amount for the expense category. You can create a view of records where the current month's expense is greater than 1/12 of the annual budget. Although monthly expenses greater than the monthly average are not necessarily problematic if the expenses are seasonal, it is easier to review this subset of the records rather than reviewing all of them for potential problems. The example variable x was arbitrarily chosen to mark the ANNUAL_AMT field. Since the purpose of this variable is to provide a reference to this field in the algebraic expression, any variable can be used as long as it meets the field name requirements and is not the same as a field name in the view or an update operation. The formula **>x/12** shown in Figure 5-28 looks for all the records where the CURRENT_M

Layout	Fields	Condition	Update	Exit	8:59:13 pm

Expenses.dbf	↓EXP_CODE	↓CURRENT_M	↓ANNUAL_AMT
		>x/12	x

Figure 5-28 Query design using example variable to use another field's value

figure is greater than the ANNUAL_AMT/12. Although it might seem that you should be able to enter the formula ANNUAL_AMT/12 without the need for an example variable, this is not possible.

Calculated Fields

Calculated fields are computed from other fields in the database. You can add up to 20 of these computed fields to the view that you create. You can also supply examples to control the records that appear in the view.

To add a Calculated field to a Query requires several steps:

1. Press ALT-F and type a **C** to select Create a calculated field for each field you add.

   If this is the first Calculated field in the query, dBASE IV adds a Calculated field area beneath the File skeleton
2. Enter the calculation in the first box.

❑ **Tip: Removing Calculated fields.**

Removing Calculated fields from the View skeleton is easy; all you need to do is press F5 a second time. Removing Calculated fields from the Calculated field skeleton is a bit more difficult. You can use CTRL-Y to delete the computation, but the Calculated field name remains if it has ever been added to a View skeleton. If you want to remove all of the Calculated fields, press ALT-L and type an **R** when the cursor is in the Calculated field skeleton.

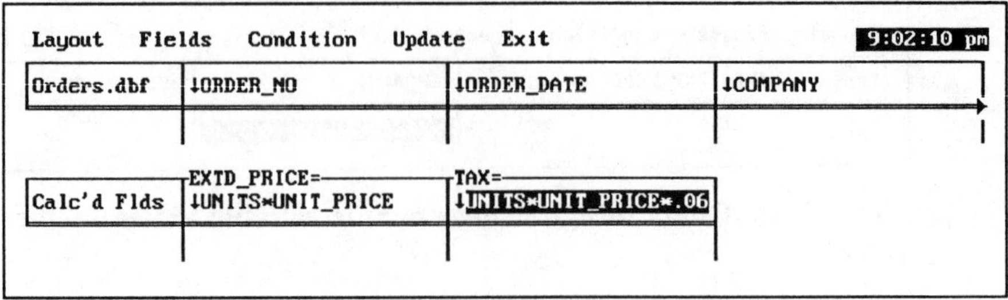

Figure 5-29 Calculated field skeleton

You can type any valid dBASE IV expression for the computation including field names, operators, constants, and functions.

3. Press the F5 Fields key, type a field name, and press ENTER to add the Calculated field to the View skeleton
4. If you want to use the Calculated field to isolate records enter an example on the row beneath the calculation.

Figure 5-29 shows two Calculated fields that appear in the View skeleton. The first entry computes an extended price by multiplying units times unit price. The second Calculated field computes the tax due on the purchase assuming a 6% tax rate. dBASE IV requires you to respecify units times unit price and does not support using EXTD_PRICE in the TAX calculation. Pressing F2 creates the view with the Calculated fields showing as part of the view. (See Figure 5-30.) Although you can change the entries for other fields in the view, Calculated fields are always Read-only.

Records Fields Go To Exit 9:02:55 pm

ITEM	UNITS	UNIT_PRICE	DELIVERY	EXTD_PRICE	TAX
Chair	10	125.98	MEMO	1259.80	75.59
Desk	5	585.95	memo	2929.75	175.79
Cabinet	3	129.95	memo	389.85	23.39
Mailers	100	1.35	memo	135.00	8.10
Chair	5	89.95	memo	449.75	26.99
Desk	5	585.95	memo	2929.75	175.79
Cabinet	2	129.95	memo	259.90	15.59
Cabinet	3	129.95	memo	389.85	23.39
Desk	4	495.00	memo	1980.00	118.80

Figure 5-30 View query of design in Figure 5-29

Tip: Use example variables to avoid repeating computations.

Although you cannot use the name of a Calculated field in the formula for another Calculated field, you can add an example variable beneath the first computation and use that variable in subsequent calculations. For example, you can place the example variable x under the EXTD_PRICE calculation, then compute TAX with the formula x*.06 rather than UNITS*UNIT_PRICE*.06.

Once you have created Calculated fields you can enter examples for them just as you do with the fields in File skeletons. Figure 5-31 shows a Query looking for records where the extended price is greater than 500. The example is entered in the same way as it would be if extended price was a database field. Since only five records match the example, the view is limited to the records shown in Figure 5-32.

If you want to modify a Calculated field, you can change most of the field's characteristics. You can change the formula by moving the highlight to the formula and modifying it. You can change the Calculated field name by pressing ALT-F and typing an E for Edit field name. When dBASE IV prompts for a new field name, type the field name you want and press ENTER. dBASE IV does not let you delete a Calculated field without deleting the entire skeleton, just as you cannot delete a field from a File skeleton.

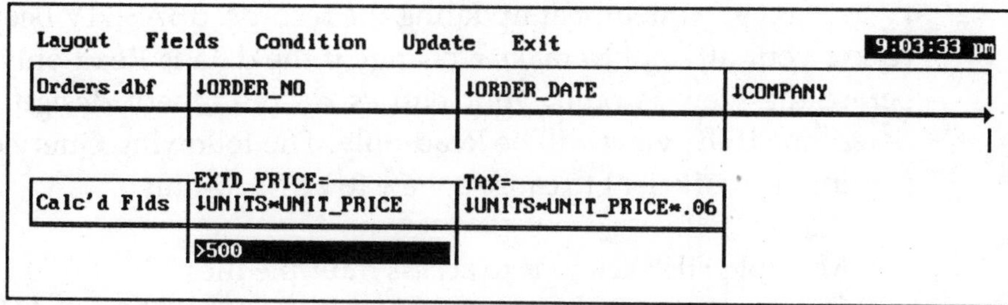

Figure 5-31 Calculated field skeleton with example

Records Fields Go To Exit 9:05:12 pm

ORDER_NO	ORDER_DATE	COMPANY	ITEM	UNITS	UNIT_PRICE	DELIVERY
453216	12/09/88	ABC Company	Chair	10	125.98	MEMO
678543	12/10/88	Baker & Associates	Desk	5	585.95	memo
001298	01/10/89	Baker & Associates	Desk	5	585.95	memo
001546	01/18/89	Smythe Company	Desk	4	495.00	memo

Figure 5-32 View query of design in Figure 5-31

Hiding Duplicates

Duplicate records are considered to be records where every field in the view is exactly the same. When you are attempting to create a list of customers or employees you may want to limit your view to records that are not duplicates of other entries. You can accomplish this by listing the word **unique** under the filename in a File skeleton. The View skeleton should be limited to fields that will contain identical values for records that you wish to treat as duplicates. For the ORDERS file this would limit the entry to the COMPANY field as shown in Figure 5-33. In the ORDERS file a unique list of companies produces the list in Figure 5-34.

Changing Data in a View

The data in a view is only available in memory, but in some situations updating this copy of the data results in an update to the database itself. In other situations, the data in the view is Read-only, causing dBASE IV to reject any attempt at updating the records. dBASE IV beeps and rejects your attempt to make a change if the data is Read-only. Even before the view is built, your entries on the Query design screen determine if the view will be Read-only. The following Query design features are sufficient to cause a view to be Read-only:

- Multiple File skeletons to access multiple files
- Queries containing summary operations like SUM and AVG
- Queries containing unique

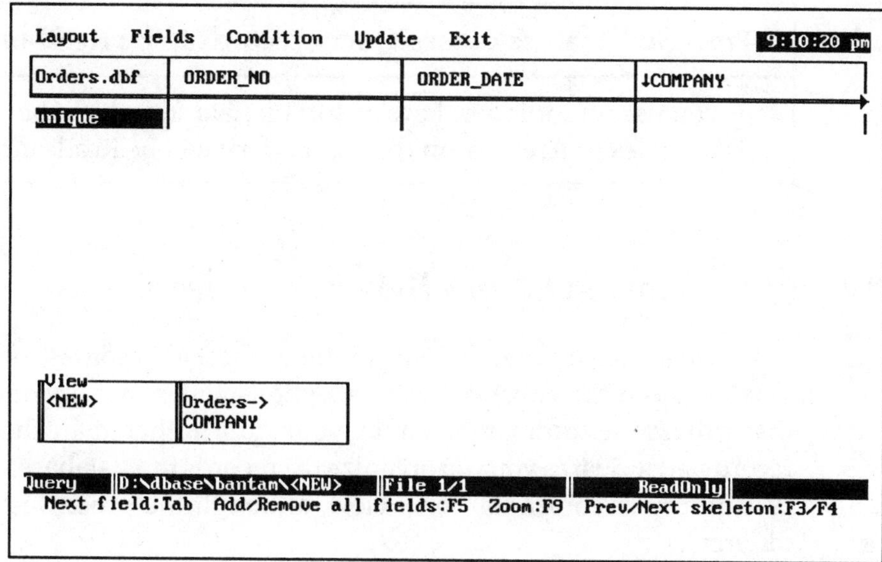

Figure 5-33 Query design using unique operator

In addition to the restrictions on updates to an entire record, records containing Calculated fields cannot have the result of the Calculated field modified.

```
Records    Fields    Go To    Exit                          9:09:20 pm
COMPANY
ABC Company
Able Bakery
BBB Bakery
Baker & Associates
Carlston & Sons
Lewis Brothers
Smythe Company
```

Figure 5-34 View query of design in Figure 5-33

Tip: Sort feature causes Query records to be Read-only.

If you use multiple sort keys or sort on field for which there is no index, the records in the View query will be Read-only.

Adding Additional Options to View Queries

Basic Query features allow you to view selected records from your database. You can enhance the basic options with summary operators that provide a summary view of your data rather than the detail records. Also, just as you can organize the records in a database, dBASE IV supports organization for a view, although the process is a little different.

Sorting a View

Just as you can sort the records in a database file, you can sort the records in a view. The same rules apply although the operation is normally less time consuming since dBASE IV only sorts the records that qualify for the view.

dBASE IV supports the same four sort sequences for a view as for a database. You can choose from ascending ASCII, descending ASCII, ascending dictionary, or descending dictionary.

You can use the Field menu command Sort on this field or type the operators you want. Asc and Dsc mark the ASCII sequences and AscDict and DscDict mark the dictionary sorts. The menu selection automatically numbers each of the sort operators by appending a number at the end after you select the sort order that you want. Figure 5-35 shows the screen that results when you select CITY as the first sort

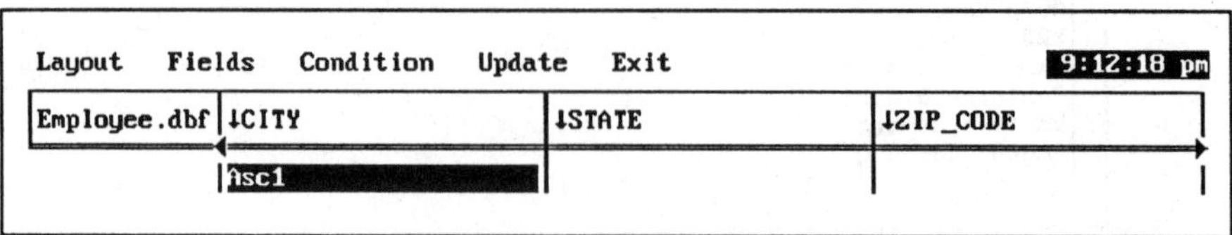

Figure 5-35 Query design that sorts records according to their CITY values

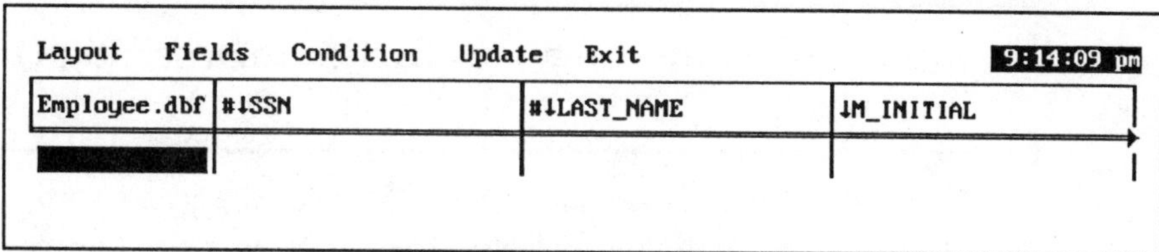

Figure 5-36 File skeleton with indexes included

field. If you elect to type the operators in yourself, you must supply a number distinguishing higher priority fields with lower numbers, as in Asc1 and Asc2.

You cannot sort on Calculated fields and are also restricted from using a sort operator in a Condition box. The sort operator does not interfere with other conditions in a File skeleton and is separated from the example by a comma, as in **>500,Asc1**. A maximum of 16 sort fields can be defined.

Using Indexes in a View

dBASE IV allows you to display index fields in your query by selecting Include indexes from the Fields menu. dBASE IV marks fields that are simple indexes with a pound sign (#). Indexes consisting of multiple fields are considered complex indexes and are listed at the end of the File skeleton. You can use these fields for listing data in a view and for sorting if you include a sort operator in the field box. Figure 5-36 shows the change to the EMPLOYEE file query after Include indexes was selected. There are two index fields marked on this screen, SSN and LAST_NAME. If the database has a complex index that includes several fields, it displays at the end of the File skeleton like the one partially visible in Figure 5-37 that contains LAST_NAME+FIRST_NAME+M_INITIAL. These index

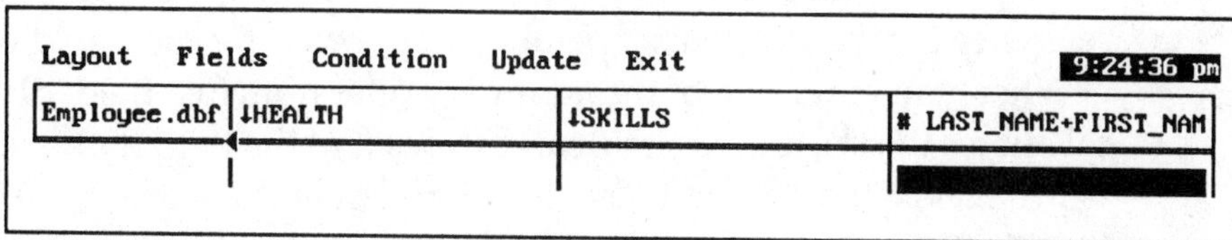

Figure 5-37 Pseudo-field in File skeleton

Tip: Indexes are still more efficient than sorting Query records.

If you include indexes on a Query form and add a sort operator under the index field, dBASE IV uses the values in the index to order the records rather than having to perform a more inefficient sort operation.

entries are called pseudo-fields. Although this index was originally created with the tag NAME, the tag is not shown on the query screen.

Placing a sorting operator beneath the pseudo-field causes dBASE IV to organize the view by the contents of the index field. Although you can add a sort operator without telling dBASE IV to include indexes, this approach is more efficient. If you tell dBASE IV to sort on a pseudo-field, it automatically uses the index values to order the records rather than actually sorting them.

With a multiple field index, you only need to add a sort operator to one pseudo-field. If the pseudo-field is composed of part number, vendor, and location information, you can enter one sort operator in the pseudo-field rather than a sort operator in each of the three fields from which the index is built.

Summarizing Data

You can use dBASE IV's summary operators to perform arithmetic operations on the records in a view. Rather than display the records, dBASE IV displays the arithmetic results in the view.

The summary operators that you can use depend on the field type with which you are working. Numeric and Float field types can support all of the summary operators, whereas Logical fields support only COUNT, and Memo fields support none. Table 5-2 provides a quick reference for the summary operators supported by each field type.

When you enter one of the summary operators in a field, dBASE IV calculates the arithmetic result and stores it in the field in the resulting view. Fields that do not use summary operators are blank in the resulting view.

Tip: Create summary queries.

Creating summary queries with AVG and SUM can provide a quick perspective of numeric entries in database. You can remove the Summary operator if you want to take a closer look at the detail records.

Figure 5-38 shows the entry of the summary operator AVG in two fields on the File skeleton. When the query is processed, an arithmetic mean is computed for these two fields by adding all the values in the field and dividing by the number of records in the field. Fields in the File skeleton without summary operators are blank in the resulting view, as shown in Figure 5-39.

You can combine summary operators with filters if the filters are not dependent on the result of a summary operator. You can summarize salaries for a specific location but you cannot display records that are greater than the average salary. The latter option would require that dBASE IV to read all the records to compute the average and then make a second pass to select those records that had a salary greater than the average. It is this second pass that cannot be automated from the menu system. Although you can accomplish this feat within a program, from the menu system you would need to compute the average in one query then perform a second query that isolated records with salaries greater than the value you supplied.

Table 5-2 Summary Operators By Field Type

Field Type	*Operator Supported*
Character	COUNT, MAX, MIN
Numeric	AVG, COUNT, MAX, MIN, SUM
Float	AVG, COUNT, MAX, MIN, SUM
Date	COUNT, MAX, MIN
Logical	COUNT
Memo	Summary operators not supported

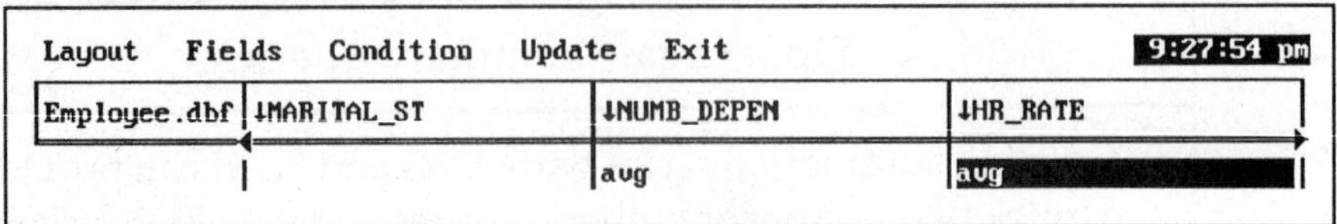

Figure 5-38 File skeletons containing summary operators

Using Group By Operators

If your records are arranged in sequence by a field you can apply the summary operators to the records having the same value for the field. You might decide to group records by CITY. As shown on Figure 5-40, the Group by entry is placed in CITY and the summary operators are placed in NUMB_DEPEN and HR_RATE. For each new value in the CITY field, dBASE IV computes the result for a summary operator in these two fields. dBASE IV lists each new value in the Group by field as well as the summary operator results when you look at the view as shown in Figure 5-41.

Using Group by in combination with the summary operator COUNT provides a frequency distribution that is a count of the number of records that contain a specific field entry. You should place the Group by operator in the field for which you need the frequency distribution. Since COUNT works with any field type you can enter COUNT in any other field. The resulting view is a frequency list.

Changing the Order for a Group dBASE IV normally orders the records in a group in ascending sequence. You can cause the group to be organized in descending sequence if you add a comma after Group by and add Dsc. The dictionary sort operators AscDict and DscDict are also acceptable entries.

Records Fields Go To Exit 9:27:13 pm

HIRE_DATE	MARITAL_ST	NUMB_DEPEN	HR_RATE	YTD_WAGES	YTD_FIT	HEALTH	SKILLS
/ /		2	12.05	.	.		memo

Figure 5-39 View query of design in Figure 5-38

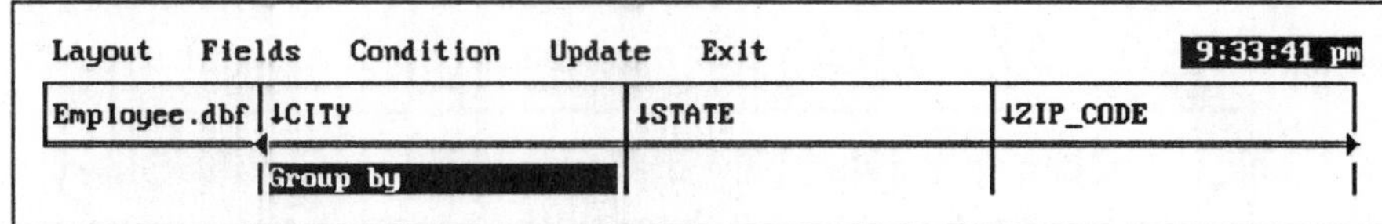

Figure 5-40 Query design using group by operator

Just as you can use sort on more than one field you can also use Group by in multiple fields. The sort operators determine the priority of the grouping.

It is possible to create a Query that uses Group by entries and regular sort operator by themselves in other fields. dBASE IV uses the grouping operator first as it filters and groups the records for the view. Next, it applies the sort operators to the resulting entries.

Creating a Database from a View

Once you have defined a view with examples or by completing a Condition box you can write this view to disk as a database file. The new file contains all of the fields shown in the view and uses the same field names. You can either enter a name for the new database file or allow dBASE IV to use the name of the view. To save the view to a database, press ALT-L and type a **W** for Write view as database file. When dBASE IV prompts for a database filename, it displays the current view name with a .DBF extension added. You can use this name or modify it to create your own and press ENTER. The maximum record length supported is 4,000 characters.

Records Fields Go To Exit 9:32:50 pm

CITY	STATE	ZIP_CODE	HOME_PHONE	HIRE_DATE	MARITAL_ST	NUMB_DEPEN	HR_RAT
Baltimore				/ /		3	12.50
Chicago				/ /		4	11.13
Cleveland				/ /		1	12.75

Figure 5-41 View query that groups records by city and averages NUMB_DEPEN and HR_RATE fields

❑ **Tip: Multiple queries can split a database.**

You can split a database into smaller files with the Query operation. Create a database with the result of View queries. After verifying that the data was split between the databases properly, delete the original file.

Since the data still resides in the original file, there are duplicate copies of the records in the smaller databases created with the View queries, unless you are creating these database extracts and eliminating these records from the database.

Creating a Quick Report from a View

If you need a quick printed copy of the contents of a view you can activate the Quick Report feature. All you need to do is display the view and press SHIFT-F9. The Quick Report print menu appears. You can display the report on your screen by typing a **V** for View report on the screen. If you would prefer a hard copy, type a **B** to send the report to your printer.

Looking at the Query File

You can look at the code that dBASE IV generates for a Query by examining the contents of the .QBE file that dBASE IV creates when you save a Query. Figure 5-42 shows the contents of the file created by the query in Figure 5-31. You can look at the contents of the file by using the TYPE command from the DOS prompt followed by the query name and .QBE. Although you do not want to change the QBE file at this time, as you migrate to the programming environment for dBASE IV it is useful to see the code that dBASE IV generates to produce query results. It also makes you appreciate the work that dBASE IV does for you when you supply the examples on the Query screen.

```
D>type calc_fld
File not found

D>type calc_fld.qbe
* dBASE IV .QBE file
SET FIELDS TO
SELECT 1
USE ORDERS.DBF AGAIN
SET EXACT ON
SET FILTER TO (((A->UNITS*A->UNIT_PRICE))>500))
GO TOP
SET FIELDS TO A->ORDER_NO,A->ORDER_DATE,A->COMPANY,A->ITEM,A->UNITS,A->;
UNIT_PRICE,A->DELIVERY,EXTD_PRICE=(A->UNITS*A->UNIT_PRICE),TAX=(;
A->UNITS*A->UNIT_PRICE*.06)
```

Figure 5-42 Program that generates Query design in Figure 5-31

Creating Queries with Multiple Files

The ability to link two or more files allows you to show data from more than one file in a View query. dBASE IV supports the addition of as many as eight File skeletons in a View query.

Establishing a Linking Field

Links are not a haphazard occurrence that allow you to join any two files. As you design your database system you must plan the structure of the files to allow common fields that will link the files. An employee ID number, a social security number, an account number, and a part number are all fields that are likely to be established as linking fields between files. They can uniquely identify entries in a file unlike fields, such as last names where duplicate entries are possible. Ideally the linking field is unique in at least one of the files.

Once you have the proper design established for multiple files, you can create views that bring together information from these files. This is accomplished through the use of example variables. You can use any entry for an example variable, as their purpose is to mark the fields in the records that you are linking. Whatever variable you choose for the linking field in the first file, you will want to use this same example variable in each of the fields that you are linking. Figure 5-43 shows the example variable **z** used to mark the VENDOR_NO in both the PARTS2 and the VENDORS files. dBASE IV displays the entries for matching

```
Layout   Fields   Condition   Update   Exit                          9:38:48 pm
Parts1.dbf | ↓PART_NO        | ↓VENDOR_NO       | ↓PRICE
           |                 | z                |
Vendor.dbf | VENDOR_NO       | VENDOR_NAM       | VEND_PHONE
           | z               |                  |
```

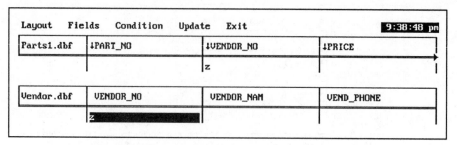

Figure 5-43 Query design with link between two File skeletons

records in the view. You can also use the Layout menu to create a link between databases by moving to the first field that you want to link, pressing an ALT-L, and typing a **C** for Create link by pointing. dBASE IV adds LINK followed by a number to the current field and then prompts you to move to the other field that is part of the link. When you move to the other field that the databases use for a link and press ENTER, dBASE IV repeats the same example variable.

In the previous example the PART_NO file controlled the sequence of the records, since it was the first File skeleton listed. If a vendor record was not referenced by a part file record, the vendor record was not shown in the view. If you want every vendor record listed you can precede the example variable with the entry Every as shown in Figure 5-44. You can use only one Every operator for each pair of linked skeletons. You can use the Every operator to identify vendors from whom you are not currently purchasing parts.

```
Layout   Fields   Condition   Update   Exit                          9:39:07 pm
Parts1.dbf | ↓PART_NO        | ↓VENDOR_NO       | ↓PRICE
           |                 | z                |
Vendor.dbf | VENDOR_NO       | VENDOR_NAM       | VEND_PHONE
           | Every z         |                  |
```

Figure 5-44 Query design with link between two File skeletons and the Every operator

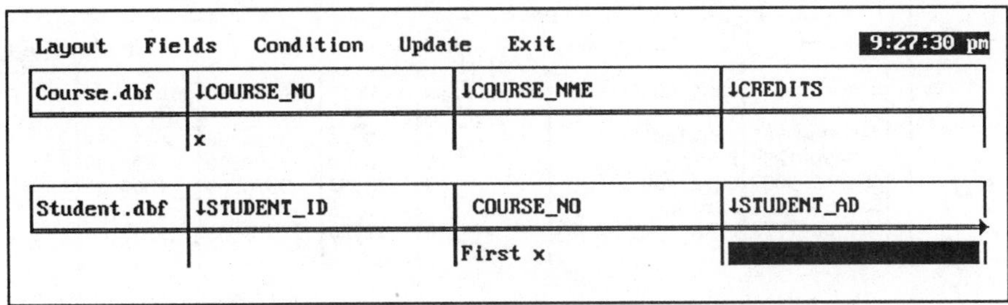

Figure 5-45 Query design with limited link

Limited Links

Limited links allow you to join records finding only one record matching the linking field in the first File skeleton. Although this type of link is specialized, in some situations it provides just the information that you need. You might have a course file and a student registration file and want to identify one student in each course. You could send course evaluations to this one student and ask the student to distribute them before the last class. Figure 5-45 shows how the First operator indicates the limited link to the student file. Only the first student record for each class displays.

When you import a dBASE III Plus view into dBASE IV, the First operator is always placed in the linking field of the dependent file. This causes the View to perform in an identical fashion to the workings of dBASE III Plus.

Self Joins

Self joins imply that a database file is being linked to itself. This linking allows you to compare all the records in the database file against all the other records. This allows you to use values in a field to filter the other records in the file.

You can use a self join to determine which employees make more than another employee. You could also determine which projects are farther over budget than a particular project or which alumni have made a larger contribution than the current president of the alumni organization.

Records Fields Go To Exit 10:55:32 pm

SSN	LAST_NAME	NUMB_DEPEN	HR_RATE	YTD_WAGES	YTD_FIT	HEALTH	SKIL
215-90-8761	Jenkins	1	9.75	3450.00	431.50	T	MEMO
675-98-1239	Foster	1	8.50	7890.00	890.00	F	MEMO
654-11-9087	Garrison	3	12.50	9875.00	1200.00	T	MEMO
888-99-7654	Larson	0	15.75	12800.00	1575.50	T	MEMO
555-66-7777	Walker	6	12.50	13575.00	1100.00	T	MEMO

Figure 5-46 EMPLOYEE database

The first File skeleton is used to filter out the one record that you want to use for comparison purposes. Enter an example variable into the linking field and assign any other variables needed for the comparison. Add another skeleton for the same file to the Query design screen and dBASE IV will mark it with a letter to distinguish it from the first skeleton. Add the same example variable under the linking field. Add any other example variables needed for the comparison. Add a Condition box to select the records using the example variables you established to the two skeletons to describe the records you need.

As an example, the EMPLOYEE file shown in Figure 5-46 will first locate the Garrison record. Next, you want to identify all the records with the same hourly rate as Garrison so the example variable **a** is arbitrarily chosen to mark the HR_RATE field. A new File skeleton is added for the same file and is also used to mark the HR_RATE field to identify those with the same hourly rate. Of these records the only ones needed are those with more dependents than Garrison. Different example variables are used to mark the NUMB_DEPEN fields in both records. The letters s and t were arbitrarily chosen. A Condition box is added to the screen and the condition t>s is entered. When F2 is pressed the resulting view produces the record for Walker, since the hourly rate is the same but Walker has six dependents rather than three, as Garrison has.

Turning Queries ON and OFF

If you save a Query you can reestablish it at any time by highlighting the name of the query in the Query panel on the Control Center menu and pressing F2. dBASE IV displays the records specified by the query. If you want to activate a Query so you can use it for a form, label, or

Tip: Closing database files.

Sometimes, after executing a Query you want to use the Query database. dBASE IV displays a message saying that the database file is open if you try to open it, yet the database name appears below the line in the Data panel. Escaping to the dot prompt and closing all files or closing databases does not solve the problem. Exiting and reentering dBASE IV is the only solution.

report, highlight the Query and press ENTER twice to open the Query without viewing the data.

To close a Query so you can use another database or query, highlight the Query and press ENTER twice. You can also close a Query when you open another database or query. For example, if you want to view the database that a Query was based on, highlight the database that you used in the query and press F2.

Update Queries

You have already seen how you can use the Edit and Browse screens to update the data in a record. In some situations you can update the data from a View query with these same screens. In both situations, you can only update one record at a time. With 10 records requiring the same change you would need to make the change 10 times.

Update queries allow you to define the records you wish to change and apply your changes to this group of records. You can replace values in records substituting a name or a part number to replace data that is no longer correct. You can also use Update queries to append selected records to the current file or to mark or unmark deleted records. In all cases you can type the operator you want to use beneath the filename in the File skeleton or use the Specify update operation option in the Update menu. Once you select Perform the update from the Update menu, dBASE IV changes the records that you have specified.

You can distinguish Update queries from View queries in the Query panel of the Control Center. Update queries are marked with an

> **Tip: Back up your database before Update queries.**
>
> Update queries that perform replace and append operations can be difficult to undo. Back up your database before executing one of these Update queries.

asterisk. If you highlight an Update query and press ENTER the menu presented differs from the View query, since it offers an option for Run update rather than Use query. The Modify and Display options are the same on both menus.

Replacing Field Entries

You can replace an entry in all the records of the database with one Update query. First, you will want to enter any examples or conditions you need to select the records you want to update. Next, the replacement operator **with** must be added to the File skeleton and followed by the replacement entry you wish to make. The replacement entry can be a fixed entry or it can be a dBASE IV expression that computes a new value.

If you want to update the UNIT_PRICE for all records in the ORDERS file for Mailers, you can move to the ITEM field and type **"Mailers**. You can move to the UNIT_PRICE field and type **with 1.50**. Invoking Update and selecting specify the update operation with a choice of Replace causes dBASE IV to place the Replace operator under the filename in the Target skeleton for ORDERS.DBF after prompting you to confirm that it can remove the File skeleton. After selecting Perform

> **Tip: Making changes to data.**
>
> The Update Replace feature offers a quick way to make changes to all the records in a database. You can even enter a unique abbreviation during data entry and update all the records with an Update query.

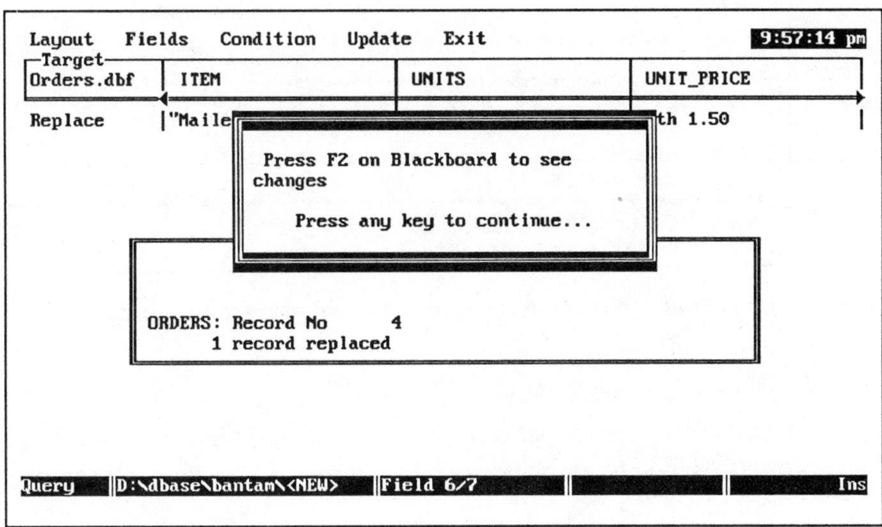

Figure 5-47 Query design screen after performing update

the update operation from the Update menu the screen looks like Figure 5-47, indicating that the Replace operation has been completed.

You can use the same field to locate records and specify a replacement. First specify the example that you want dBASE IV to match within the records. Next type a comma, press the SPACEBAR, and type with followed by the replacement value. Typing **"BBB Bakery", with "Big Blue Bird Bakery"** under the COMPANY field for the ORDERS file will locate the record for BBB Bakery and make the replacement when you perform the update.

Appending Records

The append option allows you to append all records or selected records from a file to a file that is the target of the Update operation. To use this command you will need two File skeletons on the design surface. The first skeleton is the skeleton of the file containing the records you wish to append. You can mark the example variables that will be used to match against the second file. After using the Layout command to add the target file to the screen, you can activate the Update menu and select the Append option. Place the same example variables in the Target skeleton and check to ensure the compatibility of data between the two files. Figure 5-48 shows a completed Query design form prior to

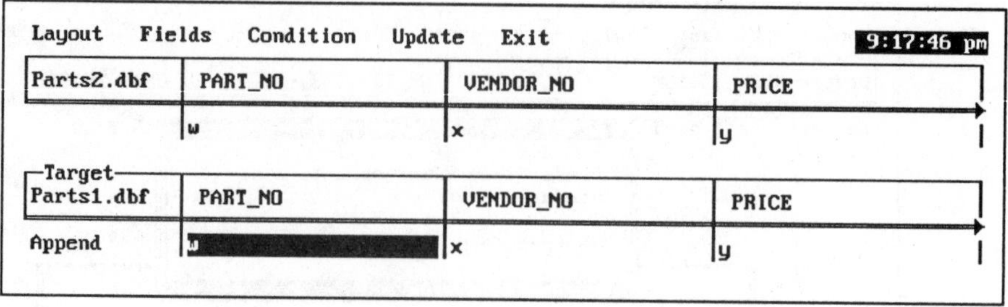

Figure 5-48 Query design screen before performing update

performing the Append operation. To execute the Append operation, press ALT-U to activate the Update menu and type a **P** to perform the update.

If you want to append only selected records, enter examples on the skeleton for the file you are appending from. These examples allow to append only the records which match your entries.

Marking and Unmarking Records for Deletion

You can use the examples you enter to establish a filter that will control records that are marked or unmarked for deletion. To use this feature press ALT-U and select either Mark or Unmark by typing an **M** or a **U**. The records that match your entries on the skeleton will be changed when you select Perform the update from the Update menu.

GETTING STARTED

➤ You will want to try some of the Query options with EMPLOYEE database. First, you will follow these steps to create several View queries:

1. With the highlight on EMPLOYEE in the Data panel of the Control Center, press ENTER twice.
2. Use the RIGHT ARROW key to move to the Query panel, highlight <create>, and press ENTER.

3. Tab to the CITY in the File skeleton, type **"Chicago"** then press F2 to view the data. Press SHIFT-F2 to return to the Query design screen.
4. Use SHIFT-TAB to move to the LAST_NAME field and type **"Foster"**. Press F2 to view the data again. This time only one record displays since both conditions must be met.
5. Press Shift-F2 to go back to the query. Press CTRL-Y to delete the LAST_NAME entry. Tab to the City field and press CTRL-Y.
6. Tab to the HR_RATE field and type **>10** then tab to the HEALTH field and type **.T.**.
7. Press F2 to see the view then press SHIFT-F2 to return to the Query design screen. Press ALT-E and type an **S** to select Save changes and exit. Type **EMPLOYEE** for the filename and press ENTER. dBASE IV saves the Query with a .QBE extension.
8. Highlight <create> in the Query panel again and press ENTER. Type an **A** to select Add file to query. Highlight EMPLOYEE and press ENTER. Press F5 to create a View skeleton with all of the fields.
9. Press ALT-C and type an **A** to select Add Condition box. Type **NUMB_DEPEN>1** then press F2 to see the records that match this specification.
10. Press SHIFT-F2, press ALT-C, and type a **D** to have dBASE IV return to the Query design screen and remove the Condition box.
11. Move to the ZIP_CODE field in the File skeleton, press F5 to remove this field from the view. Repeat this process with the remaining fields to the right of the ZIP_CODE field.
12. Use SHIFT-TAB to move to address and type **$"Lucy"** to isolate records containing Lucy. Press F2 to see the view. Press ALT-E and type an **E** to exit to the Control Center. When dBASE IV prompts if you want to save the query, type an **N**.
13. Highlight <create> in the Query panel and press ENTER. With the cursor below the database name in the File skeleton, press F5 Fields to remove all the fields from the View skeleton. Tab to STATE press F5 to add the field to the View skeleton then type **Group by**. Tab to YTD_WAGES, press F5 to add the field to the View skeleton and type **sum**. Press F2 to view the data. Press ALT-E and type an **E** to return to the Control Center. When dBASE IV prompts if you want to save the query, type an **N**.

You will also want to try an Update query for the EMPLOYEE database. You can change all the records for Chicago to the same zip code with the Replace option. You will then give each of the employees a 10% increase. Follow these steps:

1. With the EMPLOYEE file still open, highlight <create> in the Query panel and press ENTER.
2. Press ALT-U and press ENTER to specify the update operation. With the Replace option highlighted press ENTER. Type a **P** for Proceed to delete the View skeleton. This step adds Replace under the filename in the File skeleton. Tab to the CITY field and type **"Chicago"**. Tab to the zip code field and type **with 31285**. Press ALT-U and type a **P** to perform the update operation. Press F2 twice to view the updated records for Chicago.
3. Press SHIFT-F2 to return to the Query design screen. Use CTRL-Y to delete the entries under CITY and ZIP CODE. Tab to the HR_RATE field and type **with 1.1*HR_RATE**. Press ALT-U and type a P to update the records. Press F2 twice to view the result. Press ALT-E and type an E to return to the Control Center. When dBASE IV prompts if you want to save the query, type an **N**.

CHAPTER 6

Creating Reports and Labels

You have learned to use the Edit and Browse screens to view the data in your database. Although this method is convenient it will not meet your needs if you want to share the information in your database with others or access it when your computer is not on. Reports and labels allow you to create a hard copy of the information in your database.

You can create a quick report with dBASE IV's built-in reporting features. If you prefer you can build a custom report that allows you to select the fields you want to see, the order you wish to see them in, and summary statistics for the records. The options in the custom report features allow you complete flexibility in exercising your creativity to meet both summary and detail reporting needs.

The Label features in the package allow you to create mailing labels, Rolodex cards, or other abbreviated output in a consistent order. Predefined labels for the most popular label sizes make your task easy.

You can create a report or label using a database or a View query that allows you to select which data you will use to create the reports or labels.

Creating a Quick Report

You can use a Quick Report to view your data on the screen, to store the data in a file, or to print it. You can use the Quick Report to print the data that you see when you view a report. Creating a Quick Report

```
Page No.    1
01/12/90

CUST_NO  ORDER_NO  PART_NO  DESC                       QUANTITY     PRICE

 569656     21928  24-HAJ   Down Sleeping Bag                 1     65.99
 356433     41030  98-JMV   4 Man Dome Tent                   1    129.99
 253478     28691  34-RBP   Kerosene Lantern                  3     42.99
 245687     86435  25-PIC   Snow Boots                        1     67.99
 764938     17410  98-JQE   Cabin Tent                        1    149.99
 356867     41030  61-ANC   Deluxe Parka                      1     89.99
 395667     45423  73-PJW   Ground Tarp (12 X 9)              4     15.99
 320987     42290  95-XYD   Winter Jacket                     1     90.99
 878376     41478  51-EBJ   Sleeping Bag                      1     20.99
 487568     84750  71-NDB   Lightweight Backpack              1     35.99
 253478     28691  98-DZK   Deluxe Pocket Knife               1     21.99
 253478     28691  51-EBJ   Sleeping Bag                      2     20.99
 320987     42290  55-GAU   Backpacking Stove                 1     32.99
 320987     42290  53-CLN   17 Ft Canoe                       1    178.99
 320987     74406  23-MEL   Hiking Boots                      1     34.99
 764938     17410  49-HUA   First Aid Kit                     3     12.99
 569656     21928  62-RCC   Long Underwear                    6      4.99
7434168    706171                                            30   1018.83
                Cancel viewing: ESC,  Continue viewing: SPACEBAR
```

Figure 6-1 Sample Quick Report (Screen)

from a view allows you to filter the records that will appear in the report or to combine the data from multiple databases into one report. A Quick Report displays all of the data stored in the database or view.

To create a Quick Report, highlight the database or view that you want to use and press SHIFT-F9. The database or view that you want to use to create a Quick Report does not have to be active. You can also select the view or query to use by highlighting a form, label, or report that you have created for a specific database or view and pressing SHIFT-F9. dBASE IV displays the same menu box that you used to print a memo. dBASE includes an additional menu item, View report on the screen, which displays the report on the screen. When you highlight the ORDERS database, press SHIFT-F9, and type a **V**, the screen looks like Figure 6-1. When you view the report on the screen, dBASE displays the report one screen at a time. Pressing the SPACEBAR at the end of the report returns you to the Control Center.

Design of a Quick Report

The report in Figure 6-1 shows a sample Quick Report. dBASE IV includes the date and page number at the beginning of each page. In a Quick Report, dBASE displays each field in a column of the report. If the database has more fields than can fit on a line of the screen, dBASE wraps the remaining text to the next line. For each of the columns, dBASE uses the field name as a column heading. dBASE displays each field using the field width set by the database field width or the number of characters in a field name, depending on which is greater. Memo fields initially use 50 spaces across and as many lines down as necessary to fit the memo's contents. At the bottom of the report, dBASE adds a summary line. For each Numeric or Floating field, dBASE sums the numbers. For some fields, such as the CUST_NO and ORDER_NO fields, these numbers are meaningless. Some fields have asterisks in place of the total for the field. dBASE displays asterisks in a Numeric or Floating field when the field is not wide enough to display the number.

Print Menu for Reports

When you print a report, you have all of the menu options described for printing Memo fields in Chapter 3. The print options are the same for printing Quick Reports or custom reports. In addition to the options described in Chapter 3, you also have the option to view the report on the screen if you type a **V**. This option lets you preview how the report will appear when you print the report or save the report data to a file. Usually, you will type a **B** to select Begin printing to print the report. You may want to print a report to a file so you can print the report later from DOS or import the report into another computer package, such as your word processor. To print a report to a file, type a **D** for Destination from the Quick Report menu or the Print menu in the Report design screen. Then, type a **W** to switch the Write to setting from printer to file and an **N** for Name of DOS file. When dBASE prompts for a filename, modify its suggestion or enter a new one after pressing HOME and CTRL-T to remove the old filename, and press ENTER. Change the printer model dBASE will use by typing a **P** for Printer

❑

Tip: Change the width allocated to Memo fields.

You can make a quick change to the width allocated to a Memo field. See the SET MEMOWIDTH option in Chapter 8.

Tip: Printing long reports.

If you are printing a long report, you may want to print the first page to check the report's appearance. To print the first page, type an **O** for Output options, an **E** for End after page, and a **1**. Press ENTER and ESC before typing a **B** to print the report. If the first page is correct, print the entire report by typing an **O**, an **E**, and a **32767** (or an overestimation of the report's length). Press ENTER and ESC, and type a **B** to print the report.

model until the printer model (or ASCII, if you will import the report into another computer program) appears. Then, press ESC and type a **B** to start printing the report to a file.

Creating a Custom Report

While Quick Reports offer you a simple solution to displaying the information in a database or View query, you may want to make changes to the report's appearance. By designing a custom report, you can control how dBASE creates a report. Once you have selected the data that you would like to use, you can enter the Report design screen to describe how you want the report to look. Within a report, you can change the text that appears in the report, group records, and create calculated and summary fields.

Tip: Selecting the Print Model.

If your report uses different character styles, text pitch, starting codes, or ending codes, make sure that you select the printer model; otherwise, your selections may not appear correctly. To select the printer model, type a **D** for Destination and type a **P** for Printer model until your printer model appears. Then, press ESC to leave the Destination submenu.

Selecting the Data for a Report

The first step of creating a report is selecting the data that you want to use for it. You have to move to the database or view that you want and press ENTER twice. By using a view, you can limit the records that appear in the report, or you can combine the data from multiple databases in one report. dBASE IV allows you to use up to nine databases in a report by combining the databases into a view and using the view to create the report. Once you select the database or view that you want to use in the report, you can move the highlight to <create> in the Report panel and press ENTER. If you already have reports created for the active database or view, you can revise a report by highlighting it, pressing ENTER, and selecting Modify from the menu box.

Report Design Screen

Once you select <create> from the Report panel, you enter the layout menu in the Report design screen. The next step is to press ENTER again to select the Quick layout menu option. This menu option allows you to select one of three report layouts, which you can customize further. You can also press ESC to omit the quick layouts and create your own. Once you have selected Quick layout, dBASE offers the suggestions of column layout, form layout, and mailmerge layout. Selecting the column layout creates a report design identical to the Quick Report. Figure 6-2 displays a quick column layout of the ORDRLIST database. While it may extend farther to the right, you can scroll the screen to the right to see other parts of it. Selecting the form layout creates a report design like the one in Figure 6-3. This layout is similar to the Edit screen. This format might be suitable for printing confirmation copies of patient history or vendor information. The mailmerge layout is used for creating form letters and is covered in its own section later in this chapter.

A report can be 255 characters wide. Since most printers cannot print reports this wide, dBASE IV frequently moves the text that does not fit on the current line to the next line, as in the report of the EMPLOYEE database in Figure 6-4. Unless you plan to use compressed print or have a wide-carriage printer, you will want to create reports that fit within your screen width.

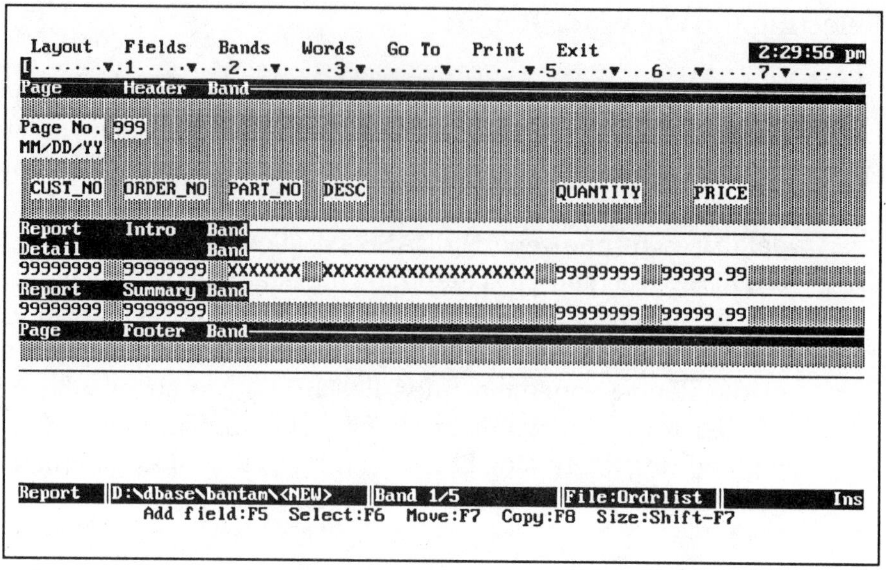

```
Layout  Fields  Bands  Words  Go To  Print  Exit                2:29:56 pm
Page      Header  Band

Page No. 999
MM/DD/YY

 CUST_NO  ORDER_NO  PART_NO  DESC                 QUANTITY    PRICE
Report    Intro   Band
Detail            Band
99999999  99999999  XXXXXXX  XXXXXXXXXXXXXXXXXXXX 99999999  99999.99
Report    Summary Band
99999999  99999999                                99999999  99999.99
Page      Footer  Band

Report  D:\dbase\bantam\<NEW>   Band 1/5     File:Ordrlist         Ins
        Add field:F5  Select:F6  Move:F7  Copy:F8  Size:Shift-F7
```

Figure 6-2 Report design using the quick column layout

In each of the layouts, dBASE IV divides the report into bands. The standard bands available to use in reports are: a Page Header Band, a

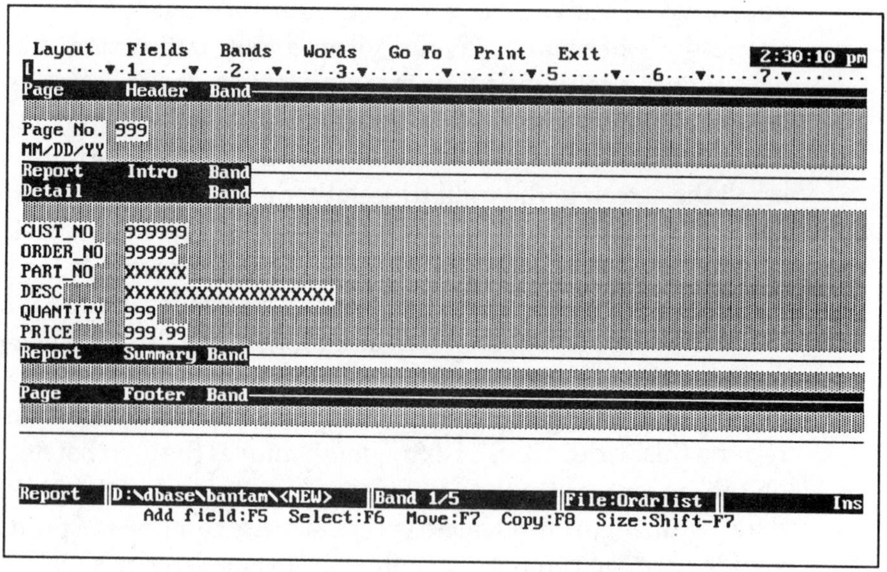

```
Layout  Fields  Bands  Words  Go To  Print  Exit                2:30:10 pm
Page      Header  Band

Page No. 999
MM/DD/YY
Report    Intro   Band
Detail            Band

CUST_NO    999999
ORDER_NO   99999
PART_NO    XXXXXX
DESC       XXXXXXXXXXXXXXXXXXXX
QUANTITY   999
PRICE      999.99
Report    Summary Band

Page      Footer  Band

Report  D:\dbase\bantam\<NEW>   Band 1/5     File:Ordrlist         Ins
        Add field:F5  Select:F6  Move:F7  Copy:F8  Size:Shift-F7
```

Figure 6-3 Report design using the quick form layout

```
Page No.   1
01/12/90

SSN            LAST_NAME         M_INITIAL  FIRST_NAME  ADDRESS           CITY
  STATE  ZIP_CODE  HOME_PHONE      HIRE_DATE  MARITAL_ST  NUMB_DEPEN   HR_RATE
 YTD_WAGES         YTD_FIT  HEALTH  SKILLS

215-90-8761  Jenkins           M            Mary        11 North St.      Cleveland
  OH        44124  (216)999-9999  12/20/88   M                       1       9.75
   3450.00         431.50  Y        Typing, Switchboard operator



                                    Some Spanish
```

Figure 6-4 Wide report wrapped to fit narrower output

Report Intro Band, a Detail Band, a Report Summary Band, and a Page Footer Band. The type of band determines where the information in the band appears in the report. For the column and form layouts, dBASE adds the date and page number in the Page Header Band to place the date and page number at the beginning of each page. A column layout also includes the field names in the Page Header Band. The templates marking the location for the fields from your dBASE records appear in the Detail Band. In form layouts, dBASE places the field names and field markers in the Detail Band. When you generate a report, dBASE creates a detail band for each of the records in the database or view. Anything entered into the Detail Band is repeated for each record. In the column layout, dBASE adds summary fields that total the Numeric and Floating fields in the Report Summary Band. This information appears at the bottom of the report.

You can remove any band by moving to the line in the Report design screen containing the band name and pressing ENTER. This closes the band. dBASE only includes open bands in a report. To open a band, move to the line containing the band name and press ENTER. dBASE remembers the band's contents that were established before you closed it. Since dBASE remembers the band's contents, you can close bands temporarily to have more room on the Report design screen for other bands. If the band is empty when you open it, dBASE inserts a blank line into the band.

For the form and column layouts, dBASE adds field markers for each of the fields in the database or view. These field markers are called field templates. The characters that dBASE uses to represent field templates indicate the type of information contained in each of them. dBASE uses

X's for Character fields since the field will contain character data. dBASE initially uses V's for Memo fields since they use as much vertical space, or lines, as their contents require. dBASE uses 9's for Numeric and Floating fields. Dates appear as MM/DD/YY, assuming you are using the default date format. Logical fields appear as Y's since dBASE will display the Logical field values as T, F, Y, or N depending on your entry. The text that dBASE adds for the field names are independent of the field templates. You can remove or modify the field names without affecting the field templates. You can also add more text to a report design. When you add text to a report design, it will appear in the report where you place it in the report design if the background of the report design is shaded. You can add text to any of the bands.

When you move the cursor to one of the field templates, dBASE displays the field name, type, length, and digits after the decimal point in the message line. Also, moving to one position in the field picture template highlights the entire template since dBASE treats the template as a unit.

In the column and form layout, the background appears shaded. This is a Layout screen. When you position text or field templates on a screen they appear in the report where you place them in the report design. The mailmerge format uses the word-wrap surface, just like the word-wrap surface that you used for entering Memo fields. When you position text and field templates in a report with a word-wrap surface, their position depends how dBASE wraps the field data and text within the margins, just as a word processor adjusts the text in a paragraph to fit the margins. You can switch between the two surfaces to have reports that have bands that wrap the text within the margins that you set and other bands that use the layout surface to position objects on the screen.

Leaving the Report Design Screen

Once you finish designing a report, you can leave the Report design screen to use other dBASE features. If you want to save the report, you can save it by pressing CTRL-W or CTRL-END, or by pressing ALT-E and typing an **S** for Save changes and exit. If it is the first time you are saving the report, dBASE prompts you for a filename. Type a filename and press ENTER. When dBASE saves the file, it generates three files that it uses for reports. These files use the filename that you provided and dBASE adds the extensions .FRG, .FRM, and .FRO. Your initial design is stored in the .FRM file. The generated code is in the .FRG file and the compiled object code file is the .FRO file. dBASE describes some of the steps it performs in the status and message line. When dBASE finishes the report generation, it returns you to the Control Center. If you have already saved the report, you can save your changes by pressing CTRL-END or CTRL-W or by pressing ALT-E and typing an **S**.

If you want to leave the Report design screen without saving the report design, press CTRL-Q or ESC, or press ALT-E and type an **A** for Abandon changes and exit. dBASE displays a confirmation box. Type a **Y** to confirm your selection and dBASE returns you to the Control Center.

If you want to save the report design using a different filename, press ALT-L and type an **S** for Save this report. Remove the existing filename by pressing HOME and CTRL-T. Type the new filename and press ENTER. dBASE saves the report design using the new filename. This menu option leaves you in the Report design screen. If you save the report design after this menu option, it will be saved using the new filename.

Saving a report can cause dBASE to generate a prompt relating to saving print settings if you have modified them. When dBASE prompts you to determine if you want to save the print settings, type a **Y** if you want to save them. dBASE prompts for a print settings file. Type a filename and press ENTER. This print settings file has a .PRF file extension. If you type an **N**, dBASE returns to the Control Center.

Once you save a report, you can modify the design by highlighting the filename in the Report panel, pressing ENTER, and typing an **M** to select Modify layout. You can also highlight the file and press SHIFT-F2. If the report filename appears above the line in the Report panel or no database or view is active, dBASE activates the Report design screen. If another database or view is active, dBASE displays a selection box to select between using the report design with the database or view that you last used to modify the design, or with the current database or view. You select one by highlighting it and pressing ENTER. If you select the current database or view, dBASE tries to match the fields in the report design with the fields in the current database or view. If the fields do not match, it displays an error message with the highlighted selection Cancel. If the fields match, dBASE activates the Report design screen, using the selected database or view.

Report Design Screen Menus

Once you learn how the Report design screen represents the report's appearance, you can use the other report features to customize your report. Most of these customization features are available using the menus.

The Layout Menu

The Layout menu contains menu options that let you change the design of the report, change the data the report uses, change the description of the report, or save the report without returning to the Control Center. All of the options are contained in the Layout menu shown in Figure 6-5 which can be accessed by pressing ALT-L.

Changing the Layout You can change the quick layout in a report design. After activating the layout menu, type a **Q** for Quick layout and the first letter of the type of layout that you want. When you change the layout, you undo any changes that you have made. You can use this menu option to set up the report when you begin a report design or when you want to change to another quick layout format if you accidentally choose the wrong one.

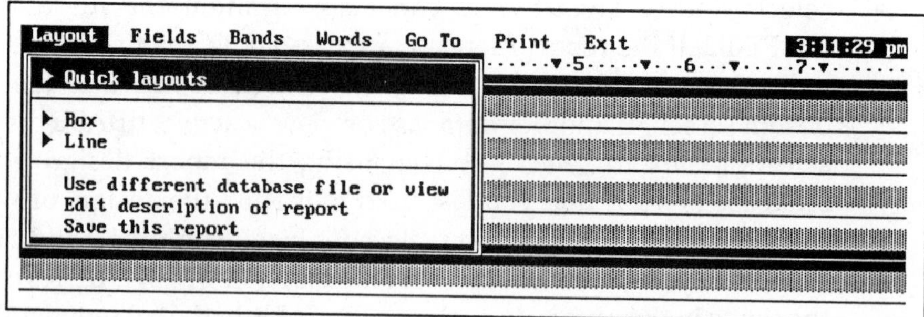

Figure 6-5 Layout menu

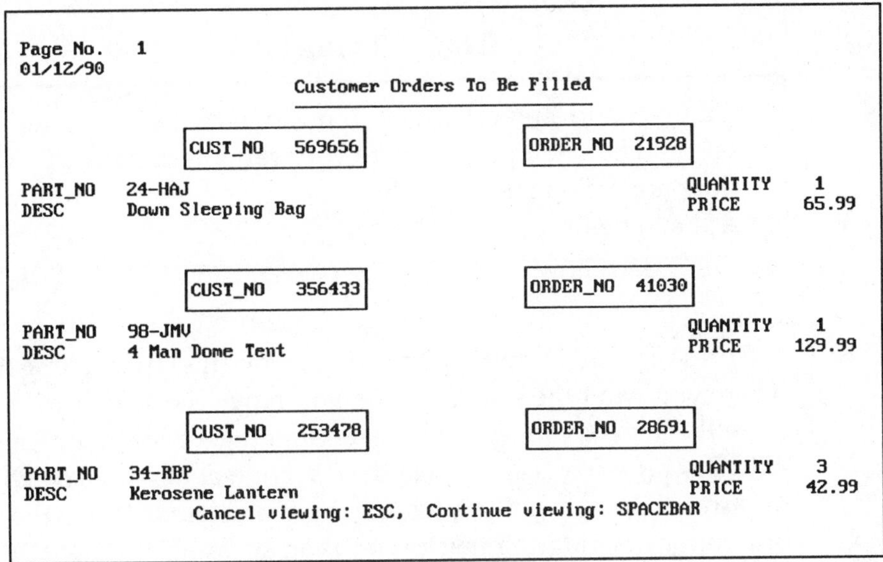

Figure 6-6 Report containing lines and boxes

Adding Boxes You can add boxes to a report to emphasize fields and text. When you type a **B** to select box from the Layout menu box, you can select whether to use a single line, double line, or another specified character to draw your lines. If you select Using specified character, you must highlight the character that you want to use from the list and press ENTER.

Once dBASE knows which character to use, move the cursor where you want the box to start and press ENTER to anchor the beginning position. Then, move the cursor to where you want the box to end and press ENTER again. As you move the cursor, dBASE draws the line or box for you. When you draw a box, you can use the TAB, SHIFT-TAB, HOME, and END keys or the ARROW keys to position the cursor. If you want to include text as part of the box, move the cursor to where you want the text to appear and type the text. The box will disappear behind the text. You can delete a box by highlighting one position of the box and pressing DEL. Figure 6-6 shows a report that uses boxes.

Adding Lines You can also add lines to a report. When you select line from the Layout menu box, you can select the character dBASE will use to draw the line just like you did for the box. Once dBASE knows which character to use, move the cursor to where you want the line to start

Tip: Moving boxes.

Add boxes to a report after you position the surrounding text and field templates where you want them, since dBASE does not include the box when you move the surrounding text and fields.

and press ENTER to start the line. Then, move the cursor along the path where you want the line to go. As you move the cursor, dBASE will draw the line for you. When you are drawing a line, you must use the ARROW keys. You can change the direction at any time by changing the arrow key that you are pressing. You can include text in the middle of a line by typing the text rather than pressing the ARROW keys. dBASE places the text that you type in the direction of the last arrow key pressed. Pressing TAB and an ARROW allows you to change the direction in which dBASE places the text that you type without redrawing the line. Figure 6-6 displays a report that uses a line. Since each position of a line is treated as an individual character, you can delete part of a line by moving to the part that you want to delete and pressing DEL. You can also delete part of a line by pressing the SPACEBAR when dBASE is in the Typeover mode.

Use Different Database or View When you enter the Report design screen, you may change your mind about the database or view that you are using for the data in the report. Also, you may have a report that you created for a database or view that you would like to use for another database or view that contains exactly the same fields and lengths. For example, if you create a report for your ORDERS database, you may want to use the same report for the ORDER_NO database that you created when you sorted the ORDERS database. When you select Use Different Database or View, dBASE lists the available databases and views in the current catalog. To select a new one to use for the report, highlight the one you want and press ENTER. If the database that you select has different field names than the current report design, dBASE lists the fields that it cannot find in the selected database. When you want to temporarily use the report with a different database or view than the one that you created it for, press ESC and type a **Y** to leave the Report design screen without saving the report. dBASE will save the database or view name with the report design.

As an alternative to using this command to use a different view or database than the one the report was designed for, you can activate the view or database that you want to use the report for. Once the view or database is active, highlight the report file in the Reports panel and press SHIFT-F2. dBASE will prompt you to select between using the current database or view, or using the database or view the report was created for. Press ENTER to select the current view or database and print the report using the Print menu that dBASE displays. This option works best when you do not want to make any changes to the existing report before using it.

Using a Report Description When you create several reports for a database or view, you may want to add a description to the report to distinguish one from the others. You can add a report description that will appear in the Description line below the panels in the Control Center. To create or modify a report description, press ALT-L to activate the Layout menu and type an **E** for Edit description of report. dBASE displays another box to enter or modify the description, displaying the report's current description. When you have entered the description or modified the existing one, press ENTER. Figure 6-7 shows a sample report description for the ORDRFILL report. To remove a report description, edit the report description and press HOME and CTRL-Y.

Saving a Report When you are working on a report design that contains several modifications, you will want to save it periodically in case you later make an error and want to return the report design to its status before the last change. You may also want to save the report under a different name. For example, you may want to modify a report design that you created using it as the basis for a new report. To save the report,

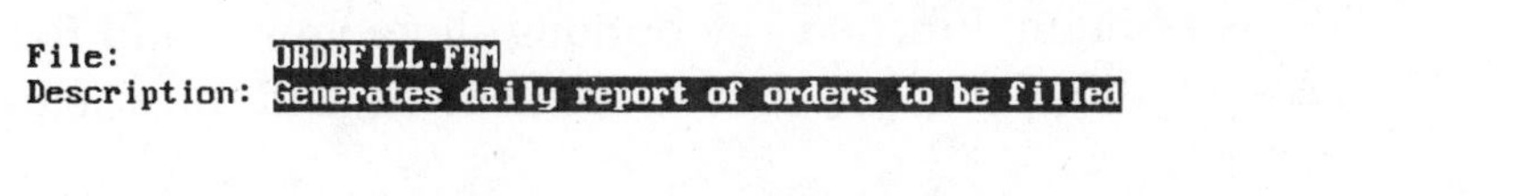

Figure 6-7 Report description displayed in Control Center

❑ **Tip: Use the same beginning characters for each report in a system.**

Assign a letter or abbreviation to all the reports in a system, then assign sequential numbers for the remaining characters. If the PAYROLL reports are PAY1001, PAY1002, and PAY1003, it will be easy to distinguish these from the reports for other dBASE systems.

press ALT-L to activate the Layout menu and type an **S** for Save this report. dBASE IV prompts you for the filename to save this report design and displays the current report design name. If this name is satisfactory, press ENTER. If you want to save the report design using a different filename, remove the old filename, type the new filename, and press ENTER. You can remove the old filename by pressing HOME and CTRL-T. If you want the report saved using a different directory than the current directory, you must also specify a path before typing the filename. After dBASE saves the report, it remains in the Report design screen. If you save the report design under a different name, the displayed report design is stored under the new filename. You can also perform this menu option by pressing CTRL-ENTER when you want to save the report design for the first time or you want to save the report using the same name. If it is the first time you are saving the file, you must enter the filename and press ENTER.

The Fields Menu

The Fields menu provides several options for defining which fields appear in a report and setting their appearance. From the Fields menu, you can add a field, remove a field, and modify a field's appearance. All of the options available from the Fields menu are shown in Figure 6-8. In addition, function key options allow you to add fields, move fields, modify their appearance, delete fields, and copy fields.

Add a Field from a Database or View When you create a report design, you may want to insert a field from the database or view that

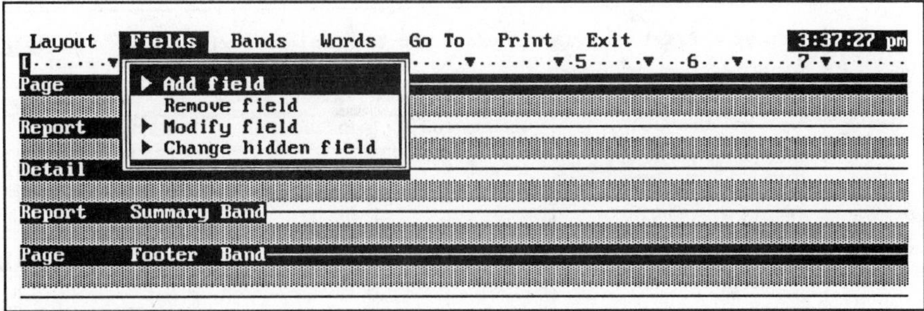

Figure 6-8 Fields menu

you are using. The first step in adding a field is moving the cursor to where you want the field to be placed.

Next, press ALT-F for the Fields menu and type an **A** for Add field, or press F5. dBASE displays a selection box like the one in Figure 6-9. The first column contains the database or View field names in alphabetical order. The other columns represent other types of fields that you can add to the report design. Select one of the fields by highlighting the field and pressing ENTER. You can also highlight a field by typing the field name, since dBASE moves the highlight to the first field that matches your keystrokes. dBASE displays a box like the one in Figure 6-10. The top half of the box lists the field characteristics. Since you cannot change these from the Report design screen, they appear in dimmed text. The other settings control how the field appears in the report. These options are described later in the chapter, with modifying fields. dBASE initially provides default settings. To accept these settings, press CTRL-END. When the box disappears from the screen, dBASE inserts a field template at the cursor's location.

Tip: Adding Fields.

When you add a field, you should check that Ins appears on the status line. If Ins does not appear on the status line, dBASE IV is in the Typeover mode. Adding a field will write over the current contents of the report design when the dBASE is in Typeover mode but will move the current contents to the right when it is in Insert mode.

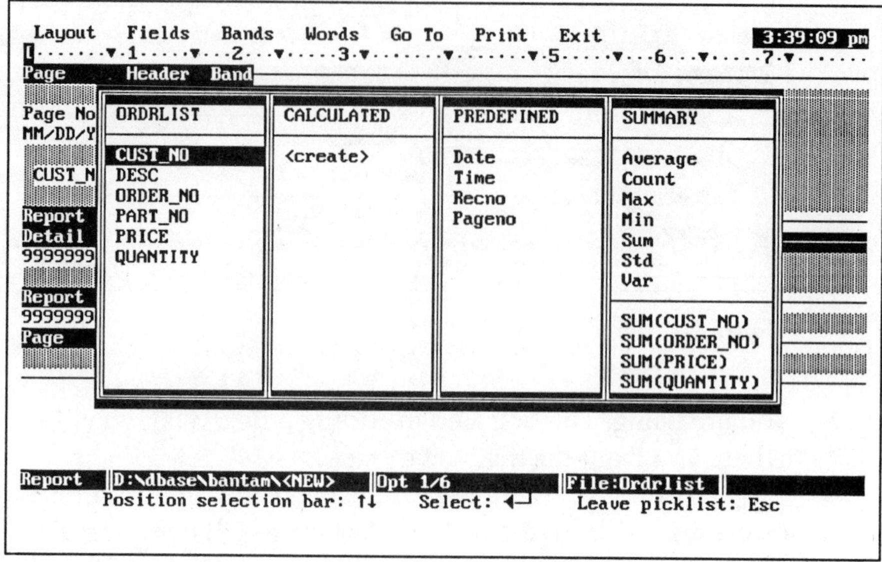

Figure 6-9 Add field selection box

Add a Calculated Field In a report, you can add Calculated fields that compute a value based on the value of other fields. To add a Calculated

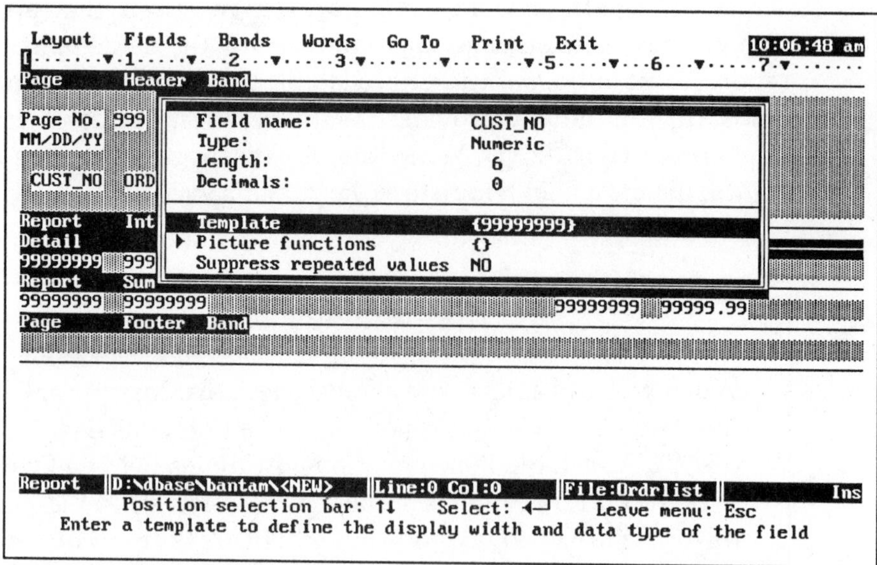

Figure 6-10 Database or View field definition box

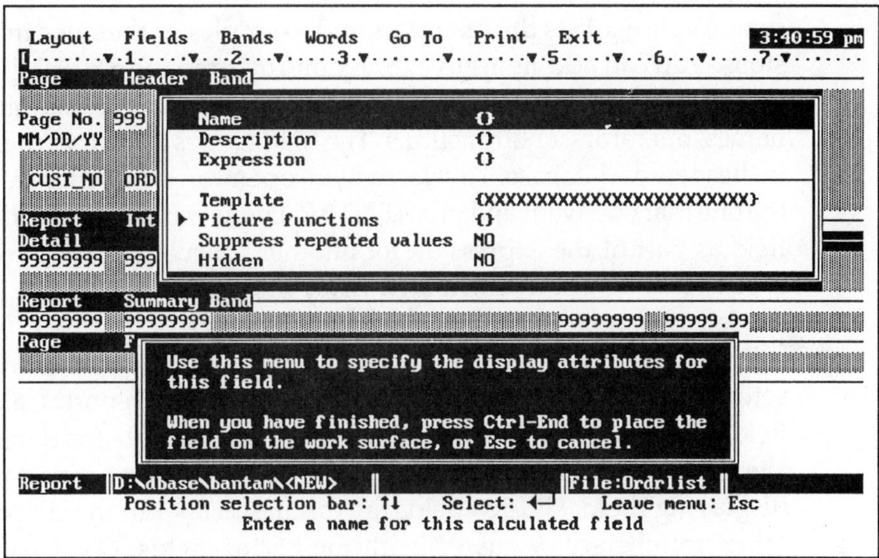

Figure 6-11 Calculated field definition box

field, move the cursor to the position where you want the Calculated field. Activate the Fields menu and select Add field, or press F5. When dBASE displays a selection box like the one in Figure 6-9, press the RIGHT ARROW and ENTER to select <create> from the Calculated field column. dBASE displays the box shown in Figure 6-11. Unlike adding a field from a database or view, the top half of the box is selectable, so you can define the Calculated field. The first option is Name. When you select this option by typing an **N**, type a name for the Calculated field and press ENTER. The Calculated field name must follow the requirements for field names. You do not have to name a Calculated field unless you want to use it in another location or you want to hide it.

The second option is Description, which allows you to describe the computation that the Calculated field is performing. To add a description, type a **D**, type a description, and press ENTER.

The third option is Expression. This is the expression that dBASE computes every time this field appears in the report. To add the expression, type an **E**, type the expression, and press ENTER. Expressions can contain fields, operators, and functions. You can use any type of data in the expression. If you use different field types in a formula, you must use one of the conversion functions so they are the same data type. Table 6-1 lists the operators and examples of their use in expressions. You can add items to expressions by pressing SHIFT-F1. When you press SHIFT-F1, dBASE displays a selection box containing field names, operators, and functions. The field names appear in their order in the view or database. To select a field, operator, or function, highlight the one that you want and press ENTER. If you want to use a Calculated field as part of the expression for another Calculated field, you must type the name of the Calculated field, since dBASE does not list it in the selection box it displays when you press SHIFT-F1.

The bottom half of the Calculated field definition box contains settings that control the field's appearance in the report. Calculated fields include a Hide field option that is unavailable for database or View fields. You can hide fields that do calculations in a report without displaying them. Hidden fields are discussed later in the chapter. The other options are discussed with modifying fields. Once you finish defining the Calculated field, press CTRL-END to return to the Report design screen and place the Calculated field at the cursor's position. The message line displays the Calculated field name and the expression. The next time you add a field, dBASE includes the Calculated field name in the Calculated field column. If you did not name the Calculated field, dBASE displays as much of the Calculated field's expression as it can fit in the column.

An example of a Calculated field is the ITEM_TOTAL Calculated field defined in Figure 6-12 that uses the ORDRLIST database. The ITEM_TOTAL field computes the item total for each item by multiply-

Table 6-1 Operators for Calculated fields

+	PRICE+15	Adds 15 to value of PRICE.
	PART_NO+DESC	Combines the text in PART_NO and DESC.
	BILL_DATE+30	
-	PRICE-5	Subtracts 5 from the value of PRICE.
*	PRICE*5	Multiplies PRICE by 5.
/	PRICE/2	Divides the PRICE by 2.
** or ^	PRICE^3	Multiplies PRICE to the third power (PRICE*PRICE*PRICE).

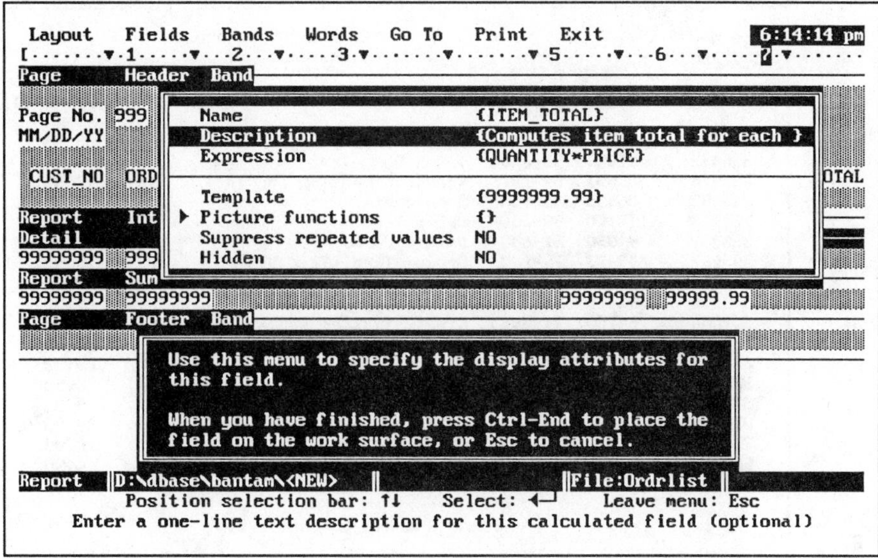

Figure 6-12 Field definition box for Calculated field

ing the unit cost by the unit price. To create this Calculated field move to the line in the Page Header Band containing the field names. Press END and the RIGHT ARROW to move to the position where the title for Calculated field should go. Type **ITEM TOTAL**. Press CTRL-LEFT ARROW twice to move to the I in Item. Press the DOWN ARROW to move to the Detail Band. Add a Calculated field by pressing F5. Name the field by typing an **N**, typing **ITEM_TOTAL**, and pressing ENTER. Add a field description by typing a **D**, typing **Computes item total for each record**, and pressing ENTER. Add an expression by typing an **E**, typing **QUANTITY*PRICE**, and pressing ENTER. When this report is printed, it looks like Figure 6-13.

Add a Predefined Field dBASE IV has four predefined fields that you can add to a report. dBASE automatically adds the date and pageno predefined field to the Page Header Band when you use the column or form quick layout. You can add a predefined field to include the date, time, record number, or page number in a report. The record number (recno) field is used primarily in the Detail Band; the date, time, and page number (pageno) fields primarily appear in the other bands. To add the predefined field, place the cursor where you want to add a predefined field. Activate the Fields menu and select Add field or press

Page No. 1
01/12/90

CUST_NO	ORDER_NO	PART_NO	DESC	QUANTITY	PRICE	ITEM TOTAL
569656	21928	24-HAJ	Down Sleeping Bag	1	65.99	65.99
356433	41030	98-JMV	4 Man Dome Tent	1	129.99	129.99
253478	28691	34-RBP	Kerosene Lantern	3	42.99	128.97
245687	86435	25-PIC	Snow Boots	1	67.99	67.99
764938	17410	98-JQE	Cabin Tent	1	149.99	149.99
356867	41030	61-ANC	Deluxe Parka	1	89.99	89.99
395667	45423	73-PJW	Ground Tarp (12 X 9)	4	15.99	63.96
320987	42290	95-XYD	Winter Jacket	1	90.99	90.99
878376	41478	51-EBJ	Sleeping Bag	1	20.99	20.99
487568	84750	71-NDB	Lightweight Backpack	1	35.99	35.99
253478	28691	98-DZK	Deluxe Pocket Knife	1	21.99	21.99
253478	28691	51-EBJ	Sleeping Bag	2	20.99	41.98
320987	42290	55-GAU	Backpacking Stove	1	32.99	32.99
320987	42290	53-CLN	17 Ft Canoe	1	178.99	178.99
320987	74406	23-MEL	Hiking Boots	1	34.99	34.99
764938	17410	49-HUA	First Aid Kit	3	12.99	38.97
569656	21928	62-RCC	Long Underwear	6	4.99	29.94
7434168	706171			30	1018.83	

Press any key to continue...

Figure 6-13 Report containing Calculated field

F5. When dBASE displays a box like the one in Figure 6-9, press the RIGHT ARROW twice to move to the Predefined field column. Highlight the predefined field that you want and press ENTER. dBASE IV displays a box like the one shown in Figure 6-14. Each time you select the Name option, dBASE changes the predefined field to another predefined field. While the bottom half of the Calculated field is identical to the field definition box for adding a database or View field, the TIME and DATE predefined fields do not let you modify the template or picture functions. These options are discussed with modifying fields. Once you finish defining the Predefined field, press CTRL-END to return to the Report design screen and place the Predefined field in the cursor's position. The message line displays the predefined field name when the cursor is on the field.

Adding a Summary Field Another type of field that you can add to a report is a Summary field. A Summary field computes a statistic for a field. You can use a Summary field to compute page totals or count the number of records in a report. By combining a Summary field with a group band, which is discussed later, you can compute the total of a field for each group.

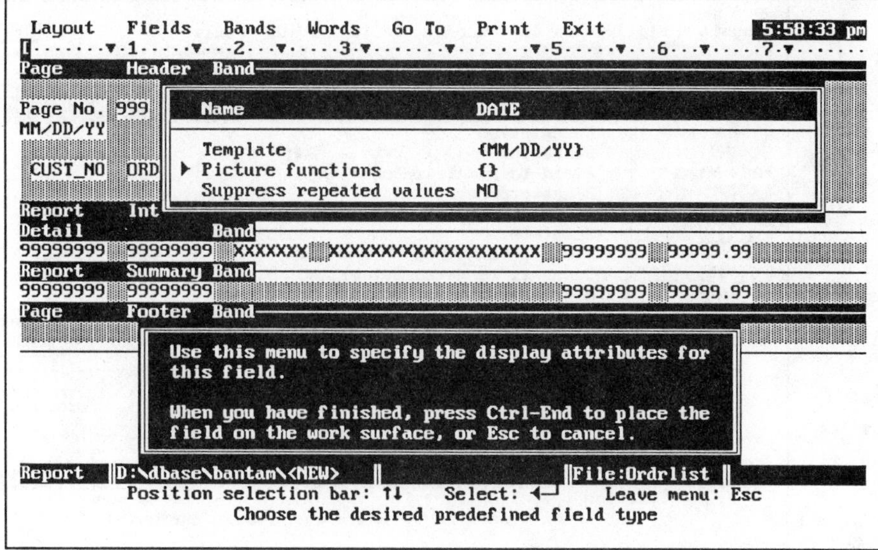

Figure 6-14 Field definition box for Predefined field

To add a Summary field, move the cursor to where you want to add the Summary field. Activate the Fields menu and select Add field or press F5. When dBASE displays a box like the one in Figure 6-9, press the LEFT ARROW to move to the Summary field column. Highlight the summary operation that you want to perform and press ENTER. dBASE displays the box shown in Figure 6-15 after you enter the summary operation. There are a number of options for you to enter that will document and control the summary operation. Although a number of entries are required, each one is easy to make:

1. The first option is Name. To name the field, type an **N**, type a field name, and press ENTER. The Summary field name must follow the requirements for field names. You do not have to name a Summary field unless you want to use it in another field or you want to hide it.
2. The Description entry allows you to describe the Summary field. To add a description, type a **D**, type a description, and press ENTER.
3. Operation is the next entry and allows you to change the operation that the Summary field performs. When you type an **O** for

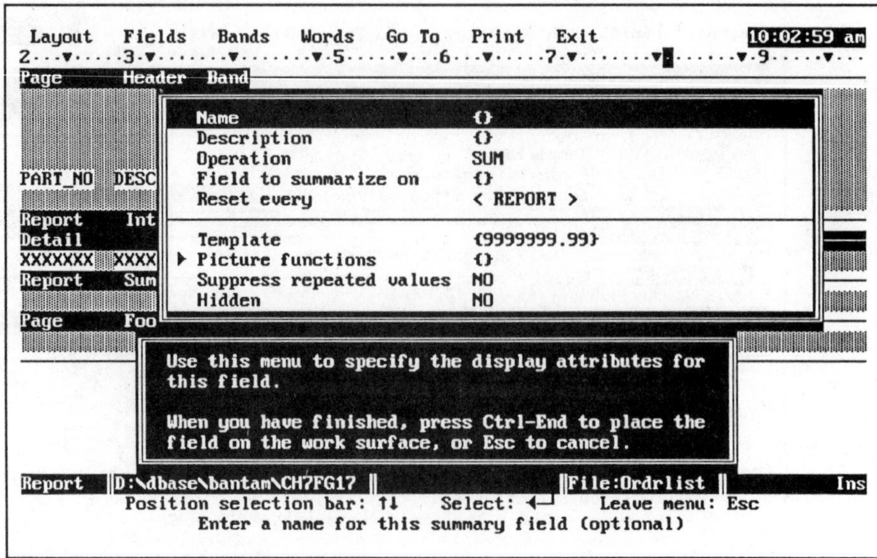

Figure 6-15 Field definition box for Summary field

Operation, dBASE lists the available operators to select by highlighting and pressing ENTER.

4. The Field to summarize on selects the field that dBASE uses as the Summary field. This option is required for all summary operators except count. Select a field by typing an **F**, highlighting the field that you want, and pressing ENTER. dBASE IV lists the fields in alphabetical order from the database or view on the left side and the named Calculated fields on the right side, dimming the fields that you cannot use. Use the LEFT and RIGHT ARROW to between the two field lists.
5. The last option in the top half of the box is Reset every, which determines when dBASE resets the Summary field to zero. dBASE sets this option to match the band that you place it in. For example, if you place the Summary field in a Page Footer Band, dBASE sets this option to reset every page. If you place the Summary field in the Report Summary Band, dBASE sets this option to reset only at the beginning of the report. If you place the Summary field in a Group Summary Band that you will learn how to create later in the chapter, dBASE sets this option to reset at the beginning of the group. You only change this setting when you want the summary field to reset at a different position. To

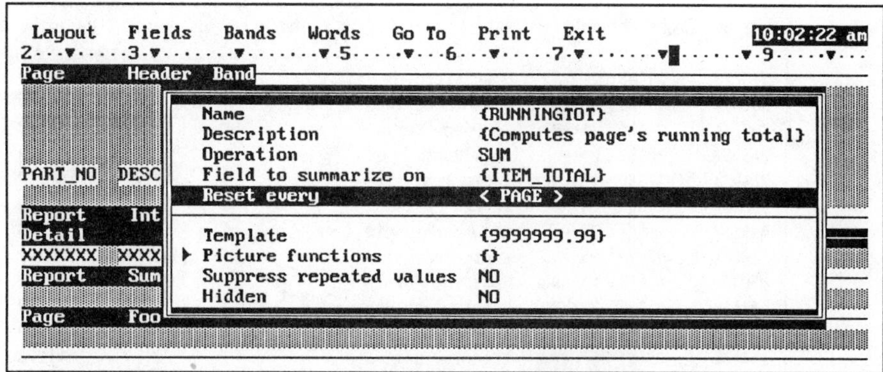

Figure 6-16 Field definition box for RUNNINGTOT Summary field

change this option, type an **R**, highlight when you want dBASE to reset the summary computation, and press ENTER. dBASE lets you select by Report, by Page, or by a group band that you have created.

6. The bottom half of the Summary field definition box is the same as the definition box for a Calculated field. The hidden field option is discussed with hiding fields. The other options are discussed with modifying fields. Once you finish defining the Summary field, press CTRL-END to return to the Report design screen and place the Summary field at the cursor's position. When the cursor is on the Summary field, the message line displays the Summary field name, the operator, and the field the Summary field uses. The next time you add a Summary field, dBASE includes the Summary field name in the bottom half of the Summary field column. If you did not name the Summary field, dBASE displays the summary operator and the field it summarizes.

An example of a Summary field using the ORDRLIST database is defined in Figure 6-16. This field is added by moving to after the ITEM_TOTAL Calculated field and pressing F5. When dBASE displays the field selection box, press the LEFT ARROW to move to the Summary field column. Highlight SUM and press ENTER. When dBASE displays the Summary field Calculation box, type an **N**, type **RUNNINGTOT** and press ENTER to name the field. Next, type a **D**, type **Computes page's running total of item total**, and press ENTER. Type

CUST_NO	ORDER_NO	PART_NO	DESC	QUANTITY	PRICE	ITEM TOTAL	RUNNINGTOT
569656	21928	24-HAJ	Down Sleeping Bag	1	65.99	65.99	65.99
356433	41030	98-JMV	4 Man Dome Tent	1	129.99	129.99	195.98
253478	28691	34-RBP	Kerosene Lantern	3	42.99	128.97	324.95
245687	86435	25-PIC	Snow Boots	1	67.99	67.99	392.94
764938	17410	98-JQE	Cabin Tent	1	149.99	149.99	542.93
356867	41030	61-ANC	Deluxe Parka	1	89.99	89.99	632.92
395667	45423	73-PJW	Ground Tarp (12 X 9)	4	15.99	63.96	696.88
320987	42290	95-XYD	Winter Jacket	1	90.99	90.99	787.87
878376	41478	51-EBJ	Sleeping Bag	1	20.99	20.99	808.86
487568	84750	71-NDB	Lightweight Backpack	1	35.99	35.99	844.85
253478	28691	98-DZK	Deluxe Pocket Knife	1	21.99	21.99	866.84
253478	28691	51-EBJ	Sleeping Bag	2	20.99	41.98	908.82
320987	42290	55-GAU	Backpacking Stove	1	32.99	32.99	941.81
320987	42290	53-CLN	17 Ft Canoe	1	178.99	178.99	1120.80
320987	74406	23-MEL	Hiking Boots	1	34.99	34.99	1155.79
764938	17410	49-HUA	First Aid Kit	3	12.99	38.97	1194.76
569656	21928	62-RCC	Long Underwear	6	4.99	29.94	1224.70
7434168	706171			30	1018.83		

Figure 6-17 Report using RUNNINGTOT Summary field

an **F** for Field to summarize on, press the RIGHT ARROW, and press ENTER to select the ITEM_TOTAL Calculated field. Type an **R** for Reset every. When dBASE displays the selections for when to reset the Summary field, highlight <PAGE> and press ENTER. Press CTRL-END to return to the Control Center. Activate the Print menu by pressing ALT-P. Change the text pitch to Elite (12 characters per inch) so the report will fit across the page by typing a **C** for Control printer, type **T** twice so Elite appears next to the Text Pitch option, and press ESC. Print the report by typing a **B**. The final report looks like Figure 6-17. Each time the report begins on a new page, the Summary field is reset to zero.

Removing Fields When you select the quick column or form layout, dBASE includes all the fields. Since you may not want all of the fields in a report, you will want to remove some fields. To remove a field, activate the Fields menu and select Remove field. dBASE displays a list of the fields in alphabetical order. Highlight the field that you want deleted and press ENTER. dBASE removes the selected field template from the Report design screen. If you perform this command when the cursor is on a field, it deletes the highlighted field. You can also remove a field by moving the cursor to the field template and pressing DEL.

Removing the field template does not remove the field name or text that accompanies the template. To remove the text, move to the text and press DEL to remove the characters. You can also remove the text using CTRL-T to delete a word at a time or CTRL-Y to delete a line at a time. You can select text and templates to delete by moving to the beginning of the text that you want to delete, pressing F6, and highlighting the text and field templates that you want to delete. Once you have selected the objects that you want to delete, press DEL. When dBASE prompts for a confirmation, type a **Y** and dBASE deletes the selected objects. When you remove a database or View field template, it is still available to add or use in Calculated or Summary fields.

Modifying Fields When you create a report, you may want to modify the option settings that dBASE IV provides for the fields. You can modify the field settings to change the field's width or appearance. You can also choose to hide fields.

You can change a field's appearance to display a dollar sign, place parentheses around negative numbers, display characters in upper case, and change the alignment. You can modify any type of field, although all options are not available for every field.

To modify a field, activate the Fields menu and type an **M** for Modify field, or press F5. If the cursor is on a template, dBASE displays the appropriate field definition box. If the cursor is not on a template, dBASE displays a list of all of the fields in alphabetical order. Highlight the field that you want and press ENTER. dBASE displays a field definition box. Once the field definition box appears, you can change the field's settings that are not dimmed.

Changing the Template You can change the template characters to change how dBASE displays the data in the report and the template's width. You can modify the template for any field type except date and

❑ **Tip: Removing fields from a form layout.**

When you create a report using the quick form layout and you want to remove the template and text for a field, move the cursor to the line containing the template and text, and press CTRL-Y.

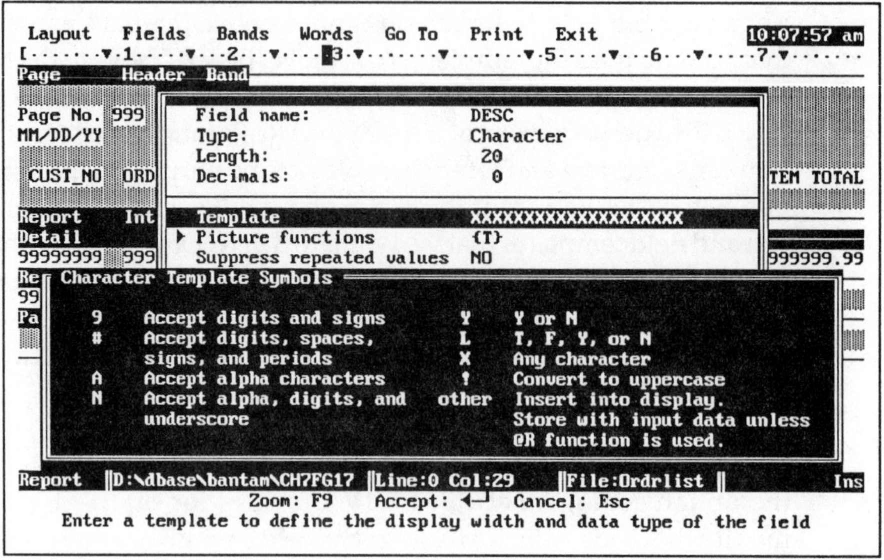

Figure 6-18 Modifying template

memo fields. To change the template, type a T for template. dBASE displays a template box like the one in Figure 6-18. Character fields can use 9, #, A, N, Y, L, X, and !. Numeric and Floating fields can use 9, #, ., comma, *, and $. Logical fields can use L and Y. When you type characters like () or - that do not appear in the bottom half of the template box, dBASE includes them in the report where they appear in the report design. Each character in the template represents a position in the report design that the field may occupy. The character determines the type of data that the report displays and the way it is displayed.

You can change the characters by moving to the character in a template and typing the new character that you want to use. For example, if you have a Character field that has a template of XXXXXXXXXX, you may change it to !XXXXXXXXX so the first letter is capitalized. You may want to change the formats of Character fields containing numeric data to include 9's instead of X's so any records that accidentally include letters will not appear. You can also add extra characters to appear, such as entering a template for a phone number Character field as (999)999-9999. For numbers, you may want the first character to be a $ so that dBASE uses a $ in the report if initial positions in the field are not used by the report data.

You can also use the template to change the amount of space that a field occupies on a report. Normally, you do this by adding more X's or 9's to the end of the template. You can also add it to the front of the template, such as adding a few 9's at the beginning to include space for more digits before a number with a decimal point not stored in the field. You may need this additional space to include the $ character in a Numeric or Floating field or to widen a numeric or floating Calculated or Summary field that appears as asterisks in the report. You can also change the size of a field using SHIFT-F7. To use this function key, move the cursor to the field that you want to change size and press SHIFT-F7. Next, press the RIGHT ARROW to increase the size or the LEFT ARROW to decrease the size until the field is the size that you want. Press ENTER. dBASE uses the first field template character for the additional characters you add. If you reduce a non-Memo field template size, dBASE omits the data beyond the characters or numbers that fit in the field template. If you increase a non-Memo field template size, dBASE uses the additional space as blanks. If you change the size of a Memo field, dBASE changes the width that it wraps the text when it prints the memo. For example, if a memo is using the default value of 50 for the memo template size, dBASE wraps the memo's contents so that it is 50 characters wide. If you change the memo template's width to 40, it fits 10 less characters on each line.

When you are finished modifying the field template, press ENTER and you return to the field definition box.

Using the Picture Functions The picture functions provide additional alterations to the field's appearance. The picture functions box that appears when you type a **P** to select picture functions from the field definition box depends on the field type that you are modifying. The picture functions box for Character and Memo fields appears in Figure

Tip: Adding template characters.

If you want to add template characters to the beginning of a template, press HOME to move to the beginning of the template. Then, press INS to switch to the Insert mode since dBASE is initially in the Overwrite mode when you edit a template.

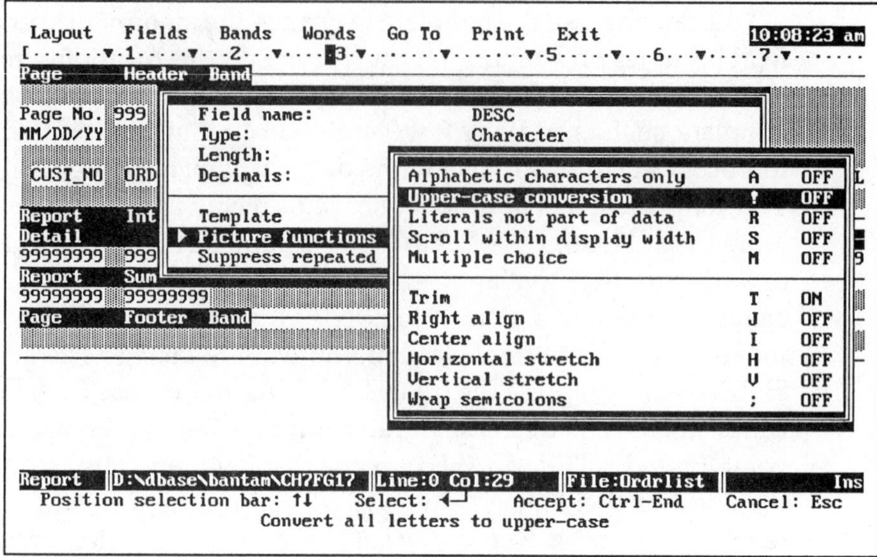

Figure 6-19 Picture functions for Character and Memo fields

6-19 and the picture functions box for Numeric and Floating fields appears in Figure 6-20. Date and Logical field types, and the Time predefined field type do not use picture functions. Since dBASE uses the same picture functions boxes for reports, labels, and forms, you will not use all of the options to create a report. Once you are finished with the picture functions, press CTRL-END to return to the field definition box. Pressing CTRL-END again returns you to the Report design screen. Each of the picture functions are either on or off. You can switch the setting for the option by typing the first letter of the function description. Some picture functions are incompatible, such as having a field left-aligned and centered. When you try to use two picture functions that are incompatible, dBASE sets the function that you are selecting on and the function that is incompatible off. When a picture function is used, the single character in the middle column of the picture function box appears in braces in the field definition box. You do not have to change the size of a field when you use a picture function that adds characters, such as the financial format, since dBASE increases the width for you if necessary. From the picture function boxes, you have the following choices:

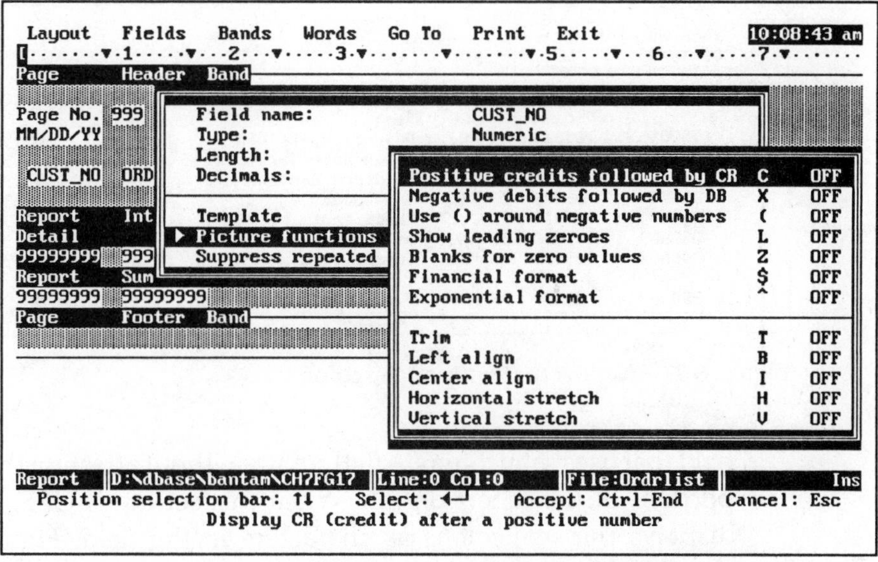

Figure 6-20 Picture functions for Numeric and Floating fields

- Uppercase conversion (Character fields) — When this option is ON, dBASE converts lowercase characters in the field to upper case. When it is OFF, dBASE IV displays the characters as they are entered in the field.
- Literals not part of data (Character and Memo fields) — Changes how dBASE IV treats characters in the field template that do not match one of the predefined template characters. For example, if you store a phone number in a Character field as 4566573490 and change the template for the phone number field to (XXX)XXX-XXXX, dBASE initially displays the phone number as (566)734-0. If you use this picture function so that the Literal characters, the parentheses and the dash, do not count as data, dBASE displays the number as (456)657-3490 since the parentheses and the dash do not count as positions to display data. If you use a picture template of (999)999-9999, dBASE will display the character data properly even if you do not use the Literals not part of data option.
- Wrap semicolons (Character and Memo fields) — When this setting is ON, dBASE displays data after a semicolon on the next line. When dBASE generates the report, dBASE adds lines below the

```
Page No.   1
01/16/90

CUST_NO  ORDER_NO  PART_NO  DESC                           QUANTITY     PRICE

 569656     21928  24-HAJ   Down Sleeping Bag                     1     65.99
 356433     41030  98-JMV   4 Man Dome Tent                       1    129.99
 253478     28691  34-RBP   Kerosene Lantern                      3     42.99
 245687     86435  25-PIC   Snow Boots                            1     67.99
 764938     17410  98-JQE   Cabin Tent                            1    149.99
 356867     41030  61-ANC   Deluxe Parka                          1     89.99
 395667     45423  73-PJW   Ground Tarp                           4     15.99
                            (12 X 9)
 320987     42290  95-XYD   Winter Jacket                         1     90.99
```

Figure 6-21 Report that wraps semicolons

field that uses semicolons to fit the data without affecting the other portions of the report design. When this setting is OFF, dBASE displays the semicolons as characters in the field. Figure 6-21 shows the beginning of a report that wraps semicolons in the DESC field. The record for the ground tarp uses two lines because the data contains a semicolon between Tarp and the dimensions.

- Right align (Character and Memo fields) — When this option is ON, dBASE displays field data so the extra spaces appear on the left side of the field. Normally, dBASE displays character data left-aligned so the extra spaces appear on the right.
- Left align (Numeric and Floating fields) — When this option is ON, dBASE displays the numbers so the extra spaces appear on the right side of the field. Normally, dBASE displays numeric data right-aligned so the extra spaces appear on the left.
- Center align (All field types except Date and Logical) — When this option is ON, dBASE displays field data centered in the field width. If this option is OFF, dBASE uses the default setting or another specified setting.
- Positive credits followed by CR (Numeric and Floating fields) — When this option is ON, dBASE displays CR after a positive number for the field. You may use this and the DB option for applications such as account balances. When this setting is OFF, dBASE does not place CR after positive numbers.
- Negative credits followed by DB (Numeric and Floating fields) — When this option is ON, dBASE displays DB after a negative number for the field. You may use this and the CR option for

applications such as account balances. When this setting is OFF, dBASE does not place DB after negative numbers.

- Use () around negative numbers (Numeric and Floating fields) — When this option is ON, dBASE encloses negative numbers in parentheses. You may use this option in financial applications to emphasize negative numbers. When this setting is OFF, dBASE precedes negative numbers with a dash.
- Show leading zeros (Numeric and Floating fields) — When this option is ON, dBASE displays blank digits to the left of a number as a zero. You may use this and the DB option for applications such as account balances. When this setting is OFF, dBASE does not place CR after positive numbers.
- Blanks for zero values (Numeric and Floating fields) — When this option is ON, dBASE leaves records with a field value of zero blank. When this option is OFF, dBASE displays zero values. You can use this function in a report listing account receivable balances so that only the records with nonzero balances appear in the report.
- Financial format (Numeric and Floating fields) — When this option is ON, dBASE places a currency symbol next to the number. When this option is OFF, dBASE does not add the currency symbol. You can use this function for monetary amounts instead of adding a dollar sign to the template since this picture function does not occupy a position in the field template. You can change the currency position and symbol using the SET CURRENCY RIGHT (or LEFT) and SET CURRENCY TO "(currency symbol)." dBASE increases the template size by one.
- Exponential format (Numeric and Floating fields) — When this option is ON, dBASE displays the numbers for the field using exponential format. Exponential format displays the first five digits starting after the first nonzero digit after a decimal point followed by an E and the power of 10 that you must multiply the number by to return to the original value. For example, 78500 appears as .78500E+05, which means .785 multiplied by 10 to the fifth power or 100000. This option only changes how the numbers appear; it does not change the numbers in the database or view. When this option is OFF, dBASE displays numbers using the format in which dBASE stores them. You can use this function in

reports containing very large or very small numbers that do not fit into the report width.

- Trim (Character, Numeric, and Floating fields) — When this option is ON, dBASE removes the blank spaces at the beginning and end of the field. When this option is OFF, dBASE includes the blank spaces and the beginning and end of the field. You can use this function to combine several fields so they appear connected, such as displaying the city, state and zip code together rather than including the blank spaces that the field data may not use. dBASE initially sets this option ON for character fields.

  When you position items in a report, having spaces between fields can have a different effect than leaving the positions blank, if you are working with trimmed fields. Trimmed fields omit their blanks or spaces at the beginning and ending of the fields. When you put two trimmed fields together, dBASE prints the trimmed first field and then prints the trimmed second field without leaving any spaces between. For example, if your report contains the templates for DESC and PART_NO next to each other and DESC is trimmed, the report displays Down Sleeping Bag24-HAJ. dBASE treats fields separated by spaces the same way. If you have a trimmed first name and last name field separated by a space, the report can generate an entry such as John Doe since it prints the first name, a space, and the last name.

  If you separate fields by pressing the arrow keys to leave a shaded position in the design screen between two fields, dBASE treats trimmed fields differently. For example, if you pressed the RIGHT ARROW instead of the SPACEBAR to separate the last name and first name fields, dBASE prints the first name, moves to the position in the report that corresponds to the last name template in the report design and prints the last name. With a name of John Doe, the report output may look like John Doe. The spaces between the first and last name are the unused positions in the first name field. If you want fields to be combined, such as the example with first and last name separated by a space, trim the fields and use spaces or other characters to separate the fields.

- Horizontal stretch (All field types except Date and Logical) — You must be in a word-wrap band on the report to use this option. It is ideally suited to the Mailmerge format where you are creating a cover letter within a band or when you are creating a form letter for each detail record in the report. When this horizontal stretch is On for a field, dBASE uses as much of the current line as it needs to display a field. A template with this option appears as HHHHH. This option allows the data to determine how much room will be required to display. The use of the H function causes dBASE to move fields that follow to the right if additional space is needed. This option is usually combined with the Trim function so that blank spaces in the field are omitted. When this option is OFF, the field can only use the width specified by the field template. This option is only available on word-wrap surfaces.

- Vertical stretch (All field types except Date and Logical) — When this option is ON, dBASE uses as many lines in the report as necessary to display all of the field data within the field width. It essentially stretches the display of the field down the page to display the entire entry. It is the default template for Memo fields. dBASE displays vertical stretch templates with V's. This allows the data to determine how many lines will be required to print the field.

  Changing the template width changes the width that dBASE uses to wrap the field data. A template width of 40 will require half as many lines as one that is only 20 characters wide. When this option is OFF, the field only uses the lines specified in the report design. This option is unavailable in word-wrap surfaces.

Suppressing Repeated Values The Suppress repeated values option can set a field to display its value only when it is different from the record above it. You can use this option to emphasize when data in the report changes. To modify a field so that its values appear only when its value is different from the record above it, type an **S** in the field definition box. Figure 6-22 displays the beginning of the report listing customer orders. Figure 6-23 displays the same report after suppressing the CUST_NO and ORDER_NO fields. By suppressing the customer number and order number when they repeat, you can quickly see when the values change. Since the report displays the fields that appear as the values change, you want the database or view records in the order of the field that you are suppressing. For example, the database in the two reports are indexed with the expression STR(CUST_NO)+STR(ORDER_NO)+PART_NO.

```
Page No.   1
01/13/90

 CUST_NO  ORDER_NO  PART_NO  DESC                          QUANTITY    PRICE

  245687     86435  25-PIC   Snow Boots                           1    67.99
  253478     28691  34-RBP   Kerosene Lantern                     3    42.99
  253478     28691  51-EBJ   Sleeping Bag                         2    20.99
  253478     28691  98-DZK   Deluxe Pocket Knife                  1    21.99
  320987     42290  53-CLN   17 Ft Canoe                          1   178.99
  320987     42290  55-GAU   Backpacking Stove                    1    32.99
  320987     42290  95-XYD   Winter Jacket                        1    90.99
  320987     74406  23-MEL   Hiking Boots                         1    34.99
  356433     41030  98-JMV   4 Man Dome Tent                      1   129.99
  356867     41030  61-ANC   Deluxe Parka                         1    89.99
  395667     45423  73-PJW   Ground Tarp (12 X 9)                 4    15.99
  487568     84750  71-NDB   Lightweight Backpack                 1    35.99
  569656     21928  24-HAJ   Down Sleeping Bag                    1    65.99
  569656     21928  62-RCC   Long Underwear                       6     4.99
  764938     17410  49-HUA   First Aid Kit                        3    12.99
  764938     17410  98-JQE   Cabin Tent                           1   149.99
  878376     41478  51-EBJ   Sleeping Bag                         1    20.99
 7434168    706171                                               30  1018.83
               Cancel viewing: ESC,  Continue viewing: SPACEBAR
```

Figure 6-22 Report of ORDRLIST with repeated values displayed

Using Hidden Fields When you use Calculated or Summary fields, you may want to hide them if they are interim steps for another field.

```
Page No.   1
01/13/90

 CUST_NO  ORDER_NO  PART_NO  DESC                          QUANTITY    PRICE

  245687     86435  25-PIC   Snow Boots                           1    67.99
  253478     28691  34-RBP   Kerosene Lantern                     3    42.99
                    51-EBJ   Sleeping Bag                         2    20.99
                    98-DZK   Deluxe Pocket Knife                  1    21.99
  320987     42290  53-CLN   17 Ft Canoe                          1   178.99
                    55-GAU   Backpacking Stove                    1    32.99
                    95-XYD   Winter Jacket                        1    90.99
             74406  23-MEL   Hiking Boots                         1    34.99
  356433     41030  98-JMV   4 Man Dome Tent                      1   129.99
  356867            61-ANC   Deluxe Parka                         1    89.99
  395667     45423  73-PJW   Ground Tarp (12 X 9)                 4    15.99
  487568     84750  71-NDB   Lightweight Backpack                 1    35.99
  569656     21928  24-HAJ   Down Sleeping Bag                    1    65.99
                    62-RCC   Long Underwear                       6     4.99
  764938     17410  49-HUA   First Aid Kit                        3    12.99
                    98-JQE   Cabin Tent                           1   149.99
  878376     41478  51-EBJ   Sleeping Bag                         1    20.99
 7434168    706171                                               30  1018.83
               Cancel viewing: ESC,  Continue viewing: SPACEBAR
```

Figure 6-23 Report of ORDRLIST with repeated values suppressed

Records   Fields   Go To   Exit   1:24:23 pm

PART_NO	DESC	QUANTITY	PRICE
24-HAJ	Down Sleeping Bag	7991	65.99
98-JMV	4 Man Dome Tent	516	129.99
34-RBP	Kerosene Lantern	4077	42.99
25-PIC	Snow Boots	8833	67.99
98-JQE	Cabin Tent	4462	149.99
61-ANC	Deluxe Parka	2556	89.99
73-PJW	Ground Tarp (12 X 9)	7215	15.99
95-XYD	Winter Jacket	1819	90.99
71-NDB	Lightweight Backpack	4458	35.99
98-DZK	Deluxe Pocket Knife	7364	21.99
51-EBJ	Sleeping Bag	7986	20.99
55-GAU	Backpacking Stove	3780	32.99
53-CLN	17 Ft Canoe	8270	178.99
23-MEL	Hiking Boots	4704	34.99
49-HUA	First Aid Kit	9584	12.99
62-RCC	Long Underwear	9556	4.99

Figure 6-24 INVENTRY database

To hide a Calculated or Summary field, modify the field and type an **H** to select Hidden field. Each time you select this option, the option switches between Yes and No. When you press CTRL-END to return to the Report design screen, the field template disappears. Since dBASE does not treat a Hidden field as a location in a report layout, you can place new text or fields in the hidden template's location. Once a field is hidden, you can modify it using the Change hidden field option in the Fields menu. To redisplay a Hidden field, move the cursor where you want the field placed, press ALT-F, type a **C**, select the field, and type an **H** to change the Hidden option to No. You can also hide a Calculated or Summary field when you create it by typing an **H**. Although a Hidden field does not have a report design position, you must be in the appropriate band when you create a Hidden field. For example, if you want a Calculated field to add three fields in the Detail Band for each record, the cursor must be in the Detail Band when you create the Hidden field.

One use of a Hidden field is when you want to perform a summary computation of a Calculated field in the Detail Band and you do not want to show the Calculated field in the report. Using the database in Figure 6-24, you can compute an item total for each item, hide the item total, and sum the item total in the Report Summary Band. To create the Hidden field in a report using the column quick layout, move to the Detail Band and press END so the cursor is not on a field. Add an

```
Page No.   1
01/13/90

PART_NO  DESC                        QUANTITY      PRICE

24-HAJ   Down Sleeping Bag               7991      65.99
98-JMV   4 Man Dome Tent                  516     129.99
34-RBP   Kerosene Lantern                4077      42.99
25-PIC   Snow Boots                      8833      67.99
98-JQE   Cabin Tent                      4462     149.99
61-ANC   Deluxe Parka                    2556      89.99
73-PJW   Ground Tarp (12 X 9)            7215      15.99
95-XYD   Winter Jacket                   1819      90.99
71-NDB   Lightweight Backpack            4458      35.99
98-DZK   Deluxe Pocket Knife             7364      21.99
51-EBJ   Sleeping Bag                    7986      20.99
55-GAU   Backpacking Stove               3780      32.99
53-CLN   17 Ft Canoe                     8270     178.99
23-MEL   Hiking Boots                    4704      34.99
49-HUA   First Aid Kit                   9584      12.99
62-RCC   Long Underwear                  9556       4.99
                                        93171     997.84
Total inventory value: 4982102.29
                  Cancel viewing: ESC,   Continue viewing: SPACEBAR
```

Figure 6-25 Report of INVENTRY database using Hidden fields

ITEM_TOTAL field by pressing F5. Name the field by typing an **N**, typing **ITEM_TOTAL**, and pressing ENTER. Add a field description by typing a **D**, typing **Computes PRICE * QUANTITY**, and pressing ENTER. Add an expression by typing an **E**, typing **PRICE*QUANTITY**, and pressing ENTER. Make the field hidden by typing an **H**. Press CTRL-END to return to the Report design screen. To summarize the Hidden field, press the DOWN ARROW until the cursor is in the Report Summary Band. Press ENTER to insert a new line. Add text by typing **Total inventory value:** and press the SPACEBAR. Press F5 to add a field. Press the LEFT ARROW to move to the Summary field column, highlight SUM, and press ENTER. When the summary definition screen appears, type an **N**, type **INV_VALUE**, and press ENTER. Add a field description by typing a **D**, typing **Computes total inventory value**, and pressing ENTER. Type an **F** for Field to summarize. Press the RIGHT ARROW and ENTER to select ITEM_TOTAL from the field list. Press CTRL-END to return to the Report design screen. When you print this report, it looks like Figure 6-25. Even though you do not see an item total, dBASE computes one for each record.

Moving Fields and Text Although you can use the quick layouts for your reports, you may want to change the report's appearance. Moving

Tip: Hidden Fields.
View a report with the fields that you intend to hide before hiding them, to check that your Calculated and Summary fields are providing the results that you expect.

text and fields allows you to customize the report's design. To move objects, text, and templates on the Report design screen, you must select the objects, move to where you want the objects placed, and move the objects. To select objects, move the cursor to the beginning of the text or templates that you want to move. Start selecting objects by pressing F6. Next, move the cursor to the bottom of the objects that you want to move. In the word-wrap surface, you are selecting all objects between the cursor's position when you pressed F6 and the cursor's current position. In the layout surface, you are selecting a rectangle of objects with the cursor's position where you pressed F6 as one corner and the cursor's position as the opposite corner. As you move the cursor, dBASE highlights the objects that it includes in the selection. To move a field name along with its template or to move several field templates at once, you must select the entire template. Once you have finished selecting objects to move, press ENTER to complete the selection. Next, move to where you want the selected objects placed. When you move the selected objects, dBASE places the upper left corner of the selection at the cursor's position. Once the cursor is in the position that you want, press F7. If you are in the word-wrap surface, dBASE inserts the selected objects in the text at the cursor's position. If you are in the layout surface, dBASE highlights the layout area where the selected objects will appear. If you are unsatisfied with the position, move the cursor and dBASE moves the highlighted area to reflect where it will move the selected objects. When you are satisfied with the position, press ENTER.

If the report design contains objects in the highlighted area, dBASE prompts for a confirmation. To confirm moving the selected objects and deleting the old ones, type a **Y** to move the objects. If the highlighted area is empty, dBASE moves the objects to the new location. dBASE adds additional lines to the report if you are moving the object to the bottom of a band.

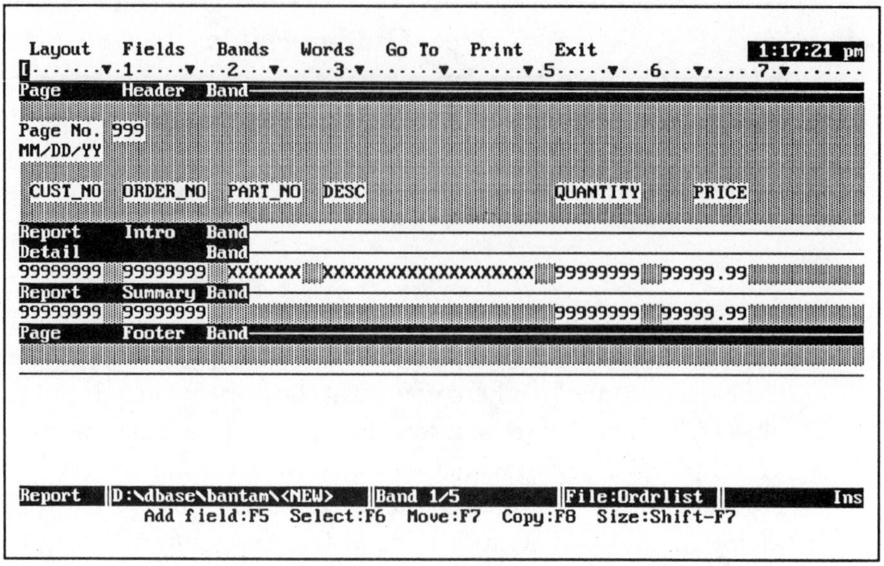

```
 Layout   Fields   Bands   Words   Go To   Print   Exit                1:17:21 pm
[·······▼·1·····▼···2···▼·····3·▼·······▼·······▼·5·····▼···6···▼·····7·▼·······
Page       Header  Band
Page No. 999
MM/DD/YY

 CUST_NO  ORDER_NO  PART_NO  DESC                     QUANTITY      PRICE
Report     Intro   Band
Detail             Band
99999999  99999999  XXXXXXX  XXXXXXXXXXXXXXXXXXXX  99999999  99999.99
Report     Summary Band
99999999  99999999                                 99999999  99999.99
Page       Footer  Band

Report  D:\dbase\bantam\<NEW>    Band 1/5        File:Ordrlist                Ins
             Add field:F5  Select:F6  Move:F7  Copy:F8  Size:Shift-F7
```

Figure 6-26 Quick column layout of ORDRLIST before moving fields

An example of objects in the column layout shown in Figure 6-26 is moving the text and templates for the last two fields so they replace the DESC field. First, move the cursor to the Q in QUANTITY in the Page Header Band. Press F6 to start selecting objects. Press END to highlight all of the text to the right of the cursor. Press ENTER to finish the selection. Move the cursor to the D in DESC. Press F7 and ENTER. When dBASE prompts for a confirmation, type a Y. dBASE moves QUANTITY and PRICE and removes DESC. To move the field templates, press the DOWN ARROW four times to move to the DESC template. Press CTRL-RIGHT ARROW to move to the QUANTITY template. Press F6, END, and ENTER to select the last two templates. Press CTRL-LEFT ARROW three times to move to the DESC template. Press F7 and ENTER. When dBASE prompts for a confirmation, type a Y. dBASE moves the QUANTITY and PRICE templates and deletes the DESC field template. To move the Summary field templates for the QUANTITY and PRICE fields, press the DOWN ARROW twice to move to the Report Summary Band. Press CTRL-RIGHT ARROW to move to the Summary field template for QUANTITY. Press F6, END, and ENTER to select the last two templates. Press the UP ARROW twice, CTRL-LEFT ARROW twice, and the DOWN ARROW twice to move below the QUANTITY

```
Page No.   1
01/13/90

 CUST_NO  ORDER_NO  PART_NO  QUANTITY      PRICE

  569656     21928  24-HAJ          1      65.99
  356433     41030  98-JMV          1     129.99
  253478     28691  34-RBP          3      42.99
  245687     86435  25-PIC          1      67.99
  764938     17410  98-JQE          1     149.99
  356867     41030  61-ANC          1      89.99
  395667     45423  73-PJW          4      15.99
  320987     42290  95-XYD          1      90.99
  878376     41478  51-EBJ          1      20.99
  487568     84750  71-NDB          1      35.99
  253478     28691  98-DZK          1      21.99
  253478     28691  51-EBJ          2      20.99
  320987     42290  55-GAU          1      32.99
  320987     42290  53-CLN          1     178.99
  320987     74406  23-MEL          1      34.99
  764938     17410  49-HUA          3      12.99
  569656     21928  62-RCC          6       4.99
 7434168    706171                 30    1018.83
                Cancel viewing: ESC,  Continue viewing: SPACEBAR
```

Figure 6-27 Report of ORDRLIST after moving fields

template in the Report Summary Band. Press F7 and ENTER to move the fields. Since the area that you are moving the objects to is blank, you do not need to type a Y. Since you cannot select objects in multiple bands, you must move the objects in each band separately. Figure 6-27 displays the report design after moving the text and templates.

Copying Fields and Text Besides moving text and templates, you can also copy text and templates. The procedure for copying fields and templates is almost identical to moving them. To copy objects on the Report design screen, you must select the objects, move to where you want the selected objects copied, and copy the objects. You can still use the F6 option for selecting the entries to be copied. Next you will move the cursor to where you want the selected objects copied and press F8. In the word-wrap surface, dBASE inserts a copy of the objects. In the layout surface, dBASE highlights where the selected objects will appear. If you are unsatisfied with the position, move the cursor and dBASE will move the highlighted area to reflect where it will place the objects. When you are satisfied with the position, press ENTER. If the report design has any objects in the highlighted area, dBASE prompts for a confirmation. To confirm copying the selected objects over the old ones, type a Y and dBASE copies the objects to their new location. If the highlighted area does not contain any objects, dBASE moves the objects to the new location. dBASE adds additional lines to the report if you are copying objects to the bottom of a band. If you are copying a named Calculated or Summary field, the new copy of the field is unnamed.

The Bands Menu

When you have a report that contains many records, you may want to group the records based on criteria arranging the detail records by job code, location, or the values in another field. The Bands menu lets you create group bands, which cause a break in the report rather than one long listing containing all the detail entries. With group bands you can arrange records on the basis of a field value, a set number of records together, or the value of a dBASE expression. Examples include placing all the accounts payable records with the same account number together, printing five records together, or arranging records for clients in sections according to their zip code. You can also have subgroups within groups, such as arranging employee records by department and within each department listing employees by job code.

You can also use the Bands menu to change a band from the layout surface to the word-wrap surface, so dBASE treats one or more bands as if it contained a word processor. You can further enhance how a band resembles a word processor by changing the size of print, the quality and the spacing that dBASE prints a band. Finally, you can use the Bands menu to change the order of the Page Header Band and the Report Intro Band. All of these options are available in the Bands menu shown in Figure 6-28.

Creating Group Bands To create a group band, you must be above the Detail Band. Next, activate the Bands menu by pressing ALT-B and add a band by typing an **A**. dBASE IV displays the box in Figure 6-29 to enter how dBASE will divide the records into groups. If you select Field value, dBASE lists the fields that you can use to group the records. This list includes the database or View fields and the Calculated fields. Highlight the one that you want and press ENTER. When you select Field value, dBASE creates a new group every time the field value changes. Therefore, dBASE creates unpredictable results if the database or view is not indexed or sorted in the same sequence that you have used for the breaks. If you select Expression, enter the expression that

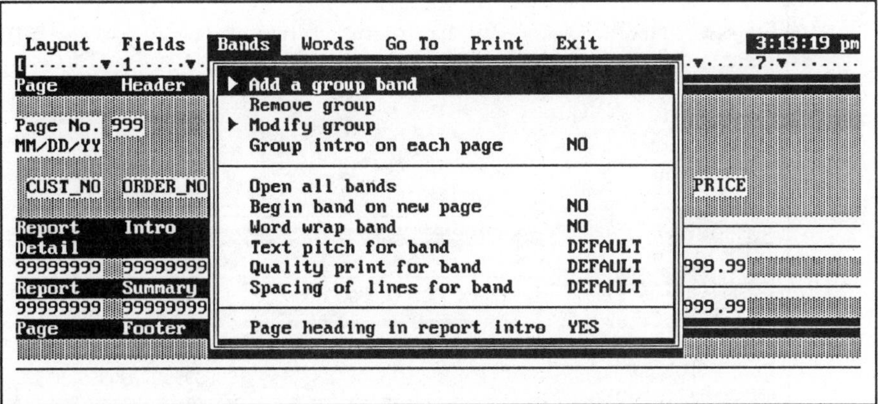

Figure 6-28 Bands menu

dBASE will evaluate, use the expression's value to group the records, and press ENTER. You can press SHIFT-F1 to display a list of database or View field names, operators, and functions to select. When you group by expression, dBASE evaluates the expression for each record and groups the records according to their expression value. For example, you can use an expression DATE()-BILLDATE to compute the days lapsed for unpaid bills and dBASE will compute the value for each record and group the records by the value. Since dBASE starts a new group every time the expression value changes, the database records should be indexed or sorted so the records are in group order. In the receivables aging example, you would index the database with the expression DATE()-BILLDATE. If you select Record count, dBASE prompts for the number of records that you want in each group. Type a number for the number of records that you want in each group and

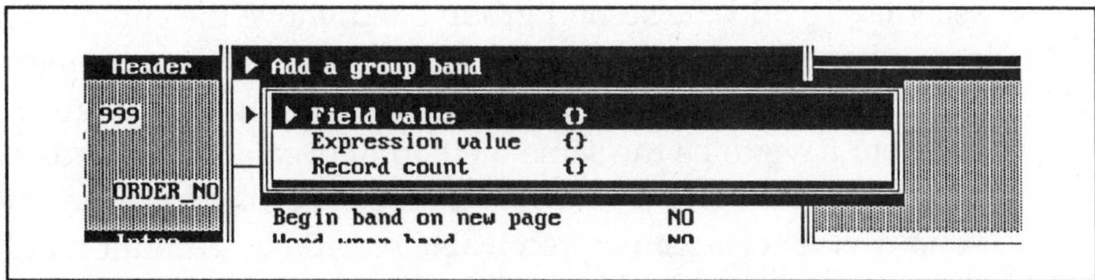

Figure 6-29 Selection box for selecting group criteria

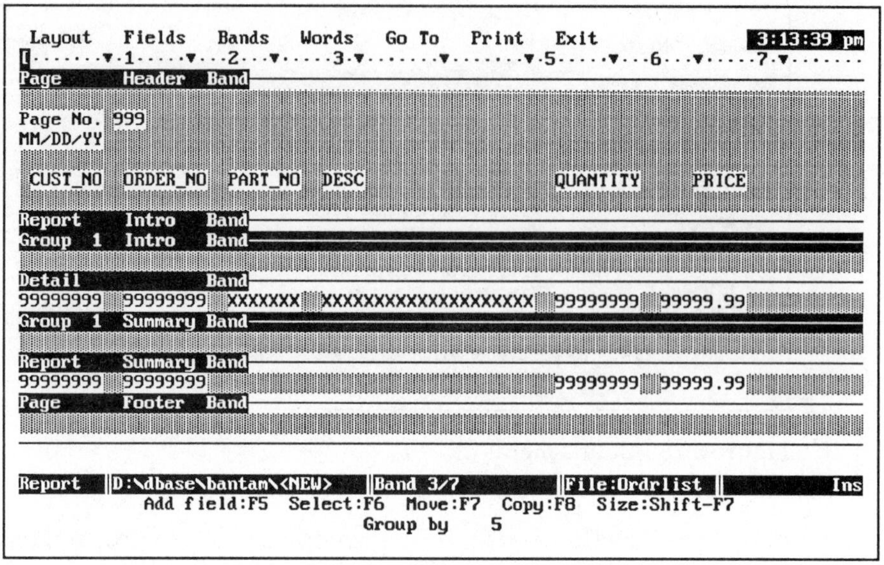

```
Layout   Fields   Bands   Words   Go To   Print   Exit              3:13:39 pm
[·······▼·1·····▼···2···▼·····3·▼·······▼·······▼·5·····▼···6···▼·····7·▼·······
Page          Header   Band
Page No. 999
MM/DD/YY

CUST_NO  ORDER_NO  PART_NO  DESC                        QUANTITY     PRICE
Report        Intro    Band
Group   1     Intro    Band
Detail                 Band
99999999 99999999  XXXXXXX  XXXXXXXXXXXXXXXXXXXX  99999999  99999.99
Group   1     Summary  Band
Report        Summary  Band
99999999 99999999                                 99999999  99999.99
Page          Footer   Band

Report  D:\dbase\bantam\<NEW>   Band 3/7        File:Ordrlist           Ins
          Add field:F5  Select:F6  Move:F7  Copy:F8  Size:Shift-F7
                              Group by    5
```

Figure 6-30 Report Design containing a group band

press ENTER. When you group records by record count, the database or view does not need to be in a specific order.

Once you decide how you want the records arranged, the report design screen changes to look like Figure 6-30. The Group Intro and Group Summary Bands appear at the beginning and end of a group. You can treat these bands like the other bands, adding text and field templates. The Group Intro Band can include descriptive information about the contents of the band and the Group Summary Band can include group totals. If you add a Summary field to the Group Summary Band, dBASE sets the Reset every option to reset at the beginning of each group.

Once you have created one group band, you can create a second group band that further divides the first set of records into smaller sections. To add the second group band, move the cursor to the first group band, press ALT-B, and type an **A** for Add group band. Next, specify how you want the band for the subgroup to arrange records. It does not have to be the same method of organizing records that you used for the first group band. For example, you can have the first group band divide the accounts receivable records by account number and then arrange the records for a particular account into sections of three records to simplify reading. Once you select how the second group will

```
Page No.   1
01/16/90

 CUST_NO  ORDER_NO  PART_NO  DESC                          QUANTITY     PRICE

Record for customer number: 569656
  569656     21928  24-HAJ   Down Sleeping Bag                    1     65.99

Record for customer number: 356433
  356433     41030  98-JMV   4 Man Dome Tent                      1    129.99

Record for customer number: 253478
  253478     28691  34-RBP   Kerosene Lantern                     3     42.99

Record for customer number: 245687
  245687     86435  25-PIC   Snow Boots                           1     67.99

Record for customer number: 764938
  764938     17410  98-JQE   Cabin Tent                           1    149.99

Record for customer number: 356867
  356867     41030  61-ANC   Deluxe Parka                         1     89.99

                Cancel viewing: ESC,  Continue viewing: SPACEBAR
```

Figure 6-31 Report grouped by CUST_NO using unindexed database

divide records, dBASE creates a Group 2 Intro Band and a Group 2 Summary Band that surround the Detail Band.

You can also add a group band outside an existing group band. To add a group band outside an existing band, move the cursor above the existing band, press ALT-B, and type an **A**. Next, specify how you want the first band to arrange records. As you add group bands, dBASE automatically numbers them. You can have as many as 44 group bands in a report.

When your report groups records by a field value or an expression, the records should be in the order in which you are requesting dBASE to arrange the report sections. You may need to sort or index the database or view. When dBASE groups the records by field value or expression, dBASE creates a new group every time the field value or expression value changes. Figure 6-31 displays the beginning of a report of the ORDRLIST database that is not indexed, which groups the records by their CUST_NO value. The four records for the 320987 customer number do not appear together since these records are not together in the database. Figure 6-32 displays the same report after indexing the database. If the report has multiple groups, the data must be in the order of the group bands. For example, if the first group band divides orders by shipping code and the second group band divides

```
Page No.   1
01/16/90

 CUST_NO  ORDER_NO  PART_NO  DESC                              QUANTITY      PRICE

Record for customer number: 245687
   245687     86435  25-PIC   Snow Boots                              1       67.99

Record for customer number: 253478
   253478     28691  34-RBP   Kerosene Lantern                        3       42.99
   253478     28691  98-DZK   Deluxe Pocket Knife                     1       21.99
   253478     28691  51-EBJ   Sleeping Bag                            2       20.99

Record for customer number: 320987
   320987     42290  95-XYD   Winter Jacket                           1       90.99
   320987     42290  55-GAU   Backpacking Stove                       1       32.99
   320987     42290  53-CLN   17 Ft Canoe                             1      178.99
   320987     74406  23-MEL   Hiking Boots                            1       34.99

Record for customer number: 356433
   356433     41030  98-JMV    4 Man Dome Tent                        1      129.99

Record for customer number: 356867
                Cancel viewing: ESC,  Continue viewing: SPACEBAR
```

Figure 6-32 Report grouped by CUST_NO using indexed database

orders by state, the database or view must have the primary index or sort key as shipping code and the secondary index or sort key as state. Another way to consider the index order is that the primary index or sort key is for the group band farthest from the Detail Band.

Remove Group Band You can remove group bands. First, move the cursor to the Group Intro or Summary Band of the group that you want to remove. Then, press ALT-B to activate the Bands menu and type an **R** for Remove group band. dBASE displays the confirmation box shown in Figure 6-33 to confirm that you want to remove the Group

❑

Tip: Indexing for reports grouped by expression.

When your report groups records using an expression, use the same expression to index the database or view. If your report contains multiple groups, combine the different fields and expressions that the report uses into an index expression. You may need to convert portions of the index expression to character types.

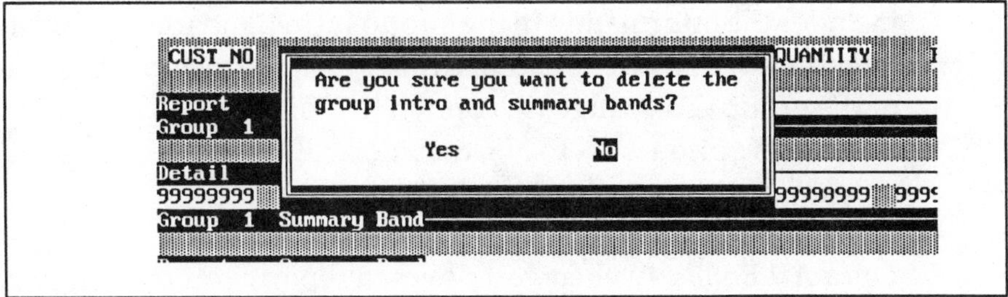

Figure 6-33 Confirmation box for deleting a group band

Intro Band and Group Summary Band. Type a **Y** to confirm and dBASE removes the group bands. You can also remove a group band by moving the cursor to the line containing the Group Intro Band or the Group Summary Band names and pressing DEL. dBASE prompts you to confirm before removing the group bands. As you remove group bands, dBASE renumbers remaining group bands. Removing group bands is different than closing bands since dBASE does not remember the group band's contents. You must recreate the group band if you want to restore it.

Modifying Group Band You can change how dBASE IV arranges records by modifying the group band. To modify a group band, move the cursor to the band that you want to modify. Then, press ALT-B to activate the Bands menu and type an **M** for Modify group band. dBASE displays the group definition box with the current group band settings. From this box, you can change how you want the records grouped or provide a new field value, expression, or record count. Once you supply the required information for grouping the records, dBASE returns to the Report design screen. Be sure to change your index expression if you are arranging records by field entries.

Placing the Group Intro Band on Each Page When you group records, you may have groups that start on one page and continue on the next page. In these cases, you may want the information in the Group Intro Band to appear at the top of the additional pages where the group appears. To include the Group Intro Band information on the top of the page for a group that began on a previous page, press ALT-B for the Bands menu and type a **G** for Group intro on each page. When this option is set to Yes, when dBASE creates the report, it includes the information in the Group Intro Band for the current group after the Page Header Band whether or not the group is the first record of the group. To change this option to No, press ALT-B and type a **G**. When this option is set to No, the information in the Group Intro Band only appears when dBASE starts a new group.

Open All Bands When you design a report, you may close bands as you finish designing them so you can focus your attention on the remaining bands. When you create your report, you will want all of the bands open so they appear in the report. To open all of the bands, press ALT-B for the Bands menu and type an **O** for Open all bands. dBASE opens every band. If a band is empty, dBASE opens that band and adds a blank line. You can continue to open and close bands by moving to the line containing the band name and pressing ENTER.

Beginning a Band on New Page You can set dBASE so every time it starts a new band it advances to the next page. To set dBASE to start a new page before it prints a band, move to the band that you want to start a new page every time dBASE includes the band in a report. Press ALT-B for the Bands menu and type a **B** for Begin band on new page to switch the setting from No to Yes. To return to the Report design screen, press ESC or CTRL-END. To return the setting to no, press ALT-B and type a **B**.

Changing the Band Between Word-wrap and Layout You can set which bands use the word-wrap editing surface and which bands use the layout editing surfaces. The layout surfaces have a shaded background. Text and templates that you place in a band using the layout surface appear in the same position in the report. The word-wrap surface has a solid background. Text and templates in a word-wrap band are word wrapped when dBASE replaces the templates with the field data when it generates a report. The word-wrap background allows you to use a band as a word processor. To switch between the two work surfaces, move to the band that you want to change. Then, press ALT-B for the Bands menu and type a **W** for Word-wrap band. Each time you select the Word-wrap band option, dBASE switches this option between No and Yes. When this option is set to No, the band uses the layout surface. When this option is set to Yes, the band uses the word-wrap surface. Changing the editing surfaces in bands that already contain text and templates, has little effect. When you change a band from the layout to the word-wrap surface, dBASE replaces the empty positions between text and templates with spaces. These spaces remain if you switch back to the layout surface.

Setting the Text Size for a Band When dBASE prints the report, it initially uses the default setting for the size of the letters in a report. You can change the size of the text by changing the text pitch if your printer supports multiple options. To change the text pitch, press ALT-B for the Bands menu and type a **T** for Type pitch for band. dBASE offers four selections for this option: Default, Pica, Elite, and Condensed. Default uses your current printer pitch setting. Pica prints 10 characters to the inch. Elite prints 12 characters to the inch. Condensed is smaller, with the exact number of characters printed determined by the printer. You can press the SPACEBAR to cycle through the available selections. Once you have the setting you want, press ESC or CTRL-END to return to the Report design screen. You can use this option to emphasize or deemphasize bands, such as printing the group heading with larger text so it stands out in the report. When you change the text pitch, dBASE does not adjust the report layout for the difference in the number of characters that it prints per inch. For example, if your report contains text that you have centered using the Position option in the Words menu, dBASE does not adjust it for a different text pitch and the text does not appear centered when you print the report. Changing the text pitch only affects how the report looks when you print it. Changing the text pitch does not change its appearance when you view the report on the screen or print the report to a file.

❑ **Tip: Using the word-wrap surface.**

If you change a band to the word-wrap surface, the next step is to set a right margin, since the initial right margin is 25 inches. Change the margin by pressing ALT-W, typing an **M**, moving on the ruler to where you want the right margin, typing a right brace (]), and pressing ENTER.

Tip: Changing the text size for a report.

When you want an entire report printed with a different text pitch, change the text pitch using the Print menu rather than changing the text pitch of the bands. To change the text size for a report, select Control of Printer from the Print menu. When dBASE displays a submenu, select the text pitch using the Text Pitch option. Press ESC to return to the Print menu.

Changing the Printing Quality of a Band When dBASE IV prints a report, it initially uses the default setting for print quality for a report. You can change the print quality of a band to emphasize or deemphasize the band if your printer supports multiple quality settings. To change the print quality, press ALT-B for the Bands menu and type a Q for Quality print for band. dBASE offers three selections for this option: Default, Yes, and No. The setting Default accepts the printer's current setting without change. A setting of Yes uses the best quality available, and No uses draft mode. You can change the setting by highlighting Quality print for band and pressing the SPACEBAR until the option you want displays. When you have the setting that you want, press CTRL-END or ESC to return to the Report design screen. This option allows you to determine whether to use a draft print quality or the best that is available. Changing the print quality only affects the report's appearance when you print it.

Setting the Line Spacing of Lines for a Band dBASE IV initially uses single spacing to print a report. You can change the spacing for band. For example, you may have a letter in the Report Intro Band that you

Tip: Changing the print quality for a report.

When you want to set the print quality for an entire report, change the print quality using the Print menu rather than setting the quality for each band. You can use the Print menu's Control of Printer Quality print option.

want double spaced. To change the spacing of a band, press ALT-B for the Bands menu, highlight the Spacing of lines for band option, and press the SPACEBAR until you see the setting you want. Each time you press the SPACEBAR, dBASE cycles through the line spacing options: single, double, and triple. Once the menu box displays the spacing you want, press CTRL-END or ESC to return to the Report design screen. This option is often used with bands that use the word-wrap surface. When you change the spacing, dBASE does not change the report design. dBASE uses the new spacing when it prints the band.

Repositioning the Report Intro Band The initial report design places the Page Header Band before the Report Intro band. You can switch these two so the Report Intro Band precedes the Page Summary Band. With the Report Intro Band first, you can add text that appears at the beginning of the report before the Page Header Band. You can use the Report Intro Band to create a letter that you need to include with the report. To switch the order of these two bands, press ALT-B for the Bands menu, and type a **P** to switch the Page Heading in report introduction setting to No. Once you switch the two bands, your report looks like Figure 6-34. To switch the two bands to their original order, press ALT-B and type a **P**. This feature is usually combined with changing the band to a word-wrap surface and adding page breaks to create a multipage letter.

The Words Menu

Each of the choices in the Bands menu affected report bands. The Words menu allows you to make other changes that can affect words or lines rather than entire bands. You can change the style or position of selected text to have text underlined or centered. You can use and

Tip: Changing the spacing for a report.

When you want to set the line spacing for an entire report, use the Print menu rather than setting the spacing for each band. To change the line spacing for an entire report, use the Print menu Page dimensions Spacing of lines option.

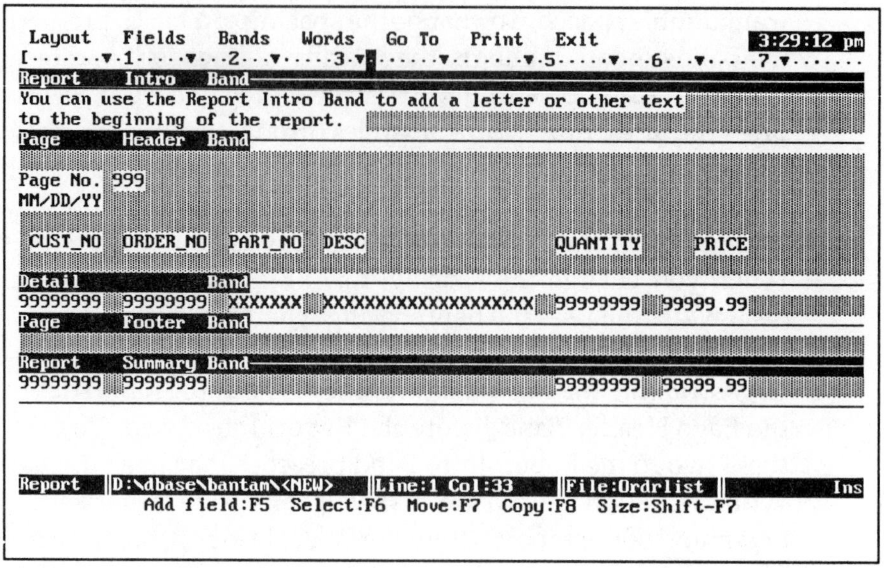

```
 Layout   Fields   Bands   Words   Go To   Print   Exit                 3:29:12 pm
[·······▼·1·····▼···2···▼·····3·▼······▼·······▼·5·····▼···6···▼·····7·▼·······
Report    Intro    Band
You can use the Report Intro Band to add a letter or other text
to the beginning of the report.
Page      Header   Band

Page No. 999
MM/DD/YY

 CUST_NO  ORDER_NO  PART_NO  DESC                        QUANTITY     PRICE

Detail             Band
99999999  99999999  XXXXXXX  XXXXXXXXXXXXXXXXXXXX        99999999   99999.99
Page      Footer   Band

Report    Summary  Band
99999999  99999999                                       99999999   99999.99


Report    D:\dbase\bantam\<NEW>    Line:1 Col:33    File:Ordrlist          Ins
           Add field:F5  Select:F6  Move:F7  Copy:F8  Size:Shift-F7
```

Figure 6-34 Report Design with Report Intro Band before Page Header Band

create ruler settings that let you change the margins that dBASE positions for you, and how dBASE wraps text in bands using the word-wrap surface. You can use the Words menu to add and remove lines from the design. You can also use the Words menu to break a band into pages if you are creating a multipage band. Finally, you can use the Words menu to bring data into the report and copy data to another file. All of these options are available using the Words menu shown in Figure 6-35.

Changing the Character Style When dBASE prints a report, it initially uses the default character style for the printer. You can change the character style to use other styles such as boldface, underline, or italics. To change the character style, you must select the objects (the text and templates) that you want to change. To select objects, move the cursor to the beginning of the text or templates that you want to select and press F6. Next, move the cursor so all of the objects that you want to select are highlighted. If you want to highlight an entire line, press F6 a second time and if you want to select the entire band, press F6 a third time. To change the style of a field's data, you must select the entire template. Next, press ALT-W for the Words menu and type an **S** for

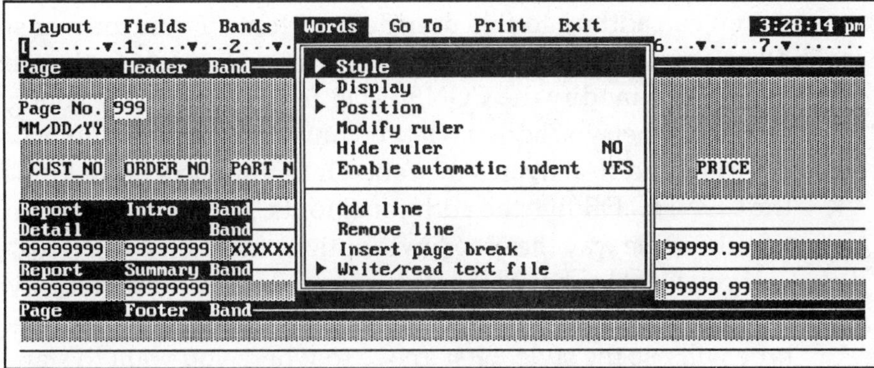

Figure 6-35 Words menu

Style. dBASE displays the selection box shown in Figure 6-36. Type the first letter of the style that you want. If you have defined a user-defined font, you can select one by typing the number next to the font that you want. When dBASE returns to the Report design screen, it displays boldface text using boldface and other styles with the color it displays on the lines containing the band names. On monochrome monitors, underlined text appears underlined. You can apply more than one style to selected text. When you use more than one style, you only have to select the objects once since dBASE remembers the selected objects when you make the second style change. If your printer cannot print the style that you select, it appears underlined.

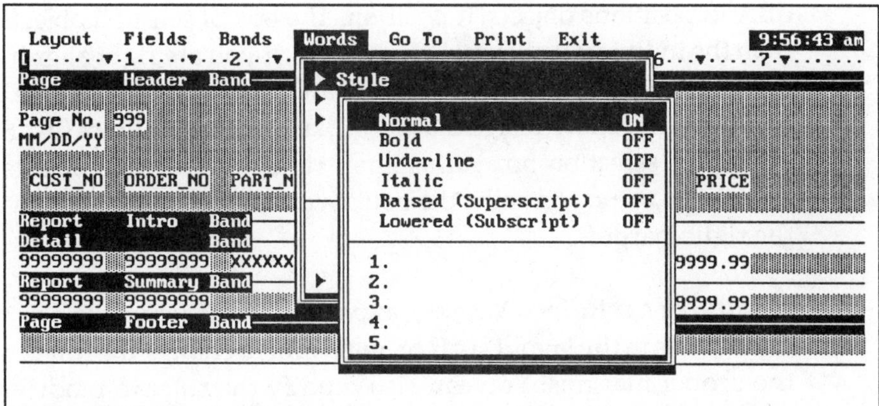

Figure 6-36 Style options

You can add up to five user-defined fonts if your printer supports other character fonts. To add a user-defined style, use the DBSETUP program to modify the CONFIG.DB file that stores the configuration settings. When you add a style, you must know the computer code that activates and deactivates the font. Once you have added the fonts to the CONFIG.DB file, the additional fonts become available and function the same way the other style options function.

If you want to change the style of text that you are about to type, you can select the style before you type and the text that you subsequently type will use the style. First, move to where you want to start typing. Next, press ALT-W, type an **S**, and select the style that you want. Next, type the text that you want in the alternate style. When you want to return to normal text, press ALT-W, type an **S** and select the option that you have finished using to switch the setting to off.

Positioning Selected Text and Template In the layout surface, you can have dBASE left align, right align, and center text and templates for you. When you position text, dBASE uses the right and left margin settings to determine the position. dBASE initially sets the left margin at 0" and the right margin at 25". Before you position objects, you probably need to modify the ruler to change the margins. To position objects, you must select the objects you want to position. Next, press ALT-W for the Words menu and type a **P** for Position. dBASE displays a box to select between left, right, and centered. Type the first letter of the option that you want. When dBASE returns to the Report design screen, it moves the selected objects to the desired position. When dBASE positions objects, it positions the box of selected objects rather than the individual objects. For example, if you are right aligning three objects that have different lengths and you select the three objects together, the report design may look like Figure 6-37. Since dBASE right aligns the selection box rather than right aligning the objects in the selection box individually, the bottom two objects are not flush against the right margin.

Modifying the Ruler When you use the word-wrap surface or position objects in the layout surface, you want to change the ruler so it uses the proper margins. You can also modify the ruler to modify the tab stops and to add paragraph indentation for a word-wrap surface.

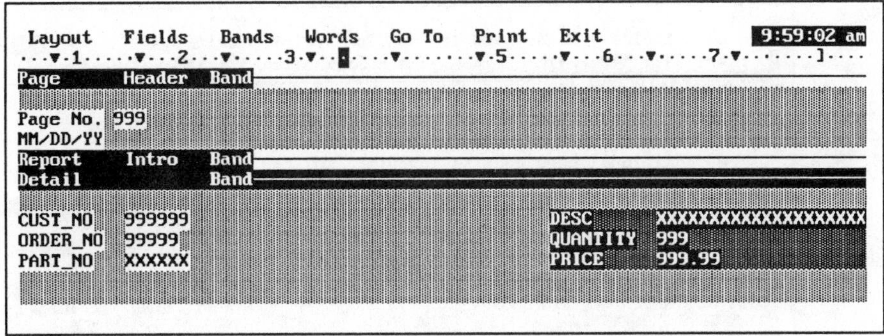

Figure 6-37 Three objects selected and right-aligned

To modify the ruler, press ALT-W and type an **M** for Modify ruler. The cursor appears in the ruler above the report design. To add symbols to the ruler, move the cursor to the ruler position where you want to add a symbol and type the symbol. You can add a tab position by typing an exclamation point (!). You can add a paragraph indent by typing a number sign (#). Typing a left brace ([) and a right brace (]) set the left and right margin. When you set the margin, dBASE removes the existing one. You can delete a character on the ruler using the DEL or BACKSPACE keys. To quickly change the left margin and paragraph indent to zero, type a **0**.

You can reset the tab stop interval by typing an equal sign. When dBASE prompts you for the number of positions that you want between tab stops, type the number of positions that you want between the tab stops and press ENTER. When you reset the tab stops dBASE removes all existing tab stops. When you have finished modifying the ruler, press ENTER to return to the Report design screen. The dBASE uses the same ruler for the entire report.

Figure 6-38 shows a report design created with a modified ruler. In this report design, the left margin is set to 0, the right margin is set to 7", the tab stops are every five positions, and the paragraph indent set for .5". With these changes, the text in the Report Intro Band is wrapped using the new margins and the title in the Page Header Band is centered. The paragraph indent, which is only used in word-wrap surfaces, causes the first line of a paragraph to be automatically indented.

```
 Layout   Fields   Bands   Words   Go To   Print   Exit              10:15:03 am
[----#....▼....▼....▼....▼....▼....▼....▼....▼....▼....▼....▼....▼....]....▼....
Report     Intro   Band
     A copy of this report goes to shipping so they can package the
items.  Once the items are packaged, they are checked against the
invoice before sealing and shipping.
     An additional copy goes to inventory so they can update their
records.
Page       Header  Band
                              DAILY ORDERS FOR MM/DD/YY

Page No. 999

 CUST_NO  ORDER_NO  PART_NO  DESC                   QUANTITY      PRICE
```

Figure 6-38 Sample report design using ruler modifications

Hiding Ruler Once you have modified the ruler for your report, you may want to hide it so the Report design screen contains an additional line of your report design. To hide the ruler, press ALT-W for the Words menu and an **H** for Hide ruler. Even when a ruler is hidden, you can still use the formatting features that the ruler contains. If you modify the ruler while it is hidden, it temporarily reappears until you press ENTER. To redisplay the ruler perform the steps that you used to hide it.

Enabling Automatic Indent Since you must use the same ruler for the entire report design, you may want to indent paragraphs in bands using the word-wrap surface. The Enable automatic indent option can create different left margins in the word-wrap bands than defined by the ruler. To change this option, move to a word-wrap surface, press ALT-W for the Words menu, and type an **E** for Enable automatic indent. Each time you select the option, the option switches between Yes and No. When this option is set to No, pressing TAB or SHIFT-TAB moves the cursor to the next or previous tab stop but does not change the left margin. When this option is set to Yes, pressing TAB or SHIFT-TAB moves the cursor to the next or previous tab stop and sets the left margin to the cursor's position. When you change the left margin with the Enable automatic indent option, the band continues to use the new margin until you change it. Figure 6-39 displays a Report Intro Band that uses the Enable automatic indent option to indent the paragraphs.

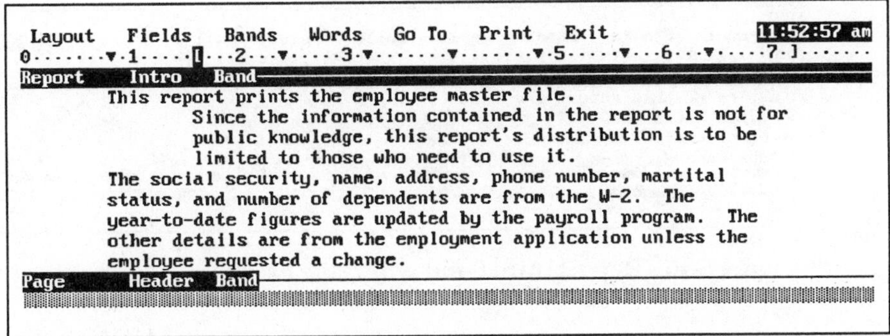

Figure 6-39 Report Intro Band using the Enable automatic indent option

Adding a Line You can add a line to the report. To add a line, move the cursor to where you want a line inserted, press ALT-W for the Words menu, and type an **A** for Add line. Everything to the right of the cursor is moved to the new line dBASE adds below the current position, with the cursor moved to the beginning of the next line. You can also add lines by pressing ENTER.

Removing a Line You can remove a line from a report. To remove a line, move the cursor to the line you want removed, press ALT-W for the Words menu, and type an **R** for Remove line. dBASE deletes everything on the line and moves the cursor to the next line. You can also add lines by pressing CTRL-Y.

Inserting a Page Break You can add a page break to a report band. You can use this feature when you are creating a cover letter for a report and you want to ensure that the report does not print on the same page as the remainder of the report. To add a page break, move the cursor to the line that you want after the page break. If the report design does not have a blank line, such as when you want to insert a page break at the bottom of the Report Intro Band, you must add one. Next, press ALT-W for the Words menu and type an **I** for Insert page break. dBASE adds a dashed line like the one in Figure 6-40. Once the page break character is added to the design, you can delete the line below it if you want. If you want to remove the page break, move the cursor to the dashed line and press DEL to delete the page break character or CTRL-Y to delete the line and page break character.

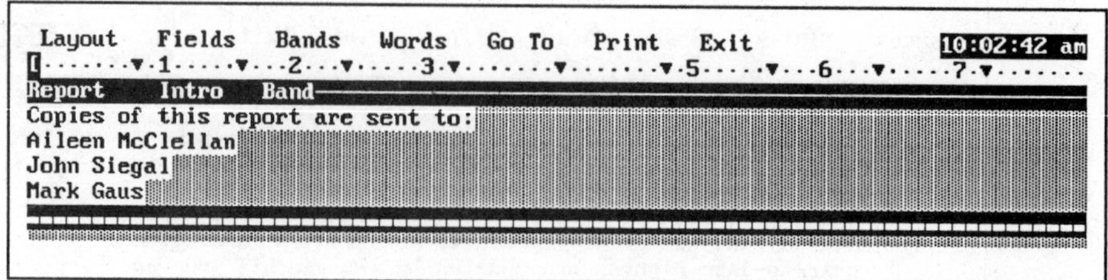

Figure 6-40 Report Intro Band with page break

Reading and Writing to a Text File Although using report bands for textual information is convenient, it is even more convenient if you have the text you want already entered. For example, if you traditionally use a word processor for your monthly report introduction letters, you would hesitate to use the Report Intro Band for them if you had to type the letter again. If you can store the word processor letter in a text file (one that does not contain special word processor symbols), you can import it into the report design. Most computer software packages can store its data in a text file. You can also copy information in a report design into a text file if you want to include it in another report or you want to import it into another software package.

To import data into a report design, move to where you want the data from the text file to appear. Then, press ALT-W for the Words menu, type a **W** for Write/Read text file, and type an **R** for Read Text from File. When dBASE prompts you for the name of the text file, type the name of the file and press ENTER. If the text file is not in the same drive or directory that you loaded dBASE, you must include the drive and directory specification. If your text file has a .TXT extension, you can press SHIFT-F1 and select the text file from the list. dBASE inserts a copy of the text file at the cursor's location.

To export data to a text file, use the F6 key to select the data that you want copied to a text file. Then, press ALT-W for the Words menu, type a **W** for Write/Read text file, and type a **W** for Write Selection to File. When dBASE prompts you for the name of the text file, type the name that you want dBASE to use to store the data and press ENTER. If you do not provide an extension, dBASE adds .TXT to the filename. If you want to use a different drive or directory, enter the drive and directory information with the filename.

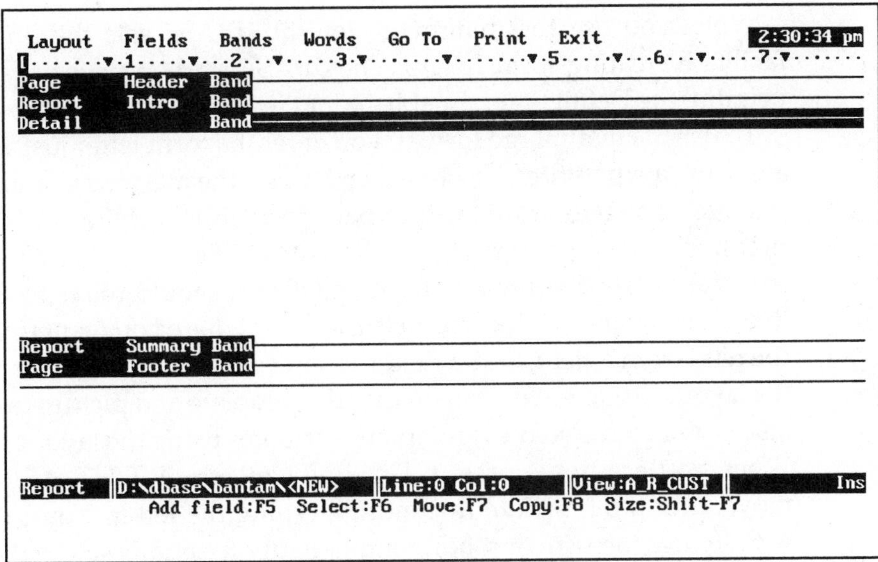

Figure 6-41 Report design using the quick mailmerge layout

The Go To Menu

The Go To menu in the report design screen is identical to the Go To menu for memos. You should be somewhat familiar with these features since you have used them for forms and memo fields on a number of occasions. You can use these features to locate specific lines in your report design or to search for specific Character strings in either a forward or backward direction.

Using the Mailmerge Layout To Create Form Letters

The mailmerge format available for the quick layout is frequently used for form letters. This option often uses different options for the different menus. When you select Quick layout and Mailmerge layout from the Layout menu, your screen looks like Figure 6-41. In this layout the design is empty, with the Detail Band in the word-wrap surface. If you open the other bands, they will use the layout surface. The mailmerge format is designed to be used like a word processor's mailmerge feature with the database data used as the variable information.

When you use the mailmerge format, dBASE sets the options to facilitate creating form letters. The dBASE starts a new page before printing the Detail Band. Enable indent is automatically set to on.

To use the mailmerge format, you enter the form letter just as if you are using a typewriter. The first step is to set the margins by modifying the ruler. You may want to add a paragraph indent character (#) so the first lines of the paragraphs are indented. Then, type the text of the letter, allowing dBASE to determine when it should move to the next line. When you reach a position in the letter where you want to include the data from a field, add a field the same way that you add a field in the layout surfaces. You can modify the template and picture functions just as you modified these template attributes using the layout surface. When you are done, press CTRL-END and the RIGHT ARROW to move after the template to continue typing the letter. You probably want to use the trim and horizontal picture functions so the data will not include unnecessary spaces and will use as much of the line as needed. You will need to modify the field definition to make these function selections. When you print the letter, dBASE substitutes the data in the fields in place of the templates. It also reformats the text to stay within the margins.

An example of a report created with the mailmerge format is the report design shown in Figure 6-42. This report contains the CUST_NAME, ADDRESS, CITY, STATE, ZIP, predefined DUE_DATE, INVOICE_NO, AMOUNT, and DAYS_PAST fields. This report is created by pressing ALT-W and typing an **M** to modify the ruler. The tab stops are changed to every five positions by typing an equal sign and a **5**, and pressing ENTER. The left margin remains at zero and the right margin is set to 6.4". The text is typed in as it appears. To add the first field, CUST_NAME, press F5, highlight CUST_NAME, and press ENTER. When the field definition box appears, press CTRL-END to return to the Report design screen. Press the RIGHT ARROW and ENTER to move past the field template and to the next line for the ADDRESS template.

All of the fields are entered this way. In the body of the letter, the letter mentions the number of days past due. To add this Calculated field, press F5, the RIGHT ARROW, and ENTER. When the Calculated field definition box appears, type an **N** for Name, type **DAYS_PAST**, and press ENTER. Type an **E** for Expression and **DATE()-DUE_DATE**, and press ENTER. This formula takes the value of the DATE function

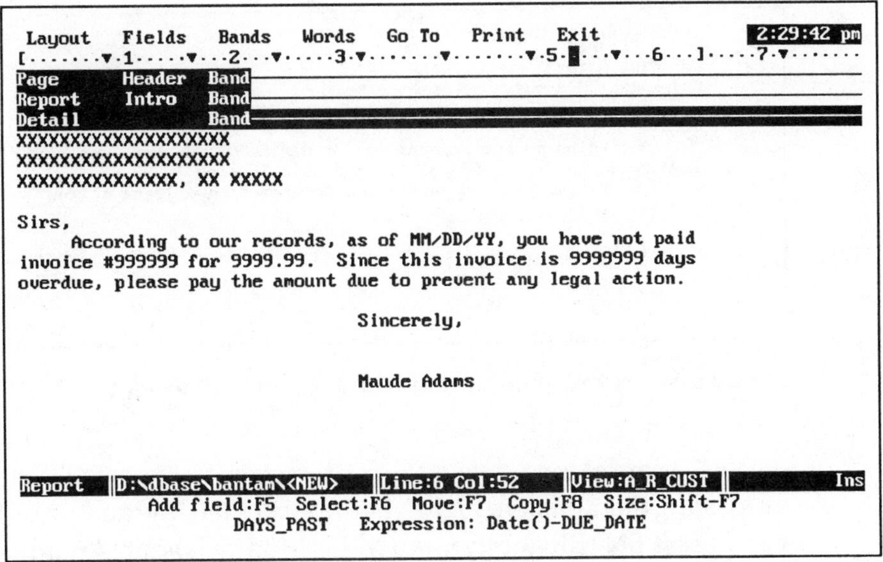

Figure 6-42 Sample mailmerge report design

(the current date) and subtracts the DUE_DATE value to compute the number of days between the two dates. Type a **T** for Template, press the BACKSPACE three times, and press ENTER to modify the template so the calculation does not display any digits after the decimal point. Press CTRL-END to return to the Report design screen. Press the RIGHT ARROW to move past the field template and continue with the letter. When you print the report, the first letter looks like Figure 6-43. In this letter, dBASE uses the database values for the templates. It adjusts how it wraps text to the next line to fit the margins.

Creating Labels

Labels are like reports since you create a design that each record uses. However, a label does not contain as many options since it is not intended to serve as many purposes as a report. You can use the label design feature to create mailing labels, package labels, and identification tags. Labels provide you with additional flexibility for sizes since dBASE adapts the Label design screen to fit one of several predefined sizes or one of your own definition. To create a label, highlight <create> in the Labels panel in the Control Center and press ENTER. To modify

```
Gem's Apparel
283 High Street
Columbus, OH 44034

Sirs,
     According to our records, as of 01/16/90, you have not paid
invoice #696967 for 8603.63.  Since this invoice is 33 days
overdue, please pay the amount due to prevent any legal action.

                                   Sincerely,


                                   Maude Adams
```

Figure 6-43 Form letter created with Figure 6-42's design

an existing label design, highlight the label filename and press SHIFT-F2 or press ENTER and type an **M** for Modify layout. An initial Label design screen is shown in Figure 6-44. The box in the middle of the screen contains the label layout. dBASE initially sets the label dimensions to 15/16" by 3 1/2" with one column of labels.

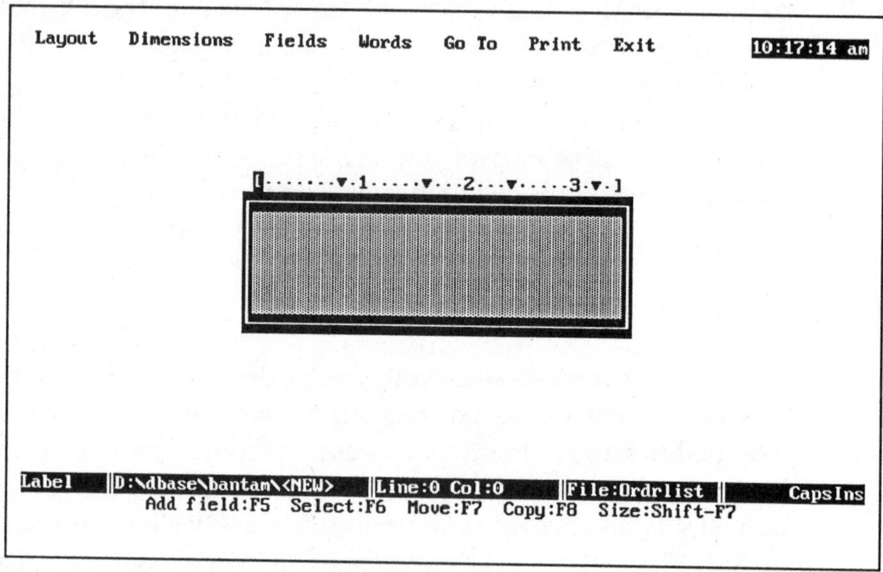

Figure 6-44 Initial label design screen

Labels Menus

Most of the label menus are identical to report menus. For most of the options you might want to use, you can use the information for the reports. Therefore, the following descriptions of the labels menus focus on the menu items that are different or not included in the report menus. Most of the additional menu options allow you to change the dimensions of the label and generate a single label before you print an entire database or view.

Differences between Menus for Reports and Labels Most of the difference between the menus for reports and the menus for labels are report features that are unavailable for labels. Since labels are not divided into bands, they do not have groups or a Bands menu. Labels also cannot have Summary fields or Hidden fields. Labels have the same options for database or View, Predefined, and Calculated fields. Labels cannot have boxes or lines. Labels also do not have a quick layout option, so you must add each field individually. Labels also do not use the word-wrap surface. If you want to join fields together, set the trim option for the fields to on and leave a space between the fields instead of pressing the RIGHT ARROW. You also cannot select Enable automatic indent, Add line, or Insert page break in labels. If you need to insert a line, press ENTER. When you insert a line, you remove the bottom line of the label and shift the remaining lines below the cursor's position down a line. dBASE lets you insert a line by pressing ENTER if the last line in the label design is empty.

Dimensions Label The dimensions label lets you describe your labels to dBASE. dBASE converts this information into a label layout box that represents the label's size. dBASE includes nine predefined sizes that are frequently used. You can also create a custom size if you are using labels that are a different size. To use a predefined label, press ALT-D to select the Dimensions menu and type a P for Predefined size. dBASE displays the list shown in Figure 6-45. All of the sizes measure labels in inches. Type the number of the size that you want or highlight your selection and press ENTER. dBASE changes the box in the Label design screen to match your selection. If you press ALT-D again, dBASE uses different numbers for the settings in the bottom half of the box. These

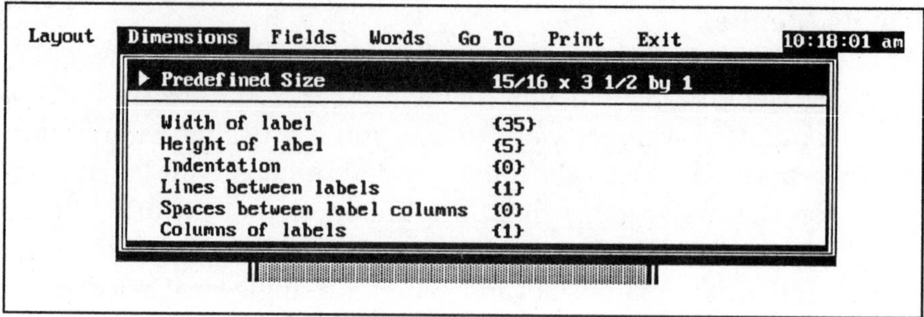

Figure 6-45 Dimensions menu

numbers are the settings for the predefined label size that you selected. Selecting a predefined label size selects the appropriate setting without having to determine the settings on your own.

If your labels do not fit one of the predefined sizes, you may need to define one. Before defining the label size, you need to measure the labels that you will use. The measurements that you need to use are shown in Figure 6-46. If you use a ruler to measure the labels, you must convert them to the number of characters and lines. dBASE assumes that it prints 10 characters to the inch and 6 lines to the inch. For example, if you measure .5" between label columns, the setting for spaces between labels is 5. If you measure .5" between labels, the setting for lines between labels is 3. If your printer prints using a different number of characters or lines per inch, you must use the printer's settings to convert the measurements to characters and lines. Once you know the number of characters or lines for the six measurements shown in Figure 6-46 (shown earlier), press ALT-D for the Dimensions menu. For each of the options in the bottom half of the box, type the first letter of the option, type the value for the option, and press ENTER. The maximum height or width is 255, the maximum indentation or spaces between labels is 190, the maximum lines between labels is 16, and the maximum column of labels is 9. When you are finished, press CTRL-END to return to the label design screen. dBASE changes the label box to match the new settings.

When you are changing the label dimensions to a different size, dBASE tries to fit the existing label design into the new label dimensions. If you are expanding the label design size, dBASE enlarges the label design box and leaves the current contents intact. The current contents have the same relative position with the upper left corner. If

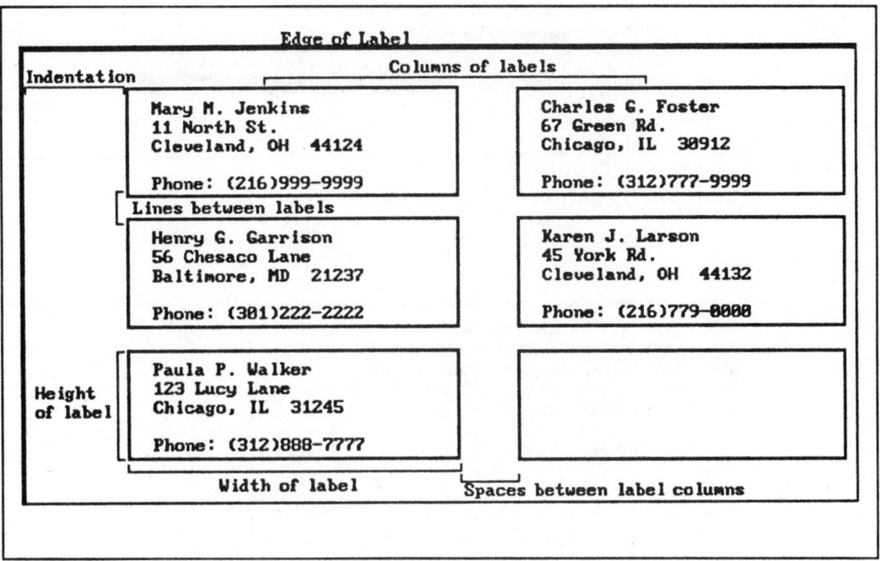

Figure 6-46 Measurements that labels use

your label has objects that are centered or right aligned, you need to realign them. If you are shrinking the label size, dBASE changes the label design box if all of the current objects can fit in the smaller size. If all of the current objects cannot fit, dBASE prompts if it can delete the objects that cannot fit in the smaller label dimensions. If you type a **Y**, dBASE deletes the objects that do not fit. If you type an **N**, dBASE aborts changing the label dimensions.

Generate Sample Label The Print menu for labels includes a Generate sample label option that does not appear in other Print menus. You can use this option to check that your labels are properly aligned in the printer before printing the labels for a database or view. When you select this option, dBASE prints a sample row of labels and then displays the prompt shown in Figure 6-47. From this prompt, you can type an **N** to print the labels for the database or view, type a **Y** to print another sample label, or press ESC to stop generating labels and leave the Print menu. When dBASE prints a sample label, it prints a box of X's the same size as the label design. If the label dimensions have several label columns, dBASE prints a row of boxes of X's. You can use these boxes to check the printer's alignment. You can also check that

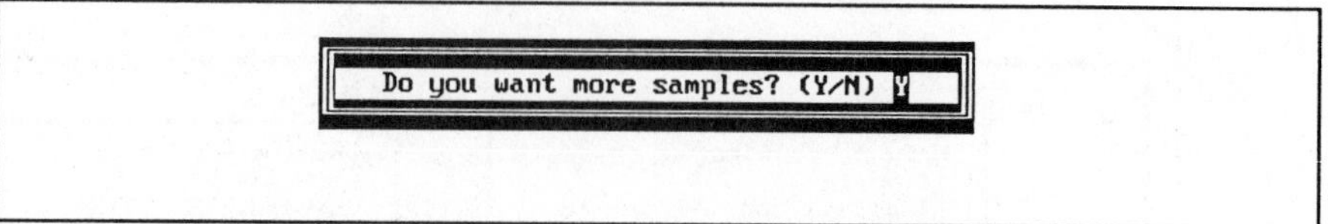

Figure 6-47 Prompt for generating another sample label

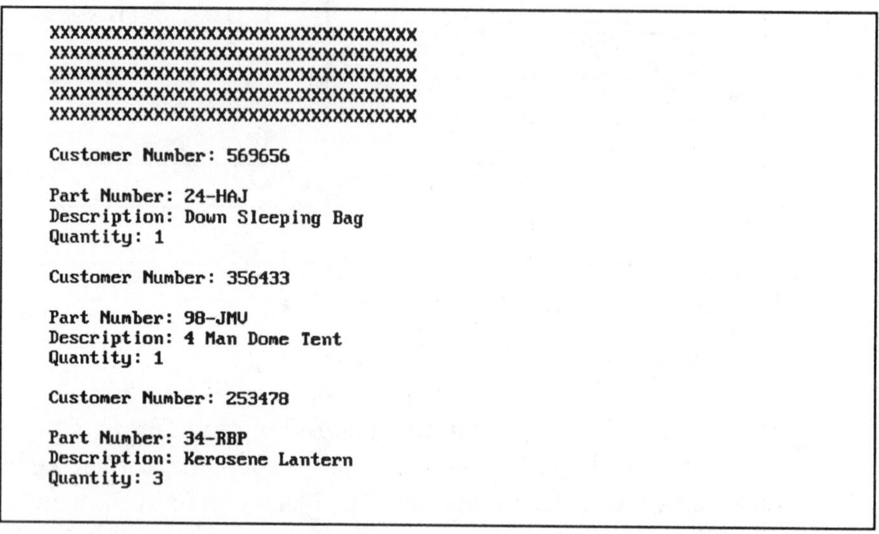

Figure 6-48 Sample generated label and beginning of creating labels

the label dimensions are correct. Figure 6-48 displays a sample label and the beginning of a report.

GETTING STARTED

➤ You will want to create a report using the EMPLOYEE database to learn how the report features work.

1. With the highlight on EMPLOYEE in the Data panel of the Control Center, press ENTER twice.
2. Use the RIGHT ARROW key to move to the Report panel, highlight <create>, and press ENTER.

3. Type a **Q** for a Quick layout from the Layout menu and type an **F** for Form layout.
4. Modify the ruler by pressing ALT-W and typing an **M**. Press the spacebar until the cursor is at the 8" position and type a right bracket (]).
5. Press the DOWN ARROW until the cursor is on the Report Intro Band. Press ENTER to open the band and type **Employee Master File** for the report title on the line below the band.
6. Center the report title by pressing F6, HOME, and ALT-W, and typing a **P** and a **C**.
7. Create a group band that groups the records into groups of three by pressing ALT-B and typing an **A**. When dBASE displays the box to enter how the records shall be grouped, type an **R** for record count and a **3**. Press ENTER.
8. Change the template of the social security number so the template automatically places the dashes in the correct location. Press the DOWN ARROW until the cursor is on the line with the SSN field. Press CTRL-RIGHT ARROW to move to the SSN template. Press F5 and type a **T** to modify the template. Press HOME to move to the beginning. Add the first dash by pressing the RIGHT ARROW three times and typing a dash (-). Add the second dash by pressing the RIGHT ARROW twice and typing a dash. Press CTRL-END twice to return to the Report design screen.
9. Change the name so that all three parts appear on the same line. Press the DOWN ARROW until the cursor is on the L in LAST_NAME. Press DEL five times to leave NAME. Press CTRL-RIGHT ARROW to move to the LAST_NAME template. Add the first name by pressing ALT-F, typing an **A**, highlighting FIRST_NAME and pressing ENTER. Press CTRL-END to return to the report design. Press the SPACEBAR to have a space between the two fields.
10. Add the middle name by pressing ALT-F, typing an **A**, highlighting M_INITIAL, and pressing ENTER. Press CTRL-END to return to the report design. Type a period and press the SPACEBAR to leave space between the middle initial and the last name.
11. Remove the original FIRST_NAME and M_INITIAL fields by pressing the DOWN ARROW and pressing CTRL-Y twice.

12. Use the financial format for the YTD_WAGES field by pressing the DOWN ARROW until the cursor is on the line with the YTD_WAGES. Press CTRL-RIGHT ARROW to move to the YTD_WAGES. Press F5 and type a **P** to change the picture functions. Type an **F** to change the financial format to on. Press CTRL-END twice to return to the Report design screen.
13. Add a Summary field to the Report Summary Band by pressing the DOWN ARROW until the cursor is on the line below the Report Summary Band. Press HOME to move to the beginning of the line. Type **TOTAL YEAR-TO-DATE WAGES:** and press the SPACEBAR. Add a Summary field by pressing F5 and the LEFT ARROW. Type an **S** to move to SUM and press ENTER. Type an **F** for Field to summarize on. Highlight YTD_WAGES and press ENTER. Press CTRL-END to return to the report design screen.
14. Print the report by pressing ALT-P. Check that dBASE is using the correct printer by typing a **D**. If the setting for Printer model is incorrect, type a **P** until dBASE displays the correct printer model. Press ESC to return to the Print menu and type a **B** to start printing.
15. Save this report by pressing ALT-E and typing an **S** for Save report and exit. Type **EMPLOY01** for a file name and press ENTER.

CHAPTER 7

Creating Forms

You have already learned how to display data records in both the Edit and Browse screens. The Browse screen always provides a tabular arrangement of fields. The Edit screen can be customized with dBASE IV's form features to enhance system flexibility and performance. Custom form features allow you to create professional screen designs that offer more than a quick way to enter and view your data. You can ensure the accuracy of the data that enters database fields with appropriate edit checks that are part of the screen design. You can offer users multiple choice selections or additional descriptive information to expedite data entry and make the system easy for even inexperienced users to work with. The ability to create multiple forms for one database allows you to use a form for data entry that matches the input document and display the data in a different format for reviewing the record entries. The arrangement of fields on the screen, the addition of color as well as lines and boxes significantly enhance dBASE IV's form features over earlier releases of the product.

In this chapter you will learn to add the five design elements for forms: database or view fields, calculated fields, text, boxes, and lines. You will also learn about each of the customization options available for the design.

Accessing the Form Design Screen

When you first create a new database or view, dBASE uses its default settings to establish the layout of the database fields on the Edit screen. The fields are always shown in the order in which they appear in the database down the left side of the screen. When the first screen is filled, dBASE IV uses the next screen to continue the field list. You can continue to use this default layout as long as you wish, but you also have the option of creating a form to customize the appearance and behavior of the Edit screen.

Once you use a form with a database, dBASE uses the form every time you activate the Edit screen. Forms are created and accessed from the Forms panel of the Control Center. To activate an existing form, highlight its name in the Forms panel and press ENTER. dBASE displays a menu as long as INSTRUCT is ON and allows you to select from Display data or Modify layout. Opening a form file with a database or View query other than the one the form was created for causes dBASE to display a menu that allows you to choose between using the current view or the one that is usually associated with the form.

To create a new form, you can highlight <create> in the Form panel and press ENTER. If a database is open, the Layout menu is displayed on the screen and Quick layout option is highlighted, and the fields in this database are available to place on the form. If no database is open, the menu is displayed on the screen and Use a different database file or view is highlighted. If you press ENTER, type the name of the database or view, and press ENTER again, dBASE makes this data available for layout on the screen.

❑

Tip: There is one difference between Edit screen and Quick layout screen for long character fields.

dBASE IV uses multiple lines on the Edit screen for long Character fields. When you use Quick layout dBASE uses only one line but sets the Edit option to scroll within the display width.

❏ **Tip: Switching between form design and data display.**

If you need to switch between making changes to an existing form and viewing the data with the changed form, open the form by moving to the form name in the Form panel and pressing SHIFT-F2. This allows you to press F2 to view the data and SHIFT-F2 to return to forms design at any time. If you enter in any other way, pressing SHIFT-F2 takes you to the Query design screen.

Using the Quick Layout Option

The Quick layout option on the Layout menu allows you to create a screen that matches the default screen layout of one field per row down the screen. Like the default layout, it skips row 0 and places data in rows 1 through 21. This allows space for the menu bar, messages, and a status line. The full screen width is accessible beginning with column 0 and extending through column 79.

Unlike the default screen format, you can modify the Quick layout. Each field name beginning with the first field in the database is placed on the form as shown in Figure 7-1. A template pattern composed of letters marks where the data is placed. Each character in the template has a special meaning that affects input and output of field entries. Table 7-1 provides a list of the default template characters for each field type. You can move fields to new locations or change the attributes of any of the fields on the screen. If you do not need a field on your form, use the Fields menu command Remove field to delete it.

Rearranging the Quick Layout Form

You can use the same techniques that you mastered in Chapter 6 for reports and labels to restructure the layout of the fields on the form. You can move both text and the templates for the fields. If you prefer, you can add new text and move just the templates. If you use the latter approach you must remove the old labels that remain in the original screen location.

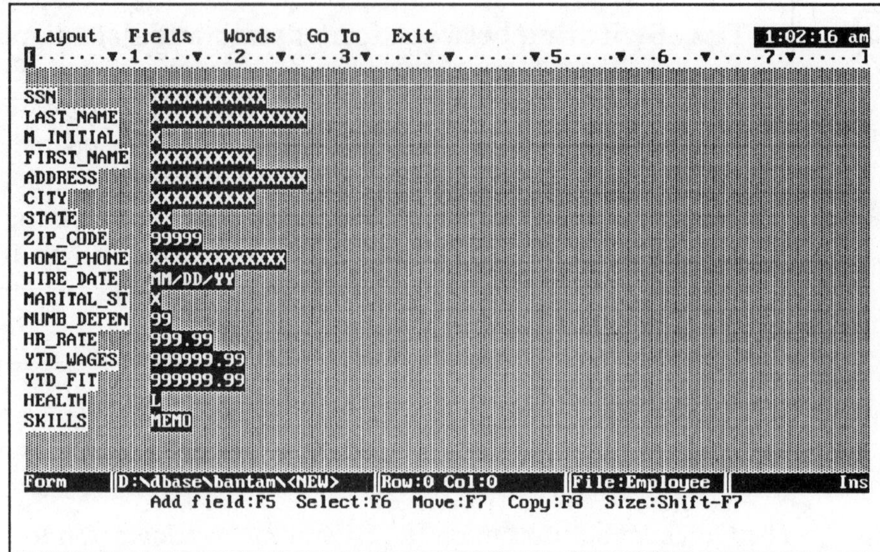

Figure 7-1 Quick layout of EMPLOYEE database

One simple change that makes the form more readable is adding blank lines between fields. Move the cursor to the first letter in the first field name and press ENTER, after verifying that Ins appears in the status line. Continue to move to the beginning of new rows and press ENTER to move the fields down a line. Figure 7-2 shows the effect of this change on the form for the ORDERS file.

Table 7-1 Default Characters Used in Templates

Character	*Field Type*
X	Character fields
9	Numeric and Float fields
L	Logical field
MM/DD/YY	Date field
MEMO Marker	Memo field

> **Tip: Quick layout is best when you need most of the fields.**
>
> The time savings realized by not having to type fields names and templates makes it easier to create a form with Quick layout if you need most of the fields. Use the ALT-F command to remove the fields you no longer need.

Moving and Adding Individual Fields and Text

Whether you start with a Quick layout and need to add back individual fields that you removed or decide to create your own layout, you can position the cursor and add a field to the Form design screen. You can remove fields when you do not want them to appear. You can add text to provide additional descriptive information. You can also rearrange the fields on a form to follow a source document or a preferred way of viewing information rather than the order of the fields in the database.

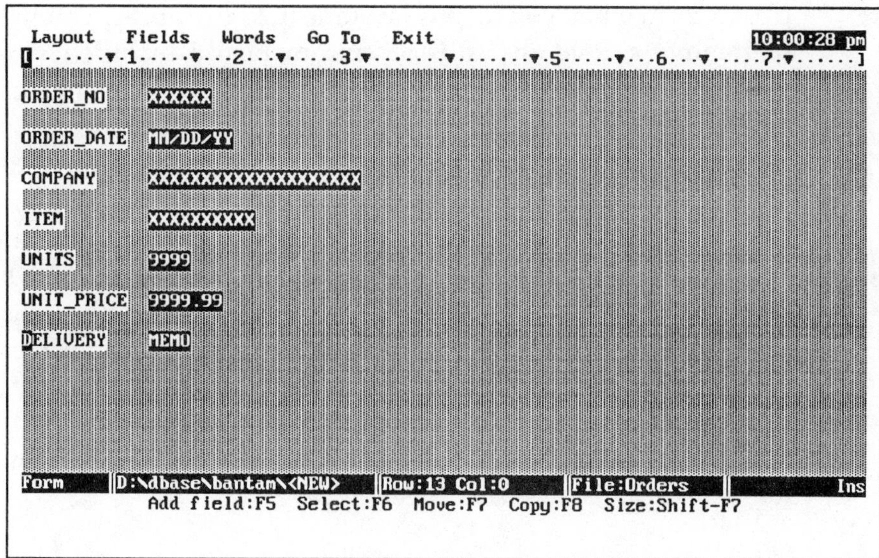

Figure 7-2 Form design after insertion of blank lines

Later in the chapter you will learn that you can even create multipage forms and display some of the fields on screens.

Adding Fields Templates Fields templates can be added at any location on the screen. You can add a field template to a form to include a field that does not appear. To add a field template from a database or view, move the cursor to where you want the field to appear. Using the form for the ORDERS database, move to row 1 column 30. Then use the Fields menu and select Add field. You can also press F5 (Field) provided the cursor is not on another field template when you press F5. dBASE displays a field selection box. This field selection box is identical to the field selection box you used for reports except the summary field column is missing. Select a field by highlighting it and pressing ENTER. Then the field description box appears. You can use the options in this box to change how the field's values appear. When you are finished with this box, press CTRL-END. dBASE removes the field description box and places a field template for the field that you selected at the cursor's location. dBASE did not add the field name as it did when you selected Quick layout from the Layout menu.

Removing Fields Templates Field templates can also be removed from a form when you do not want the field to appear. You may want to remove a field that dBASE automatically included when you selected Quick layout from the Layout menu. To remove a field template from a form, move the cursor to the template you want to remove. Using the form for the ORDERS database, move to row 1 column 30. To remove a field, activate the Fields menu and select Remove field. You can also press the DEL key to remove the highlighted field template. If the cursor is not on a field template when you select Remove field from the Fields menu, dBASE displays a list of the fields in alphabetical order. Highlight the field that you want deleted and press ENTER. dBASE removes the selected field template from the Report design screen. Removing the field template does not remove the field name or text that accompanies the template. To remove the text, use the DEL and BACKSPACE keys.

Adding Text Text can also be added at any location on the screen. You can use text entries to title the screen, to provide specific instructions to the operator who uses the screen, or to use different descriptors with

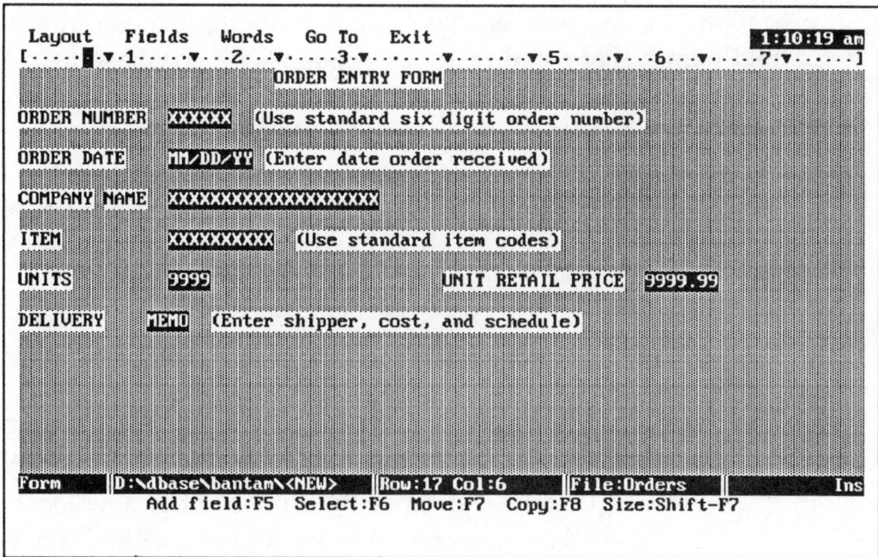

Figure 7-3 Form design with text added

the field templates in place of the field names. Figure 7-3 provides an example of text used for all three functions. The title ORDER ENTRY FORM is created with a text entry. The entries ORDER NUMBER, ORDER DATE, COMPANY NAME, and UNIT RETAIL PRICE are text entries replacing the actual field names that were shown on the screen. Also, entries such as (Use standard six-digit order number) are text entries to specify what must be placed in the fields. You can also use the Edit option Message from the Modify field option in the Fields menu for these entries. This latter approach is preferable since the message only appears when the cursor is on the field, eliminating the cluttered effect that results from all the messages on the screen at once.

Before adding text or field to the screen, check to see if the Insert mode is on. If it is on, Ins appears in the status line. If Ins is off, press the Ins key to toggle it back on. The text ORDER ENTRY SCREEN can be added to the top of the ORDERS form by moving to row 1 column 30 and typing the text.

You can type text to replace the field names on the screen. This removes the 10-character limitation and allows you to provide a clearer description for users of the form. The ORDER_NO field can be changed to eliminate the abbreviation and the underscore. You can eliminate the underscores in the other two names as well. dBASE still knows where to place the database entries since it is the templates rather than the field names that are directly associated with database fields. Before making any additions, you will want to move existing entries so that your entries do not overlay existing fields.

Moving Screen Entries Moving entries is a multistep process. The order of the steps is crucial to achieving the desired results. You will want to follow these steps:

1. Move the cursor to the first character that will be moved.
2. Press F6 (Select) to begin the selection process.
3. Move the cursor to the last position to be moved and press ENTER. The area being moved is highlighted.
4. Press F7 (Move) and move the cursor to the new location. The highlighted box moves to the new location without the information that was originally highlighted. To copy the selected area, press F8 (Copy) instead.
5. Press ENTER to finalize the move. Note that the highlighting remains and the entries are moved.
6. Press ESC to remove the highlighting.

You can apply this procedure to the form for the ORDERS file. Before the entry for ORDER_NO can be lengthened, the template for the fields must be moved to the right. To maintain the alignment of all the field templates, they can all be moved to column 20. To effect the change, the cursor is moved to row 1 column 12 and F6 is pressed. The arrow keys are used to move down to row 13 and right to column 31. ENTER is pressed to finalize the selection and the cursor is moved to row 1 column 20. After pressing F7 (Move) the highlighted box moves to look like Figure 7-4. When ENTER is pressed, the screen changes to match Figure 7-5. After pressing ESC, the highlight area disappears from around the relocated entries. Once the field templates are moved, you can modify the form text. The completed entries match Figure 7-6.

Rearranging Field Descriptions and Templates You are not limited to moving templates. Field names or descriptions can be moved just as easily. You may want to transform the form for ORDERS to match the form in Figure 7-7. The procedure used is the same as moving the

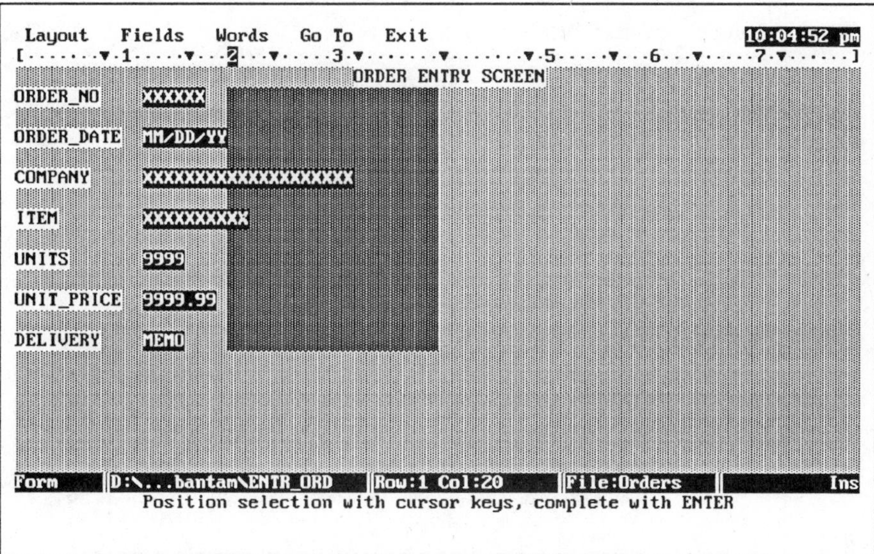

Figure 7-4 Highlighted box indicates where selected templates will be moved

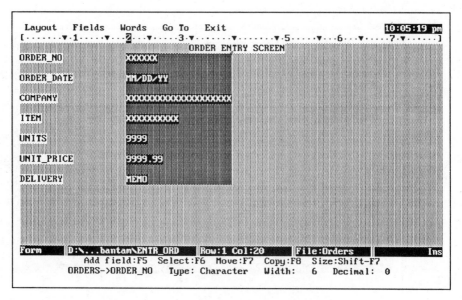

Figure 7-5 Form design after moving field templates

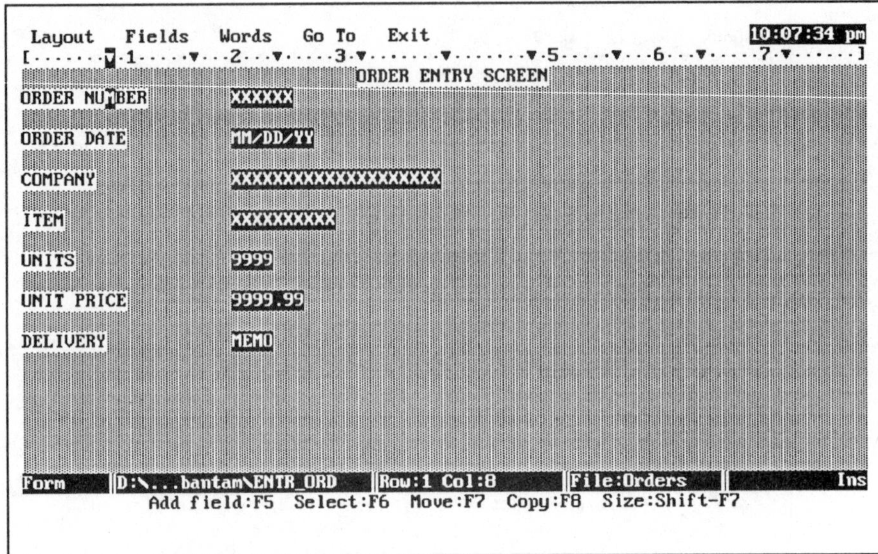

Figure 7-6 Form design with text added after moving field templates

templates. To move the ORDER DATE entry and the associated field to the same row as ORDER NUMBER, the cursor is placed at O in

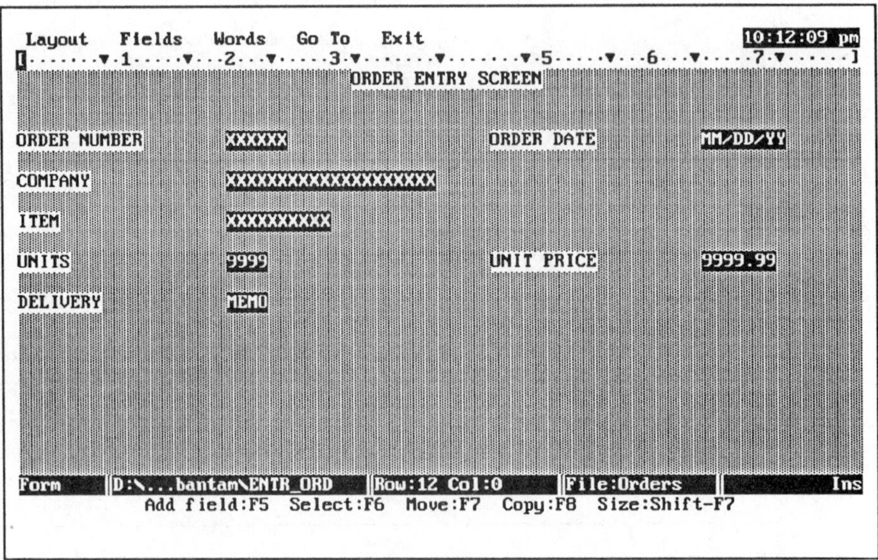

Figure 7-7 Form design after moving text and templates

ORDER. F6 (Select) is pressed and the END key is pressed to move to the end of the entry. Since it moves one position beyond the Y, you can use the LEFT ARROW once to change it. ENTER is pressed to finalize the selection. Next F7 (Move) is pressed. You must move the cursor to the position where you want the field to begin. For the ORDER_DATE this would be row 3 column 45. The ENTER key is pressed to finalize the location and the ESC key is pressed to remove the highlighting.

Adding and Removing Lines with Menu Commands

You have already seen how you can use ENTER to add a new row to a form. You can accomplish this same task by pressing ALT-W and typing an **A** to select Add a line. The line is inserted below the cursor when the command is requested.

You either use the menu or CTRL-Y to remove a line. To remove a line with the menu command, press ALT-W and type an **R** to select Remove a line.

After moving the entries in Figure 7-7, another line was added at the top of the form beneath ORDER ENTRY SCREEN and several lines that were no longer needed were removed.

Using the Go To Menu to Position and Replace

The Go To menu for forms is shown in Figure 7-8. It is identical to the Go To menus in Report and Label design screens. You can use these selections to position the cursor on a specific line on the screen. You

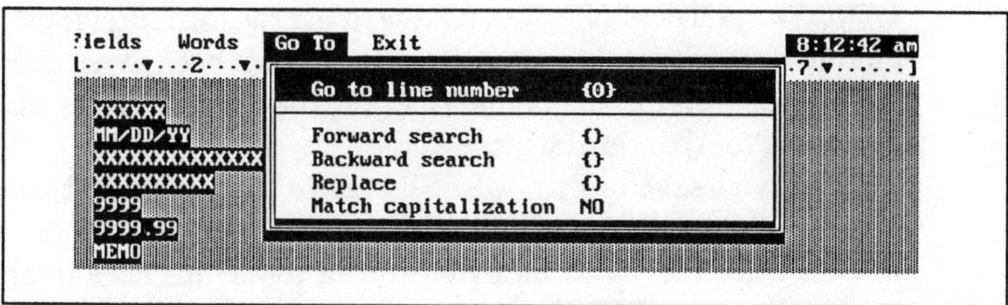

Figure 7-8 Go To menu

can also use it to do a forward or backward search for a specific entry. As in the Report and Label design screens, you can also use it to replace a word or phrase throughout a form design. You will find additional information about the Go To menu options in Chapter 5.

Saving and Using a Custom Form

Once you create a new form you can save it to disk. You can add a description for the form that is saved with the current catalog. You should exercise this option for each of your forms since the descriptions display on the Control Center screen when you highlight the form name. These descriptions can help you decide which form you want to use. You can enter a description by pressing ALT-L and typing an **E** for Edit description of form. You can type a description up to a maximum of 80 characters and press ENTER.

To save the form, you can also use the Layout menu option if you need to make additional changes. To do this, you press ALT-L and type an **S** to select Save this form. dBASE prompts you for a filename, displaying the current filename, if any. Type a name of up to eight characters and press ENTER. dBASE creates a file with this name after adding the filename extension .SCR. Once a form is saved to disk, dBASE automatically uses the same name each time you save it if you press ENTER when it prompts with the original name. CTRL-ENTER provides another way to save the form without leaving the design itself. Pressing CTRL-ENTER only prompts for the filename if you have not saved the design before.

You can also save a form and exit from Form design. To do this press ALT-E and type an **S** for Save changes and exit. You can also press CTRL-W or CTRL-END. If you have saved the form previously, it will automatically reuse this name. If the file has not been saved previously, dBASE prompts for a filename. To exit without saving press ALT-E and type an **A** to Abandon changes and exit.

When you save a form, dBASE creates three different files. Your original design entries are saved in a file with an extension of .SCR. dBASE code files with an extension of .FMT are also created. The compiled version of these files are the .FMO files.

❑

Tip: Be careful which form files you provide.
You can provide users who do not need to modify screens the .FMO files. If you provide .SCR files they must edit the screen design and save this design before the other required files are generated.

Customizing Field Displays and Entries

dBASE IV provides a number of options for customizing both the entry and display of database fields. You can change the picture templates that are automatically created when you add a field to the Form design screen. You can also use picture functions that operate on an entire field at once. Edit options offer another way to alter field characteristics and values.

Picture Templates

A picture template is like a pattern that represents a field on the Form design screen. Each character in the template represents one position in the field. By changing the characters in the template you can change the type of data that a field accepts and the way that the field displays on the screen. All field types with the exception of Date and Memo fields allow you to customize the field template. Although form templates are similar in concept to report and label templates, templates are more important for forms since they can restrict data entry as well as display the data.

Changing a Picture Template To change a picture template the first step is to place the cursor on the template. You can either press ALT-F to activate the Field menu and type an **M** for Modify field or press F5 (Field). If you press ALT-F and type an **M** when the cursor is not on a field, dBASE displays a list from which you can select the field you want to modify. dBASE displays the field description menu box. The upper portion of the box is fixed and displays information specific to the database definition of the field.

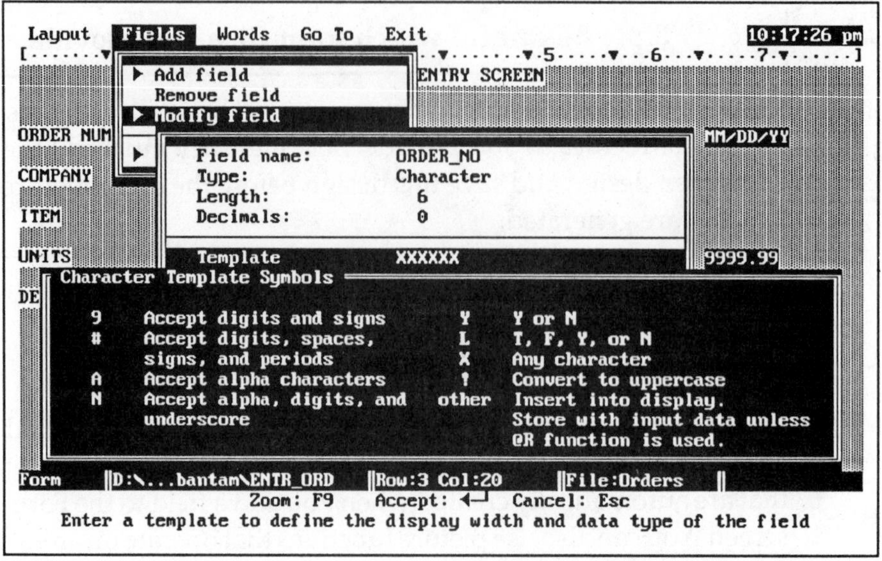

Figure 7-9 Field description menu box while entering a template

The first entry in the lower portion of the box is Template. If you highlight this and press ENTER, dBASE displays a box similar to the one in Figure 7-9 for a Character field. The entries depend on the field type that you are working with. You can use these template characters to type a new template. After creating a template that you want, press ENTER.

Although you cannot change the template for a Date type field in the Forms design screen, you can change it by changing the Date order setting. From the Control Center, press ALT-T to select Tools then type an S to select Settings. Change the Date order setting for the type of date display that you want. This change affects the date displayed in new forms. To change an existing form, delete the date and add it back.

Template Characters for Various Field Types Regardless of which template character you use, you are ultimately limited by the field type. You can choose template characters that add additional restrictions to the field type but there is no way to eliminate any of the restrictions implied by the field type. For example, using a template character that permits alphabetic characters for a Numeric field does not allow you to enter alphabetic characters in this field. Table 7-2 shows the charac-

Table 7-2 Characters Used In Picture Templates

Character	*Effect*
!	Converts entry to upper case.
#	Restricts input to numeric digits, blanks, and signs.
9	Restricts input to numeric digits and signs.
A	Restricts entries to A through Z.
L	Restricts entry to Y, N, T, or F in either upper or lower case.
N	Restricts entry to letters and digits.
X	Any character.
Y	Restricts entry to Y or N.

ters that are acceptable in picture templates for Character fields. You can also use a period, comma, or other symbols in a template.

Character fields You can use templates to restrict the entries placed in Character fields or to convert the data they contain to upper case. Character fields accept each of the characters shown in Table 7-2 even though some of the options are more restrictive than what is allowed for a Character field.

You may choose to use a Character field for an entry such as zip code, which contains numeric digits in order not to have dBASE remove leading zeros. To prevent the entry of other characters into this field you can provide a picture template of 99999. This allows the same entries as a field that was originally defined as numeric but does not truncate the leading zeros. The character 9 is also used for fields like social security number or phone number.

Using the Character field type allows you to supply the special characters such as - and (but limits the other entries. You can use a picture template of 999-99-9999 for social security number and (999)999-9999 for the phone number. When the user types the entry for the field the special Edit characters are automatically supplied. All the user types are the digits. Also there is no possibility of an alphabetic character being entered, as would be the case with the default picture template of X's.

For some fields like names and states you may only want to accept characters. To restrict the entry to alphabetic characters enter A's for the template. Other fields may require a combination of numeric and alphabetic characters. To restrict entries to appropriate characters for a seven-position field that always looks like the sample part number PW-8765, use the picture template AA-9999. The user types the first two letters followed by the four digits. dBASE supplies the dash.

Numeric Fields The default template for Numeric and Float fields is 9's. The number of 9's in Numeric and Float fields is exactly the same as the field length if there are no decimal positions. Since the decimal point requires a position, this will make the number of 9's one less than the field length when the numbers contain decimal digits. The addition of commas also requires space and must be considered when selecting a field template width in the form.

You can change the template for Numeric or Float fields to display leading zeros as either an asterisk or a dollar sign. A template of $$$$.99 displays .59 as $$$$.59 and 13.20 as $$$13.20. If the asterisk is in this position it changes the leading character to *.

Another popular change for numeric field types is to add a comma in the thousands position. 99,999.99 displays the comma on the screen if the number is 1,000 or larger. The comma requires one position of the display field width.

Logical Fields The default template for a logical field is an L. With this setting, dBASE will accept T, t, F, f, Y, y, N, or n. You can restrict the entries for a logical field to Y, y, N or n by changing the template character to a Y. If you enter a T, t, F, or f, the character is converted to a Y or N.

Picture Functions

Unlike the picture template feature, which required one template character for each position in the field length, the picture function

❑

Tip: Watch out for problems with floating currency symbols.

If you are using a multicharacter currency indicator, the floating indicator may cause problems by repeating the first character as a floating symbol.

affects the entire field entry. Each picture function entry may consist of multiple symbols indicating that several functions were selected for a field, although each one applies to the entire field. As an example you can use a picture template to convert each of the characters in a six-character field to upper case by entering a template of !!!!!!. You can accomplish the same effect with a picture function of ! since one exclamation point affects the entire entry. Where the same options exist for both features you will find that the picture template offers additional flexibility, since you can define the options for each individual character. On the other hand, if you want the same feature for the entire entry, the picture function requires a much shorter entry to handle the task.

Changing the Picture Function To alter the picture function for a field, highlight the field template and press the F5 key. The curly braces next to the picture function option display the currently assigned functions. To change any of these you will need to highlight the Picture function in the field description menu box and press ENTER. The options available for the current field type will display like the options for a Character field type shown in Figure 7-10. Each of the options function on a toggle switch basis allowing you to highlight the option and press the SPACEBAR to change the current selection. By looking at the menu you can tell if the setting is ON or OFF. Since an ON setting causes dBASE IV to place the associated character in the picture function, you can look at this function to tell which features are ON. To return to the field description menu box, press CTRL-END.

Alphabetic Characters Only Toggling this option ON prevents the entry of any characters other than A through Z. Punctuation, blank spaces, and numeric digits are all rejected from a field that has this setting ON.

❑

Tip: Use picture functions to save time.

You can alter all the characters in a field with a one-character entry in a picture function. A template requires one character for each position in the field width.

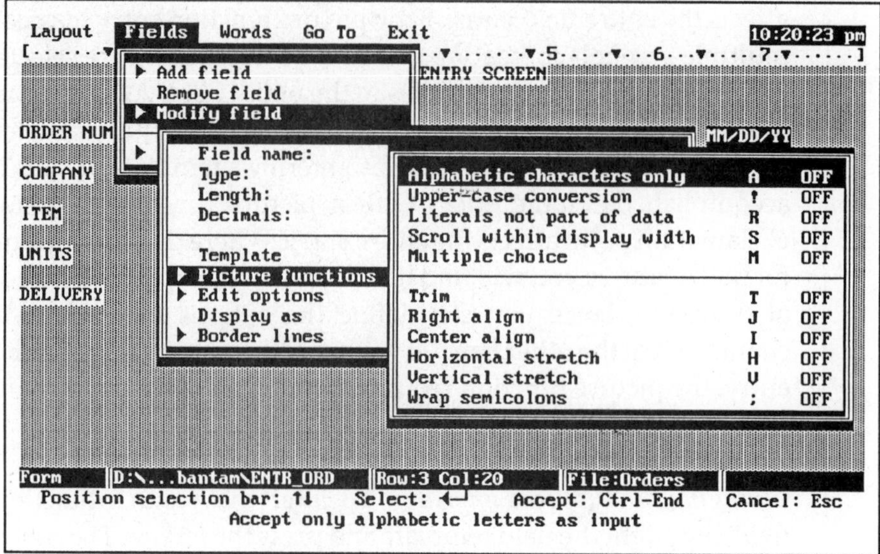

Figure 7-10 Picture functions for Character field type

Uppercase Conversion You can convert the alphabetic characters in an entry to upper case by toggling the uppercase conversion setting ON. Nonalphabetic characters are unaffected by the conversion. This means that an entry of 123 Smith ave. becomes 123 SMITH AVE., but an entry of 546 remains as 546. Use this type of conversion if you want to store name and address information in upper case or to convert the letters in alphanumeric part codes to upper case.

Literals Not Part of Data This setting allows you to determine whether the special editing characters that are typed on a form are stored in the database. Creating a form with a template of 999-99-9999 for the social security number field stores nine digits if the setting for Literals not part of data is set ON. With a setting of OFF, the entire entry is stored.

With a large database the saved characters can make a noticeable reduction in the storage requirements for a database field. If record 1 has a social security number of 555-77-8888, the database contains either 555778888 or 555-77-8888. The two character saving for not storing the hyphens in the file can be multiplied by the number of records in the file. As long as the hyphens remain in the form they

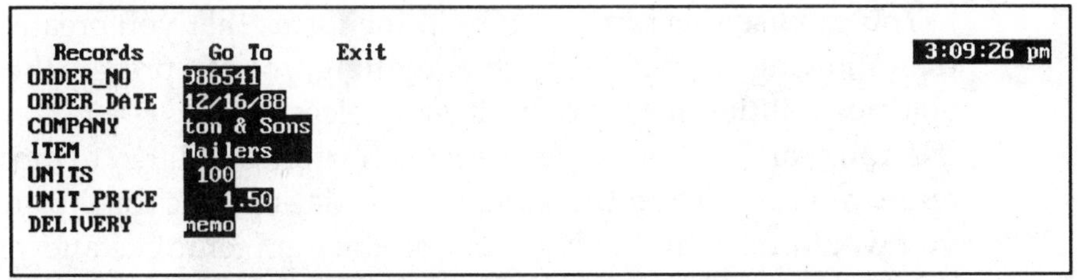
Records Go To Exit 3:09:26 pm
ORDER_NO 986541
ORDER_DATE 12/16/88
COMPANY ton & Sons
ITEM Mailers
UNITS 100
UNIT_PRICE 1.50
DELIVERY memo

Figure 7-11 COMPANY field scrolled to show second half of entry

display when you review the data, as the template definition adds them to the display each time.

Scroll within Display Width The Scroll within display width option allows you to create picture templates that are narrower than the actual field width. You can set this option to ON and by using the arrow keys to scroll the data that displays within the template area on the screen.

This feature is particularly useful for descriptive information that is longer than the template area you are setting. A Character field defined at the maximum width of 254 characters can never fit within the maximum screen width of 80. dBASE IV automatically uses this feature and provides the remaining space on the line with the field name for your entry.

You can use a narrower width with smaller fields. A field containing special handling instructions may have a width of 25 yet your screen design may only accommodate 15 characters easily. If most entries for this field are less than 15 characters, the Scroll within display width option may provide a very workable solution. First, highlight the field template then press F5 (Fields). Type a **P** for picture function then type an **S** for scroll within display width. Type the width that you want to use and press ENTER. Figure 7-11 shows the second portion of the field entry in the display width for the 20-character COMPANY field that has had its scroll width narrowed to 10.

Multiple Choice You have selected many options from dBASE menus by cycling through the possible selections with the SPACEBAR. The options you are presented were multiple choice options for the particular entry. This method saves typing time and limits your entries to a fixed set of options.

You can use this same feature in the forms that you create. Rather than allowing an operator to type anything, you can present the acceptable possibilities in a list of multiple choices.

As an example, you might want to limit items ordered to those on an approved list. To add these multiple choice options for the order file, you would position the highlight on the item template and press F5. After selecting Picture function, you would move to the Multiple choice option and press ENTER. Next, the options for the field are typed and separated by commas. Typing **Chair, Computer, Credenza, Desk, File cabinet, Table** limits acceptable entries to this list. Note that quotation marks are not used with the list entries. When you press ENTER followed by CTRL-END, the multiple choice list is finalized. When you use the form, the first multiple choice is always visible, as shown in Figure 7-12. Any of the other options are accessed with the SPACEBAR or by typing the first letter. Entries outside this acceptable list are rejected.

Edit Options

The dBASE IV edit options provide additional ways that you can customize a form. Like picture templates and functions, these features are selected for a specific field. Also like the other field modifications, more than one change can be chosen for a field.

To change an Edit option for a field, highlight the field template and press F5 or press ALT-F and type an **M**. Highlight Edit options and press ENTER. Most of the selections on this Edit options menu require more than the ON/OFF toggle used with picture templates and functions.

❑ **Tip: Consider the order of multiple choice entries carefully.**

When entering multiple choice entries for fields, one of two options probably meet your needs for organizing the entries. If one or two of the choices are used more than the others, place them at the beginning of the list. If all choices are used equally, alphabetize them to make it easy to locate each selection.

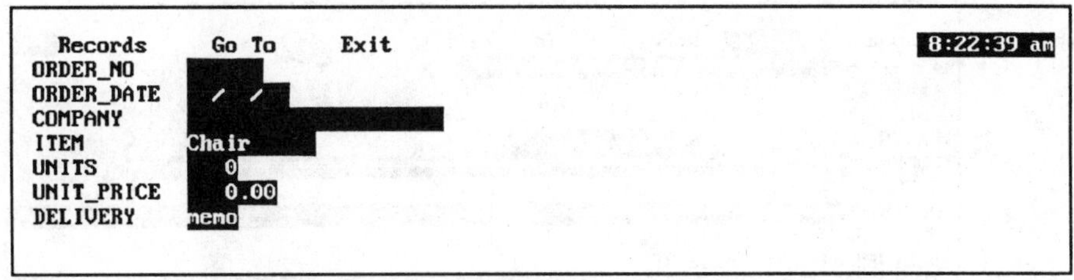

Figure 7-12 ITEM field displaying first multiple choice selection

Editing Allowed Up to now any field that appeared on a screen could be changed. This is due to the default setting for Editing allowed is Yes. If you highlight this option and press the SPACEBAR, dBASE prevents editing for this field, effectively making it read-only. Since dBASE does not update values until you move to the next record, you could place a second copy of a field on the current screen to allow you to see the before and after values for a field. Once the screen is saved, both copies of the field display the same entry.

Permit Edit If This option allows you to establish a condition to determine whether or not this field can be edited. The condition is established with an expression just like the ones you use in Condition boxes in Chapter 5.

If you are making the records in the order file available to the companies that order from you, you can tailor each company's version of the order entry form to allow them to edit orders for their company but not the orders of other companies. If you are designing a screen for BBB Bakery, you could enter this expression in the Permit edit if option: **COMPANY="BBB Bakery"**. If the company matches this entry, the field can be edited.

❑ **Tip: Permit edit if it is not a substitute for system security.**

If the expression you use to determine whether a field is Read-only is another field in the record, the user can change this field until it meets the qualifications for editing the second field.

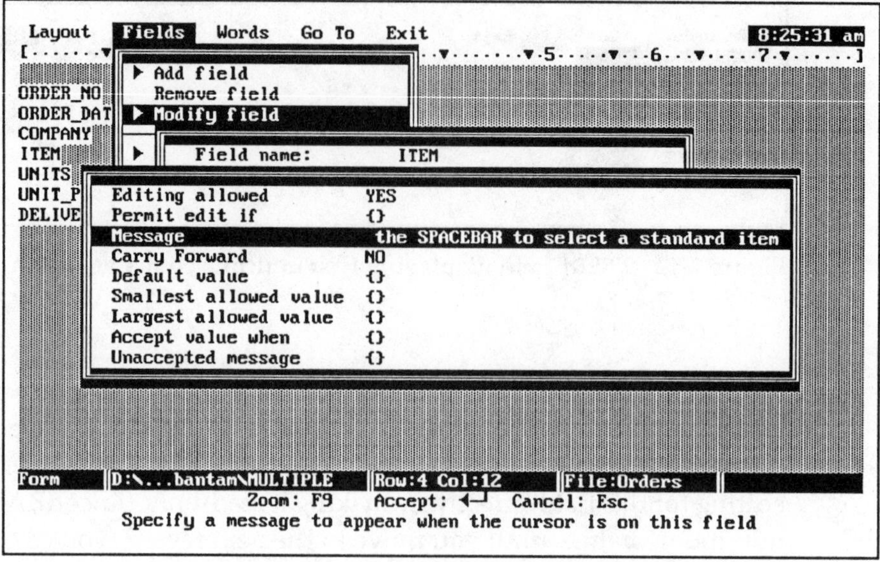

Figure 7-13 Edit options

Fields that are dependent on other fields in the form should always be located below or to the right of the field they depend on. You want the entries placed in the independent field before you allow it to affect whether or not you can edit a second field.

Message dBASE allows you to supply a prompt to the user for each field on a form. The entry that you make in the message option displays when the cursor is on the field.

The message that you enter can define the format or contents of a field entry. If you have a field for name, your message might be "Enter last name followed by a comma and the first name." If you are entering a part number, you might want to provide a sample, e.g., "Enter part number as in KU-5643." You can use as many as 79 characters, but avoid quotation marks in your entry. Figure 7-13 shows the end of the message entry for the ITEM field. Figure 7-14 shows the bottom of the screen with the first multiple choice option for this field.

Carry Forward When you add records, dBASE begins each new record without entries in any of the fields. You can set CARRY to ON and have every new record begin with all of the field entries from the previous record. This all or nothing approach may not be the solution

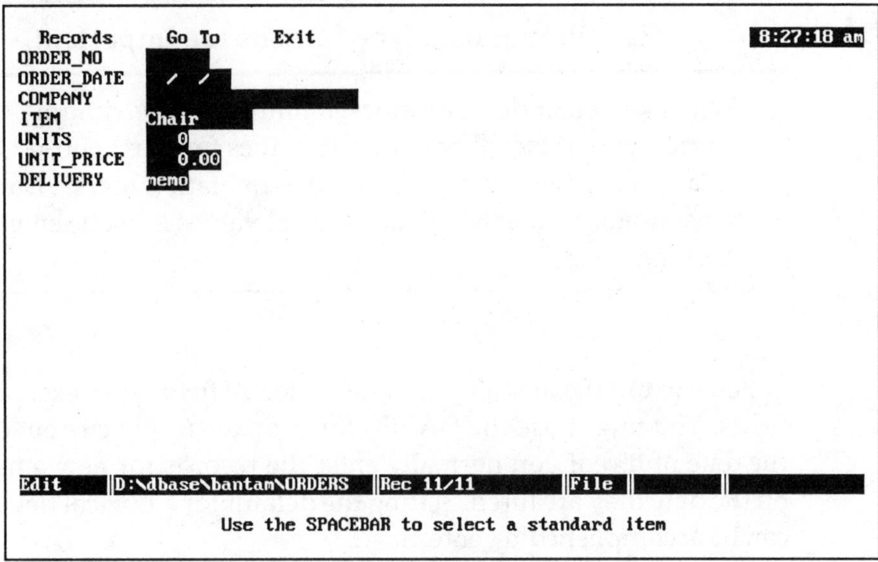

Figure 7-14 Message line displaying when ITEM field is highlighted

you need. If you have a field or two that is the same, having all the fields carry forward can be confusing.

dBASE IV allows you to use the Carry Forward option at the field level through the Edit option Carry forward. If you highlight this option in the Edit options menu, it toggles the setting for the field.

If you organize your data entry, this option can save a significant number of keystrokes. If you have ten records to enter for one company and they are grouped together, with the Carry forward option set to On for the COMPANY field, you can enter the company in the first record and not need to change it until you begin entering records for the second company. Once you replace the company field entry, this new value carries forward to subsequent records until you make another change.

Default Value The default value setting allows you to establish a default value for a field. This entry always appears in the field for a new record. If you have a location in the employee file and most of the records entered are for the location Chicago, you can establish Chicago as the default for this field by entering **"Chicago"** in the Default value entry. For records where you wish to override the default, type the replacement value for the field.

Tip: Proper data type formats are important.

When you enter default values, minimum or maximum entries, you must adhere to dBASE rules for these entries. Character strings must be encased in quotation marks. Dates must be encased in braces and logical values must be entered as .T. and .F..

You can use the default value option for all field types except Memo fields. You might use the DATE() function to supply current date for the date of hire if you normally enter the records for new employees on the date they are hired. Setting the default for a Logical field to true can be accomplished by entering .T..

Smallest Allowed Value Another way to trap errors before they become part of the database is to establish a minimum acceptable value for a cell. If the lowest unit price on any item in stock is $2.95, you can enter 2.95 as the smallest value. For a Character field, quotation marks are required around the entry.

Largest Allowed Value The Largest allowed value options establishes a cap for the largest entry that can be entered into a field. If valid part numbers for a company are in the range BA-0000 and ST-9999, you might want to set a Smallest value entry of **BA-0000** and the highest entry to **ST-9999**. Entries that are either greater than or less than the range are rejected.

Accept Value When This option determines whether dBASE accepts or rejects entries for the field based on whether a condition is true or false. If the expression is evaluated as false the entry is rejected and if true, your entry is stored in the database. Rather than looking at the contents of another field to make the determination, this option looks at the entry you are placing in the current field and determines whether it evaluates as true or false. Even though you always reference the current field you still need to use the field name in the expression. In some cases you can use the range options or multiple choice as another way of accomplishing the same thing.

You can use this option to check to see if the STATE is equal to MD or VA. The expression you would enter is STATE="MD" .OR. STATE="VA". Another option can require that the ORDER_DATE is greater than or equal to today's date. This is accomplished with an expression entry of ORDER_DATE>=DATE(). This would prevent a user from entering an order as if it had been in the system for several weeks. They must date the order with today's date or a future date. If the entry does not meet the condition established, dBASE displays a message and requests that you press the SPACEBAR.

Unaccepted Message This option is a partner to the preceding option. If you use Accept value when and the expression is false for a field, dBASE looks in the Unaccepted message option and displays the message it finds at this location. The message displays in the message line and can be removed with the SPACEBAR. The maximum length for the message is 79 characters and cannot include quotation marks. In the first example in the preceding section a message of **STATE entry must be MD or VA** would highlight a user's mistake immediately.

Using Words Features to Affect the Display

The Words menu offers features to enhance the appearance of your screens and make the design process easier. To enhance the appearance of the screen there are options like Display, which allow you to modify the intensity or color of any selectable item on a screen. You can also change the position of fields from the left to the right or center of the screen.

Tip: Think of Accept value when and Unaccepted message as an inseparable pair.

Whenever you establish an expression that might reject an entry, use the Unacceptable message option to explain the reason for the rejection to the user. Otherwise, they may continue to try other incorrect options with their frustration level growing.

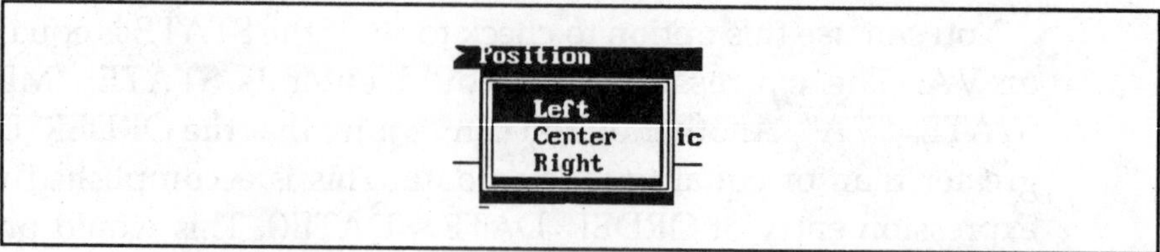

Figure 7-15 Selection box for positioning selected text and templates

Changing Position

The Position option allows you to change the position of the current field template and name on the screen. To use these options select Position from the Words menu. The selections in Figure 7-15 can be used to make the change.

Controlling Color

Depending on the type of monitor you are using, you can use the color options to change either the color or intensity of selected information. To change the color or intensity follow these steps:

1. Press F6 (Select) to begin selecting the area you wish to change.
2. Use the ARROW keys to highlight all the text, fields, lines or boxes you wish to change.
3. Press ALT-W to select the Words menu.
4. Type a **D** to select Display.
5. Depending on your monitor type, either select from the Intensity or Colors options. The Colors menu options are shown in Figure 7-16.
6. Press CTRL-END after making your selection.
7. Press ESC to remove the highlighting still over the selected area when you return to the Form design screen.

Reading and Writing Form Text

You can save all the text on a Form design screen to a text file. This text can be retrieved for use in another program or by dBASE when you are designing a new screen. Field names and special on-screen documentation can be used for multiple forms easily, using this approach.

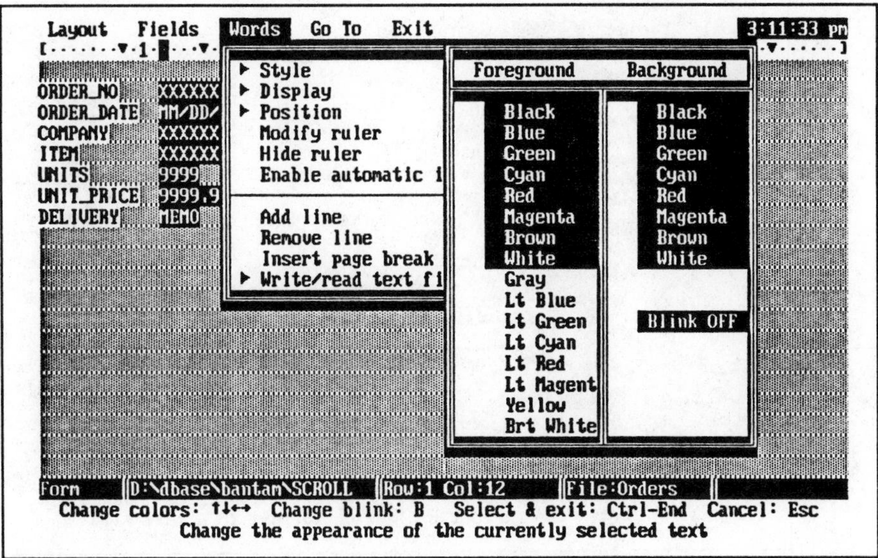

Figure 7-16 Selection box for selecting colors

To save the text on a form in a file, press ALT-W for the Words menu. Type a **W** to select Write/read text file. Highlight Write selection to file and press ENTER. Type the name of the file you wish to use for saving the information. If you save the text from the screen in Figure 7-17, the text from this ORDERS form is saved. If you do not provide an extension, dBASE adds a .TXT extension.

To retrieve the information into another file, press ALT-W and type a **W**. Highlight Read text from file and press ENTER. Type the filename you wish to read and press ENTER. dBASE reads the text from the file and adds it to the screen at the cursor's position as shown by the addition of the text from the ORDERS form to the current screen in Figure 7-18.

Ruler Line Options

The ruler line is the same one that appears at the top of the Report design screen. The options are the same as the ruler line options covered in Chapter 6. You can hide this line or modify the margins or tab stops with the same techniques you use in the Report design screen.

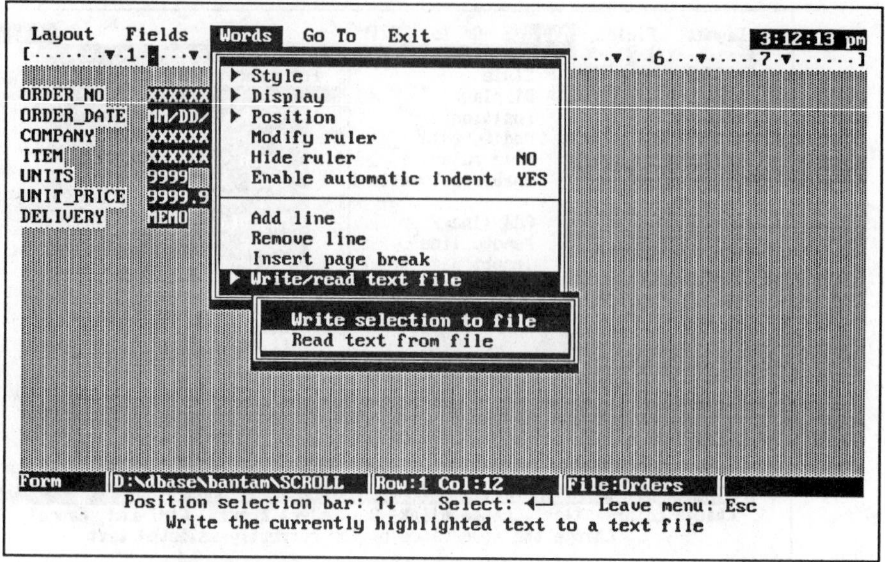

Figure 7-17 Words menu

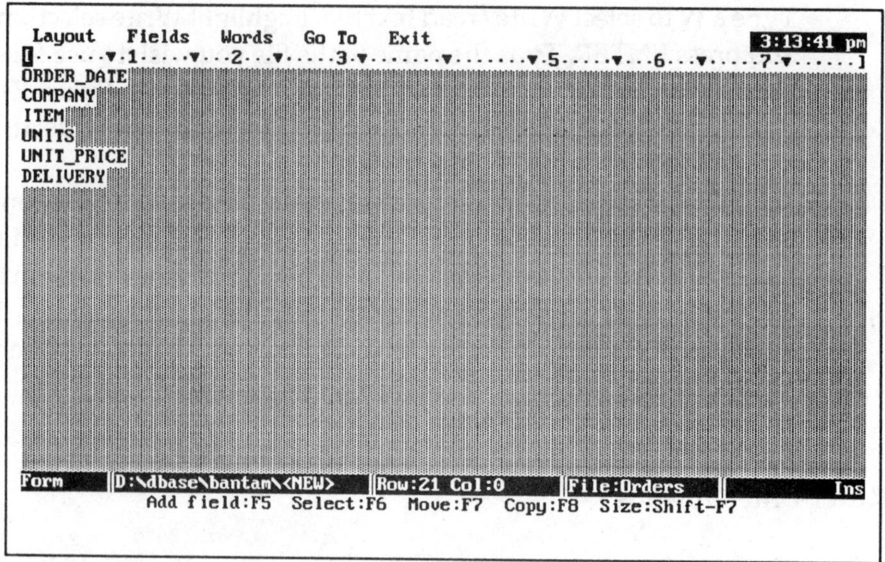

Figure 7-18 File read into form design

Memo Fields

The default within dBASE is to show a marker on the Edit screen to indicate the location of the Memo field. The marker is shown on the Form design work surface as MEMO. When data is displayed with this form, the marker appears as memo if the memo field is empty and MEMO if it contains an entry. To make an entry in the Memo field, you have learned to highlight the field and press CTRL-HOME.

dBASE IV offers another option in allowing you to create a window on the screen for a Memo field. The default width of this window is 50 characters, although once it is created you can size and move the window. The advantage of a Memo field window is that the memo field entries in existing records are immediately visible in this window.

To change a Memo field marker into a window, highlight the Memo field and press F5 (Field). Type **D** to select Display as and press ENTER to toggle the setting to Window. You can also use the Borders option to place a specific type of box around the window. The default is a single line, but you can change it to a double line or a specific character. Figure 7-19 shows the box that displays when the Delivery field in the ORDERS file is changed to a window.

The box for the window is filled with X's and currently overlays other important information on the design screen. Since the cursor is on the box you can move it by pressing F7 (Move) and placing the cursor in the new location. For the ORDERS file you might want to move to row 11 column 14. Press ENTER and the box is repositioned. To shrink the box press SHIFT-F7 (Size) and move the cursor to row 15 column 65. The final result looks like Figure 7-20.

Adding Calculated Fields

Calculated fields on a form allow you to perform computations with the data in existing database records. They do not serve as a "what-if" feature that can evaluate many different options for you since Calculated fields are not recalculated when you change the database values used by the Calculated field. It is not until you store the data record and review it again that the Calculated field is recalculated.

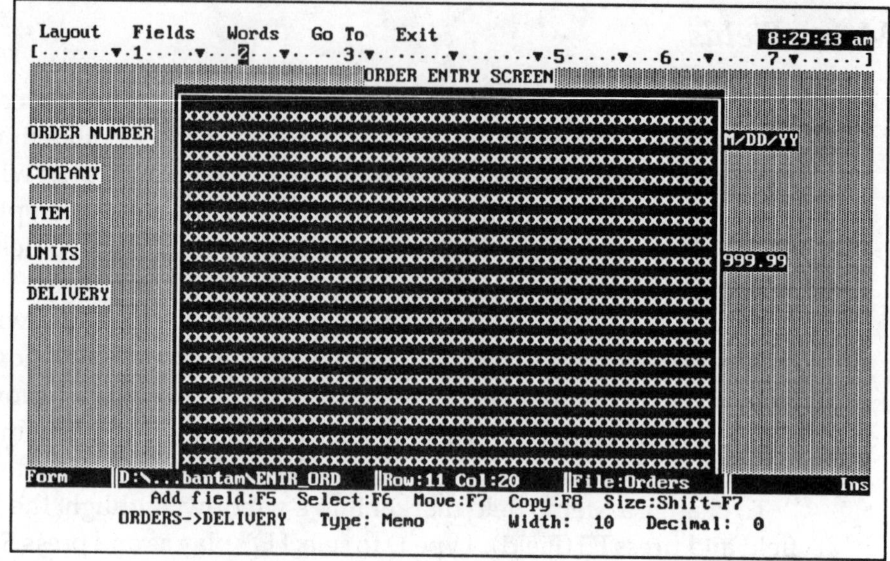

Figure 7-19 Memo window box

To add a Calculated field to your form, move the cursor to the location where you want the Calculated field template to be positioned.

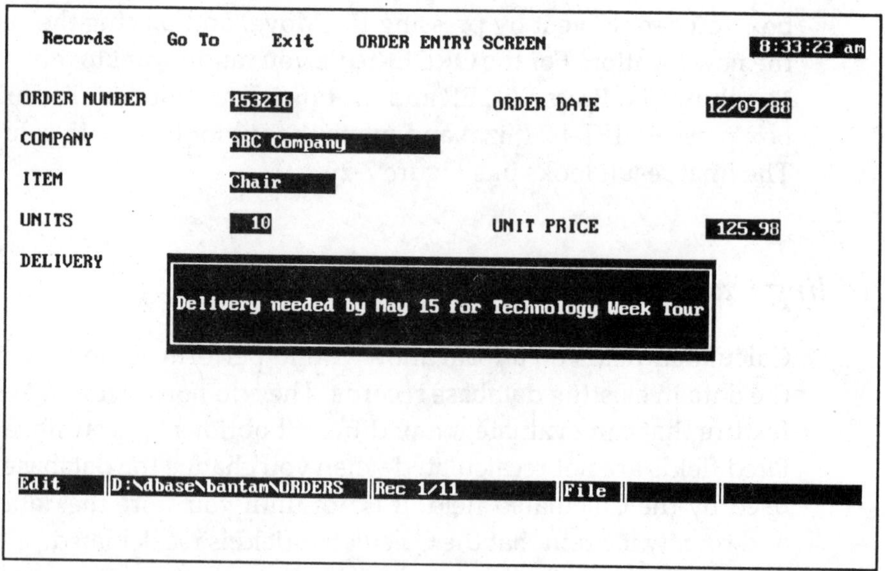

Figure 7-20 ORDERS database using form with a memo window box

Press F5 to add a field. Choose <create> from the Calculated column shown in Figure 7-21. The resulting menu has many of the same options already provided for existing fields as well as entries for a name, a description, and an expression. Select Name and type **TAX**. Press ENTER then press the DOWN ARROW to move to Description. Press ENTER and type **State tax on order**. Press ENTER and use the DOWN ARROW to move to Expression. Press ENTER and type **UNITS*UNIT_PRICE*.07**. Press ENTER and CTRL-END. You can use SHIFT-F1 to generate the pick box and select field names, functions, and operators from this box. You must press SHIFT-F1 for each entry that you need; otherwise, you can type the expression.

Figure 7-22 shows the field description menu box that defines the tax calculation for each order. Figure 7-23 shows the Calculated field on the screen. Note the distinctive lack of highlighting on a Calculated field, since you cannot edit it.

Using Lines and Boxes

You can enhance the appearance of a custom screen with the addition of lines and boxes. Boxes can group similar types of data or make a screen look more like the source document from which the data is being entered. You can draw single-line boxes, double-line boxes, or you can use any of the special graphics characters to draw a box. Normally you complete most of the form design and add lines or boxes once the text and field templates are positioned.

❑ **Tip: Use PGUP and PGDN as a quick recall.**

Calculated fields on a form do not automatically recalculate when you enter or change data. To have dBASE recalculate the screen for the current record, press PGUP followed by PGDN. As soon as you move to the preceding record, dBASE stores the entries for the current record. When you return again, dBASE recalculates the Calculated fields for your new entries.

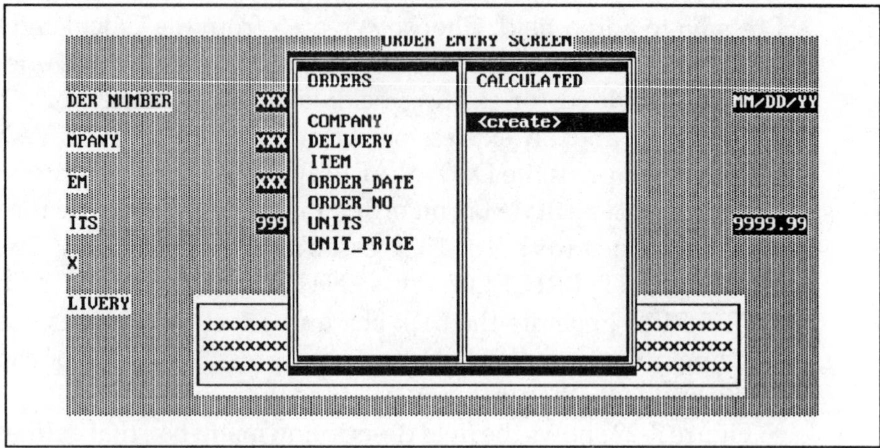

Figure 7-21 Field selection box

The line draw feature can highlight a screen title or provide a separation between two areas of the screen in much the same way as the dBASE IV menu boxes are often divided. You can also use the line draw feature to create a simple logo on the screen or to draw a special symbol. If you study the graphics characters that you can use for lines, you can often create what you need by changing the graphics symbol.

To add either a line or a box, the process is almost the same:

1. Position the cursor on the position where you want to begin drawing. For a box this should be the upper left corner.
2. Press ALT-L for Layout and type an **L** or a **B** depending upon whether you want a line or a box. Choose the type of line from Single, double, or character.
3. Move the highlight to the upper left position for the line or box. Press ENTER.
4. Move to the lower right corner of the box or line. Press ENTER to finalize the line or box positioning.

When you draw a line, you can change the direction by changing which arrow key you press. You can also include text in the line by typing the text after the line has started in the direction you want. When you draw a box, you have more keys you can use to draw the box since you can use HOME, END, TAB, and SHIFT-TAB.

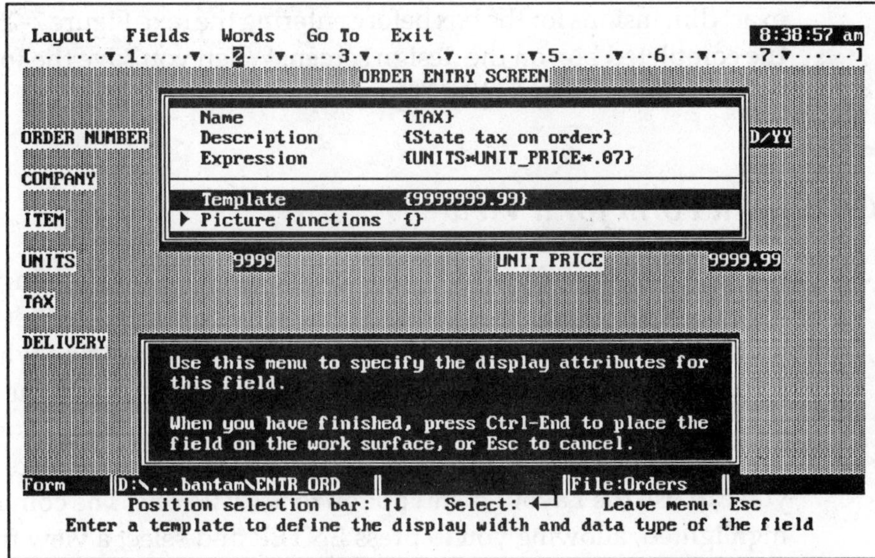

Figure 7-22 Completed field description box for TAX Calculated field

Figure 7-24 shows text that was typed for inclusion in a box. It is easier to type the text and draw the box around it than to decide the

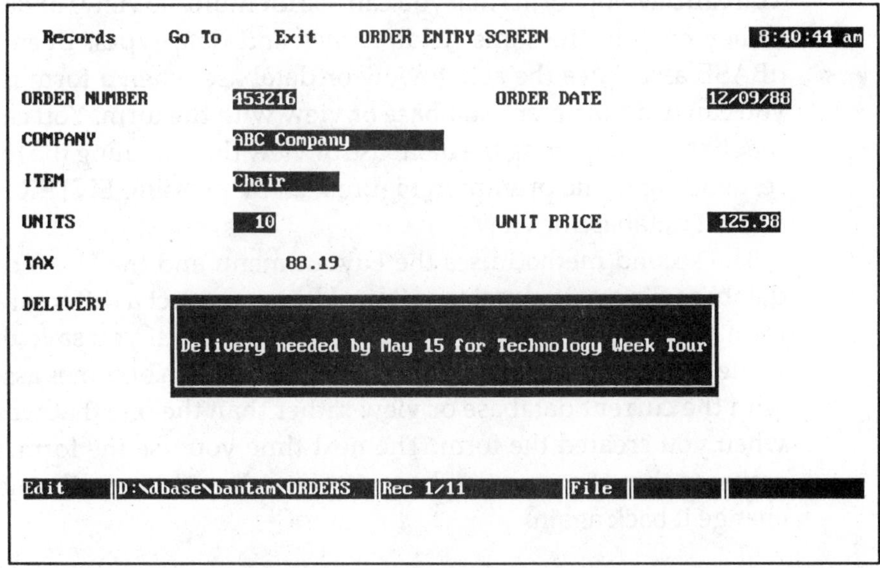

Figure 7-23 ORDERS database using form with a Calculated field

exact dimensions for the box before entering the text. Figure 7-25 shows the completed box on the design screen. When you save the form and use it for entry, it looks like Figure 7-26.

Creating a Form for a View

Creating a custom form for a view is no different than creating a form for a database. You can activate the view by selecting the View query that selects the appropriate records. If this view is active when you select <create> from the Forms panel, dBASE assumes that the form is being created for the view.

If there is no database or view open when you begin to create a form, you can use the Layout menu option to activate one. The command is highlighted, allowing you to press ENTER and select a view from the list of databases and views. If the view that you select is a composite of two or more databases, ReadOnly appears in the status line and you cannot change the data.

Using a Form with Another Database

You can develop forms that you can use for multiple views or databases if they contain the same fields names and data types. Even though dBASE associates the active view or database when a form is saved, you can use a different database or view with the form. You can make the change by opening the database or view then opening the form and responding to the prompt in Figure 7-27 by pressing ENTER to select current database or view.

The second method uses the Layout menu and the Use a different database file or view menu option. After you select a different file, the form continues to use the new database or view. If you save the form while the other database or view is active, the form becomes associated with the current database or view rather than the one that was active when you created the form. The next time you use the form, dBASE assumes that the new database or view should be used unless you change it back again.

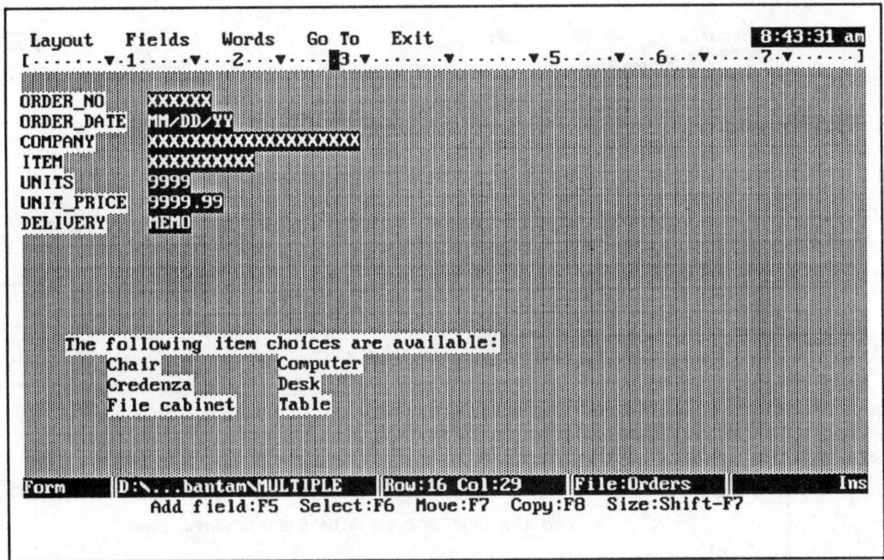

Figure 7-24 Text in a form before adding a box

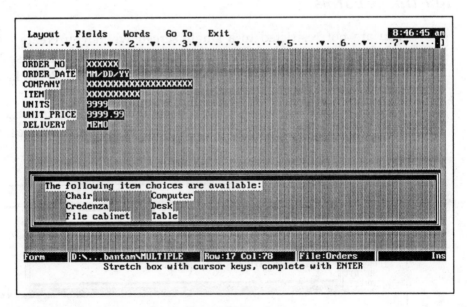

```
Layout   Fields   Words   Go To   Exit                       8:46:45 am
ORDER_NO      XXXXXX
ORDER_DATE    MM/DD/YY
COMPANY       XXXXXXXXXXXXXXXXXXXX
ITEM          XXXXXXXXXX
UNITS         9999
UNIT_PRICE    9999.99
DELIVERY      MEMO

   The following item choices are available:
         Chair            Computer
         Credenza         Desk
         File cabinet     Table

Form  D:\...bantam\MULTIPLE  Row:17 Col:78  File:Orders  Ins
        Stretch box with cursor keys, complete with ENTER
```

Figure 7-25 Text in a form after adding a box

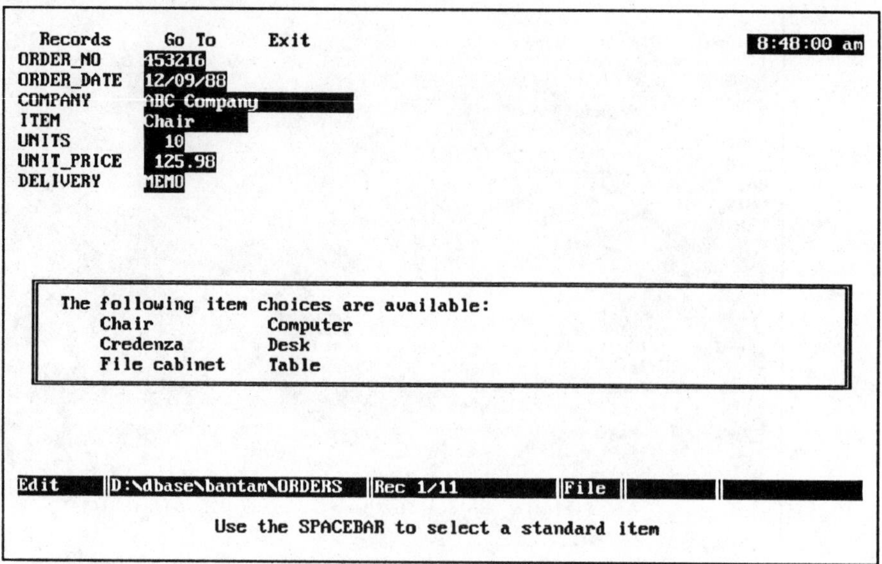

Figure 7-26 ORDERS database using form with text in a box

Multipage Forms

You are not restricted to a single screen when you create a form. Although you are always limited to a width of 80, you can use 32,767 rows when designing a custom form. The PgUp and PgDn keys are used to move from screen to screen.

Since you are limited to 255 fields in a database, all this extra space is not needed to list the fields. You can feel free to add as much

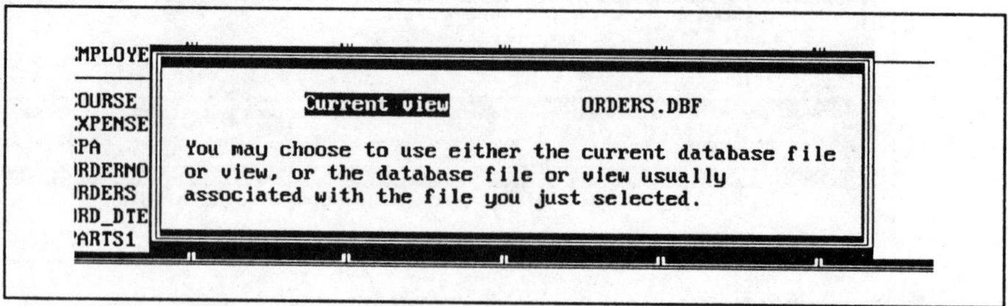

Figure 7-27 Selection box between current view and database form was created for

descriptive information as necessary to assist the operator in completing the form. You can even repeat fields on multiple pages of the form. After the data is entered on the first screen, listing the field again with Edit allowed set to Off will prevent the cursor from moving to this field. PgUp and PgDn does not move you from record to record until you are on the first or last screen in a multiscreen form.

GETTING STARTED

➤ You will want to try out some of the custom form features by creating a form for the EMPLOYEE file. Follow these steps to open the EMPLOYEE file and rearrange the fields on the form:

1. Highlight EMPLOYEE in the Data panel and press ENTER twice.
2. Press the RIGHT ARROW key twice. If there are existing form names above the line, press HOME to highlight <create>. Press ENTER to move to the forms design screen.
3. Press ENTER with Quick layout highlighted.
4. Press the DOWN ARROW to move to the LAST_NAME field. Press ENTER to move this entry down one line.
5. Press the DOWN ARROW to move to the M_INITIAL field. Press F6 (Select). Press the END key followed by the LEFT ARROW to highlight the field and template then press ENTER. Press F7 (Move). Move the cursor to row 3 column 30 and press ENTER.
6. Press the DOWN ARROW twice and HOME once to move to the F in the FIRST_NAME field. Press F6 (Select). Press END and ENTER. Press F7 (Move). Press the UP ARROW twice. Press the RIGHT ARROW until the cursor is in column 46 of row 3. Press ENTER.
7. Press the DOWN ARROW. Press CTRL-Y to delete a blank line.
8. Press the DOWN ARROW twice then press HOME so the cursor is on the C in CITY. Press ENTER to move CITY down a line.
9. Press the DOWN ARROW to move to the S in STATE. Press F6 (Select). Press END and ENTER. Press F7 (Move), press the UP ARROW followed by the RIGHT ARROW until the cursor is in column 30 of row 7. Press ENTER.

10. Press the DOWN ARROW twice, press HOME once to place the cursor on the Z in ZIP_CODE. Press F6 (Select). Press END and ENTER. Press F7 (Move). Press the UP ARROW twice followed by pressing the RIGHT ARROW to move to column 46 of row 7. Press ENTER.
11. Press the DOWN ARROW then press CTRL-Y. Press the DOWN ARROW. Press ENTER.
12. Press the DOWN ARROW twice to move to the M in MARITAL_ST. Press F6 (Select). Press END and ENTER. Press F7 (Move) and move the cursor to column 30 in row 11. Press ENTER.
13. Press the DOWN ARROW twice, press CTRL-A twice to move to the N in NUMB_DEPEN. Press F6 (Select). Next, press END, LEFT ARROW, and ENTER. Press F7 (Move), move the cursor to row 11 column 46 and press ENTER.
14. Press the DOWN ARROW twice. Press CTRL_Y to delete an extra line.
15. Press the DOWN ARROW to move to the line with YTD_WAGES. Press HOME to move to the Y. Press F6 (Select). Press END and ENTER. Press F7 (Move) and move the cursor to row 14 column 30 and press ENTER.
16. Repeat step 12 for YTD_FIT but place it in row 15 column 30.
17. Move to the S in SKILLS and press ENTER to move down a line.

Adding custom templates, picture functions, and edit options can improve the appearance and performance of the form further. Follow these steps to save the current design and continue modifications:

1. To save the design as it exists and continue, press ALT-L, type **S**, type **ENTEREMP**, and press ENTER.
2. Move to the SSN template in row 1 column 12. Press F5 (Fields). Press ENTER to select Template. Press HOME. Type **999-99-9999**. Press ENTER and CTRL-END.
3. Move to row 3 column 12 in the template for the LAST_NAME. Press F5 (Fields). Press the DOWN ARROW to move to Picture function. Press ENTER. Press the DOWN ARROW to move to upper case. Press ENTER followed by CTRL-END twice.
4. Move to row 3 column 42 and repeat the actions in step 3 to convert the M_INITIAL field to upper case.

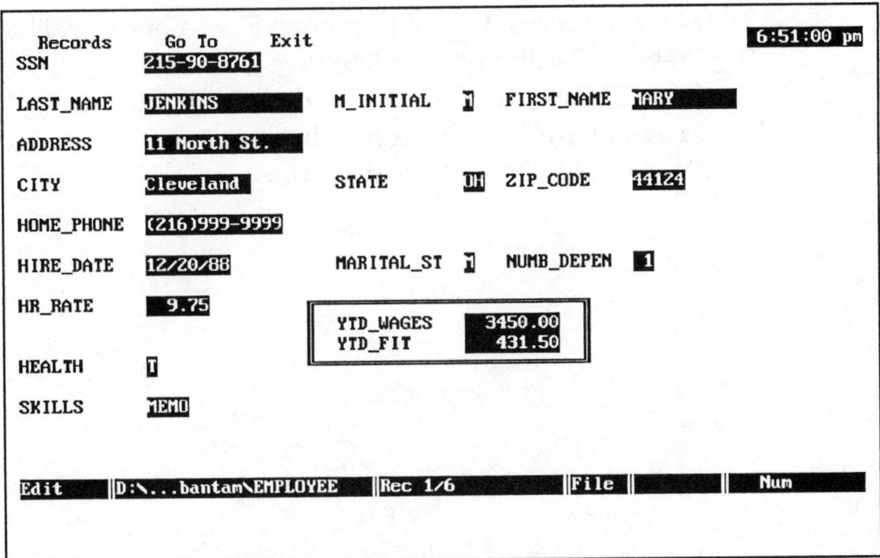

Figure 7-28 ENTEREMP form for EMPLOYEE database

5. Repeat step 3 for the FIRST_NAME field in row 3 column 58.
6. Move to the HOME_PHONE field template and press F5 (Field). Press ENTER to select Template, press HOME and type **(999)999-9999**. Press ENTER followed by CTRL-END.
7. Move to the template for the HIRE_DATE field. Press F5 (Fields). Press ENTER to select Edit options. Move the Default value choice and press ENTER. Type **DATE()** and press ENTER. Press CTRL-END twice to finalize.
8. Move to the HR_RATE field in row 13 column 12. Press F5 (Fields). Type an **E** for Edit options. Type an **S** for smallest value. Type **3.35** and press ENTER. Press the DOWN ARROW key to largest allowed value. Press ENTER, type a **50** and press ENTER. Press CTRL-END twice to finalize.

As a final step, you can add a box around two of the fields on the form. Follow these steps to finalize a design that matches Figure 7-28.

1. Move the cursor to row 13 column 27.
2. Press ALT-L and type a **B** for Box. Type a **D** for Double line.
3. Press ENTER to lock the current position as the upper left corner of the box.

4. Move the cursor to row 16 column 53 and press ENTER.
5. Press ALT-E and type an **S** to save the form.
6. Press ENTER twice to display the existing data with the form. Press PgUp and PgDn to switch between records.
7. Press CTRL-END to save the form.

PART III

Working with dBASE Files

CHAPTER 8

Using File Utilities and Customization Options

dBASE IV creates many files as you develop applications. There are files for databases, indexes, reports, labels, forms, and programs. All of these require multiple files to contain data, object design, code files, and compiled code files. Although most of your file tasks are handled by dBASE IV automatically, you will want to be familiar with the file-handling options that dBASE IV offers. Using the dBASE file utilities provides a time savings when compared with exiting dBASE to use DOS and returning when you are finished. dBASE IV provides commands that allow you to copy, sort, and rename files. In addition dBASE IV provides a way to transfer data between dBASE IV and other programs.

You can access dBASE IV settings to customize some of your activities with the program. The program provides several ways to change the settings. The method you choose determines the permanency of the change and the number of options that you can alter.

dBASE IV FILES

dBASE IV filenames must follow the rules established by the disk operating system. This means they are composed of two parts separated by a period. The first part is the filename itself. This name can consist of from one to eight characters. Alphabetic characters, numeric digits, and some of the special symbols are acceptable. You can use either upper or lower case when you enter the filename but should never include spaces.

The second part of the filename is the filename extension. It can consist of from zero to three characters. dBASE IV automatically assigns a unique filename extension for each type of file that it creates. The only time that you will need to enter a filename extension for dBASE files is when you are working with the files directly from the operating system.

You must understand dBASE filename extensions to work effectively with the package. In addition to the files that you are aware of, like database files, dBASE IV creates other files for storing related information. For example, the creation of a database results in the creation of a .DBF file for the database itself, an .MDX file for database indexes, and a .DBT file to store Memo field data. The filenames are the same for the three files. It is the filename extension that distinguishes the files and indicates the type of data they contain. Also, since the database contains pointers to these filenames, when you create a copy of the database, it is important that you copy all three files and leave their filenames unchanged.

The other types of information that dBASE stores in files also require multiple files but for a different reason. When you create queries, forms, reports, and labels, dBASE stores your original design in a file. These design files can be modified if you decide to change the way that your database information is presented. You can also present these

❑

Tip: Limit special symbols in filenames.

Limit special symbols in filenames to the underscore (_). This character is universally accepted as a separator character and does not cause compatibility problems with later releases of the operating system.

❑ **Tip: Establish file-naming standards.**

Developing a standard set of rules for naming dBASE files makes the package easier to use. You may want to consider using the same first letter for each file in the system; a file list sorted by filename will place all the files from one system together if you employ this technique.

design files to someone else, who could alter the design to meet their exact needs.

dBASE takes design files and creates code files. These code files convert your design into instructions that dBASE can interpret. dBASE then takes these code files and creates the compiled files that dBASE uses to generate your reports, forms, and labels.

Like the database files, the filenames used for queries, forms, reports, and labels retain their original filename in all formats. It is only the filename extensions that distinguish one type from another. Table 8-1 presents a list of all the filename extensions that dBASE IV uses.

dBASE IV often creates temporary files when it generates a query, form, report, or label that has not been saved. Random numbers are used for the filenames, although the standard filename extensions are appended to these names.

❑ **Tip: Support files are essential for database files.**

Both .MDX and .DBT files are essential to maintain index and Memo field information. If you copy a database, you must also copy these files. Renaming any of the three files does not work since the database stores pointers to the Memo field and production index fields using the original file names. To use a different name you must use the COPY STRUCTURE and APPEND commands covered in Chapter 10.

Table 8-1 List of Filename Extensions

Type of File	*Type of Data*	*Filename Extension*
Database	Design	.DBF
Database	Index	.MDX
Database	Memo fields	.DBT
View query	Design	.QBE
View query	Compiled	.QBO
Update query	Design	.UPD
Update query	Compiled	.DBO/.UPO
dBASE III PLUS view	Design	.VUE
Form	Design	.SCR
Form	Code	.FMT
Form	Compiled	.FMO
Report	Design	.FRM
Report	Code	.FRG
Report	Compiled	.FRO
Label	Design	.LBL
Label	Code	.LBG
Label	Compiled	.LBO
Program	Code	.PRG
Program	Compiled	.DBO
dBASE/SQL Program	Code	.PRS
dBASE/SQL Program	Compiled	.DBO
Applications Generator	Design	.APP
Applications Generator	Code	.PRG
Applications Generator	Compiled	.DBO

❑ **Tip: Copying files.**

To copy the files for a database, query, form, report, or label, enter the design screen for the object, press ALT-L, and type an **S**. Type a new filename and press ENTER. Copying a file with the Layout menu from the design screen copies the files connected with the object and changes the pointers in the copy so they refer to the associated files of the new copy.

❑ **Tip: dBASE IV forgets to delete temporary files.**

The files with a sequence of numbers for names are temporary but dBASE IV often leaves them on your disk. Periodically you want to check the file list and delete these files. The only ones that you cannot remove immediately are the ones that are currently open.

Directories Versus Catalogs

Directories and catalogs offer you a way to work with dBASE IV files more efficiently. There are similarities in these two logical ways of organizing data but there are also differences.

Directories

You are probably already familiar with the logical divisions called subdirectories that help to organize the files on your hard disk. Subdirectories allow you to maintain many programs on your hard disk and organize the information that is used with each of them. They are not physical divisions of the disk but are actually files that contain entries for each of the files they manage.

You can have several levels of entries in a directory. The highest level is called the root directory. You can create several levels of directories beneath it as shown in Figure 8-1. The DOS MD command creates and names these new directories. Follow the same naming rules that you use for filenames except do not use any filename extensions.

Reading the directory entry tells DOS the size of the file and its location on the hard disk. If the directory entry for a file is removed from the directory, the file becomes inaccessible since DOS does not know where to find it. It considers the disk area used by the file to be empty space and may write other information over it.

When you work with dBASE IV you can define a default directory that dBASE uses when saving or retrieving files. You can override the default directory at any time by supplying a full pathname for any file, including the disk and directory. If you want to change to the default

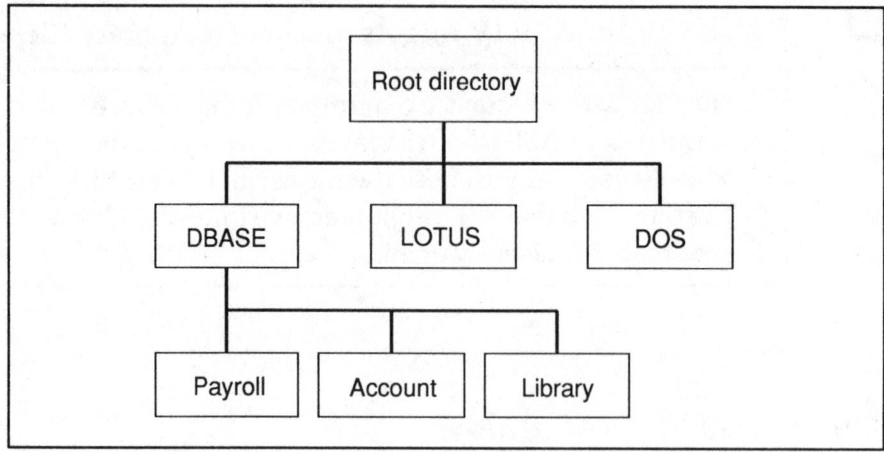

Figure 8-1 Example of multiple subdirectories

directory in effect for the current session, you can use the Tools DOS utilities, DOS Change directory command sequence, or the SET DEFAULT TO command discussed later in this chapter. You can make a permanent change to the default directory with the DBSETUP command Files Path.

Catalogs

Catalogs also provide a way to organize dBASE IV information. The influence of catalogs does not extend beyond dBASE. They are designed to organize all the information connected with one application and make it easy to select any of the associated files from the Control Center.

As you create new files in dBASE, a catalog entry is created for the new file. These catalog entries associate the supporting files with a database. Unlike directories they are not designed to record the physical device addresses for the data that they manage, only its relationship to other dBASE files. Deleting a catalog entry does not affect a file the way that deleting a directory entry does. If you delete a catalog entry, the file is still available on the disk. You can always add the file back to the current catalog if you want to work with it again. You can also include the same file in several catalogs. You will look at catalogs in a more in-depth fashion in the next chapter.

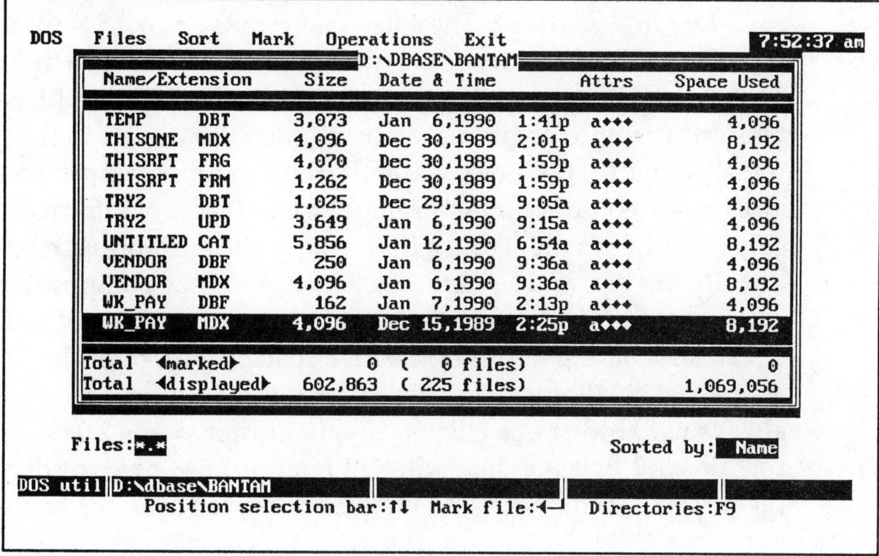

Figure 8-2 Files List screen

DOS Utilities

The DOS utilities make the commands of the DOS operating system available from within dBASE IV. To copy or rename a file quickly it is easier to work with these commands from within dBASE. You can also mark files and work with a group of files rather than entering commands repeatedly. These commands also provide a way to sort the file display easily and to change the current directory.

To access the DOS utilities, you will want to press ALT-T from the Control Center menu to select Tools. Next type a **D** to select DOS utilities. The Files List screen appears.

Working with the Files List

The Files List screen provides a list of files from the current directory. You can move through the list selecting files by pressing ENTER or select commands from the menu shown in Figure 8-2. The options in this menu can be selected by pressing the ALT key in combination with the first letter in the selection, or by pressing F10 and highlighting the desired option.

Files List Information The Files List display provides information found in a DOS directory listing with a few additions. The first column contains the filenames. The second column displays the filename extension. The third column contains the amount of data in the file. The fourth and fifth columns contain the date and time, respectively.

The sixth column contains four different pieces of information. This column displays the settings for the DOS file attributes Archive, Hidden, Read-only, and System. Each attribute uses one position in the column and is shown as a diamond if the attribute has not been set.

The last column indicates the disk space required for the file. Since disk space is allocated in clusters, a file no matter how small, will always use at least one cluster. If your cluster size is 2,048, a file that contains 512 bytes of data will still require 2,048 bytes of disk space. Likewise a file requiring 2,049 bytes will need two clusters or 4,096 bytes.

The lower part of this screen contains selected summary information. This includes the total number of files that are marked and their total size, and the total number of files displayed and their total size.

Moving Around in the Files List You can use the UP and DOWN ARROW keys to move from name to name in the Files List. If you prefer to move faster, the PGUP and PGDN keys moves from screen to screen in this listing. You can also use the HOME and END keys to move to the top or bottom of the list.

You can use the ENTER key to mark any file in the list once you highlight the filename. Pressing ENTER a second time unmarks the name. Once marked, you can enter other commands once and the commands affect all the marked files.

Moving to a Higher Level View If you press F9 (Zoom), dBASE will immediately move you to a higher view of the data on your disk with a directory tree like the one shown in Figure 8-3. If you press SHIFT-F1, dBASE will allow you to select another disk on your system and produce a directory for it like the C drive directory in Figure 8-4. If you highlight a directory path and press F9 or ENTER, dBASE displays the files in this directory.

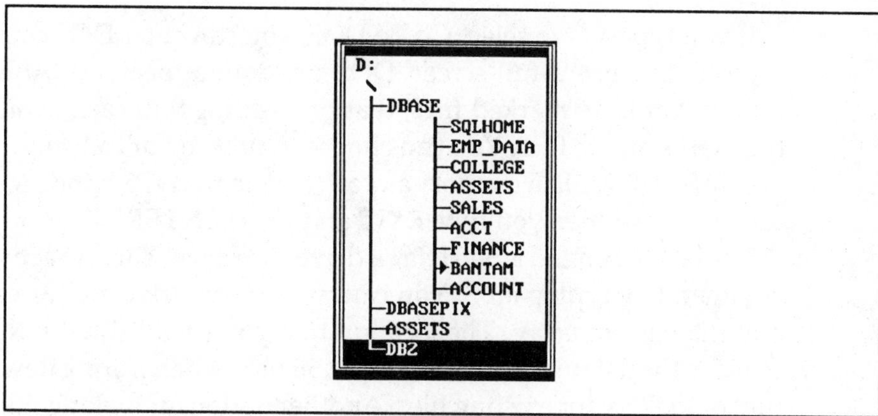

Figure 8-3 Pick list for selecting directory

The DOS Option

If you select the DOS option, dBASE IV presents a menu with three choices. If you select Perform DOS command by typing a **P**, dBASE allows you to enter a DOS command for immediate execution. You might enter **COPY DENVER.DBF A:** and press ENTER to have DOS complete the copy operation for you.

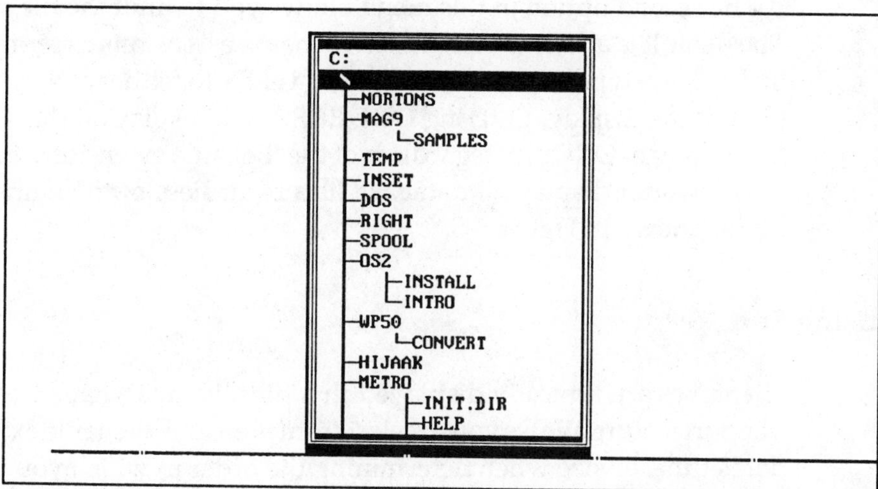

Figure 8-4 Pick list after changing drive

If you type a **G** to select Go To DOS, you can enter DOS commands repeatedly since a full-screen DOS window appears. dBASE warns you, if you have marked files, that proceeding will cause you to lose the marks on the files. You can choose to proceed or cancel.

dBASE IV is still in memory as you work in the DOS window. dBASE returns fully when you type **EXIT** and press ENTER.

The last command is Set default drive:directory. You can activate this command by typing an **S**. You can type a new drive and directory or edit the current entry. The location that you establish with this command is the default location that dBASE uses when storing new dBASE files or looking for existing files. Another option for making the change is to press SHIFT-F1 (Pick) and select from the directory tree.

The Files Option

The Files menu offers two options. The first command allows you to change the drive or directory for the Files List that is displayed on the screen. After pressing ALT-F to invoke Files and typing a **C**, you can enter a new drive and directory or edit the existing entry. The SHIFT-F1 (Pick) option also works with this command. You can also change the Files List by highlighting the subdirectory name or parent directory name in the current Files List and pressing ENTER.

The second option in this menu allows you to limit the file display. The default is all filenames and all filename extensions as represented by *.*. If you type a **D**, you can supply an entry for either of the asterisks to limit the display. Entering **ORDERS.*** will display all the files that had names of ORDERS regardless of the filename extensions. Entering ***.DBF** would display all database files regardless of the name of the file, as shown in Figure 8-5.

Using Sort

Filenames are typically displayed in a files list in alphabetical order. The Sort feature allows you to select from filename, filename extension, date&time, or size when determining the order in which you want to organize your data. The default setting is Name order indicated by the ON next to this entry. You can type the letter at the front of any of the entries to create a new sequence.

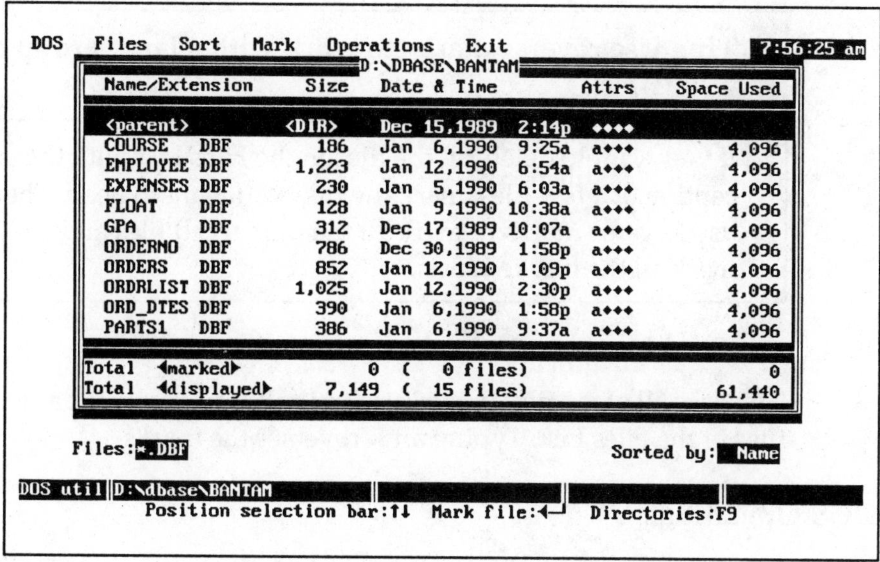

Figure 8-5 Files List limited to database files

If you use the Display only option under Files to limit the display, dBASE only needs to sort the files that display. If you need only a subset of the files, exclude them first with an appropriate entry.

Marking Files

There are two ways to mark files. You can mark them individually by highlighting file names and pressing the ENTER. This marks the highlighted file by placing a triangle at the left side of the filename in the list.

You can also mark and unmark groups of files from the menu commands. Pressing ALT-M to activate the Mark menu and typing an

❑

Tip: Use Date & time to isolate problems.

You can sort files by date and time when you are testing programs. This allows you to take a quick look at files that were created by the test since they all appear together in the list.

> **Tip: Use reverse marks to work with a large group of files.**
>
> If you want to delete all the files in the Files List with the exception of a few files, mark the files you want to keep. Then use Reverse marks to mark all the unmarked files and unmark all the marked files.

M marks all of the files in the list. Typing a **U** will unmark any marked files in the Files List. Typing an **R** reverses the marks.

DOS Operations

The menu-selectable DOS commands that you can execute from dBASE are located in the Operations menu. Delete, Copy, Move, and Rename are all available on this menu. These commands are accessed by pressing ALT-O and typing the first letter of the command. A second menu appears for each of these commands to allow you to select from Single file, Marked files, or Displayed files.

The View option allows you to look at the contents of text files. Although dBASE filters out nonprintable ASCII characters in this display, normally you only want to use it to look at text files that do not contain these characters. Figure 8-6 provides a quick look at data in a database file. If you were trying to decide which files to delete, View can help you identify the correct ones. Figure 8-7 provides a view of the first part of a report .FRG file. This information is ideally suited for the View command since it is stored as text.

```
                                                                      7:59:50 am
Z         BORDER_NOC
S}ORDER_DATEDS}COMPANYCS}ITEMC/S}UNITSN9S}UNIT_PRICEN=S}DELIVERYMDS}
 45321619881209ABC Company          Chair       10 125.980000000001 678543198812
10Baker & Associates  Desk          5 585.95          78965419881215ABC Company
          Cabinet     3 129.95          98654119881216Carlston & Sons      Mail
ers    100    1.50          00125419890103Lewis Brothers        Chair        5  8
9.95        00129819890110Baker & Associates  Desk            5 585.95
  00132519890115Able Bakery          Cabinet      2 129.95              00135919890
117BBB Bakery          Cabinet      3 129.95          00154619890118Smythe Com
pany      Desk          4 495.00
```

Figure 8-6 ORDERS.DBF displayed with View from Operations menu

```
                                                                    8:00:43 am
* Program............: D:\DBASE\BANTAM\THISRPT.FRG
* Date...............: 12-30-89
* Versions...........: dBASE IV, Report 1
*
* Notes:
* ------
* Prior to running this procedure with the DO command
* it is necessary use LOCATE because the CONTINUE
* statement is in the main loop.
*
*-- Parameters
PARAMETERS gl_noeject, gl_plain, gl_summary, gc_heading, gc_extra
** The first three parameters are of type Logical.
** The fourth parameter is a string.  The fifth is extra.
PRIVATE _peject, _wrap

*-- Test for no records found
IF EOF() .OR. .NOT. FOUND()
   RETURN
ENDIF


                                    -- 13% --
      Display control: SPACEBAR:Next screenful,  RETURN:Start/stop scroll.
```

Figure 8-7 THISRPT.PRG displayed with View from Operations menu

The Edit option allows you to use the program editor to change the contents of the current file. This approach is appropriate for creating a quick DOS batch file, but for most dBASE IV files you should not forego the safeguards that dBASE applies when you create the files through dBASE menus and commands.

Exiting

You can exit from the Dos utilities by pressing ALT-E and pressing ENTER. dBASE IV will return you to the Control Center menu.

Importing and Exporting Data

Importing and exporting data can save a significant amount of time if you are using the same data with multiple software packages. Many applications use data in a database context and also need some of the same data in a spreadsheet for financial projections. dBASE supports the transfer of information to and from spreadsheet files as well as other databases. Because dBASE is such a popular program, many programs

Tip: Creative thinking may locate an import/export solution.

If the type of import/export option you need is not listed as a menu option, there may still be a solution. You can use the Append command to add non-dBASE records stored in a text file to a database. To export data to a program that accepts ASCII text data you can print a dBASE report to a text file.

also offer the ability to transfer their data to a format that dBASE can understand.

Figure 8-8 shows the Tools Import menu with the filename extension that dBASE looks for when attempting to convert these file types. If you have data in these other formats with a different filename extension, you need to rename these files to the extensions that dBASE expects.

Importing a Foreign File

The Lotus 1-2-3 data shown in Figure 8-9 provides an example of the conversion process. This data is stored in the tabular-type arrangement that is needed for a successful transfer to dBASE. A worksheet file that contains extraneous information can still be used but you may want to create a temporary copy and delete the unneeded information, or use 1-2-3's File Xtract feature to save a portion of the work sheet to a separate file. The 1-2-3 data shown in Figure 8-9 is stored as NEW_HIRE.WK1. The fields in this file represent name, date of hire, salary, job code, and location.

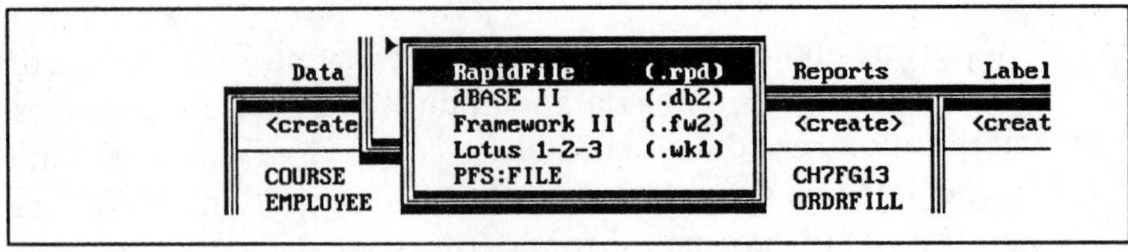

Figure 8-8 Import format selection box

	A	B	C	D	E	F	G
1	Brown, Jim	15-Jan-89	25600	1401	Chicago		
2	Cabbott, Mary	29-Jan-82	32900	3219	Dallas		
3	Deaver, Sue	23-Dec-84	38000	1401	New York		
4	Larkin, Steve	16-May-83	14600	2301	Chicago		
5	Royster, Paul	17-Feb-89	17500	1901	Dallas		
6	Walker, Jane	24-Nov-84	12500	2301	New York		

Figure 8-9 Lotus 1-2-3 file

To import Lotus 1-2-3 data into dBASE follow these steps:

1. Press ALT-T to activate the Tools menu.
2. Type a **I** to select Import.
3. Type an **L** to select Lotus 1-2-3.
4. Highlight the name of the 1-2-3 file that you wish to translate and press ENTER. You may need to use the parent option in the Files List to access a different directory unless you copied the 1-2-3 file to the dBASE directory. dBASE creates a database with the same name as the 1-2-3 file with a .DBF extension. If a file with this name exists, you can overwrite it or cancel the request.
5. Press SHIFT-F2 to review the structure of the file when dBASE finishes or press F2 to view the data. Figure 8-10 displays the dBASE file structure that the import feature creates for the NEW_HIRE.WK1 data. Figure 8-11 displays some of the data in the file NEW_HIRE.DBF.

Tip: You may need to use a little trial and error to determine how to handle different types of data.

Each program you work with may have its own idiosyncrasies that affect the proper translation of certain field types. When storing dates in Lotus 1-2-3 you will want to use @DATE to record your dates and format them with Date Format 1. All dates are initially transferred as characters, but when the field type is changed to Date in dBASE, the dates convert to dates for dBASE. The long international format date (Date Format 4) is not handled in the same fashion as Date Format 1 for transferring dates.

Layout Organize Append Go To Exit 5:15:30 pm

Bytes remaining: 3950

Num	Field Name	Field Type	Width	Dec	Index
1	A	Character	15		N
2	B	Date	8		N
3	C	Numeric	9	2	N
4	D	Numeric	9	2	N
5	E	Character	9		N

Figure 8-10 Database structure of Lotus 1-2-3 file imported into dBASE IV

6. Make appropriate field name and type changes.

   All of the field names need to be changed. Also the data types for the date of hire and the job codes should be altered. Figure 8-12 shows the revised structure.

Importing by Appending

You can also import data by creating the data structure and then appending the data to the database. By appending records, you may not have to convert the data to another format since dBASE offers more selections for appending records from an external file than for importing an external file. To append records, create the database structure. The fields in the database structure must match the field order in the external file. If you are uncertain about the field type to use, select Character. Then select Copy records from non-dBASE file from the Append menu in the Database design screen. When dBASE displays a list of the available file types, select the file type. Then select the file name from the list, switching between directories if necessary.

Records Fields Go To Exit 5:16:04 pm

A	B	C	D	E
Brown, Jim	01/15/89	25600.00	1401.00	Chicago
Cabbott, Mary	01/29/82	32900.00	3219.00	Dallas
Deaver, Sue	12/23/84	38000.00	1401.00	New York
Larkin, Steve	05/16/83	14600.00	2301.00	Chicago
Royster, Paul	02/17/89	17500.00	1901.00	Dallas
Walker, Jane	11/24/84	12500.00	2301.00	New York

Figure 8-11 Database data of Lotus 1-2-3 file imported into dBASE IV

Tip: Retain your original file until verifying the translate process.

You should not delete your original file until after you have had the opportunity to review the data, revise the field names and structure, and review the data with the new structure. If anything happens to your translated file, you can go back to the original file and create a new translated copy.

Exporting Data to a Foreign File

As an example of exporting dBASE data, you might want to transfer the data in the EMPLOYEE database to a Lotus 1-2-3 spreadsheet. As you transfer the data, each dBASE field is placed in a column of the spreadsheet and each dBASE record is entered across a row. To export the dBASE data follow these steps:

1. Press ALT-T to activate the Tools menu and type an E to select Export.
2. Highlight Lotus 1-2-3 from the options shown in Figure 8-13 and press ENTER.
3. Highlight EMPLOYEE and press ENTER.

dBASE creates the file EMPLOYEE.WKS. If you activate Lotus 1-2-3 and retrieve this file, you will notice that the columns are too narrow

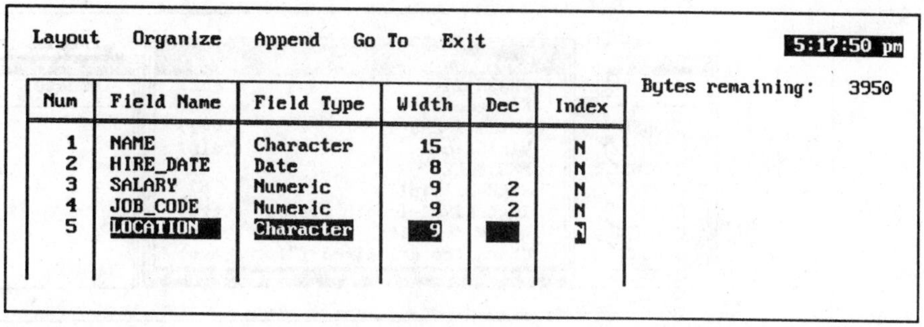

Layout Organize Append Go To Exit 5:17:50 pm

Bytes remaining: 3950

Num	Field Name	Field Type	Width	Dec	Index
1	NAME	Character	15		N
2	HIRE_DATE	Date	8		N
3	SALARY	Numeric	9	2	N
4	JOB_CODE	Numeric	9	2	N
5	LOCATION	Character	9		N

Figure 8-12 Revised database structure

Tip: Use the Translate Features of Lotus 1-2-3 to change 1-2-3 formats.

dBASE supports Lotus 1-2-3 files stored with the .WK1 extension. To translate an older Lotus 1-2-3 file with a .WKS extension, use the 1-2-3 Translate feature to convert the spreadsheet to a .WK1 file.

to display the complete entries in the column. You can use the **/Worksheet Column Set-Width** command in 1-2-3 to expand the width. Figures 8-14 and 8-15 shows some of the fields from the EMPLOYEE.WKS file after widening the columns and formatting the data. dBASE displays the Numeric fields in unprotected columns. On a color monitor, these fields are distinguished from the other data since they appear in green.

Changing the Settings

When you install dBASE you make some custom selections, but many default options are automatically chosen for you. The longer you work with the program, the more you will find that some of the default settings are not as appropriate for your needs as some of the custom options.

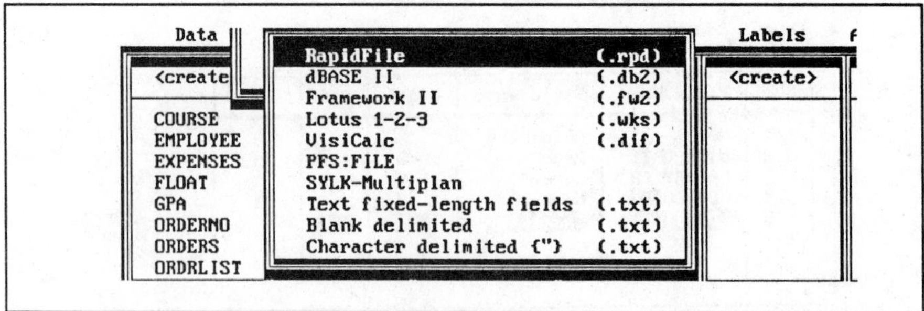

Figure 8-13 Export format selection box

```
A1: [W13] 'SSN                                                    READY

          A          B              C           D           E
1  SSN          LAST_NAME      M_INITIAL  FIRST_NAME  ADDRESS
2  215-90-8761  Jenkins        M          Mary        11 North St.
3  675-98-1239  Foster         G          Charles     67 Green Rd.
4  654-11-9087  Garrison       G          Henry       56 Chesaco Lane
5  888-99-7654  Larson         J          Karen       45 York Rd.
6  555-66-7777  Walker         P          Paula       123 Lucy Lane
```

Figure 8-14 Database exported to Lotus 1-2-3

You can make changes to both the operating system and dBASE defaults to customize your environment. If you make changes to the DOS environment, you will store these changes in the file CONFIG.SYS. DOS reads this file every time you start your computer.

Other customization changes are made to dBASE IV. These changes become permanent if you alter the CONFIG.DB file that sets the defaults each time dBASE is loaded into the machine. Other changes may only be required on a temporary basis. Rather than store the temporary changes in CONFIG.DB, they are made in dBASE through menu selections.

Changing CONFIG.SYS

You may already have a CONFIG.SYS file on your system. If so, you can make additional changes to it for dBASE IV requirements. If there is not a copy of CONFIG.SYS on the disk, you can create a new copy with the dBASE IV installation program or any editor that creates an

```
H1: [W10] 'ZIP_CODE                                                   READY

       H           I            J         K            L          M
1  ZIP_CODE  HOME_PHONE     HIRE_DATE MARITAL_ST  NUMB_DEPEN  HR_RATE
2     44124  (216)999-9999  20-Dec-88 M                    1     9.75
3     30912  (312)777-9999  24-Jan-89 S                    1     8.50
4     21237  (301)222-2222  05-Feb-87 M                    3    12.50
5     44132  (216)779-0000  07-Jul-82 M                    0    15.75
6     31245  (312)888-7777  15-Mar-84 M                    6    12.50
7
8
```

Figure 8-15 Database exported to Lotus 1-2-3

Tip: Check protection status before implementing protection.

Since Lotus 1-2-3 has a two-procedure protection process that involves selecting a protection status for cells and enabling protection, the actions taken by dBASE IV may conflict with your needs. You may want to reestablish the protect status for some of the Numeric fields if you plan to enable Lotus 1-2-3's protection, to safeguard your data.

ASCII text file. This file is stored on the root directory of your boot disk or hard disk. If you are not familiar with an editor, you can use the dBASE Tools Operations Edit command or simply use **COPY CON CONFIG.SYS** from DOS to copy each keystroke you enter to the file CONFIG.SYS. If you use the DOS approach when you finish entering commands, move to a new line and press F6 to generate ^Z. Press ENTER and DOS closes the file. You must reboot your system before the new options take effect.

The DOS default for the number of files open at one time may not be sufficient for a typical dBASE application that requires a database in addition to reports, indexes, and dBASE program files. To increase the files that can be open, Ashton-Tate recommends that you include a line in the CONFIG.SYS file that reads **FILES=40**. Although DOS accepts any number up to 255, it is unlikely that you will need this many. In addition, dBASE IV does not support any more than 99, making this the effective limit. Buffers supply space in memory that is reserved for reading and writing file information. Additional buffers speed the transfer of data between memory and disk. Enter the command **BUFFERS=15**.

Changing CONFIG.DB and Making Temporary Settings Changes to dBASE IV

The CONFIG.DB file is similar to CONFIG.SYS except that the parameters it contains pertain to dBASE rather than DOS. Like the CONFIG.SYS file, it is a text file. This means that you can create it with any editor, although dBASE supports a number of options that will automatically generate the command lines for you. You can select menu options during installation or by running a program called DBSETUP that makes changes to this file. Options like color, function key definitions, and memory allocation are stored in this file as parameters and configure dBASE each time it is loaded. You can also change some of these settings for the current session without affecting CONFIG.DB.

The entries in the CONFIG.DB file look just like the entries in CONFIG.SYS. They consist of a keyword, an equal sign, and the setting for the keyword.

The settings options offer a significant level of flexibility in the way that dBASE operates. The changes that you can make are beyond cosmetic changes that affect the appearance of the screen. The full complement of settings options that dBASE IV offers makes almost every aspect of the package customizable.

dBASE IV often provides several ways to make your changes. It can be a little confusing to remember which options are available for a given change. The main section on settings presented later in this chapter arranges them according to dot prompt SET commands. Although most of these commands change dBASE settings, there are a few SET commands that perform tasks, such as SET FILTER TO and SET INDEX TO, that you can perform through ASSIST selections. Table 8-2 allows you to determine the other methods available for each of these options. SET commands without entries in any of the columns are ones that are not generally thought of as true settings options. An example is the SET FILTER command that specifies which records appear.

Some settings cannot be changed unless the CONFIG.DB file is modified. The settings changes that are not supported through the dot prompt commands are covered with the options for making the changes. Settings for changing the key assignments and the display are also covered in more detail under the section discussing the method of changing the specific setting.

Options for Making Settings Changes

One method for changing settings is to access dBASE settings through the same Tools menu that you use to perform file tasks. After selecting Tools and Settings, you can decide whether deleted records should display, the format of the date display, whether the exact match feature

Table 8-2

	DBSETUP	*TOOLS SETUP*	*SET*
ALTERNATE	Files		Options/Files
AUTOSAVE	Database		Options
BELL	General	Options	Options
BLOCKSIZE	Database		
BORDER			
CARRY	Database	Options	Options
CATALOG	Files		Options
CENTURY	General	Options	Options
CLOCK	General		
COLOR			
CONFIRM	General	Options	Options
CONSOLE	Output		
CURRENCY	General	Options	
DATE	General	Options	Options
DEBUG	General		
DECIMALS	Output	Options	Options
DEFAULT	Files		
DELETED	Database	Options	Options
DELIMITERS	General		Options
DESIGN	General		
DEVELOPMENT	General		Options
DEVICE	Output		Options/Files
DISPLAY			
DOHISTORY			
ECHO	Output		
ENCRYPTION	Database		Options
ESCAPE	General		Options
EXACT	Database	Options	Options
EXCLUSIVE	Database	Options	Options
FIELDS	Display	Display	Options/Display
FILTER			
FIXED			
FORMAT			Files
FULLPATH	Database		Options
FUNCTION			
HEADING	Output		Options
HELP	General		Options
HISTORY	General		Options
HOURS	General		Options
INDEX			Files
INSTRUCT	General	Options	Options
INTENSITY	Output		Options
LOCK	Database		Options
MARGIN	Output	Options	Options
MEMOWIDTH	General	Options	Options
MENU			
MESSAGE	Display	Display	Display
NEAR	Database		Options

(continued)

Table 8-2 ***(continued)***

	DBSETUP	*TOOLS SETUP*	*SET*
ODOMETER	Output		
ORDER			
PATH	Files		
PAUSE	Output		Options
POINT	General		
PRECISION	General		Options
PRINTER	Output		Options
PROCEDURE			
REFRESH	Memory		
RELATION			
REPROCESS	Memory		
SAFETY	Files	Options	Options
SCOREBOARD	Output		Options
SEPARATOR	General		
SKIP			
SPACE	Output		Options
SQL	General		
STATUS	General		Options
STEP	General		
TALK	General	Options	Options
TITLE	Display	Display	Options
TRAP	General	Options	Options
TYPEHEAD	General		
UNIQUE	Database		Options
VIEW	Files		
WINDOW			

is in effect, and many other features that affect the way that dBASE IV works.

By exiting dBASE and executing the utility program DBSETUP you can access an even larger number of settings. The changes made through DBSETUP are permanent, whereas the ones made through the Tools menu are in effect only for the current session.

A third way to change the settings is to use the dot prompt command SET. This option allows changes beyond the Tools Setup menu features. Like the changes made through the Tools menu, these changes are temporary and are not available beyond the current session. Each command is entered using the keyword in the following section, such as SET DELETED ON or SET CARRY OFF.

The fourth option for making changes is entering SET at the dot prompt. dBASE displays a menu system, shown in Figure 8-16, that

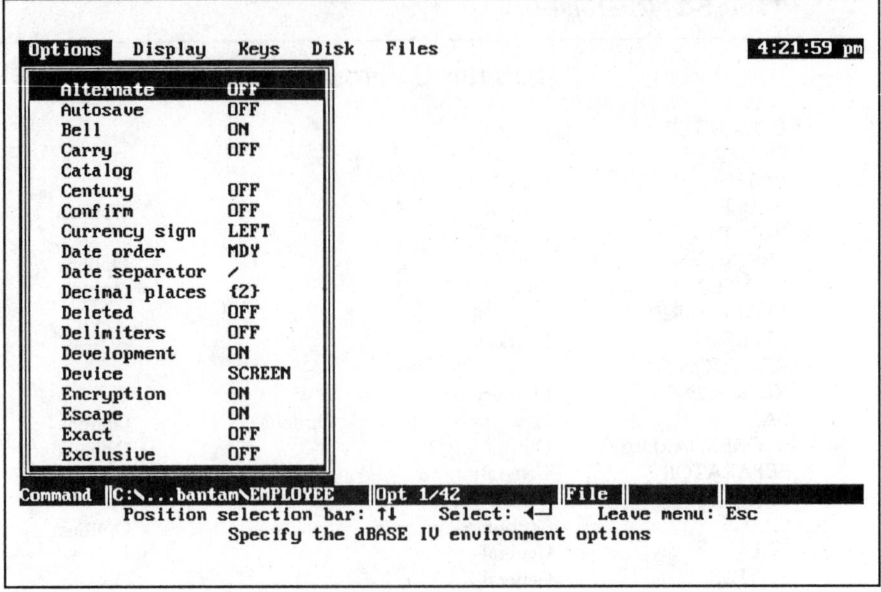

Figure 8-16 Initial SET command screen

allows you to change many of dBASE's settings. For now all you need to know is how to get to the dot prompt from the Control Center and how to return when you are through with the dot prompt entries.

The fifth way changes can be made is by inserting instructions in programs. The same SET commands that are entered at the dot prompt can be lines of program code. This technique is covered in detail in Chapter 16.

Making Changes to Settings from the Tools Menu You can change a subset of the settings through the Tools menu. The changes that you make to these settings are in effect until you exit dBASE. When you reload dBASE the default values for the settings established in installation or through DBSETUP changes are again in effect.

To change a setting option through the Tools menu follow these steps:

1. Press ALT-T from the Control Center to activate the Tools menu.
2. Type an **S** to select Settings. dBASE displays the menu shown in Figure 8-17.

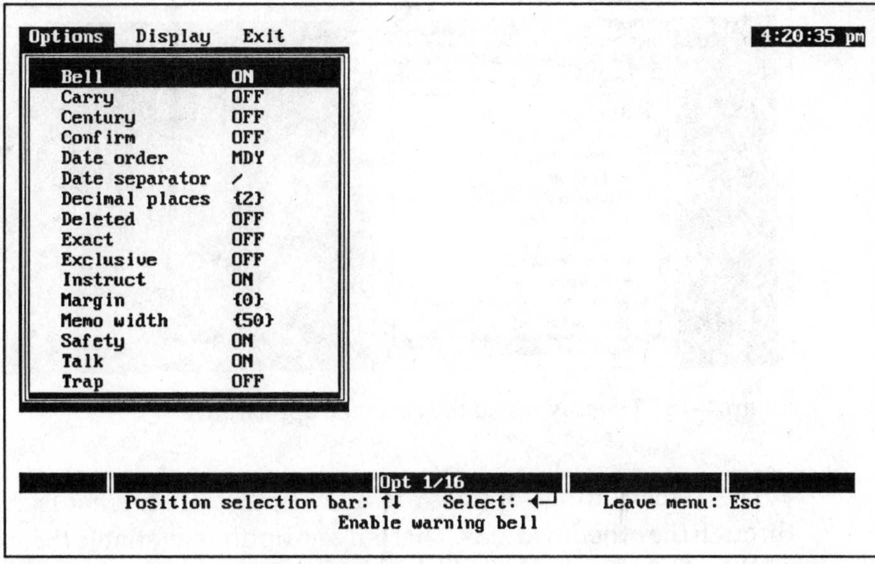

Figure 8-17 Tools Setting menus

3. To change one of the settings options, highlight the option and press ENTER. This will change it if it is a toggle switch setting of on and off. For other types of settings like number of decimal places, type the new entry and press ENTER.
4. Press ALT-E and ENTER to save the change and return to the Control Center.

The Tools Settings menu has a special menu for making changes to display options. The options are shown in Figure 8-18. To change a display setting through the Tools option:

1. Press ALT-T and type an **S** to select Tools Settings.
2. Press ALT-D and highlight the option that you wish to change and press ENTER. dBASE displays the menu shown in Figure 8-19 if you have a color monitor. With a monochrome monitor your selections are limited to Intensity, Underline, Reverse, and Blink.
3. Highlight the foreground and background option that you want, pressing TAB to switch between columns.
4. Press CTRL-END to finalize your selection.

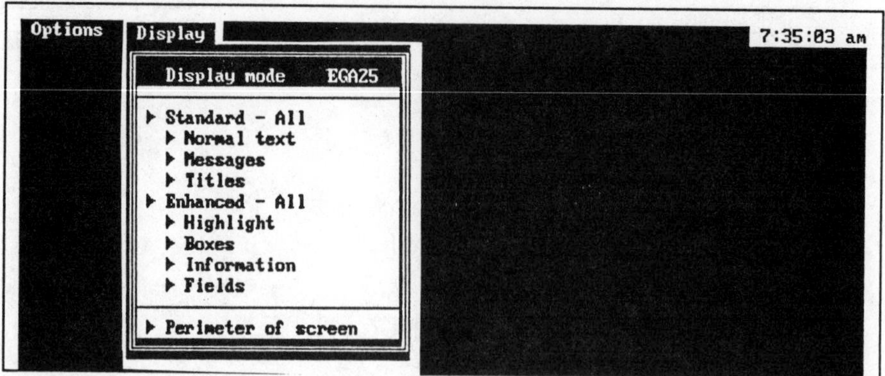

Figure 8-18 Display menu to set screen appearance

The Tools Settings options are more limited than what is available through the other methods. There are no options available through this method that are not available through other options for making settings changes. Since the options that are available from the Tools Settings menu are more limited than the other options, these options are marked with an asterisk in the section that shows the settings options.

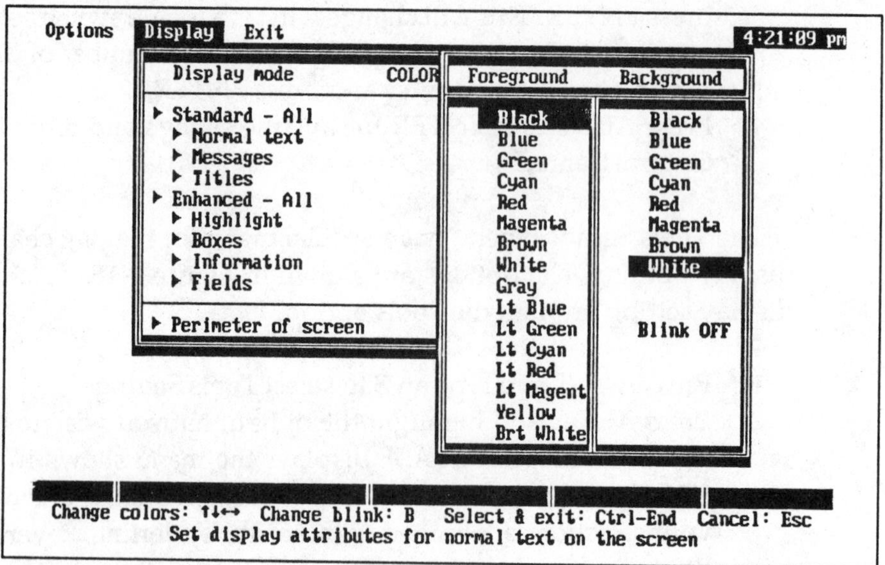

Figure 8-19 Selection box to set screen appearance

Using DBSETUP to Change Settings The changes that you make to the settings from the DBSETUP program remain in effect until you change them again. Using DBSETUP to make the changes alters the file CONFIG.DB that determines default settings each time dBASE is loaded.

Some settings can only be changed by altering CONFIG.DB. Table 8-3 lists these options along with the default value, an acceptable range of entries, and a brief description. You can either make the appropriate menu selections in DBSETUP to alter the default or add commands to the CONFIG.DB file that equate the keyword to a setting as in **WP=\WS\WS** which equates the word processor used to edit Memo fields to the Wordstar program file WS in the WS directory.

To run DBSETUP you must exit dBASE. Activate the main dBASE directory, unless you have placed DBSETUP in a different directory. Type **DBSETUP** and press ENTER. The menu shown in Figure 8-20 will appear. This menu allows you to access utilities, installation, an the option to change the CONFIG.DB file. If you decide to modify the existing configuration, the additional menu options shown in Figure 8-21 group many of the same settings that are available through the SET command. Changes are made with the same methods used for changing settings through the Tools menu.

Making Dot Prompt Entries to Change Settings The dot prompt is covered in detail in Chapter 10. For now, all you need to know is how to activate the dot prompt and enter your requests and return to the Control Center. To exit the Control Center to the dot prompt, press ESC and type a **Y**. Alternately, you can press ALT-E and type a **E**. To return to the Control Center, type **ASSIST** and press ENTER.

Commands are simply typed at the dot prompt. To use the SET option you type **SET** and press ENTER. The menu shown in Figure 8-16 displays to allow you to select the type of setting change you wish to make through the pull-down menus. A few of the options allow entries, but most toggle a setting on and off as you select them.

To use a specific SET command at the dot prompt, you type the command as in **SET DELETED OFF**. Any of the options in the list of SET commands can be entered at the dot prompt.

Table 8-3 Settings Changes that Must Be Made to CONFIG.DB

Setting	*Current Default*	*Acceptable Entry*	*Effect*
BUCKET	2K	1K to 31K	Change memory allocation block size.
COMMAND		any command	Starts dBASE and executes the command.
CTMAXSYMS	500	1 to 5,000	Sets number of compile symbols.
DO	20	1 to 256	Limits nested DOs.
EEMS	ON	ON/OFF	Accesses extended or expanded memory.
EXPSIZE	100	100 to 2,000	Size of memory buffer for compiled expressions.
FASTCRT	ON	ON/OFF	Eliminates "snow."
FILES	99	15 to 99	Max number open files.
GETS	128	35 to 1,023	Number of active @...GETs.
INDEXBYTES	2K	2K to 128K	Memory allocated to index buffers.
MVBLKSIZE	50	25 to 100	Sets memory variables to a block.
MVMAXBLKS	10	1 to 150	Blocks available for memory variables.
PDRIVER		any printer driver	Sets print driver.
PRINTER		4 printers	Configures up to 4 printers, 1 to 5 fonts.
PROMPT		19 characters	Changes dot prompt.
RESETCRT	ON	ON/OFF	Resets screen mode.
RTBLKSIZE	50	25 to 100	Run-time blocks for memory variables.
RTMAXBLKS	10	1 to 150	Run-time blocks available for memory variables.
SQLDATABASE		SQL database name	Designates SQL database.
SQLHOME		SQL path	SQL directory.
TEDIT		ASCII editor	Text editor.
WP		ASCII editor	Memo field editor.

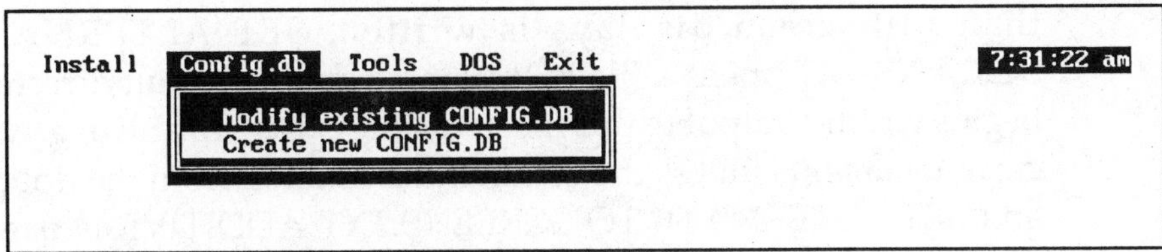

Figure 8-20 DBSETUP menus

Setting Options

The Settings options that follow are organized in alphabetical order and match the settings entries supported through dot prompt entries. In many cases these are identical to menu selections, although there are a few differences. For example, through DBSETUP and the Tools Setup option you can change the date separator character. This is not an option through the dot prompt. Another difference is the number of date order changes supported. Fewer options are available through Tools Setup than an alternative like SET.

ALTERNATE There are two Alternate commands. The first command SET ALTERNATE TO establishes a text file where output other

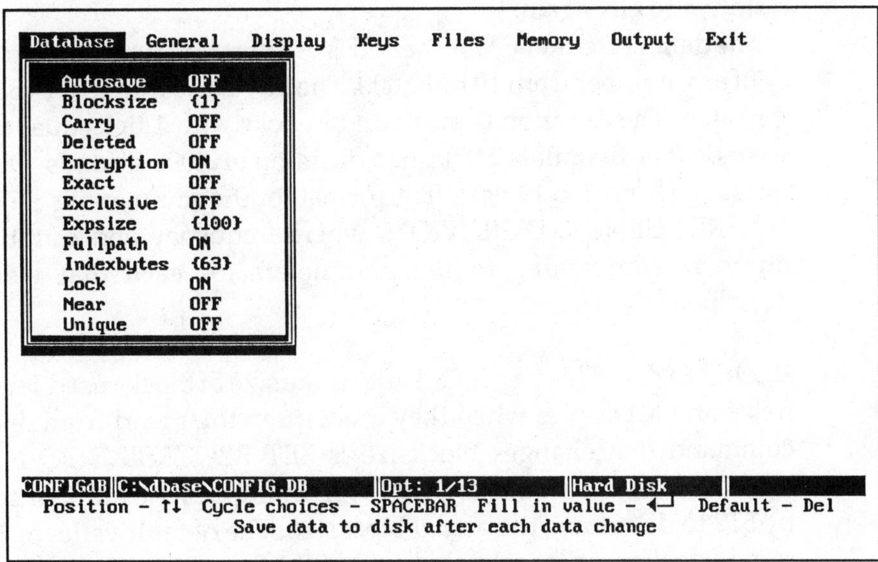

Figure 8-21 Menus for modifying CONFIG.DB

than full-screen displays is written. SET ALTERNATE TO SCREENS.TXT opens a file of this name on the default directory and begins writing output to this file. If the file exists, dBASE overwrites its current contents unless the command is entered from the dot prompt and SET ALTERNATE TO SCREENS.TXT ADDITIVE is used. This causes dBASE to add new data to the end of the file rather than overwrite it.

The actual recording of data in the field does not occur until the second command SET ALTERNATE ON is executed. You can stop recording output to the file with SET ALTERNATE OFF but the file remains open. To close the file, enter SET ALTERNATE TO and leave the filename blank. The file is also closed when you exit from dBASE.

AUTOSAVE The Autosave feature determines whether or not records are saved after each change to the record. With the default setting of OFF, changes are not saved until the record buffer is full. If you change the setting for Autosave to ON, records are saved after each change.

***BELL* Two commands affect the bell. You can turn it off or on, or set the tone for the bell. There is no need to change the tone unless the bell is on. If the default setting of ON has been changed to OFF, you can restore it to ON again.

The default frequency for the bell is 512 hertz. You can use a frequency of any number from 19 to 10,000. The lower the frequency the lower the pitch. The duration is measured in ticks with 1 tick equal to .0549 seconds. The default is 2 ticks or a duration of .1098 seconds. Duration can range from 2 to 19 ticks. The format for the command is SET BELL TO FREQUENCY, DURATION, where frequency and duration are numbers conforming to the parameters for each that were just described.

BLOCKSIZE This command affects the size of blocks used for Memo fields and MDX files when they are written to or read from disk. The command that changes blocksize is SET BLOCKSIZE TO Number where Number is from 1 to 32. dBASE multiplies the number selected by 512 to determine the actual blocksize. The default value of 1 is the same size that earlier releases of dBASE use.

BORDER The SET BORDER command changes the borders around menus, windows, and @ commands. The default is a single-line box but it can be changed to double lines, inverse video, customized, or none. To use double lines you would enter SET BORDER TO DOUBLE. For reverse video, the word PANEL is substituted for DOUBLE; to eliminate the lines, NONE is substituted.

You can also specify a border string that uses a different ASCII character for the four sides and the four corners. The ASCII character numbers are provided in the sequence needed to define top, bottom, left, right, upper left corner, upper right corner, lower left corner, and lower right corner with commas separating them. The entry might appear as SET BORDER TO 205,205,179,179,213,184,212,190.

****CARRY*** The Carry option allows you to carry entry values from one record to the next when you are adding records to a file. It functions the same as the Carry Edit option in custom forms except the SET CARRY ON command performs this carry function for every field in the record. The default is OFF.

You can also use the command SET CARRY TO and specify a list of field names separated by commas. This command automatically changes the Carry setting to ON and carries forward the fields in the list. If the word ADDITIVE is added to the end of the field list, the fields that are set ON are added to any other fields established with earlier commands.

CATALOG There are two commands that affect the use of a catalog to manage files in your dBASE system. The SET CATALOG ON command determines whether new files are automatically added to the current catalog. The SET CATALOG TO command allows you to specify the name of the catalog that you wish to use.

The default setting for SET CATALOG is OFF. As soon as you set a catalog to a specific catalog filename, this setting is changed to ON.

****CENTURY*** You can change whether the century portion of years are entered and displayed with the SET CENTURY command. The default setting is OFF, causing dBASE to use only two digits for the display and entry of years. If you change this setting to ON, a four-digit year is used.

CLOCK Two commands which affect the clock position and display. The clock always displays with full-screen commands in row 0 column 69. In other commands, you can change the default setting of OFF by entering SET CLOCK ON. You can use the SET CLOCK TO Row, Column to supply a row and column location. If entered without a row and column, the location 0,69 is used.

COLOR There are two Color options. One switches between monochrome and black & white if the system is equipped with both options. The other command makes specific color projections. Display options are probably better set from the Menu options for this purpose rather than the Set options, as color selections must be supplied with letter codes and the application of each code is dependent on the code's position within a list.

****CONFIRM*** The default setting of OFF for Confirm causes dBASE to move to the next field at the end of an entry if the field completely fills the width for the field. Setting it to ON causes the cursor to remain in the last position in an entry field until ENTER is pressed, even if the field completely fills the field width.

CONSOLE The SET CONSOLE command only works from within a program. It sets the screen display off when OFF is chosen for the setting. With the default setting of ON, all data displays on the screen. Even with Console set to OFF, error messages and safety prompts still display.

CURRENCY The SET CURRENCY TO command allows you to change the currency symbol from the default of $. You can use as many as nine characters to describe the new currency symbol. SET CURRENCY TO "YEN" uses YEN as the currency symbol. Storing and printing a number as currency may result in YEN567.8 You may also want to change the decimal point to a comma in your picture clause for consistency with foreign currency representations.

Displaying the currency symbol at the left side of a number is the default. You can use SET CURRENCY RIGHT to change the entry to the other side. You would then have 567.8YEN as the representation.

****DATE*** The format of this command is dependent on where you use it. At the dot prompt and in programs you will type SET DATE

Tip: Floating dollar sign can cause double letters.

If you plan to use a picture with floating dollar signs you will want to enter a blank as the first position in the currency entry; otherwise, dBASE will repeat the first letter as the float character. You might see a display like YYYYen6,78 without the blank in the first position of the currency definition.

followed by one of the date types from Table 8-4. If you select Tools Settings or DBSETUP for your change you can choose from a limited set of offerings with the option SET DATE ORDER. The default date is AMERICAN with the format mm/dd/yy.

The menu options also allow you to select Date Separator to change the character that separates the various parts of a date. You may prefer to use a hyphen (-) rather than a slash.

DEBUG The SET DEBUG command determines whether SET ECHO output goes to the screen or the printer. With the default setting of OFF, output is routed to the screen. If you set it to ON, output is routed to the printer.

**DECIMALS* The default setting is two decimal places. You can use the SET DECIMALS command with any number from 0 to 18. In Tools

Table 8-4 Date types supported

Date Setting	*Date Appearance*
American	mm/dd/yy
Ansi	yy.mm.dd
British/French	dd/mm/yy
DMY	dd/mm/yy
German	dd.mm.yy
Italian	dd-mm-yy
Japan	yy/mm/dd
MDY	mm/dd/yy
USA	mm-dd-yy
YMD	yy/mm/dd

Settings and DBSETUP the menu selection that you need to change is Decimal places.

DEFAULT The SET DEFAULT command establishes the default drive that controls the location where file operations for files without pathnames are saved and retrieved. This command is used from the dot prompt and programs. DBSETUP and Tools Settings use PATH and Change drive: directory respectively to make this change.

DELETED The Deleted setting determines how dBASE treats deleted records. With the default setting of OFF, dBASE displays deleted records with the other records. With DELETED ON, deleted records do not appear on the Edit or Browse screens or in reports.

DELIMITERS The Delimiters commands determine how field widths are shown in full screen mode. With the default setting of OFF, inverse video is used. If you enter SET DELIMITED ON, colons (:) mark the field width. If you prefer another character like braces, you can enter the characters as in SET DELIMITERS TO "{}". You must SET DELIMITERS ON before you see these special characters on the entry screen.

DESIGN The SET DESIGN option is ON as the default allowing you to press SHIFT-F2 to transfer to the design screen. If you enter SET DESIGN OFF, SHIFT-F2 no longer has this effect. Also, dBASE will not let you create or design objects.

DEVELOPMENT The default setting for DEVELOPMENT is ON, causing dBASE to check the creation dates and times on program files and compiled object files. With this setting ON, dBASE recompiles a program file to create a new object file if the object file is outdated. Using SET DEVELOPMENT OFF, causes dBASE to stop performing this check.

DEVICE The @...SAY commands are used to display output. They are entered in programs and are also created by dBASE as you create reports and forms. The SET DEVICE command allows you to direct the output of @..SAY commands to different devices. SET DEVICE TO SCREEN displays the output on the console. SET DEVICE TO

PRINTER prints the output. SET DEVICE TO FILE OUT.TXT writes the output to a text file, OUT.TXT.

DISPLAY The SET DISPLAY command performs two functions. It can select between a monochrome and color monitor as in SET DISPLAY TO COLOR or SET DISPLAY TO MONOCHROME. The command can also be used if you have a graphics card that supports either 25 or 43 lines of output. SET DISPLAY TO EGA25, SET DISPLAY TO EGA43, or SET DISPLAY TO MONO43 are all options.

DOHISTORY The SET DOHISTORY command has been maintained in dBASE IV for compatibility with earlier releases. The default setting is OFF.

ECHO The Echo command controls what happens when command lines are executed from a program or the dot prompt. The default setting is OFF. If you SET ECHO ON and SET DEBUG is off, the command lines display on the screen. If both commands are set to ON, the command lines are echoed to the printer.

ENCRYPTION Encryption is a method that stores data so that it is coded and not readable if the file is accessed from another program. In dBASE IV, Encryption is always used in conjunction with Protect. In fact, changing the default setting for Encryption to ON has no effect if the PROTECT command is not used. This feature is designed for multiuser systems where you need to hide the contents of files from others on the network.

ESCAPE SET ESCAPE has a default setting of ON. This allows you to press ESC to stop the execution of a program. SET ESCAPE OFF disables ESC and CTRL-S. If you want to leave a program without quitting, you must reboot your computer, which can damage dBASE files.

****EXACT*** Normally dBASE does not require two Character strings being compared to have the same length to be considered equal. With SET EXACT OFF, the strings "Smith" and "Smithe" are equal. As long as the first string matches the second string beginning on the left, it is not a problem that the second string has additional characters. SET

EXACT ON requires that two strings match from the left and have the same number of characters to be considered equal.

EXCLUSIVE The EXCLUSIVE option allows a user to request a file for exclusive use on a multiuser system. If SET EXCLUSIVE is set to ON for a file, no one else can use the file. With the default setting of OFF, multiple users can request the same file.

FIELDS The set commands for fields allow you to restrict access to all fields that are not supplied in a field list. This command can be applied to Calculated fields and can establish a Read-only status for a field.

dBASE has two field commands. The first, SET FIELDS, has a default value of OFF. With this setting in effect, dBASE does not even look for a field list. Before changing the setting to ON, you must enter one or more SET FIELDS LIST TO commands to make data available.

The list of fields are separated by commas. Each field that you wish to establish as Read-only is followed by a /R. SET FIELDS TO LAST_NAME, SSN, SALARY /R makes three fields available but salary cannot be changed since it is marked as Read-only. To restore all fields you can use SET FIELDS TO ALL.

FILTER The SET FILTER command applies a condition to control which database records display. The default is not to have a Query file active for the current database since initially no database is active. You can set the filter to a condition or to a Query file containing one or more conditions. To set the filter to a condition you might enter **SET FILTER TO HIRE_DATE > {01/15/89}**. In ASSIST mode, filters are established with View queries. Although these queries affect the other dBASE tasks you perform, they are not considered settings.

❑

Tip: File pointer must be moved to activate a filter in an open file.
Use the GO TOP, GOTO BOTTOM, or SKIP commands to move the pointer. This activates the current filter condition.

FIXED SET FIXED is another command that was retained in dBASE IV for compatibility with earlier releases of the product. The default setting is OFF.

FORMAT This command activates a format file to a custom screen for a database. SET FORMAT is a customization option that can be accessed easily from the Control Center Forms panel.

FULLPATH The SET FULLPATH command determines whether functions that return filename return the path as well as the drive and filename. The default setting is OFF, which does not include a path. If you change it to ON, this makes dBASE III+ code compatible with dBASE IV since it includes the paths for functions like MDX() and NDX().

FUNCTION The SET FUNCTION command is used at the dot prompt or within a program to program characters to a function key or key combination. From DBSETUP, SET, and the Tools Setup command, menu options support these assignments. To cause CTRL-F8 to generate the SET command you would enter SET FUNCTION Ctrl-F10 TO "SET;". The semicolon at the end is equivalent to pressing ENTER.

HEADING The SET HEADING option has a default entry of ON causing dBASE to place headings above output from the DISPLAY, LIST, AVERAGE, and SUM commands. Changing it to OFF eliminates the headings.

HELP The SET HELP command controls whether help screens offer assistance in the dot prompt mode. The default is ON, making help available. If you SET HELP OFF, mistakes do not activate help information.

HISTORY There are two history commands that affect whether dBASE stores commands in a history buffer and the number of commands that are stored. The defaults are SET HISTORY ON and SET HISTORY TO 20, which retains the last 20 commands in the buffer.

HOURS This option allows you to select from a 12- or 24-hour time display. The default setting is 12. To change this command you would enter SET HOURS TO 24.

INDEX This command can serve several purposes, both opening index files and establishing the index tag, or controlling NDX file. To open an index file, the syntax is SET INDEX TO CITY where CITY is the name of the index file that you wish to open. To open the MDX file EMPLOYEE and use the tag LAST_NAME you can enter SET INDEX TO EMPLOYEE ORDER LAST_NAME. If you want to open multiple index files, list the files separated by commas before you specify the order.

**INSTRUCT* This feature is set at ON initially to allow the display of menu boxes when panel entries are selected. If you set INSTRUCT to OFF, no prompts appear.

INTENSITY The default setting on allows for intensity differences between data that is displayed and data that is entered. If you use SET INTENSITY OFF, there is no difference in the data displayed by dBASE and the data that you enter.

LOCK The default setting is ON for SET LOCK to ensure that locks are applied to records in multiuser systems. These locks allow only one user to update a file at once, in an effort to prevent data collisions. SET LOCK OFF is not effective for all commands that access data. Some commands still restrict access even if the setting is OFF.

**MARGIN* The SET MARGIN command allows you to establish the left margin offset for printing. The default setting is 0. If you make a change, your change affects all dBASE output.

MARK This command changes the Date Separator character. You can effect this same change with the Tools Settings menu option Date Separator. Changing the date format to different countries can automatically change this indicator. SET MARK TO "-" changes the separator to a -.

**MEMOWIDTH* The default width of Memo field output is 50. With SET MEMOWIDTH to you can change the width to any number from 8 to 32000.

MENU SET MENU is ignored in dBASE IV. In dBASE III+, it determined whether or not cursor movement keys appeared on full screen displays. The default setting is Yes for dBASE III+.

MESSAGE This command allows you to display a custom message in line 23 of the screen display if SET STATUS is ON. You can enter a message of up to 79 characters. If you define this message line by entering SET MESSAGE TO and providing an expression, the message displays as soon as you enter SET STATUS ON. Full screens, such as ASSIST and EDIT, override your message and display their own message.

NEAR This command affects the way dBASE works when you cannot find an exact match for a record key. The default is OFF, requiring an EXACT match. If you enter SET NEAR ON, dBASE positions the record pointer on the record after the potential position of where a record would appear that matches the expression you are looking for.

ODOMETER Normally dBASE displays a record count on the screen. You can use SET ODOMETER to define the frequency with which this counter is updated for commands such as COPY and RECALL. The default value is 1 with a maximum setting of 200 allowed.

ORDER The SET ORDER command is used from the dot prompt to change the index file or tag that controls the order of the records. Rather than make this change from the Settings when using ASSIST, you can use the Organize menu from the database design screen that allows you to select Order records by. Entering SET ORDER TO without an entry restores the natural order.

PATH This command allows you to establish the path that dBASE follows to search for files that are not in the current directory. The DOS PATH command and the SET PATH TO command in dBASE are not

Tip: Don't overwrite message data.
You need to be sure that you do not define fields for line 23 in customized forms if you plan to use the message feature.

PATH command and the SET PATH TO command in dBASE are not the same since neither uses the other. This command does not affect the current directory or where newly created files are stored. If you are working in the directory C:\DBASE and enter SET PATH TO C:\DBASE\BANTAM, dBASE will look in C:\DBASE\BANTAM for files it cannot find in C:\DBASE.

PAUSE This command controls dBASE SQL commands. It stops the display of data after SQL Select has returned a screen full of information if it is set ON.

POINT The default character used for a decimal point is a period (.). You can change it to a comma or other symbol compatible with foreign numeric standards with this command.

PRECISION The default precision for the storage of numbers used in computations is 16. You can change this precision by entering SET PRECISION TO and following it with a number from 10 to 20.

PRINTER There are several print set changes. You can direct all output not created with @...SAY commands to a printer with SET PRINTER ON. To direct print output to a specific device you can enter SET PRINTER TO Device where Device is a printer port like LPT1 or COM1. You can also use SET PRINTER TO to direct output to a file.

When you redirect output you may also want to change the print driver that dBASE is using. You can change the print driver used by entering PDRIVER=Driver name where Driver name represents a print driver like ASCII.PR2 or HPLAS100.PR2.

PROCEDURE This command opens a procedure file. Although a procedure file can have many routines in it, only one procedure file can be open at one time. Entering SET PROCEDURE TO and supplying a filename opens the procedure file in the current directory. If the file is not in the current directory, you must specify the path. Entering SET PROCEDURE TO or CLOSE PROCEDURE closes the current procedure file.

REFRESH This command pertains to converted files on a network and allows you to determine the time interval between file checks when the file is edited or browsed.

RELATION The SET RELATION command is not a setting, it links two databases. When you create a View query that links two databases, a SET RELATION command is generated. Chapter 5 discussed linked files and they are also discussed in Chapters 10 and 16.

REPROCESS The reprocess option allows you to control the number of times that dBASE tries a network or record lock. With the default setting of zero and no ON ERROR command, dBASE retries indefinitely to lock the record or file. You can set this command to any value from -1 to 32,000. The -1 option also allows unlimited tries.

SAFETY This option can prevent you from accidentally overwriting a file. With the default setting ON, you receive a message to cancel or overwrite if the file already exists. If you enter SET SAFETY OFF, you disable dBASE's warning messages.

SCOREBOARD SET SCOREBOARD and SET STATUS can control the appearance of the keyboard indicators on the screen. With both set to OFF, the indicators do not display. With SET SCOREBOARD ON and SET STATUS OFF, line 0 is used for indicators like Ins, Del, Caps, and Num.

SEPARATOR The default setting uses a comma for a numeric separator. You can change it to a period or other character to conform with foreign currency requirements. SET SEPARATOR TO "." would provide a suitable separator for recording British pounds.

SKIP You can use the SET SKIP to use all the matching records in a detail file that is related to a master file.

SPACE The SET SPACE command controls the operation of the dot prompt commands ? and ??. The default setting is ON, which means that entering ?LAST_NAME, F_NAME displays as Smith Mary. If you enter SET SPACE OFF and repeat the command, the data displays as SmithMary.

SQL This command is not a setting but the way that SQL is activated. The default is OFF. Once SET SQL ON is entered, only SQL commands and a limited number of dBASE commands are supported.

STATUS The SET STATUS command controls the display of the status bar when you work from full-screen Edit commands, the dot prompt, or a program. If you use a CONFIG.DB file, the default is ON. Otherwise, the default is OFF.

STEP This command is used in debugging to halt program execution after each step. The default is OFF. You are given the option to proceed with the next step, suspend execution, or cancel execution after each step.

**TALK* The default setting for Talk is ON to allow you to see record numbers, memory variables and command results from APPEND, PACK, STORE and SUM operations. If you enter SET TALK OFF, command responses, compiler warnings, and other information are not displayed.

TITLE This option controls the catalog file title prompt. The default setting is ON, causing dBASE to prompt for a file description each time a file is added to a catalog. If you enter SET TITLE OFF, dBASE does not prompt for file descriptions.

**TRAP* This option has a default value of OFF. If you set it ON, a program error or pressing ESC automatically activates the debugger.

TYPEAHEAD The default size for the typeahead buffer is 20. This is the number of keystrokes you can enter before dBASE is ready to process them. You can set it to any number from 0 to 32,000.

UNIQUE This setting determines whether all records that match on key values are displayed. The default setting is OFF, which displays all records. Enter SET UNIQUE ON if you want to exclude duplicates.

VIEW The SET VIEW command is not a setting. It performs a View query.

Tip: Enlarge buffer if you hear a frequent beep.

If you type fast, 20 may not be large enough for the buffer. Increasing the buffer size to 50 should be more than adequate for your needs.

WINDOW The SET WINDOW command is used from the dot prompt to establish a default window for Memo fields. When working from ASSIST, this activity is handled in a forms design with the Display As option in the field description menu box.

Programming the Function Keys

You can assign commands to any of the function keys. These assignments function from the dot prompt mode but do not affect tasks in the ASSIST mode. You can change the keys from DBSETUP or by making changes to the CONFIG.DB file. To place the value in the CONFIG.DB file you would type the key, an equal sign, and an expression representing one of the valid dBASE commands that will be covered in greater detail in Chapter 10. You can assign F2–F10, SHIFT-F1–SHIFT-F9, and CTRL-F1–CTRL-F10. Examples are provided in Chapter 10 with dot prompt entries.

Configuring Print Drivers

You set the CONFIG.DB file to use the correct print drivers. You can do this during installation, during DBSETUP, or by editing the CONFIG.DB file. Although you were introduced to this idea earlier in a brief review of the DBSETUP options, you will want to spend a little more time on this important activity to take advantage of the ability to configure up to four print drivers with as many as five fonts available for each one. Once you have established the configuration for each of your printers, choosing the correct one for any print job can be accomplished with a simple selection from the print menu.

You can choose printers from DBSETUP's Hardware or Modify CONFIG.DB OUTPUT menus. The Printer option in the Output menu has four selections. Printer determines if the output default is the printer. The Driver option is the same as the Printer option for Modify hardware setup from the Install menu. You can select up to four print drivers. The PDriver option selects the default print driver. The Fonts option lets you enter up to five font names, begin codes, and end codes. The begin and end codes are in your printer manual.

Other DBSETUP Options

DBSETUP provides several useful utilities under its Tools menu. You can use these options to review the configuration for your system, check disk usage, and test disk performance.

The Configuration options are especially useful if you are designing applications to work on client's systems. At a glance you can check the total memory, parallel and serial ports, the current video mode, the central processor chip, and other configuration options without opening the machine.

The Tools command to display the disk usage provides the sector byte size, the number of disk surfaces, and the sectors per track. It also tells you the number of tracks, cluster size, number of sectors per cluster, the operating system used to format the disk, and the root directory's capacity for file entries. The size of the disk system area, boot area, file allocation table, and root directory are provided. The space in use, available, and unavailable due to bad sectors are also listed.

The Tools option for testing disk performance is a test that is beneficial when used on a regular basis. You will want to compare current times against previous performance checks. As the information on your disk becomes increasingly fragmented, performance can decline by 50% or more. A utility program like MACE Utilities can help you eliminate this problem.

GETTING STARTED

➤ You will want to try a few of the Tools commands as well as some customization options. First try the Tools options that allow you to access DOS by following these steps:

1. From the Control Center press ALT-T to select the Tools menu.
2. Type a **D** to select the DOS utilities.
3. Press ALT-D to select DOS.
4. Type a **P** to select Perform a DOS command.
5. Type **TYPE C:\DBASE\CONFIG.DB** and press ENTER substituting your drive and directory where CONFIG.DB is stored in place of C:\DBASE.

   The contents of CONFIG.DB will list on the screen or DOS will return the message File not found if you have not created the file.
6. Press ENTER to return to the menu.
7. Press ALT-D to select DOS again.
8. Type **G** to select Go to DOS.
9. Type **TYPE C:\DBASE\CONFIG.DB** and press ENTER substituting your drive and directory where CONFIG.DB is stored in place of C:\DBASE.

   The contents of CONFIG.DB will be listed on the screen, or DOS will return the message File not found if you have not created the file. The DOS prompt C> returns to the screen when DOS finishes processing your current request. You can continue to enter DOS requests.
10. Type **EXIT** to return to the menu.

You will want to try the file-marking capabilities available with the Files List screen. You will use these features to mark and copy files. Follow these steps:

1. If the Tools DOS utilities menu is not on the screen, press ALT-T and type a **D**.
2. Press ALT-F to select the Files menu.
3. Type a **D** to select Display only.
4. Type **EMP*.*** and press ENTER.

   The Files List displayed on the screen changes to display only those files that begin with EMP.
5. Move the highlight to EMPLOYEE.DBF and press ENTER to mark the file.
6. Repeat step 5 for EMPLOYEE.DBT and EMPLOYEE.MDX.
7. Press ALT-O to select Operations.
8. Type a **C** to select Copy and an **M** to select Marked files.

9. Place a blank formatted disk in your A or B drive and type **A:** or **B:** depending on which drive you are using. Press CTRL-T to remove the remaining entry.
10. Press ENTER and type **EMPLOYEE.*** and press CTRL-END.
11. If the files that you are copying exist on the target disk you will be prompted to determine whether you want to overwrite each one. Type an **O** to overwrite each file.
12. Press ALT-E and ENTER to Exit from the DOS utilities menu.

Although settings changes are normally best done to meet your own needs, try a few to ensure that you can access the various options for making changes. You will start with the Tools Settings option since dBASE is active. Follow these steps:

1. Press ALT-T and type an **S** to select settings.
2. Use the RIGHT ARROW key to move across the options reading through the lists.
3. With Exit highlighted press ENTER.
4. Press ESC to exit to the dot prompt and type a **Y**.
5. Type **SET** and press ENTER.
6. Highlight each of the menu options to see the types of settings that are accessible from these menus.
7. Press ESC.
8. Type **QUIT** and press ENTER.
9. Change directories if you are not in the directory that contains DBSETUP. For example if the directory with this program is C:\DBASE and you are in another directory on drive C, type **CD \DBASE** and press ENTER.
10. Type **DBSETUP** and press ENTER. Press ENTER a second time after viewing the copyright notice.
11. Highlight the various menu options to see the options available.
12. With the Config.db option highlighted, type an **M** to modify the existing Config.db file. Press ENTER to accept the drive and directory to read CONFIG.DB from or enter a new drive and directory and press ENTER.
13. Highlight the menu options to see the available selections.
14. Press ALT-E and type an **A** to select Abandon changes and exit.
15. Press ALT-E and ENTER to exit the program.

CHAPTER 9

Working with Catalogs

In the preceding chapter you learned about dBASE IV files. Catalogs are one type of dBASE file that can help you organize all of your other dBASE files. Like the file directories you learned about in Chapter 8, catalogs help you organize your information. Unlike directories, their influence does not extend beyond the dBASE program.

In this chapter you will learn about the features that catalogs offer and how to use them effectively. You will learn about some of the problems that can occur with catalogs so that you will be prepared to prevent or correct them.

What Catalogs Offer

A catalog is nothing more than a special type of database file that contains entries about a related group of databases, views, reports, forms, and other dBASE objects.

Catalogs use the file directories you learned about in the last chapter to locate the files on a disk. A file can only be in one directory, but it can have an entry in multiple catalogs. As an example, you might have a file for labels that can be used with your personnel application for the mailing of W2 forms that can also be used to generate mailing labels for your accounts receivable application. Since you will probably have two catalogs to group the information by application, it would be appropriate to have an entry for the label file in both catalogs.

Catalogs can contain entries for files that are stored on different drives or directories. When you alter a catalog entry, you are not changing the actual file, only the entry in the catalog file. When you change the directory where a file is stored, you are changing important information about the file that will affect where DOS looks for the file on your hard disk. When you place a file in another catalog, you still have only one copy of the file. When you place a file in another directory, you must create another copy.

Catalogs provide a way to organize all the information related to one dBASE application. As you create new files in dBASE, a catalog entry is created for the new file. These catalog entries associate the supporting files with a database. Unlike directories, catalogs do not record where the data is stored. Catalogs record only the filename and other related information. When a catalog records information for a form, label, or report file, the catalog also records the database or view that the form or report was used with last.

Deleting a catalog entry only removes the name of the file from the Control Center panels. The entry is still stored on a disk so you can use the file in another catalog. Also, you can always add the file back to the current catalog if you want to work with it again.

Organizing Your Data

Once you have an idea of the applications that you want to implement with dBASE, you can create catalogs to organize your files. Using a catalog for each application limits the files that the catalog must keep track of to the minimum needed to perform the application tasks.

Minimizing the number of entries in a catalog allows you to load dBASE more quickly and improve its performance with many tasks. Also, if you are sharing the computer with others, maintaining separate catalogs allows each person to focus on the information that they need for their applications and minimizes accidental changes or deletions to files that pertain to an other individual's applications.

Creating Catalogs

Once you decide on the catalogs that you want to create, the actual creation is a simple process. To create a catalog, press ALT-C for catalog

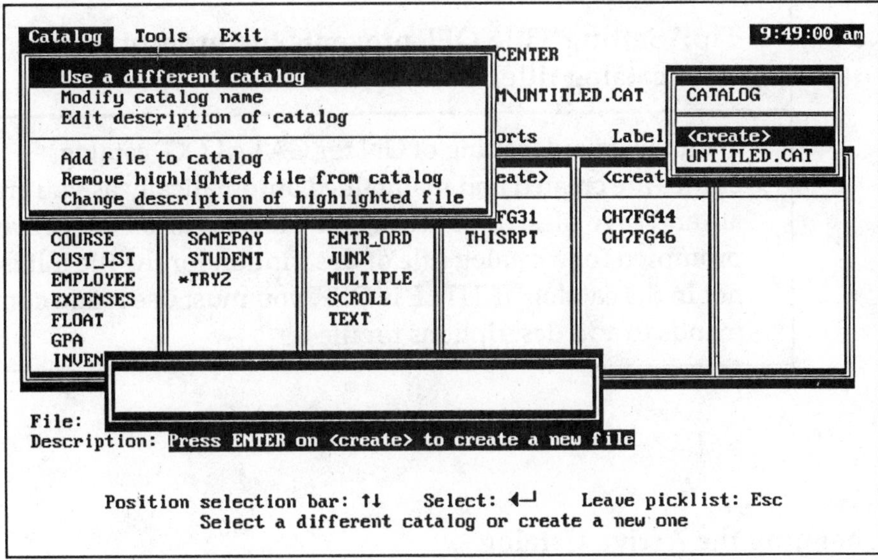

Figure 9-1 Selection box for using a different catalog

and type a U for Use a different catalog. dBASE displays the box shown in Figure 9-1. Press ENTER to select <create>. dBASE displays the box shown in Figure 9-2. Enter the catalog name and press ENTER. Since dBASE stores catalog information in a file, the filename must follow the DOS conventions for filenames. A catalog filename can consist of one to eight letters, numbers, or underscores. While you can use other symbols, the underscore can act like a space in the filename and does not conflict with DOS's use of other symbols. dBASE creates an empty catalog.

When you create objects, dBASE adds them to the current catalog. The catalog automatically keeps track of which forms, labels, and reports belongs with the databases and views.

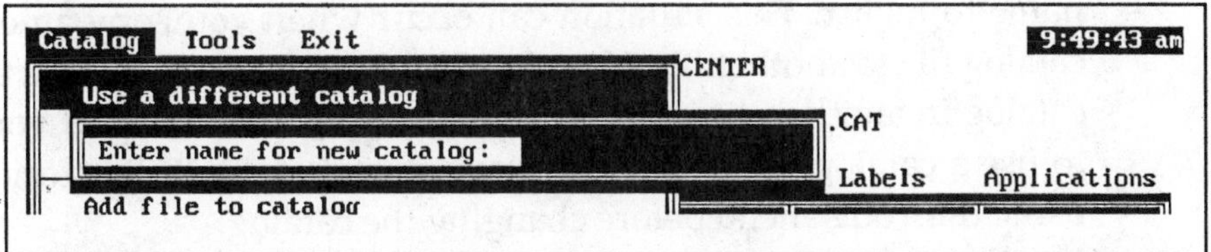

Figure 9-2 Prompt for catalog name

Tip: Setting Title OFF prevents the prompt for a catalog title.

With the default setting of ON for CATALOG, catalog entries are created and maintained automatically as you create and save files. If the setting for TITLE is also ON, you are prompted for a catalog title or description for the file if it is not in the catalog. If TITLE is OFF, you must use menu commands to add descriptions for files.

Changing the Active Catalog

To switch to an existing catalog, press ALT-C for the Catalog menu and type a **U** for Use a different catalog. dBASE IV displays a list of the catalogs. When you highlight a catalog that contains a catalog description, dBASE displays the description in the horizontal box like the one in Figure 9-3. Highlight the one that you want and press ENTER.

dBASE knows which catalogs are available by looking at the entries in CATALOG.CAT. This is a special catalog that keeps track of the other catalogs. You do not use this catalog directly, but as you add and delete catalogs, dBASE updates this one. dBASE automatically creates CATALOG.CAT when it creates UNTITLED.CAT, when you initially load dBASE.

If a catalog does not appear in the list but you know it is in the current directory, you can activate the catalog by selecting <create> when dBASE prompts for the category name and typing the name of the existing catalog name. dBASE finds the existing catalog and makes it active. Once you have activated a catalog, dBASE adds the catalog name to its list. This situation can occur when you copy an existing catalog file to another file. You should not perform these steps to use a catalog in another directory since it corrupts the catalog. If you want to use a catalog in another directory, switch default directories first, using the Tools menu before changing the catalog.

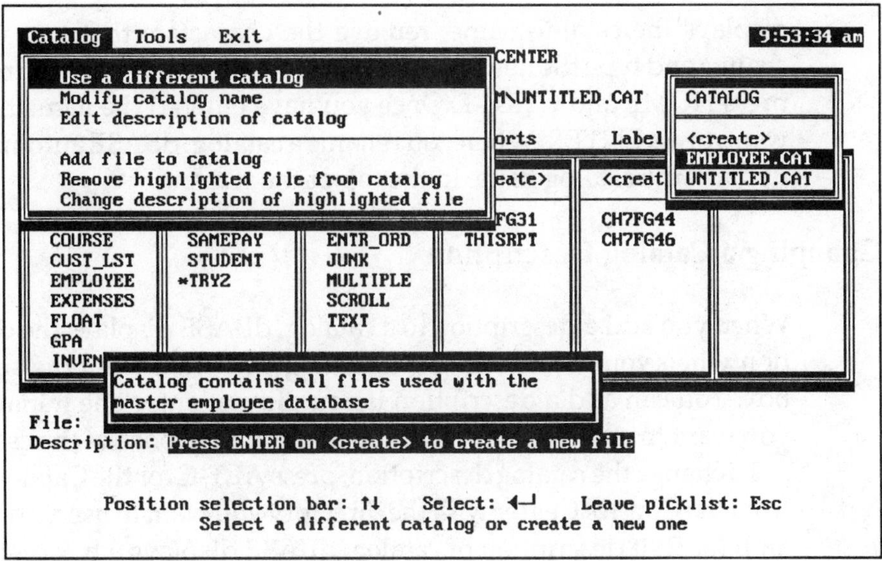

Figure 9-3 Catalog description

Modifying Names and Descriptions

The first catalog that dBASE creates is called UNTITLED. You can change the name of this catalog and other catalogs that you create to ensure that the catalog's names provide information about the files they manage. You can also add a catalog description, which appears when you change catalogs.

Renaming a Catalog

When you rename a catalog, you are renaming the file that contains the catalog information. Just like renaming other files, renaming a catalog keeps the catalog contents the same but changes the name that you use to refer to a catalog. Therefore, all of the files listed in the original catalog and all of the associations between databases or views and forms, labels, and reports automatically appear in the renamed catalog. The renamed catalog is actually the same catalog with a different name. To change a catalog name, press ALT-C for the Catalog menu in the Control Center and type an **M** for Modify catalog name. When dBASE displays the catalog name, remove the characters that you want to change and type the new letters. If you want to remove the entire entry, press HOME and CTRL-T. Once you have entered the name that you want, press ENTER. When you rename a catalog, dBASE automatically updates the catalog name in the top of the screen.

Changing a Catalog Description

When you add a description to a catalog, dBASE displays the description when you are selecting the catalog you want from the selection box. You can add a description if you did not enter one initially or if you want to change it to reflect the changing purpose of the catalog.

To change the catalog description, press ALT-C for the Catalog menu from the Control Center with the directory you want to use active. Type an **E** for Edit description of catalog. dBASE displays a box displaying the current catalog description, if one exists. Type or modify the description. Once you have the description that you want, press ENTER to finalize it and return to the Control Center. If you want to remove the original entry, press HOME and CTRL-Y. You can press DEL or CTRL-T to delete a character or word at a time. Pressing INS switches you between Insert and Typeover mode.

Adding and Removing Files

As you build catalogs for your applications, you will want to change which files appear in a catalog. You will want to add and remove files. When you add files from a catalog, dBASE also lets you add a file description. When you remove files from a catalog, you can also delete the files from the disk.

Adding Files to a Catalog

When you create databases, views, forms, reports, and labels, dBASE creates other types of files that it uses for these objects. When you add files to a catalog, dBASE only lets you add database files, or the design and compiled files of other objects. For example, when you create a form, you create files with .SCR, .FMT, and .FMO extensions. If you add this form to a catalog, dBASE only lets you add the .SCR or .FMO file. The one that you select depends upon whether you want to modify the design.

Catalogs can include up to 200 files. To add a file to a catalog, move the highlight in the Control Center to the panel where you want to add a file. Press ALT-C for the Catalog menu and type an **A** for Add file to catalog. dBASE displays all of the files in the current directory with the default extensions for the current panel. The default extensions that dBASE uses for each panel are shown in Table 9-1. If you want a file that is in another directory, you can select the parent directory or another level of subdirectory from the list of file names. Once you highlight the directory entry and press ENTER, a list of the appropriate file types from this other directory is displayed. When you have highlighted the file that you would like to add, press ENTER. dBASE displays a box for you to enter the filename description. Enter the description that you want to appear when the added file is highlighted and press ENTER.

When you add forms, labels, query, or reports, you can add either a design or a compiled file. dBASE also has code files that you cannot select since dBASE automatically uses them when you select the design or compiled file. When you have both the design and the compiled file, you normally should select the design file. Although you can add both the design and compiled files to a catalog, the compiled file is replaced if the design file is recompiled. After the design file is recompiled, the compiled selection becomes unavailable. You may want to select the

Table 9-1 Default Extensions Shown in the Control Center

Panel	*Extension*	*File Type*
Data	.DBF	Database
Queries	.QBE .QBO	View Query
Queries	.UPD .UPO	Update Query
Queries	.VUEd	BASE III+ view
Forms	.SCR .FMO	Form
Reports	.FRM .FRO	Report
Labels	.LBL .LBO	Label
Applications	.APP .PRG .DBO .PRS .EXE .COM	Applications Generator

❑ **Tip: Number of files in a catalog affect performance.**

Every time you change catalogs or load dBASE, dBASE loads the catalog information and confirms that each file exists. Keeping the number of files in a catalog small reduces the time you must wait for dBASE to set up a catalog.

compiled version of the query, form, label, or report if you do not want it to be changed. For example, if you are creating a catalog for someone and you want to prevent them from changing a form, label, or report, you would add the compiled version, since they can use the form, label, or report but they cannot change it. If you have included the compiled and the design files of the same form, label, or report, you will want to remove one of them from the panel.

Changing and Adding File Descriptions You may want to add file descriptions to files in a catalog that do not have a file description. You may also want to modify an existing file description as the file's purpose in a catalog changes. Since file descriptions are stored with the catalog, a file can have a different description for each catalog the file is in. To change or add a file description, highlight the file where you want to add a description or modify the existing one. Then, press ALT-C for the Catalog menu and type a **C** for Change description of highlighted file. dBASE displays a box displaying the current file description, if one exists. Type or modify the description. Once you have the description that you want, press ENTER to finalize it and return to the Control Center. You can remove the original entry by pressing HOME and CTRL-Y. You can press DEL or CTRL-T to delete a character or word at a time. Pressing INS switches you between Insert and Typeover mode.

Removing Catalog Entries

To remove a file from a catalog, move the highlight in the Control Center to the file. Then, press ALT-C for Catalog and type an **R** for Remove file from catalog. dBASE will prompt you with the box shown in Figure 9-4. Type a **Y** to remove the file from the catalog. Then dBASE

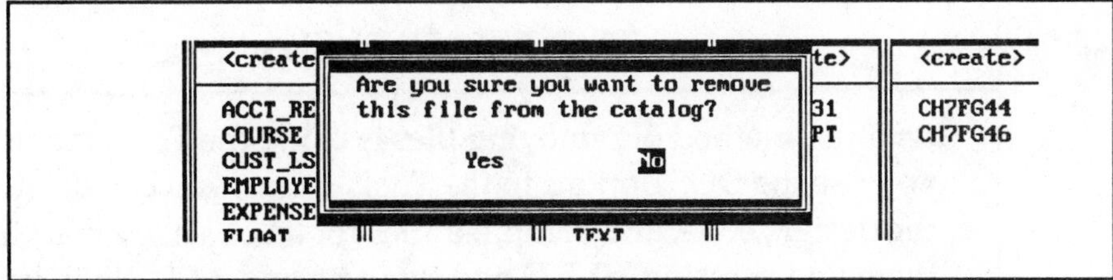

Figure 9-4 First confirmation box for removing a file from a catalog

displays the box shown in Figure 9-5. Type an **N** if you want the file to remain on the disk. Type a **Y** if you want to delete the file. If you delete the file, you cannot retrieve it unless you have a utility program that restores files that you have erased. You can also remove a file from a catalog by highlighting the file that you want to remove and pressing the DEL key. Then type a **Y** to remove the file from the catalog and an **N** or a **Y** to keep or delete the file on the disk. When you delete a file, you are only deleting the filename shown below the Control Center panels when you highlight the file. The disk may still contain code or compiled object files.

File Changes that Affect Catalogs

When you delete a file other than by deleting it from the current catalog, dBASE updates the catalogs the next time the catalog is used. When dBASE loads a catalog, it looks for each file. If dBASE cannot find a file in a catalog when it loads or changes catalogs, it removes the file's information from the catalog. For the same reason, catalogs loose track of files when they are renamed. Since dBASE does not update the

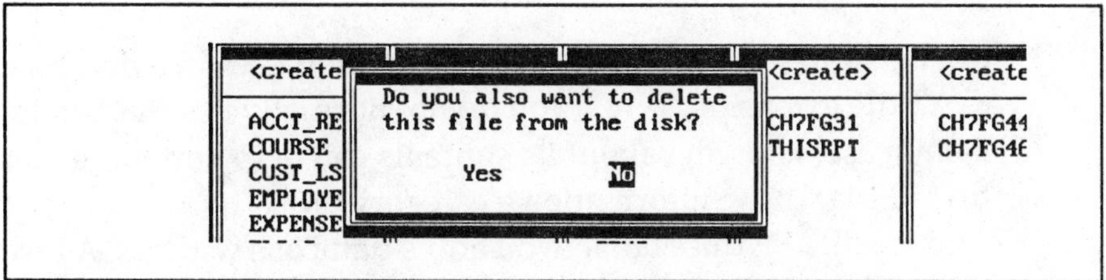

Figure 9-5 Second confirmation box for removing a file from a catalog

❑

Tip: Removing files.
Another method of removing files is using the Tools menu. If you use the DOS options in the Tools menu, you can delete the design, code, and compiled files for an object by marking them and pressing ALT-O and typing a and a **M**. When you return to the Control Center, dBASE removes the catalog entry.

catalogs for the new filenames (even when you use the Tools menu to rename them), renaming files removes their references in catalogs.

One way of renaming a file so a catalog keeps track of the file is by copying the object to a new filename and deleting the old object. To rename a file this way, highlight the file that you want to rename in the Control Center and press SHIFT-F2. When the design screen appears, press ALT-L for the Layout menu and type an **S** for the Save option. While each object uses a different name for this option, they all start with S and they all perform the same function. When dBASE displays a filename, press the BACKSPACE to remove the old filename and type a new one. Press ENTER. dBASE saves the object using the new name. Once dBASE is finished, press ESC and type a **Y** to return to the Control Center. Then, highlight the old name, press DEL, and type a **Y** twice. Renaming a file this way maintains the catalog entry. If you use this option to copy a database, you also copy the Memo field file and any production indexes. If you use this option to copy a query, form, report, or label, you also copy the code and compiled files.

Catalog File Structure

dBASE stores the information that a catalog uses in a database with a .CAT file extension. While you do not normally use this catalog file as a database, knowing about its contents can help you understand how dBASE stores the information a category uses.

Since dBASE does not let you add a database with a .CAT extension in the Control Center, you must use the dot prompt to view this file. To view this file, press ESC and type a **Y** to leave the Control Center.

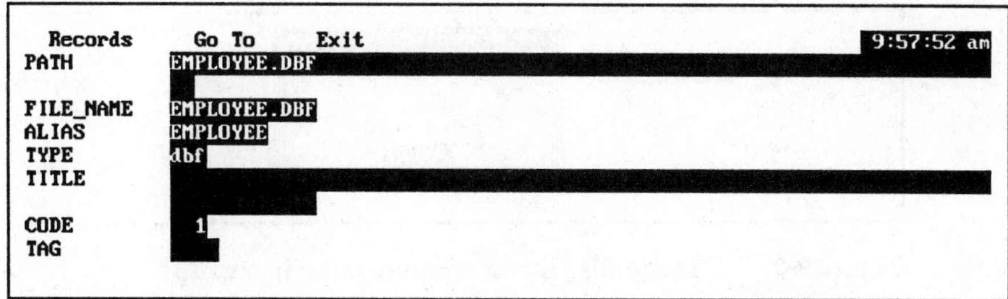

Figure 9-6 Sample record in a catalog

Then, type **SET CATALOG TO** and the catalog name, and press ENTER to select the catalog. Since dBASE provides 10 different areas to work with databases and it uses the tenth one for the current catalog, type **SELECT 10** and press ENTER to switch to the work area containing the catalog. To look at the data, type **EDIT** and press ENTER. The screen looks like Figure 9-6 which shows the record for one object dBASE includes in the catalog.

The PATH field describes the DOS path statement dBASE uses if the object is not contained in the same directory as the catalog. The FILE_NAME field is the DOS filename. It includes the filename and the extension. The ALIAS field stores the database filename or the database's alias if one is assigned. For other objects, this field is blank. The TYPE field stores the default extension for the object. For example, if the object is a report, the TYPE field contains .FRM even if the filename uses the extension .TMP. The TITLE field contains the file description. The CODE field contains a number that describes the database or view associated with the object. dBASE assigns a unique non-zero number to each database or view. This number also appears in records for forms, labels, or reports associated with the database or view. This number tells dBASE which files dBASE places above the line in each panel when you activate a database. This number is 0 for application programs and forms, labels, and reports that are not associated with a database. The most frequent reason forms, labels, and reports are not associated with a database is that they are added to the catalog and their design has not been modified while this catalog is open. The TAG field is not used.

Press ESC to return to the dot prompt. You do not want to change the data unless you are correcting a mistake, such as reestablishing a link between a form, label, or report and the database or view it uses.

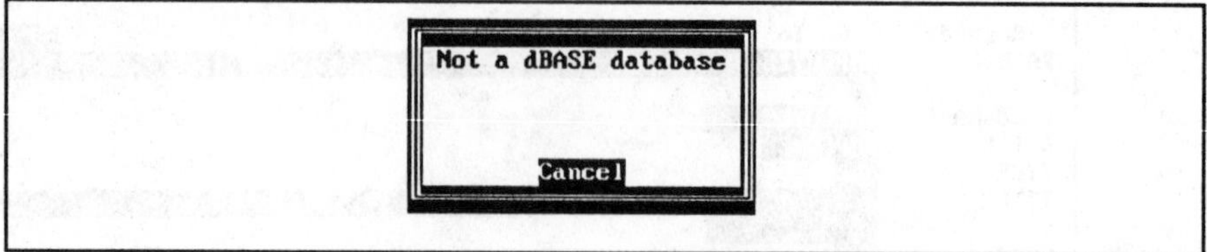

Figure 9-7 Message displayed when catalog is corrupt

Type **SELECT 1** and press ENTER to return to the first work area. Type **ASSIST** and press ENTER to return to the Control Center.

If a Catalog File becomes Corrupt

A catalog can become corrupted, such as by trying to use a catalog in another directory or editing and saving the catalog file using an editor that adds special characters, or that removes special characters that dBASE needs. dBASE lets you know the catalog is corrupted by displaying the message in Figure 9-7. If you do not have a backup, you may need to re-create a catalog. You can use one of two steps to re-create a catalog. When you re-create a catalog, you lose the file associations between the database or views and its forms, labels, and reports since dBASE sets the value for Code in the catalog to 0. You can use one of two steps to re-create the associations. The steps that you select depend upon the number of files involved in a catalog.

If your catalog contains only a few files, re-create the catalog by creating a catalog and adding the files to it. To create a catalog, press ALT-C and type a **U** for Use a different catalog. Press ENTER to select <create>. Type the catalog name and press ENTER. Add a catalog description and press ENTER. Once you have created the initial blank catalog, you can add the files that you want to the catalog by pressing ALT-C, typing an **A** for Add file to catalog, highlighting the file you want, and pressing ENTER. If you want to add a description, type the description in the box dBASE displays. Press ENTER.

If your catalog contains many files and they are primarily in one directory, you can add all the files in the directory to an UNTITLED catalog, delete the ones that you do not want, and rename the catalog. First, rename the existing catalogs in the directory to use a different extension, such as CT1. Then load dBASE and let dBASE create a new UNTITLED catalog for you that contains the database files, the design and code files for forms, labels, and reports, and the larger application-generated files with .APP file extensions. Once dBASE has created a new UNTITLED catalog, rename the catalog by pressing ALT-C and typing an **M** for Modify catalog name. Replace UNTITLED with the new catalog name and press ENTER. Then, remove the files in the catalog that you do not want to include by highlighting the file, pressing DEL, and typing a **Y** and an **N** to remove the file from the catalog without deleting the file from the directory. If you use this method to re-create the directory, you must add the file descriptions later. After you create this UNTITLED catalog, rename the catalog files with a different extension to the .CAT extension, using the Tools menu or the DOS RENAME command.

One method of reestablishing the associations between databases or views and their forms, reports, and labels is saving the files again. To reassociate reports, labels, and forms with a database or view by saving the files again, activate the database that you want to associate the files with. Then, move to the report, label, or form that you want to associate with the database or view and press SHIFT-F2 to enter the design screen. When the design screen appears, press CTRL-END to save the file. When you return to the Control Center, the form, label, or report appears above the line in the panel. You must repeat this step for each file that you want to reassociate.

To reassociate forms, labels, and reports by modifying the catalog file, press ESC and type a **Y** to leave the Control Center. When the dot prompt appears, type **SET CATALOG TO** and the catalog name. Press ENTER. This activates the catalog and puts it in the tenth work area. Then, type **SELECT 10** and press ENTER to switch to the tenth work area. Since the catalog file is a database, you use the same steps you use to modify a database.

To re-create the associations between objects, you must know code numbers that dBASE assigns to the databases and views since they are unique to each catalog. You can quickly print a list of the objects in the catalog by typing **LIST FIELDS FILE_NAME, CODE TO PRINT** and pressing ENTER. dBASE prints a list of the object filenames and the codes they use. When the dot prompt reappears, type **EDIT** and press ENTER. The screen looks like Figure 9-6. To re-create the file associations, move to the record for the record for the form, label, or report that you want to reassociate with a database or view and replace the 0 in the CODE field with the CODE for the appropriate database or view.

You must perform this step for each object that you want to reassociate with a database or view. If you want to add file descriptions at this time, move to the TITLE field and enter the filename description for the current object. When you are done, press CTRL-END. When the dot prompt returns, type **SELECT 1** and press ENTER return to the first work area. To return to the Control Center, type **ASSIST** and press ENTER. dBASE updated the catalog to include the changes that you have made while out of the Control Center.

GETTING STARTED

➤ You will want to try a few of the Catalog commands to build a catalog to contain your files for the EMPLOYEE database. To create an EMPLOY catalog and add a description, follow these steps:

1. From the Control Center press ALT-C to select the Catalog menu.
2. Type a **U** to select Use a different catalog.
3. Press ENTER to select <create>.
4. Type **EMPLOY** for the catalog name and press ENTER.
5. Press ALT-C to select the Catalog menu.
6. Type an **E** to select Edit description of catalog.
7. Type **Catalog contains all files used with the employee master database** and press ENTER for the catalog description.
8. Press ALT-C, type a **U**, and type an **E** to highlight the EMPLOY catalog. Notice the description appears in the box at the bottom of the screen. Press ESC twice to remove the Catalog menu box.

Once you have created a catalog, you will want to add files to it. To add files to the EMPLOY database, follow these steps:

1. Move the highlight to the Data panel
2. Press ALT-C to select the Catalog menu.
3. Type an **A** to select Add file to catalog.
4. Highlight EMPLOYEE.DBF and press ENTER.
5. Type **Employee master database** when dBASE prompts for a file description and press ENTER.
6. To add a query file, press the RIGHT ARROW to move to the Query panel, press ALT-C, type an **A**, highlight a file, and press

ENTER. Since you will remove this file from the catalog later, it does not matter which one you add. Press ENTER again when dBASE prompts you for a file description.

7. To add a form design file, press the RIGHT ARROW to move to the Forms panel, press ALT-C, type an **A**, highlight ENTEREMP.SCR, and press ENTER. Press ENTER again when dBASE prompts you for a file description.
8. To add a report design file, press the RIGHT ARROW to move to the Reports panel, press ALT-C, type an **A**, highlight EMPLOY01.FRM, and press ENTER. Press ENTER again when dBASE prompts you for a file description.

Once the catalog contains some files, you can start to use them. You can make additional enhancements to the catalog by following these steps:

1. Move to the Data panel.
2. Activate the EMPLOYEE database by pressing the DOWN ARROW once and ENTER twice. Notice that the ENTEREMP form and the EMPLOY01 report are not automatically activated for the database.
3. Press the RIGHT ARROW twice and the DOWN ARROW once to move to the ENTEREMP form.
4. Press SHIFT-F2 and CTRL-END to save this form while the EMPLOYEE database is activated.
5. Press the RIGHT ARROW and the DOWN ARROW to move to the EMPLOY01 report.
6. Press SHIFT-F2 and CTRL-END to save this form while the EMPLOYEE database is activated.
7. Press the LEFT ARROW twice and the DOWN ARROW once to highlight the Query file. Since this Query is not needed for the EMPLOYEE database, press DEL. When dBASE prompts if it should remove the file from the catalog, type a **Y**. When dBASE prompts if it should remove the file from the disk, type an **N**.
8. Rename the catalog by pressing ALT-C and typing an **M** for Modify catalog name. Press the BACKSPACE four times to remove .CAT. Type **EE** and press ENTER to change the catalog name to EMPLOYEE.

PART IV

Using Advanced dBASE IV Techniques

CHAPTER 10

Using Dot Prompt Entries

All of the tasks you have asked dBASE to complete to this point have been requested through the Control Center and other menu entries. This method of interfacing with dBASE IV is frequently referred to as the ASSIST mode.

dBASE IV offers a second method of making requests that can provide both flexibility and time savings. This method is referred to as the dot prompt mode. It is called the dot prompt mode because the screen on which you make your entries is blank except for a dot (.) and the status line. You can complete any of the tasks you have accomplished through the menu system and many others, through the use of dot prompt entries.

The full set of commands that are acceptable at the dot prompt are listed in Appendix C. The commands that correspond to frequently used Control Center options are shown in Table 10-1. Beginning to familiarize yourself with these commands can be the first step toward dBASE programming since the commands and syntax in dBASE programs are exactly the same.

Basics of Dot Prompt Entries

Once you master the syntax of dot prompt entries you will find that they are easy to use. You will have many more options for dBASE requests than presented with the menu system. You will also be able to

Table 10-1 Menu Options and Associated Dot Prompt Commands

Menu Task	*Sample Dot Prompt Command*
Add records	APPEND
Browse or edit	EDIT or BROWSE
Create database	CREATE EMPLOYEE.DBF
Modify database	MODIFY STRUCTURE
Use a database	USE EMPLOYEE
Order records	USE EMPLOYEE ORDER SSN
Create or modify a report	CREATE REPORT LIST_EMP
Print a defined report	REPORT FORM LIST_EMP
Create or modify labels	CREATE LABELS MONTHLY
Create an index	INDEX ON LAST_NAME TO LSTNME
Create or modify a query	CREATE QUERY OVER_50
Create or modify a screen	CREATE SCREEN NEW_EMP
Sort a database	SORT ON SSN TO NEWFILE
Draw a box	DEFINE BOX FROM 3 TO 30 HEIGHT 5 AT LINE 12
Mark records for deletion	DELETE FOR SALARY > 90000
Unmark records for deletion	RECALL ALL
Remove a file from	ERASE EMPLOYEE.DBF
Search for an index	FIND Smith SEEK "SMITH"
Position on top record	GO TOP
Execute a macro key	PLAY MACRO
Seek a match for a key	SEEK "Smith"

reuse previous requests by reviewing the last 20 requests entered or by saving the entries and executing them as a program.

The Dot Prompt Screen

The dBASE screen with the dot prompt visible is shown in Figure 10-1. You can access this screen from the ASSIST mode by pressing ESC and typing a Y. Another option is pressing ALT-E and pressing ENTER to exit to the dot prompt.

To return to the Control Center from dot prompt mode, type **ASSIST** or **ASSI** and press ENTER. To exit to DOS, type **QUIT**.

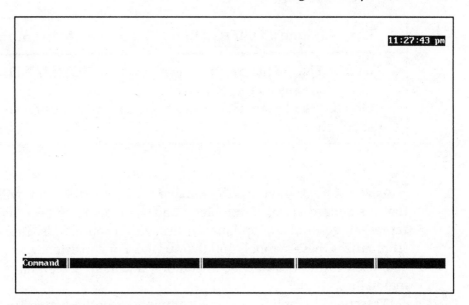

Figure 10-1 Dot prompt screen

Syntax of dBASE IV Commands

The syntax of the commands that you enter at the dot prompt range from a simple one-word entry to a complex phrase. At a minimum, each request must contain a verb or a command. For some requests like ASSIST this is sufficient. There are no options to add to the basic request. Other requests support the use of either required or optional parameters to more explicitly define your requirements to dBASE.

If you make a mistake when entering a command at the dot prompt dBASE presents the box in Figure 10-2. You can choose to cancel your entry, edit the entry, or see a help screen. If dBASE can determine the command you were trying to use, a help box with the proper command syntax will display. Otherwise, it will present a help menu for your selection.

For some of the commands, you can use the command by itself to perform one task, yet combine it with parameters to perform a completely different action. The command DISPLAY works like this. When used alone it displays the current record in the active database. When used with one of its optional parameters it can display all the records in the database, display a specific group of fields, or display only those records that meet your specifications.

Tip: Change CONFIG.DB to start at the dot prompt.

The CONFIG.DB file contains the instruction, COMMAND = ASSIST. Use any editor to remove this line from the CONFIG.DB file and dBASE will begin each new session at the dot prompt.

As you study the syntax of commands in Appendix C you will find that a standard set of terminology and symbols have been used to represent required and optional entries within commands. Table 10-2 summarizes these symbols and their usage. For consistency, the symbols used in the dBASE documentation and help screen have been maintained.

Dissecting the options for one command may be helpful in comprehending the many variations offered by just one command. Figure 10-3 shows the help screen that dBASE provides for the TOTAL command. This screen shows the full range of parameters that can be used with the command. In addition to the many variations taken individually, it is possible to combine options in many different ways.

For the command shown in Figure 10-4, **TOTAL ON** is the command verb. The entry **<key field>** indicates that the entry is required and must be for a field used to sort or index the database. All the records with the same value in the key field will be used when computing totals. The next required word is **TO**, which must be followed by a filename. The file will have the same structure as the current database and will contain one record for each new entry in the key field.

Tip: Change the appearance of the dot prompt.

Although the dot is the standard prompt for dot prompt mode you can use any character or phrase that you wish. You can change the prompt by entering **PROMPT=** in your CONFIG.DB file and following it with from 1 to 19 characters.

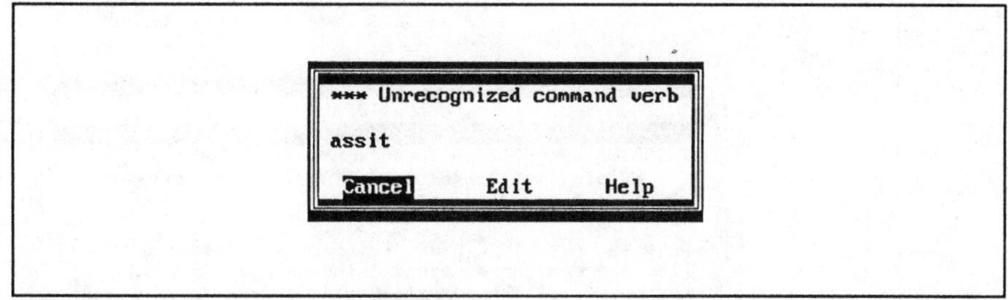

Figure 10-2 dBASE response to dot command

Table 10-2 Symbols and Other Substitutions for dBASE Commands

Command Symbol	*Meaning*
[]	Encase an optional entry.
<>	Encase a required entry.
/	Separates either or choices.
alias name	The work area being used for a database.
array name	The name assigned to a one- or two-dimensional array with a DECLARE statement.
condition	A logical expression or a comparison.
expC	Character expression.
expD	Date expression.
expF	Float expression.
expN	Numeric expression.
expression list	One or more expressions separated by commas.
field list	A list of valid field names from the current database or view separated by commas.
filename	A one- to eight-character name for an existing file or one you plan to create.
key field	A field used to sort or index the database.
list	A group of entries separated by commas.
literal key	An entry used for an index key.
mdx file list	A list of .MDX files for the current database.
mdx tag	The tag assigned for the MDX index.
memvars	Memory variables.
record number	A record number
window name	A name assigned to a window

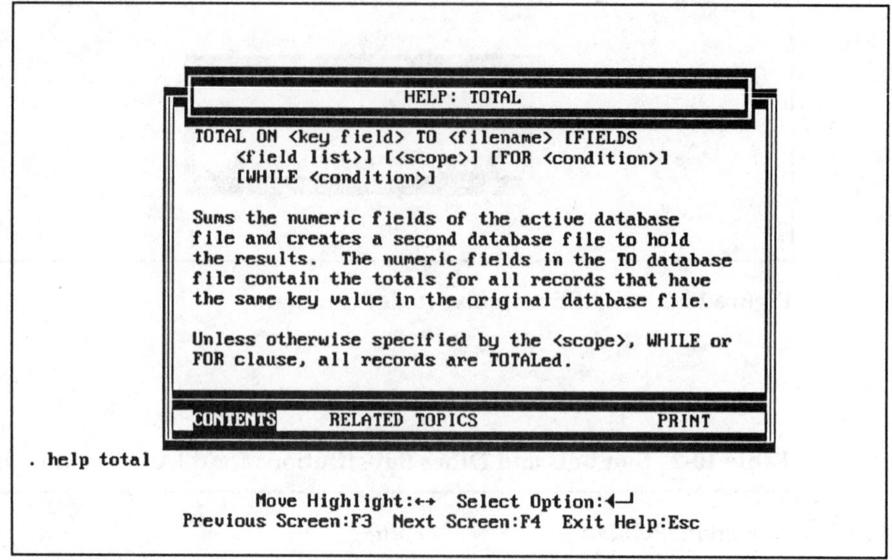
HELP: TOTAL
TOTAL ON <key field> TO <filename> [FIELDS
<field list>] [<scope>] [FOR <condition>]
[WHILE <condition>]
Sums the numeric fields of the active database
file and creates a second database file to hold
the results. The numeric fields in the TO database
file contain the totals for all records that have
the same key value in the original database file.
Unless otherwise specified by the <scope>, WHILE or
FOR clause, all records are TOTALed.
CONTENTS
RELATED TOPICS
PRINT
. help total
Move Highlight:←→ Select Option:←┘
Previous Screen:F3 Next Screen:F4 Exit Help:Esc

Figure 10-3 Help screen for TOTAL

The command will total all the Numeric fields in the database unless the **Fields <field list>** option is used. If you use a field list, it should contain fields that are Numeric or Float with each name separated from the others by commas.

The optional **<scope>** entry allows you to control the records that are affected by the command. You can use ALL, RECORD x for a single record, NEXT x to specify x records beginning with the current record, or REST to include all the records from the current position to the end of the file.

The **FOR <condition>** option can be a logical expression or a comparison to process records for which the condition is true. If a logical expression is used, dBASE will perform the command for all records where the expression is evaluated as true. Entering .NOT. EOF() will cause dBASE to execute the condition until the end of file is reached. If a comparison like SALARY > 50000 is used, the command will also be performed for each record that satisfies the condition.

The **WHILE <condition>** causes dBASE to repeat the command until the first occurrence of a false condition. It will not check the remaining records after the first false is encountered.

```
Programmable function keys:
F2        - assist;
F3        - list;
F4        - dir;
F5        - display structure;
F6        - display status;
F7        - display memory;
F8        - display;
F9        - append;
F10       - edit;
Press any key to continue...
Command  D:\...bantam\EMPLOYEE    Rec 1/5         File
```

Figure 10-4 Assigning commands to function keys

Using the Function Keys at the Dot Prompt

You have used the function keys to perform many tasks in dBASE. Now that you are working at the dot prompt you will find that these keys have new functionality that conforms with your needs in this environment. The keys shown in Figure 10-4 have each been assigned a command. When you press the key it enters the command shown in the figure, at the dot prompt. You can continue typing to add additional entries to the line or press ENTER to have dBASE process the command. Later you will learn how to assign additional commands to key combinations that are not being used.

Making Long Dot Prompt Entries

Entries made at the dot prompt cannot exceed 255 characters. If you want to continue an entry to a second line you can use a semicolon at the end of the first line to serve as a continuation indicator. If you need to make longer entries you can use up to a maximum of 1,024, if you open an edit window while at the dot prompt. To open this window, press CTRL-HOME. A window like the one in Figure 10-5 will appear for your entries. You will find this window convenient for entries between 70 and 255 characters in length as well. Even though they can be accommodated at the dot prompt, the window makes it much easier since you can see the entire entry on the screen at one time. You also

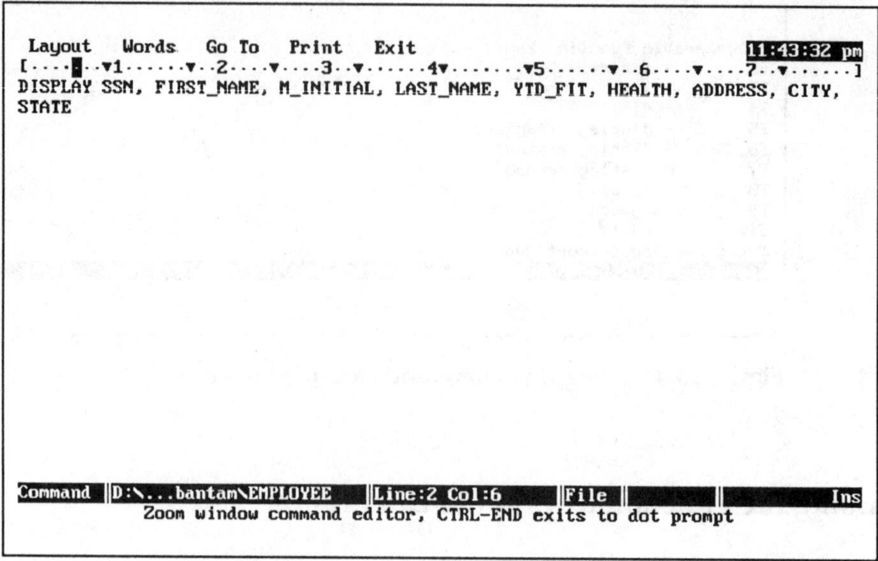

Figure 10-5 Window for long entries

have the menu options available through the edit window that can search and perform other tasks. When you are ready to execute the entry in the edit window press CTRL-END.

Performing Computations at the Dot Prompt

dBASE also supports calculations at the dot prompt. To tell dBASE that you want to display the value of one or more expressions, start your entry with ? or ??. When you use the single question mark, dBASE displays the expression list that you enter then generates a carriage return and line feed, and displays the result on the next line. When you use a double question mark, dBASE displays the expression you type then prints the results without generating a line feed or carriage return.

You can use any of the standard dBASE arithmetic or logical symbols in your computations. The priority of these operators is shown in Table 10-3. For more complex expressions you might want to use parentheses for grouping, since operations within parentheses are always performed first. You can use constants, field names, and functions. Memory variables are also supported, but they will be introduced later.

Table 10-3 dBASE Operators in Priority Sequence

Type	*Operator*	*Meaning*
Math	+ -	Positive and negative
	^	Exponentiation
	* /	Multiplication and division
	+ -	Addition and subtraction
String	+	Joins strings with trailing spaces between strings left intact.
	-	Joins strings with trailing spaces added at the end of the last string.
Relational	<	Less than
	>	Greater than
	=	Equal
	# or <>	Not equal
	<=	Less than or equal to
	>=	Greater than or equal to
	$	Contains
Logical	.AND.	Logical and
	.OR.	Logical or
	.NOT.	Logical not

Expressions using a combination of operators will treat Math or String as the highest priority followed by Relational then Logical operators.

Relational operators all have the same priority.

Parentheses are not actually operators but can be used for grouping to change the priority. Operators within the innermost parentheses are performed first.

An expression containing several operators with the same priority will be evaluated from left to right.

As an example of a computation with constants, you can calculate a price extension for 25 items at $4.29. You enter ? 25*4.29 and press ENTER. dBASE displays 107.25.

Reviewing and Reexecuting Commands

dBASE maintains a history of the dot prompt entries that you make. The default setting is to store the last 20 entries. You can review these entries by pressing the UP ARROW key to move from the most recent to the earliest command maintained within the 20 entries. If you want to move back down through the list toward the more recent entries, you can press the DOWN ARROW key.

When a command from the dot prompt history is displayed on the line with the dot prompt, you can execute it again. The only step required is to press ENTER. This allows you to reexecute any of the last 20 commands entered by using the UP ARROW until the desired command is current and then pressing ENTER. You can also modify any of these commands before executing them.

To see the entire set of history entries, type DISPLAY HISTORY and press ENTER. Commands from this display cannot be executed unless you use the ARROW keys to make them active on the dot prompt line. As you review the commands you will find that commands that you canceled or edited when prompted for a correction by dBASE will still appear in the history along with the corrected command.

Storing Dot Prompt Entries

A little advanced planning will allow you to store the dot prompt entries in a file. This will allow you to review the commands at a later time. You may even decide to use some of your entries as a basis for a program later.

To store the commands follow this procedure:

❑

Tip: Change the default for the number of history commands stored.

You can use the SET HISTORY command to alter the number of commands stored in the history buffer to any number from 0 to 16,000. Using SET HISTORY to 0 clears the history buffer.

1. Enter SET ALTERNATE TO PROGFILE where PROGFILE is the name of the .TXT file that dBASE will use to store you entries.
2. Enter SET ALTERNATE ON.
3. Enter SET TALK OFF to prevent the recording of record numbers, memory variables, and the results of commands like APPEND.
4. When you are finished recording, enter SET ALTERNATE OFF and SET TALK ON.

Using Dot Prompt Entries to Create Databases and Display Data

You can perform all of the Assist tasks for creating and modifying databases that you have used in previous chapters. Many of the menus that are presented are identical to the screens that you used with commands that performed the identical tasks from Assist.

Creating a New Database

To create a new database, you enter **CREATE <filename>** at the dot prompt. If you want the file in the current directory, only the filename needs to be specified, as in CREATE EMPLOYEE. If you want the file in a directory other than the current directory, the entire path should be specified as in CREATE D:\DBASE\PAYROLL\EMPLOYEE. dBASE displays the design screen shown in Figure 10-6.

❏ **Tip: Edit commands to create executable instructions.**

> You need to use the editor to remove the dots at the beginning of each command before attempting to execute the file with DO. Change each dot to a blank space. You will also want to change the filename extension to .PRG with the DOS or dBASE RENAME command.

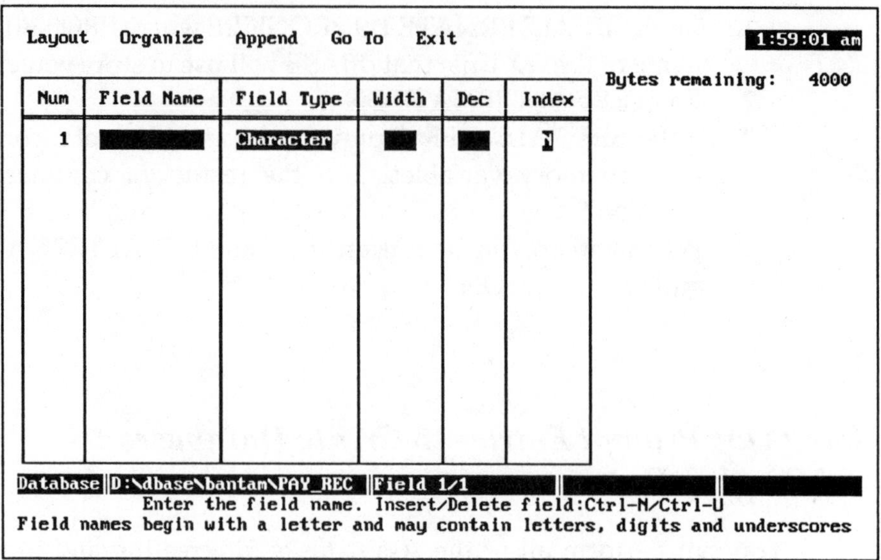

Figure 10-6 Design screen for creating a database

Once the database design screen is on the screen, you proceed exactly as you did when designing a database from ASSIST mode. When you are finished entering fields and definitions, you should press CTRL-END or select Exit and Save. dBASE will prompt you concerning adding records just as it does when you create a new structure from ASSIST mode. If you type a Y, you will be able to add records immediately. When you finish entering the last record, press CTRL-END to return to the dot prompt. If you do not wish to enter records immediately you can type an N.

Opening and Closing a Database

Just as when you use the ASSIST mode, certain commands required that a database be open. The USE command will open a database and close a database that may be open in the current work area. If you are working in the default work area 1, it will close the database in this area leaving open databases in areas 2, 3, and 4. This is consistent with selecting another database file to use from Assist mode since you are automatically working in work area 1. It is entered as **USE <database filename>**. The current drive, directory, and the .DBF extension are assumed. As with the ASSIST mode, the .DBT file for memo fields is automatically opened if it exists. The production .MDX file will be available as soon as you open the database but the database will be in natural order or the order in which you entered the records. To use one of the index tags in the production MDX file you can use the ORDER clause as in USE EMPLOYEE ORDER SSN to use the SSN tag. If you wish to open an index file other than the production MDX file you must always specify the file you wish to use with the INDEX clause, **INDEX <.mdx or .ndx file list>**, as in USE EMPLOYEE INDEX EMPLOYEE.MDX. If you want a specific index tag to control the order of the file, you can make the change when opening the file rather than using an Organize command like you do in ASSIST mode. The syntax addition is **ORDER <.mdx tag> [OF <.mdx filename>]** as in USE EMPLOYEE INDEX EMPLOYEE.MDX ORDER SSN. The use of [OF <.mdx filename>] is optional. If you are using the .ndx files from dBASE III+ you can enter **ORDER <.ndx filename>**.

You can use the CLOSE command to close open files. You must select one of the following keywords to specify which files you want dBASE to close: ALL/ALTERNATE/DATABASES/FORMAT/INDEX/PROCEDURE. To close all databases, you would enter CLOSE DATABASES.

Modifying a Database

To modify the structure of a database, the file must be open. Once opened, the MODIFY STRUCTURE command can be used to modify a database structure. Like most other commands, this command can be abbreviated as the first four letters of each command word, MODI STRU.

The same precautions concerning changing field names and other field attributes apply to the dot prompt entries as to changes made through ASSIST. You will use the same full-screen window for your changes as you used with ASSIST.

To review the structure of the current database, type LIST STRUCTURE or DISPLAY STRUCTURE. You can also use the abbreviation DISP STRU. Adding TO PRINTER or TO FILE allows you to direct the output of this command to a printer or file. The TO FILE option requires a filename.

Adding Records and Changing Records

There are a number of options for entering and reviewing data when you work at the dot prompt. These options parallel the ones available from the ASSIST menus.

APPEND The APPEND command allows you to add records to the end of the active database. The syntax of the command is APPEND [BLANK]. The one optional parameter is used when you want to add a blank record to the end of the database.

With the exception of the BLANK option, the APPEND command presents the same full-screen editor for entering new records that the ASSIST mode does. You can move between records with the PgUp and PgDn keys. Press CTRL-END to save the current record before exiting from APPEND. Press CTRL-HOME to open a Memo field for entry. The other special keys also operate in the same fashion that they do when adding records from ASSIST.

BROWSE The BROWSE command provides access to records for review or update in the familiar tabular structure. It provides many more options than it does from ASSIST mode. The syntax of the command is

```
BROWSE [NOINIT] [NO FOLLOW] [NO APPEND] [NOMENU] [NOEDIT]
     [NODELETE] [NOCLEAR] [COMPRESS] [FORMAT] [LOCK <expN>]
     [WIDTH <expN>] [FREEZE <field name>] [WINDOW <window
     name>] [FIELDS <field name 1> [/R] [/ <column width>]
     / <calculated field name 1> = <expression 1> [, <field
     name 2> [/R] [/ <column width>] / <calculated field
     name 2> = <expression 2>] ....]
```

Entering BROWSE without any of the optional arguments is the simplest form of the command that is acceptable. It will cause dBASE to display the Browse screen for the current database. You can add a list of fields to it by entering BROWSE FIELDS SSN, LAST_NAME, FIRST_NAME. This will restrict the entries in the Browse table to the fields specified. At any time you can switch to Edit mode by pressing F2, just as you can from ASSIST mode. If you want to see a set of fields but update a single field, you might enter something like this: BROWSE

FIELDS SSN, LAST_NAME, FIRST_NAME FREEZE SSN. Three fields will display in the Browse table but the highlight will be confined to the SSN field. As you press the TAB key it moves you to the SSN in the next record, since this is the only field that can be changed. Entering BROWSE by itself will restore the display of all the fields with none of them frozen.

The option NOINIT instructs Browse to use the same browse table used for the previous Browse operation. Entering BROWSE NOINIT generates the same Browse table used earlier. NOFOLLOW tells dBASE not to follow indexed records to their new position in a file. If you change a record's index value rather than following this record to obtain the next record, the current position in the database is maintained. NOAPPEND prevents the addition of new records from Browse mode. NOMENU deactivates the menu bar at the top of the screen. NOEDIT makes the Browse data Read-only. NODELETE does not allow you to delete the records in the Browse table with CTRL-U. NOCLEAR keeps the Browse table on the screen after you leave Browse. COMPRESS displays two additional records on the Browse screen. FORMAT causes Browse to use the @ commands in the active format file. LOCK specifies the number of fields frozen at the left side of the table. WIDTH places an upper limit on field width for all fields but Logical and Memo fields. WINDOW activates a window area on the screen for Browse. You can change individual fields with the /R option that makes them Read-only or the /<column width> option that defines the width for the field. You can use any number from 4 to 100 for character fields and 8 to 100 for Date and Numeric fields.

EDIT The EDIT command provides many of the same options as BROWSE. In addition it allows you to limit the records that are accessible with a scope, a FOR condition, or a WHILE condition. It is synonymous with the CHANGE command. Its syntax is

```
EDIT [NOINIT] [NOFOLLOW] [NOAPPEND] [NOMENU] [NOEDIT]
     [NODELETE] [NOCLEAR] [<record number>] [FIELDS <field
     list>] [<scope>] [FOR <condition>] [WHILE <condition>]
```

Entering EDIT will place you in Edit mode for the current record. EDIT 4 will place record 4 on the Edit screen. The other options work the same as they do in the APPEND and BROWSE commands.

Reviewing Records

There are also commands that display information on the screen without allowing you to change it. These commands use LIST and DISPLAY interchangeably. These words can be used alone to look at records in the current database or combined with other keywords to look at other information.

DISPLAY/LIST This command is used for displaying fields and expressions. The command displays an unformatted list of fields unless you build an expression with the STR and SPACE functions to control the layout. The syntax for the instruction is

```
LIST/DISPLAY [[FIELDS] <expression list>] [OFF] [<scope>]
      [FOR <condition>] [WHILE <condition>]
      [TO PRINTER/FILE <filename>]
```

LIST shows all the records in the file and DISPLAY shows the current record unless you use a limiting option like scope, FOR, or WHILE. DISPLAY will pause after each screen but LIST does not. Adding the option OFF suppresses record numbers. The Printer and File options direct the output to devices other than the screen.

To view all the fields in all the records you might enter DISPLAY ALL to see the information one screen at a time. To display all the fields from the current record, type DISPLAY. To see SSN and SALARY with lowercase headings you would enter DISPLAY ssn, salary. To see the LAST_NAME and SALARY fields you might enter DISPLAY LAST_NAME + SPACE(10) + STR(SALARY,8,2) to lay out the appearance of the output.

To position on a specific record before displaying the data you might use GO TOP or GO BOTTOM. You can also use GO 4 to position on record 4. To position the record pointer on a record meeting a specific condition you might enter LOCATE LAST_NAME="Smith".

DISPLAY/LIST STATUS The DISPLAY STATUS command has only one optional parameter. If desired you can route the output to a printer or a file. DISPLAY STATUS TO PRINTER prints the output and DISPLAY STATUS TO FILE PRTSTAT writes the output of the commands to a disk file. As with the other DISPLAY/LIST options, DISPLAY

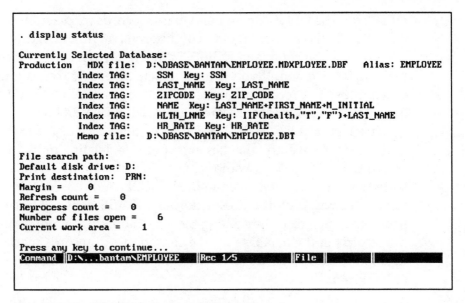

```
. display status

Currently Selected Database:
Production    MDX file:   D:\DBASE\BANTAM\EMPLOYEE.MDXPLOYEE.DBF    Alias: EMPLOYEE
              Index TAG:      SSN  Key: SSN
              Index TAG:      LAST_NAME  Key: LAST_NAME
              Index TAG:      ZIPCODE  Key: ZIP_CODE
              Index TAG:      NAME  Key: LAST_NAME+FIRST_NAME+M_INITIAL
              Index TAG:      HLTH_LNME  Key: IIF(health,"T","F")+LAST_NAME
              Index TAG:      HR_RATE  Key: HR_RATE
              Memo file:   D:\DBASE\BANTAM\EMPLOYEE.DBT

File search path:
Default disk drive: D:
Print destination:  PRN:
Margin =      0
Refresh count =     0
Reprocess count =    0
Number of files open =     6
Current work area =    1

Press any key to continue...
Command  ║D:\...bantam\EMPLOYEE   ║Rec 1/5          ║File ║     ║
```

Figure 10-7 Displaying status information

STATUS pauses after each screen that displays and allows you to press a key to continue, but the LIST command continues to scroll the output on the screen. This command provides many different pieces of information about the current dBASE session. Figure 10-7 shows the first screen of information presented.

DISPLAY/LIST STRUCTURE This command displays the database structure for the active file. Its syntax is simple and consists of

```
LIST/DISPLAY STRUCTURE [IN <alias name>] [TO PRINTER/
     FILE <filename>]
```

The only new parameter is the IN option, which allows you to specify a work area when you are working with multiple databases.

Deleting Records

You can remove records from the database while in the dot prompt environment. These records will remain in the database and can be recalled until the database is packed.

DELETE The DELETE command marks records for deletion. Its syntax is DELETE [<scope>] [FOR <condition>] [WHILE <condition>].

If you use the command DELETE alone, only the current record is marked for deletion. If you want to delete a specific record number, you can specify a record number for the scope as in DELETE RECORD 3. To delete the next three records, enter DELETE NEXT 3.

DELETE WHILE COMPANY="PARTIES INC." will delete the current record if the entry matches and continue deleting until it finds a record that differs. You would want to have the database indexed or sorted by the field referenced in the WHILE condition for this option to be effective. With the FOR condition, dBASE does not have to be positioned on a record matching the condition; dBASE will search all the records in the database for the condition. All records marked for deletion will display with an asterisk at the left when viewed with LIST or DISPLAY.

RECALL The RECALL command unmarks records that have been marked for deletion. The syntax of the command is RECALL [<scope>] [FOR <condition>] [WHILE <condition>]. The optional parameters are identical to the ones described for DELETE.

Only the current record is recalled unless you use one of the optional parameters. It is important to note that the DELETE command does not change the record pointer when you use it to delete records. If you DELETE NEXT 3, you can use RECALL NEXT 3 to bring them back.

❑ **Tip: Do not pack until reviewing the records marked for deletion.**

When you use a condition to specify the records to be removed, you would be well advised to review the records before removing them. If you pack the database before reviewing the marked records, you risk eliminating many records unintentionally if there is an error in the condition you specified.

> **Tip: SET DELETED ON has an effect on RECALL.**
>
> If SET DELETED is ON, RECALL will not unmark records unless you specify the record number. You will want to check that your records have been unmarked before proceeding with PACK unless you are certain that DELETED is set OFF.

PACK The PACK command removes records marked for deletion from the current database. Active indexed files are automatically updated. There are no optional parameters for this command.

Replacing Entries

The REPLACE command is equivalent to an update query in ASSIST mode. You can change the contents of one or more fields with this instruction. To increase all hourly rates by 5 percent you might enter the following command with the EMPLOYEE file active:

```
REPLACE ALL HR_RATE WITH HR_RATE*1.05
```

The syntax of the command is

```
REPLACE <field> WITH <exp> [ADDITIVE] [,<field> WITH <exp>
[ADDITIVE]] [<scope>] [FOR <condition>] [WHILE <condition>]
```

ADDITIVE is ignored unless the field is a Memo field. For Memo fields, it allows you to build the field from several Character strings.

Using Dot Prompt Entries to Organize Data

You can use dot prompt commands to organize data on the screen in a custom format. There are also dot prompt commands that organize the records in the database for presentation in a more meaningful order.

Creating Forms

CREATE/MODIFY SCREEN The CREATE/MODIFY SCREEN command presents the Form design screen that you have used from Assist mode. You can either enter a filename or a ? as the only parameter for the command. If you enter CREATE SCREEN SCRFILE, dBASE will allow you to either create or modify the forms file SCRFILE. If you use the ?, dBASE will display the list of existing .SCR files in the current catalog if one is open. If no catalog is open, dBASE will present the .SCR files in the current directory.

SET FORMAT TO This command will cause dBASE to use the screen file that you specify for commands like APPEND and EDIT.

Sorting

When you sort a database, a new database is created. Using the options available from the dot prompt, you can place all the records in the original database in the new sorted database, or you can select the ones to be placed in the sorted file.

The records will be written to the new sorted database in sequence based on the values in from 1 to 10 fields. Although you can specify up to 10 fields, dBASE does not look at higher-numbered sort fields unless it finds duplicate entries in earlier fields. If you use the command SORT ON LAST_NAME, FIRST_NAME TO TEMP_EMP, dBASE will not look at FIRST_NAME unless there are duplicate entries for the LAST_NAME field.

The syntax of the command is:

```
SORT TO <filename> ON <field1> [/A] [/C] [/D] [,<field2>
     [/A] [/C] [/D]...] [ASCENDING]/[DESCENDING] [<scope>]
     [FOR <condition>] [WHILE <condition>]
```

The / options are entered on a field basis with A representing ascending, D representing descending, and C indicating that the sort is not case sensitive (a dictionary sort). You can combine C with either A or D and will need only one slash, as in /AC or /CA. ASCENDING and DESCENDING applies to all the sort fields that do not have individual slash (/) settings.

Indexing

INDEX ON This command is used to create both dBASE III+ .NDX style indexes and TAG entries in an MDX file. The syntax of the command is

```
INDEX ON <key expression> TO <ndx filename>/TAG <tagname>
     [OF <mdx filename>] [UNIQUE] [DESCENDING]
```

You can enter the command as simply as INDEX. dBASE will prompt for the expression that follows ON. Your key expression from which the index is built can be a simple as a single field name or a more complicated expression that requires calculations and functions to convert field types before combining them.

If you enter the command as INDEX ON SSN TO NDXFILE, an .NDX style index file will be created. Using the alternate format of INDEX ON SSN TAG SSN will create the index in the production .MDX file. To write the index to an .MDX file other than the production one the format of the entry is INDEX ON SSN TAG SSN OF OTHERMDX where OTHERMDX is the name of an .MDX file other than the production .MDX file.

The UNIQUE option is the same as using SET UNIQUE ON. Only the first record with the index value is indexed. Reindexing a file that was originally indexed with UNIQUE will always maintain unique entries, even if SET UNIQUE is changed to OFF.

DESCENDING causes entries in an .MDX file to be recorded in descending order. It must apply to the entire index expression.

Using an Index You can use the INDEX and ORDER clauses in the USE command to open .MDX and .NDX files and establish the controlling index. Opening an .MDX index file will cause dBASE to maintain each of these indexes, although the database will remain in natural order. For .NDX files, each index file must be listed with the first file listed controlling the order of the records. If you are using NDX files you might enter **USE EMPLOYEE ORDER Ssn.ndx, Last_name.ndx, Zip.ndx** and the records will be in Ssn order.

The SET ORDER command will switch controlling indexes to another index tag in an MDX file. You can also use SET ORDER with open NDX files. Enter **SET ORDER TO Last_name.ndx** to use the Last_name index to control the record sequence.

To open a closed indexed file, type SET INDEX TO INDXFLE where INDXFLE is the index file that you want to open. This command will close other index files that may be open as it opens the new one.

SEEK This command is used to locate index entries that match an expression. The expression can be a Character string, date, or number. The data type that you supply must match the index expression and must use the proper characters like " or { to encase entries like characters or dates. To seek a date of 01/19/89 in a date index you would enter SEEK {01/19/89}. To seek an entry of Jones in an index of last names type SEEK "Jones".

FIND The FIND command searches the index for the first Character string or number to match your entry. The syntax is FIND <literal key>. Since the command will accept a Character string, quotes are not required to search for an entry of Jones in an index built with last names. FIND Jones will locate your entry.

Using Dot Prompt Entries to Filter and Summarize Data

You can use dot prompt commands to avoid the drudgery of reviewing your database records one by one. Rather than reviewing each record you can review exception or summary statistics for the database information.

Creating Queries

Many commands at the dot prompt allow you to limit the display of fields and records. With a field list you can restrict the data presented to less than full database records. With the scope, FOR, and WHILE clauses you can control the number of records presented. These are not the same as Queries that can be used with any task that you perform. You can continue to create Queries but with dot prompt commands. You can use other commands that provide a summary calculation for the records in your database.

CREATE QUERY The CREATE QUERY command activates the same Query design screen that you used from ASSIST mode. The syntax of the command is CREATE/MODIFY QUERY <filename>/? or CREATE/MODIFY VIEW <filename>/?

SET FILTER TO This command is retained in dBASE IV for compatibility with earlier releases. It is designed to establish a filter for database records by using the contents of a QRY file or a condition in the command.

To specify a condition you might enter: SET FILTER TO LAST_NAME="Smith". Records with entries other than Smith will not be available for display or edit while this filter is in effect.

SET VIEW TO This command uses the contents of a QBE file created with CREATE/MODIFY VIEW or CREATE/MODIFY QUERY to control the records available for display and edit.

Adding Entries

TOTAL The TOTAL command creates a database with records that contain the total of numeric fields for each value of the index key. The second database has the same structure as the original file. The syntax of the instruction is described in detail early in this chapter as an example of the various types of parameters that dBASE commands support.

SUM The SUM command also totals numbers but they are stored to memory variables or array lists rather than another database file. Memory variables and array lists are storage locations in memory. Arrays differ from memory variables in that they have a series of locations or compartments where numbers can be stored. If you plan to use an array you must declare the array before entering the SUM command. The DECLARE statement is used to determine the size of the array. Memory variables can only store one entry at a time.

The syntax of the command is

```
SUM [<exp N list>] [TO <memvar list>/TO ARRAY <array name>]
     [<scope>] [FOR <condition>] [WHILE <condition>]
```

If you use this command without an expression list, dBASE will sum all the numeric variables in the database. If you use an array in the command you will need to declare it first. This is accomplished with the DECLARE command. To establish a one-dimensional array named NUMSUM with four locations for sum entries type DECLARE NUMSUM[4]. Next, you can type SUM SALARY, NUMB_DEPEN, YTD_FIT, YTD_FICA TO ARRAY NUMSUM. dBASE displays the sum for each of the four fields. If you want to access them individually you can use the ? command referencing the various locations as NUMSUM[1], NUMSUM[2], NUMSUM[3], and NUMSUM[4].

Creating and Modifying Reports

You may find it difficult to envision creating reports from the dot prompt but actually it is just as easy as from ASSIST. DBASE makes available the same design screens used from the ASSIST mode so you are able to fill in the bands with entries just as you have learned to do.

CREATE REPORT The CREATE REPORT command takes you to the same Report design screen that you use from ASSIST mode. The syntax of the command is

```
CREATE/MODIFY REPORT <filename>/?
```

If you use the question mark option, dBASE will display the .FRM files in the current catalog. If no catalog is open, dBASE displays the .FRM files in the current directory.

REPORT FORM The REPORT FORM command is used to generate a report developed with CREATE REPORT. The syntax of the command is

```
REPORT FORM <report form filename>/? [PLAIN] [HEADING
    <expC>] [NOEJECT] [SUMMARY] [<scope>] [FOR <condition>]
    [WHILE <condition>] [TO PRINTER/TO FILE <filename>]
```

The PLAIN option removes the system date and page numbers from the report. HEADING prints these entries and allows you to specify an optional Character string containing additional heading information.

```
. use order.dbf
. disp stru
Structure for database: D:\DBASE\BANTAM\ORDER.DBF
Number of data records:        9
Date of last update   : 01/22/90
Field  Field Name  Type        Width    Dec    Index
    1  ORDER_NO    Character       6               N
    2  ORDER_DATE  Date            8               N
    3  CUST_NO     Character       8               Y
    4  ITEM        Character      10               N
    5  UNITS       Numeric         4               N
    6  UNIT_PRICE  Numeric         7      2        N
    7  DELIVERY    Memo           10               N
** Total **                       54
```

Figure 10-8 Customer file structure

When you choose the option TO PRINTER and use NOEJECT, the initial form-feed that normally occurs before printing starts is not used. Using neither TO FILE nor TO PRINTER causes dBASE to display the report on the screen.

The SUMMARY option suppresses all the detail lines in a report. Only subtotals and totals display with this option.

Using Dot Prompt Entries to Relate Files

Using dot prompt entries to relate files is a little more cumbersome than performing the same commands with the Query design screen. When you use the dot prompt you must explicitly assign each open file work area before establishing the link.

Given that you have two files, a CUSTOMER file and an ORDER file, with structures that match the ones shown in Figure 10-8 and Figure 10-9, you have files that can be linked by CUST_NO. If you want to list order information for each customer who has placed an order, you will want to use the ORDERS file indexed by CUST_NO and show fields from it along with fields from the CUSTOMER file. First activate the first work area with the entry SELECT 1. Next, tell dBASE what database to use in this work area, by entering USE CUSTOMER ORDER CUST_NO. dBASE will display the message Master index: CUST_NO to let you know that CUST_NO will control the order of the records from this file.

The second file needs to be opened. First you will want to select the second work area by entering SELECT 2 and USE ORDER.DBF ORDER

```
. use customer
. list stru
Structure for database: D:\DBASE\BANTAM\CUSTOMER.DBF
Number of data records:       3
Date of last update   : 01/21/90
Field  Field Name  Type       Width    Dec    Index
    1  CUST_NO     Character      8               Y
    2  NAME        Character     20               N
    3  COMPANY     Character     20               N
    4  ADDRESS     Character     20               N
    5  CITY        Character     15               N
    6  STATE       Character      2               N
    7  ZIP         Character      5               N
    8  PHONE       Character     13               N
** Total **                     104
```

Figure 10-9 Order file structure

CUST_NO. To establish a relation from work area 2 into work area 1, type SET RELATION TO CUST_NO INTO CUSTOMER. This establishes ORDER as the controlling or parent file and CUSTOMER as the child.

Sometimes you may want to open files in a different work area than the one that is current but would prefer to remain in the current work area. The IN option allows you to do this without activating the work area. Rather than using a select statement you would enter the USE command as USE EMPLOYEE IN 1. This tells dBASE to use work area 1 for this file but it still leaves your current work area active.

The USE command is the same command you have used to open a database that is used by itself. The full syntax of the other two commands are listed here. The syntax for SELECT is SELECT <work area name/alias>. Work area can be any number from 1 to 10, although 10 is reserved for the open catalog. If you have assigned an alias to a file with the USE command you can change areas by entering SELECT work area name or alias.

The syntax of SET RELATION is

```
SET RELATION TO <expN> INTO <alias> [, <expN> INTO
    <alias>]...
```

Once linked you can display or list fields from both files. The field shared in common between the files can be displayed by listing its field name, if it is the same in the two files. Fields from the file in the active work area can also be listed with just a field name. Fields from other work areas require the addition of the filename or alias followed by a hyphen and a greater than symbol, as in EMPLOYEE->LAST_NAME. To avoid confusion you may want to use the filename or alias entry along with each field that you show. Entering DISPLAY ALL ORDER->ORDER_NO, CUST_NO, UNITS*UNIT_PRICE, CUSTOMER->COMPANY will display the fields shown for all the records in the View created by the joined files.

Using Dot Prompt Entries to Change Settings

In Chapter 8, you learned about the five different ways to change dBASE settings. Now that you know a little more about dot prompt entries you will want to examine a few of the options in more detail.

Using the SET Command

You can always enter SET at the dot prompt to use a menu-driven system to change dBASE set options. The changes that you make will only be in effect for the current session. If you only need to make one change you might find it more convenient to enter the specific set option at the dot prompt.

Chapter 8 includes a reference to SET commands that are entered with one or more keywords to change a specific dBASE setting. Like the changes made through the SET command, these changes are only in effect for the current session. Many of these commands like SET DEBUG have a single ON/OFF setting and are entered as SET DEBUG ON or SET DEBUG OFF. Other SET entries require a value or expression like SET PRINTER TO LPT1 where a DOS device is expected.

Other set entries allow you to activate objects like Views and Queries created with other commands. You can use SET FILTER TO QRYFILE to activate the Query file QRYFILE. If you want a view to be active you can use SET VIEW TO VIEWFILE where VIEWFILE is the name of the View that you created.

Other SET commands can make your work with the dot prompt easier. Rather than entering a series of display commands for a specific group of fields, use the SET FIELDS TO command and specify the Fields List that you want to use. The fields in this list will be the only fields available. If you enter CLEAR FIELDS or SET FIELDS OFF, the

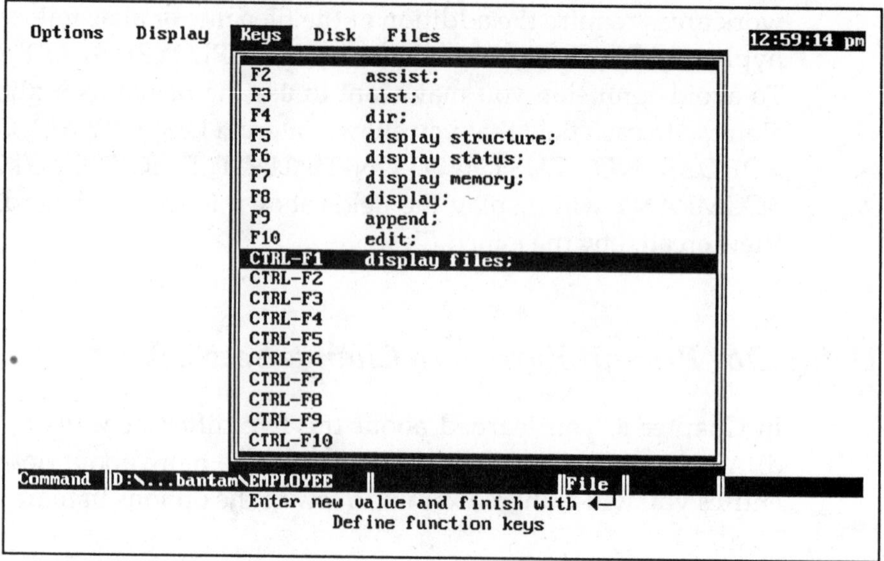

Figure 10-10 Assigning a command to CTRL-F1

Fields List established with SET FIELDS TO will be ignored and all fields will again be available.

Changing Key Assignments

You can use the SET command to change the assigned function of keys when working from dot prompt mode. Type **SET** at the dot prompt and press ENTER. Press ALT-K to select Keys and move to the key assignment you wish to enter or change.

To assign an entry to CTRL-F1, move to this entry and press ENTER. Type the command you wish to assign followed by a semicolon (;). Figure 10-10 shows **display files;** as the entry for CTRL-F1. Once you return to the dot prompt, pressing these two keys simultaneously will generate this command on the dot prompt line.

Memory Variables

Memory variables are names assigned to locations in memory where data can be stored. Unless you take some special action, memory variables are temporary and are lost when you exit dBASE.

Although memory variables have been mentioned in some of the earlier dot prompt commands you will want to look at them close-up. There are several types that you can create. Also, you can store them to disk for later use. The time invested to learn how to use them from the dot prompt is well spent since they are an essential part of any programming you do later.

Types

There are several classifications for memory variables. You can classify them by the type of data they contain. Memory variables are initialized to the data type of the information that you store in them.

Memory variables are created and initialized with a data type in one step. You can use names of from 1 to 10 characters. You can use the STORE command to name a memory variable and place a value in it or you can use the equal sign (=). You might enter STORE 1 TO MCOUNT or MCOUNT=1. If you need to place the same value in several variables you will want to use the STORE command. The entry STORE 1 TO MCOUNTA, MCOUNT2, MCOUNT3 initializes all three variables.

You can create logical-type memory variables with an entry like STORE .T. to MMATCHED. Date-type variables require braces around the initial value as it MCUT_DATE={04/15/89}. STORE SPACE(15) to MCITY and STORE "Smith" TO MLAST_NAME are two instructions that initialize character memory variables.

The other classification for memory variables is whether they are public or private. This distinction is important when you are using them in a programming environment. The default is private, which means that the variable will not be defined beyond the bounds of the

Tip: Start each memory variable name with the letter m.
To distinguish memory variable names from field names, you may want to place an m at the beginning of every memory variable name. If the corresponding field name begins with an m, the memory variable will start with a double m.

current program and any programs it may call. Public memory variables are available to all the programs within your application. To declare a memory variable public you enter PUBLIC followed by the name of the memory variable. The next instruction can initialize the variable as in

```
PUBLIC MCOUNT
STORE 0 to MCOUNT
```

You will have an opportunity to look at this aspect of memory variables in more detail in the programming chapters.

If you do not want public variables or private variables from a higher- level procedure available in the current procedure you can hide them. To hide a variable you must explicitly declare it private as in

```
PRIVATE   mstate
STORE "OH" to mstate
```

When you return to a higher level program, the original memory variable will again be in effect.

Purpose

Memory variables are convenient since you can continue to change the values they contain, yet refer to them by the same name. You can use them in Condition test to select records that you want to work with or to supply variable information for any task.

Looking at the Contents of Memory Variables

You can look at the contents of memory variables with the same commands that you use to evaluate an expression. Typing ? followed by a list of memory variables separated by commas will display the contents of each on the next line. Using ?? followed by a list of variables will begin printing the contents of memory variables on the same line as the ?? command, as it does not generate a carriage return or a line feed. Figure 10-11 shows several command entries at the dot prompt to assign and display memory variables.

```
. STORE 5*6 TO PAY
        30
. ?PAY
        30
. STORE 11 to RATE
        11
. ?(40*RATE)+(1.5*RATE*10)
      605
. STORE 12 to OVT_HOURS
        12
. STORE 11 TO RATE
        11
. ?(40*RATE)+(1.5*RATE*OVT_HOURS)
      638
.
Command  D:\...bantam\EMPLOYEE   Rec EOF/5   File
```

Figure 10-11 Assigning and displaying memory variables

Entering DISPLAY MEMORY will display a list of the current memory variables defined as well as their contents. The display will look something like Figure 10-12 depending on the variables you have defined.

Erasing Memory Variables

When you exit from dBASE, all memory variables are cleared. They will not be available during your next session. If you are using private memory variables in a program, they are cleared when the program ends. Public memory will remain and must be explicitly erased if you no longer need the entries.

The command that you use to erase memory variables depends on whether you want to eliminate all the variables at once. To erase all public memory variables, enter **CLEAR MEMORY**. CLEAR ALL erases memory variables but also erases the screen, releases windows and pending GET instructions, eliminates a field list, clears the typeahead buffer, and deactivates menus and pop ups. To erase a single memory variable, use the RELEASE command with the name of the variable as in RELEASE MCOUNT.

There are two options for RELEASE that can be used to clear a portion of the private variables. When used with LIKE, the command

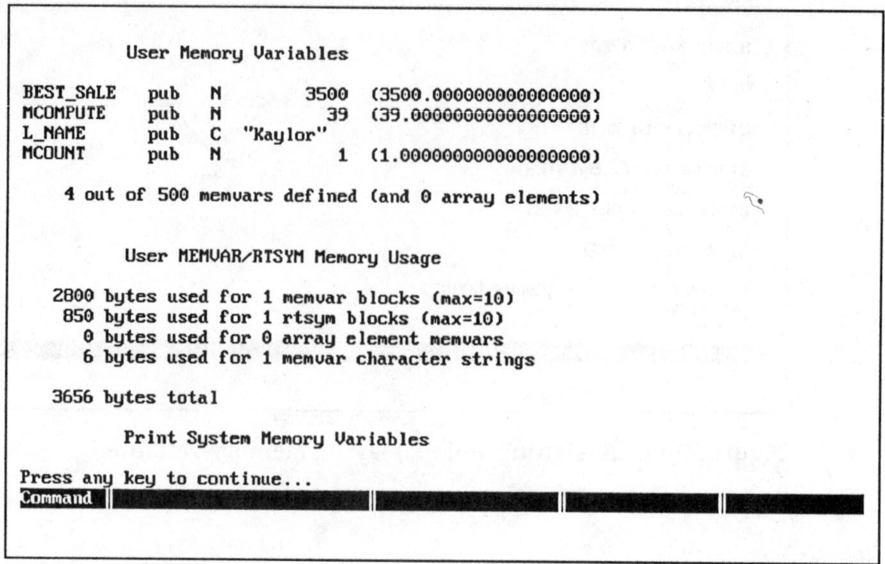

User Memory Variables
BEST_SALE pub N 3500 (3500.000000000000000)
MCOMPUTE pub N 39 (39.0000000000000000)
L_NAME pub C "Kaylor"
MCOUNT pub N 1 (1.00000000000000000)
4 out of 500 memvars defined (and 0 array elements)
User MEMVAR/RTSYM Memory Usage
2800 bytes used for 1 memvar blocks (max=10)
850 bytes used for 1 rtsym blocks (max=10)
0 bytes used for 0 array element memvars
6 bytes used for 1 memvar character strings
3656 bytes total
Print System Memory Variables
Press any key to continue...
Command

Figure 10-12 Displaying memory

will erase all the private variables that match the established pattern. RELEASE LIKE MCOUNT* would erase MCOUNTA, MCOUNTB, and MCOUNTC. The EXCEPT option is similar but uses the opposite approach, erasing all records that do not match the pattern provided. RELEASE ALL EXCEPT M* would release all the private memory variables that started with any letter except M.

Storing Memory Variables to a Memory File

If you enter SAVE TO MFILE, where MFILE is the name you want to use when saving the memory variables and values, you can enter RESTORE FROM MFILE to place the variables in memory again. When you use this command, dBASE clears all the memory variables currently in memory. You can overcome this problem by adding ADDITIVE if you want to retain existing variable values. The only ones that will be overwritten if you take this approach are the ones with the same names as the stored variables.

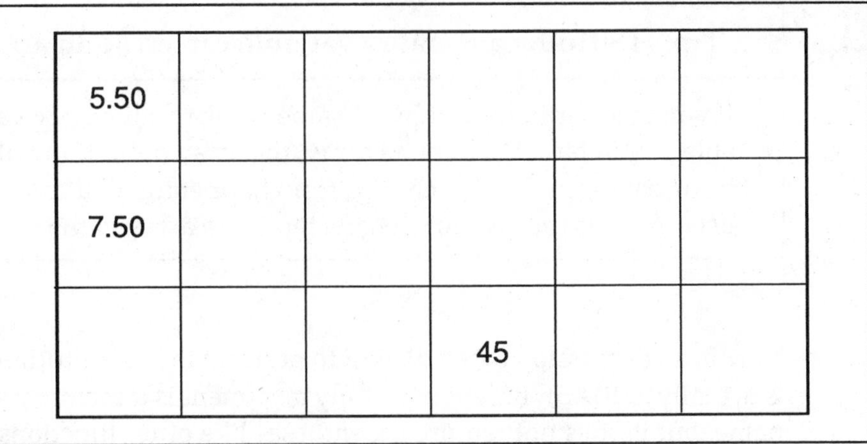

Figure 10-13 Array entries

Memory Variable Arrays

Memory variable arrays provide multiple locations for the storage of information. They can be either one or two dimensional. A one-dimensional array is like a column of storage locations and a two-dimensional array is a tabular arrangement that has both multiple rows and columns. Arrays must be declared to establish their size.

The DECLARE command is used to establish the size of the array. For a one-dimensional array you state the number of rows in the array and dBASE assumes there is only one column, as in DECLARE M_RATES[5]. The statement DECLARE M_RATES[5,6] tells dBASE there are five rows and six columns allowing for a maximum of 30 entries in the array.

After you declare the size of the array you are ready to initialize the entries. M_RATES[1;1]=5.50, M_RATES[2,1]=7.50, M_RATES[3,4]=45 initialize three locations in the array. The array entries would be placed as shown in Figure 10-13.

Macro Substitution

You can use the macro substitution feature to substitute the contents of a memory variable for its name. The memory variable name is preceded

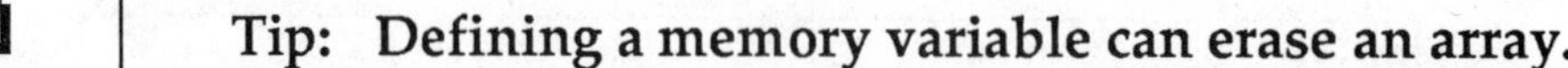

Tip: Defining a memory variable can erase an array.

If you inadvertently assign the same name to a memory variable as you have used for an array, the array definition will be overwritten. To prevent this from happening you can used ARY as the last three characters in an array name.

by & in an expression to tell dBASE to perform the substitution. The & is actually a dBASE function. Its only argument is a memory variable name, but it does not require parentheses like other functions. It will only operate with character variables since the variable is supposed to represent a memory variable name.

You might use these instructions:

```
STORE "SSN, LAST_NAME, FIRST_NAME" TO FLDS
LIST &FLDS
```

dBASE lists the field entries for SSN, LAST_NAME, and FIRST_NAME since it substitutes the current value of FLDS.

GETTING STARTED

➤ You will want to try some of the options covered in this chapter by making entries at the dot prompt. Follow these instructions to use the dot prompt for appending records to the employee database and creating a report:

1. Start dBASE and exit to the dot prompt. If the Control Center is on your screen you need to press ESC and type a **Y** to use the dot prompt.
2. Type **USE EMPLOYEE** and press ENTER.
3. Type **APPEND** and press ENTER.
4. Complete the new employee record. Type **111-55-1111**. Type **York** and press ENTER. Type **J**. Type **Sally** and press ENTER. Type **1119 Oak Way** and press ENTER. Type **Baltimore** and press ENTER. Type **MD**. Type **21237**. Type **(301)880-6633**. Type

```
Page No.    1
01/22/90

SSN          LAST_NAME          NUMB_DEPEN HR_RATE

215-90-8761  Jenkins                     1    9.75
675-98-1239  Foster                      1    8.50
654-11-9087  Garrison                    3   12.50
888-99-7654  Larson                      0   15.75
555-66-7777  Walker                      6   12.50
111-55-1111  York                        1    9.00
                                        12   68.00
```

Figure 10-14 Report display

110988. Type **M**. Type **1** and press ENTER. Type **9** and press ENTER. Type **4000** and press ENTER. Type **400** and press ENTER. Type **450** and press ENTER. Type **T**. Press CTRL-END to end the record and stop appending.

5. Press ALT-L and press Q for Quick layouts and press ENTER twice. Type **CREATE REPORT PAY_INFO** and press ENTER.
6. Use the Layout option to create a quick column layout.
7. Move to the Page Header Band. Place the cursor on the field name M_INITIAL. Press CTRL-T nine times. Move two spaces to the right of NUMB_DEPEN. Press CTRL-T to eliminate all the extra space which precedes HR_RATE. Move to after the "E" in HR_RATE. Press CTRL-T five times. The only field names remaining are SSN, LAST_NAME, NUMB_DEPEN, and HR_RATE. You could have chosen to add these fields individually rather than creating a column layout and deleting the unneeded fields.
8. Move to the Detail Band. Place the cursor on the template that follows the LAST_NAME template. This is actually the template for M_INITIAL. Press CTRL-T nine times. The proper template for NUMB_DEPEN will appear. Move two spaces to the right of this template and press CTRL-T to eliminate the space preceding the HR_RATE template. Move to the right of this template and press CTRL_T five times.
9. Press ALT-P and type a **V** to view the report on the screen. The report will look like Figure 10-14. You will notice that the numeric columns are added, telling you the total number of dependents your employees have and the total cost per hour if all of your employees are working. If these totals are not needed,

the templates representing them can be eliminated from the report total band before creating the report again. Press the SPACEBAR three times to return to the design screen.

10. Press ALT-E and type an **S** to save the report design.

You can use the dot prompt entries to establish a link between two files. First, you will create a second file that contains weekly payroll information on the number of hours each employee worked, if you did not create it in Chapter 2. Next, you will link the two files and display data from both files. Follow these steps to link the EMPLOYEE file with WEEK_PAY:

1. Type **CLOSE ALL** and press ENTER to close all the databases.
2. If you did not create the database in the Getting Started for Chapter 2, type **CREATE WEEK_PAY** and press ENTER.
3. Enter the following structure on the design screen dBASE presents:

Field Name	*Field Type*	*Width*	*Dec*	*Index*
SSN	Character	11		Y
PAY_DATE	Date	8		N
REG_HRS	Numeric	5	2	N
OVTME_HRS	Numeric	5	2	N

4. Press CTRL-END when you complete the design entries and type a **Y** to enter records immediately.
5. Enter these records:

	Record 1	*Record 2*	*Record 3*
SSN	555-66-7777	111-55-1111	215-90-8761
PAY_DATE	071489	071489	071489
REG_HRS	40	35	40
OVT_HRS	10		5

	Record 4	*Record 5*	*Record 6*
SSN	888-99-7654	675-98-1239	654-11-9087
PAY_DATE	071489	071489	071489
REG_HRS	30	40	40
OVT_HRS		7.5	2

6. Press CTRL-END to save the database.
7. Type **CLOSE DATABASES** and press ENTER.
8. With the files you need available type **SELECT 1**. Type **USE WEEK_PAY ORDER SSN**. This will use work area 1 for the WEEK_PAY file and will establish the TAG SSN as the controlling order for the records.
9. Type **USE EMPLOYEE IN 2 ORDER SSN**. This opens the EMPLOYEE file in work area 2 with the TAG SSN. Since the IN 2 option was used with the USE command, work area 1 is still active.
10. Type **SET RELATION TO SSN INTO EMPLOYEE** to establish the link between the two files.
11. Type **DISP ALL SSN, EMPLOYEE->LAST_NAME, EMPLOYEE->HR_RATE, WEEK_PAY->REG_HRS**. dBASE displays data from the two linked files.

Display the history file with these steps:

1. Press the UP ARROW key to review the previous command. Press it again to move farther back in the history. Press the DOWN ARROW twice.
2. Type **DISPLAY HISTORY** and press ENTER. dBASE displays the last 20 commands entered at the dot prompt.

You can combine the use of memory variables with dot prompt instructions. Follow these steps to use memory variables to control the records displayed from the EMPLOYEE file:

1. Type **SELECT 2** to make the work area containing the EMPLOYEE file active.

2. Type **STORE "L" TO NME** and press ENTER.
3. Type **DISPLAY LAST_NAME, SSN, HR_RATE FOR LAST_NAME<NME** and press ENTER. dBASE displays the entries for Jenkins, Garrison, and Foster.
4. Type **STORE 9 to RATE** and press ENTER.
5. Type **DISPLAY LAST_NAME, SSN, HR_RATE FOR HR_RATE>RATE** and press ENTER. dBASE displays the entries for Jenkins, Walker, Garrison, and Larson.
6. Type **?NME, RATE** and press ENTER to display the contents of the memory variables.
7. Type **Quit** to exit dBASE.

CHAPTER 11

Macros

Macros are recorded keystrokes that are assigned a name to allow you to replay the keystrokes as often as you like. Most of the popular packages today have some type of macro capability to allow users to perform a task once while saving it for later use. Some packages record their macros in a programming language of sorts and do not capture the keystrokes automatically for the user. The macro features added to dBASE IV have the automatic recorder feature, allowing you to concentrate on the task you are trying to accomplish rather than the syntax of macro commands.

Macros are an excellent solution for short, repetitive tasks. For example, you can use a macro to modify a ruler, print the report on a specific printer, or activate a database and print a report. If the task is only required once, it makes no sense to store it as a macro. If it is lengthy, a dBASE IV program may provide a more flexible solution. Also, with longer tasks you are likely to need decision-making ability in your code. Logic processing commands are easier to add in the programming environment than in a macro.

You may already be using a memory resident utility that captures keystrokes. There are many on the market that can capture keystrokes across application environments, including Lotus' Metro and Borland's SuperKey. If you are already familiar with one of these utilities, you can give it a try. dBASE IV's memory requirements and the fact that Ashton-Tate does not promise compatibility with these products may mean that you will need to use the dBASE macro features. Since dBASE IV provides the same basic functionality as these other products, the only requirement is adjusting to a few new commands.

It is important to note that macros and the macro substitution used with memory variables are quite different. Macro substitution, which is represented by the ampersand symbol (&) in front of a variable name, causes dBASE to substitute the current variable contents in the command. This feature was available in dBASE III+ and continues to be available in dBASE IV. It is distinct from the new macro features that are designed exclusively for capturing instructions and providing a way to execute them again. Macro substitution is discussed briefly in Chapter 10 and is used more extensively in the programming chapters.

Macro Basics

Macros record every keystroke that you type, once you start the record process. If you follow a few simple rules you will find macros almost effortless to create, since you are performing a task with them the first time you use them. The only extra work required is naming the macro and correcting any mistakes that you make while recording the keystrokes.

Creating a Macro

Creating a macro is as simple as telling dBASE that you want to record the keystrokes that you are about to press. Once you record the macro, you can modify it to make it run more efficiently. You can also add to an existing macro or replace it.

To begin recording a macro, follow these steps:

1. Press ALT-T to select the Tools menu and type an **M** to select Macros to display the Macros menu box shown in Figure 11-1. You can also press SHIFT-F10 to display the box shown in Figure 11-2.
2. Type a **B** to select Begin recording. If you used the Tools menu to start recording the macro, dBASE displays the macro display box shown in Figure 11-3, which lists each of the keys and macros

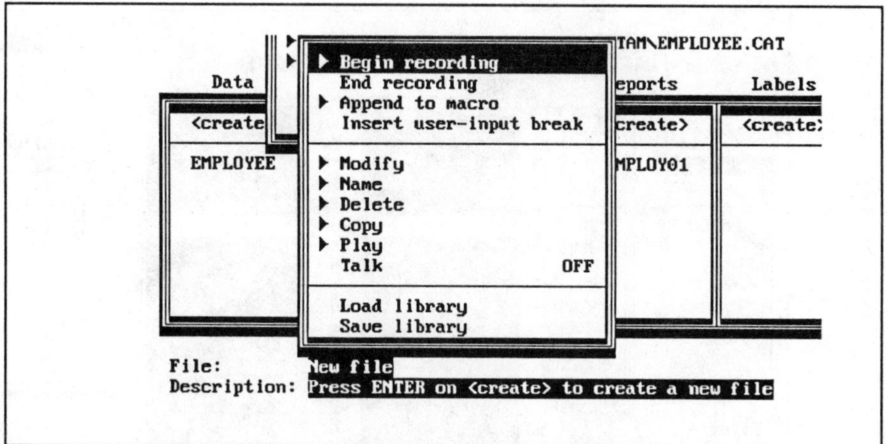

Figure 11-1 Macros menu box

assigned to them. If you used SHIFT-F10 to start recording the macro, dBASE displays the prompt shown in Figure 11-4.

3. Type the letter or function key that you will use to activate the macro. It can be any letter or any function key except F10.

Once dBASE knows the key to assign the macro to, it displays the message shown in Figure 11-5 in the navigation line. If you have already assigned a macro to the key you entered in step 3, dBASE prompts you with the message shown in Figure 11-6. If you want to replace the existing macro, type a Y. If you want to keep the existing macro and cancel creating a new macro, type an N. Once dBASE starts recording a macro, every key you press is recorded. Since you may press unnecessary keys when you record a macro, you will want to modify it.

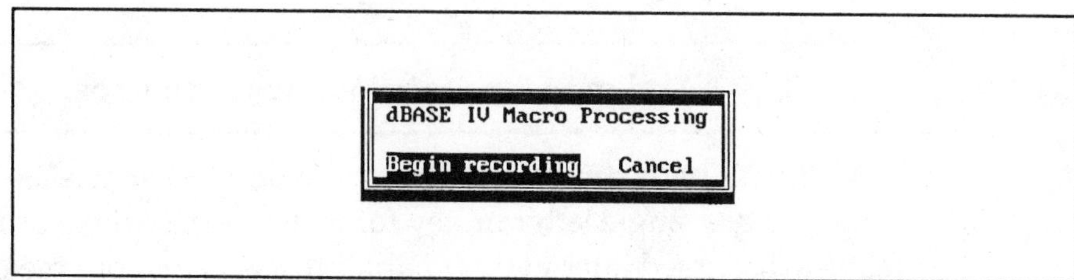

Figure 11-2 Macros prompt box

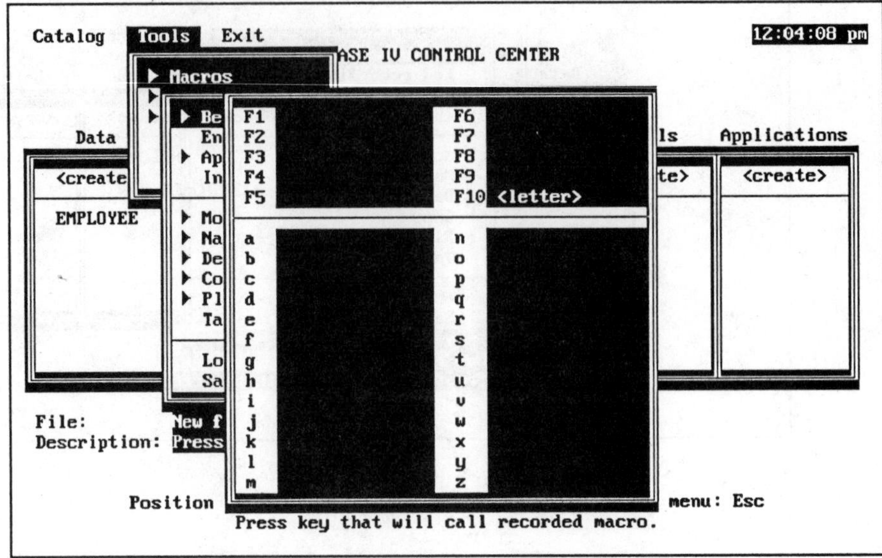

Figure 11-3 Macro display box

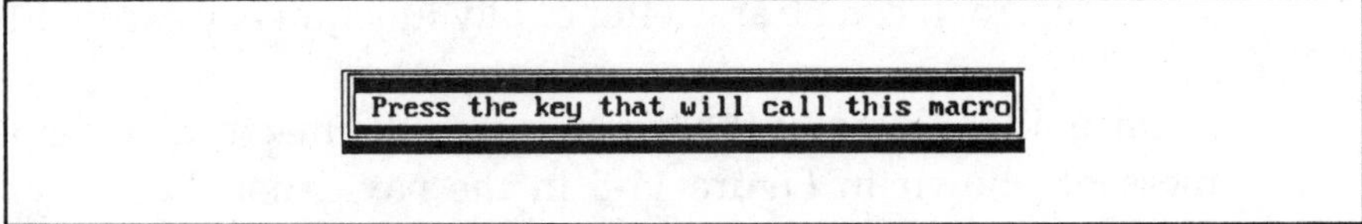

Figure 11-4 Prompt for selecting macro to record

```
Recording Macro; Press Shift-F10 E to end.
```

Figure 11-5 Message during recording a macro

❑

Tip: Assign meaningful names to macros.

It is difficult to remember what a macro does when it is assigned only a single letter or key for its name. Use the Name feature discussed later in this chapter to assign a more meaningful name.

```
Do you really want to overwrite A ? (Y/N)
```

Figure 11-6 Prompt if creating a macro that already exists

When you are creating a macro, you can execute another macro. When you execute another macro while you are creating one, dBASE includes the steps to execute the other macro in the one that you are creating. When you execute the macro, this executes a second macro. dBASE performs the keystrokes in the macro you have just created; when it reaches the steps that perform the other macro, it performs the second macro and then continues to perform the remaining keystrokes in the macro you just created.

When you finish adding keystrokes to the macro, press ALT-T and type an **M** to select Macros and an **E** to select End recording. dBASE remains in the Macros menu box and records these final keystrokes in the macro. You can also end recording a macro by pressing SHIFT-F10 and typing an E. SHIFT-F10 and the E are not recorded as part of the macro. The second alternative leaves you in your current position and does not have to be performed in the Control Center. When you finish recording a macro, dBASE displays the message shown in Figure 11-7 in the navigation line to indicate that subsequent keystrokes are not part of the macro.

The macro shown in Figure 11-8 shows the keystrokes for a macro that adds Acme Company and Employee File, and centers them. You can use a macro like this for the beginning of forms, labels, and reports. Notice that dBASE records the letters that you press rather than the menu options you select, like the p and c for Position and Center in the Words menu, and how dBASE records the keys that you press with keywords in braces.

Tip: Recursive execution of a macro is not allowed.
Although you can execute another macro from within a macro, the macro cannot execute itself.

```
Macro recording has been finished.
```

Figure 11-7 Message after recording a macro

If you are using an external program for the Memo field or text editor, dBASE will not record keystrokes that you press after entering this external program. It will record all of the keystrokes before you enter and after you leave the external program.

Suggestions for Creating Problem-free Macros

Since dBASE macros record keystrokes rather than the functions that the keystrokes perform, you will want to follow these suggestions to create error-free macros:

- When you select menu options, type the first letter rather than highlighting the option and pressing ENTER. Since dBASE remembers the last menu option you selected when you return to a menu, using the arrow keys to make a menu selection is likely to result in incorrect selections when you execute the macro a second time.
- This advice also applies to selecting menu boxes. Use the ALT and letter key approach since pressing F10 activates the last menu box you used.
- Select filenames by typing the entire entry. For example, if you have a macro that selects the file EMPLOYEE and you also have a

```
 Layout   Words   Go To   Print   Exit                              11:10:40 am
[·······▼1······▼··2····▼····3··▼·······4▼·······▼5·······▼··6····▼····7··▼·······
Acme Company{Enter}
Employee File{Enter}
{uparrow}{uparrow}{F6}{downarrow}{End}{Enter}
{Alt-w}pc
```

Figure 11-8 Macro that enters and centers text

```
Press an alphabetic key of macro to playback.
```

Figure 11-9 Prompt for playing back a macro by pressing ALT-F10

file called EMPLOY, typing only part of the filename will cause dBASE to use the wrong file.

- Use a building-block approach to make testing easy. Create several small macros and join them after they are tested. You can include steps in one macro to execute others. This lets you combine several smaller macros into a larger one, which facilitates testing since it is easier to test several small macros than one large one.

Executing the Macro

Although you saw the results of the macro code as you entered it, when you are finished you will want to try it again. This ensures that you have recorded the keystrokes properly and that the macro will continue to provide consistent results time after time.

To execute a macro, press ALT-T, and type an **M** for Macros and a **P** to select Play. When dBASE displays the macro display box, press the key assigned to the macro you want to execute. dBASE returns to the Control Center and performs the macro. If a macro is assigned to a letter, you can also execute the macro by pressing ALT-F10 and typing the letter the macro is assigned to when dBASE displays the prompt shown in Figure 11-9. If a macro is assigned to one of the first nine function keys, you can execute the macro by holding down ALT while you press the function key the macro is assigned to. Using ALT-F10 to execute a macro allows you to start a macro at a position other than the Control Center.

You can stop a macro before it finishes if it does not seem to be operating correctly. If the macro is not performing the steps you expect, you need to stop the macro so you can modify it. Press ESC, type a **Y**, and press ENTER to halt the macro. Since dBASE leaves you at the position where the macro stopped, you may have to return to the Control Center to modify the macro.

❑ **Tip: Be careful of changing settings in a macro.**

The toggle switch settings used by many dBASE IV options can cause problems in a macro setting. If you have a macro that changes a menu option with two settings, check that the option will be selected when you are sure what the setting for the option is, such as changing settings at the beginning of a form, label, or report design.

Modifying a Macro

As you enter a macro, you may enter keystrokes that are unnecessary or you may notice an error and correct it. Since dBASE records every keystroke, unnecessary entries are recorded as well as any errors you make and the keystrokes that you use to correct them.

You can remove these unnecessary keystrokes. This will make the macro run better. Eliminating unnecessary keystrokes also eliminates any confusion that may result from macro code that contains superfluous instructions.

To modify a macro, press ALT-T for the Tools menu and type an **M** for Macros and an **M** for Modify. dBASE displays the macro display box that lists the macro names and the number of keystrokes in each macro next to the macro's key assignment. The highlighted letters are the macro names. dBASE initially uses the assigned key as the name of the macro.

How dBASE Records Your Instructions

To modify a macro, type or press the assigned key of the macro that you want to modify. dBASE displays a macro edit screen like the one in Figure 11-10, which is for a macro that sets the right margin to 8" and hides the ruler. For each of the keystrokes stored in the macro, dBASE displays a keyword representing the keystroke. Table 11-1 lists keystrokes and the keywords associated with them.

dBASE uses braces for other types of entries in a macro besides keywords. You can include a character by typing the ASCII number

> **Tip: Choice of an editor for changes can affect your ability to record macros.**
>
> When you edit a macro, dBASE uses the same editor that it uses for editing text. If you want to use a different editor, you must change the setting for Tedit in the General column of CONFIG.DB options in DBSETUP. Since this also sets the editor used with the MODIFY COMMAND command, you will not be able to record macros that use this command.

inside curly braces. For example, if you want a macro to enter a , you would type {171}. You can see all of the characters and their ASCII codes when you select Use specified character for drawing a box or line in a form or report. dBASE also places braces around dates automatically. For example, if a macro contains <01/01/90 as an example for a Query that you are recording, the example appears as <{01/01/90} in the macro.

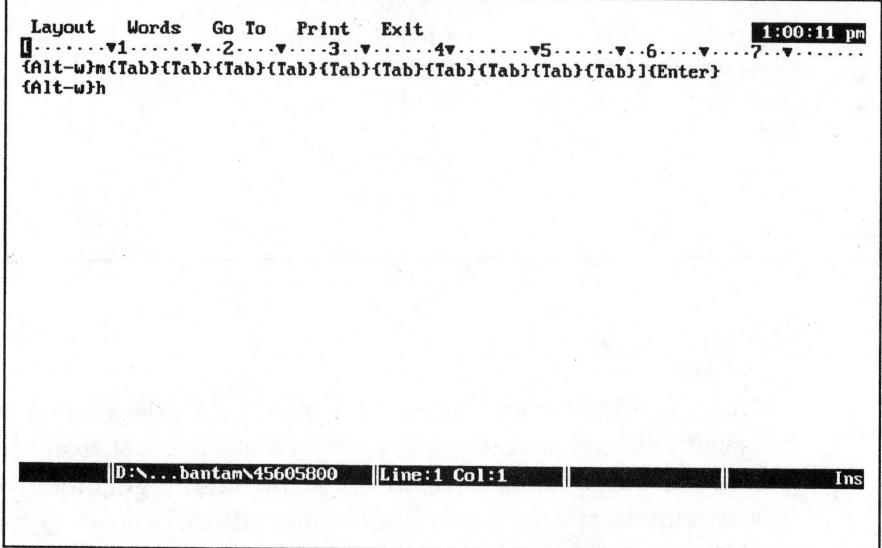

Figure 11-10 Macro screen

Table 11-1 Macro keywords

Keyword	*Key Represented by Keyword*
{Alt-letter}	ALT-letter
{Backspace}	BACKSPACE
{Ctrl-Backspace}	CTRL-BACKSPACE
{Ctrl-End}	CTRL-END
{Ctrl-Enter}	CTRL-ENTER
{Ctrl-Home}	CTRL-HOME
{Ctrl-leftarrow}	CTRL-LEFT ARROW
{Ctrl-letter}	CTRL-letter
{Ctrl-PgDn}	CTRL-PGDN
{Ctrl-PgUp}	CTRL-PGUP
{Ctrl-PrtSc}	CTRL-PRTSC
{Ctrl-rightarrow}	CTRL-RIGHT ARROW
{Del}	DEL
{downarrow}	DOWN ARROW
{End}	END
{Enter}	ENTER
{Esc}	ESC
{Home}	HOME
{Ins}	INS
{leftarrow}	LEFT ARROW
{PgDn}	PGDN
{PgUp}	PGUP
{PrtSc}	PRTSC
{rightarrow}	RIGHT ARROW
{Shift-function key}	SHIFT-function key
{Shift-Tab}	SHIFT-TAB
{Tab}	TAB
{uparrow}	UP ARROW
{InpBreak}	User-input break

Since the dBASE uses braces for macro keywords, you must enter curly left braces that you want typed in a macro by surrounding the left brace in a set of braces like this {{}. To include a right brace, you can type it without special treatment because dBASE knows to treat the right brace as a literal character since it will not match with a left brace of a keyword.

```
 Layout   Words   Go To   Print   Exit                                   1:08:11 pm
[·······▼1······▼··2····▼····3··▼······4▼·······▼5······▼··6····▼····7··▼·······
{Alt-c}ua{Enter}
acct_rec{Shift-F2}o{Enter}
{Esc}ycust{Enter}
{Enter}
{Shift-F2}o{Enter}
{Esc}y{rightarrow}a_r_cust{Enter}
{Enter}
{rightarrow}{rightarrow}arletter{Enter}
pb
```

Figure 11-11 Macro that activates a view and prints a report

Adding or Removing Keystrokes

When you edit a macro, you may want to change the keystrokes stored. Your modifications may include adding, removing, copying, and moving keystrokes. Your reasons for changing the keystrokes may include removing unnecessary keystrokes or providing more keystrokes, such as complete database names rather than the first few letters.

Figure 11-11 shows a macro that activates the A_R_CUST view and prints a report. The macro must activate the ACCT_REC and CUST_LST database and activate the CUST_NO index tag so that the records can be properly combined when you use the A_R_CUST view. Then it activates the A_R_CUST view and prints the report in ARLETTER. This macro contains two keystrokes that are unnecessary. The {Enter}'s at the end of the third and fourth lines are unnecessary since the database is activated when you press SHIFT-F2. This macro also lacks other keystrokes that may prevent the macro from working correctly as more catalogs, databases, and index tags are added. For example, if you add an index tag that appears before CUST_NO in the index list in the ACCT_REC or CUST_LST databases, you will select the wrong index. You can include the index tag names, complete file names, and complete catalog names. Figure 11-12 shows the same macro after the {Enter} ending; the third and fourth lines are deleted and the index tags, filenames, and catalog name are filled in.

When you modify a macro, you can use the F6, F7, and F8 function keys to select, move, and copy macro text. These three function keys operate identically to their use in word-wrap bands in reports and

```
 Layout   Words   Go To   Print   Exit                                    2:35:11 pm
[·······▼1······▼··2···▼····3··▼······4▼·······▼5······▼··6···▼····7··▼·······
{Alt-c}uacct_rec{Enter}
acct_rec{Shift-F2}ocust_no{Enter}
{Esc}ycust_lst{Shift-F2}ocust_no{Enter}
{Esc}y{rightarrow}a_r_cust{Enter}
{Enter}
{rightarrow}{rightarrow}arletter{Enter}
pb
```

Figure 11-12 Macro in Figure 11-11 with characters added and deleted

editing Memo fields. To move text in a macro, move to the beginning of the text you want to move and press F6. Then, highlight all of the text you want to move. Press ENTER. Next, move the cursor to where you want the selected text moved. Press F7 and dBASE moves the selected text from its current location to the cursor's position. To copy text in a macro, move to the beginning of the text you want to copy and press F6. Then, highlight all of the text you want to copy. Press ENTER. Next, move the cursor to where you want the selected text copied. Press F8 and dBASE copies the selected text to the cursor's position.

Improving the Appearance

A few changes can make your macro code a little easier to read and will not adversely affect its performance. When you edit macros, you can press ENTER and TAB to arrange the keystrokes. Figure 11-13 displays a macro that has been rearranged. Since the order of the keystrokes is unchanged, it performs the same steps as the macro in Figure 11-12.

Unfortunately, when you save the macro, dBASE removes the ENTERs and TABs, providing only a temporary improvement in readability. Adding spaces to a macro produces a different result since dBASE includes them in the macro. The added spaces are pressed when the macro executes and will normally adversely affect the results.

Saving the Modified Macro

When you finish modifying the macro, press ALT-E and type an **S** to select Save changes and exit. dBASE returns to the Control Center. You can also press CTRL-END or CTRL-W. dBASE reviews the macro's contents. If it finds a macro keyword that it does not understand, such

```
 Layout   Words   Go To   Print   Exit                                    2:36:39 pm
[·······▼1······▼··2····▼····3··▼······4▼·······▼5······▼··6····▼····7··▼·······
{Alt-c}uacct_rec{Enter}

acct_rec{Shift-F2}
ocust_no{Enter}
{Esc}y

cust_lst{Shift-F2}
ocust_no{Enter}
{Esc}y

{rightarrow}a_r_cust{Enter}{Enter}

{rightarrow}{rightarrow}arletter{Enter}pb
```

Figure 11-13 Macro in Figure 11-12 with ENTER pressed to increase readability

as if you delete the e in {Enter}, it displays a box like Figure 11-14. You can reedit the macro or abandon the changes. Abandoning the changes returns the macro to its state before you modified it. If you do not want to save your changes, press ALT-E, type an **A** to select Abandon changes and exit, and a **Y** to confirm. You can also press ESC and type a **Y**. dBASE returns to the Control Center. dBASE stores the macro in a temporary file that it deletes when you exit dBASE. If you want to save the macro for later use, you must save the macro in a macro library.

Assigning a Longer Name to a Macro

When you initially create a macro, dBASE names the macro using the assigned key. You can change the macro name so the name describes the task that the macro performs. To rename a macro, press ALT-T for the Tools menu, type an **M** to select Macros, and an **N** to select Name.

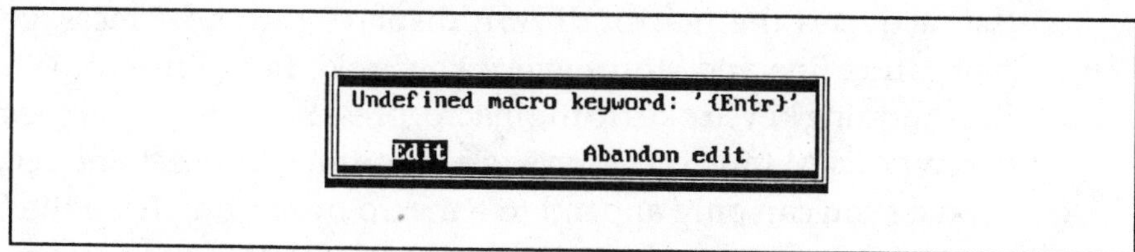

Figure 11-14 Error message for an improper keyword

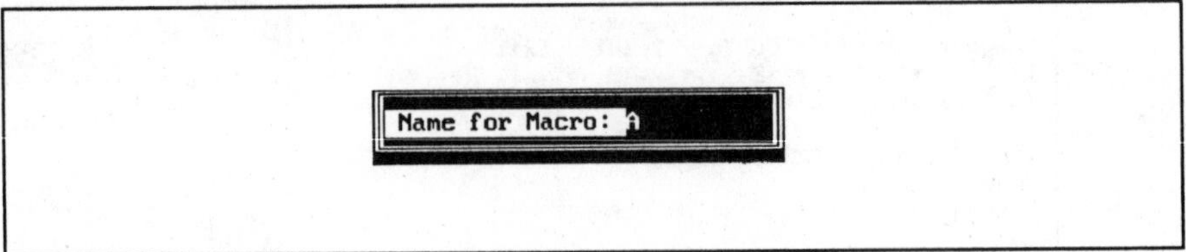

Figure 11-15 Prompt for macro name

When dBASE displays the macro display table, press the key that activates the macro. dBASE displays the prompt shown in Figure 11-15. Enter a macro name and press ENTER. Macro names follow the same requirements for field names, which are unique, start with a letter, and contain up to 10 letters, numbers, or underscores. When you rename a macro, you remain in the Macros menu box. If you execute the macro from the dot prompt, you must use this name when you use the PLAY MACRO command.

Appending Keystrokes to a Macro

Once you record a macro, you may want to add other keystrokes to it. Rather than modifying the macro and entering the letters and keywords that you want the macro to perform, you can append additional keystrokes to the end of the macro. Appending the macro is better than modifying the macro since appending automatically records the correct keystrokes as you walk through the remaining steps you wish to include. If you modify the macro and type the keywords and letters that you want the macro to perform, you may forget a keystroke.

To append keystrokes to a macro, press ALT-T to select the Tools menu and type an **M** to select Macros and an **A** to select Append to macro. When dBASE displays the macro display table, type the letter that activates the macro. dBASE displays the same message in the navigation line and stores every keystroke in the macro. When you finish adding keystrokes to the macro, press SHIFT-F10, or press ALT-T and type an **M** to select Macros, and type an **E** to select End recording.

Since you can only append to a macro by starting from the Control Center, you may need to modify the macro to remove unnecessary steps if the new commands require starting at a different location. For example, if you are entering the keystrokes for a macro that creates a report with group bands and you realize that the database must be sorted for the report to group the records properly, you may terminate the macro, exit the report design and put the database records in order. Once the records are in order, you can move back to the Report panel and start recording the macro again. Press ALT-T, type an **M** for Macros and an **A** for Append to macro, and type the letter or key assigned to the macro. Then, press SHIFT-F2 and move to where you left the report design and complete the design process. When you finish the report and return to the Control Center, press ALT-T for the Tools menu, type an **M** for Macros and an **M** for Modify, and type the letter or key assigned to the macro. Next, move in the macro to where you began appending steps. You will need to remove the {Shift-F2} and the keystrokes that you pressed to return to where you left the report design the first time. Then press CTRL-END to save the macro and return to the Control Center.

Deleting Macros

When you have macros that you do not need any more, you may want to delete them to make room for additional macros. To delete a macro, press ALT-T for the Tools menu, and type an **M** for Macros and a **D** for Delete. When dBASE displays the macro display box, type the letter or function key of the macro that you want to delete. When dBASE prompts for a confirmation, type a **Y** and press ENTER. Once dBASE copies the macro, it remains in the Macros menu box.

Copying Macros

Another way of creating macros is by copying existing ones. You may want to copy a macro so you can reassign the key that you use to execute the macro. Also, you may want to copy a macro so you can modify it and use it for a different purpose. To delete a macro, press ALT-T for the Tools menu, and type an **M** for Macros and a **C** for Copy. When dBASE displays the macro display box, type the letter or function key of the macro that you want to copy. Then type the letter or function key where you want the macro copied. If a macro is already assigned to the copy's destination, dBASE prompts for confirmation to overwrite the existing macro. If you type a **Y**, dBASE continues and will copy the macro to the destination. If you type an **N**, dBASE aborts the menu option. dBASE displays the original macro name and prompts for you to enter a new one. Enter a new macro name, delete the old one if necessary, and press ENTER. Once dBASE copies the macro, it appears in the Macros menu box.

Displaying the Macro Keystrokes as a Macro is Executed

When you create a macro that does not perform the tasks that you expect, you can change how dBASE performs the macro. Since a macro often executes instructions faster than you can follow, you will want to slow the macro's execution speed. Also, you will want to display the keystrokes as the macro performs them. To display the keystrokes a macro is performing, press ALT-T for the Tools menu, and type an **M** for Macros and a T for Talk to switch the Talk setting from OFF to ON. Since dBASE remains in the Macros screen, type a **P** and the key assigned to the macro to start executing the macro. When you execute a macro with Talk set to ON, dBASE displays the steps at the bottom of the screen. Figure 11-16 displays the bottom lines of the screen as dBASE performs the macro shown in Figure 11-13. You can change the speed that dBASE performs these steps as the macro executes by typing < and >. When you type <, dBASE slows the speed with which it executes the macro keystrokes. When you type >, dBASE increases the speed with which it executes the macro. You do not have to press SHIFT when you type these keys. For most keyboards, you are actually typing a comma or period to change the macro's speed, which are the keys below the < and >. It is just easier to remember < and >.

```
{Alt-c}uacct_rec{Enter}acct_rec{Shift-F2}ocust_no{Enter}{Esc}ycust_l
```

Figure 11-16 Bottom of the screen during macro execution when Talk is set to ON

Adding a User-Input Break

When you create a macro, you may need the user to provide information. The information may be a filename that you want to use to save a report or your name. When you play a macro with a user-input break, dBASE suspends performing the macro until you press SHIFT-F10. To include a user-input break in a macro, start recording the macro. When you reach the point where you want the user-input break, press SHIFT-F10 and type an **I** for Insert user-input break. If you are in the Control Center, you can press ALT-T and type an **M** for Macros and an **I** for Insert user-input break, although your macro will contain {Alt-t}mi. Continue recording the macro. You can include as many user-input breaks as you want. When you have finished recording the macro, press SHIFT-F10 and type an **E** for End recording. Next, modify the macro by pressing ALT-T for the Tools menu and type an **M** for Macros and an **M** for Modify. Type the key that the macro you have just created is assigned to. Move the cursor to the {InpBreak} keyword. This is the keyword for the user-input break. As you can see from the text and keywords that follow, dBASE continued recording every keystroke after the user-input break. Some of the text and keywords may need to be deleted since they contain information that the user will enter when the user executes the macro. After you modify the macro, press CTRL-END to return to the Control Center.

When you execute a macro with a user-input break, dBASE performs the keystrokes in the macro until it reaches the user-input break. Then it displays the message shown in Figure 11-17. Once the user presses a key, the message box disappears and the message shown in Figure 11-18 appears in the navigation line. When the user finishes entering information, the user presses SHIFT-F10. Then the macro continues executing until it reaches the end of the macro or the next user-input break.

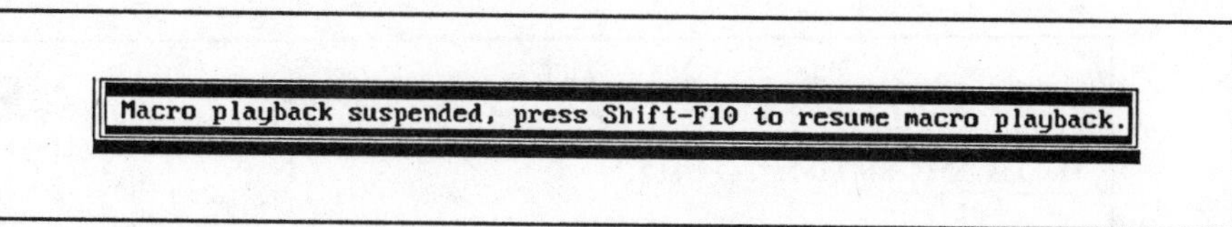

Figure 11-17 Message displayed when a macro reaches a user-input break

```
Press Shift-F10 to resume macro playback.
```

Figure 11-18 Message in navigation line during user-input break

Figure 11-19 displays a macro that uses a user-input break. This macro must be started in the SKILLS field in the Browse or Edit screen for the EMPLOYEE database. The macro activates the SKILLS Memo field and writes it to a file. When dBASE prompts for a filename, the macro suspends operation, which allows the user to type a different filename for each Memo field. After the user types the filename and presses ENTER, the user presses SHIFT-F10 and the macro closes the Memo field and moves to the next one. The user-input break is designed to continue after the text file is written so if the user enters an existing filename, the user can decide whether to overwrite or cancel writing to the specified file. If the user cancels, the user will have to press ALT-W, type two W's and a filename, and press ENTER. The macro uses TABs instead of END so the macro will perform identically if you execute this macro in the Edit or Browse screen.

Macro Libraries

When you create macros, dBASE deletes them when you exit dBASE. Rather than enter new macros each time, you can save a group of macros in a macro library. When you need to use a macro in a library, you retrieve the library and all of the macros are immediately available. Since you can create as many macro libraries as you want, you can save as many macros as you want. dBASE allows you to have only one library open at a time. Macro libraries are not part of a catalog.

```
Layout   Words   Go To   Print   Exit                              2:47:13 pm
[·······▼1······▼··2····▼····3··▼······4▼·······▼5······▼··6····▼····7··▼······
{F9}{Alt-w}ww{InpBreak}{F9}{Tab}{Tab}{Tab}{Tab}{Tab}{Tab}{Tab}{Tab}{Tab}{Tab}{Tab}
{Tab}{Tab}{Tab}{Tab}{Tab}{Tab}
```

Figure 11-19 Macro containing user-input break

To save a macro library, press ALT-T for the Tools menu and type an **M** for Macros and an **S** for Save library. When dBASE prompts for a filename, enter a filename and press ENTER. Do not enter a file extension since dBASE adds .KEY to the file. If you saved the macro library previously, dBASE prompts you that the file already exists and asks if it should overwrite the file or cancel the request to save the library. Type an **O** for Overwrite if you want dBASE to replace the file's contents with the macro library's contents or a **C** to cancel saving the library. Since dBASE does not save the macros unless you explicitly save them, you will want to save the macro library whenever you make a change that you want to be permanent. After saving the macros into a library, you remain in the Macros menu box.

The next time you want to use a macro in the macro library, you must load it into dBASE's memory first. Each time you exit dBASE, dBASE removes the macros from its memory. When you load dBASE again, the macro display box is empty. To load a macro library, press ALT-T for the Tools menu and type an **M** for Macros and an **L** for Load library. When dBASE displays a list of macro library names, highlight the one you want and press ENTER. After loading the macro library, you remain in the Macros menu box. Once you load the macro library, you can use any of the macros in the library. If you try to load another macro library after you have changed a macro in the current macro library, dBASE will prompt you to confirm that you want to replace the current library. Type a **Y** if you want to replace the current library and lose the changes that you have made since saving the library or an **N** to cancel the menu option for loading another library. If you have a macro library loaded when you load another macro library, dBASE combines the two. If both libraries contain macros that use the same key, dBASE uses the one in the library that you loaded last.

Transferring Macros between Libraries

Since dBASE does not have a menu option for transferring macros between libraries, you must use the Words menu. To transfer a macro between libraries, you must load the library with the macro that you want to transfer, modify the macro, write the macro to a text file, load the library from which you want to add the macro, create an empty macro, and read the text file into the macro.

Since transferring a macro between libraries involves many steps, you can follow the steps listed below which transfer the macro in Figure 11-19 from the GENERAL macro library to the EMPLOYEE library. In the GENERAL macro library, this macro is assigned to F3. In the EMPLOYEE macro library, this macro will be assigned to F3. While you do not have to use the same assigned key for both libraries, it prevents confusion. To transfer the macro, follow these steps:

1. Load the GENERAL library by pressing ALT-T and typing an **M** for Macros and an **L** for Load library. Highlight GENERAL.KEY and press ENTER.
2. Modify the macro in Figure 11-19. Type an **M** for Modify and press F3 to modify the macro assigned to F3.
3. Save the macro to a text file. Press ALT-W, and type a **W** for Write/Read Text file and a **W** for Write selection to file. When dBASE prompts for a filename, type **TRANSFER** and press ENTER.
4. Leave the macro by pressing ESC.
5. Load the EMPLOYEE library by pressing ALT-T and typing an **M** for Macros and an **L** for Load library. Highlight EMPLOYEE.KEY and press ENTER.
6. Create an empty macro by typing a **B** for Begin recording and pressing F3 for the key to assign the macro. When the Macros and Tools menu disappears, press SHIFT-F10 and type an **E**. This creates an empty macro. Since dBASE does not let you modify a macro that you have not created, this step provides a macro to add the text file.
7. Modify the F3 macro by pressing ALT-T for the Tools menu and typing an **M** for Macros and an **M** for Modify. When dBASE displays the macro display box, press F3.
8. Read the macro in the text file into the macro. Press ALT-W, and type a **W** for Write/Read Text file and an **R** for Read text from file. When dBASE prompts for a filename, press SHIFT-F1, highlight TRANSFER and press ENTER.
9. Save the macro by pressing CTRL-END. Now, you have a copy of the macro in the GENERAL macro library and the EMPLOYEE macro library.

Using Macros from the Dot Prompt

You can also use macros from the dot prompt. You can use macros to store commands. Storing dot prompt commands in a macro is inefficient. You would only want to create a macro that includes dot prompt commands if the macro performs tasks from the Command Center and the dot prompt and switches between the two. To use a macro from the dot prompt you must use dot prompt commands to play a macro and to load or save a macro library. While you can still use SHIFT-F10 for some macro options, other options are unavailable from the dot prompt.

When you want to store a group of commands that you enter from the dot prompt, you will want to store them in a program or another file. In Chapter 14, you will learn how to create programs. Chapter 10 described how you can store the dot prompt history in a file using SET ALTERNATE commands.

A program also behaves differently from a macro when dBASE encounters an error, such as that a file that you are creating already exists in the directory. When a program encounters an error such as file overwriting, dBASE temporarily suspends the program until you enter a response. When a macro contains an error such as file overwriting, dBASE continues executing the macro.

The dot prompt command does not use the key assigned to the macro, although it is the same as the name unless you rename the macro. To load a macro library, you must type **RESTORE MACROS FROM** followed by a space and the macro name. To save a macro library, you must type **SAVE MACROS TO** followed by a space and the macro name. To run a macro from the dot prompt, you must type **PLAY MACRO** followed by a space and a macro name. You can also use ALT-F10 to play a macro. If you want to edit a macro, you must enter the Control Center first.

Macro Editor Options

By now you are probably an expert with many of the dBASE editor features as you have used them in a number of places. There are a number of options that will make your work with macros much easier. These menu options are similar to the menu options that you use for modifying forms, labels, memo fields, and reports. These options are discussed in detail in earlier chapters but they are quickly covered here to provide a one-stop source for macro information and to provide the specifics for their use with macros.

Saving the Macro from the Layout Menu

As you modify a macro, you may want to save it periodically. This way you can restore the macro as it existed before the change if you make a mistake. To save the macro, press ALT-L for the Layout menu and type an **S** to select Save this macro. After dBASE saves the macro, it remains in the macro editor.

Hiding the Ruler Line

When you edit macros, you may use the ruler at the top of the screen to judge where you want to press ENTER and TAB, if you plan to print the macro or write part of it to a file. You can use the Words menu option to hide the ruler.

Enabling Automatic Indentation

Another feature that you may use if you will be printing or exporting the macro is to indent portions of the macro. The Enable automatic indent option allows you to change the left margin to indent portions of the macro. The Words menu is again the source for the menu option that will make this change.

Adding a Blank Line

You can add a blank line to a macro to improve readability or to allow room for the addition of instructions. Adding a line has no effect on a macro's performance since dBASE removes all ENTERs when it saves the macro. To add a line, use the same ALT-W and **A** entry that works on the other design screens.

Removing Macro Lines

You can remove a line from a macro if it is not needed. When you remove a line from a macro, you remove any keystrokes displayed on the line. Again it is the Words menu that provides the required Remove command.

Inserting a Page Break

You can add a page break to a macro to split a macro into pages for printing. To add a page break, move the cursor to the line that you want after the page break, adding a line if necessary. Next, press ALT-W for the Words menu and type an **I** for Insert page break. dBASE removes page break characters from the macro when you save it.

Data Transfer Features

You can copy part of the macro to a file or copy from an external file into the macro. Writing a macro to a file provides an easy way to transfer a macro from one macro library to another. You may also want a copy of the macro for documentation purposes. When you read text from a file into a macro, the file must contain macro instructions or other text that you would want to include as part of another macro. Use the Words menu option to read and write text file information.

Positioning on a Specific Line Number

You can move the cursor to a specific line in the macro by pressing ALT-G for the Go To menu and typing a **G** for Go to line number. When dBASE prompts for a line number, enter the line number that you want to move to and press ENTER.

Using Search Features

You can perform a forward or backward search to find text in a macro. You have used the Go To menu features to perform this task in Report designs, Form designs, and Memo fields. Just as in those environments, you have the option to search for the text or to supply a replacement string. You also have the option to consider or ignore capitalization. If you need a refresher on the mechanics of these options you can refer to the discussions in earlier chapters.

Printing the Macro

When you want to print a macro, press ALT-P and type a **B**. You can make changes that will affect the print output after invoking the Print menu. Be sure to complete all your changes before typing **B** to begin printing.

The Line numbers option lets you select whether dBASE prints line numbers next to each line of the macro. This lets you quickly match the lines in the printout to the editing screen.

GETTING STARTED

➤ To learn about macros, you will want to create a macro. Follow these steps to create a macro that activates the EMPLOYEE catalog, selects the NAME index tag, and prints the EMPLOY01 report.

1. Move to the Data panel since you want the macro to start from here.
2. To start the macro recording, press SHIFT-F10 and type a **B** for Begin recording. Press F1 when dBASE prompts for the key to assign the macro.
3. Change the catalog to EMPLOYEE by pressing ALT-C and typing a **U** for Use a different catalog. Type an **E** and press ENTER to select EMPLOYEE.CAT.
4. Select the EMPLOYEE database by typing **EMPLOYEE**. Press SHIFT-F2 to enter the database design screen.
5. Select the NAME index tag. When the Organize menu appears, type an **O** for Order records by index tag and **NAME**, and press ENTER.
6. Press ESC and type a **Y** to return to the Control Center.
7. Select the EMPLOY01 report. Press the RIGHT ARROW three times to move to the Report panel.

8. Print the report. Press ENTER and type a **P**. When the Print menu appears type a **B**.
9. End the macro by pressing SHIFT-F10 and typing an **E** for End recording.
10. View the macro. Press ALT-T, type an **M** twice, and press F1.
11. Change the macro by pressing the RIGHT ARROW nine times to move to the left brace in the first {Enter}. Type **Employee.**
12. Save the macro by pressing ALT-E and typing an **S**.
13. Rename the macro by pressing ALT-T for the Tools menu, typing an **M** for Macros and an **N** for Name, and press F1 for the macro key assignment. When dBASE prompts for a macro name, press the BACKSPACE key twice, type **EMPLOY_REP**, and press ENTER.
14. Save the macro in a macro library called EMPLOYEE by typing an **S** for Save library. When dBASE prompts for a library name, type **EMPLOYEE** and press ENTER. Press CTRL-END to return to the Control Center. You can use this macro when the macro library is loaded by pressing ALT-F10.

CHAPTER 12

Using the Applications Generator

An application is a series of programs to handle your processing needs. If you need to maintain a base of information and use it to create reports and labels, your application will include the programs needed to handle each of these tasks. Part of the process required to develop the programs is designing the input and output the application will need to work with.

You have already created most of the components of a complete application as you have designed databases, reports, labels, and custom forms. What is needed is a link that can join each of these objects into a unified system. The dBASE IV Applications Generator is designed to provide that link without the need for programming.

The fact that you can create a complete application system by making menu selections rather than programming is an important timesaving feature of the applications generator. Although code will ultimately be generated, your focus will be on the objects that make up the application. This means that you will concentrate on the design of reports, databases, labels, forms, menus, and other information sources. From your perspective creating the application will consist of defining the system components or objects. Some of these objects are developed with the Applications Generator and others are developed through commands at the dot prompt or through the ASSIST menus.

You have already seen that objects like databases, reports, forms, and labels are essential components of meeting your application needs. The Applications Generator allows you to design objects like pop-up menus and entry screens. When combined with existing objects these features can be used to create an application for users who do not know any dBASE commands. The menus that you design from the application generator will contain elements that represent business tasks. Although selecting these items will cause the execution of dBASE commands, the user does not need to be aware of the work that is taking place behind the scenes.

Defining Your dBASE Application

The Applications Generator can construct an application from a series of design object files and your definitions, but it cannot design an application for you. Designing an application requires some of your time. The design itself is often an iterative process created by producing a rough draft and critiquing it to refine the components.

Although many users think they can hire a consultant to create a design for them, it is not possible to delegate the entire process and come up with a system that will meet your needs. You must play an active role in the needs analysis if you hope to be pleased with the final system results. Keep in mind that the outside resources can facilitate the process, bring a fresh perspective, and guide you in the right direction, but they cannot possibly know all that you need the system to do unless you tell them.

Performing a Needs Analysis

To create a system that will assist you in your business and provide a competitive edge, you need to take a close look at the tasks that you must perform and the information that you manage in doing so. You must also look beyond the current day-to-day operation of your business and focus on improvements that are needed to make your operation more effective.

The steps that are described in the needs analysis will work regardless of whether you are a business person attempting to automate your inventory system, a professor desiring to create a student information system, or a librarian wishing to put together an acquisitions and holdings system. The purpose of the system does not dictate the process since the same steps are required regardless of the purpose of the application.

Recording the Results of Your Analysis

Many of the steps that you will perform in the needs analysis should be recorded as you complete them. Although you may feel it is sufficient to focus on each area, you are likely to have a vague and fuzzy definition of your system unless you record the work as you progress from step to step. Also, recording the information allows you to share it with others to obtain their input. The importance of this last step as you proceed through the process cannot be overemphasized. Support for the system will be required if it is to be successful. There is no better way to ensure success than to allow all those whose cooperation is needed some role in the design of the system. Likewise, there is no better way to ensure failure and lack of acceptance for the new system than to design it on your own, operating in a vacuum.

Create an Overall Definition of the System

At a high level, without getting too involved in the details, you need to establish the parameters in which the system will operate. The essence of what you are doing is defining the scope of the system. If the system is an inventory system what data will the system manage and at what point will data become part of the system? Will the system monitor only inventory on hand or will it also process orders for items whose quantity is running low? Although it may seem obvious that it should do both, if you are the warehouse manager and another manager is in charge of ordering, you will need the other manager's support and involvement before even considering a system that will automate both sets of tasks.

If you are analyzing an accounts receivable system there are similar questions to ask. At what point are accounts flagged as overdue? Are customers notified immediately? Does the same individual who handles regular billing handle the collection of overdue accounts? Figure 12-1 provides one possible overview of an accounts receivable system.

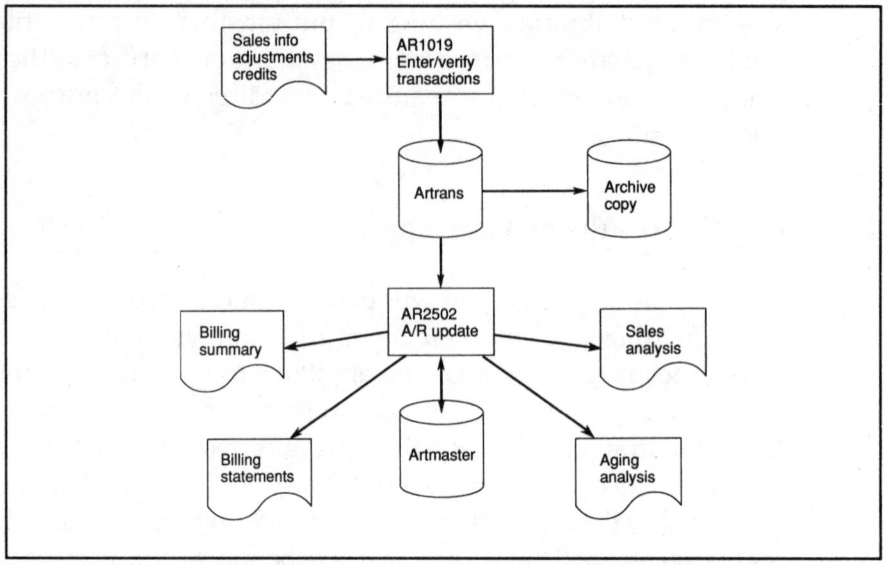

Figure 12-1 System overview of an accounts receivable application

This establishment of the boundaries of the system is important for all systems. You must understand the scope before you begin to define the subtasks that comprise the system.

Define System Components

With the overall definition established you will want to define the system components. If there is an existing system you will want to look at the system inputs, reports, and other outputs from this system. You can incorporate aspects of the existing system that are meeting your needs well and also focus on the shortcomings of the current system.

At this point you do not want to be designing system output on a line by line basis. You want to make decisions like whether or not you need a special quarterly or year-end report and whether or not both a summary and a detail version of daily reports are needed.

Examine the current processing carefully. Look for tasks that are handled by the formal system as well as informal activities that staff members have assumed. You want to consider both formal and informal processes for inclusion in the new system.

Interview Staff Members

Although you can start the process with interviews to obtain all the information, you may want to obtain an overview of the system and its components first. If written documentation on the existing system is available it is usually advisable to obtain an overview with this method. Although you want to be open to the ideas of the staff members you interview, you need to be prepared for the fact that some will need to be drawn out to obtain the information you need. Others will have a tendency to ramble in their discussions of the system. A base of knowledge will help you deal with both situations effectively and may prevent the need for a second interview as you will be able to guide the discussion with a conceptual understanding of the current system.

Interview the staff performing system tasks. Focus on input forms, notebooks they maintain, reports they prepare, and any other physical components of the system. Center your discussions around these items and attempt to expand the horizons of individuals using the system to determine expanded features that would make a new system better than existing methods.

Document the Interview Results

Document the results of each interview. Although copious notes are not required, trusting all this important information to memory will result in the loss of important information. Also, if you review your interview notes soon after the discussion, it will only take a few minutes to fill in missing points.

If the user does not object, you may prefer to record the discussion. This will free you to participate fully in the discussion, rather than having to be concerned with note-taking.

Create a System Diagram

Create a flow chart of the information flow within the system. All tangible input forms and reports should be shown on the chart. It should also include reports that are needed but not currently a part of the system. If data from outside sources is required or if forms flow from department to department before entry, these flows should also be recorded in the diagram. You do not need to be concerned with using the standard flowchart symbols or using a flowchart template to draw the appropriate symbols. Just be sure you use the same symbol for identical activities like calculations, reports, input forms, and other processes.

Review the System Flowchart

Once you draft the overall system flow, ask others to review the chart for changes. Be prepared for an iterative process and don't try to freeze the design at this point. Often important insights occur for staff members that work with the system once they see things mapped out. Ask for ideas that will make the process more efficient and fill in any major areas that were overlooked. In addition to adding components to the system, you may be able to identify processes that are useless or reports that are seldom used in their current form. Attempt to solicit agreement to eliminate as much of this overhead as possible.

Dissect the Enhanced Design into Smaller Components

Once you establish the overall system flow and identify the components you can begin to focus on the individual components. You can determine each of the components of the system that will need to be created. You can sketch items like reports, menus, and entry screens on paper.

Determine the databases that are needed to support the system and sketch out the design elements that each will contain. You can review the discussions of database design earlier in the book for additional assistance with this task.

Using dBASE IV as a Prototyping Tool

Once you identify the major components you are ready to call on dBASE IV for help. Rather than build the entire system, enter all the real data, and present it to the user for final testing, you can use dBASE as a prototyping tool. You can add a few records to the database design and build rough reports and entry forms that can be enhanced later. These quick versions can form the basis of your final system and will involve the user in the design process while it is still easy to make changes. The process of actually seeing a screen and reviewing a sample report often encourages the user to make new suggestions, causing further iteration in the system design. This should not be thought of as a step backward but rather a further step toward the design of a system that will adequately meet the user's needs. A system built with this additional iteration often has a longer life after implementation before requiring major changes.

The Design Process

There are a number of techniques that you can use to successfully design an application with the Applications Generator.

The objects that you combine in an application can be created in the Assist mode, the dot prompt, or from within the Applications Generator. Most of the objects are created with the first two options since you want to view the object's appearance before incorporating it into an application.

Design Files, Reports, and Screens

You can switch back and forth between the generator and the dot prompt or Assist mode in designing objects. A better approach is to create all the objects that require Assist or the dot prompt first. This is a good idea for several reasons. First, objects like the screen design, labels, and reports are the backbone of your application since they represent your system inputs and outputs. Creating these objects first allows you to circulate them for user approval while you are designing the menu and other components that will link all the components together. Second, finishing with the Control Center options first minimizes moving in and out of the Applications Generator and ensures that you have all the components you need to build your system.

You can also create objects within the Applications Generator. You may use this feature when you are in the middle of creating an applications file and realize that you have not created an object that you want to use. When you select a form, label, or report and use the F1 (Pick) key to select one, dBASE displays <create> at the top of the list. If you select <create>, dBASE enters the design screen for the form, label, report, or database. Since dBASE reduces the memory the Applications Generator uses when you are creating an object, you can print or view the object to ensure that you are pleased with its appearance. When you finish designing the object and save it, dBASE returns you to your position in the Applications Generator.

Create Design Objects with the Applications Generator

The Applications Generator can create menus, lists, and batch processes. It also allows you to place design objects like menus and lists on the application screen from which users will make selections.

There are three menu styles supported. You can have bar menus at the top of the screen. You can also have pull-down menus that are attached to bar menus. These menus look like dBASE menus on the Control Center and other design screens. Pop-up style menus are the last choice and allow you to place a menu box anywhere on the screen. For each of the menu styles, you will add menu items. Menu items are descriptions of a task dBASE will perform just the way Use a different catalog is a menu item for the dBASE Catalog menu.

The list types supported are file lists, structure lists, and values lists. File lists allow users of the completed application to select from a list of files. Structure lists look like file lists except they display the field names in a database or view for selection. Values lists allow a user to select from field values or contents for a field within an application database or view.

Assign Actions to Menu Items

Once you add menu items, you can assign actions to them. A menu item's action is the task dBASE performs when you select the menu item. dBASE lets you select these tasks from menus. Examples of actions that a menu item can perform are displaying another menu, printing labels or a report, displaying the records using a custom form, and executing another dBASE program.

Once you create the menu and assign actions to the menu items, you can change the menu's appearance to control what the user sees. Layout options include changing the size of boxes, their color, and the placement of these boxes on the screen. Once you combine the application menus and the other design objects, and select their appearance, you are ready to convert the application into code so you can execute it.

Document the Application

When you create the application, document it for future reference. When you need to make a change to the application at a later date, the documentation will save you time and make your job easier. dBASE has a template that you can use to generate object documentation for your application. When you generate object documentation, dBASE stores information about the application in a file. The object documentation displays the colors selected, the settings, the menus, and the menus' layouts. Figure 12-2 shows a page of the documentation from the accounts receivable application.

Generating the Application

Your next task is converting the application design into code that dBASE can execute. Using another template, dBASE generates the code for the application. This code can be executed whenever you want to work with the application.

Once you convert the application design into dBASE code, you must test it. Even though you may have tested individual components like reports and labels separately, testing an application is a necessary step to uncover any design elements you overlooked. Adequate testing prevents problems from surfacing after you give the application to someone else to use.

Working with the Applications Generator

When you create an application in dBASE, you will use the Applications Generator to combine the different objects you have created. You will need to learn how to start the Applications Generator from the dot prompt or Assist mode. You will also want to learn more about the desktop service that you will use to create the application design.

Starting and Stopping the Applications Generator

You can start the Applications Generator from the dot prompt or the assist menu. To start it from the dot prompt, type CREATE APPLICATION APPNAME where APPNAME is the name of the application that

```
Application Documentation for System: ACCT_REC.PRG


Display Application Sign-On Banner: Yes

Screen Image:
    0         10        20        30        40        50        60
   >....+....|....+....|....+....|....+....|....+....|....+....|....+
00:
01:
02:
03:
04:
05:
06:            Accounts Receivable Application
07:
08:            This application is used for generating
09:            aging analysis, data entry, and labels
10:            using the data in the accounts
11:            receivable database.
12:
13:
14:
15:
16:
17:
18:
19:
20:
21:
22:
23:
24:
   >....+....|....+....|....+....|....+....|....+....|....+....|....+
Main Menu to Open after Sign-On: A_R_MENU.POP

Sets for Application:
---------------------
  Bell          ON
  Carry         OFF
  Centry        OFF
  Confirm       OFF
  Delimiters    OFF
  Display Size  25 lines
  Drive
  Escape        ON
  Path
  Safety        ON

Starting Colors for Application:
--------------------------------
 Color Settings:
   Text          : W/N
   Heading       : W/N
   Highlight     : N/W
```

Figure 12-2 Page of documentation generated for the accounts receivable application

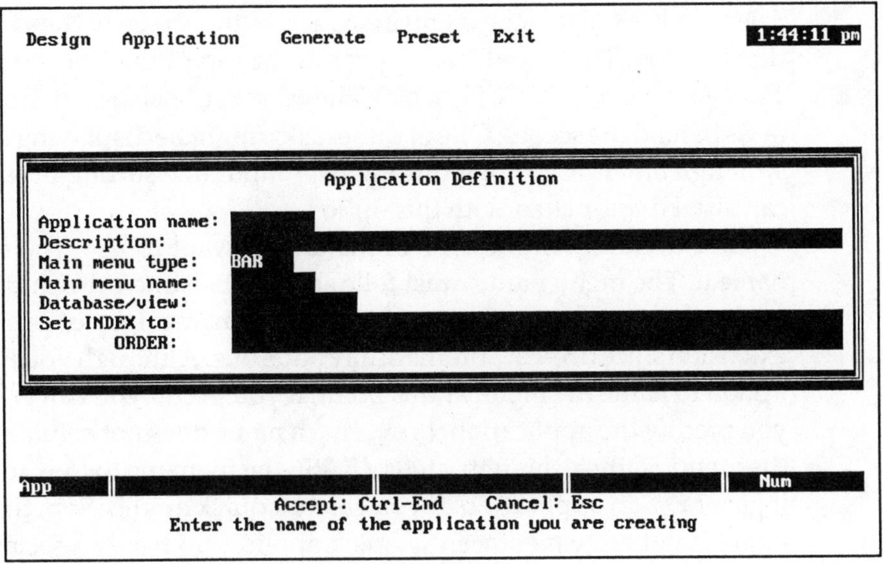

Figure 12-3 Application definition screen

you want to create. The application name must follow the rules for DOS filenames. You do not need to add an extension since dBASE will add one for you.

To start from the Control Center, move the highlight to the Application panel. Highlight <create> and press ENTER. You will be given a choice of writing a dBASE program or using the Applications Generator. Highlight the Applications Generator and press ENTER.

With either approach the application definition box shown in Figure 12-3 must be completed. The first entry is for the application name. When you enter from the dot prompt, this entry has already been completed with the application name that you typed. It is blank if you entered through the Control Center. Your entry must follow the rules for DOS filenames. The next entry is the description that appears in the application code and the object documentation. This description appears as the file description below the filename when the application name is highlighted in the Application panel in the Control Center.

The next box shows the type of the main menu. The default is for a bar-style menu like the one at the top of the Applications Generator screen. Once the cursor is in this field, you can change the menu type by pressing the SPACEBAR. Selecting POP-UP provides the pull-down style and vertical menus that you use for dBASE menu selections.

Selecting BAR places the menu items across the screen in the same way that Catalog, Tools, and Exit appear at the top of the Control Center. The last option is BATCH, which allows you to perform a number of tasks behind the scenes. One of these tasks might be displaying a menu, although other tasks not requiring user input like sorting or indexing can also be completed with this option.

After deciding on the type of menu you want to use, you need to name it. The menu name must follow DOS filename rules and cannot be the same as another menu or application name. Do not provide an extension since dBASE automatically adds one. Although you have the option to name the menu at this point, if you prefer you can wait until you modify the application. Providing a name does not actually create the menu. Rather, this entry tells dBASE the filename to look for when it generates an application. If you create a quick application, the menu name is not relevant since the quick application uses a special menu file.

The database name or view is the next entry. The database or view must be from the current catalog or directory. If you press SHIFT-F1, dBASE lists the databases and views (QBE extension) in the current catalog. If you type a filename, you must include the extension if it is for a view. The extension is not necessary for a database. The Set INDEX to field is used to enter the names of the indexes that you want active in the application. You can include up to 10 index files although you are limited to 58 characters. You can also specify indexes that the application uses later in the application design process. If you use the F1 (Pick) key, dBASE only lists the files with an .NDX extension. The last entry is for ORDER. You can skip this entry or include the controlling index for the application. Since you can select different indexes in each portion of the application, you probably will leave this field blank at this time.

To leave the application definition screen, press CTRL-END to save the definition and continue working on the application. If you want to abandon the application definition, press ESC and type a **Y**. Once you press CTRL-END, dBASE displays the desktop shown in Figure 12-4. This is the design surface you will use to place menus and other text that will appear in the application. To leave the Applications Generator, you can press ALT-E to select the Exit menu. Next, choose Save changes and exit or Abandon changes and exit. If you entered the Applications Generator from the dot prompt you will be returned there; if you

Tip: Location of files used in applications.

All of the database, view, forms, reports and labels files should be in the same directory as the application. dBASE cannot find files used in an application if they are in another directory. You can eliminate this problem by specifying the directory containing the files for the PATH setting in DBSETUP.

entered from the Control Panel, you will be back in the Control Center when you exit. When you want to modify an application you can highlight the application name in the Application panel, press ENTER, and type an **M**.

The Desktop

The desktop is the surface you use for creating your applications. Menus allow you to define the design objects. You can position these

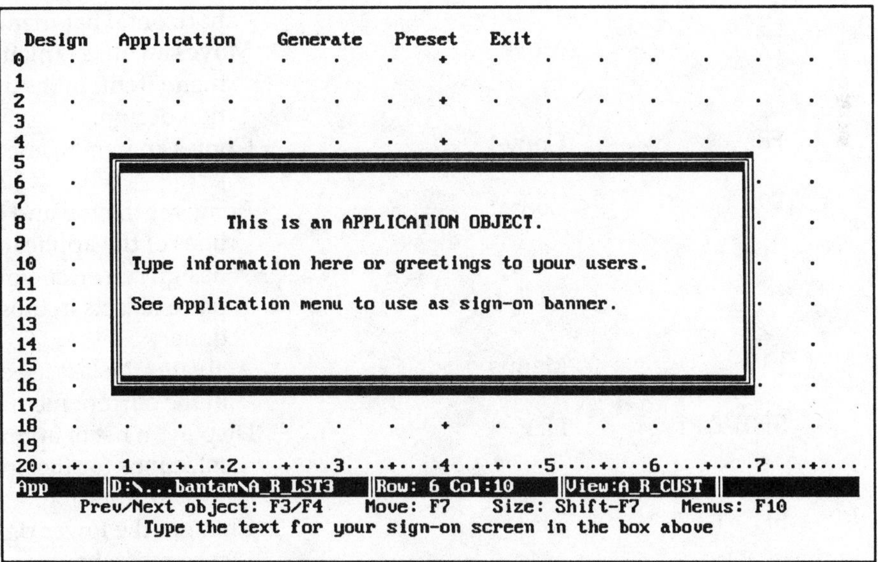

Figure 12-4 Initial application design screen

objects on the surface of the desktop in the position you want them when your application runs. Menu selections, special key assignments, and the help system will make your job easy.

Navigating within the Applications Generator A number of special keys can help you navigate within the Applications Generator. The function key assignments are identical to their use in other design screens. They are summarized for your convenience in Table 12-1.

Table 12-2 summarizes the other key assignments. You will notice that these are either identical or very similar to their use in other parts

Table 12-1 Function Keys in the Applications Generator

Key	*Name*	*Description of function*
F1	Help	Displays help on current task.
F3	Previous	Moves to previous object (menu, sign-on banner) so you can work on it.
F4	Next	Moves to next object (menu, sign-on banner) so you can work on it.
F5	Field	Marks beginning and end of horizontal bar menu items.
F7	Move	Moves an object (menu box, menu item) in the application design.
F8	Copy	Copies an item to another object.
F9	Zoom	Removes the top and bottom lines of the application design screen so you can place objects in those locations.
F10	Menus	Activates the last used menu in the current menu bar.
SHIFT-F1	Pick	Displays a list of appropriate selections for the option you are entering.
SHIFT-F7	Size	Changes the lower right corner of a box.

Table 12-2 Movement Keys in the Applications Generator

Key	*Description of function*
INS	Switches between Typeover and Overwrite mode.
HOME	Moves to beginning of line of an entry or first option in a dialog box.
END	Moves to end of line of an entry or first option in a dialog box.
DEL	Deletes the highlighted character.
BACKSPACE	Deletes the previous character.
UP ARROW	Moves the cursor up one row.
DOWN ARROW	Moves the cursor down one row.
RIGHT ARROW	Moves the cursor to the right or to the next menu bar option.
LEFT ARROW	Moves the cursor to the left or to the previous menu bar option.
PGUP	Moves the cursor to the next page in a list or next item in the Item menu.
PGDN	Moves the cursor to the previous page in a list or previous item in the Item menu.

of dBASE. Naturally since you are designing objects some of these keys have specific assignments that move them within an object or from item to item in the object.

The Menu Bar Figure 12-5 shows the first menu bar that you see after starting the Applications Generator. The second item on the menu is Application since the application itself is being designed. As you move to other objects on the work surface this option will alternate among Menu, List, and Batch depending on the object you are working on.

You can activate the menu by pressing F10 or by pressing the ALT key in combination with one of the letters that start a menu selection. As with other dBASE menus you can make a selection from one of the pull-down menus by highlighting the option and pressing ENTER or by typing the first letter of the option.

The other menu bar in the Applications Generator is used when you are working on an object. Figure 12-6 shows the menu bar when you are working on an application menu with the Item menu box displayed.

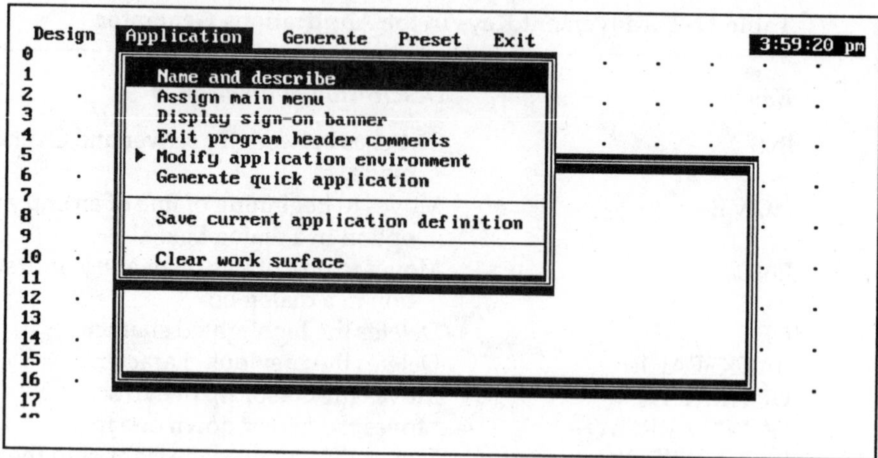

Figure 12-5 Initial Applications Generator menu bar

Help The help provided in the Applications Generator is similar to the help provided throughout dBASE. It is context-sensitive and provides the same button options at the bottom of the box for printing or moving to related topics or an overview of available help options.

Creating Sample Applications

The Applications Generator has a diverse feature set that will allow you to create applications that are diverse in appearance. If you need a quick application that can fit within the limitations of the automatic

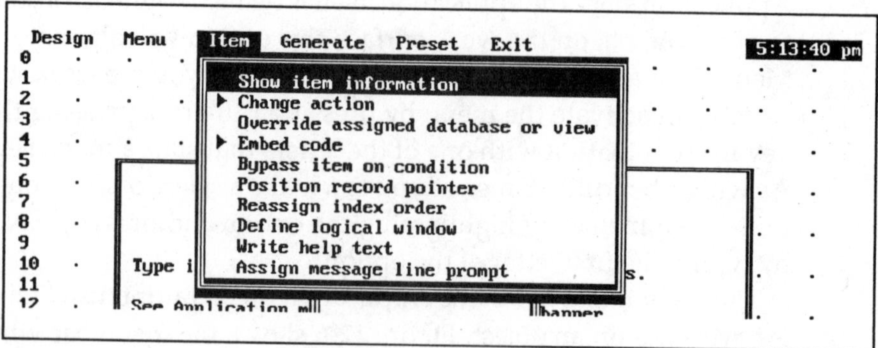

Figure 12-6 Menu Bar for designing menus

application generation, very little work is involved since even the menu is predefined. If you are building a large system, more time will be required. There is not a step-by-step procedure that can be followed for the more complex applications since the steps are driven by the composition of the system you are attempting to design. Once you become comfortable with the options, you will not have a problem making selections for your own application.

Since the easiest way to learn how to use the Applications Generator is by creating applications, you will follow the creation of two different applications. The first application takes advantage of the quick application option in the Application menu box. This example discusses the basic steps that you perform when you create an application. When you use the quick application option, you are limited to one database, one form, one report, and one label form. Since you will want to enhance some applications, the quick application option may not always meet your needs. The second application creates an application that uses more of dBASE's features.

Creating a Quick Application

If you want to create a simple application that combines a database or view, a form, a report, and a label form, dBASE can generate the application for you. This will allow you to build a professional-looking menu-driven system with very little effort. You can have dBASE generate a quick application for an accounts receivable system. The system will use a view created from the accounts receivable and customer files, A_R_CUST view. You need to start the Applications Generator and enter the data in the application definition screen. Since dBASE automatically includes a menu for quick applications in the same file containing the other portions of the application design, ignore the menu type or menu name fields. Once you finish the application definition, press CTRL-END to save this information and enter the desktop screen.

To generate the application, press ALT-A for the Application menu and type a **G** for Generate quick application. dBASE displays a dialog box for the quick application. Figure 12-7 shows a completed one for the A_R_CUST view. This box contains the same settings for the database file, Set INDEX to, and ORDER in the application definition screen. The database file must contain the database or view the applica-

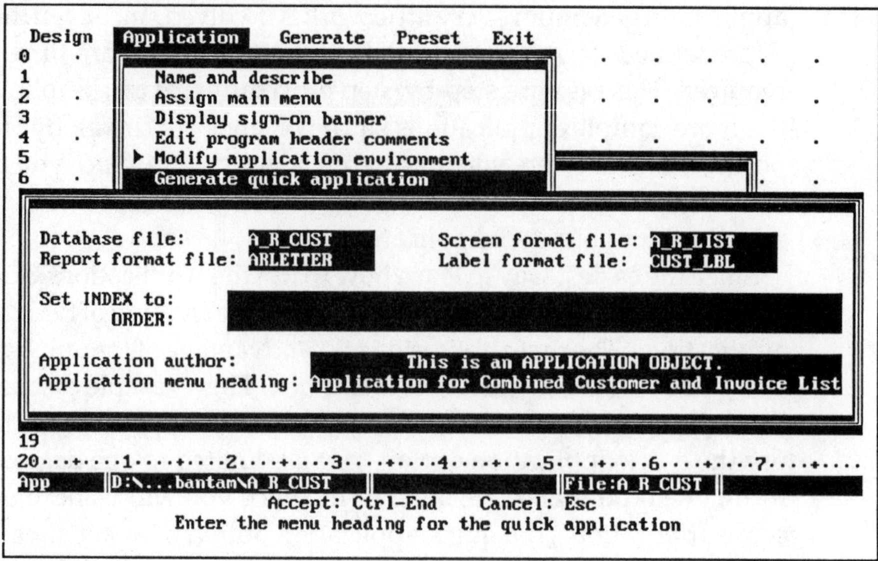

Figure 12-7 Generate quick application dialog box

tion will use. Since dBASE assumes that this file has a .DBF extension unless you provide an extension, you must include a .QBE extension for views. For the screen format file, enter **A_R_LIST** as the form file the application will use when you edit the database or view. This form contains fields from the accounts receivable and customer databases. For the report format file, enter **ARLETTER** as the Report design file the application will use. This report is a form letter that will be sent to individuals with overdue accounts. For the label format file, enter **CUST_LBL** as the Label design file the application will use. These labels are suitable for use on the envelopes that will be used to mail the late notice letters.

You can use SHIFT-F1 to list the appropriate files in the current catalog for each file. You do not have to include the extension if you type the name unless it is different from the default. From the files list, you can select <create> if you want to create a database, form, label, or report. Once you finish creating the database, form, label, or report, dBASE returns to the Applications Generator and includes the file you created in the quick application. If you do not include an entry for the report or label format file, dBASE omits reports or labels in the quick application. If you do not include a screen format file, dBASE uses the default screen for editing records.

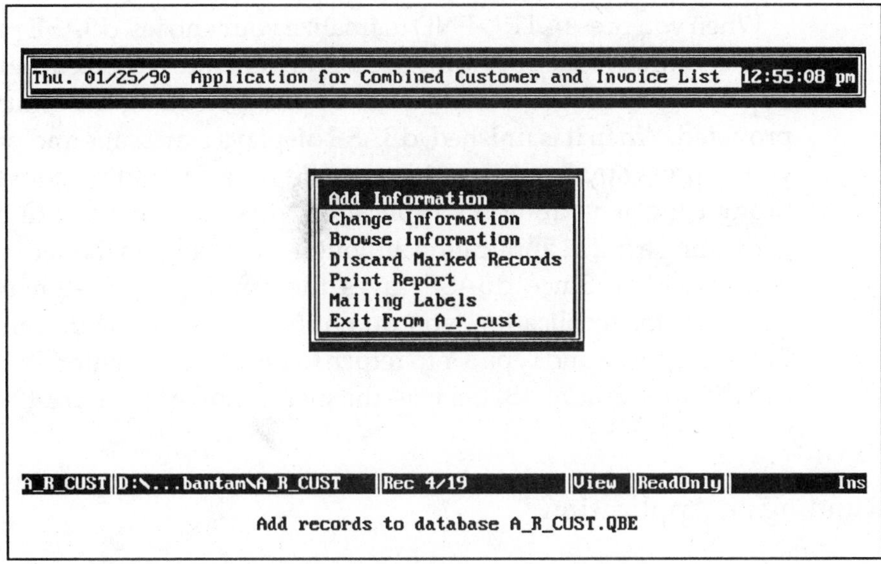

Figure 12-8 Main menu of quick application

The Set INDEX to option can include the index filenames that the application will use. You must include the .MDX or .NDX filename extension. You must include the production index file, the .MDX file with the same filename as the database, in the list if you want to use it. If you are using multiple index files, separate the filenames with commas. If you do not include any index files, the application does not use an index to order the records and the quick application does not include Reindex Database in the menu. For the ORDER option, you must enter the index filename or index tag that you want to control the order for the application. If you do not specify an order, the records in the application will be presented in their natural database order.

Since the Applications Generator is designed to create professional applications, there are options for entering descriptive text. For the application author option, enter text that you want included in the dBASE instructions for the quick application. dBASE initially displays the first line of the default sign-on banner, which is the entry screen for the application. For the application menu heading, enter the text that you want at the top of the application screen. Figure 12-8 displays the A_R_CUST quick application screen with an application menu heading.

When you press CTRL-END to finalize your entries, dBASE prompts you to confirm that you want dBASE to generate a quick application. Type a **Y**. dBASE generates a quick application using the information provided. When it is finished, dBASE displays a message and prompts you to press any key to continue. If you type an **N** in response to the prompt for generating an application, dBASE removes the box for generating a quick application although it remembers the settings that you provided. Since dBASE saves the application design when it generates the application, you do not have to save the design again. Press ESC twice and type a **Y** to return to the Control Center. When you run the application, dBASE uses the menu shown in Figure 12-8.

Running an Application

Once you generate an application, you can run it. The steps are the same whether you direct dBASE to generate a quick application or you design a custom one. From the dot prompt, type **DO**, a space, and the application name. From the Control Center, highlight the application name in the Application panel and press ENTER. If the INSTRUCT setting is ON, dBASE prompts you to select between running the application and modifying the application. Highlight Run application and press ENTER, or type an **R**. dBASE prompts for a confirmation that you want to run the program. Type a **Y**. If this is the first time that you are executing the latest version of the application, dBASE compiles the application creating .DBO files that it uses to execute the application and begins running the application. If the application contains a sign-on screen, dBASE displays the sign-on screen and waits a few seconds or until you press ENTER to display the main menu.

Figure 12-8 shows the main menu of a quick application that uses the A_R_CUST view. Since this view is a combination of two databases, ReadOnly appears in the status line to indicate you cannot change the data. You can use the Edit and Browse screens to view the data. When you select Change information, dBASE displays the current record with the A_R_LIST form specified when you generated the quick application.

If you select Add information or Discard marked records, dBASE displays an error message since you cannot do either in this application. To continue using the application, press a key.

When you highlight Print report or Mailing labels, the Report or Label design file the application uses appears in the message line. When you select one of these, dBASE displays the first 16 fields in the database or view. Then it prompts you for the record that you want to see in the database or view. If you want to change the current record position, select the appropriate menu items. When you finish, or if you do not want to change the current record position, type an **R** to select Return. Next, dBASE displays the output options for the report or labels. Make a selection, or type an **R** to abort printing a report or labels. If an application prints reports or labels to a disk file, it uses the report or label design filename with a .PRT extension. If the file already exists, it prompts you to select between overwriting the disk file or canceling printing the labels or reports. If an application uses an indexed database, you can reindex the database with the Reindex database menu option to update the index file entries. The Exit from option followed by the database or view name lets you leave the application program.

In an application, you can select menu items from pop-up menus, like the one in Figure 12-8, by typing the first letter of the item you want. For pop-up and horizontal bar menus, you can select a menu item by highlighting it and pressing ENTER. If you press F1 in a quick application, the application ignores the keystroke since a quick application does not have help screens. Also, the quick application is set to ignore ESC. Therefore, you must use menu items to leave the application.

To leave an application, you can select Exit, Quit or another appropriately named menu item. In some applications, you can also press ESC and type a **Y** when dBASE prompts you if you want to exit the program. You will be returned to either the Control Center or to the dot prompt, depending on your location before starting.

Modifying an Application

Once you save an application, you may want to return to the design to make a few changes. To modify a design from the dot prompt type **MODIFY APPLICATION,** a space, and the application name. To modify a design from the Control Center, highlight the application name in the Application panel. If the INSTRUCT setting is ON, you can modify the design by pressing ENTER and selecting Modify application. You can also modify the application by pressing SHIFT-F2. When you generate the application again to incorporate your changes, dBASE warns you that an application with a .PRG extension already exists and allows you to type a Y to replace the old version. If you type an **N**, dBASE does not generate the application although it saves the new application design. When dBASE finishes saving and generating the application, dBASE displays a message on the bottom of the screen. You can press a key to remove the message and continue with the application design.

If you modify a quick application, you will not be able to modify the menu design. The menu design within a quick application is fixed. The application design must retain the same menu settings provided by the Generate quick application menu option.

Building Your Own Application

The quick application creates most of the application design for you. When you design your own application, you need to perform these steps yourself. However, when you design the application, you can take advantage of features the quick application did not use. You can use multiple forms, reports, and labels. You can select which database, view, index, or index tag is used for each section. You can provide more meaningful menu item descriptions. You can perform additional tasks like update queries and reindexing a database. You can add help screens and define the colors for the application.

Following the steps for generalizing the ACCT_REC application for the ACCT_REC database will introduce you to many new options. This application can add records using the AR_ENTER form design, edit existing records using the default Edit screen, or browse the records but not allow changes. The application uses the ACCT_REC database to print aging reports using the AR_AGING report design, or labels using the AR_LABEL label design. The application also contains an Other menu item, which displays another level of menu selections that perform an update query to delete records, pack the database, reindex a database, or return to the original menu. The original menu also contains a Quit menu item that returns to the dot prompt or Control Center. By building this application, you can learn about application design features that you can use when you are designing your own applications. The ACCT_REC application uses the application definition shown in Figure 12-9.

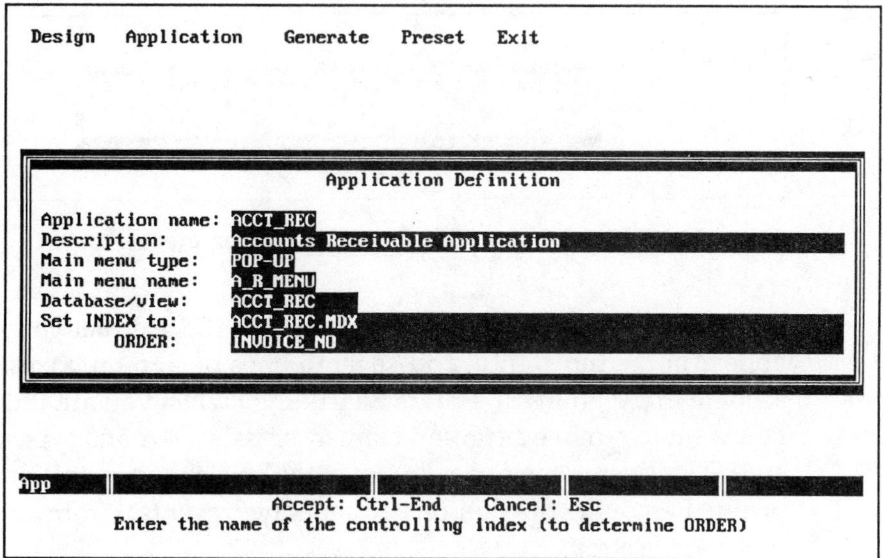

Figure 12-9 Application definition screen for ACCT_REC

Adding a Sign-On Screen

When you execute an application, you may want to see a screen indicating that you have activated the correct application before you begin making menu selections. A screen containing textual information about the application is typically called a sign-on screen. For example, when you load dBASE, the opening screen is dBASE's sign-on screen. With the sign-on screen dBASE displays, you can proceed to the next screen by pressing ENTER or waiting until the box disappears after a few seconds.

You can add a sign-on screen to an application built with the Applications Generator. To create a sign-on banner, press ALT-A and type a **D** for Display sign-on banner. When dBASE displays the prompt shown in Figure 12-10, type a **Y**. When the application displays a sign-banner, it displays the information in the first box in the application design screen like the box in Figure 12-11. You can change the text in the sign-on banner by typing the text directly into the box. Working in this box is like working in the Label design screen since you can add and remove lines using CTRL-Y and CTRL-N.

You can permanently alter the default signs on banner by pressing ALT-P for the Preset menu and typing an **S** for Sign-on defaults. When

Display frame as "sign-on banner" at run time?

Yes No

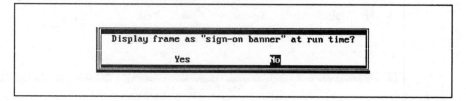

Figure 12-10 Selecting if frame is the sign-on banner

dBASE displays a box with three lines, type the text that you want to appear in the third, fifth, and seventh lines of sign-on boxes in subsequent applications and press CTRL-END when you are finished. If you want to remove a sign-on banner, press ALT-A and type a **D** and an **N**. This does not remove the text in the box in the application design screen. Removing the sign-on banner only prevents it from appearing in the application.

When you run an application with a sign-on banner, dBASE displays the sign-on banner. The sign-on banner has the same size, contents, and position on the screen that it has in the application design. If you do not press ENTER to remove the sign-on banner, is disappears after a few seconds. Once the sign-on banner disappears, the main menu appears.

Changing the Size of Boxes

Once you add the text that you want in the sign-on banner or a menu box, you can reduce the box size to eliminate the blank space or enlarge

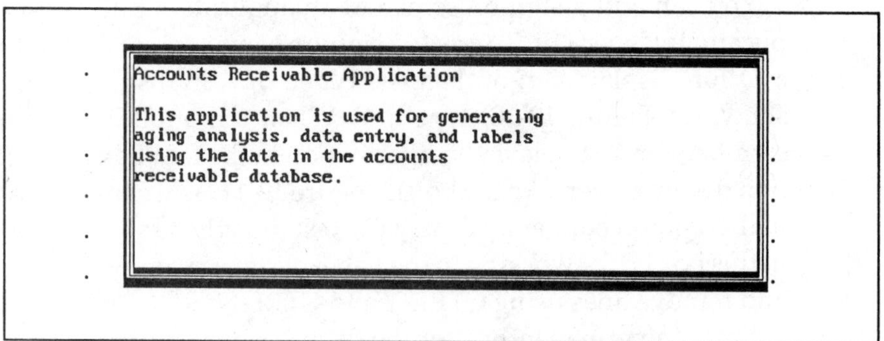

Figure 12-11 Frame for ACCT_REC used as sign-on banner

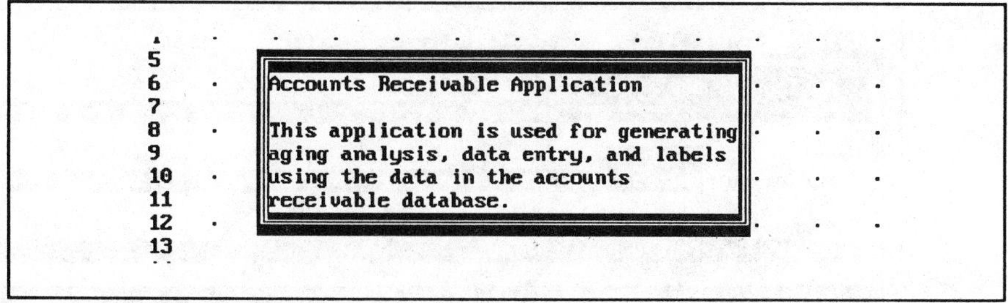

Figure 12-12 Resized frame for ACCT_REC used as sign-on banner

the box so you can enter more text. To change a box size, press the SHIFT-F7 (Size) key. The black line defining the box becomes bright white and flashes. When you change the box size, you are changing the position of the lower right corner of the box. You can press the arrow keys to adjust the box size. As you press the arrow keys, dBASE adjusts the box size to display the box's new size. You cannot reduce the box size to make it smaller than its contents. When you position the lower right corner of the box, press ENTER and the line defining the box size returns to normal. Figure 12-12 shows the sign-on banner after the size is changed. If you want to change the upper left corner, move the entire box so the upper left corner is where you want it. dBASE always keeps the text in the box in the same relative position to the upper left corner when you change the box size.

Creating a Pop-up Menu

If you want to create an application to perform multiple tasks, you must create a main menu to select the tasks that you want the application to perform. From this main menu, you can add additional menus to create submenus.

You can add horizontal bar and pop-up menus to an application. Since the main menu in the Accounts Receivable Application is a pop-up, horizontal bar menu options are discussed when the second menu is created.

Pop-up menus list each menu item on a different line in the same way that the Display sign-on banner and Generate quick application appear on different lines in the Application menu box. You create a pop-up menu using the Design menu.

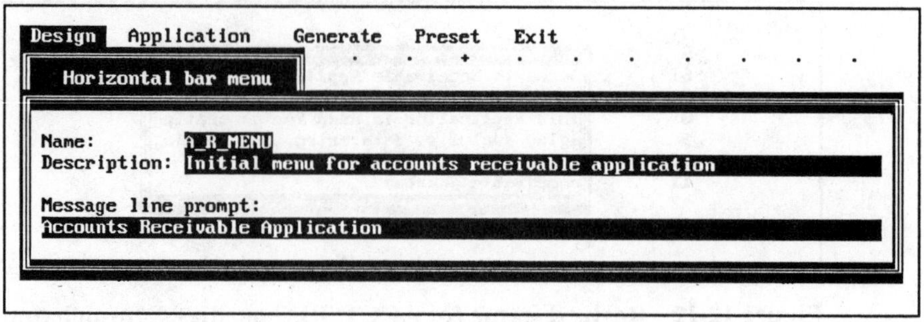

```
Design  Application   Generate   Preset   Exit

  Horizontal bar menu

 Name:          A_R_MENU
 Description:   Initial menu for accounts receivable application

 Message line prompt:
 Accounts Receivable Application
```

Figure 12-13 Dialog box for creating a menu

When you create a menu, it must be the same type menu that you selected in the application design screen. For example, in the applications definition screen for this application, the main menu type is pop-up. If you create the A_R_MENU as a horizontal bar menu, dBASE cannot find the menu design file since the pop-up and horizontal bar design files have different file name extensions. To change the main menu type, press ALT-A for Application and type an **A** for Assign main menu. From this menu you can enter a new main menu name and type before pressing CTRL-END to return to the application design screen.

To create a pop-up menu, press ALT-D for Design and type a **P** for Pop-up menu. dBASE lists the existing menu files for the menu type. You can select <create> to create a new one. When you select <create>, dBASE displays the dialog box for creating a menu. Figure 12-13 shows the completed box for A_R_MENU in the ACCT_REC application. The menu name can consist of up to eight letters, numbers, or underscores that must be different from existing menu, application, or program names. The menu description appears in the object documentation. The message line prompt appears in the message line when the menu appears unless the highlighted menu item has its own message line prompt. When you enter the information for the menu, press CTRL-END. dBASE adds a blank menu box to the application design screen. Figure 12-14 displays an empty box for a pop-up menu. As you can see from the figure, when you add a menu box, the menu box is placed on top of the other application boxes. The one on the top is the current one. Since dBASE remembers each box, you can continue to add new boxes. Later you will learn how to switch between the boxes.

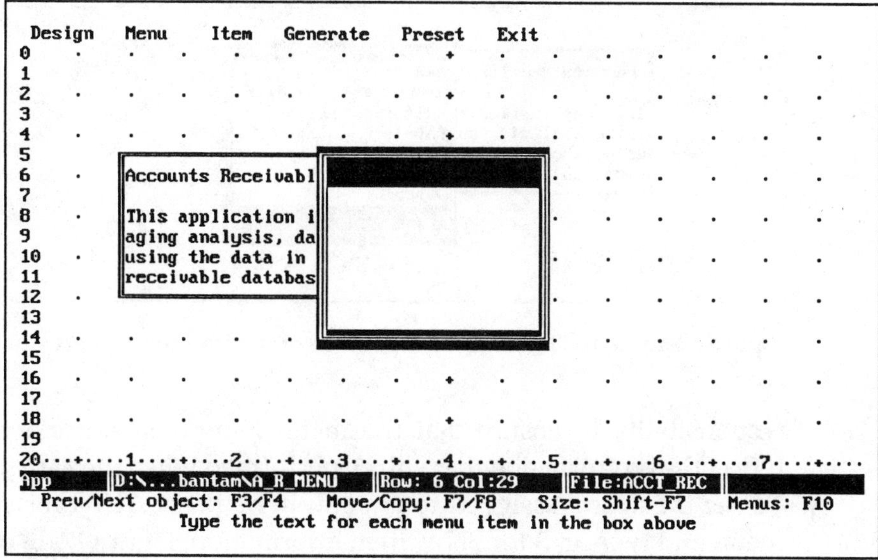

Figure 12-14 Initial pop-up menu box

Adding Menu Items

Once you create the pop-up menu, you can add the menu items. When you first add a menu, the cursor is in the upper left corner in the box. From this position you can start typing menu items. To enter the menu item text, type the text and press ENTER to move to the next line before typing the next menu item. With a pop-up menu, you want each menu item to start with a different letter. When you run an application and have a pop-up menu, typing a letter selects the first menu item that starts with the letter. Once you enter the menu item text, you can change it by moving to where you want to make a change and entering the new characters. Figure 12-15 displays the pop-up menu for the ACCT_REC application.

Adding Actions to Menu Items

When you add menu items to a menu, dBASE does not interpret the text to determine what it should do when you select a menu item. Initially, each menu item performs no task. To convert the menu items into actions, you must assign an action to each menu item. It is your

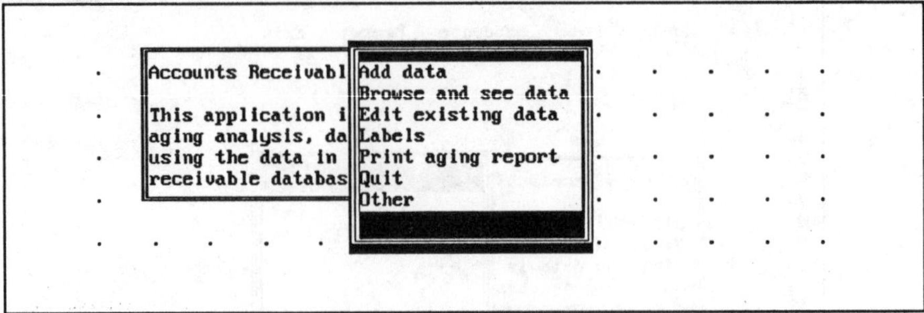

Figure 12-15 ACCT_REC pop-up menu box with menu items

responsibility to ensure that the menu items you show accurately reflect the type of action that will be performed when they are selected. To see the action assigned to a menu item, press ALT-I for the Item menu and type an **S** for Show item information. Figure 12-16 displays the item information for Print aging report menu item in the A_R_MENU. To change the menu item's action, press ENTER to leave the item information screen and type a **C** for Change action. dBASE displays the selection box in Figure 12-17. You assign actions to each menu item by selecting the action you want the item to perform and entering the additional information that each selection requires.

You can use menu items to provide multiple options for the same task. For example, in the ACCT_REC application, you can assign one menu item to enter new accounts receivable data and another menu item to modify existing data but not permit the addition of new records. You can also use menu items to extend the Quick Application limita-

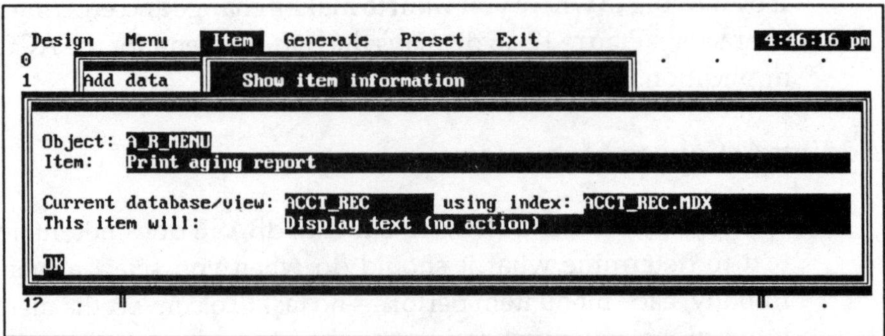

Figure 12-16 Dialog box for describing menu item's action

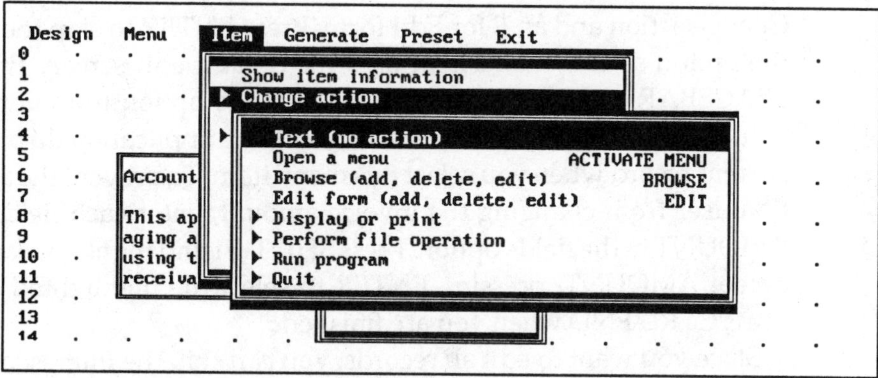

Figure 12-17 Selection box for selecting menu item action

tions of one database or view, one form, one report, and one label. For example, one menu item can print the AR_AGING report and another menu item can print the ACCOUNTS report.

Editing Records with a Menu Item You can assign a menu item to edit records and use other settings to limit the editing features available. To assign a menu item to Add data in the ACCT_REC application, press ALT-I for the Item menu and type a **C** for Change action and an **E** for Edit form. For the Format file, type **AR_ENTER**. Since AR_ENTER has an .SCR extension, you do not need to include it. You can also press SHIFT-F1 and select from the list. If you select <create>, you can create a screen form that is included in the dialog box when you save and exit the design screen. Since you want to add records, leave the mode option at Append. This option moves the record pointer to the end of the database so you can add new records. When the mode is set to Append, you can only modify the first three options. The fields option allows you to select which fields you can add. Since you are using a form to enter data, leave this field blank. The format file is the only setting changed for the Add records menu item. Press CTRL-END to save the menu action. Type an **S** for Show item information. As the dialog box indicates, this item is now assigned to use a form to edit a database or view. Press ENTER to select OK and remove the dialog box. Press CTRL-END to remove the Item menu. Press the DOWN ARROW twice to move to the Edit existing data.

For the Edit existing data menu item, you want to create limits on the editing features. First, press ALT-I for the Item menu and type a **C** for

Change action and an **E** for Edit form. Press ENTER to skip the format file option so this menu item uses the default edit screen. Press the SPACEBAR and ENTER to change the mode option from append to edit. When the mode option is set to Edit, the application displays the current record when you select this menu item. To prevent the application user from changing the invoice amount, enter each field except AMOUNT in the fields option. Press SHIFT-F1 and highlight each field except AMOUNT, pressing ENTER to select the highlighted option. Press CTRL-END when you are finished.

Since you want to edit all records, you can skip the filter, scope, for, and while options by pressing ENTER until you reach the Allow record add option. This option, like all of the options below the While option, switch between Yes and No when you press the SPACEBAR. Press the SPACEBAR to change the Allow record add option to No to prevent the user from adding new records when this menu item is selected. You want to maintain the settings for the other options so the user can edit records, delete records, use the Edit screen menus, and reposition the record in the index if you change the index field value. Since the Keep image on exit option is set to No, dBASE will clear the screen when you exit the edit screen. Figure 12-18 displays the completed the dialog box for the Edit existing data menu item. Press CTRL-END twice to save the menu item action and remove the menu items from the screen. Press the UP ARROW to move to the Browse and see data menu item.

Browsing Records with a Menu Item You can assign a menu item to use dBASE's Browse screen and place limitations on the Browse screen features. To assign the Browse and see data menu item to use the Browse screen, press ALT-I for the Item menu and type a **C** for Change action and a **B** for Browse. The fields, filter, and format file options are identical to the options that you used for the Add data and Edit existing data menu options. The fields to lock on and freeze edit for field options are identical to the Freeze field and Lock fields on left option available in the Fields menu in the Browse screen. The maximum field column width places an upper limit on every Character field column so more columns can appear on the screen. The options in the third group except for the Compress display option are identical to the options for using the Edit screen. The compress display option changes the Browse screen table to show two more records. Figure 12-19 displays the completed dialog box for the Browse and see data menu item. This

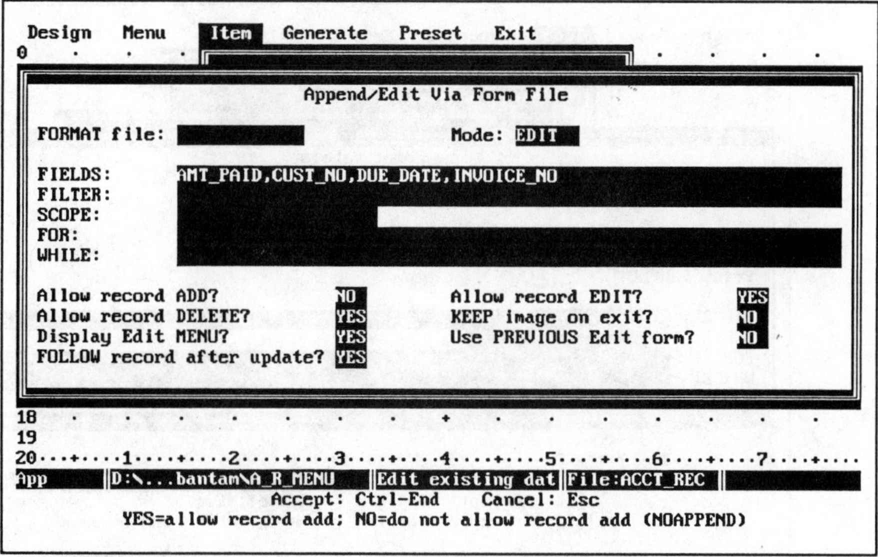

Figure 12-18 Filled-in box for Edit existing data menu item

menu item only allows users to view data. Therefore, settings for the Allow record add, Allow record edit, and Allow record delete are No.

```
Design   Menu   Item  Generate   Preset   Exit                1:45:04 pm
                 Show item information
                Browse a Database file or View
FIELDS:
FILTER:
Fields to LOCK onscreen:    0       FREEZE edit for field:
Maximum column WIDTH:       0       FORMAT file:

Allow record ADD?           NO      Allow record EDIT?          NO
Allow record DELETE?        NO      KEEP image on exit?         NO
Display Browse MENU?        NO      Use PREVIOUS Browse table?  NO
FOLLOW record after update? YES     COMPRESS display?           NO
App   D:\...bantam\A_R_MENU   Browse and see da   File:ACCT_REC
                    Accept: Ctrl-End     Cancel: Esc
      YES=display Browse menu; NO=do not display Browse menu (NOMENU)
```

Figure 12-19 Filled-in box for Browse and see data menu item

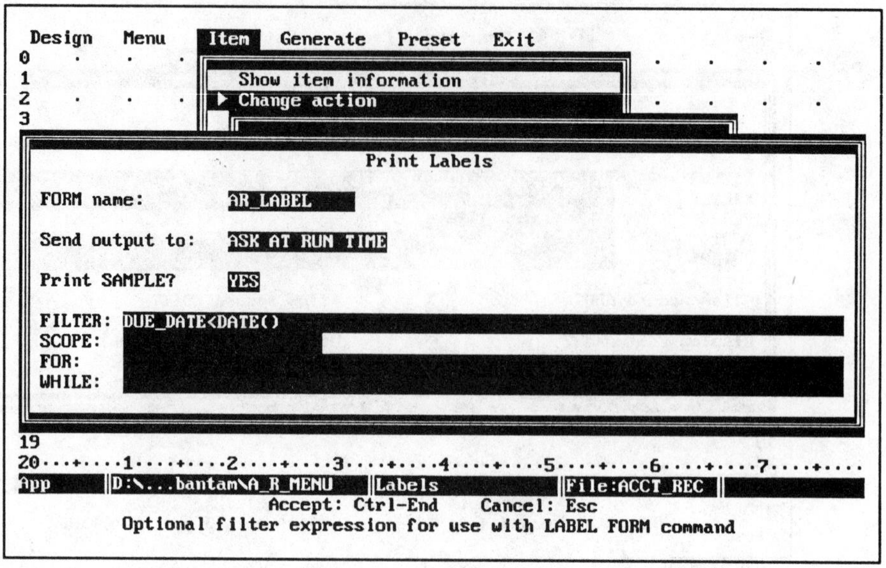

```
 Design   Menu    Item   Generate   Preset   Exit
0   .     .    .
1               Show item information
2   .     .    . ▶ Change action                          .    .    .    .
3
                            Print Labels

 FORM name:            AR_LABEL

 Send output to:       ASK AT RUN TIME

 Print SAMPLE?         YES

 FILTER: DUE_DATE<DATE()
 SCOPE:
 FOR:
 WHILE:

19
20···+····1····+····2····+····3····+····4····+····5····+····6····+····7····+····
App      ║D:\...bantam\A_R_MENU  ║Labels            ║File:ACCT_REC ║
                  Accept: Ctrl-End    Cancel: Esc
          Optional filter expression for use with LABEL FORM command
```

Figure 12-20 Filled-in box for Labels menu item

The menus are hidden and unavailable since the display browse menu is set to No. Press CTRL-END to return to the Item menu box and CTRL-END again to remove the Item menu box from the screen. Press the DOWN ARROW twice to move to the Labels menu item.

Printing Labels from a Menu Item You can assign a menu item to print labels and provide other selections to determine how the labels are printed. To assign the Labels menu item to print labels, press ALT-I for the Item menu and type a **C** for Change action. From the selection box for Change action, type a **D** for Display or print. When dBASE prompts you to select between reports, labels, or display/list, type an **L** for Labels. dBASE displays a dialog box like the one in Figure 12-20 which is completed for the ACCT_REC application. For the Form name, type **AR_LABEL** as the label design filename. You can also press SHIFT-F1 and select AR_LABEL from the list. You do not need a file extension since AR_LABEL uses the default label extension. If you select <create>, dBASE allows you to create a label design that is included in the dialog box when you save the design and exit the Label design screen.

You can specify an output location for the labels or request that dBase ask you at run time. The send output to option determines where the application prints the labels and can be changed with the SPACEBAR. Select Ask at run time by pressing the SPACEBAR three times. When you run this application and select Labels, the application displays a selection box containing the locations where it can print the labels. dBASE creates this selection box for you. The other options, printer, disk file, or screen are other places where the application can print the labels. The Print sample option selects whether the application prints a sample label for alignment purposes before it prints the labels. Leave this option at Yes so it will print a sample label and then prompt you if you want another until you type an **N**, when it will print the labels.

The filter, scope, for, and while options let you select which records dBASE uses to print labels. In this application, you want to print labels for the records from the ACCT_REC database where the due date for the invoice is prior to the current date. In the FILTER option, type **DUE_DATE<DATE()**. Since this completes this dialog box, press CTRL-END twice to leave the menus. Press the DOWN ARROW to move to the Print aging report.

Printing A Report from a Menu Item Just as you can print labels with a menu item, you can also print a report from a menu item. You can even switch to design mode and create the report that you want to use. For the Print aging report, press ALT-I for Item and type a **C** for Change action and a **D** for Display or print. When dBASE prompts you to select between reports, labels, or display/list, type an **R** for Report. dBASE displays the dialog box like the one shown in Figure 12-21 which is completed for the Print aging report item. For the Form name, type **AR_AGING** as the Report design filename. You can press SHIFT-F1 and select from the list. If you select <create> from the list, dBASE enters the Report design screen. When you finish designing the report, save and exit the report design to include the report design in the dialog box. For the Heading option, enter the text that you want to appear at the top of the report. This heading appears on each page before the Page Header Band or Report Intro Band.

The next four options determine which parts of the report the application prints. You can change these options by moving to the option and pressing the SPACEBAR to change the setting. Leave the report format setting at full detail by pressing ENTER to move to the next option. The Full detail setting includes the Detail Band in the report. The other setting, Summary only, omits the Detail Band from the

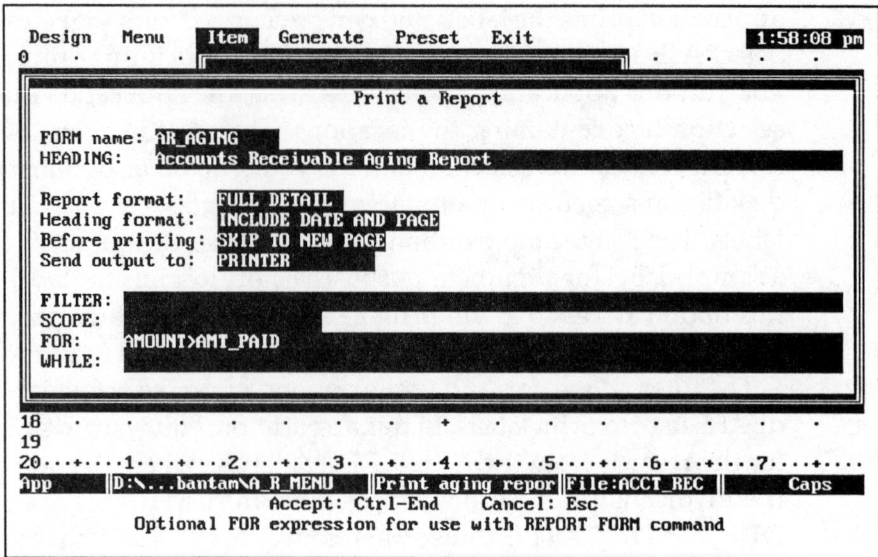

```
Design  Menu  Item  Generate  Preset  Exit                        1:58:08 pm
                         Print a Report
FORM name:  AR_AGING
HEADING:    Accounts Receivable Aging Report

Report format:      FULL DETAIL
Heading format:     INCLUDE DATE AND PAGE
Before printing:    SKIP TO NEW PAGE
Send output to:     PRINTER

FILTER:
SCOPE:
FOR:        AMOUNT>AMT_PAID
WHILE:

18
19
20
App  D:\...bantam\A_R_MENU  Print aging repor  File:ACCT_REC  Caps
                 Accept: Ctrl-End    Cancel: Esc
        Optional FOR expression for use with REPORT FORM command
```

Figure 12-21 Filled-in box for Print aging report menu item

report. Change the heading format to include page and date by pressing the SPACEBAR before pressing ENTER to move to the next setting. When an application prints a report, it omits the lines containing the page number and date from the Page Header Band. By setting the header format option to include page and date, the report will include the page, the heading entered in the dialog box, and the date where the date and page number appear in the Page Header Band. If you select plain, the Page Header Band only appears at the beginning of the report and the Page Footer band does not appear. For the ACCT_REC application, you can leave the remaining settings as they appear. If you changed the Before printing option from Skip to new page to Do not eject, dBASE would not advance the printer to the next page before printing the report. You can select from Printer, Disk file, Screen, or ask at run time for print locations.

The filter, scope, for, and while options let you select the records dBASE includes in the report. To limit the report to records where the AMOUNT is greater than the AMT_PAID, enter AMOUNT>AMT_PAID for the For option. Press CTRL-END twice to save the menu item action and remove the Applications Generator menus from the screen. Press the DOWN ARROW to move to the Quit menu item.

Quitting the Application from a Menu Item When you are executing an application, you can leave the program using a menu option or by pressing ESC and typing a **Y**. Pressing ESC is not a good solution for someone who does not know dBASE. Also, the application may change some settings and not return them to their original settings if you terminate the application with ESC. A better solution is to include a menu option that returns to the previous menu or exits the program. If you provide menu items to leave the program or a menu, you can alter the application so the user cannot press ESC to leave the program. For the Quit menu item in the ACCT_REC application, press ALT-I for the Item menu and type a **C** for Change action and a **Q** for Quit. dBASE displays a box that lets you select between returning to the calling program (RETURN) or quitting to DOS (QUIT). For the ACCT_REC application, type an **R** for Return. Next, dBASE displays a confirmation box to confirm that you want the menu item to return control to the program that called the menu with the highlighted menu item. Press ENTER. Since dBASE returns to the Item menu, press CTRL-END once to remove the menus. Press the DOWN ARROW to move to the Other menu item.

If you assign Return as a menu item action in the main menu, the application stops when you select the menu item. If you assign Return as a menu item action for a menu that is not the main menu, the application returns to the menu that invoked the menu with the Return menu action. If you assign Quit to DOS for any menu item, the application stops when you select the menu item and exits dBASE. The Quit to DOS option performs the same way regardless of which menu calls it.

Activating Another Menu from a Menu Item You can have a menu item activate another menu. For example, when you select Change action from the Item menu, the Applications Generator displays another menu box. To have the Other menu item activate a menu called AR_OTHER, press ALT-I for the Item menu and type a **C** for Change menu and an **O** for Open a menu. dBASE displays a dialog box for you to use when entering the menu type and name. For the menu type, press ENTER to select BAR. Type **AR_OTHER** for the menu name. Just as when specifying the menu name and type in the applications definition screen, entering the type and name only describe the menu name to find when you generate an application. To create the menu, you must perform the steps that you performed for the main menu to design the menu, enter menu items, and assign actions to the menu items. Since this is the only action you are assigning to this menu item, press CTRL-END twice to remove the menus from the screen.

Adding a Horizontal Bar Menu

The discussion on creating the ACCT_REC application main menu describes how to create a pop-up menu, enter menu items, and assign actions to the menu items. The Other menu item in the main menu activates a horizontal bar menu. Creating this menu and adding the menu items and their actions will illustrate the steps you perform when you create your own horizontal bar menus. A horizontal bar menu lists each menu item across the top in the way that Design, Application, Generate, Preset, and Exit appear at the top of the application design screen.

To create a horizontal bar menu, press ALT-D for the Design menu and type an **H** for Horizontal bar menu. dBASE displays a list containing <create> and existing horizontal bar menu files. To create a new menu, highlight <create> and press ENTER. dBASE displays the same dialog box for entering the menu name, description, and message line prompt that you filled in when you created the pop-up main menu. For the menu name, type **AR_OTHER** and press ENTER. For the message that will appear in the object documentation, type **Menu when you select Other from main menu**. Leave the message line prompt blank. Press CTRL-END to finish the initial menu dialog box and create the horizontal bar menu.

When dBASE adds a blank horizontal bar menu to the top of your screen like the one shown in Figure 12-22, you can add menu items, but dBASE must know where each one starts and stops. To start a menu item, you position the cursor, press F5, and type the menu item text. For the first menu item, you would press F5, with the cursor at the beginning of the line, type **Delete paid invoices**, and press F5 again. The entire menu item is highlighted when you enter the menu item text or when you move the cursor to a character in the menu text. Since the menu is easier to read if the menu items have spaces between them, the SPACEBAR is pressed five times. You can also use ENTER instead of the second F5. For the second menu item, you would press F5, type **Pack database**, and press ENTER. The SPACEBAR is pressed five times

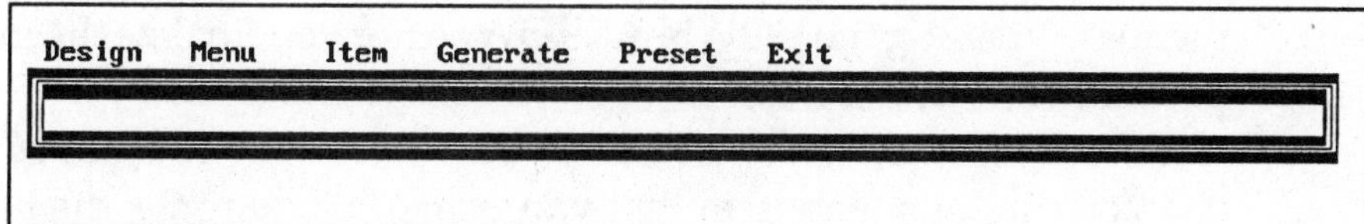

Figure 12-22 Initial horizontal bar menu box

to add spaces between the second and third menu items. dBASE also stops adding text to a menu item when you use the arrow keys. For the third menu item, you would press F5, type **Reindex**, and press the LEFT ARROW. You can edit the text by moving the cursor to where you want to add, delete, or change the text and make the appropriate changes. If Insert mode is On, the menu item text to the right of the cursor will shift to the right as you add characters. You cannot add characters if the Menu bar is full. dBASE also does not let you add text on the menu bar unless the cursor is on a menu item. To insert text at the end of a menu item, move to the last character in the menu item, press INS if Ins does not appear in the status line, and type the letter you are highlighting and the letters you want to add.

When you are done, press DEL to delete the current character. For example, to change Reindex to Reindex database, move the cursor to the x in Reindex, type **x database**, and press DEL to remove the extra x. If you try to add characters after the x, dBASE will not let you unless you press F5. If you use this approach, dBASE will treat the characters that you add as a new menu item if you press F5. To add a final entry, press the SPACEBAR five times. You can add a Quit menu item by pressing F5, typing **Quit**, and pressing F5 again.

If you need to fit more menu items into a horizontal menu bar than can fit into a single line, you can change the menu size to include multiple lines. When you press SHIFT-F7, you can add lines to the

Tip: Horizontal bar menu items.

Menu items in a horizontal bar menu are easier to read when each item is separated from the other by several spaces. Also, menu items are easier to read if only the first letter of each menu item is capitalized.

menu by pressing the DOWN ARROW. After you finalize the menu by pressing ENTER, you can enter additional menu items.

To assign an action to an item, you must move the cursor to any character in the menu item that you want. For example, the first step of assigning an action to the Pack database menu item is moving the cursor to any character in Pack database. dBASE highlights all of the text in the menu item the cursor is on.

Assigning Menu Items to Perform File Operations

When you assigned tasks to the menu items in the ACCT_REC application, you did not assign any tasks that perform file operations. File operations include update queries, indexing and sorting databases, reindexing database, importing and exporting files, and copying files. All of these are tasks that you performed in the Assist mode or the dot prompt. When you select one of these file operations, dBASE displays a dialog box that you fill in with the same information that you provide when you perform the task using the Assist mode or dot prompt. For the Deleted paid invoices menu item, you want the application to perform an Update query that marks records for deletion that have the same values for the AMOUNT and AMT_PAID fields. If you convert this task into a dot prompt command, the dot prompt command is DELETE FOR AMOUNT=AMT_PAID. To assign this task to the Delete paid invoices menu item, you would press ALT-I for the Item menu and type a **C** for Change action, a **P** for Perform file operation, and an **M** for Mark records for deletion. When dBASE displays a dialog box for you to enter how the application will determine which records are marked, you would move to the For setting and type **AMOUNT=AMT_PAID**. CTRL-END is pressed twice to return to the horizontal bar menu. For the Pack database menu item, you would move to a letter in the menu item, press ALT-I for the Item menu, and type a **C** for Change action, a **P** for Perform file operation, and a **D** for Discard marked records. dBASE displays a confirmation box that you accept by pressing ENTER. Press CTRL-END to return to the horizontal bar menu. For the Reindex database, you would move to the menu item, press ALT-I for the Item menu, and type a **C** for Change action, a **P** for Perform file operation, and an **R** for Reindex database, and press ENTER to confirm the menu item action. Again pressing, CTRL-END returns to the horizontal bar menu. When you build an application menu that uses other file operations, the basic steps are the same although the information that you provide in a dialog box changes to match the task that you are selecting. To assign an action to Quit, you perform the same steps that you performed for the Quit menu item in the A_R_MENU menu. This Quit menu item returns control to the A_R_MENU.

Switching between Application Design Boxes

Once you create the menus and assigned actions to the menu items, you can add other features that improve your application's appearance. However, the box that you want to modify may not be the one at the top of the screen. For example, you may want to move the sign-on banner or you may want to change the size of the main menu. To switch between boxes, press F3 or F4. When you press F3, dBASE makes the last box that you used current. When you press F4, dBASE makes the next box current. If you do not have a box designed for use after the current one, pressing F4 makes the first box (sign-on) current. As you change the box that is current, dBASE places the current box on top of the others and highlights the box's border. dBASE remembers the contents of the other boxes, allowing you to switch between boxes without losing information. In the ACCT_REC application, press F3 to make the A_R_MENU current. By making this menu box current, you can add other features to A_R_MENU.

Setting the Index

When you use the database in the ACCT_REC application, you can use a different sort order for portions of the application. For example, the primary index tag for the application is INVOICE_NO. For the AR_AGING report, that index is inappropriate since you want the records in order of the invoice due date to allow the report to group the records by the number of days the payment is overdue. To change the index the application uses to print the report, highlight the Print aging report menu item. Press ALT-I for the Item menu and type an **R** for Reassign index. When dBASE prompts with set ORDER to, you would type **DUE_DATE** and press CTRL-END twice to save the index tag for the aging report and return to the menu design. When you run the application, the application uses the INVOICE_NO index tag for each task except for printing the report when it uses the DUE_DATE index tag.

Moving Menu Items and Boxes

Another feature that improves the application's appearance is the position of the menu items and boxes on the screen. You can reposition boxes so a menu box does not cover another one when you activate the menu. You can reposition menu items to place them in a different order. When you move a box or menu item, the box or item maintains its characteristics. For example, if you move Quit to another line in a menu box, it still performs the same function.

The A_R_MENU menu in the ACCT_REC application is almost in alphabetical order. You can rearrange Print aging report, Quit and Other to appear in alphabetical order. When you move menu items, you cannot place a menu item on top of another menu item. To move menu items, you need a blank line in the menu box. Since A_R_MENU has a blank line, you do not have to change the box's size. First, highlight the Other menu item and press F7. dBASE lets you select between moving the entire box and moving the menu item. You would type an **I** to select Item, then press the DOWN ARROW to move to the blank line. Pressing ENTER moves the menu item to this position. Next, you would highlight the Quit menu item, press F7, type an **I** for Item, press the DOWN ARROW and press ENTER. The step is repeated for the Print aging report menu item. Finally, move the Other menu item by highlighting it, pressing F7, typing an **I** for Item, pressing the UP ARROW three times, and pressing ENTER once. With the last three items in alphabetical order, you can reduce the menu box size. This can be accomplished by pressing SHIFT-F7, the UP ARROW, and ENTER. The main menu now looks like Figure 12-23.

When you move a menu box, you are not limited in its screen placement. You can move the horizontal bar menu below the pop-up menu. First, you would press F4 to make the horizontal bar menu current, then press F7. When dBASE prompts you to choose between moving the box of the menu item, you type an **E** for Entire box. The DOWN ARROW is pressed until the horizontal bar menu is below the pop-up box, then it is finalized with ENTER. With the horizontal bar menu in this position, you can still see the main menu when you run the application and select Other.

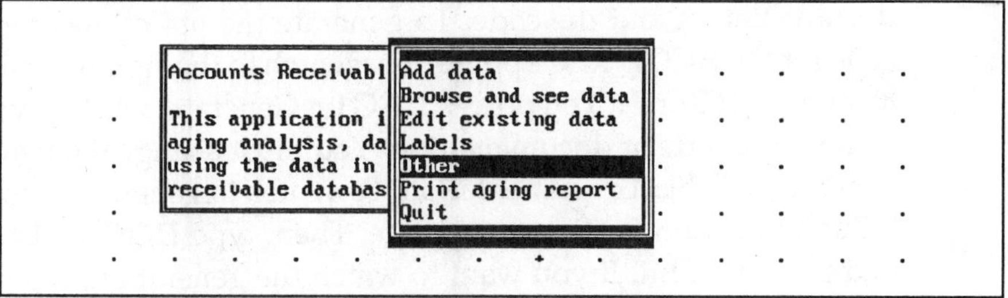

Figure 12-23 A_R_MENU after moving menu items

Creating a Help Facility for the Application

When you perform tasks from the dot prompt or ASSIST mode, you can always activate Help and display context-sensitive help for the current task. You can add a similar help screen to an application. You can add help text to a menu or a menu item. When you run an application and press F1, the application displays the help text for the menu item. If the menu item does not have help text, the application displays the help text for the menu. If the menu item and menu do not have help text, the application displays **No help defined.** To add help text to a menu, press ALT-M for the Menu menu when the menu requiring help text is current. To add help text to a menu item, highlight the menu item requiring help text and press ALT-I for the Item menu. Then, type a **W** for Write help text. dBASE displays a blank box where you can enter the help text. For the ACCT_REC application, you can add help text to the AR_OTHER menu. Press ALT-M and type a **W.** When the help box appears, type **This menu performs commands on the entire database. You can use this menu**. When you get to the end of the line, you must press ENTER since dBASE does not wrap the text to the next line. After you press ENTER, type **to delete paid invoices, pack, or reindex the database.** Once you are finished, press CTRL-END to leave the help text screen. Press CTRL-END again to leave the Menu menu. If you need to change the help text, repeat the steps that you performed to add help text.

Generating the Application

When you are finished designing the application, you can generate the application. When you generate the application, you generate object documentation and the code. To generate the object documentation code for the ACCT_REC application, switch to the sign-on banner box by pressing F3 or F4. You press ALT-G for Generate, whether you want to generate code or documentation. You must change the template to generate the object documentation. To switch to generating documentation, type an **S** for Select template. Then, type **DOCUMENT.GEN** and press ENTER. If you want to watch the generation, type a **D** for Display during generation, a **Y** for Yes, and a **B** for Begin generating. dBASE prompts you to determine if you have an IBM graphics compatible printer. If your printer can print the characters dBASE uses as borders for the menu boxes, type a **Y**. Otherwise, type an **N**. As dBASE generates the object documentation, it displays the object documentation in a box on the screen. Also, dBASE describes the steps it performs in the message line. When dBASE generates an application, it saves the application and menu design files, generates the code, then reads the application and menu design files back into the Applications Generator. When dBASE finishes, dBASE displays a message to press a key to continue. After you press a key, you can generate the application code.

To generate the application code for the ACCT_REC application, you must follow the steps just described. After you generate documentation, you can generate the application code. Since dBASE saves the application when you generate the code, press ESC twice and type a **Y** to leave the application if you don't want to save it.

Running the Accounts Receivable Application

Once you have generated ACCT_REC, you can run it. To execute the application from the dot prompt, type **DO ACCT_REC** and press ENTER. To execute the application from the Control Center, if you are in the Control Center, highlight ACCT_REC in the Applications panel and press ENTER. If dBASE prompts you to select between running the application and modifying the application, type an **R**. When dBASE displays a prompt to confirm that you want to run the program, type a **Y**. The first time that you execute the application, dBASE compiles the application and stores the compiled version using a .DBO extension. Then, dBASE displays the sign-on screen and waits a few seconds or until you press ENTER to display the main menu.

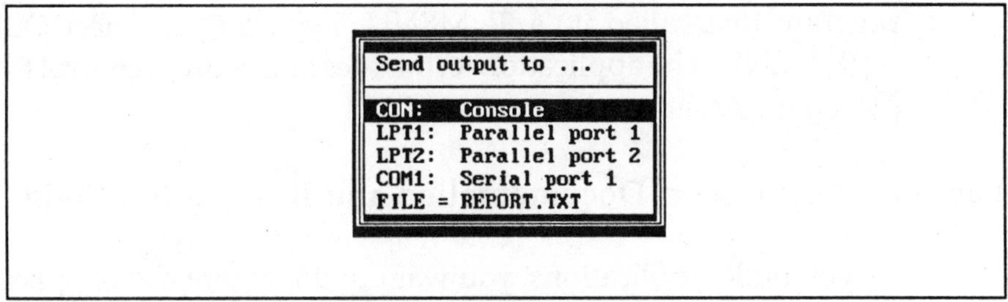

Figure 12-24 Selection box for label output

When you run ACCT_REC, once you see the main menu, you can type a **B** to view the data in the Browse screen. When you press F10, notice how nothing happens, since the Browse menus are disabled. After pressing ESC to return to the A_R_MENU menu, type an **E** for Edit existing data. This screen lists the fields in alphabetical order and omits the AMOUNT field. This time when you press F10, the Records menu appears although the Add new records menu item is dimmed. After pressing ESC twice to return to the A_R_MENU menu, type an **A** to select the Add data menu item. The application displays a form for you to fill with new data. Press ESC to return to the A_R_MENU menu. Try the Labels option by typing an **L**. dBASE displays the box in Figure 12-24. LPT1, LPT2, and COM1 print the labels to the printer devices called LPT1, LPT2, or COM1 (Most printers are LPT1). File prints the report to the REPORT.TXT file. To print the labels to the screen, type a **C** for Console. dBASE prints a sample label. When the application prompts if you want another sample label, type an **N**. The application prints all of the labels to the screen and returns to the A_R_MENU menu.

To try the report, turn on your printer and type a **P** for Print aging report. Since you set this menu item to print to the printer, it immediately prints the aging report and then returns to the A_R_MENU menu.

To look at the options in the Option menu, type an **O** for Other. dBASE displays the AR_OTHER menu below the A_R_MENU menu. Press the RIGHT ARROW and LEFT ARROW keys. Notice how pressing the arrow keys moves the highlight from menu item to menu item rather than from character to character. When you type a **Q**, you will notice that the application does not return to the A_R_MENU menu since typing the first letter of a menu item does nothing in a horizontal bar menu. Highlight Quit and press ENTER. dBASE returns you to the program that called it, A_R_MENU. Type a **Q** to select Quit from A_R_MENU. The application terminates and returns control to the dot prompt or Assist mode.

Looking at the Object Documentation and Application Code

As you build applications, you want to document each application so you know the application's function and appearance. After you generate an application, you have two files that document the steps the application performs. The object documentation describes each object in the application. The code contains the dBASE instructions that dBASE performs when you perform the application. To view either of these, you can use the same screens that you will use to create programs. You can use these screens to print the object documentation as well.

The object documentation is in a file with the application name followed by a .DOC extension. If you are in the Control Center, press ESC and type a **Y** to switch to the dot prompt. To view and print the object documentation for the ACCT_REC application, type **MODIFY COMMAND ACCT_REC.DOC** and press ENTER. When dBASE displays the object documentation, you can view it by pressing PGUP and PGDN keys. To print the object documentation, press ALT-P for the Print menu and type a **B** to begin printing. When you finish printing and viewing the object documentation, abandon the file by pressing ESC and typing a **Y**, if necessary.

The code is in a file with the application name followed by a .PRG extension. From the dot prompt, type **MODIFY COMMAND ACCT_REC** and press ENTER. When dBASE displays the code, you can view it by pressing PGUP and PGDN keys. While some of the commands in the code are familiar from Chapter 10, many of them will

Tip: Running an Application.

To immediately execute a application when you load dBASE, type the application name after dBASE. For example, for the ACCT_REC application, type **DBASE ACCT_REC**. Once dBASE is loaded, it runs the application.

be unfamiliar. These are dBASE commands that you use for programming; these commands are covered in Chapters 14 through 18 and the Command Reference in Appendix C. To print the code, press ALT-P for the Print menu and type a **B** to begin printing. When you have finished printing and viewing the object documentation, abandon the file by pressing ESC and typing a **Y**, if necessary. Since this code only includes the main application design, you must repeat these steps for A_R_MENU.PRG and AR_OTHER.PRG which contain the code the application uses for the menus.

Other Important Options

Although creating the ACCT_REC application showcases many Applications Generator features, the Applications Generator contains other features that you may want to include in an application. Some of these features include embedding code into the application, bypassing a menu item when a condition is met, using color, and saving the menus as you work on them.

Embed Code

You can embed code for a menu item to perform dBASE commands before or after dBASE performs a menu item action. To embed code, highlight the menu item, press ALT-I for Item, type an **E** for Embed code, and type a **B** if you want the embedded code before the menu item action or an **A** if you want the embedded code after the menu item action. When dBASE displays the editing screen, type the dBASE commands that you want performed with each command on a separate line. An example of embedded code is shown in Figure 12-25, where code is embedded before the Edit existing data menu item action. After it is entered, press CTRL-END three times to return to the Item menu. When the application is run, this code prompts the user for a password. After the user enters the password, the code converts it to upper case and compares it to CONTROL. If you enter the wrong password, the code ends the application and leaves dBASE. If you enter the correct password, application continues with the menu item action. You will use this option as you learn more about dBASE programming.

```
Design   Menu   Item   Generate   Preset   Exit

STORE "          " TO Password
@ 20,20 SAY "Enter password"
@ 20,35 GET Password
READ
IF .NOT. UPPER(Password)="CONTROL"
  QUIT
ENDIF
```

Figure 12-25 Sample of embedded code

Bypass Item on Condition

When you use dBASE menus, some menu items are unavailable. For example, when the highlight is on <create> in a panel in the Control Center, you cannot select Remove file from Catalog in the Catalog menu. You can add this same feature to an application. To bypass an item on a condition, highlight the menu item, press ALT-I, and type a **B** for Bypass item on condition. When dBASE displays the Skip this item if prompt, type the condition that must be met for the application to be skipped. For example, if you are operating an the ACCT_REC application on a network, you would not want to reindex the database. For the Skip item if prompt, type **NETWORK()** and press ENTER. When you run the application, dBASE dims menu items that you cannot select.

Change the Database or View of a Menu or Menu Item

Just as you can change the index tag of a menu item, you can also change the database or view for a menu item. To change the database or view for a menu or menu item, press ALT-M to change the menu database or view or ALT-I to change the menu item or view. When dBASE displays a dialog box, type the new database or view (with a .QBE extension) and press ENTER. If you want a new index file or tag, enter the index file name or index tag in the appropriate lines below. When you are finished, press CTRL-END to return to the Menu or Item menu. When you execute the application, dBASE changes the database or view when you select the menu or menu item, then changes to the original database or view when you leave the menu or menu item.

Using Color

You can select the colors a menu uses. To change the color, press ALT-M and type an **M** for Modify display options. Then select the screen attribute that you want to change. When dBASE displays the color selections, select the colors you want to use the same way you selected colors for form objects. When you have selected the colors you want, press CTRL-END twice to return to the menu you are designing. If you want to change the default colors, change the color settings by pressing ALT-P for Preset and type a **D** for Display options to have the same screen attribute selection box.

Pull-down Menus

When a horizontal bar menu is the current object, a menu option appears for attaching a pull-down menu. If you select this item and respond to the prompt with Yes, you can make the pull-down entries under each menu option as you move the cursor between horizontal bar menu selections.

Saving a Menu and Putting the Menu Away

As you work on the menu, you may want to save it. If you make mistakes as you progress through the design, you can revert to the copy of the design that you saved to eliminate the mistakes. To save the current menu, press ALT-M for Menu and type an **S** for Save current menu. dBASE saves the menu and leaves the Menu menu on the screen.

If you want to remove the menu from the application design screen, type a **P** for Put menu away. If you have not changed it, dBASE removes it from the screen. If you have changed the current menu design, dBASE prompts you to select between saving changes and abandoning changes. If you type an **S** for Save changes, dBASE saves the menu design before removing it from the screen. If you type an **A** for Abandon changes, dBASE removes the menu design from the screen. You may want to abandon the menu design if you have made a change you do not want to keep. Once a menu design is removed from the screen, you can return it to the application design using the Design menu.

GETTING STARTED

➤ You will want to create an application using the employee database and the related files you have created. Since you have only one view, one report, and one form, you can create a quick report to quickly generate your own application. To create a quick application of the employee database, follow these steps:

1. From the dot prompt type **MODIFY APPLICATION EMPLOYEE**. From the ASSIST mode, highlight <create> in the Applications panel, press ENTER. Type an **A** for Applications Generator, type **EMPLOYEE** and press ENTER again.
2. Move to the Description option and type **Employee Database Application**.
3. Move to the database name and type **EMPLOYEE** and press ENTER.
4. Enter **EMPLOYEE.MDX** for Set INDEX to and press ENTER.
5. Enter **SSN** for the ORDER option.
6. Press CTRL-END to save the settings and enter the application design screen. For the EMPLOYEE application, you can create a sign-on banner that appears when you run this application.

To create a sign-on banner, follow these steps:

1. Press CTRL-Y until the existing text in the sign-on banner is removed.
2. Type **EMPLOYEE MASTER DATABASE** and press ENTER twice
3. Type **ACME Company** and press ENTER twice.
4. Type your name.
5. Change the size of the box by pressing SHIFT-F7. Press the UP ARROW and the LEFT ARROW until the box is reduced to its minimum size. Press ENTER.
6. Specify this box as the sign-on banner by pressing ALT-A for the Application menu and typing a **D** for Display sign-on banner. When dBASE prompts for whether you want the box's contents as the sign-on banner, type a **Y**.

Now that you have added the sign-on banner, you can add the menu for application. Since this is a quick application, you will have dBASE generate the menu for you. To create a quick application, follow these steps:

1. Type a **G** for Generate quick application from the Application menu. This generates the quick application dialog box that dBASE uses to generate the quick application. To complete the dialog box, follow these steps:
2. Press ENTER to accept EMPLOYEE for the database file.
3. Type **ENTEREMP** as the screen format file and press ENTER.
4. Type **EMPLOY01** as the report design file and press ENTER.
5. Move to the Application menu heading and type **Employee Database application.**
6. Press CTRL-END to finalize these entries and begin generating a quick application.
7. Type a **Y** when dBASE prompts for confirmation to create a quick application. dBASE generates the quick application.
8. Press a key when dBASE is finished.
9. Leave the Applications Generator by pressing ESC twice, typing a **Y**, and pressing ENTER.

Now that you have created a quick application, you can start using it. To use the application, follow these steps:

1. Type **DO EMPLOYEE** from the dot prompt. From the ASSIST mode, highlight <create> in the Application panel, press ENTER, type an **R** for Run Application, type a **Y** and press ENTER again.
2. When the sign-on banner appears, press ENTER.
3. Type a **C** to select Change information. Notice how dBASE uses the form you created in ENTEREMP. Press ESC to return to the main menu.
4. Highlight Print Report. Notice EMPLOY01 appears in the message line. Press ENTER. When dBASE displays a selection box, type an **R** for Return. When dBASE displays the selection box for where to print the report, type a **P** for Printer. The application prints the report using the design created in EMPLOY01.

5. Type an E to select Exit from Employee. The application returns to the dot prompt or Control Center.

As you use this application, you may want to make enhancements. You can continue to modify the application to try various application features. For example, you may want to create an application for the employee files like the ACCT_REC application. You can follow the steps performed for the ACCT_REC application using the information for the EMPLOYEE database and the related files.

CHAPTER 13

Customizing with the Template Language

The template language is a separate program that works with the design for objects like reports, forms, and menus. Working with your definitions, the program will create either documentation or programs from the design for these objects. You can work with one component or can modify the templates for several and generate new code for an entire application or just a report or label design.

You can use the template language to make many versions of a design or your can alter all the label designs created to meet corporate standards and include a special code or a return address. Although it provides the ultimate in customization, it is not for the novice user. The commands and functions that you must use to define your desires to the template language are similar to dBASE programming language commands. Although similar to the options in the dBASE language, they are distinct command and function entries that use different keywords and parameters.

If you purchased the Developer's Edition of dBASE IV, you automatically received a copy of the template language and template language compiler in your dBASE package. If you purchased another version of dBASE, the template language is not included although you can contact Ashton-Tate for information on purchasing the product. Examples of where the product might be an appropriate acquisition would be for users who require a high degree of customization, users who need to develop systems for different hardware but don't want to code each application separately, or users who must supply documentation to subsidiaries in a number of foreign languages.

The template language is an exciting new tool providing customization possibilities that you never thought possible without unlimited time for coding. It is designed for corporate or professional developers and would be frustrating for someone without programming experience. Also, the start-up time required to master its features would not be warranted if you only plan to use it once or twice.

The Concept of Design Objects

When you create a report, label, or form with the Control Center commands or dot prompt entries, you are creating a dBASE design object. Likewise when you create a menu, application, file, database structure list, file list, values list, or a batch process with the Applications Generator you are creating a design object. A description of this design object is stored in a file that has a unique extension depending on the type of design object you created.

Each report, form, and label that you create has only one file containing design data. Applications created with the Applications Generator may be composed of many different files depending on the number of pop-up menus, bar menus, and other components used in the application.

The design files are composed of design elements. These elements vary depending on the type of design file involved but may include elements like a ruler, page break, field, band, box, or group. The various design elements each have attributes that describe them further. Attributes are either strings or numbers representing things like colors, row numbers, and column numbers. You will reference design elements, attributes, and elements with symbols called selectors when you create a template. The DEF files provided on the template language disks provide the selectors that you need for each type of design object. By using these selectors in the template you can incorporate the value for this attribute or element in the final template file.

The Concept of Templates

A template is a file that dBASE IV uses to convert your design object file into dBASE code for the object. When you change the template file, you change how dBASE converts the object designs into program code files. The entries in the template file include text that is carried forward to the code for the object and commands and functions that format, validate, and insert data into the code for the object. The template language allows you to access the design elements in reports, labels, forms, and menus and to manipulate the attributes that comprise these elements. Included in the disks dBASE IV provides for the template language are the template files that dBASE uses to generate code files for its objects. When you change templates, you will modify dBASE's existing templates to customize how you want dBASE to convert design object files into code files for the object.

When you create your own template files, you must perform several steps. First, you need to create a COD file consisting of text and template commands and functions. This file is the source code file for the template. Although the COD files supplied with dBASE have more features than you are likely to need they are a good starting place for your first few attempts. Just be sure that you make a copy of these files and modify the copy in case you encounter problems; you will always be able to start over with a fresh copy. You will also want the original file in the event that you want to use the default .COD file. Next, enter the changes into the .COD file with the new filename. Once you have saved the new .COD file, you must compile it using the DTC.EXE program. Compiling the template file creates a .GEN file with the same filename. You can use this file to convert design files into code files. The compiler uses the .DEF files to define the data that the template will find in the object design file. If you look at the .GEN files in your dBASE directory, you can see that dBASE already has .GEN files for the different objects.

After you create your own template files, you can use them on new and existing design files. You can use the DGEN program that comes with the template language files or change the default template dBASE uses to generate an object. You must use the DGEN program if you want to use a template other than the default. For example, if you have

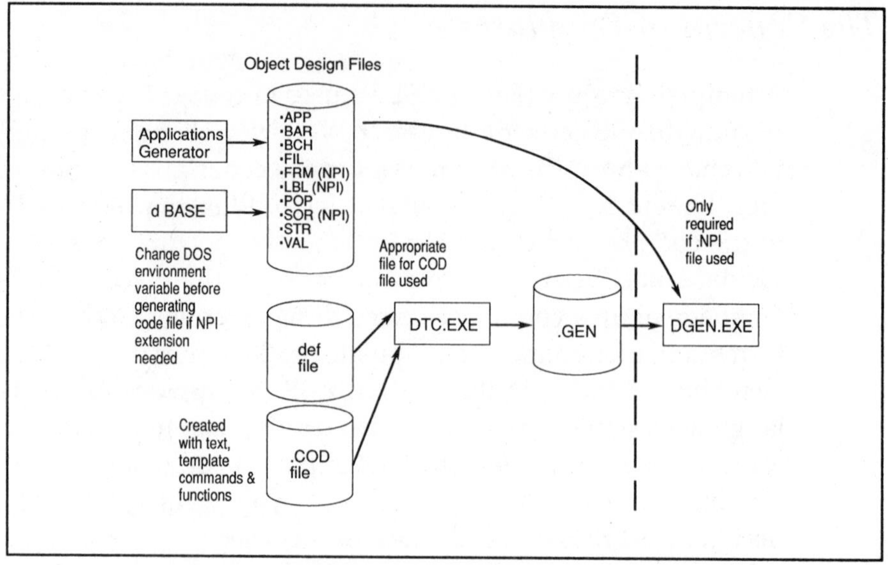

Figure 13-1 File types that can be used with the template language

two templates for reports, one is your default and for the other you must use the DGEN program to use the template.

Template Components

Understanding the raw material required to create a template and the end products created is helpful in conceptualizing the overall process that takes place when you create a template. Figure 13-1 shows the various file types representing design objects that can be processed by the template you create. The stages in the development of the final program are also shown in this figure. Note the .NPI files that are required for report, label, and forms data if they are to be processed by DGEN interpreter to create the final template files. If you change the default template for an object, you do not need to create .NPI files.

Creating A Template (.COD) File

You can use a standard text editor to create a template source file. dBASE's program editor (MODIFY COMMAND), DOS's EDLIN, and

Wordstar's nondocument mode are three possibilities for text editors you can use. When you edit a template file, you will use text and the commands and functions in the template language book to create your entries. Since a template is lengthy, you may prefer to modify a copy of an existing one rather than creating a new one.

The .COD source template files provide examples of a template structure. A source template file contains an introduction, comments, commands, and text.

In a template source code, the introduction provides information like the template name, the date created, it purpose, and a change history. If the line contains a double slash (//), the text to the right of the double slash is comments that do not appear in the compiled template. A template source file can include comments in any location if the line starts with a double slash. Text that is entered without a double slash but before the first left brace ({) appears on the screen when you use the DOS TYPE command. You can include up to 4K (or 4096) bytes of introduction.

The actual template code starts with the first left brace. After the first left brace, all of the information is either comments, text directly transferred to the compiled template, or a template command or function. Template commands are enclosed in curly braces. You can have multiple template commands within a set of braces if they are separated by semicolons. A few commands such as ENDIF and NEXT do not need semicolons. Template functions follow the same rules as commands except they include parentheses. Text directly transferred to the compiled template is text that is not part of a command or function.

Before you create or modify a template code file, you should print several files. Printing these files provides you sample files to follow and describes the variable names you will use. First, print BUILTIN.DEF. This file contains many of the built-in template functions and the ENUM declarations that you use to determine environment features. Next, print the .DEF file for the object that you are modifying or creating a template for. This lists the names of the elements in objects that the template can use. Then, print the .COD file of the object that you are modifying or creating the template source file. This lists the steps the template currently performs when it generates the code file for the object. Finally, print one or more code files for the object. By seeing the output of what the template generates, it is easier to follow the steps that the template performs. Once you print these files, you can use them to follow the steps a template currently performs and plan the steps that you want it to perform.

Template Commands and Functions

The syntax of the template commands and functions are similar to the commands and functions in the dBASE language. The angle brackets in the dBASE documentation indicate required items and the [] Square brackets indicate optional items in the commands. Unlike dBASE commands, you can enter multiple commands on the same line if they are separated by braces or by semicolons.

There are four types of commands that are used in the template language. These are compiler commands, definition commands, program flow commands, and loop commands.

Compiler commands define your needs to the compiler. A template normally includes two INCLUDE statements that include information in another file. These INCLUDE statements include the BUILTIN.DEF and the .DEF file for the object. These .DEF files list the selectors that the template can use. The codes should not be changed. You can use an INCLUDE statement to include information from an external file. You can choose to include or exclude assembly language statements with the compiled file with commands like #CODON and #CODOFF, which is the default.

Definition commands allow you to define both variables and user-defined functions. ENUM is one command in this section. It is used frequently since it can perform substitutions of values for the symbol names. VAR is another command that declares the variables the template uses. DEFINE and ENDDEF mark the beginning and end of a function defined within the template.

Program commands allow you to change the steps the template performs when it generates code for the object. These commands work similar to dBASE commands with some differences. The template language CASE command must use numeric selectors unless an ENUM variable precedes it. GOTO changes the order of the steps the compiled template performs by switching control to a label. RETURN in a user-defined function returns a function value when it returns control to the position in the template called the user-defined function.

Loop commands can repeat a section of template instructions. The FOREACH and NEXT command performs a group of template commands for a group of files, elements, or attributes. Commands like DO WHILE and ENDDO perform like the dBASE commands with the same names. The EXIT command stop performing the current loop and switches control to the next template instruction after the loop. The LOOP command switches control to the FOREACH, DO WHILE, DO UNTIL, or FOR command of the current loop.

Suggestions for Template Changes

While changing template source files can include involved template commands, you can make editing template source files easier by following these guidelines:

- If you want the template to include a design change that you can enter into an object design, create the object without the feature that you want the template to add and print the code file. Then, create the object again including the feature that you want the object to add and print the code file. Having the two program files and knowing where they differ can indicate where the template code needs to be changed. For example, if you want a report to include a specific heading, create a report without it and print the .FRO file. Then modify the report and add the heading and print the .FRO file. By comparing the two files, you can discover that the report heading needs to be included near the Pghead procedure.
- Focus on keywords such as variable names, selector, and procedures to locate the template source code that you want to modify. For example, if you wanted to change the sign-on banner, you would look in APPLCTN.DEF, find that DISP_SIGN is the selector that indicates whether the sign-on banner appears, and look in the AS_MENU.COD file for DISP_SIGN to find where you want to make changes.
- Make one change at a time and test each change. If you make several changes then test the template by compiling the template and generating a code file for an object, you may have difficulty locating the cause of an error if the template does not provide the results you expect.
- Use comment lines frequently to document the lines you have changed. Later if you need to modify the template, you can quickly

see which lines have been changed and the reason they were changed.

Compiling and Using Templates

The .COD file that you create must be processed before it is a working file that can produce programs or documentation. When you compile the template source file, you convert it to a .GEN file. This .GEN file is just like the .GEN files that dBASE already uses to generate code files for an object. This step processes the .COD files with the program DTC.EXE. To compile the template source file, type **DTC -i TRYTHIS.COD** and press ENTER. Compiling a template source file checks the command and function statements to ensure that they are free of syntax errors. The compiler does not catch all errors. Some errors can be caught when you use the code file for the object that you create with the template. The object file output from this process is stored in TRYTHIS.GEN unless you specify a different name for the output file with the -o option as in DTC -i TRYTHIS.COD -o WRTOUT.GEN. A third option allows you to specify a file to retain a copy of the source listing. Otherwise, the output is displayed on the console.

Using the Template

Once you have the file compiled, you can use the template to generate documentation or code files for object designs. The steps you perform to use the new template depends upon the object and how many template files you want to use.

If the template is designed for the Applications Generator, you can use the new template from within the Applications Generator by pressing ALT-G for Generate and type an **S** for Select template. When dBASE lists the templates you can use, select the one you created. When you type a **B** for Begin generating, dBASE uses the template you have selected to convert the application design into application code or documentation.

If you want to use the new template in place of the old template dBASE used to generate the form, label, or report, you need to tell dBASE to use the new template. To describe which template dBASE should use for a form, label, or report, you must create a DOS environment variable. From the DOS prompt, type **SET DTL_** followed by FORM, LABEL, or REPORT, as appropriate. Then type an equal sign (=) and then the template filename and a .GEN extension. Press ENTER. If you type **SET** and press ENTER, DOS displays the environment variables. DOS environment variables last until you reload DOS. Once you have this environment variable, enter dBASE and design the forms, reports, or labels. When you save a new design or a modified existing design, dBASE uses the new template file.

If you want to select which template you use to generate a form, label, or report, you need to tell dBASE not to generate the code file when you save the object design. Also, you must tell dBASE to save the design in an .NPI file, which stores the design information differently. First, from the DOS prompt, type **SET DTL_TRANSLATE=ON** and press ENTER. Once you set this environment variable, enter dBASE and design the forms, reports, or labels. When you save a new design or a modified existing design, dBASE saves the design using an .NPI extension. When you want to create a code file from the object design file, exit dBASE. The template language disks include an interpreter that performs the code generation that dBASE automatically performs when DTL_TRANSLATE is not set to ON. To use the interpreter, you must provide the template that you want to use and the input file you want interpreted. For example, to interpret MAILING.NPI using the FORMS.GEN template, type: **DGEN -t FORMS.GEN -i MAILING.NPI**

When DGEN interprets the input file it returns to the DOS prompt. The output filename is determined by the template commands. If you are creating a code file, you can use the new code file when you are in dBASE, using the same dot prompt commands or keystrokes in the ASSIST mode, as when you use dBASE's default templates.

❑ **Tip: Using a different template permanently.**

If you want to permanently use another template for forms, labels, or reports, include the SET command for the environment variable in the AUTOEXEC.BAT file.

Testing the Template

The final and most important step of using new templates is testing them. If your template creates documentation for an object, print the object out, making sure that the documentation file displays the information you expect. If the template creates code for the object, use the new template to create code for the object. For example, if the new template automatically inserts a new header into a report, create and print the report making sure the header appears as expected.

Creating a Template to Add Return Addresses to Mailing Labels

While creating templates can involve many steps, a quick example of a small change will give you an idea of what you are working with as you change and create templates. You can see some of the basic features by changing the label template so it automatically changes the label size to envelope size and includes the return address. If this new template is used to generate the code for all the labels you create, all of them will be the new size regardless of your selections in label design; and they will all have a return address added automatically. The new label template that the rest of the chapter develops only requires that the initial label design include the forwarding address as it should appear. The template used for this example modifies a copy of the LABEL.COD file.

Copying the .COD File

Before you modify a template, you should check to ensure that you have a copy of the original file. Copy the original file to another file rather than applying your changes to the original. For the envelope template file, enter **COPY LABEL.COD ADDRESS.COD** from the DOS prompt and press ENTER.

Printing Files

Before you modify the ADDRESS.COD template source file, you will want printouts of a few files. Since these files are standard text files, you can use the DOS PRINT command to print the files. You can also use dBASE's MODIFY COMMAND command to view and print the files. The advantage of using MODIFY COMMAND is you can print line numbers. Also, you can use dBASE's program editor to edit ADDRESS.COD. For modifying the ADDRESS.COD template source file, you want to print BUILTIN.DEF, LABEL.DEF, ADDRESS.COD, and a label code file that has a .LBG file extension. If you do not have a label design file, create a simple one and print the .LBG file.

Editing the .COD File

Once you have copied the LABEL.COD file to the ADDRESS.COD file, you can edit the ADDRESS.COD file. The editor you use does not matter if it is a standard text editor. You can determine if it is a standard text editor by typing one of the files. If the file contains characters that do not appear when you view the file with the editor, it is not a straight text editor. You want to use an editor that has a search feature. With a search feature, you can quickly find a command, variable or selector. The complete text of the LABEL.COD file is included at the end of the chapter so that you can follow the changes by line number if you do not as yet have a copy of the template language.

To have the template convert the label design from mailing labels to envelope addresses, enter the following changes:

- Change LABEL.COD in line 2 to ADDRESS.COD. Next time you view this file, the text will describe the file you are editing.
- Change the description in line 3 to Define label generator for addressing envelopes. This changes the description to match the actions of the template.
- Change the width the template uses for the labels by moving to line 69, which contains lbl_wide = LABEL_WIDE;. Replace LABEL_WIDE with 78. You can change the value of variables

within the template source code if it is declared with a VAR command, such as in line 39. When the template source file has the variable lbl_wide, it uses the value of 78.

- Change the height the template uses by moving to the text in the template source file that contains the introductory information that will appear in the .LBG file this template creates. Since this is the first line that starts with the asterisk, you can use the editor's search feature to find this character. Move to the line that displays * Tall - {label_tall} in line 150. Replace the braces and label_tall with 17, the envelope's height. Since label_tall is a selector defined in LABEL.DEF, you cannot change the value like you changed the label's width. Use the editor's search (and replace, if available) features to replace label_tall with 17 in lines 738, 744, and 831.
- Change the LABEL_WIDE in line 834 to 78. Since this uses the selector rather than the template variable, lbl_wide, you must replace the selector with the value.
- Move the forwarding address 30 positions to the right. Note by looking at a label .LBG file, the code uses the AT command to horizontally position text. Use the editor's search feature to find AT followed by a space. The line that horizontally positions the label fields looks like this:

```
AT {Col_Positn+(mrows*(lbl_wide+lbl_hspace))+30} \
```

Since you want to add 30 to the final value in the expression in brackets, move to the right brace in the line and type +30.

- Add the return address. By looking at an .LBG label file, you can notice that the actual loop in the dBASE code that the template places into the .LBG file starts with this code:

```
DO WHILE FOUND() .AND. .NOT. EOF() .AND. gl_prntflg
```

Using the editor's search features, you can look for the first DO WHILE in the .COD file to find this code in the template source file. Move to the end of the line and press ENTER. Then type the following lines into the template source code as they appear:

```
? "Acme Company"
? "5384 Main Street"
```

```
? "Cleveland, OH 44106"
?
?
?
```

Since the text does not include template commands or functions, the compiler includes them as they appear. When you generate the .LBG file with this template, the template includes these lines immediately after the DO WHILE command. The return address appears next to the left margin since these dBASE commands do not include AT.

- Since you have added six lines for the return address, you must reduce the number of blank lines the label code will print to advance to the next envelope. If you look at a .LBG label code file, you will notice these lines below the DO WHILE command where you inserted the return address:

```
DO WHILE gn_line < 9
   ?
   gn_line=gn_line+1
ENDDO
```

These lines print a blank line the number of times necessary to advance to the next page. Since you have added six lines at the beginning of the label, you must reduce this number by six. Move to the line that says DO WHILE gn_line < {17+lbl_vspace}. Move to the right brace and add **-6**. This reduces the number of blank lines the label prints by six.

- Comment the changes that you have made. For example, above the return address, enter:

```
// The next six lines provide a return address
```

Add comments to the other changes you have made by pressing ENTER to start a new line, typing two slashes, and typing the comment.

Since these are all of the changes necessary to change the label size to envelopes and include a return address, save ADDRESS.COD.

Compiling ADDRESS.COD

When you exit the editor and enter DOS, you are ready to compile the template. To compile the template, switch to your dBASE directory. Then, type **DTC -i ADDRESS.COD** and press ENTER. The space after the i and before the A is optional. When the compiler is complete, the compiler displays a message and the DOS prompt returns. If you type **DIR ADDRESS** and press ENTER, DOS lists ADDRESS.COD and ADDRESS.GEN. This .GEN file is the file you use to create labels that print envelopes from a label design.

Setting DOS Environment Variables

As mentioned earlier, when you use a form, label, or report design, dBASE checks the DOS environment variables. For the ADDRESS.GEN template, you must add the DTL_TRANSLATE environment variable. To set the DOS environment variable so you can select the template you will use, type **SET DTL_TRANSLATE=ON** and press ENTER. Now when you create a form, label, or report, dBASE stores the design in a .NPI file and does not create a code file for the object or an object compiled file. To see how the new DOS environment variable affects objects, you can create a label to see how it works. The disadvantage of using the DTL_TRANSLATE variable and setting it to ON is that you must use DGEN to generate object files for forms and reports as well as labels.

Creating an Object with the ADDRESS.COD Template

To see how the new DOS environmental variable and the ADDRESS.COD file works, create a label file using the EMPLOYEE database. First, load dBASE. Activate the EMPLOYEE database. Enter the label design screen. Add a few fields. Figure 13-2 shows a sample label design that creates labels like this:

Mary Jenkins
11 North St.
Cleveland, OH 44124

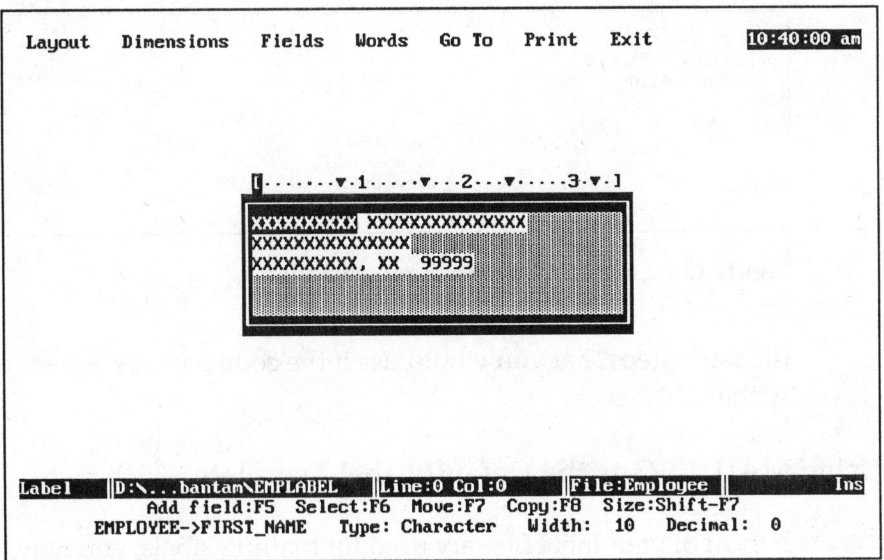

Figure 13-2 Sample label design

Press CTRL-END to save the file. Type **MAIL** as a filename and press ENTER. Look at the message line and notice how dBASE is saving the label design to MAIL.NPI. When dBASE returns to the Control Center or dot prompt, exit dBASE. You can leave dBASE and use the ADDRESS.GEN template to create an label code file.

Generating Code Files with ADDRESS.GEN

Once you have exited dBASE, you can use the DGEN program to create .LBG files from .NPI files. To create MAIL.LBG, type **DGEN -T ADDRESS.GEN -I MAIL.NPI**. The spaces between the T and A and between the I and M are optional. The file extensions are not. Press ENTER. dBASE creates MAIL.LBG using the instructions in ADDRESS.GEN. When DGEN finishes and the DOS prompt returns, you can reload dBASE to use the label file.

Using MAIL.LBG

Once you have loaded dBASE, you can print the labels using the MAIL.LBG file that you created using the design in MAIL.NPI as modified by ADDRESS.GEN. To print labels using MAIL.LBG file, use

```
Acme Company
5384 Main Street
Cleveland, OH 44106

                         Mary Jenkins
                         11 North St.
                         Cleveland,  OH  44124
```

Figure 13-3 Sample label with return address

the same steps that you would use if the code file was generated from within dBASE.

Using MAIL.LBG as the Default Label Template

If most of your label files are used for mailing labels, you may want to make MAIL.LBG the default label template. When you set the default label template, you eliminate the steps that you perform to generate the forms, labels, and reports. First, exit dBASE. When the DOS prompt appears type **SET DTL_TRANSLATE=** and press ENTER. This removes the DTL_TRANSLATE variable. Then type **SET DTL_LABEL=ADDRESS.GEN** and press ENTER. After these two changes, when dBASE generates the label code file, it uses the template in ADDRESS.GEN. When dBASE generates the code file for a form or report, it uses the default template for forms and reports. When you modify the MAIL label design and save the label design, you will notice by observing the status line that dBASE automatically uses ADDRESS.GEN to generate the label code file. When you print these labels or view them on the screen, they look just like Figure 13-3.

Making Other .COD File Modifications

When you change other templates, the process will be slightly different. For example, in the ADDRESS.COD file, you made many changes at once. When you make your own modifications, you only want to make one or two changes at a time. Then you compile the .COD file, generate a code file with the template, and view the code file output when you use it. If the changes you have made appear in the object's output as expected, you can modify the file again and add the next change. You will repeat the modify, compile, generate, and test steps for each change. When the object output does not have the appearance you want, check the object code file and then go back to the .COD file to find why it did not perform as expected. By constantly checking the .COD file as you make modifications, you can quickly find the source of an error.

```
//
// Module Name: LABEL.COD
// Description: Define Application menus and program structure.
//

Label (.lbg) Program Template
-----------------------------
Version 1.0
Ashton-Tate (c) 1987

{include "label.def";
 include "builtin.def";
 //
 // Enum string constants for international translation
 //
 enum wrong_class = "Can't use LABEL.GEN on non-label objects. ",
      label_empty = "Label design was empty. ",
     more_samples = "Do you want more samples? (Y/N)",
     gen_request  = "Generation request cancelled. ",
  temp_file_error =
"File $$$LAB.TMP already exists. Possible file lock collision.
Retry? ";
 //
 if frame_class != label then
   pause(wrong_class + any_key);
   return 0;
 endif

 //----------------------------
 // Declare working variables
 //----------------------------
 var lblname,        // Name of label file program
     default_drive, // dBASE default drive
```

```
     crlf,            // line feed
     line,            // Line counter for outputing number of "?'s"
     isfirst,         // Logical work variable
     mrows,           // Number of rows that the label uses
     mcolumns,        // Number of columns in label
     lbl_vspace,      // Number of characters between labels
     lbl_wide,        // Label width
     lbl_hspace,      // How tall the label is
     numflds,         // Number of fields used in label
     style,           // Style attribute assigned to the field/text
    current_column,   // Current column number
     first_combine,   // text or field first in combined data chain
     combine,         // combine fields flag

     new_line,        // is the next field on a new line
 i, j, x, temp, ni,   // temporary usage variables
     first_item,      // relative element number repeating columns
     item_number,     // current item number
     count,           // number of text and field items
   current_row,
  previous_row,
    next_row,
   blank_line,
  printed_lines,
previous_set_was_blank,
number_of_blankable_lines,
   current_element,
      response
;
 //-----------------------------------------------
 // Assign starting values to some of the variables
 //-----------------------------------------------
 crlf = chr(10);
 current_element=2;
 item_number = isfirst = mcolumns = first_combine = new_line =
next_row = 1;
 count = line = mrows = numflds = current_column = combine = 0;
 lbl_vspace = nul2zero(LABEL_VSPACE);
 lbl_wide = LABEL_WIDE;
```

```
lbl_hspace = nul2zero(LABEL_HSPACE);

blank_line = 1;
current_row = 0;
previous_row = -1;
printed_lines = 0;
number_of_blankable_lines=0;

foreach ELEMENT ecursor
  if COUNTC(ecursor) > 1 && !eoc(ecursor) then
    previous_row = current_row = Row_Positn;
    do while !eoc(ecursor)
      if Row_Positn > previous_row then
        number_of_blankable_lines=number_of_blank-
able_lines+blank_line;
        blank_line=1;
        previous_row=Row_Positn;
        ++printed_lines;
      endif
      if blank_line then
        if FLD_VALUE_TYPE == 78 then
          if not AT("Z",FLD_PICFUN) then
            blank_line=0;
          endif
        else
          if Text_Item then
            blank_line=0;
          endif
          if FLD_VALUE_TYPE != 67 then
            blank_line=0;
          endif
        endif
      endif
      ++ecursor;
    enddo
    number_of_blankable_lines=number_of_blankable_lines+blank_line;
    ++printed_lines;
    --ecursor;
    previous_row=Row_Positn+1;
```

```
    endif
  next
  blank_line=0;

  if number_of_blankable_lines then
    response="Y";
    do while FILEEXIST("$$$LAB.TMP") && upper(response) == "Y";
      response=ASKUSER(temp_file_error,"Y",1);
    enddo
    if upper(response) == "Y" then
      if not CREATE("$$$LAB.TMP") then;
        PAUSE("$$$LAB.TMP"+".LBG"+read_only+any_key);
        response="N";
      endif
    endif
    if upper(response) != "Y" then
      PAUSE(gen_request+any_key);
      return 0;
    endif
  endif

  default_drive = STRSET(_defdrive);
  lblname = FRAME_PATH + NAME;
  if not FILEOK(lblname) then
    if FILEDRIVE(NAME) || !default_drive then
      lblname=NAME;
    else
      lblname=default_drive + ":" + NAME;
    endif
  endif

  if not CREATE(lblname+".LBG") then;
    PAUSE(fileroot(lblname)+".LBG"+read_only+any_key);
    return 0;
  endif
}
* Program............: {lblname}.LBG
* Date...............: {LTRIM(SUBSTR(DATE(),1,8))}
* Version............: dBASE IV, Label {FRAME_VER}
```

```
*
* Label Specifics:
*    Wide - {lbl_wide}
*    Tall - {label_tall}
*    Indentation - {nul2zero(label_lmarg)}
*    Number across - {label_nup}
*    Space between - {lbl_hspace}
*    Lines between - {lbl_vspace}
*    Blankable lines - {number_of_blankable_lines}
*    Print formatted - {printed_lines}
*
PARAMETER ll_sample
*-- Set printer variables for this procedure only
PRIVATE _peject, _ploffset, _wrap

*-- Test for End of file
IF EOF()
   RETURN
ENDIF

IF SET("TALK")="ON"
   SET TALK OFF
   gc_talk="ON"
ELSE
   gc_talk="OFF"
ENDIF
gc_space = SET("SPACE")
SET SPACE OFF
gc_time=TIME()       && system time for predefined field
gd_date=DATE()       && system date  "    "    "     "
gl_fandl=.F.        && first and last record flag
gl_prntflg=.T.      && Continue printing flag
gn_column=1
gn_element=0
gn_line=1
gn_memowid=SET("MEMOWIDTH")
SET MEMOWIDTH TO 254
gn_page=_pageno      && capture page number for multiple copies
_plineno=0
```

```
{if LABEL_LMARG then}
_ploffset = _ploffset + {LABEL_LMARG}
{endif}
_wrap = .F.

IF ll_sample
   DO Sample
   IF LASTKEY() = 27
      RETURN
   ENDIF
ENDIF

*-- Setup Environment
ON ESCAPE DO prnabort

{numflds=FRAME_NUM_OF_FIELDS;}
{if LABEL_NUP > 1 && numflds then}
*-- Initialize array(s) for {LABEL_NUP} across labels
DECLARE isfound[{LABEL_NUP-1}]
DECLARE tmp4lbl[{LABEL_NUP-1},{numflds}]
{endif}
{if number_of_blankable_lines then}
DECLARE gn_line2[{label_nup}]
{endif}

PRINTJOB

{x=0;}
{foreach FLD_ELEMENT k}
//
// only if there is a fieldname assigned to the calculated field
//
{if FLD_FIELDTYPE == Calc_data && FLD_FIELDNAME then}
{  if !x then}
*-- Initialize calculated variables.
{  endif}
{FLD_FIELDNAME}=\
{case FLD_VALUE_TYPE of}
{68: // Date   }CTOD(SPACE(8))
```

```
{70: // Float   }FLOAT(0)
{76: // Logical}.F.
{78: // Numeric}INT(0)
{otherwise:}""
{endcase}
{  ++x;}
{endif}
{next k;}

*-- set page number for multiple copies
_pageno=gn_page

DO WHILE FOUND() .AND. .NOT. EOF() .AND. gl_prntflg
{LMARG(4);}
{if LABEL_NUP > 1 and numflds then}
{isfirst=1;}
{x=1;}
STORE .F. TO \
{init_array:}
{if isfirst then}
{  isfirst=0;}
{else}
,\
{endif}
isfound[{x}]\
{++x;}
{if x < LABEL_NUP then goto init_array endif}

{x=0;}
{i=1;}
{arcopy:}
{  if x then}
IF FOUND() .AND. .NOT. EOF()
{     LMARG(7);}
{  endif}
{  calcflds();}
//
{foreach FLD_ELEMENT i}
tmp4lbl[{x+1},{i}]=\
```

```
{case FLD_FIELDTYPE of}
{Tabl_data:}
{  if FLD_VALUE_TYPE == 77 then}
MLINE({FLD_FIELDNAME},1)
{  else}
{    FLD_FIELDNAME}

{  endif}
{Calc_data:}
{  if FLD_FIELDNAME then}
{    FLD_FIELDNAME}

{  else}
{    foreach FLD_EXPRESSION exp in i}
{      FLD_EXPRESSION}\
{    next}

{  endif}
{Pred_data:}
{  case FLD_PREDEFINE of}
{  0: // Date}
gd_date
{  1: // Time}
gc_time
{  2: // Recno}
RECNO()
{  3: // Pageno}
_pageno
{  endcase}
{endcase}
{next i;}
//
{  if x then}
isfound[{x}]=.T.
{  endif}
CONTINUE
{  if x then}
{    LMARG(4);}
ENDIF
```

```
{   endif}
{   ++x;}
{   if x < LABEL_NUP-1 then
       goto arcopy;
    endif
}
IF FOUND() .AND. .NOT. EOF'
{LMARG(7);}
{calcflds();}
isfound[{x}]=.T.
{LMARG(4);}
ENDIF
{else}
{calcflds();}
{endif}
//
{if number_of_blankable_lines then}
gn_line=\
{   if previous_row - number_of_blankable_lines > 0 then
       previous_row - number_of_blankable_lines}

{   else}
0
{   endif
 endif
 blank_line=0;
 printed_lines=0;
 previous_set_was_blank=0;}
//
// Main loop (inner loop handles fields on each line by # of cols.)
//
{foreach ELEMENT k}
{   if ELEMENT_TYPE == @Band_Element then}
{     ++k; ++item_number;}
{     if eoc(k) then}
{       exit;}
{     endif}
{   endif}
{   ++count;}
```

```
{  LMARG(4);}
//
{  check4_blank_line:

   if !blank_line then
     blank_line=1;
     current_element=COUNTC(k);
     previous_row=Row_Positn;
     previous_set_was_blank=0;
     printed_lines=0;

     do while !eoc(k);
       if Row_Positn > previous_row then
         ++printed_lines;
         previous_set_was_blank=previous_set_was_blank+blank_line;
         if Row_Positn > previous_row+1 then
           blank_line=0;
         else
           blank_line=1;
           previous_row=Row_Positn;
         endif
       endif
       if blank_line then
         if FLD_VALUE_TYPE == 78 then
           if not AT("Z",FLD_PICFUN) then
             blank_line=0;
           endif
         else
           if Text_Item then
             blank_line=0;
           endif
           if FLD_VALUE_TYPE != 67 then
             blank_line=0;
           endif
         endif
       endif
       if !blank_line then
         exit
       endif
```

```
        ++k;
      enddo
      if eoc(k) then
        --k;
        ++printed_lines;
        if blank_line then
          previous_set_was_blank=previous_set_was_blank+blank_line;
          previous_row=Row_Positn;
        endif
      endif

      do while COUNTC(k) > current_element;
        --k;
      enddo

      if previous_set_was_blank then
        blank_line=previous_set_was_blank;
      else
        blank_line=0;
        printed_lines=0;
      endif
    else}
{     if blank_line then
        --blank_line;
      endif}
{     if label_nup > 1 then}
{LMARG(4);}
{     else}
{LMARG(1);}
{     endif}
{     if blank_line then}
ELSE
   lc_ret=.T.
{     endif}
{     if label_nup > 1 then}
ENDIF
{     endif}
{LMARG(1);}
ENDIF
```

```
RETURN lc_ret

{    if blank_line > 0 then}
FUNCTION ___{nul2zero(Row_Positn)}1
lc_ret=.F.

{       if label_nup > 1 && mrows then
          conditional_if_for_blank_line(k, 7);
        else
          conditional_if_for_blank_line(k, 4);
        endif
      endif
      if !blank_line then
        ++line;
        LMARG(4);
        APPEND(lblname+".LBG");
      endif
   endif
}
//---------------------
// Process blank lines
//---------------------
{  nextline:}
{  if line < Row_Positn then}
{    if !blank_line || blank_line == printed_lines then}
?
{    endif}
{    ++line; goto nextline;}
{  endif}
//--------------------
// End of blank lines
//--------------------
{  if previous_set_was_blank && !blank_line then goto
check4_blank_line endif
   if previous_set_was_blank && blank_line &&
blank_line==printed_lines then}

*-- Check for blank lines
DO chk4null WITH {line}, {printed_lines}, {printed_lines*label_nup}
```

```
{    APPEND("$$$LAB.TMP");}
{LMARG(1);}
*
*-- The next\
{if printed_lines*label_nup > 1 then}
 {printed_lines*label_nup}\
{endif}
 function file\
{if number_of_blankable_lines > 1 then}s{endif} are for blank line
checking

FUNCTION ___{line}1
lc_ret=.F.

{    conditional_if_for_blank_line(k, 4);}
{  endif}
//
{  mrows = 0;}
{  first_item = item_number;}
//
{  repeat:}
//
{  if new_line then}
{    if !mrows then}
{      if !blank_line then}
{LMARG(4);}
{      endif}
{    else}
{      if blank_line then}
{        if mrows < label_nup then}
{          if mrows > 1 then LMARG(4); else LMARG(1); endif}
{          if blank_line > 1 then}
ELSE
   lc_ret=.T.
{          endif}
ENDIF
{        endif}
{        if mrows > 1 then}
{LMARG(1);}
```

```
ENDIF
{        endif}

RETURN lc_ret

FUNCTION ___{nul2zero(Row_Positn)}{mrows+1}
lc_ret=.F.

{        if mrows then}
*-- Column {mrows+1}
IF isfound[{mrows}]
{LMARG(4);}
{        endif}
{        if mrows then}
{          conditional_if_for_blank_line(k,7);}
{        else}
{          conditional_if_for_blank_line(k,4);}
{        endif}
{      endif}
{    endif}
{    if LABEL_NUP > 1 && first_item == item_number then}
{      if !blank_line then}
*-- Column {mrows+1}
{        if mrows then}
IF isfound[{mrows}]
{          if !blank_line then}
{LMARG(7);}
{          endif}
{        endif}
{      endif}
{    endif}
?? \
{  else}
,\
{  endif}
//
{ni=0;}
{  case ELEMENT_TYPE of}
//
```

```
{  @Text_Element:}
//
{x=Col_Positn;}
{i=LEN(Text_Item);}
{if i == 237 then}
{  foreach Text_Item fcursor in k}
{    if ni then}
{      i=i+LEN(Text_Item);}
{      temp=Text_Item;}
{    endif}
{    ++ni;}
{  next}
{endif}
{current_column=x+i;}
//
{  @Fld_Element:}
//
{x=Col_Positn;}
{i=FLD_REPWIDTH;}
{if i > 237 then}
{  foreach FLD_TEMPLATE fcursor in k}
{    if ni then}
{      temp=FLD_TEMPLATE;}
{    endif}
{    ++ni;}
{  next}
{endif}
{current_column=x+i;}
//
{  endcase}
//
// is the next element on the same line
//
{  ++k;}
{  if (not EOC(k)) && line == Row_Positn then}
{    new_line=0;}
//
// is the next element flush with previous element
//
```

```
{     if current_column == Col_Positn then}
{       combine=1;}
{     else}
{       combine=0;}
{     endif}
{  else}
{     new_line=1;}
{     next_row=Row_Positn;}
{  endif}
{  --k;}
//---------------------------------------------
// Determine what type of data we are processing
//---------------------------------------------
{  case ELEMENT_TYPE of}
//
{  @Text_Element:}
//
{if i > 70 then}
;
{  seperate(Text_Item);}
{  if ni then}
+ "{temp}";
{  endif}
{else}
"{Text_Item}" \
{endif}
//
{  @Fld_Element:}
//
{     if mrows+1 < LABEL_NUP then}
tmp4lbl[{mrows+1},{mcolumns}] \
{     else}
{       putfld(k);}
{     endif}
{     ++mcolumns;}
{  endcase}
//
{  if ELEMENT_TYPE == @Fld_Element then}
//
```

```
{     if !FLD_FIELDTYPE || FLD_FIELDTYPE == Calc_data ||
         (FLD_FIELDTYPE == Pred_data && FLD_PREDEFINE > 1) then}
//
{       if FLD_VALUE_TYPE == 67 then
          j=FLD_TEMPLATE+temp;
          if FLD_LENGTH == FLD_REPWIDTH && j == REPLI-
CATE("X",FLD_LENGTH) then
            j="";
          endif
        else
          j="1";
        endif}
//
{       if FLD_PICFUN || j then}
PICTURE \
{       endif}
//
{       if FLD_PICFUN then}
"@{FLD_PICFUN}\
{         if j then}
 \
{         else}
" \
{         endif}
{       endif}
//
{       if j then}
{         if i > 70 then}
{           if FLD_PICFUN then}
"+;
{           else}
;
{           endif}
{           seperate(FLD_TEMPLATE);}
{           if ni then}
+ "{temp}";
{           endif}
{         else}
{           if !FLD_PICFUN then}
```

```
"\
{          endif}
{FLD_TEMPLATE}" \
{        endif}
{      endif}
{    endif}
//
{  endif}
//
{  if FLD_STYLE then}
{    style=getstyle(FLD_STYLE);}
STYLE "{style}" \
{  endif}
{  if first_combine then}
AT {Col_Positn+(mrows*(lbl_wide+lbl_hspace))} \
{    if combine then}
{      first_combine=0;}
{    endif}
{  else}
{    if not combine then first_combine=1; endif}
{  endif}
//
// position to next element
//
{  ++k; ++item_number;}
//
{  if !new_line || (!EOC(k) && line == Row_Positn) then
     if !new_line then}
;
{    else}
,
{    endif
     if !EOC(k) then
       goto repeat;
     endif
   endif}
//
{  combine=0;}
{  first_combine=1;}
```

```
//
{  if LABEL_NUP-1 > mrows then}
,
{    if mrows && !blank_line then}
{        LMARG(4);}
ENDIF
{    endif}
{    ++mrows;}
{    backup_cursor:}
{    if item_number > first_item then}
{      --k; --item_number;}
{      if ELEMENT_TYPE == @Fld_Element then}
{        --mcolumns;}
{      endif}
{      goto backup_cursor;}
{    endif}
{    new_line=1;}
{    goto repeat;}
{  else}

{    if mrows && !blank_line then}
{        LMARG(4);}
ENDIF
{    endif}
{    mrows=0;}
{    --k; --item_number;}
{  endif}
//
{next k;}
{if blank_line then}
{  if label_nup > 1 then}
{LMARG(4);}
ENDIF

{  endif}
{LMARG(1);}
ENDIF

RETURN lc_ret
```

```
{endif}
{LMARG(4);}
{APPEND(lblname+".LBG");}
{if number_of_blankable_lines then}
{  if !blank_line then}
?
{  endif}
DO WHILE gn_line < {label_tall+lbl_vspace}
   ?
   gn_line=gn_line+1
ENDDO
{else
   lastline:
   if line < LABEL_TALL+lbl_vspace then}
?
{     ++line;
      goto lastline;
   endif
 endif}
CONTINUE
{LMARG(1);}
ENDDO

IF .NOT. gl_prntflg
   SET MEMOWIDTH TO gn_memowid
   SET SPACE &gc_space.
   SET TALK &gc_talk.
   ON ESCAPE
   RETURN
ENDIF

ENDPRINTJOB

SET MEMOWIDTH TO gn_memowid
SET SPACE &gc_space.
SET TALK &gc_talk.
ON ESCAPE
RETURN
* EOP: {lblname}.LBG
```

```
PROCEDURE prnabort
gl_prntflg=.F.
RETURN
* EOP: prnabort

{if number_of_blankable_lines then
   COPY("$$$LAB.TMP");
   FILEERASE("$$$LAB.TMP");
   APPEND(lblname+".LBG");
 endif}
{if number_of_blankable_lines then}
PROCEDURE chk4null
*-- Parameters:
*
*-- 1) line number on the design surface
*-- 2) maximum number of printable lines
*-- 3) parameter 2 times number of labels across
*
PARAMETERS ln_line, ln_nolines, ln_element
gn_element=0
{    x=1;
     do while x <= label_nup}
gn_line2[{x}]=ln_line
{       ++x;
     enddo}
lc_temp=SPACE(7)
ll_output=.F.
DO WHILE gn_element < ln_element
   gn_column=1
   ll_output=.F.
   DO WHILE gn_column <= {label_nup}
      IF gn_line2[gn_column] < ln_line+ln_nolines

lc_temp=LTRIM(STR(gn_line2[gn_column]))+LTRIM(STR(gn_column))
         DO WHILE ___&lc_temp.()
            gn_element=gn_element+1
            gn_line2[gn_column]=gn_line2[gn_column]+1

c_temp=LTRIM(STR(gn_line2[gn_column]))+LTRIM(STR(gn_column))
```

```
            ENDDO
            gn_element=gn_element+1
            gn_line2[gn_column]=gn_line2[gn_column]+1
         ENDIF
         gn_column=gn_column+1
      ENDDO
      IF ll_output
        ?
        gn_line=gn_line+1
      ENDIF
ENDDO
RETURN
* EOP: chk4null

{endif}
PROCEDURE SAMPLE
PRIVATE x,y,choice
DEFINE WINDOW w4sample FROM 15,20 TO 17,60 DOUBLE
choice="Y"
x=0
DO WHILE choice = "Y"
   y=0
   ?
   DO WHILE y < {LABEL_TALL}
      x=0
      DO WHILE x < {LABEL_NUP}
         ?? REPLICATE("X",{LABEL_WIDE})\
{if LABEL_HSPACE then}
+SPACE({LABEL_HSPACE})
{else}

{endif}
         x=x+1
      ENDDO
      ?
      y=y+1
   ENDDO
{if LABEL_VSPACE then}
   x=0
```

```
    DO WHILE x < {LABEL_VSPACE}
       ?
       x=x+1
    ENDDO
{endif}
    ACTIVATE WINDOW w4sample
    @ 0,3 SAY "{more_samples}";
    GET choice PICTURE "!" VALID choice $ "NY"
    READ
    DEACTIVATE WINDOW w4sample
    IF LASTKEY() = 27
       EXIT
    ENDIF
ENDDO
RELEASE WINDOW w4sample
RETURN
* EOP: SAMPLE
{if !count then pause(label_empty + any_key); endif}
{return 0;}
//----------------------------------
// End of main template procedure
// User defined function follows
//----------------------------------
{
 define getstyle(mstyle);
  var outstyle;
  outstyle="";
  if Bold        & mstyle then outstyle=outstyle+"B"; endif
  if Italic      & mstyle then outstyle=outstyle+"I"; endif
  if Underline   & mstyle then outstyle=outstyle+"U"; endif
  if Superscript & mstyle then outstyle=outstyle+"R"; endif
  if Subscript   & mstyle then outstyle=outstyle+"L"; endif
  if User_Font   & mstyle then
    if  1 & mstyle then outstyle=outstyle+"1"; endif
    if  2 & mstyle then outstyle=outstyle+"2"; endif
    if  4 & mstyle then outstyle=outstyle+"3"; endif
    if  8 & mstyle then outstyle=outstyle+"4"; endif
    if 16 & mstyle then outstyle=outstyle+"5"; endif
  endif
```

```
return outstyle;
enddef;
}
{define putfld(cursor);
 var value,value2;
 value=cursor.FLD_FIELDTYPE;}
{          if mrows+1 < LABEL_NUP then}
tmp4lbl[{mrows+1},{mcolumns}] \
{          else}
{case value of}
{Tabl_data:}
{  if cursor.FLD_VALUE_TYPE == 77 then}
MLINE({cursor.FLD_FIELDNAME},1)\
{  else}
{    cursor.FLD_FIELDNAME}\
{  endif}
{Calc_data:}
{  if cursor.FLD_FIELDNAME then}
{    cursor.FLD_FIELDNAME }\
{  else}
{    foreach FLD_EXPRESSION exp in cursor}
{      FLD_EXPRESSION}\
{    next}
 ;
{    new_line=1;}
{  endif}
{Pred_data:}
{  value2=cursor.FLD_PREDEFINE;}
{  case value2 of}
{  0: // Date}
gd_date\
{  1: // Time}
gc_time\
{  2: // Recno}
RECNO()\
{  3: // Pageno}
_pageno\
{  endcase}
{endcase}
```

```
 \
{          endif}
{return;
enddef;
}
{
 define conditional_if_for_blank_line(cursor2, page_offset);
 var current_column, current_row;
}
*-- Test for blank line
IF LEN(TRIM( \
{      current_column=cursor2.Col_Positn;
       current_element=COUNTC(cursor2);
       current_row=cursor2.Row_Positn;
       do while !eoc(cursor2) && cursor2.Row_Positn == current_row}
{        if cursor2.Col_Positn > current_column then}+ {endif}\
{        if cursor2.FLD_VALUE_TYPE == 78 then}
TRANSFORM(\
{          if mrows+1 < LABEL_NUP then}
tmp4lbl[{mrows+1},{mcolumns}],"\
{          else}
{            if cursor2.FLD_FIELDNAME then}
{cursor2.FLD_FIELDNAME},"\
{            else}
{              foreach FLD_EXPRESSION exp in cursor2}
{                FLD_EXPRESSION}\
{              next}
 ;
{            endif}
{          endif}
{          if cursor2.FLD_PICFUN then}
{            if not cursor2.FLD_FIELDNAME then}
,"\
{            endif}
@{CURSOR2.FLD_ = FUN} \
{          endif}
{cursor2.FLD_TEMPLATE}") \
{//
        else
```

```
          putfld(cursor2);
        endif
        ++cursor2;
        ++mcolumns;
      enddo
      do while eoc(cursor2) || COUNTC(cursor2) > current_element;
        --cursor2;
        --mcolumns;
      enddo}
)) > 0
{LMARG(page_offset);}
ll_output=.T.
{  return;
 enddef
}
{
define nul2zero(numbr);
//
// if number is null convert to 0
//
if !numbr then numbr=0 endif;
 return numbr;
 enddef
}
{define calcflds();}
{foreach FLD_ELEMENT k}
{  if FLD_FIELDNAME && FLD_FIELDTYPE == Calc_data then}
{FLD_FIELDNAME}=\
{foreach FLD_EXPRESSION j in k}
{FLD_EXPRESSION}
{next}

{  endif}
{next k;}
{return;}
{enddef}
{
 define seperate(string);
 var x,y,length;
```

```
 x=1;
 length=LEN(string);
 moreleft:
 if x < length then
   if x != 1 then}
+ \
{  endif
   if x+70 <= length then y=70; else y=length-x+1; endif}
"{SUBSTR(string,x,y)}";
{  x=x+70;
   goto moreleft;
 endif
 return;
 enddef
}
// EOP: LABEL.COD
```

PART V

dBASE IV Programming

CHAPTER 14

Programming Basics

If you worked through the examples in Chapter 10, making entries at the dot prompt you have taken the first step toward writing a dBASE program. In fact, the command syntax that you used in the dot prompt environment is identical to the command syntax used in dBASE programs.

Dot prompt entries are appropriate for quick one-time needs. Programs offer the advantage of allowing you to store the commands. This means that you can reuse these instructions whenever you need to perform the task again. With dot prompt entries, you would need to retype them.

With dot prompt entries you must complete the entire task from start to finish in one session since the history is not stored when you turn off the system. With programs, you can break a task into parts and complete a part or a portion of it. Since you can save your entries at any point, you can resume work on your program at a later time without losing any of the work accomplished in earlier sessions.

Another difference in the use of commands in the dot prompt and programming environment is that commands in the dot prompt environment are mostly used on a stand-alone basis. Normally a program is a planned succession of commands that are performing related tasks. Also, commands in programs are often organized in logical constructs that perform tasks repetitively, sequentially, or based on a selection from a set of choices. Some dBASE commands like IF and SCAN create a logical construct and can only be used within a program.

You don't have to be a professional programmer to successfully write simple dBASE programs. You do need to be committed to plan out your task before starting. You also need to be attentive to detail as you enter the required commands. Last, a little patience goes a long way. If your program doesn't work correctly the first time, use the tools available to help you find the problem. If you are unsuccessful and find your frustration mounting, focusing on other tasks for a period of time frequently provides a needed change of perspective when you come back to the program. With a little persistence you will soon find that the programming environment is also a comfortable arena for creating solutions and it provides you the ultimate in control over the system you are creating.

Planning the Program

You learned about designing an application system in Chapter 12, which taught you how to create applications with the Applications Generator. The Applications Generator uses a building-block approach allowing you to connect various objects in the system through the use of menus or batch processes. The Applications Generator produces all the required dBASE code for you. If you are going to do all the programming yourself you want to approach the process with the same logical techniques, applying the system design concepts presented in Chapter 12 to lay out your application.

Using Modular Programming

A large application can contain thousands of lines of code. Even if you create the entire program yourself, it can be difficult to keep the flow of logic for the entire system in your memory. You need to find a way of breaking the program design down into pieces that are more manageable in size.

A page of code or approximately 50 lines of code has been found to be the optimal size for program modules by individuals whose career is programming. You are well advised to adopt this size guideline as you approach the design of your program. As you look at the functions the program must perform, such as displaying a menu, printing a report, and updating the database, you will see tasks that can logically be separated from the whole and handled as either internal or external program modules. Internal modules are sections of the main program, and external modules are programs that are stored in separate procedures.

The advantage of this approach is that this approach looks at the final product as a number of subtasks. Each subtask is dealt with separately and is more manageable in size than one large mass of code. If a group of programmers are available, the modules can be divided so that each can work on some of the system components. Even if you need to do the entire system yourself, you can test each of the modules separately before combining them, simplifying the testing process.

Top–Down Design

As you examine your application to determine where the logical breaks occur you will want to use a top–down approach that places the main menu as the central element in the system. The main program can provide the code that is needed to display this menu. The other modules can be added hierarchically as you pursue the various paths down from the main menu to the actual tasks that need to be performed. The separate modules that you define as you walk down the menu tree can provide all the functionality you need to perform the system tasks.

The top–down approach allows you to create higher level modules first and test the upper-level system functions before all the modules are complete. Dummy or stub modules can be developed for the ones that are incomplete to allow a user to walk through as much of the system as possible while it is still being developed.

Planning the Modules

The single most important step to creating programs that run error-free in minimum time is planning the steps that are required to complete the task. Sketch these steps on paper so you can walk through the steps before beginning to code the program. You can use any method you like for recording the steps. Some choose to use a set of graphic symbols with the steps inside to show the flow of the program. These are referred to as flowcharts. Figure 14-1 provides an example of a flowchart showing the processing of the Employee file and the printing of

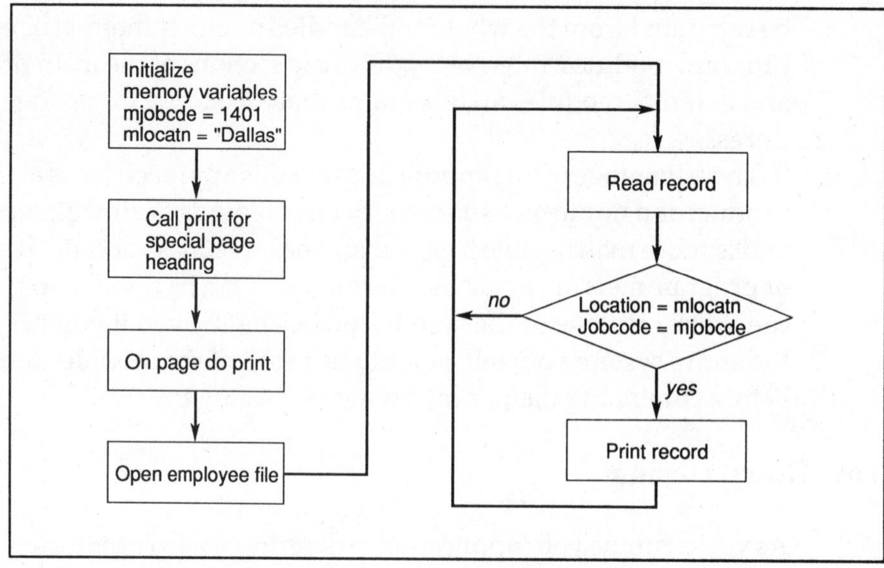

Figure 14-1 Flowchart of tasks for processing Employee file

selected information from the file. Others prefer to avoid the time-consuming process of drawing the symbols and will record their steps in pseudo-code. Pseudo-code is nothing more than abbreviated English language statements representing each of the steps that might look something like Figure 14-2.

Neither neatness nor grammar are important as you attempt to document the program steps. What you are attempting to capture are the steps and the way in which they are logically connected. Once you are convinced that you have recorded the logic correctly you can begin to convert your plan into dBASE code.

```
Initialize mjobcde to 1401
Initialize mlocatn to Dallas
Print page heading
Open employee file
Do until end of file is reached
     Write report line for locatn=mlocatn and jobcode=mjobcde
     If end of page, print heading
Repeat Do loop
Close files
```

Figure 14-2 Pseudo-code of tasks for processing Employee file

Command Syntax

The dBASE programming language is like any other programming language in that it has a syntax for its commands that must be followed. Although you might prefer to make your requests in free-form English sentences, dBASE will not honor any of them. If you want dBASE to do your bidding, your concession is to enter requests in the exact form required for each command.

You were introduced to the syntax of dBASE commands in Chapter 10 with dot prompt entries. The same rules apply to the entry of commands in dBASE programs. In addition to following the correct syntax for commands, it is also important that you consider organization and readability more when a large number of dBASE commands are stored as a program.

Adding Comments to the Code

At the time that you enter a line of code, your reasoning for its use is always clear to you. When you look back at the program in a day, a week, or a month, the clarity of your prior decision is often not there. You find yourself having to think back through the lines of code to remember what your reasoning process was. If you add comments to the code at the time that you create it, this additional time is not needed to determine what at one time was completely clear to you.

You can add comments in two different ways. The comments can be placed on the code line or on a separate line at any location in a program.

Including a comment within a code line is a good idea if the instruction includes computations that are difficult to understand or a condition test that you wish to document. All program lines do not need

❑

Tip: Use full commands.

Do not try to save time by abbreviating command entries. Since the full command words are easier to understand it saves you time in the long run to spell out each of the command entries.

```
 Layout   Words   Go To   Print   Exit                                        4:24:24 pm
[·······▼1······▼··2····▼····3··▼······4▼·······▼5······▼··6····▼····7··▼·······
SET TALK OFF                                              &&Disable display
SET ECHO OFF                                              &&Disable command display
SET PATH TO \DBASE\BANTAM                                 &&Default directory
mstate="OH"                                               &&Variable for state
msalary=15000                                             &&Variable for salary
SET PRINTER ON                                            &&Enable printer
Use Employee                                              &&Open Employee file
DO WHILE .NOT. EOF()                                      &&Begin repetitive process
        IF HR_RATE*40>msalary                             &&Condition test
                ?LASTNAME                                 &&Display LASTNAME if true
        ENDIF                                             &&End if statement
        SKIP                                              &&Move to the next record
ENDDO                                                     &&End repetitive process
RETURN

Program  |D:\dbase\bantam\FIG15_3 |Line:1 Col:1 |                          | Num    Ins
```

Figure 14-3 Comments on lines containing code

these comments since some lines do not require interpretation to understand their meaning. To include comments in the same line with code, type the code, type a &&, then type the comments. Figure 14-3 provides an example of a program with comments documenting each of the lines. Although this approach is excellent, it is not always used throughout the book due to the width required to show both the code and the comments.

Adding comments on a separate line is a good approach when you want to document the code in the section that follows. You might have a section that checks for records that match a specific condition and updates several fields in these records or that uses a series of several statements to calculate the proper federal withholding tax for a payroll

❑ **Tip: Start all comments in the same location.**

Consider starting all comments at a set location on a line. Although this shortens the amount of code that you can enter in one line, it makes it easy to read the comments down the right side of the page or screen.

```
 Layout   Words   Go To   Print   Exit                                6:17:10 pm
[·······▼1······▼··2····▼····3··▼······4▼·······▼5······▼··6····▼····7··▼·······
*Establish memory variable for testing menu entry
mchoice = "D"
*Case construct to process menu selection
DO CASE
*The following case traps invalid entries
        CASE .NOT. mchoice $ "ABC"
             ? "Unacceptable entry"
        CASE mchoice="A"
             ? "Entry is A"
        CASE mchoice="B"
             ? "Entry is B"
        CASE mchoice="C"
             ? "Entry is C"
ENDCASE
*End of case construct to process menu selection
RETURN
```

Figure 14-4 Comments on separate lines

report. A comment preceding this section makes its purpose clear to anyone reading the program. You can add comments on a separate line by entering an asterisk at the beginning of the line. dBASE ignores everything on a line that begins with an asterisk. Figure 14-4 shows some program code that contains comments on separate lines. This type of entry is especially valuable at the beginning or end of a section to focus attention on the purpose of the code in the section. You can also add comments on the same line of commands that end constructs like loops and if statements without entering the && symbols first. Although these entries are ignored and do not affect execution, the compiler flags entries on the same line as ENDIF, ENDDO, and similar commands.

Developing Your Own Programming Standards

Establishing conventions that apply to all the dBASE programming that you do makes your life easier. Doing things the same way from program to program allows you to skim through certain sections of a program quickly since you know from past experience that it contains certain types of instructions. Using rules for naming files and variables also allows you to make assessments concerning the system that these programs or variables are used in.

You can establish your own rules or use some of the ones that Ashton-Tate uses throughout their sample programs. Although the important thing is having rules almost without regard to what they are, there is some advantage in adopting the same ones used by Ashton-Tate. If you decide to adapt some of their sample program code for your own use, the standards within it are compatible with what you are using. In this section, the capitalization and structure rules are the same as those used by Ashton-Tate. Where possible the rules covered are maintained throughout the programming chapters that follow. In the case of added spacing this rule has not been adopted for the book due to the space limitations within a printed line of the book.

Capitalization Consistent use of capitalization makes it clear which words in a line are command words and which ones represent field or file names. Within the sample code provided by Ashton-Tate, all command words appear in upper case. Memory variables, menu names, and window names appear in lower case. File names, field names, procedures, and index tags appear in proper case with the first letter capitalized and the remaining letters in lower case.

You can adopt these same standards or create your own. The important point is consistency. This helps you categorize entries you see instantly by the capitalization that you use.

Naming Standards As a first step you should ensure that the name that you assign to fields, files, windows, memory variables, index tags, and menus convey as much meaning as possible. A file named D with fields of X, Y, and Z conveys no information; whereas, a filename of ACCOUNT with fields of CUST_NO, BALANCE, and PAYMENT tell you something about the file and the information it contains.

If you are creating a large system you might want to choose a letter to identify the system like R for Receivables and P for Payables. You can begin the names of all the system files with this letter. Although it uses one of the eight allowable characters in file names, it allows you to see which databases, reports, forms, labels, and application programs are part of the system. In addition you can easily copy groups of the system files with the wildcard characters such as entering the DOS command **COPY R*.SCR B:** to copy all the custom forms for the Receivables system.

Using the same name for the same type of information in different files may make it possible to share forms, reports, and labels between

❑ **Tip: Avoid the use of command words when naming.**

Do not use the words in the dBASE language when assigning any name. The use of these words can cause problems and confusion. If you name a file Order, you will need to open the file by entering USE Order.dbf. dBASE would not recognize USE Order since ORDER is a word representing one of the parameters for the USE command.

files. If you call a field containing the zip code, Zip_code, continue this practice rather than calling it Zip or Z_code in another database design.

Spacing Extra spaces can be added in an expression to make it easier to read the expression. The arithmetic operators are clearer when spaces are added.

Spacing can also be added to a program in the form of blank lines. These blank lines can be used to set off a section code, making it easier to read.

Line length also affects the amount of space shown with the code. Although dBASE allows you to enter lines that are 1,024 characters long, this length capability should be reserved for special situations.

Figure 14-5 shows a few entries that were made at the dot prompt without any extra spacing. The last few lines of this code are particularly crowded. The appearance of these lines is improved by spacing within the lines as shown in Figure 14-6. The problem of no spacing within expressions is magnified in a program where you may have many lines with expressions that are even more complex. Extra spaces make it easier to see the distinct components of the calculation. When there are no spaces all the computations run together and it is easy to miss an arithmetic operator sandwiched between two variables if you read the line quickly. The latter example is much easier to read. Blank lines can also be used to separate distinct sections of the code to make the divisions more obvious.

Indentation You can use indentation to offset sections of code that are logically related. In Chapter 16 you will learn about programming

```
. mhours=45
        45
. mrate=10
        10
. mpay=(40*mrate)+((mhours-40)*1.5*mrate)
        475
. mdepend=4
        4
. mtype=2
        2
. minsur=(mdepend*50)+(mtype*25)
        250
. mpay=(40*mrate)+((mhours-40)*1.5*mrate)
        475
. minsur=(mdepend*50)+(mtype*25)
        250
.
```

Figure 14-5 Formulas

constructions that test a condition or perform code repetitively. The code within these constructs is related and should be indented to show that all of the indented instructions are executed while a condition is true. Since these constructs can be used together, multiple indentation levels are sometimes needed to show the relationship between various lines of code. Figure 14-7 shows a section of code that does not use indentation. The same code with indentation is shown in Figure 14-8. The indentation makes it easier to see the logical grouping between lines of code.

Entering the Program Code

dBASE supplies a program editor that you can use for entering your code line by line. It works almost identically to the word-wrap editor that you have used for memo fields and report word-wrap bands.

```
. mpay = (40 * mrate) + ((mhours - 40) * 1.5 * mrate)
        475
. minsur = (mdepend * 50) + (mtype * 25)
        250
```

Figure 14-6 Formulas with spaces added

```
Layout   Words   Go To   Print   Exit                                    9:18:34 am
[····▼··▼1······▼··2····▼····3··▼······4▼········▼5······▼··6····▼····7··▼·······
DO WHILE .NOT. EOF()
IF Qtr_sales >= 50000
DO CASE
CASE Qtr_sales > 500000
DO Super
CASE Qtr_sales > 250000
DO Great
CASE Qtr_sales > 100000
DO Good
OTHERWISE
DO Ok
ENDCASE
ELSE
IF Qtr_sales < 10000
DO Fired
ELSE
DO Probatn
ENDIF
ENDIF
ENDDO
Program  D:\dbase\bantam\B15_8      Line:20 Col:6                               Ins
```

Figure 14-7 Program code

The size limitation of 5,000 bytes that applied to earlier dBASE releases has been expanded to 32,000 lines of code. With this increase

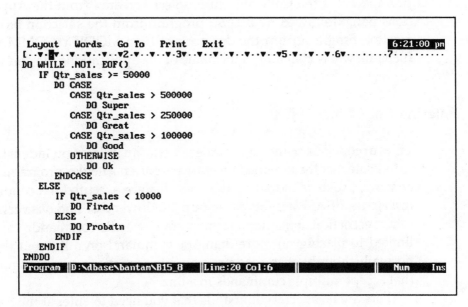

```
Layout   Words   Go To   Print   Exit                                    6:21:00 pm
[··▼·▼▼··▼··▼··▼··▼2·▼··▼··▼·3▼··▼··▼··▼··▼··▼··▼··▼5·▼··▼··▼·6▼········7·········
DO WHILE .NOT. EOF()
   IF Qtr_sales >= 50000
      DO CASE
         CASE Qtr_sales > 500000
            DO Super
         CASE Qtr_sales > 250000
            DO Great
         CASE Qtr_sales > 100000
            DO Good
         OTHERWISE
            DO Ok
      ENDCASE
   ELSE
      IF Qtr_sales < 10000
         DO Fired
      ELSE
         DO Probatn
      ENDIF
   ENDIF
ENDDO
Program  D:\dbase\bantam\B15_8      Line:20 Col:6                         Num   Ins
```

Figure 14-8 Program code using indentation

❑

Tip: Establish evenly spaced indentation.

Use the _tab system variable discussed later in the chapter under Enabling Automatic Indentation to create tab locations that are evenly spaced every two or three positions across the line.

your available disk space may be more of a limiting factor for large programs than the upper limit imposed by dBASE.

Lines of code in a program can also be longer with the limit increased to 1,024 characters. If you prefer to continue lines of code rather than enter long lines you can use the semicolon as a continuation symbol on each line but the last line. Since SQL regards the semicolon as a request to execute the previous command, you cannot use a semicolon to indicate continuation in SQL code.

Starting the Program Editor

You can access the program editor from the Control Center or the dot prompt. From the Control Center, select <create> from the Applications panel followed by dBASE program from the selection box. To create a program from the dot prompt type MODIFY COMMAND filename where filename is the name of the applications file you want to create.

Entering Code Lines

Lines of code normally begin at the left margin unless you indent them to indicate that the indented lines are part of a particular programming construct, such as indenting the lines that are executed if a condition test is true. dBASE accepts either upper or lower case and has very few other restrictions outside the syntax for a specific command. You are limited to placing no more than one command on a line but this is normally thought of as good programming practice even in languages that accept multiple commands to a line.

There are no special commands that you need to enter at the beginning of a program. You will want to review the section on program

```
 Layout   Words   Go To   Print   Exit                                   9:24:10 am
[·····█·▼1······▼··2····▼····3··▼······4▼·······▼5······▼··6····▼····7··▼·······
USE Employee ORDER Ssn
DO Rpt_frm
DO Lkup
CLOSE ALL
RETURN

PROCEDURE Rpt_frm
 .
 .
 .
RETURN

PROCEDURE Lkup
 .
 .
 .
RETURN
```

Figure 14-9 Program containing several procedures

structure later in this chapter for some helpful suggestions on establishing conventions that apply to every program that you create. dBASE IV supports the entry of multiple procedure within one program file. Each procedure should end with a RETURN statement. All procedures with the exception of the first must start with a PROCEDURE statement. Figure 14-9 provides an example of how these would appear within a program.

Indenting Code

The indentation features of the editor are especially useful for program code. It is good programming practice to indent code that falls within the bounds of a particular program construct.

You want to establish tab settings that are close enough to allow a number of nested levels of indentation on the screen. Three spaces apart is sufficient to show the difference distinctively but allow more levels of indentation on the screen than the eight spaces between levels provided by the default tab settings. To change the tab settings that are three units apart set the system variable _tabs to 3,6,9, etc with this entry at the dot prompt:

_tabs="3,6,9,12,15,18,21,24,27,30,33,36,39,42,45,48,51,54,57,60"

When you enter the program editor, the new tab settings appear on the ruler line. These tab settings also apply to other dBASE editing screens such as Memo fields and Report designs. If you want to make this change permanent, enter the tab locations separated by commas for the TABS setting in the OUTPUT menu for modifying the CONFIG.DB file in DBSETUP.

In the program editor, check the status of Enable automatic indent to ensure that it is set to YES. When Enable automatic indent is set to YES, pressing TAB or SHIFT-TAB moves the cursor to the next or previous tab stop and sets the left margin to the cursor's position. Each time you want to indent to the next tab stop, press the TAB key. The code for the statement you type starts at this location. dBASE also maintains this level of indentation for all subsequent lines. You can press the TAB key to indent to the next tab stop or use SHIFT-TAB to move to tab settings to the left.

Printing the Code

The print features are identical to the ones that you use to print Memo fields and macros. Although printing with line numbers is available, it is seldom used with Memo fields. With a program, the line numbers are helpful when walking through a program with someone else or trying to debug the program yourself.

Saving and Executing Programs

You can save a program without exiting if you use the Layout Save option. It is a good idea to do this periodically so you do not risk losing the code that you have entered in the event of a system crash.

You can also use the Save and exit option available through the Exit menu. This returns you to either the dot prompt or the Control Center depending on how you entered the program editor.

Additional options on the Exit menu allow you to run the program or use the dBASE debugger. Although these two options save the .PRG file containing the source code they do not recompile the program into a .DBO file. Since this is the file that dBASE executes, using these two options to run your program does not update the compiled file. If you use the Save changes option and choose highlight the file in the Applications panel and press ENTER twice to select Run application from the Instruct box, dBASE recompiles the source code as long as SET DEVELOPMENT IS ON. The DEVELOPMENT setting causes dBASE to check the time stamps on the compiled file and the source file and recompile if the source is more recent. From the dot prompt, the DO and COMPILE commands recompile your program.

Testing and Debugging a Program

If your program is short and simple, it is likely that it works the first time you try it. Even if the program produces the expected results you have not finished testing it. You need to check the program under a variety of conditions to ensure that it always produces the correct results.

Designing Test Scripts or Transactions

The easiest approach for programs to be used on a long-term basis is to develop a set of test data that checks for all conditions. The test data set can contain examples of expected entries, unexpected entries, and entries designed to "break" the system. This way, anytime you change a program, you can process this script or set of transactions and you know that you have tested all aspects of the program.

It is a good idea to involve the users of the system in helping you develop this test data. They are aware of the expected inputs. They may also recall instances in the past where problem data caused problems for their existing system. You may also need to elicit the cooperation of users in testing the system, especially if it is a multiuser system where part of the testing necessitates having a number of users working on the system at the same time.

Using the Debugger

Once you recognize that there is a problem with the system, you may want some help in isolating the source of the problem. dBASE IV has a built-in debugger feature that you can use for this purpose. The debugger provides several windows with each providing vital information on the status of your program. It is interactive in that it allows you to enter a number of commands to control the way in which it operates.

You can choose to start the debugger before beginning the execution of your program. To do this you can choose Debug from the Exit menu

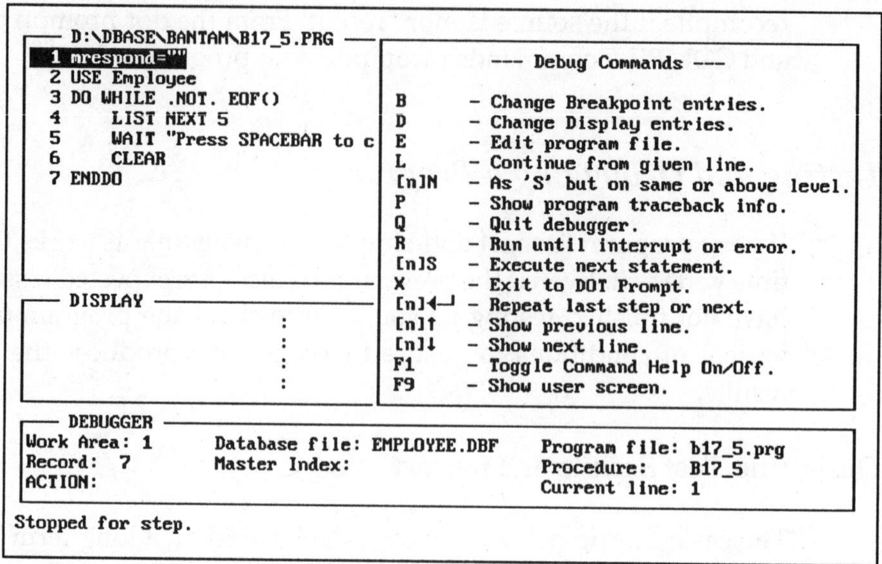

Figure 14-10 Debug screen

of the program editor or type DEBUG filename at the dot prompt. Figure 14-10 shows the initial debugger display partially overlaid with a help window showing the debugger actions. The other option is turning the debugger on and off from with your program. The command to activate the debugger is SET TRAP ON. This command causes the debugger to start as soon as an error is encountered. If SET ESCAPE is ON and the program does not have an ON ESCAPE command, the debugger starts when you press ESC during the execution of a program.

Debugger Windows When the debugger is active, it uses four windows on your screen. If the help display is overlaying part of the display, you can press ESC to see all four windows. The first window is the edit window in the upper part of the screen. This window displays your program code and can be activated by typing an E in the debugger window's action code. The line numbers that display at the beginning of this file are offsets from the beginning of the file rather than any procedure that may be active within the file. You can make changes to the lines of code from this window and save them with CTRL-END, although they do not execute until the program is compiled.

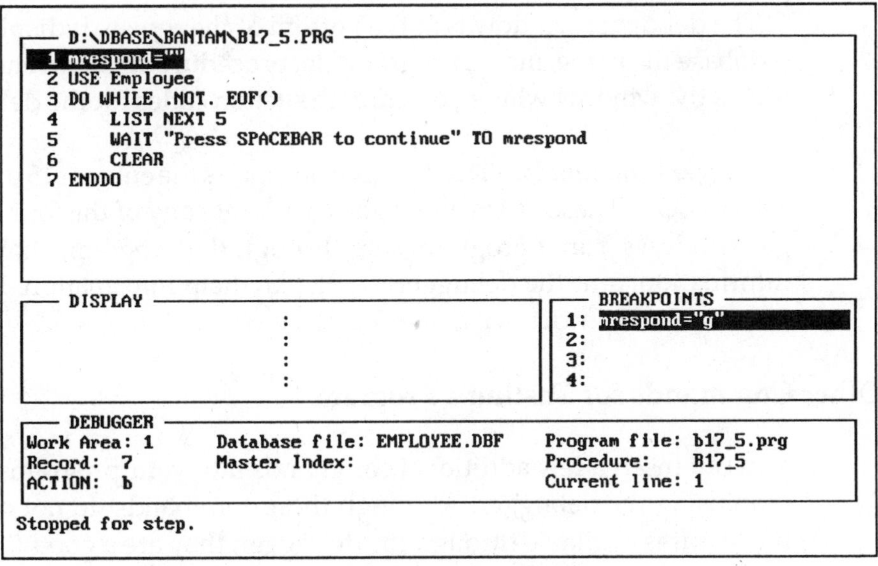

Figure 14-11 Debug screen using breakpoints

The display window can be activated to show the status of the program. You can enter expressions in this window and have dBASE evaluate them based on the current record and memory variables values. Any valid dBASE expression or memory variable can be entered into the left side of each line with the right side showing the results.

The breakpoint window is next to the display window on the debugger layout. It allows you to establish the condition under which you want to halt program execution. You might as an example elect to halt execution when the Location is equal to Dallas or the Salary is greater than 50,000. After each line of code is executed, the breakpoints are evaluated. The debug window is activated as soon as any one of the breakpoint conditions evaluate as true. The halt allows you to enter action codes that permit you to slow down execution at this point to a step-by-step approach or to take some other action that helps you determine errors that you noticed in the processing for records that meet a certain set of conditions. Up to 10 different breakpoints are supported. Figure 14-11 shows an entry in the debugger window that stops the program if the user types a g rather than pressing the SPACEBAR. This allows you to interrupt the program and switch to a step-by-step execution or another action.

The debugger window is at the bottom of the screen. It displays the database file name, index, program file, procedure, and current line. It is also the window where you enter the action codes for the debugger.

Debugger Commands The debugger supports the entry of 15 different action codes. These codes allow you to activate any of the four debugger windows, run a program, step through the program, show trace information, quit the debugger, or display help information. Each of the command entries is listed in Table 14-1.

Other Commands for Testing a Program

You can insert a few additional commands into your programs rather than using the debugger. Although these commands do not offer all the features available through the debugger, they are a good first step when you are attempting to isolate problems.

The SET TALK and SET ECHO commands can be useful in program debugging. With SET ECHO ON, each of your dBASE command lines display on the screen as they are executed. With SET TALK ON, memory variables, record numbers, and the results of commands like APPEND, COPY, and STORE display on the screen. Although you normally want both of these settings at OFF, you can use the SET commands within your program to monitor the processing. If you know that no problems exist in the early part of the code, you can begin the program with both options set at OFF and insert the SET commands before the area where you think the problem exists.

❑ **Tip: Debugger is still in memory if you use the X option.**

If you use the X action to go to the dot prompt the debugger is still in memory. You can enter dot prompt commands and return to the full use of the debugger by typing RESUME. If you attempt to execute the debugger again it is not reloaded but operates as if you had SET STEP ON.

Table 14-1 Debugger Options

Option Code	*Action Taken*
B	Moves to the breakpoint window.
D	Moves to the display window.
E	Moves to the edit window.
L	Begins execution at specified line.
[<n>]N	Steps through program <n> steps at a time at current or higher level only.
P	Displays trace of calling programs/procedures.
Q	Quits the debugger and cancels program.
R	Executes the program until breakpoint or error occurs.
[<n>]S	Steps through program <n> steps at a time.
X	Suspends program and exits to dot prompt.
Enter	Issues a 1S or 1N, whichever is most recent.
[<n>]DOWN ARROW	Moves to next instruction.
[<n>]UP ARROW	Moves to previous instruction.
F1	Displays Help menu of debugger commands.
F9	Toggles the debugger windows on and off.

Modifying a Program

To modify an existing program, you can highlight the program name in the Application panel, press ENTER and type an **M** to select Modify program. To work at the dot prompt you would type **MODI COMM** or **MODIFY COMMAND** followed by the name of the program and press ENTER. You can add new lines, delete lines, or change existing entries by editing them.

The same features are available as for original program entry. If you wish to save the modified version under a new name, use the Layout option to save the program and edit the existing name or type a new one. Save the program changes by pressing ALT-E and typing an **S**. If you choose run from the Control panel Instruct box, dBASE recompiles the source code before executing the program.

> **Tip: Make sure the code is compiled again after making changes.**
>
> From the dot prompt you can use the DO or COMPILE commands to recompile the code file. From the ASSIST mode, save the changes and highlight the program name from the Control panel and select Run to perform the same task.

Program Structure

To apply the concepts of modular programming discussed earlier, you want to create separate procedures for some of the tasks required by your application. There are other components of a program that are not directly related to a single task that you need to handle. Some of these tasks might appropriately be labeled housekeeping activities since they establish the proper environment for the rest of the application.

Some programming languages like COBOL require a structure for any program you create. COBOL programs have Identification, Environment, Data, and Procedure sections with special entries in each type of section. Programs written in the dBASE language do not have this requirement although you should adopt a certain amount of this structure in each of the programs that you create. You can use comments and separate procedures to achieve the same effect.

Creating an Identification Header

The first entries in a program should be identifying information. Entries like the program name, its purpose, the programmer, and a change history are important entries in this section. Ashton-Tate refers to this section as a preamble but reserves the change history for a program footer at the very end of the program.

Each entry in the identification header should begin with an asterisk so that dBASE recognizes it as a comment and skips over the line when it compiles the source code entries to create the object code. The entries in a typical program might look like this:

```
*PROGRAM NAME: RPROCPAY
*PROGRAM PURPOSE: Process customer payments
*PROGRAMMER: Carol Hanson
*CHANGE HISTORY:
*Add limits on amount without override CVH 12/31/88

*Add summary reportTLL 2/15/89
*Revise interest calculationCVH 4/10/89
```

The change history is especially valuable if you have a problem with a program that has been in use for some time. It can help you isolate the first areas of a program to look at in the event of a problem. A recent change may unexpectedly cause a problem when a particular type of entry is processed by the system.

Establish the Settings and Initial Variable Values

dBASE provides numerous SET commands and system memory variables that allow you to customize the dBASE environment. In addition you will want to create your own memory variables for counters or other tasks. Depending on the extensiveness of your changes you might want to include the SET commands immediately after the comments in the identification header or you might want to store them in a separate procedure. If you are defining screen colors and key definitions you will definitely want to use a separate procedure since your objective should be to maintain the 50-line limit on the length of the main program as well as other modules.

Defining Set Options Figure 14-12 shows a series of SET commands stored in the procedure Set_up. Note the word PROCEDURE followed by the procedure name in the first line. You can execute this series of commands from within the main program with the entry DO Set_up.

If you want to save the current settings for any of the set commands you can equate a memory variable to the SET function with an argument of the setting you want to store. An entry of carry = SET("CARRY") will store either ON or OFF depending on the value of CARRY. You can use these entries to reestablish the settings before leaving a program with the entry SET CARRY &carry.

```
PROCEDURE Set_up
PUBLIC mstate, mzip
mstate="OH"
mzip=44040
SET TALK OFF
SET ECHO OFF
SET PRINTER ON
SET STATUS OFF
SET DECIMALS TO 2
SET EXACT OFF
RETURN
```

Figure 14-12 Procedure that sets SET command settings for program

Defining System Variables The SET commands can be supplemented by assigning values to the system variables. You can change tab settings, the default printer, the quality of print, and the page number with these settings. Table 14-2 summarizes the various system variable options. Figure 14-13 shows the addition of a few system variables to the Set_up procedure.

Initializing Memory Variables Although you may alter the values in memory variables throughout a program, you want to establish an initial value for each one at the beginning of the program. Also, you must declare which memory variables are public, which means that they are available to all program modules. Public, or global, variables should be declared and initialized first. The private or local variables

```
PROCEDURE Set_up
PUBLIC mstate, mzip
mstate="OH"
mzip=44040
SET TALK OFF
SET ECHO OFF
SET PRINTER ON
SET STATUS OFF
SET DECIMALS TO 2
SET EXACT OFF
_box=.T.
_tabs="3,6,9,12,15,18,21,24,27,30,33,36,39,42,45,48,51,54,57,60,63"
_pquality=.T.
_peject="NONE"
RETURN
```

Figure 14-13 Set_up procedure with system variables added

Table 14-2 System Variables

Variable	*Usage*	*Default*
_alignment	Alignment of output for ?/?? commands.	Left
_box	Determines whether boxes created with DEFINE BOX display.	.T.
_indent	Indentation for the first line of paragraphs printed with ?	0
_lmargin	Left margin for output created with ?	0
_padvance	Determines whether form feeds or line feeds advance the paper.	FORMFEED
_pageno	Sets the current page number.	1
_pbpage	Specifies beginning page for print.	1
_pcolno	Positions on a specific column before printing streaming output from commands like LIST and DISPLAY.	current column
_pcopies	Sets number of copies for print.	1
_pdriver	Activates a print driver.	default chosen by install
_pecode	Provides ending codes for printer.	null string
_peject	Controls page eject before and after printing.	BEFORE
_pepage	Specifies the ending page for print.	32,767
_pform	Activates the print form file.	Null string
_plength	Sets page length.	66
_plineno	Assigns a line number for streaming print output.	0

(continued)

Table 14-2 System Variables *(continued)*

Variable	*Usage*	*Default*
_ploffset	Sets the page left offset.	0
_ppitch	Sets the printer pitch.	DEFAULT
_pquality	Selects the quality for print.	.F. for draft
_pscode	Provides beginning print codes.	Null string
_pspacing	Sets line spacing.	1
_pwait	Determines whether the printer waits after each page.	.F.

that are only available in the current program or any dependent programs should be initialized next. You can place the declaration and initialization of memory variable arrays either after public or private variables.

When you declare and initialize private variables in subprograms or lower-level system modules, these variables are cleared when the RETURN statement for the subprogram is executed.

Figure 14-14 shows the initialization of the memory variables for a program. The public variables are declared then initialized. Next the private variables are initialized. It is not necessary to indicate that these are private since any variable not declared as public is automatically private.

The Initial Program Code

The first code in the program should display the menu of choices for the user. Using one menu as a launching pad for any of the applications activities means that you can return to this point when a user finishes one task to see if the user has other tasks to be accomplished. It also allows you to control entry and exit to the system from this one location. The code for the menu definition does not need to be in the main

```
 Layout   Words   Go To   Print   Exit                                     5:31:12 pm
[·····█·▼1·····▼··2····▼····3··▼······4▼·······▼5······▼··6····▼····7··▼·······
PUBLIC mzip, mlast_nme, mhr_rate
PUBLIC ARRAY M_table[4]
STORE 21237 TO mzip
STORE "" TO mlast_nme
STORE 15 to mhr_rate
STORE "OH" TO mstate
STORE "Cleveland" to mcity
STORE " " TO M_table[1],M_table[2],M_table[3],M_table[4]
DECLARE M_counter[5]
STORE 5 TO M_counter[1],M_counter[2],M_counter[3],M_counter[4],M_counter[5]
RETURN
```

Figure 14-14 Declaring and initializing memory variables

routine. You will want to create a procedure that contains the definition of your main menu. Your first entry in the main program can be DO Main_menu.

Processing main menu selections is the next task. The procedures that handle each of the subtasks have their own sections for initializing memory variables if additional ones are required. In addition, it is normally at this second level where you begin to open files since you have defined a task at this point. Opening files in the main routine frequently results in files being opened unnecessarily. This may place your data at risk in the event of a system crash.

Final Cleanup

Just as there are housekeeping activities at the beginning of a program, there is housekeeping at the end to restore original settings to the SET options and system memory variables. You want to be certain that you have cleared all windows, menus, and public memory variables, and closed all databases as well.

To restore SET commands to their original entries requires some planning. You want to store the setting to memory variables when you begin. At the end of the program you can use the macro substitution feature to use the values in the variables to reestablish the correct setting. If you stored the setting for CARRY in carry, you can enter SET CARRY &carry to restore it.

GETTING STARTED

➤ You will want to try the program editor and debugger to see how they work. To create a program that displays information from a few of the Employee records follow these instructions:

1. Highlight <create> in the Application panel of the Control Center. Press ENTER twice to begin creating a dBASE program.
2. Type **SET TALK OFF** and press ENTER.
3. Type **SET ECHO OFF** and press ENTER.
4. Type **USE Employee** and press ENTER.
5. Type **DISPLAY Last_name, Ssn, Hr_rate**. and press ENTER.
6. Type **SKIP 2** and press ENTER.
7. Type **DISPLAY Last_name, Ssn, City** and press ENTER.
8. Type **GO BOTTOM** and press ENTER.
9. Type **DISPLAY Last_name, Hr_rate, Ytd_fit** and press ENTER.
10. Type **CLOSE ALL** and press ENTER.
11. Type **SET TALK ON** and press ENTER. Type **SET ECHO ON** and press ENTER.
12. Press ALT-E and press ENTER. Type **Random** and press ENTER to save the program as Random and exit.

You can execute the program with the Run option or you can use the debugger. First take a look at how the program executes with the run command:

1. Highlight Random and press twice to run the program.
2. dBASE will compile and then execute the program, displaying the information on the screen.

To use the debugger to slow down execution:

1. Highlight Random in the Applications panel and press ENTER. Type an **M** for Modify application.
2. Press ALT-E and type a **D** to select Debug.
3. When prompted for a parameter, press Enter.
4. When the debug window appears continue to press ENTER or type an **S** to walk through the application step by step.
5. When you reach the last step type a **Q** to quit the debugger.

CHAPTER 15

Functions and Expressions

Functions are predefined operations that supplement the tasks that can be performed with the dBASE IV commands. Some dBASE functions perform calculations, such as calculating a payment that would be time-consuming if you needed to enter the formula. Other functions return information about dBASE like the name of the current MDX file or the name assigned to a function key. Still other functions convert data into a different format to extend its usefulness.

dBASE IV provides 128 of these functions and arranges them in alphabetical order within the dBASE manual. These functions can be classified in a number of different groups according to the tasks that they perform for you and are shown in this way within the chapter. Appendix D provides an alphabetical listing of all the functions.

Expressions are a combination of various types of dBASE information that can be substituted for one entry. In other words if dBASE is expecting a number, in many cases it will accept an expression like 5+7 since this expression evaluates to the number 12. Entering the expression is equivalent to entering the number 12.

Expressions allow you to combine field entries, function results, memory variables, array elements, constants, and operators. When you combine these elements in an expression you must confine your entries in a single expression to one data type. You can enter 5+4 or "ABC"+"XYZ" but you cannot enter "ABC"+3 without using a function to convert 3 to a character string.

dBASE IV Expressions

dBASE IV expressions can be used to compute a calculated field, provide entries from which to build an index, create lines or a label, compute a counter value in a program, or to perform any of a number of other activities. You have already used some of them when exploring various dBASE features. This section provides more exhaustive coverage of the function options, including all the operators that they support and the priority sequence used when expressions are evaluated.

Types of Expressions

dBASE IV supports character expressions, numeric expressions, floating-point numeric expressions, date expressions, and logical expressions that are better known as conditions. Each of the elements that you use to build an expression must fit within the expression type that you have selected or they must be converted to this type of entry before being used in the expression. You can use expressions to supply an entry in a report or compute a calculated field. You can also use expressions to supply a value for a memory variable as in mnewdate =today()+5 where you are computing a newdate and placing this entry in a memory variable. In this case it may not look as if the two entries in the expression are of the same type since dates are normally entered as {07/31/89} and a number is being added to it. Actually you cannot add two dates in the format {02/15/89}+{07/31/89} and arrive at anything that makes sense. With dates you have to think about the way the data is stored as a numeric value and add or subtract the number of days desired.

Character Type Expressions Character type expressions are composed of fields or variables containing characters, functions that return character expressions, or character constants. If you use a character constant in a character expression you must enclose it within delimiters. You can use double quotes, single quotes, or square brackets to enclose character constants but most use the same character on both sides of the constant. In other words, "Last name", 'Last Name', and [Last name] are all acceptable but "Last name' is not.

Numeric Expression Types dBASE support two types of numeric expressions. The first type supports type N or Numeric entries and is useful when a decimal representation is needed. The second type, the Float type, is used in scientific calculations for very large and small numbers. These types of expression can consist of field variables, or functions that return numbers as well as numeric constants. Numeric constants do not need to be encased in any type of special delimiter.

Date Type Expressions Date expression can consist of fields and variables that contain dates, functions that return date expressions, and date constants. Date constants must be enclosed in curly braces as in {02/15/89}.

Logical Expressions Logical expressions are better known as conditions and are normally represented using variables, functions, and the relational operators. They return a .T. for true or an .F. for false. It is important that the data types on both sides of a relational operator be the same. Expressions also evaluate as .F. when they are not valid expressions.

Expression Operators

Expression operators allow you to join or compare two or more variables, constants, or fields. There are four different types of operators. There is also an established precedence for the order in which these operators are evaluated.

Mathematical Operators The mathematical operators provide standard numerical capabilities. In addition they offer the parentheses for grouping. The mathematical operators in priority order are

()	Parentheses for grouping
+ -	Positive and negative indicators
** or ^	Exponentiation
* /	Multiplication and division
+ -	Addition and subtraction

Relational Operators The relational operators allow you to test two expressions and produce a .T. or .F. value. They can be used with expressions that return characters, numeric data, logical data, or dates as long as the expressions on both sides of the relational operator are the same type of expression. All the relational operators have the same precedence level. If an expression contains more than one joined by a logical operator they are evaluated from left to right. The relational operators are

Operator	Meaning
=	Equal
<> or #	Not equal
<	Less than
<=	Less than or equal to
>	Greater than
>=	Greater than or equal to
$	Contains; "ABC"$"ABCD" returns true since ABC is contained in ABCD

Logical Operators The logical operators return a logical result as they join two or more expressions. Like the mathematical operators, they support parentheses to support overriding the default priority sequence. The operators in priority order are

Operator	Meaning
.NOT.	Logical not
.AND.	Logical and to join two expressions; will return .T. only if both expressions are true.
.OR.	Logical or; will return .T. if either expression is true.

String Operators The string operators allow you to join two or more strings. Like mathematical and logical operators they support parentheses, although both operators have the same priority and are evaluated from left to right. The string operators are

Operator	Meaning
+	Strings are joined with trailing spaces left intact.
-	Strings are joined with trailing spaces moved to the end of the last string.

Precedence of Operators in Mixed Expressions When an expression contains more than one type of operator a set order is used to evaluate the different types. Within each type the priority sequence previously discussed is still maintained. Parentheses can be used to override the order. The sequence from highest to lowest priority is

Mathematical and string operators
Relational operators
Logical operators

Defining Expressions

You can define expressions at the dot prompt to see immediate results. You can also use them with dBASE functions and any command expecting an expression. First, we will look at a few entries at the dot prompt to see the result achieved with different types of operators. Entering ? 3+4*5 produces the result 23, not 35. The entry ? 5<3 returns .F. as does ? 5<3 .AND. 17>8 since both relational expressions must be true to return .T.. Changing the logical operator to .OR. as in ? 5<3 .OR> 17>8 returns .T. since only one of the relational expressions needs to be true to return .T..

The string expression ?"abc   "+"def   " returns "abc   def   ". The string expression ?"abc   "-"def   " returns "abcdef   ".

Functions

You can use functions to customize your use of the dbASE IV environment. All of the functions have names and a set of parentheses following the name. The only exception to this is the macro substitution & feature that dBASE lists with the functions. This special feature is in the same category as the other function entries and is covered with memory variables. Some of the functions also have parameters that define the specific use you wish to make of the function. When parameters exist, they are placed inside the parentheses separated by commas.

Types of Functions

dBASE IV provides a number of different categories of built-in functions. Although the classifications are somewhat arbitrary and arguments could be made for showing some of the functions in any one of several categories, each are shown in only one. Having the categories is helpful with such a wealth of functions available. It will allow you to focus on one or two categories to explore the options available rather than having to read through all the descriptions to see if there is a function to meet your needs. The categories that have been used are date, character, testing, conversion, math, financial, network, identification, input, special, and the macro substitution function that cannot be categorized with any of the others.

dBASE IV provides another type of function in its user-defined functions (UDFs). With these a user can create functions that are not a part of the dBASE function set. User-defined functions are a special type of procedure, that is written to do the work of a function. Once you write the special procedure, a user-defined function is invoked in the same way as other functions and follows the same syntax rules.

Function Format

Each of the dBASE functions with the exception of the macro substitution function consists of a special keyword followed by a set of parentheses. The keywords are shown in upper case in this book but are recognized by dBASE regardless of the case used. Within the parentheses you may find arguments that define your particular use of the function to dBASE.

Optional arguments are shown in square brackets ([]). Required arguments are shown in angle brackets (<>). The slash is used to show a selection that can be made from among two or more choices.

Application for Functions

Functions can be used within dBASE expressions to perform computations, to convert data, or to provide additional information. They are used to supplement the commands of the dBASE programming language and can check various dBASE values and settings and control subsequent actions of programs. As an example you can use a function to access the current date and compare it to the date entry in the current record. If the comparison condition is true, you can process the current record and if it is false you can read the next record.

Date Functions

The date functions all relate to the current date or time. They may provide the value of the current system date or time, convert the date to a different format, or extract a portion of the date. There are thirteen functions in this category.

CDOW(<expD>) The CDOW function returns a character string containing the day of the week when you supply a date expression. The syntax is CDOW(<expD>). You can store the date expression in a memory variable, a field, or produce it as the result of another function. If you include the date directly as an argument you must place it within curly braces.

Examples:

`CDOW({1/31/89})` returns Tuesday

`?"Today is "+CDOW(DATE())` returns Today is Tuesday if the date is 1/31/89.

CMONTH(<expD>) This function returns the name of the month from the date supplied by a date expression. You can use a memory variables, field, or another function to supply this date or enter it directly within the function if you prefer. Note the required use of curly braces if you decide to enter a date directly.

Example:

`CMONTH(DATE())` returns August if the current date is 8/20/89.

CTOD(<expC>)/{expC} This function converts the character expression into a date. You can use a memory variable, field name or another function to supply the character string or enter it directly within the function if you prefer. If you enter the character string containing the date as the function's argument, the character string must be enclosed in quotes. If you use the curly braces, you must enter the date directly although you do not need the quotes. The format of date in the character string must match date format of the SET DATE and SET CENTURY commands.

Examples:

`STORE CTOD("05/31/88") TO DATESTRING` stores 05/31/88 in the DATESTRING variable.
`CTOD(DATE_OUT)+30` returns a date thirty days after the date stored in the character variable DATE_OUT.
`{05/31/88}+30` returns 06/30/89.

DATE() This function returns the current date. Since this uses the date set by the operating system, if it is incorrect, you must change the date from DOS. This function does not use any arguments. The date returned uses the date format set by the SET CENTURY, SET DATE, and SET MARK commands.

Example:

`DATE()` returns 08/20/89 if the current date is 8/20/89.

DAY(<expD>) This function returns the day of the month from the date supplied by a date expression. You can use a memory variable, field, or another function to supply this date or enter it directly within the function if you enclose the date in curly braces.

Example:

`DAY(DATE())` returns 20 if the current date is 8/20/89.

DMY(<expD>) This function returns a character string containing the day of the month, the name of the month, and the year from the date supplied by a date expression. You can use a memory variable, field, or another function to supply this date or enter it directly by enclosing it in curly braces.

Example:

`? "Todays date is "+DMY(DATE())` returns Todays date is 20 August 89 if the current date is 8/20/89.

DOW(<expD>) The DOW function returns a number representing the day of the week when you supply a date expression. The date expression can be a memory variable, a field, the result of another function, or entered directly by enclosing the date in curly braces. Each day of the week uses a different number with Sunday represented as a 1.

Example:

`DOW({1/31/89})` returns 3.

DTOC(<expD>) This function converts a date to a character string. This function is like the DMY function except the format of the date returned in the DTOC function uses the date format set with the SET CENTURY and SET MARK commands. You can use a memory variable, field, or another function to supply this date or enter it directly by enclosing it in curly braces.

Example:

`? "Todays date is "+DTOC(DATE())` returns Todays date is 08/20/89 if the current date is 8/20/89.

DTOS(<expD>) This function converts a date to a character string in the format YYYYMMDD. This function is like the DTOC function except the two functions return the date in a different format. You can use a memory variable, field, or another function to supply this date or enter it directly by enclosing it in curly braces. This function is normally used as part of an index expression.

Examples:

`? DTOS({08/20/89})` returns 19890820

`INDEX ON DTOS(HIRE_DATE) + LAST_NAME` indexes the database in ascending order according to the HIRE field with the LAST_NAME field deciding the order for records with the same HIRE_DATE.

MDY(<expD>) This function returns a character string containing the name of the month, the day of the month, and the year from the date supplied by a date expression. You can use a memory variable, field, or another function to supply this date or enter it directly by enclosing it in curly braces.

Example:

`? "Todays date is "+MDY(DATE())` returns Todays date is August 20, 89 if the current date is 8/20/89.

MONTH(<expD>) The MONTH function returns a number representing the month when you supply a date expression. The date expression can be a memory variable, a field, the result of another function, or entered directly by enclosing the date in curly braces. Each month uses a different number ranging from 1 for January to 12 for December.

Example:

`MONTH({1/31/89})` returns 1.

TIME() This function returns a string containing the current time in a HH:MM:SS format. Since the function uses the operating system time, if it is incorrect, you must change the time from DOS. This function does not use any arguments. This function uses a 24-hour clock which represents times in the afternoon as the hour plus 12.

Example:

`TIME()` returns 12:51:49 if the current time is 12:51:49 pm.

YEAR(<expD>) The YEAR function returns a number representing the year when you supply a date expression. The number returned is a four-digit number that includes the century. The date expression can be a memory variable, a field, the result of another function, or entered directly by enclosing the date in curly braces.

Example:

`YEAR({1/31/89})` returns 1989.

Character Functions

Each of the character functions performs actions with character type data. Some of these functions change the case of a character string.

Some trim excess blank characters from the function and others extract a portion of a character entry.

AT(<expC>,<expC>/<memofield name>) The AT function returns a number representing the starting position of the first string within the second string or Memo field name. The character expressions can be memory variables, fields, the results of another function, or entered directly by enclosing the characters in quotes. The function returns a 0 if the first string is not contained in the second string. The AT function is case sensitive.

Examples:

AT("Sold","Cost of Goods Sold") returns 15.
AT("SOLD","Cost of Goods Sold") returns 0.
AT("Spanish",SKILLS) returns 36 if the EMPLOYEE database is active and Mary Jenkins' record is current.

LEFT(<expC>/<memofield name>,<expN>) The LEFT function returns the number of characters from the character expression or current Memo field detailed by the numeric expression. The character expression can be a memory variable, field, the result of another function, Memo field name, or entered directly by enclosing the characters in quotes. The numeric expression can be a memory variable, field, the result of another function, or entered directly.

Examples:

LEFT("Sales - 1989",5) returns the characters Sales.
LEFT("Cost of Goods Sold",55) returns the character string Cost of Goods Sold
LEFT(SKILLS,25) returns Typing, Switchboard operator if the EMPLOYEE database is active and Mary Jenkins' record is current.

LOWER(<expC>) This function converts a string to lower case. The character expression can be a memory variable, a field, the results of another function, or entered directly by enclosing it in quotes.

Example:

LOWER("HELLO") returns hello.

LTRIM(<expC>) This function returns the original string after removing any spaces at the beginning. The character expression can be a memory variable, a field, the results of another function, or entered directly by enclosing it in quotes.

Examples:

`LTRIM("        A string with extra spaces")` returns "A string with extra spaces".
`LTRIM(STR(66.5,11,2))` removes the extra spaces the STR function places to the left of 66.50.

MLINE(<memo field name>,<expN>) The MLINE function returns a specified line of a Memo field. The Memo field name must be in the active database. The numeric expression can be a memory variable, a field containing a number, the result of another function, or a number. The memo is divided into lines according to the SET MEMOWIDTH setting and the carriage returns entered in the memo text.

Examples:

`MLINE(SKILLS,2)` returns Switchboard when the EMPLOYEE database is active and Mary Jenkins' record is current if MEMOWIDTH is set to 15.
`MLINE(SKILLS,2)` returns Some Spanish when the EMPLOYEE database is active and Mary Jenkins' record is current if MEMOWIDTH is set to 65.

REPLICATE(<expC>,<expN>) The REPLICATE function returns a specified string repeated the number of times specified in the second argument. The character expression can be a memory variable, field, the result of another function, memo field name or entered directly by enclosing the characters in quotes. The numeric expression can be a memory variable, a field containing a number, the result of another function, or a number. The resulting string must be less than 255 characters. You can use this function to create bar graphs and screen borders.

Examples:

`REPLICATE("=",20)` returns ====================.
`REPLICATE("~^",4)` returns ~^~^~^~^.

RIGHT(<expC>/<variable>,<expN>) The RIGHT function returns the number of characters from the right side of a character expression or the Memo field specified by the numeric expression. The character expression can be a memory variable, a character or memo field name, the result of another function, or entered directly by enclosing the characters in quotes. The numeric expression can be a memory variable, field, the result of another function, or entered directly.

Examples:

`RIGHT("Sales - 1989",4)` returns the characters STRING 1989.

`RIGHT("Cost of Goods Sold",55)` returns the character string Cost of Goods Sold

`RIGHT(SKILLS,10)` returns Spanish if the EMPLOYEE database is active and Mary Jenkins' record is current. The right arrow symbol is the end of the memo field character.

RTRIM(<expC>) This function returns the original string after removing any spaces at the end. The character expression can be a memory variable, a field, the results of another function, or entered directly by enclosing it in quotes.

Examples:

`RTRIM("A string with extra spaces      ")` returns "A string with extra spaces".

`RTRIM(FIRST_NAME)+" "+RTRIM(LAST_NAME)` returns Mary Jenkins if the EMPLOYEE database is active and the first record is current.

SOUNDEX(<expC>) This function returns the four-character soundex code dBASE IV uses. This is the code used when you look for a match based on sound. This function is primarily used in an index expression. The character expression can be a memory variable, a Character field name, the result of another function, or entered directly by enclosing the characters in quotes.

Examples:

`SOUNDEX("Jenkins")` returns J525

`INDEX ON SOUNDEX(LAST_NAME)` indexes the EMPLOYEE database based on the sound of the last name.

SPACE(<expN>) This function returns a string containing the number of spaces specified by the function's argument. The numeric expression is a memory variable, a Numeric field, the result of another function, or a number that must be less than 255.

Example:

`SPACE(10)` returns "   ".

STUFF(<expC1>,<expN1>,<expN2>,<expC2>) This function inserts and removes characters in a string. The first character expression is the character string that is acted upon. The first numeric expression is the position where characters are inserted and/or deleted. The second numeric expression is the number of characters deleted. The second character expression is the characters that are inserted. The character expressions are memory variables, character fields, the results of another function, or entered directly by enclosing the characters in quotes. The numeric expressions are memory variables, numeric fields, the results of another function, or a number. You can use zeros for the numeric expressions if you want to use the beginning position or do not want to remove any characters. You can use an empty string for the second character expression if you do not want to insert any characters.

Examples:

`STUFF("Have a wonderful, nice day",8,11,"")` returns Have a nice day.
`STUFF("Have a nice day",8,0,"very ")` returns Have a very nice day.
`STUFF("Have a wonderful, nice day",8,11,"very ")` returns Have a very nice day.

SUBSTR(<expC>/<memo field name>,<starting position> [,<number of characters>]) This function returns a specified number of characters from the part of a character expression or current Memo field. The character expression can be a memory variable, character or Memo field name, the result of another function, or entered directly by enclosing the characters in quotes. The starting position and the number of characters are numeric expressions from a memory variable, field, the result of another function, or entered directly. If the number of characters is missing, the function returns all of the characters after the starting position.

Examples:

`SUBSTR("Sales - 1989",5)` returns "s - 1989".
`SUBSTR("Cost of Goods Sold",9,5)` returns Goods.
`SUBSTR(SKILLS,9,20)` returns Switchboard operator if the EMPLOYEE database is active and Mary Jenkins' record is current.

TRANSFORM(<exp>,<expC>) This function returns a string containing the original expression after it is formatted using the character expression. The first expression is a memory variable, a field name, the result of another function, or entered directly by enclosing it in quotes if it is a character string or curly braces if it is a date. The character expression can be a memory variable, the results of another function, or entered directly by enclosing it in quotes. The character expression contains template characters and picture functions.

Examples:

`TRANSFORM("Have a nice day","@!")` returns HAVE A NICE DAY.
`TRANSFORM(HOME_PHONE,"(999)999-9999")` returns (216)999-9999 if the first record of the EMPLOYEE database is current.

TRIM(<expC>) This function is the same as the RTRIM function, which removes trailing blanks from a character expression.

UPPER(<expC>) This function converts a character expression to upper case. The character expression can be a memory variable, a Character field name, the results of another function, or entered directly by enclosing it in quotes.

Example:

`UPPER("hello")` returns HELLO.

Financial Functions

Financial functions are new to dBASE IV. Although a full set of the many functions available within a spreadsheet are not present, some of the most popular options are available. You can use the financial functions to compute a future value of an annuity, a present value of an annuity, or a loan payment. You can always create a user-defined function for any of the other financial functions that you might need.

FV(<payment>,<rate>,<periods>) This function returns the future value of a series of equal cash flows, each earning interest. This function treats cash flows like an ordinary annuity. An ordinary annuity is an investment where you put in a fixed amount every period and at the end of a fixed number of periods, you receive the amount that you have saved plus the interest earned on all of the money invested. The payment, rate, and periods arguments are numeric expressions from memory variables, field names, the results of other functions, or entered directly. The values used for the payment, rate and periods must use the same time periods. For example, if you are using an annual rate, you must provide the annual payment and the number of years.

Examples:

`FV(3120,.08,18)` returns 116844.76 assuming 18 years, a 8% interest rate and a 3120 annual payment.

`FV(60,.08/52,18*52)` returns 125425.09 with the same assumptions as above but changing from annually to weekly payments, interest rates, and periods. The difference is due to the difference in number of periods that the interest is compounded.

PAYMENT(<principal>,<rate>,<periods>) This function computes a payment based on the principal, an interest rate, and a number of periods. The payment, rate, and periods arguments are numeric expressions from memory variables, field names, the results of other functions, or entered directly. Like the FV function, the values used for the interest rate and periods must use the same time periods.

Examples:

`PAYMENT(20000,.13,30)` returns 2668.21 as a yearly payment on a $20,000 loan for 30 years at a 13% interest rate.
`PAYMENT(20000,.13/12,30*12)` returns 221.24 as a monthly payment on a $20,000 loan for 30 years at a 13% interest rate. The difference between 2668.21 and 2654.88 (221.24*12) is due to the difference in number of periods that the interest is compounded.

PV(<payment>,<rate>,<periods>) This function returns the present value of an annuity, or series of equal cash flows, invested at a certain interest rate for a number of periods. The payment, rate, and periods arguments are numeric expressions from memory variables, field names, the results of other functions, or entered directly. Like the FV function, the values used for the payment, rate, and periods must use the same time periods.

Example:

`PV(50000,.08,20)` returns 490907.37 as the present value of receiving $50,000 for the next 20 years assuming an 8% interest rate.

Math Functions

The math functions provide basic mathematical features like determining the absolute value or rounding a number. They perform computations like maximum and minimum. The math functions provide access to trigonometric capabilities like sine and cosine as well as logarithmic functions.

Trigonometric functions involve the relationships of the sides and angles of triangles. They provide information about one part of a triangle if you provide information about another part of the triangle.

The trigonometric angle ratios can be understood by inscribing an angle in one of the four quadrants of a circle, as shown in Figure 15-1. The angle in this circle, which is the focus of trigonometric function examples, is angle YXZ (an angle is described by listing the letters representing the points on the two lines that create the angle with the center letter being the pivot point for the two lines that form the angle). Angle YXZ is created by the rotation of the line XY to point Z on the circle's circumference.

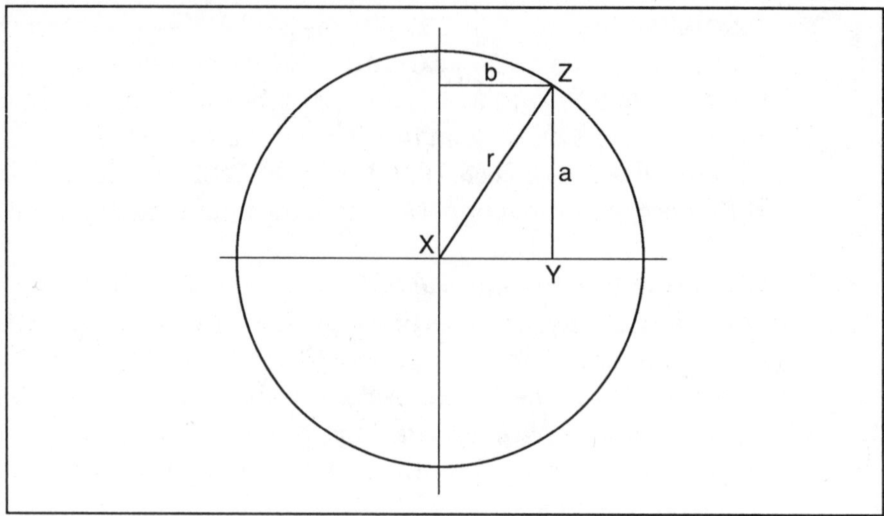

Figure 15-1 Diagram of trigonometric ratios

By dropping a perpendicular line from Z to the horizontal axis, you create a right triangle. This triangle has several key measurements used in trigonometric calculations. The hypotenuse is the distance from Z to X and is described as *r*. This is the longest side of the triangle. The distance from Z to the vertical axis is *b* and is the same whether it is measured from Z to the vertical line or from X to the point where the dropped line meets the horizontal axis. The distance from the horizontal axis to Z is *a*. By comparing these three sides to one another, you create ratios that are dependent upon the size of the triangle's angles. These ratios remain the same as the triangle is enlarged or contracted as long as the triangle's angles remain the same. Thus, if you know the ratio between two sides of a triangle, you can determine the angles of the triangle.

In any right triangle, if you know the length of any two sides you can determine the length of the third side using the Pythagorean theorem. The Pythagorean theorem is $a^2 + b^2 = r^2$ using letters in the triangle described previously.

ABS(<expN>) This function returns the absolute value of a number that is the value of the number without a plus or minus sign. The numeric expression is a memory variable, a field name, the result of another function, or entered directly.

Example:

`ABS(-5)` returns a 5.

ACOS(<expN>) This function returns the angle measured in radians that has a cosine of the specified ratio. The numeric expression is a value between -1 and 1 contained in a memory variable, a field name, the result of another function, or entered directly. The SET DECIMALS and SET PRECISION commands determine the number of digits after the decimal point.

Example:

`ACOS(.5)` returns 1.05, which is the angle measured in radians that has a cosine equal to .5.

ASIN(<expN>) This function returns the angle measured in radians that has a sine of the specified ratio. The numeric expression is a value between -1 and 1 contained in a memory variable, a field name, the result of another function, or entered directly. The SET DECIMALS and SET PRECISION commands determine the number of digits after the decimal point.

Example:

`ASIN(.87)` returns 1.06, which is the angle measured in radians that has a sine equal to .87.

ATAN(<expN>) This function returns the angle measured in radians that has a tangent of the specified ratio. The numeric expression is a memory variable, a field name, the result of another function, or entered directly. The SET DECIMALS and SET PRECISION commands determine the number of digits after the decimal point.

Example:

`ATAN(1.73)` returns 1.05 which is the angle measured in radians that has a tangent equal to 1.73.

ATN2(expN1>,<expN2>) This function returns the angle measured in radians that has a tangent of the specified ratio. This function expects the *x* and *y* coordinates of the point that you want the arctangent. The numeric expressions are memory variables, field names, the results of other functions, or entered directly. Their ratio must be less than or equal to the absolute value of π. The SET DECIMALS and SET PRECISION commands determine the number of digits after the decimal point.

Example:

`ATN2(5.2,3)` returns 1.05, which is the angle measured in radians that has a tangent equal to 1.73.

CEILING(<expN>) This function returns the smallest integer greater than or equal to the numeric expression. The numeric expression is a memory variable, a field name, the result of another function, or entered directly.

Examples:

`CEILING(5)` returns 5.

`CEILING(5.999)` returns 6 since 6 is the smallest integer greater than or equal to 5.999.

`CEILING(-7.2)` returns -7 since -7 is the smallest integer greater than or equal to -7.2.

COS(<expN>) This function returns the cosine of an angle measured in radians. The numeric expression is a memory variable, a field name, the result of another function, or entered directly. The SET DECIMALS and SET PRECISION commands determine the number of digits after the decimal point.

Example:

`COS(1.05)` returns .5, which is the cosine of 1.05 radians.

DTOR(<expN>) This function returns the radians of an angle measured in degrees. This function is often used to convert degree measurements to a value other functions can use. The numeric expression is a memory variable, a field name, the result of another function, or entered directly.

Example:

DTOR(45) returns .79 which is the number of radians in 45 degrees.

EXP(<expN>) This function returns the value of raising the numeric expression to the constant e (about 2.718). The numeric expression is a memory variable, field name, the result of another function, or entered directly. The SET DECIMALS command determines the number of digits after the decimal point.

Example:

EXP(1) returns 2.72, which is the rounded value of e.
EXP(5) returns 148.41, which is e raised to the fifth power.

FIXED(<expN>) This function converts a real floating number to a binary-coded decimal number. This function is often used to convert Floating field type values into Numeric field type values. The numeric expression is a memory variable, a field name, the result of another function, or entered directly.

Example:

FIXED(5.43) returns 5.43 stored as a binary coded decimal number.

FLOAT(<expN>) This function converts a binary-coded decimal number to a real floating number. This function is often used to convert Numeric field type values into Floating field type values. The numeric expression is a memory variable, a field name, the result of another function, or entered directly.

Example:

FLOAT(5.43) returns 5.43 stored as a real floating number.

FLOOR(<expN>) This function returns the largest integer less than or equal to the numeric expression. The numeric expression is a memory variable, a field name, the result of another function, or entered directly.

Examples:

`FLOOR(5)` returns 5.

`FLOOR(5.999)` returns 5 since 5 is the largest integer less than or equal to 5.999.

`FLOOR(-7.2)` returns -8 since 8 is the largest integer less than or equal to -7.2.

INT(<expN>) This function returns the integer portion of the numeric expression. The numeric expression is a memory variable, a field name, the result of another function, or entered directly.

Examples:

`INT(5)` returns 5.

`NT(5.999)` returns 5 since 5 is the integer portion of 5.999.

LOG(<expN>) This function returns the natural logarithm of the numeric expression. The numeric expression is a memory variable, field name, the result of another function, or entered directly. This function returns a real floating number.

Examples:

`LOG(100)` returns 4.61.

`EXP(LOG(6500)` returns 6500 since raising e to the natural logarithm of a number returns the original number.

LOG10(<expN>) This function returns the common logarithm (base 10) of the numeric expression. The numeric expression is a memory variable, field name, the result of another function, or entered directly. The natural logarithm is a real floating number.

Examples:

`LOG10(100000)` returns 5.

`LOG10(6500)` returns 3.81 since raising 10 to the 3.81 power equals 6500.

MAX(<expC1>/<expN1>/<expD1>,<expC2>/<expN2>/<expD2>)
This function returns the larger of the two character, date, or numeric expressions. The expressions are memory variables, field names, the results of other functions, or entered directly. If you enter dates directly,

the dates must be enclosed in curly braces. If you enter character strings directly, the strings must be enclosed in quotes. The two expressions must be the same data type. Character comparisons use the ASCII values of the characters.

Examples:

`MAX("Alphabetical","Numerical")` returns Numerical.
`MAX(134,356)` returns 356.
`MAX({03/28/90},{04/02/89})` returns 03/28/90.

MIN(<expC1>/<expN1>/<expD1>,<expC2>/<expN2>/<expD2>)
This function returns the smaller of the two character, date, or numeric expressions. The expressions are memory variables, field names, the results of other functions, or entered directly. If you enter dates directly, the dates must be enclosed in curly braces. If you enter character strings directly, the strings must be enclosed in quotes. The two expressions must be the same data type. Character comparisons use the ASCII values of the characters.

Examples:

`MIN("Alphabetical","Numerical")` returns Alphabetical.
`MIN(134,356)` returns 134.
`MIN({03/28/90},{04/02/89})` returns 04/02/89.

MOD(expN1>,<expN2>) This function returns the remainder from the division of two numeric expressions. This remainder is called the modulus. The numeric expressions are memory variables, field names, the results of other functions, or entered directly.

Examples:

`MOD(18,5)` returns 3, which is the remainder when you divide 18 by 5.

PI() This function returns the value of π (approximately 3.14159), which is the ratio between the circumference and diameter of a circle.

This function does not use any arguments. This function is usually combined with other functions.

Example:

`PI()*4` returns 12.57 as the circumference of a circle with a diameter of 4.

RAND([<expN>]) This function returns a random number between 0 and .999999. You can provide a numeric expression that is used as a basis for computing the random number. If the numeric expression is negative, dBASE uses the system clock. The numeric expression is a memory variable, field name, the result of another function, or entered directly.

Examples:

`RAND()` can return .5767865
`RAND()*50` returns a number between 0 and 50.

ROUND(<expN1>,<expN2>) This function rounds the first numeric expression. The second numeric expression is the number of digits to the right of the decimal point that the first numeric expression is rounded. The numeric expressions are memory variables, field names, the results of another functions, or entered directly.

Examples:

`ROUND(5.3,0)` returns 5.
`ROUND(5.919,2)` returns 5.92.
`ROUND(24923,-3)` returns 25000.

RTOD(<expN>) This function returns the degrees of an angle measured in radians. This function is often used to convert radian measurements from other functions' output to degrees. The numeric expression is a memory variable, a field name, the result of another function, or entered directly.

Example:

`RTOD(1.05)` returns 45, which is the number of degrees in 1.05 radians.

SIGN(<expN>) This function returns a -1, 0 or 1 based upon the sign of the numeric expression. A negative value returns a -1. A zero value returns 0. A positive value returns a 1. The numeric expression is a memory variable, a field name, the result of another function, or entered directly.

Examples:

`SIGN(6573)` returns 1 since it is a positive value.
`SIGN(0)` returns 0 since it is a zero value.
`SIGN(-6573)` returns -1 since it is a negative value.

SIN(<expN>) This function returns the sine of an angle measured in radians. The numeric expression is a memory variable, a field name, the result of another function, or entered directly. This function returns a real floating number.

Example:

`SIN(1.05)` returns .87, which is the sine of 1.05 radians.

SQRT(<expN>) This function returns the square root of the numeric expression. The numeric expression is a memory variable, a field name, the result of another function, or entered directly. This function returns a real floating number.

Example:

`SQRT(625)` returns 25.

TAN(<expN>) This function returns the tangent of an angle measured in radians. The numeric expression is a memory variable, a field name, the result of another function, or entered directly. This function returns a real floating number.

Example:

`TAN(1.05)` returns 1.73, which is the tangent of 1.05 radians.

Conversion Functions

Each of the conversion functions changes the data that you provide as an argument. They can convert numeric data into character strings to allow you to combine it with other character strings. They can also provide the ASCII code for a character or convert a character string that looks like a value into a number.

ASC(<expC>) This function returns the ASCII code for the first character in the character expression. The character expression is a memory variable, a field name, the result of another function, or entered directly enclosed in quotes.

Example:

`ASC("Mary")` returns 77, which is the ASCII code for M.
`ASC("5")` returns 53, which is the ASCII code for the character, not number, 5.

CHR(<expN>) This function returns the character for the ASCII value contained in the numeric expression. The numeric expression is a memory variable, a field name, the result of another function, or entered directly.

Example:

`CHR(77)` returns M.
`CHR(7)` sounds the bell, which is ASCII code 7.

STR(<expN> [,<length>][<decimal>]) This function returns the value in the numeric expression as a string. The numeric expression and the length and decimal values are memory variables, field names, the results of other functions, or entered directly. The default values for length and digits after the decimal point that are used if not provided are 10 and 0. The decimal point counts as a position in the number's length. If the specified length is inadequate for the number, the function returns asterisks.

Example:

`STR(569.34,6,2)` returns the character string 569.34.
`STR(569.34)` returns the character string "   569".
`STR(569.34,2,0)` returns the character string **.

VAL(<expC>) This function returns the numeric value in the character expression as a string. The numeric expression and the length and decimal values are memory variables, field names, the results of other functions, or entered directly. The function ignores leading blanks. When the function encounters the first nonnumeric character, other than spaces, it stops changing numbers into values.

Example:

`VAL("  569.34")` returns the numeric value 569.34.
`VAL("569.34 Total")` returns the numeric value 569.34.
`VAL(Total is 569.34")` returns the numeric value 0.

Testing Functions

The testing functions evaluate the arguments you provide or conditions in the dBASE environment to perform a test. You can check for an end of file condition, a color monitor, or a deleted record among other things.

BOF([<alias>]) This function returns .T. if the record pointer is at the beginning of the file and .F. otherwise. The alias is a numeric expression that evaluates to a number from 1 to 10 or a character expression that evaluates A to J or that contains an alias name. The alias is a memory variable, the result of another function, or entered directly, using quotes for a character expression. The alias argument lets you select which work area you are testing for the beginning of the file.

Example:

```
USE EMPLOYEE
? BOF()          && returns .F.
SKIP -1
? BOF()          && returns .T.
USE
```

COL() This function returns the current column position which is a number between 0 and 79. This function does not use any arguments.

Example:

```
@ 1,1 SAY "First Name:"
@ 1,COL()+25 SAY "Last Name:"
* leaves 25 spaces between First Name and Last Name
```

DELETED([<alias>]) This function returns .T. if the current record is marked for deletion and .F. otherwise. The alias is a numeric expression that evaluates to a number from 1 to 10 or a character expression that evaluates A to J, or that contains the alias name. The expression is a memory variable, field name, the result of another function, or entered directly, using quotes for a character expression. The alias argument lets you select which work area you are testing for the beginning of the file.

Example:

```
USE EMPLOYEE
DELETE
? DELETED()            && returns .T.
RECALL
? DELETED()            && returns .F.
USE
```

DIFFERENCE(<expC>,<expC>) This function returns a number between 0 and 4 based on the difference between the Soundex codes for the two-character expressions. The higher the number the closer their Soundex codes. The character expressions are memory variables, field names, the results of other functions, or entered directly enclosed in quotes.

Examples:

`DIFFERENCE(LAST_NAME,"Jonas")` returns 3 when the EMPLOYEE database is open and the first record is current.
`DIFFERENCE("Jonas","Smith")` returns 2.

DISKSPACE() This function returns the amount of diskspace on the default drive. This function does not use any arguments. You can use this function to determine if the disk has enough room before you begin a file operation.

Example:

`DISKSPACE()` returns 966656 if the default drive has 966656 bytes left.

EOF([<alias>]) This function returns .T. if the record pointer is past the last record in the database and .F. otherwise. The alias is a numeric expression that evaluates to a number from 1 to 10 or a character expression that evaluates A to J, or that contains an alias name. The numeric expression is a memory variable, field name, the result of another function, or entered directly, using quotes for a character expression. The alias argument lets you select a work area other than the current one.

Example:

```
USE EMPLOYEE
? EOF()           && returns .F.
GOTO BOTTOM
? EOF()           && returns .T.
USE
```

ERROR() This function returns the dBASE IV error number of an error trapped with the ON ERROR command. This function does not use any arguments.

Example:

```
ON ERROR ? ERROR ()     && displays error # if error occurs
SELECT 9                && purposefully opens the same
USE EMPLOYEE            && database without using different
SELECT 1                && aliases so the ON ERROR command
USE EMPLOYEE            && displays error number 3
```

FILE(<expC>) This function returns .T. if the filename in the character expression exists and .F. if the filename does not exist. The character expression is a memory variable, field name, the result of another function, or entered directly, using quotes for a character expression. The character expression must include the file extension. If the file is not in the current directory, it must include the path name.

Example:

`FILE("EMPLOYEE")` returns .F. since no extension is provided.
`FILE("EMPLOYEE"+".DBF")` returns .T.
`FILE("YYYY")` returns .F. since the file does not exist.
`FILE("D:\DBASE\BANTAM\EMPLOYEE.DBF")` returns .T. even when the current directory is not D:\DBASE\BANTAM.

FOUND([<alias>]) This function returns .T. if the last FIND, LOCATE, SEEK, or CONTINUE command was successful and .F. otherwise. The alias is a numeric expression that evaluates to a number from 1 to 10 or a character expression that evaluates between A and J, or that contains an alias name. The expression is a memory variable, field name, the result of another function, or entered directly, using quotes for a character expression. The alias argument lets you select a work area other than the current one.

Example:

```
USE EMPLOYEE
LOCATE FOR LAST_NAME="Jenkins"
? FOUND()        && returns .T.
LOCATE FOR LAST_NAME="Henley"
? FOUND()        && returns .F.
USE
```

IIF(<condition>,<exp1>,<exp2>) This function evaluates an expression and provides one of two expressions depending on the results of the condition test. You can use the command from the dot prompt or embedded in program code. Depending on the application you wish to make of this function, the returned expressions are character, numeric, logical, or date expressions as long as they are both the same type of expressions.

Example:

```
?"The account is " +
    IIF(Due_date<DATE(),"overdue.","current.")
```

returns either The account is current. or The account is overdue, depending on the Due_date in the current record.

ISALPHA(<expC>) This function returns .T. if the first character in the character expression is an alphabetical character, or .F. otherwise. The character expression is a memory variable, field name, the result of another function, or entered directly, using quotes for a character expression.

Example:

`ISALPHA("String")` returns .T. since the character expression starts with an S.
`ISALPHA("869.34 Total")` returns .F. since the character expression starts with an 8.

ISCOLOR() This function returns .T. if the monitor can display colors, or .F. otherwise. This function does not use any arguments. You can use this command to perform one set of instructions for color monitors and another for monochrome monitors.

Example:

`ISCOLOR()` returns .T. if your monitor can display colors.

ISLOWER(<expC>) This function returns .T. if the first character in the character expression is a lowercase letter or .F. otherwise. The character expression is a memory variable, field name, the result of another function, or entered directly, using quotes for a character expression.

Example:

`ISLOWER("String")` returns .F. since the character expression starts with an S.
`ISLOWER("string")` returns .T. since the character expression starts with an s.
`ISLOWER("869.34 Total")` returns .F. since the character expression starts with an 8.

ISUPPER(<expC>) This function returns .T. if the first character in the character expression is an uppercase letter, or .F. otherwise. The character expression is a memory variable, field name, the result of another function, or entered directly, using quotes for a character expression.

Example:

ISUPPER("String") returns .T. since the character expression starts with an S.

ISUPPER("string") returns .F. since the character expression starts with an s.

ISUPPER("869.34 Total") returns .F. since the character expression starts with an 8.

LEN(<expC>/<memofield name>) This function returns the number of characters in a character expression or Memo field. The character expression is a memory variable, Character or Memo field name, the result of another function, or entered directly, using quotes for a character expression. The LEN function includes spaces at the beginning and end of the character expression.

Example:

LEN("String") returns 6

LEN(" String ") returns 10 since the length includes the two spaces at the beginning and end of the String.

LEN(SKILLS) returns 45 if the EMPLOYEE database is active and Mary Jenkins' record is current.

LIKE(<pattern>,<expC>) This function supports wildcard comparisons between two character strings and returns .T. if they match and .F if they do not. The first string argument supplies a pattern including *'s and ?'s. The second string is compared with this pattern. Where a ? occurs in the first string, the second can have any character; and where an * is used, any number of characters can be in the second string.

Example:

LIKE("*tion",Company) returns .T. if the entry in Company ends in tion.

`LIKE("?m?th","Smith")` returns .T.

`LIKE("?m?th","Smythe")` returns .F.

LINENO() This function returns the program line number that is about to be executed. This function does not use any arguments.

Example:

```
? "You can use the LINENO function to determine"
? "which line in your program you are performing."
? LINENO()           && returns 3
? "If your program does not work properly, you can use"
? "this function to find the error."
```

LOOKUP(<return field>,<look-for exp>,<look-in field>) This function returns the value of the expression in the return field when it finds the value of the look-for expression in a look-in field in the current database. The return field and look-for expression are memory variables, dBASE expressions, or the results of other functions. The look-in field and return field can also be fields of the current database.

Example:

`LOOKUP(City,"Jenkins",LAST_NAME)` returns Cleveland when the EMPLOYEE database is open.

LUPDATE([<alias>]) This function returns the date of the last update. The date of the last update is the date the file was last saved. The alias is a numeric expression that evaluates to a number from 1 to 10 or a character expression that evaluates into a letter from A to J, or an alias name. The alias argument lets you select a work area other than the current one.

Example:

`LUPDATE()` returns the date that the current database was last saved.

MEMLINES(<memo field name>) This function returns the number of lines in the specified Memo field for the current record. The number of lines in the Memo field is controlled by the SET MEMOWIDTH command and the locations where you pressed ENTER.

Examples:

`MLINE(SKILLS)` returns 5 when the EMPLOYEE database is active and Mary Jenkins record is current if MEMOWIDTH is set to 15.
`MLINE(SKILLS)` returns 3 when the EMPLOYEE database is active and Mary Jenkins record is current if MEMOWIDTH is set to 65. Since there were five lines in the preceding example, it might seem like the answer for this exercise should be 2 but the location of an ENTER causes it to require three lines.

MEMORY([0]) This function returns the amount of unused kilobytes of RAM. The 0 function argument is optional and does not affect the function's output. You can use this function to determine if the computer has enough memory before you begin an operation.

Example:

`MEMORY()` can return 144 when you load dBASE without ASSIST on a machine with 640K of RAM.

MESSAGE() This function returns the message for the error number trapped with the ON ERROR command. This function does not use any arguments.

Example:

```
ON ERROR ? MESSAGE()     && displays error message if error
SELECT 9                 && occurs. Purposefully opens the
USE EMPLOYEE             && same database so the ON ERROR
SELECT 1                 && command displays error message
USE EMPLOYEE             && File already open
```

PCOL() This function returns the current column position of the printer. This function does not use any arguments.

Example:

```
SET DEVICE TO PRINTER
@ 1,1 SAY "Acme Company"
@ 1,PCOL()+20 SAY "Accounts Receivable Aging Report"
SET DEVICE TO SCREEN
```

PRINTSTATUS() This function returns .T. if the printer is ready to accept input, or .F. otherwise. This function does not use any arguments. You can use this command to tell a user if the user needs to turn the printer on.

Example:

```
IF .NOT. PRINTSTATUS()
     ? "Your printer is not ready for the report"
ELSE
     REPORT FORM EMPLOY01 TO PRINT
ENDIF
```

PROW() This function returns the current row position or the printer. This function does not use any arguments.

Example:

```
SET DEVICE TO PRINTER
@ 1,1 SAY "Acme Company"
@ PROW+2,1 SAY "Accounts Receivable Aging Report"
SET DEVICE TO SCREEN
```

RECCOUNT([<alias>]) This function returns the number of records in the specified database. The record count includes records marked for deletion and records filtered from appearing in the view. The alias is a numeric expression that evaluates to a number from 1 to 10 or a character expression that evaluates A to J or that contains an alias name. The alias is a memory variable, field name, the result of another function, or entered directly, using quotes for a character expression. The alias argument lets you select which work area you are testing for the beginning of the file.

Example:

`RECCOUNT()` returns 6 if the EMPLOYEE database is active.

RECNO([<alias>]) This function returns the current record number of the database specified with the alias argument. The alias is a numeric expression that evaluates to a number from 1 to 10 or a character expression that evaluates to a letter from A to J or that contains an alias name. The alias argument is a memory variable, the result of another function, or entered directly, using quotes for a character expression. The alias argument lets you select which work area you are testing for the beginning of the file.

Examples:

`RECNO()` returns 0 if no database is open.
`RECNO()` returns 1 if the open database does not contain any records.
`RECNO()` returns 3 if the EMPLOYEE database is open and Henry Garrison's record is current.

RECSIZE([<alias>]) This function returns the record size of a record in the database currently in use. The alias is a numeric expression that evaluates to a number from 1 to 10 or a character expression that contains an alias name or a letter from A to J. The alias is a memory variable, the result of another function, or entered directly, using quotes for a character expression. The alias argument lets you select which work area you are testing for the beginning of the file. This does not include the current record's Memo field data, only the ten characters used for the memo marker. The record size is the same for each record in the database.

Examples:

`RECSIZE()` returns 0 if no database is open.
`RECSIZE()` returns 129 if the EMPLOYEE database is open.

ROW() This function returns the current row position on the screen, which is a number between 0 and 24. This function does not use any arguments.

Example:

```
@ 1,1 SAY "The date is: "+DTOC(DATE())
@ ROW()+2,1 SA = The time is: "+TIME()
```

SEEK(<exp>,[<alias>]) This function finds the expression in the indexed database specified by the alias. If it finds the expression, it moves the record pointer to the record containing the expression and returns a .T.. If the function does not find the expression, it returns an .F.. The expression is the dBASE expression that the function looks for. The alias is a numeric expression that evaluates to a number from 1 to 10 or a character expression that evaluates to an alias name or a letter between A and J. The numeric expression is a memory variable, field name, the result of another function, or entered directly, using quotes for a character expression. The alias argument lets you select which work area you are testing for the beginning of the file.

Example:

`SEEK("Larson")` returns .T. and changes the record pointer to record number 4 if the EMPLOYEE database is open and the LAST_NAME index tag is active.
`SEEK("888-99-7654")` returns .F. if the EMPLOYEE database is open and the LAST_NAME index tag is active since the function's expression is inappropriate for the current index tag.

SET(<expC>) This function returns the string "ON" or "OFF" or a numeric value that represents the setting of the status of the SET command. The character expression is a memory variable, the result of another function, or entered directly when enclosed in quotes, which is a keyword for a SET command.

Examples:

`SET("Bell")` returns the string ON if SET BELL is ON.
`SET("Memowidth")` returns 50 if SET MEMOWIDTH is set to 50.

TYPE(<expC>) This function returns a single letter representing the type of data contained in the character expression. The function returns C for Character, N for Numeric, L for Logical, M for Memo, D for Date, F for Float, or U for Undefined. The character expression is a memory variable, field name, the result of another function, entered directly enclosed in quotes, or the memory variable or field name enclosed in quotes.

Examples:

`TYPE(569.34)` returns Invalid function argument since the function's argument is not a character expression.
`TYPE("569.34")` returns N since the string contains numeric characters.

Special Functions

The special functions are a small group. They provide a group for two functions that do not properly fit with any of the other groups. These functions are the CALL function, which executes binary programs, and the macro substitution function, which substitutes the current value of a memory variable for the variable name.

CALL(<expC>,<expC>/<memvar name>) This function executes the binary file described in the first character expression and passes the second character expression to the binary file. This function returns any value the binary file is designed to return. You can use this function to incorporate programs written in another language with a dBASE program. Before you can perform this command, you must load the binary file and declare the variables that you will pass to the binary file.

Example:

```
    LOAD MYPROG
    ? "The file is "
+IIF(CALL("MYPROG","EMPLOYEE")="Y","","not ")+"intact.
```

&<character variable>[.] This function substitutes the variable value that follows as the variable name where this function appears. The period is optional but is used to distinguish the &'s function argument from the text that follows. This macro substitution function is the only function that does not use parentheses. This function is often used for other functions' and commands' input.

Example:

```
USE EMPLOYEE INDEX EMPLOYEE ORDER TAG LAST_NAME
STORE "Larson" TO Findname
FIND &Findname      && equivalent to Find Larson
```

Identification Functions

Each of the Identification functions provide some information concerning your current place in the dBASE environment. They are used to identify a current alias, the current index used, the last tag used, or the current version.

ALIAS([expN>]) This function returns the alias name of the work area specified by the numeric expression. If a numeric expression is not provided, the function uses the current work area. The numeric expression is a memory variable, result of another function, or entered directly that evaluates to a number from 1 to 10.

Examples:

`ALIAS()` returns EMPLOYEE if the EMPLOYEE database is open in the first work surface.
`ALIAS(10)` returns CATALOG if a catalog is open.

BAR() This function returns the bar number of the last selected bar from a pop-up menu. Each bar in a pop-up menu is numbered starting with 1. This function lets you determine which menu item was selected. This function does not use any function arguments. The function returns 0 when there is no active pop-up menu, no pop-up menu is defined, or ESC is pressed to leave the pop-up menu.

Example:

Figure 15-2 shows a portion of the POPUP program that uses the BAR() function to determine which menu item in the pop-up menu is selected.

DBF([<alias>]) This function returns the active database name in the work area specified by the alias. If an alias is not provided, the function uses the current work area. The alias is a numeric expression that evaluates to a number from 1 to 10 or a character expression that evaluates into an alias name or a letter from A to J. The expression is a memory variable, the result of another function, or entered directly, using quotes for a character expression. The alias argument lets you select which work area you are testing for the beginning of the file.

Example:

`DBF()` returns EMPLOYEE if the EMPLOYEE database is open in the current work surface.

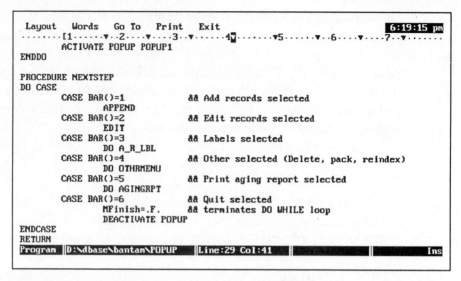

```
 Layout   Words   Go To   Print   Exit                                  6:19:15 pm
········[1·····▼··2····▼····3··▼······4▼·······▼5······▼··6····▼····7··▼·······
        ACTIVATE POPUP POPUP1
ENDDO

PROCEDURE NEXTSTEP
DO CASE
        CASE BAR()=1            && Add records selected
                APPEND
        CASE BAR()=2            && Edit records selected
                EDIT
        CASE BAR()=3            && Labels selected
                DO A_R_LBL
        CASE BAR()=4            && Other selected (Delete, pack, reindex)
                DO OTHRMENU
        CASE BAR()=5            && Print aging report selected
                DO AGINGRPT
        CASE BAR()=6            && Quit selected
                MFinish=.F.     && terminates DO WHILE loop
                DEACTIVATE POPUP
ENDCASE
RETURN
Program  D:\dbase\bantam\POPUP   Line:29 Col:41                          Ins
```

Figure 15-2 NEXTSTEP procedure using BAR() function to select menu item action

FIELD(<expN>[,<alias>]) This function returns a field name from the active database in the work area specified by the alias. Each field has a number that dBASE displays when you display or modify the database structure. The field name returned is specified by the numeric expression. The alias is a numeric expression that evaluates to a number from 1 to 10 or a character expression that evaluates to an alias name or a letter from A to J. The alias and numeric expression are memory variables, the results of other functions, or entered directly, using quotes for a character expression. The alias argument lets you select which work area you are testing for the beginning of the file. If an alias is not provided, the function uses the current work area. This function returns a empty string if the value of the numeric expression is not between 1 and 255, or is greater than the number of fields in the database.

Example:

`FIELD(1)` returns SSN if the EMPLOYEE database is open.
`FIELD(10)` returns HIRE_DATE if the EMPLOYEE database is open.

FKLABEL(<expN>) This function returns the name assigned to a function key. Each of the programmable function keys is assigned a number. F2 through F10 are 1 through 9. CTRL-F1 through CTRL-F10 are 10 through 19. SHIFT-F1 through SHIFT-F9 are 20 through 28. The numeric expression is a memory variable, result of another function, or entered directly.

Example:

`FKLABEL(25)` returns SHIFT-F6.

FKMAX() This function returns the maximum number of function keys you can program. This function does not use any function arguments.

Example:

`FKMAX()` returns 28.

GETENV(<expC>) This function returns the value of the DOS environment variable specified by the character expression. Examples of DOS environment variables are PATH, COMSPEC, and DTL_TRANSLATE. The character expression is a memory variable, result of another function, or entered directly by enclosing it in quotes.

Example:

`GETENV("dtl_translate")` returns "ON" if you have used the SET DTL_TRANSLATE=ON command from DOS to use your own template.

KEY([<.mdxfilename>,]<expN>[,<alias>]) This function returns a character string containing the index expression for the index file described by the numeric expression. The alias selects the work area the function uses. If none is specified, the function uses the current one. The .MDX filename selects which .MDX filename is used. If none is specified, the function uses all open indexes. The numeric expression represents the number assigned to a particular .ndx file or tag name.

```
Master index: SSN
. disp stat

Currently Selected Database:
           Index file:  D:\DBASE\BANTAM\LASTNAME.NDX  Key: last_nameas: EMPLOYEE
           Index file:  D:\DBASE\BANTAM\CITY.NDX  Key: city
Production   MDX file:  D:\DBASE\BANTAM\EMPLOYEE.MDX
    Master Index TAG:     SSN  Key: SSN
           Index TAG:     LAST_NAME  Key: LAST_NAME
           Index TAG:     STATE  Key: State
           Index TAG:     NAME  Key: LAST_NAME+FIRST_NAME+M_INITIAL
           Index TAG:     HLTH_LNME  Key: IIF(health,"T","F")+LAST_NAME
           Index TAG:     HR_RATE  Key: HR_RATE
           Index TAG:     ZIP_CODE  Key: ZIP_CODE
             MDX file:  D:\DBASE\BANTAM\EMPINDEX.MDX
           Index TAG:     LOCATION  Key: city+state+str(zip_code,5)
           Index TAG:     SORTORDER  Key: trim(last_name)+ssn
           Memo file:   D:\DBASE\BANTAM\EMPLOYEE.DBT

File search path:
Default disk drive: D:
Print destination:  PRN:
Command  ║D:\...bantam\EMPLOYEE  ║Rec 1/6           ║File ║
             Type a dBASE IV command and press the ENTER key (◄─┘)
```

Figure 15-3 EMPLOYEE database used with multiple indexes (a)

Examples using the database and indexes in Figure 15-3:

```
KEY(1) returns last_name.
KEY(4) returns LAST_NAME.
KEY("EMPLOYEE",4) returns
LAST_NAME+FIRST_NAME+M_INITIAL.
```

MDX(<expN>[,<alias>]) This function returns a character string containing an .mdx index filename. The alias selects the work area the function uses. If none is specified, the function uses the current one. The numeric expression represents the number assigned to a particular .mdx file. If the number exceeds the open .mdx index files, the function includes .ndx and .mdx files.

Examples using the database and indexes in Figure 15-3:

`MDX(1)` returns C:EMPLOYEE.MDX.

`MDX(2)` returns C:EMPINDEX.MDX.

`MDX(3)` returns nothing since the database only uses two .MDX files.

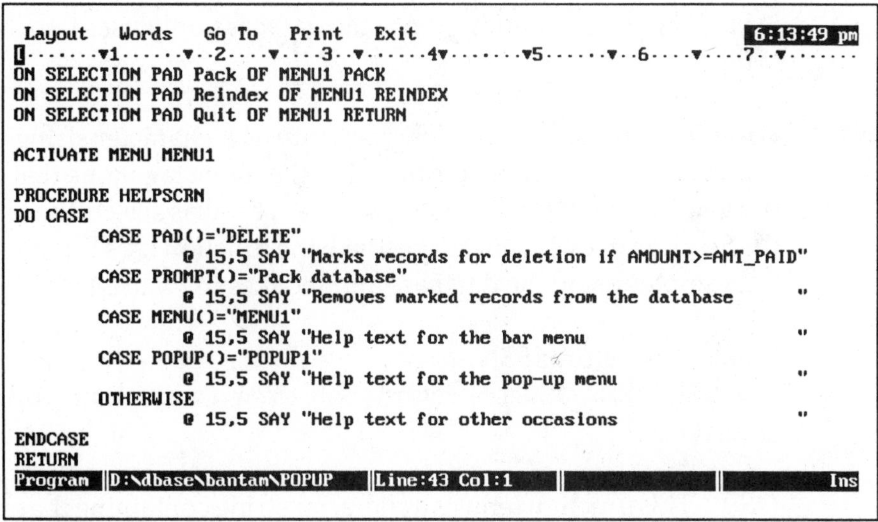

```
Layout   Words   Go To   Print   Exit                                6:13:49 pm
ON SELECTION PAD Pack OF MENU1 PACK
ON SELECTION PAD Reindex OF MENU1 REINDEX
ON SELECTION PAD Quit OF MENU1 RETURN

ACTIVATE MENU MENU1

PROCEDURE HELPSCRN
DO CASE
        CASE PAD()="DELETE"
                @ 15,5 SAY "Marks records for deletion if AMOUNT>=AMT_PAID"
        CASE PROMPT()="Pack database"
                @ 15,5 SAY "Removes marked records from the database       "
        CASE MENU()="MENU1"
                @ 15,5 SAY "Help text for the bar menu                     "
        CASE POPUP()="POPUP1"
                @ 15,5 SAY "Help text for the pop-up menu                  "
        OTHERWISE
                @ 15,5 SAY "Help text for other occasions                  "
ENDCASE
RETURN
Program  D:\dbase\bantam\POPUP   Line:43 Col:1                               Ins
```

Figure 15-4 HELPSCRN procedure using functions to display context sensitive help (b)

MENU() This function returns a character string containing the name of the active horizontal menu. This function does not use any arguments.

Example:

Figure 15-4 shows a portion of the POPUP program that uses the MENU() function to determine if the current menu when F2 is pressed is MENU1. The program has ON KEY LABEL F2 DO HELPSCRN as the first line of the program.

NDX(<expN>[,<alias>]) This function returns a character string containing an .NDX index filename. The alias selects the work area the function uses. If none is specified, the function uses the current one. The numeric expression represents the number assigned to a particular .NDX file in the order the .NDX files are opened. If the number exceeds the open .NDX index files, the function includes .NDX and .MDX files.

Examples using the database and indexes in Figure 15-3:

`NDX(1)` returns LAST_NAME.

`NDX(2)` returns CITY.

`NDX(3)` returns nothing since the database only uses two .NDX files.

ORDER([<alias>]) This function returns a character string containing an .NDX index filename or .MDX file index tag name that controls the database in the specified work area. The alias selects the work area the function uses. If none is specified, the function uses the current one.

Examples using the database and indexes in Figure 15-3:

`ORDER()` returns SSN.
`ORDER("EMP_MAST")` returns SSN even if a different work area is current.

OS() This function returns a character string containing the operating system name. This function does not use any function arguments.

Example:

`OS()` returns DOS 3.30 if your machine is using DOS version 3.30.

PAD()

This function returns a character string containing the name of the active menu pad. This function does not use any function arguments.

Example:

Figure 15-4 shows a portion of the POPUP program that uses the PAD() function to determine if the current pad in the bar menu when F2 is pressed is Delete. The program has ON KEY LABEL F2 DO HELPSCRN as the first line of the program.

POPUP() This function returns a character string containing the name of the active pop-up menu. This function does not use any function arguments.

Example:

Figure 15-4 shows a portion of the MENU program that uses the POPUP() function to determine if the current menu is POPUP1 when F2 is pressed. The program has ON KEY LABEL F2 DO HELPSCRN as the first line of the program.

PROGRAM() This function returns a character string containing the program name dBASE was executing when an error occurred. This function does not use any function arguments.

Example:

`? "An error occurred in the "+PROGRAM()` returns the character string followed by the name of the program where an error occurred. . This command would appear in a procedure that a program executes with an ON ERROR command.

PROMPT() This function returns a character string containing the menu item text of the last pop-up or menu item selected. This function does not use any arguments.

Example:

Figure 15-4 shows a portion of the POPUP program that uses the PROMPT() function to determine if the current menu item is Pack database when F2 is pressed. This procedure is performed when the user presses F2 since the program has ON KEY LABEL F2 DO HELPSCRN as the first line of the program.

SELECT() This function returns the number of the highest unused work area. This function does not use any function arguments. You can use this function to assign databases to work areas starting with the higher number work areas and working downward.

Examples:

`SELECT()` returns 10 if a catalog is not open and no databases are assigned to the tenth work area.

`SELECT()` returns 9 if a catalog is open and no databases are assigned to the ninth work area.

TAG([<.mdx filename>,]<expN>[,<alias>]) This function returns a character string containing an .NDX index filename or .MDX file index tag name. The alias selects the work area the function uses. If none is specified, the function uses the current one. The .MDX filename selects which .MDX filename is used. If none is specified, the function uses all open indexes. The numeric expression represents the number assigned to a particular .NDX file or tag name.

Examples using the database and indexes in Figure 15-3:

`TAG(1)` returns LASTNAME.
`TAG(4)` returns LAST_NAME.
`TAG("EMPLOYEE",4)` returns NAME.

VARREAD() This function returns the field or memory variable edited when this function is performed. This function does not use any function arguments. This function is used to create context-sensitive help screens.

Example:

`? "An error while editing the "+VARREAD()+" field."`
returns the character string followed by the name of the memory variable or field the user was editing when an error occurred. This command would appear in a procedure that a program performs with an ON ERROR command.

VERSION() This function returns a character string containing the version of dBASE IV in use. This function does not use any function arguments.

Example:

`VERSION()` returns dBASE IV 1.0 if you are using dBASE IV 1.0.

Input Functions

The three input functions are used to process user input. You can use INKEY to store a keystroke from the input buffer. LASTKEY and READKEY tell you the keystrokes a user presses while editing a program. These functions are primarily used in programs.

INKEY([n]) This function returns a number representing the next keystroke to be processed in the keyboard buffer. All keystrokes are stored in the keyboard buffer. Most of the time, dBASE immediately converts these keystrokes into actions. If dBASE cannot immediately convert these keystrokes into actions, such as when you must wait for dBASE to generate a report, it keeps the keystrokes in the buffer. This function returns the numeric value of the next keystroke in the keyboard buffer to be processed. The numeric values for most keys are the keystroke's ASCII codes. Certain combination keystrokes and function keys return negative numbers. CTRL-S and CTRL-ESC are not evaluated with INKEY. The optional number in this function is the number of seconds the function waits. If the waiting period is exceeded, INKEY() returns a 0 and dBASE performs the next command.

Examples:

`INKEY()` returns 65 if the next key to be processed is an A.
`INKEY()` returns -402 if the next key to be processed is CTRL-ENTER.
`INKEY(5)` returns 0 if no key is waiting to be processed or is pressed after five seconds. Otherwise, INKEY returns the numeric value of the key pressed.

LASTKEY() This function returns a number representing the last keystroke pressed. The numeric values for most keys are the keystroke's ASCII code. Certain combination keystrokes and function keys return negative numbers. CTRL-S and CTRL-ESC are not evaluated with LASTKEY. If the keyboard buffer contains several keystrokes, LASTKEY() processes the last key, unlike INKEY, which processes the first key in the buffer.

Examples:

Figure 15-5 shows a program that uses LASTKEY to determine which key the user pressed to activate AID.

READKEY() This function returns a number representing the key pressed to exit from a full-screen command. The numeric values for the potential keys are shown in Table 15-1. As the table shows, the number returned is determined by whether any data is changed. You can use the two ranges of values to determine whether data has changed.

Example:

```
IF READKEY()>255
     DO CHANGE_REC              && selection if data changes
ELSE
     DO NO_CHANGE               && selection if data unaltered
ENDIF
```

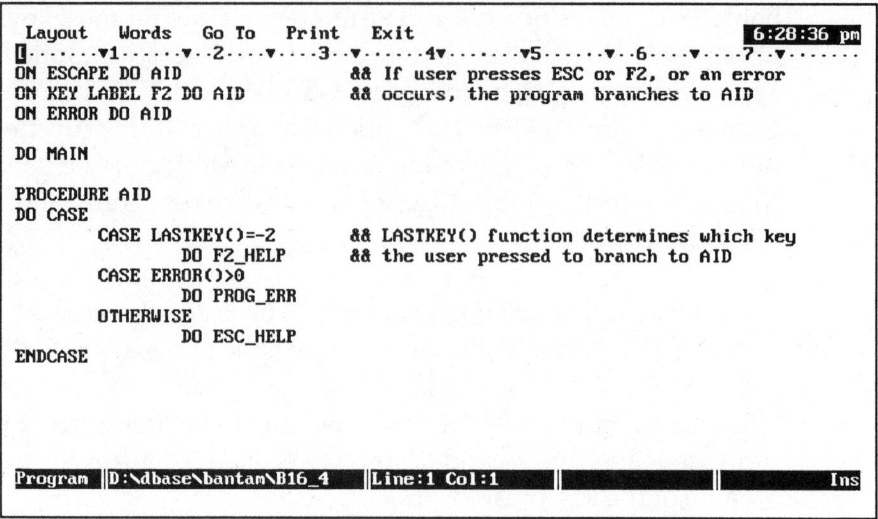

```
 Layout   Words   Go To   Print   Exit                                   6:28:36 pm
[·······▼1······▼··2····▼····3··▼······4▼·······▼5······▼··6····▼····7··▼·······
ON ESCAPE DO AID                     && If user presses ESC or F2, or an error
ON KEY LABEL F2 DO AID               && occurs, the program branches to AID
ON ERROR DO AID

DO MAIN

PROCEDURE AID
DO CASE
        CASE LASTKEY()=-2            && LASTKEY() function determines which key
                DO F2_HELP           && the user pressed to branch to AID
        CASE ERROR()>0
                DO PROG_ERR
        OTHERWISE
                DO ESC_HELP
ENDCASE

Program ||D:\dbase\bantam\B16_4   ||Line:1 Col:1   ||   ||   Ins
```

Figure 15-5 Program using LASTKEY() function to determine which key activated the AID procedure

Network Functions

The network functions include a group of functions that are beneficial in a multiuser environment. They allow you to lock files and records, confirm whether a transaction is entered properly, and receive information about locked records. These functions have no impact on single-user versions of dBASE IV.

ACCESS() This function returns the number for the access level of the current user. This access level is determined when the user logs in. You can use this function to decide whether to display a message indicating that the user does not have access to a program or data.

Example:

`ACCESS()` returns 2 if the user logged in has an access level of 2.
`ACCESS()` returns 0 in a single-user environment or if the user has entered dBASE without logging in, such as when DBSYSTEM.DB is missing.

Table 15-1 Values Returned by READKEY()

Key Pressed	*Value if Record is Not Updated*	*Value if Record is Updated*
BACKSPACE, LEFT ARROW, CTRL-S, CTRL-H	0	256
RIGHT ARROW CTRL-D, CTRL-L	1	257
UP ARROW, CTRL-E, CTRL-K	4	260
DOWN ARROW, CTRL-J, CTRL-X	5	261
PgUp, CTRL-R	6	262
PgDn, CTRL-C	7	263
ESC, CTRL-Q	12	
CTRL-END, CTRL-W		270
ENTER, CTRL-M	15,16	271
CTRL-HOME	33	289
CTRL-PgUp	34	290
CTRL-PgDn	35	291
F1	36	292

Note: ENTER and CTRL-M return the second number if you append in an Edit or Browse screen by pressing ENTER at the beginning of a blank record. The first number is returned in other cases.

CHANGE() This function returns .T. if the current record has been changed, or .F. otherwise. It only works on records that have been converted with the CONVERT command. This function does not use any arguments. This function cannot determine that a record has not changed if its original values are restored with the ROLLBACK command.

Example:

`CHANGE()` returns .T. if the current record has been changed.

COMPLETED() This function returns .T. if an END TRANSACTION or ROLLBACK command has successfully been completed after a

BEGIN TRANSACTION command, or .F. otherwise. This function does not use any arguments.

Example:

```
ON ESCAPE DO leave_early
BEGIN TRANSACTION
     REPLACE ALL HR_RATE WITH HR_RATE*1.1
END TRANSACTION

PROCEDURE leave_early
ROLLBACK
IF .NOT. COMPLETED()
     ? "Database problem"
     ? "Contact database administrator"
ENDIF
```

FLOCK([alias]) This function locks the active database name in the work area specified by the alias and returns .T.. If dBASE cannot lock the file, the function returns .F.. If an alias is not provided, the function uses the current work area. The alias is a numeric expression that evaluates to a number from 1 to 10, a character expression that evaluates to a letter from A to J, or an alias name. The expression is a memory variable, the result of another function, or entered directly, using quotes for a character expression. When you lock a file, other users have read-only access to the data. The file remains locked until you use the UNLOCK command, close the file, or quit dBASE. If the locked file is related to other files, the other files become locked.

Example:

`FLOCK()` returns .T. and locks the file if the database in the current work area is locked.

ISMARKED([<alias>]) This function returns .T. if the function is in a state of change, or .F. otherwise. Examples of states of change are indexing the database or performing an update query. If an alias is not provided, the function uses the current work area. The alias is a numeric expression that evaluates to a number from 1 to 10 or a character expression that contains an alias name or a letter between A and J. The expression is a memory variable, the result of another function, or entered directly, using quotes for a character expression.

Example:

```
IF .NOT. ISMARKED        && Makes sure the database is not
DO Temp_Proc             && changing before performing
ENDIF                    && Temp_Proc
```

LKSYS(n) This function returns a character string containing the time, date, or log-in name of the user who locked a file or record. The n is a numeric expression that equals 0, 1, or 2. A 0 function argument returns the time a user has locked the current record or file. A 1 function argument returns the date a user has locked the current record or file. A 2 function argument returns the log-in name of the user who locked the current record or file.

Examples:

`LKSYS(0)` returns 12:41 if 12:41 is the time a user locks the current file or record.
`LKSYS(1)` returns 06/02/89 if 06/02/89 is the date a user locks the current file or record.
`LKSYS(2)` returns WILLIAM if WILLIAM is the log-in name for the user who locked the current file or record.

LOCK([<expC list>,<alias>]/[<alias>]) This function is the same as the RLOCK function that locks individual records.

NETWORK() This function returns a .T. logical value if you are using a networked version of dBASE, or .F. if you are using a single-user version of dBASE IV. This function has no arguments.

Example:

`NETWORK()` returns .T. if you are using a networked version of dBASE.

RLOCK([<expC list>,<alias>]/[<alias>]) This function locks specified records in the database in the specified work area. If the function successfully locks the records, it returns .T.. If the function cannot lock the records, it returns .F.. If an alias is not provided, the function uses the current work area. The alias is a numeric expression that evaluates to a number from 1 to 10 or a character expression that evaluates A to J, or the alias name. The expression is a memory variable, the result of another function, or entered directly, using quotes for a character expression. When you lock records, other users have read-only access to the data but can change other records. The record remains locked until you use the UNLOCK command, close the file, or quit dBASE. If the locked records are related to other records, the other records become locked.

Examples:

`RLOCK()` returns .T. after locking the current record in the database in the current work area.

`RLOCK("1,3")` returns .T. after locking the first and third records in the database in the current work area.

`RLOCK("2,6","PAY_RECORD")` returns .T. after locking the second and sixth records in the database with an alias of PAY_RECORD.

`RLOCK("PAY_RECORD")` returns .T. after locking the current record in the database with an alias of PAY_RECORD.

ROLLBACK() This function returns .T. if the last ROLLBACK command was successful, or .F. otherwise. This function does not use any arguments.

Example:

```
BEGIN TRANSACTION
     REPLACE ALL HR_RATE WITH HR_RATE*1.1
     SUM YTD_WAGE TO TOTAL_WAGE
     IF TOTAL_WAGE>100000
          ROLLBACK
     ENDIF
     IF .NOT. ROLLBACK() .AND. TOTAL_WAGE>100000
          ? "Database problem"
          ? "Contact database administrator"
     ENDIF
END TRANSACTION
```

USER() This function returns a character string containing the log-in name of the user logged into a protected system. This function has no arguments.

Examples:

`USER()` returns WILLIAM if WILLIAM is the log-in name for user logged into a protected system.

User-Defined Functions (UDFs)

You can create your own functions to perform computations and manipulations that are not supported as part of dBASE IV's basic group of functions. The functions that you create are similar to procedures that you write to handle part of a program's processing. There are a few important differences between procedures and user-defined functions.

The first rule of creating a UDF is that it must start with the word FUNCTION followed by with the function name. The function name cannot be the same as an existing dBASE function name or any of the dBASE commands. It is also restricted in its ability to use certain dBASE commands. You can only use the READ command when no format file is active. The CLEAR command can only be used without any of its optional parameters. All of the commands in Table 15-2 are not allowed in UDFs and cause an error message if used. UDFs cannot use macro substitution.

You will find that many of your UDFs consist of expressions used to manipulate data or perform a computation that dBASE cannot ordinarily handle. All of the dBASE functions are available to you from within a UDF and are frequently used in expression-building.

UDFs have one final area where they differ from normal procedures. They must return a value and accomplish this by adding an expression to the RETURN command.

To use a UDF you write the function entry in much the same way that you would use a dBASE function. You enter UDFNAME(parameter list) where UDFNAME is the name of the function that you created and parameter list is the argument that this function needs.

Table 15-2 Commands Not Allowed in UDFs

APPEND
APPEND FROM
APPEND FROM ARRAY
APPEND MEMO
ASSIST
BEGIN TRANSACTION/END TRANSACTION
BROWSE
CANCEL
CHANGE
CLEAR ALL/FIELDS
CLOSE
CLOSE ALTERNATE
CLOSE FORMAT
CLOSE PROCEDURE
COMPILE
CONVERT
COPY
COPY FILE
COPY INDEXES
COPY MEMO
COPY STRUCTURE
COPY STRUCTURE EXTENDED
COPY TAG
COPY TO ARRAY
CREATE or MODIFY STRUCTURE
CREATE FROM
CREATE VIEW FROM ENVIRONMENT
CREATE/MODIFY APPLICATION
CREATE/MODIFY LABEL
CREATE/MODIFY QUERY/VIEW
CREATE/MODIFY REPORT
CREATE/MODIFY SCREEN
DEBUG
DEFINE BAR
DEFINE BOX
DEFINE MENU
DEFINE PAD
DEFINE POPUP
DEFINE WINDOW
DELETE TAG
DIR
EDIT
ERASE or DELETE FILE
EXPORT
HELP
IMPORT
INDEX
INSERT
JOIN
LABEL FORM
LOAD
LOGOUT
MODIFY COMMAND/FILE
MOVE WINDOW
ON ERROR/ESCAPE/KEY
ON PAD
ON PAGE
ON READERROR
ON SELECTION PAD
ON SELECTION POPUP
PACK
PRINTJOB/ENDPRINTJOB
PROTECT
QUIT
REINDEX
REPORT FORM
RESTORE
RESTORE MACROS
RESTORE WINDOW
RESUME
ROLLBACK
SAVE
SAVE MACROS
SAVE WINDOW
SET
SET CATALOG
SET DEBUG
SET DEVICE

(continued)

Table 15-2 Commands Not Allowed in UDFs *(continued)*

SET FIELDS	SET VIEW
SET FORMAT	SET WINDOW
SET PROCEDURE	SORT
SET RELATION	SUSPEND
SET SKIP	TOTAL
SET SQL	TYPE
SET STEP	UPDATE
SET TRAP	ZAP

Figure 15-6 shows a UDF that computes the sum-of-the-years'-digits depreciation given a cost, salvage value, useful life and depreciation period. The UDF must be defined in a FUNCTION rather than a procedure. It can be included in the main program file or a separate file. If you store it in a separate file you must compile it before attempting to access it. You must also include the SET PROCEDURE TO

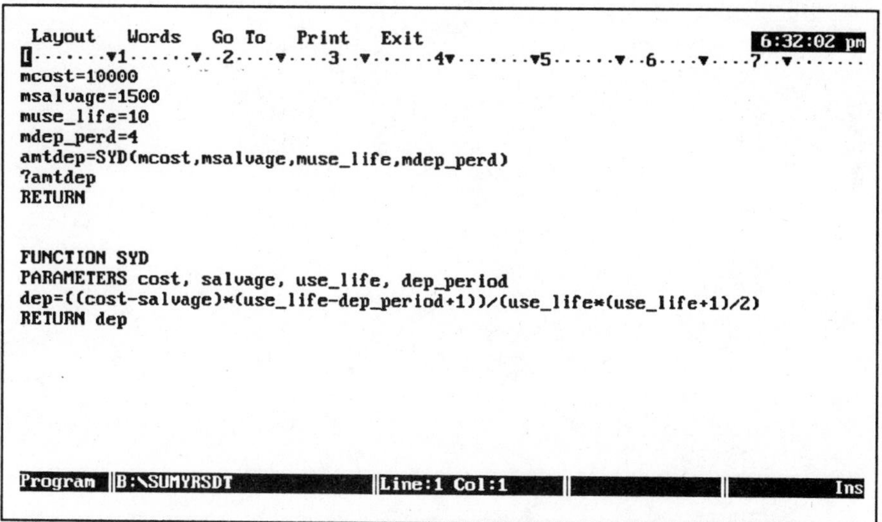

Figure 15-6 UDF that computes sum-of-the-years'-digits depreciation

filename where filename is the name of the file containing the function. Only one procedure file can be open at a time but it can contain as many as 963 procedures. With the function and the instruction that uses it in the same file as shown in Figure 15-6, these additional steps are not necessary. The result 1081.82 is computed when the cost is 10,000, the salvage value is 1500, the useful life is 10 years and the depreciation period is 4.

You can create UDFs for all the calculations and other operations that dBASE does not perform for you. Since you can also use any of the dBASE functions within your UDF you can create tailored versions of these functions that manipulate character strings in a specific way or alter the computations performed by dBASE functions. You can even create UDFs to perform elaborate data validations and use them with the VALID option of @SAY...GET as long as you have the UDF return a logical .T. or .F..

CHAPTER 16

Conditions, Branches, and Loops

In its simplest form, a program is a series of commands that are processed one after the other from the beginning to the end. This simple form of sequential processing works fine if you never need to perform repetitive processing or select from multiple conditions. It also works if you do not need to reuse a series of program lines in different situations or deal with error situations. But all of these conditions exist, and if programming is to provide practical solutions to business problems it must support the development of solutions that can deal with these more complex situations.

With the use of program constructs, you can control the flow of logic in a program. These constructs allow you to change the flow of the program, executing some instructions repetitively, others under certain conditions, and still others only if an error occurs. Since programmers have the same requirements regardless of the programming language they use, a common set of constructs is found in almost all programming languages. The exact commands and syntax structures differ, but the end result is the ability to accomplish the same types of tasks.

dBASE Constructs

The four constructs that dBASE IV supports are sequential processing, repetitive processing, choice selection, and program interrupts. The last category includes error handling and recognition for other types of conditions, such as the end of a page.

Sequential processing allows you to execute a specific program once from start to finish. This construct includes the entries that you make at the dot prompt but can also offer more. A program that you execute sequentially may be part of the current program file or in a separate file.

Repetitive constructs allow you to execute the same set of instructions repeatedly. Stopping the execution of these instructions may be triggered by a condition being met or the execution of the instructions a specific number of times.

Choice constructs allow you to select which instructions execute based upon conditions. You can select from two or more courses of action based on the values of variables or conditions in the dBASE file or environment.

Program interrupt constructs allow you to interrupt the current program processing when certain conditions exist. These conditions can include errors, environmental conditions, or actions taken by the operator.

Sequential Processing Constructs

A simple start-to-finish execution of a program uses a sequential programming construct. In this situation execution starts at the top of the program and continues downward until the last instruction is reached. The commands at the beginning of Figure 16-1 are sequential and are executed from top to bottom. Near the bottom of these entries is a DO command. This causes dBASE IV to begin executing the instructions within the new procedure. Control returns to the instruction following the DO command when the RETURN statement at the end of the new procedure is executed. The DO command for calling one program from another fits within the model for sequential processing and is a construct that you want to examine more closely. It lets you

```
 Layout   Words   Go To   Print   Exit                                      12:02:21 pm
[·······▼1······▼··2····▼····3··▼·······4▼·······▼5······▼··6····▼····7··▼·······
STORE "" to mssn
USE Employee ORDER Ssn
@ 10,10 SAY "Enter Social security number for employee: " GET Ssn
READ
mssn=Ssn
SEEK mssn
DISPLAY Ssn, Last_name, First_name, Hr_rate
DO Wait
RETURN
```

Figure 16-1 Sample sequential program

build modular programs with the code in each program kept to a manageable level.

Using the DO command

When you create and save program code, dBASE IV compiles this code and saves an object code version of it for execution. Part of the object code file is a list of procedures contained in the program. By default, there is at least one procedure in every program, and it has the same name as the program file. This procedure continues from the beginning of the program until the RETURN statement for the program.

It is possible to add additional procedures to a program. Once you end the main program with a RETURN statement, you can add a Procedure Statement and follow it with the name of the procedure. This procedure becomes part of the procedure list that keeps track of all the procedures within an object file. Program statements that fall between the RETURN statement that ends one procedure and the PROCEDURE statement that starts the next procedure are prohibited and cause compile-time errors.

The DO command's syntax is DO <program filename>/<procedure name> [WITH <parameter list>]. You can use either an external program file or an internal procedure as a method of employing the sequential processing construct. You can use a second program to call yet another program establishing a *call chain* from which dBASE IV eventually returns to the original program or procedure.

The option WITH allows you to pass a list of as many as 64 parameters. They can be memory variables, field names, and constants. If a memory variable and field name use the same name, the field name

```
 Layout   Words   Go To   Print   Exit                                              3:09:13 pm
[·······▼1·······▼··2····▼····3··▼·······4▼········▼5·······▼··6····▼····7··▼·······
DO Read_nxt
DO Basic WITH mrate
DO Complex WITH mrate
DO Prt_one WITH mselect,msize
DO Wrt_prt1
DO Wrt_prt2
DO Last_prt
```

Figure 16-2 Sample sequential program that calls other procedures

is used unless you use a M-> designator to indicate that you want to use the memory variable instead.

Executing a Procedure When you execute a DO command, dBASE calls the procedure and performs the instructions that it contains until encountering a RETURN. When it finishes executing the instruction, it returns to the routine that originally called it and executes the instruction following the DO instruction. Figure 16-2 shows some program code that consists of a series of DO commands. A main routine coded in this fashion allows you to obtain an overview of the program by reading through the names of the routines it calls. Although this does not provide the detail, if you have assigned meaningful procedure names within the limitations of an eight-character name you can at least determine the major program activities. You can explore the details of any model that you need to examine more closely.

Search for Procedures dBASE IV has a set order in which it searches for a procedure named in a DO command. First it looks in the current DBO file, if one is active. Next it searches for a procedure in an active procedure file. Other open DBO files are checked next. DBO files with the same name as the procedure are the next target. If it still has not located the file, it searches for a .PRG file with the same name and compiles it before executing it. The last check is a .PRS file with the same name. It too is compiled and executed.

All procedures within an active file are available for the DO command. If program MAIN calls procedure LEVEL2 in a separate file, which in turn calls another separate procedure, LEVEL3, you can execute any procedure in MAIN, LEVEL2 or LEVEL3 while in LEVEL3.

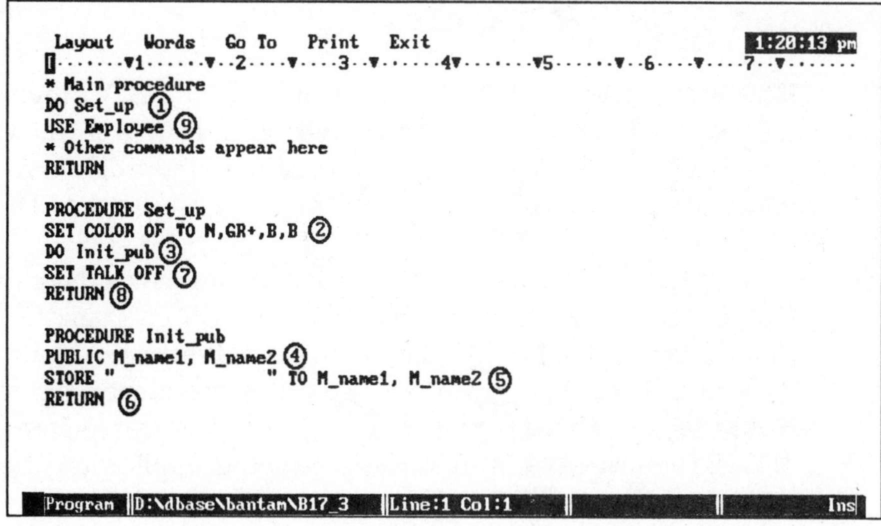

Figure 16-3 Order of instructions with nested DO loops

dBASE IV still supports the SET PROCEDURE command from earlier releases, which makes procedures from a named inactive file available.

The object files used with the DO command have an extension of DBO. If dBASE cannot find a DBO file when searching for a filename used in a DO command, it uses other extensions; it is important to maintain distinct names for each of your programs. If SET DEVELOPMENT is ON, dBASE recompiles the source file to create a new DBO file if the DBO file is older than the source file. The maximum number of DBO files that can be open at one time is 32.

Instruction Execution Order When dBASE completes the execution of the file called by the DO command, control returns to the calling location. This may be the dot prompt or a calling program. With nested DO commands, completing each one is like a backward walk through the call chain. Figure 16-3 shows the order of instruction execution in a series of nested DO procedures.

Recursively executing a procedure occurs when you call procedure B from procedure A then call procedure A from procedure B. It eventually causes dBASE to display the message DO's nested too deep, or too many files open. Although you can increase the number assigned to DO = in the CONFIG.DB file, the real solution is to avoid recursive calls.

Using RUN for External Programs

If the program you want to execute is another dBASE IV program you can execute it with the DO command whether it is in the current program file or stored as a separate procedure. If the program you want to execute is a non-dBASE IV program you must use the RUN command.

This capability allows you to execute both resident and nonresident DOS programs. You can run the resident DOS program, COPY, to create a copy of a file, or DIR, for a listing of a directory. As long as you have sufficient memory you can also run nonresident programs like FORMAT, if you need to prepare a disk. Batch files that contain a series of DOS commands can also be run as can other application programs.

You must have sufficient memory for the program that you want to execute in addition to COMMAND.COM. A message indicating insufficient memory appears if there is not enough memory to handle the RUN request. Unless you indicate otherwise with COMSPEC, DOS must reside in the root directory of the disk you use when booting your system.

The syntax of the RUN command is RUN/! <DOS command or program>. The exclamation point is an abbreviated form of the RUN command. Entering ! DIR lists the current directory just as RUN DIR does.

Using CALL to Execute a Binary Program

Binary programs are treated differently from other external programs. Binary programs are written in C or assembly language. For example, you can use a function written in C language rather than rewriting it in dBASE for greater efficiency. C and assembly language programs can perform some tasks that dBASE is unable to perform, such as

❑ **Tip: Avoid running programs that remain in memory.**

Some DOS programs like PRINT remain in memory after execution. You should not attempt to execute these programs with the RUN command.

checking whether a disk drive is ready to be written to. Binary programs are loaded into memory as if they were dBASE modules. They are executed from memory with a CALL command rather than RUN.

The first step to executing a binary program is to load it into memory. This is accomplished with the LOAD command. The syntax is LOAD <binary file>. Multiple binary files can be loaded into memory as long as there is sufficient memory and you do not exceed the maximum of 16 files. Each binary file can contain as many as 32,000 bytes.

Each binary file that you load must have a unique name. Since dBASE uses the filename as the module name without regard to its extension, loading a file with the same name but a different extension than an existing file still replaces the original file.

There are several conventions that you must adhere to in your assembly language program if you wish to use the LOAD/RUN option:

- Since LOAD uses the program size to determine memory allocation, the assembly language program cannot use memory beyond its size.
- The program should not alter the size of memory variables passed with CALL.
- The program must have its ORG at zero.
- Code Segment and Stack Segment registers must be restored before returning to dBASE with a RET FAR (return far).

Loaded programs remain in memory until you clear them with RELEASE MODULE <module name list>. To execute a loaded program you use the CALL command. You can enter CALL <module name>. If you want, you can also pass up to seven arguments to the program using the WITH <expression list>. The entries in the expression list can consist of character expressions, memory variables, or field names. You can also use the CALL() function to execute a loaded program. The CALL function uses one to eight arguments. The first argument is the loaded module name, and the remaining arguments are the parameters that the function passes to the module. Figure 16-4 shows the use of all three commands that work with assembly language routines. After the RELEASE module statement, the only program that you can call without loading is Get_prt.

```
 Layout   Words   Go To   Print   Exit                                3:07:55 pm
[·······▼1······▼··2····▼····3··▼······4▼·······▼5······▼··6····▼····7··▼·······
LOAD Get_mntr
LOAD Get_dsk
LOAD Get_prt
CALL Get_mntr WITH mcnt
CALL Get_dsk WITH mdrive
CALL Get_prt WITH mlist
RELEASE MODULE Get_mntr,Get_dsk
```

Figure 16-4 Program using binary programs

Repetitive Programming Constructs

Most of the processing that you do in database applications is repetitive. This is part of what makes the computer an attractive solution for meeting your needs. dBASE IV provides two commands that fit within the repetitive processing construct. With these repetitive constructs, marking the end of the construct with the ENDDO and ENDSCAN commands is just as important as putting the correct command at the beginning.

Using DO WHILE

DO WHILE is a powerful command that allows you to execute a group of commands repetitively. It continues to execute the sequence of commands as long as the condition specified in the command is true. When the condition is no longer true, dBASE changes the execution flow to the statement following the required ENDDO statement.

The syntax of DO WHILE is

```
DO WHILE <condition>
      <commands>
      [LOOP]
      [EXIT]
ENDDO
```

dBASE continues to execute commands as long as there is a true condition. When the LOOP option is encountered, execution returns to the beginning of the loop even if there are additional commands before

```
 Layout   Words   Go To   Print   Exit                                    12:53:43 pm
[··▼··▼··▼··▼··▼··▼··▼2·▼··▼··▼·3▼··▼··▼··▼··▼··▼··▼5·▼··▼··▼·6▼········7··········
mrespond=""
USE Employee
DO WHILE .NOT. EOF()
   LIST NEXT 5
   WAIT "Press SPACEBAR to continue"
   CLEAR
ENDDO
```

Figure 16-5 Simple DO WHILE loop

the ENDDO statement. The EXIT command also changes the execution flow by ending the instructions within the loop and executing the instruction following ENDDO.

If the first condition test for the DO WHILE is false, none of the DO WHILE instructions are executed. dBASE executes the instruction following the ENDDO instead.

Figure 16-5 shows a simple DO WHILE command. In this example the DO WHILE construct processes records until an end of file condition is reached. As long as it is not the end of file, dBASE continues to process instructions within the DO WHILE construct repeatedly allowing you to view five records and control when the processing continues by typing a response to the WAIT statement.

Figure 16-6 shows another popular use of the DO WHILE instruction. The seek instruction positions the file on the first occurrence of an index entry. dBASE continues to process the records with this index entry until a record is read with a location different from Chicago. At this point dBASE looks for instructions following the ENDDO.

Figure 16-7 shows a popular counter application used with the DO WHILE instruction. The counter, mcount, is initialized to 1. As long as the value in the counter is less than or equal to 5, dBASE displays the Last_name from the record, increments the counter, and reads the next record. When mcount is greater than 5, dBASE executes SET PRINT OFF.

You can nest DO WHILE instructions or nest other instructions, like IF and DO CASE, within a DO WHILE instruction. Figure 16-8 provides a more complex example that nests an IF statement within the DO WHILE loop. The group of instructions between DO and ENDDO are executed repeatedly as long as an end-of-file condition is not present.

```
Layout   Words   Go To   Print   Exit                                   12:55:06 pm
[··▼··▼··▼··▼··▼··▼2·▼··▼··▼·3▼··▼··▼··▼··▼··▼··▼5·▼··▼··▼·6▼········7··········
Use Employee ORDER Location
SEEK "Chicago"
DO WHILE Location="Chicago"
   DISPLAY Last_name, Ssn, Hr_rate
   WAIT "Press SPACEBAR to continue" TO mrespond
   SKIP
ENDDO
```

Figure 16-6 DO WHILE command limiting which records are used

Within these instructions are instructions that use a logical IF construct to test the truth or falsity of a particular condition.

Macro substitution within a DO WHILE condition causes problems if you plan to update the memory variable in the macro substitution and the DO WHILE loop contains another DO WHILE or a DO procedure name, since dBASE only evaluates the macro substitution the first time through the loop. Figure 16-9 equates the memory variable muse to a condition. The DO WHILE command uses this memory variable in a macro substitution and the end of file indication for the condition to control the execution of the DO WHILE instructions.

Using SCAN

The SCAN command is new in dBASE IV. Although its syntax seems more cumbersome, it is actually a simplified and more flexible approach to completing repetitive tasks.

```
Layout   Words   Go To   Print   Exit                                   3:37:34 pm
[··▼··▼··▼··▼··▼··▼2·▼··▼··▼·3▼··▼··▼··▼··▼··▼··▼5·▼··▼··▼·6▼··▼·····7··········
USE EMPLOYEE
SET PRINT ON
mcount=1
DO WHILE mcount<=5
   DISPLAY Last_name
   STORE mcount+1 TO mcount
   SKIP
ENDDO
SET PRINT OFF
```

Figure 16-7 DO WHILE command used as a counter

```
 Layout   Words   Go To   Print   Exit                                    3:44:
[··▼··▼··▼··▼··▼··▼··▼2·▼··▼··▼·3▼··▼··▼··▼··▼··▼··▼5·▼··▼··▼·6▼··▼·····7·····
USE EMPLOYEE
SET PRINT ON
DO WHILE .NOT. EOF()
   IF Hr_rate>15
      SKIP
      LOOP
   ELSE
      DISPLAY Last_name,Hr_rate
      SKIP
   ENDIF
ENDDO
SET PRINT OFF
```

Figure 16-8 Nested IF command in a DO WHILE loop

DO WHILE allows you to specify a WHILE condition, but SCAN also permits a scope and a FOR condition. The commands placed between the SCAN and ENDSCAN commands are executed as long as the records meet the scope and other conditions specified.

The full syntax of SCAN is

```
SCAN [<scope>] {FOR <condition>] [WHILE <condition>]
     [<commands>]
     [LOOP]
     [EXIT]
ENDSCAN
```

You can use any scope option, like NEXT 10 or RECORD 6. If you do not specify scope, dBASE assumes every record in the file. When working with a subset of the records, the pointer starts at the current

```
 Layout   Words   Go To   Print   Exit                                 3:54:15 pm
[··▼·▼··▼··▼··▼··▼··▼2·▼··▼··▼·3▼··▼··▼··▼··▼··▼··▼5·▼··▼··▼·6▼··▼·····7·········
muse=[SUBSTR(Part_no,5,3)="DAL"]
DO WHILE &muse .AND. .NOT. EOF()
   ?Part_no, Unit_price, Quantity
   SKIP
ENDDO
```

Figure 16-9 DO WHILE using macro substitution

```
 Layout   Words   Go To   Print   Exit                                          4:00:51 pm
[··▼··▼·▼··▼··▼··▼2·▼··▼··▼·3▼··▼··▼··▼··▼··▼··▼5·▼··▼··▼·6▼··▼·····7··········
Use Employee ORDER Location
SCAN FOR .NOT. Medical
   ?Ssn, Last_name
ENDSCAN

SEEK "Dallas"
SCAN WHILE Location="Dallas"
   LIST OFF Last_name,Hr_rate
ENDSCAN
```

Figure 16-10 Two SCAN constructs

record. It moves toward the end of the records and remains at its final location when processing stops.

Once records pass your scope selection, you can limit them further with a condition for the FOR clause. The WHILE condition option excepts records that continue to match a condition.

The two optional parameters LOOP and EXIT change the flow of control within the repetitive loop established. LOOP causes control to return to the beginning of the SCAN process. Exit causes the SCAN process to end. The next command executed is the command that follows ENDSCAN.

Figure 16-10 shows two SCAN constructs. The first scans the Employee file for all the employees not subscribing to medical insurance. The field Medical is a logical field and contains either a true or a false. If true, the individual has subscribed to insurance. If false, you might want to include them in future mailings that discuss the various medical plans available.

The second SCAN seeks the index value Dallas. It lists information from the record while Dallas is the active index entry.

Choice Constructs

In everyday business situations you not only encounter different choices but at times are almost overwhelmed by the range of options. At times there are exceptions to exceptions as you attempt to tie down the rules for processing and calculations. dBASE IV provides you two

```
 Layout   Words   Go To   Print   Exit                                      4:07:25 pm
[··▼·▼··▼··▼··▼··▼2·▼··▼··▼·3▼··▼··▼··▼··▼··▼··▼··▼5·▼··▼··▼·6▼··▼·····7··········
IF Qtr_sales>=Quota
   DO Bonus
ENDIF

IF Qtr_sales>=Quota
   DO Bonus
ELSE
   DO Regular
ENDIF
```

Figure 16-11 Two IF constructs

specific instructions designed specifically for handling situations where different conditions may prevail.

Using IF

The IF command enables you to select from two or more options based on conditional processing. You can use IF to execute a set of commands if a condition is true. If you use the ELSE option you can also provide a series of commands for execution when the condition is false.

The syntax of IF is

```
IF <condition>
        <commands>
[ELSE
        <commands>]
ENDIF
```

Although the indentation is not a required part of the syntax it helps make your program more readable and emphasizes the beginning and end of the commands within each component. It is important to note that IF cannot be executed from the dot prompt and can only be used in dBASE programs.

Figure 16-11 provides two examples of the IF command. The first IF construct checks to see if quarterly sales are greater than or equal to Quota. If they are, the Bonus routine is executed. If not, the IF construct ends without executing Bonus. The second entry for IF also contains an

```
 Layout   Words   Go To   Print   Exit                                              4:14:34 pm
[··▼·▼··▼··▼··▼··▼2·▼··▼··▼·3▼··▼··▼··▼··▼··▼··▼5·▼··▼··▼·6▼··▼·····7·········
IF Job_code=1401
   IF Hr_rate>15
      IF Out_hrs>5
         DO High_cst
      ELSE
         DO High_pay
      ENDIF
   ENDIF
   SKIP
ELSE
   DO Oth_job
   SKIP
ENDIF
```

Figure 16-12 Nested IF commands

ELSE clause. The true and false conditions allow you to execute either Bonus or Regular depending on the number of hours worked.

You can nest IF statements by including a second IF in the commands under either IF or ELSE. Each IF statement must have an ENDIF. dBASE matches the innermost IF with the innermost ENDIF and ELSE entries. Figure 16-12 provides an example of a nested IF statement. The first IF tests the Job_code. If it is equal to 1401, the second IF determines if their hourly rate is greater than $15 hour. The third IF is only executed if the conditions in the first two IF statements are true.

When you have a condition that is either true or false, IF is the solution of choice. As the options grow, the number of levels of nesting

❑

Tip: Mismatched ENDIF statements cause undesirable results.

Carefully check the beginning and end of all IF statements. Although nested IF's can provide an excellent solution for many problems, missing or misplaced ENDIF statements have been known to cause more than their share of problems. If you have a problem with mismatched ENDIF (or other construct END) commands, print the program and draw lines like the ones shown in Figure 16-8 to connect the beginning and ending of each construct.

Tip: Limit nesting to three levels.

A rule of thumb in many professional programming shops is to limit nesting to no more than three levels. Although dBASE and other languages support additional levels, there are more program bugs when this level is exceeded.

required to solve the problem may exceed your ability to manage the complexity involved.

Using DO CASE

The DO CASE command allows you to specify a set of conditions with actions for each of them. The first condition that is true determines the actions that are executed.

The syntax of DO CASE is

```
DO CASE
     CASE <condition>
          <commands>
     .
     .
     [CASE <condition>
          <commands>]
     [OTHERWISE
          <commands>]
ENDCASE
```

The ENDCASE statement is required. The OTHERWISE option specifies the actions to occur when none of the CASE conditions are met. Once a CASE condition is met, the commands for this case are executed, the DO CASE construct ends, and dBASE transfers control to the first statement following ENDCASE. This is also the command executed next if no CASE statements are true and the optional OTHERWISE entry is absent.

```
 Layout   Words   Go To   Print   Exit                                          4:21:37 pm
[··▼··▼·▼··▼··▼··▼2·▼··▼··▼·3▼··▼··▼··▼··▼··▼··▼5·▼··▼··▼·6▼··▼·····7··········
DO CASE
   CASE BAR()=1
      DO Prt_emp
   CASE BAR()=2
      DO Chg_slry
   CASE BAR()=3
      DO Chg_name
   CASE BAR()=4
      DO Lst_dltd
   CASE BAR()=5
      DO Skills
ENDCASE
```

Figure 16-13 DO CASE construct

When a CASE condition is true, the commands that follow are executed until an OTHERWISE, ENDCASE, or CASE statement is encountered. You can nest DO CASE commands if you wish and may also nest IF and DO WHILE within the commands for a case.

Figure 16-13 provides an example of a simple case construct that checks the value of a pop-up menu bar to see its current position. Depending on the location within this menu, a routine associated with the specific selection is executed. If none of the conditions in the case construct are met, it executes without performing a routine since the OTHERWISE option is absent.

Figure 16-14 shows another case construct. In this example, the variable mchoice is first checked to see if it is contained within a list of the acceptable choices. If it is not, a message indicating an unacceptable entry appears. All of the other case options display messages indicating the entry. Although this program lacks the routines to be executed for each case at this time, it provides an example of a simple way to test complex logic within a program. Before adding all the detail, quick messages are included within the code to help you follow the execution of a program that may follow a complex path.

Program Interrupt Constructs

Program interrupts allow you to alter program flow when a special condition occurs. dBASE provides interrupts for the ESC key, errors, read errors, page breaks, and pressing any key. Once you execute the

```
 Layout   Words   Go To   Print   Exit                                      3:05:24 pm
[·······▼1·····▼··2····▼····3··▼······4▼·······▼5·····▼··6····▼····7··▼·······
*Establish memory variable for testing menu entry
mchoice = "D"
*Case construct to process menu selection
DO CASE
*The following case traps invalid entries
        CASE .NOT. mchoice $ "ABC"
                ? "Unacceptable entry"
        CASE mchoice="A"
                ? "Entry is A"
        CASE mchoice="B"
                ? "Entry is B"
        CASE mchoice="C"
                ? "Entry is C"
ENDCASE
*End of case construct to process menu selection
RETURN
```

Figure 16-14 DO CASE construct

ON statement, dBASE waits constantly for the situation to occur. If the condition does not occur, program execution continues uninterrupted. When the condition occurs, dBASE performs the code that you establish with the ON command.

Using ON ESCAPE

You can include the ON ESCAPE command in your program to allow you to recognize that the user has pressed the ESC key. You can develop a special program to end the current activity or program or to display a message asking the user to confirm that you wish to escape.

Following ON ESCAPE you need to provide the command that you wish to have executed when the ESC key is pressed. Figure 14-4 provides an example of this routine. The End routine only executes when ESC is pressed.

If you have the ON KEY option in effect at the same time as the ON ESCAPE command, ON ESCAPE has priority. Since it is the more specific of the two commands, dBASE executes the ON ESCAPE command rather than the ON KEY option. If you SET ESCAPE OFF, you can recognize the ESC key being pressed with the ON KEY command.

Using ON KEY

The ON KEY routine allows you to recognize that a specific key is pressed. With a change in the command syntax, ON KEY also allows

```
 Layout   Words   Go To   Print   Exit                                  1:02:15 pm
[··▼··▼··▼··▼··▼··▼2·▼··▼··▼·3▼··▼··▼··▼··▼··▼··▼5·▼··▼··▼·6▼········7·········
ON KEY DO End_pgm
Display Last_name, First_name, Hr_Rate
* Other commands appear here
RETURN

Procedure End_pgm
   mkey = INKEY()
   IF mkey="S"
      WAIT "Type a Y to confirm" TO mconfirm
      IF mconfirm = "Y"
         RETURN TO MAIN
      ENDIF
   ENDIF
RETURN
```

Figure 16-15 Program using ON KEY

you to recognize that any key is pressed rather than focusing on a specific key.

If you use ON KEY [LABEL <key label>], dBASE executes a procedure when the user presses the key indicated by the key label. Entering **ON KEY LABEL F3 DO Report** executes the procedure named Report if the user presses F3. The entries are not case sensitive and for the most part the entries are intuitive, with ALT-A represented by alt-a and HOME represented by home. The arrow key representations are leftarrow, rightarrow, dnarrow, and uparrow.

The ON KEY command without a key label executes the command that you specify as soon as the user presses any key. If you are displaying information you might use the ON KEY option to allow the user to press any key when through looking at the information.

You might include an ON KEY command in the main program. From that point on it traps any input from the keyboard. When it recognizes that a key is pressed, it finishes the current instruction then passes control to the routine in the ON KEY command. You can use the INKEY() function to determine the value of this keystroke and assign it to a memory variable. You can test its value for certain conditions and base your actions on these results. Figure 16-15 presents a program that employs this construct.

There are a number of dBASE commands that cannot be used by the ON KEY command. These are summarized in Table 16-1.

Table 16-1 Commands Excluded from the ON KEY Command

APPEND
APPEND FROM
APPEND FROM ARRAY
APPEND MEMO
ASSIST
BEGIN TRANSACTION/END TRANSACTION
BROWSE
CANCEL
CHANGE
CLEAR ALL/FIELDS
CLOSE
CLOSE ALTERNATE
CLOSE FORMAT
CLOSE PROCEDURE
COMPILE
CONVERT
COPY
COPY FILE
COPY INDEXES
COPY MEMO
COPY STRUCTURE
COPY STRUCTURE EXTENDED
COPY TAG
COPY TO ARRAY
CREATE or MODIFY STRUCTURE
CREATE FROM
CREATE VIEW FROM ENVIRONMENT
CREATE/MODIFY APPLICATION
CREATE/MODIFY LABEL
CREATE/MODIFY QUERY/VIEW
CREATE/MODIFY REPORT
CREATE/MODIFY SCREEN
DEBUG
DEFINE BAR
DEFINE BOX
DEFINE MENU
DEFINE PAD
DEFINE POPUP
DEFINE WINDOW
DELETE TAG
DIR
DISPLAY
EDIT
ERASE or DELETE FILE
EXPORT
HELP
IMPORT
INDEX
INSERT
JOIN
LABEL FORM
LIST
LOAD
LOGOUT
MODIFY COMMAND/FILE
MOVE WINDOW
ON ERROR/ESCAPE/KEY
ON PAD
ON PAGE
ON READERROR
ON SELECTION PAD
ON SELECTION POPUP
PACK
PRINTJOB/ENDPRINTJOB
PROTECT
QUIT
REINDEX
REPORT FORM
RESTORE
RESTORE MACROS
RESTORE WINDOW
RESUME
ROLLBACK
SAVE
SAVE MACROS
SAVE WINDOW
SET
SET CATALOG

(continued)

Table 16-1 Commands Excluded from the ON KEY Command *(continued)*

SET DEBUG	SET TRAP
SET DEVICE	SET VIEW
SET FIELDS	SET WINDOW
SET FORMAT	SORT
SET PROCEDURE	SUSPEND
SET RELATION	TOTAL
SET SKIP	TYPE
SET SQL	UPDATE
SET STEP	ZAP

Using ON PAGE

The ON PAGE command allows you to handle headers and footers and any other requirements for streaming output when you reach a specific line on the current page. Streaming output is produced as a data stream by commands like LIST, DISPLAY, LABEL FORM, REPORT FORM, DIR, TEXT, and TYPE.

The syntax of the command is

```
ON PAGE [AT LINE <expN> <command>]
```

The AT LINE option allows you to specify how many lines of output you want on a page. You should calculate an appropriate value by subtracting both the top and bottom margin depths from the actual length of the paper. dBASE checks the system variables _plineno to keep track of the number of lines printed. Using ON PAGE without a command disables the end-of-page processing.

You can create headers and footers with the ON PAGE option. Figure 16-16 shows the ON PAGE command. It executes Page_end as soon as it encounters the end-of-page. The Page_end procedure aligns the page number at the center of the page in the footer. Next, it ejects the page and places a company name and date at the top of the following page, using left alignment.

```
 Layout   Words   Go To   Print   Exit                                        1:00:41 pm
[··▼··▼··▼··▼··▼··▼2·▼··▼··▼·3▼··▼··▼··▼··▼··▼··▼5·▼··▼··▼·6▼········7··········
ON PAGE DO Page_end
* Other commands appear here
RETURN

Procedure Page_end
_alignment="center"
?pageno
EJECT PAGE
_alignment="left"
?Prepared by Campbell & Associates"
?DATE()
RETURN
```

Figure 16-16 Program using ON PAGE

Using ON ERROR or ON READERROR

dBASE IV provides two error traps. Neither command intercepts errors at the operating system level, confining their responses to dBASE errors. ON ERROR traps general dBASE IV errors, whereas ON READERROR traps errors during full-screen operations like invalid dates, range specifications, or a VALID <condition> that is unmet.

Both error-trapping commands can be used to perform routines when errors are encountered. There are no restrictions on the commands that you can execute in the ON ERROR routines unless it is a descendent of a user-defined function or ON PAGE, ON KEY, or ON READERROR. ON READERROR has the same restrictions as the ON KEY command prohibiting the commands in Table 16-1. The syntax of both commands are identical; the command word is followed by the command you wish to execute.

Multiple Levels of Structures

The concept of using one structure within another is referred to as nesting. The individual sections of the nested code may all be the same constructs or they may be different.

This means that an IF construct can contain another IF construct or a DO WHILE construct can contain another DO WHILE construct. It

```
 Layout   Words   Go To   Print   Exit                                    4:33:11 pm
[··▼·▼··▼··▼··▼··▼2·▼··▼··▼·3▼··▼··▼··▼··▼··▼··▼5·▼··▼··▼·6▼··▼·····7·········
DO WHILE .NOT. EOF()
   IF Qtr_sales >= 50000
      DO CASE
         CASE Qtr_sales > 500000
            DO Super
         CASE Qtr_sales > 250000
            DO Great
         CASE Qtr_sales > 100000
            DO Good
         OTHERWISE
            DO Ok
      ENDCASE
   ELSE
      IF Qtr_sales < 10000
         DO Fired
      ELSE
         DO Probatn
      ENDIF
   ENDIF
ENDDO
Program  D:\dbase\bantam\<NEW>   Line:20 Col:6                                  Ins
```

Figure 16-17 Nesting multiple constructs

also means that an IF construct can contain a DO WHILE construct and vice versa, since one type of construct can be nested inside another.

Figure 16-17 provides an example of nesting several constructs. Within the DO WHILE instruction, an IF instruction is introduced. Within the true portion of the IF, a CASE statement is introduced. Within the false portion of the IF, a second IF statement is introduced. Note the location of the ENDCASE, ENDIF, and ENDDO ending each construct in the proper location.

GETTING STARTED

➤ You want to try several quick programs to see how to implement some of the constructs covered in this chapter. Follow these steps to create a program that uses the DO WHILE command:

1. Highlight <create> in the Application panel of the Control Center and press ENTER.
2. With dBASE IV program highlighted in the instruct box, press ENTER.

```
USE Employee ORDER Zip_code
SEEK 21237
DO WHILE Zip_code=21237 .AND. .NOT. EOF()
       DISPLAY Last_name, First_name, Zip_code, City
       SKIP
ENDDO
RETURN
```

Figure 16-18 Sample program with DO WHILE construct

3. Type the following **USE Employee ORDER Zip_code** to add a command that activates the Employee file and use the index tag Zip_code. Press ENTER.
4. Type **SEEK 21237**. Press ENTER.
5. Type **DO WHILE Zip_code=21237 .AND. .NOT. EOF()**. Press ENTER.
6. Press the TAB key then type **DISPLAY Last_name, First_name, Zip_code, City**. Press ENTER.
7. Type **SKIP** and press ENTER.
8. Press SHIFT-TAB, then type **ENDDO** and press ENTER.
9. Type **RETURN** and press ENTER. Press ALT-P followed by ENTER. Press ALT-P and type an **E** to eject the page. Your program will look like Figure 16-18. Press ESC.
10. Press ALT-E and press ENTER. Type **DOWHLE** and press ENTER. Highlight DOWHLE in the Application panel and press ENTER. Press ENTER again to select Run application. Type a **Y** to confirm that you want to run the program. Two records from the Employee database appear on the screen briefly after the program is compiled.

You can modify the program to write the output to the printer. Follow these steps to write the output to a printer:

1. Highlight DOWHLE in the Application panel and press ENTER. Type an **M** to select Modify application.
2. Move to the line containing DO WHILE, press ENTER. Use the Up ARROW key to move to the blank line, type **SET PRINTER ON.**
3. Move to the end of the line containing ENDDO and press ENTER. Type **SET PRINTER OFF**. Press ALT-L and type an **S**.

```
USE Employee ORDER Zip_code
SEEK 21237
SET PRINTER ON
SCAN WHILE Zip_code=21237
        DISPLAY Last_name, First_name, Zip_code, City
ENDSCAN
SET PRINTER OFF
RETURN
```

Figure 16-19 Sample program with SCAN construct

Edit the file name so it reads DOWHLEPT and press ENTER. Press ALT-E and type an **R** to run the application.

Alter the program to use the SCAN command rather than DO WHILE. This means you do not need SKIP since SCAN automatically advances the record pointer. You also do not need to check for the end-of-file condition. Follow these steps to make the change:

1. Press ESC then type a **Y** to move to the dot prompt.
2. Type **MODI COMM DOWHLEPT** and press ENTER.
3. Move to the line containing DO WHILE and replace DO with SCAN. Move to the period in .AND. and delete the remaining characters on the line.
4. Move to the line containing the SKIP instruction and press CTRL-Y to delete it.
5. Move to the line containing ENDDO and with Insert still off type **ENDSCAN**. The program looks like Figure 16-19.
6. Press ALT-L and type an **S** (if you attempt to use the ALT-E save option, you cannot change the name). Edit the name of the file to read **SCANEMP** and press ENTER. Press ALT-E and type an **A**. Since you saved the file with the Save this program option, you do not need to save it again.
7. Type **DO SCANEMP** and press ENTER to execute the program.

You can use the LOCATE AND CONTINUE instructions within a DO WHILE loop to locate information without an index. Follow these steps to alter your original program:

1. Type **MODI COMM DOWHLE** and press ENTER.

```
USE Employee ORDER Zip_code
LOCATE FOR State="OH"
DO WHILE .NOT. EOF()
       DISPLAY Last_name, First_name, Zip_code, City
       CONTINUE
ENDDO
RETURN
```

Figure 16-20 Sample program with DO WHILE construct

2. Move to the line containing SEEK and with Insert off, type **LOCATE FOR State="OH"**.
3. Move to the Z in Zip_code and press CTRL-T until the DO WHILE instruction reads **DO WHILE .NOT. EOF()**.
4. Move to SKIP and with Insert off, type **CONTINUE**. The program looks like Figure 16-20.
5. Press ALT-L and type an **S**. Press HOME and CTRL-Y to remove the old program name. Type **LOC_ST** and press ENTER. Press ALT-E and type an **R** to run the application.

CHAPTER 17

Writing Programs to Handle Input and Output

You have looked at dBASE IV code for handling popular programming constructs like repetition and choice selection. You have also looked at some of the functions that can be used to handle data manipulation or other processing for your data. dBASE IV provides programming commands specifically designed to handle all your needs, including the nuts and bolts aspects of input and output.

In this chapter you will have an opportunity to look at some of the commands that are used for building screens. You can create screens that allow the user to make menu selections or screens that support the user's input or editing of data records. dBASE also supports various types of output but this chapter will focus on the tabular reports that are so popular in presenting dBASE output.

If you have created reports, forms, labels, or any of the objects you can create with the Applications Generator, you have a wealth of dBASE source code that you can examine. dBASE stores this source code in files with the following extensions: .prg, .fmt, .lbg, and .frg. You can use MODIFY COMMAND to examine it or just use the DOS PRINT command to produce a hard copy for your review.

Creating Data Entry Screens

There are a variety of commands that allow you to use the screen as a communication medium with a user. You can display information on the screen or accept information that the user types in response to your display. The commands that you choose to handle your work will in part depend on the complexity of the task that you are trying to handle. A sampling of some of the most popular commands for handling screen input and output are shown in this section.

Screen Coordinates

The screen is composed of a grid of rows and columns. You can think of its locations as the boxes on a sheet of graph paper where you can place any one character in a box. Depending on the type of monitor you are using there are either 25 or 43 rows on the screen. There are always 80 columns. Each position on the screen can be uniquely identified by its row and column number.

Figure 17-1 shows a portion of the grid that makes up a dBASE screen. Note that dBASE begins counting both rows and columns with 0 rather than 1. To indicate a specific position on the screen grid you would state the row number followed by the column number, as in 10,25 to specify row number 10 and column number 25. Actually these are the eleventh row and the twenty-sixth column from the upper left corner of the screen but you must always refer to them with dBASE's numbering scheme rather than using your own counting methods.

You can ask dBASE to position character strings, fields, variables, or expressions at any location on the screen. The location that you specify will be the beginning location for the information.

dBASE also supports the use of relative addressing through the use of the functions ROW() and COL(). These functions represent the current row and column on the screen. You can compute locations based on offsets from the current position by adding an offset to the current position. ROW(),COL() indicates the current position but ROW()+5,COL()+10 indicates 5 rows down and 10 columns to the right of the current positions. dBASE also supports the use of negative offsets. Both ROW() and COL() can be abbreviated as $ making allowing you to specify the last offset as $+5,$+10.

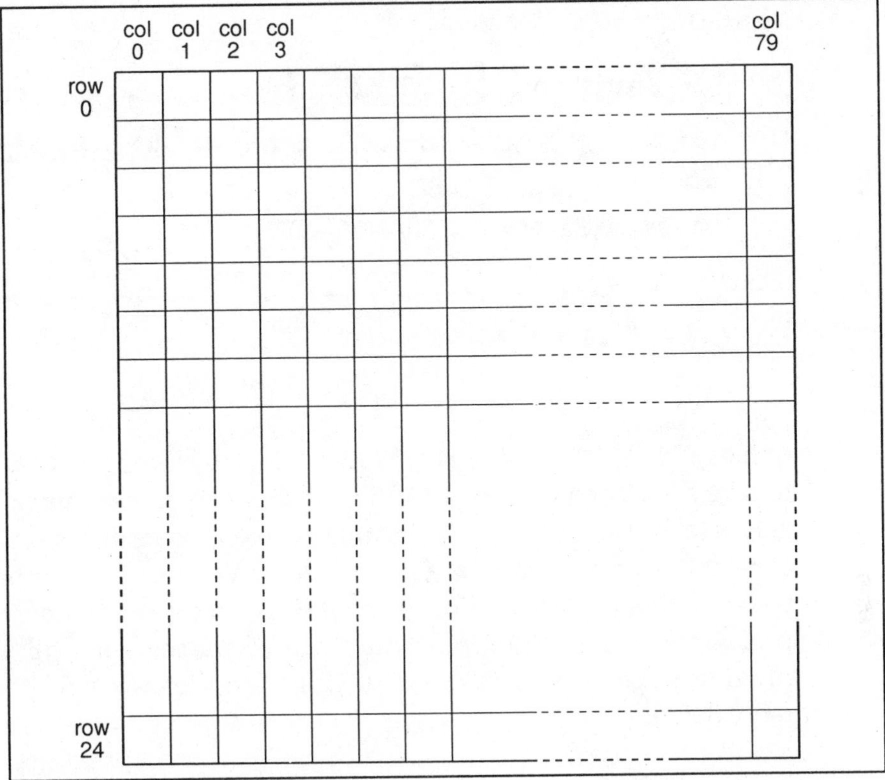

Figure 17-1 Screen grid

dBASE Form Files

dBASE uses the @SAY..GET command as a building block for the custom forms that you create from the Form panel of the Control Center

❑

Tip: Exceeding the screen boundaries will not produce the correct result.

Using relative addressing can lead to creating coordinates that are not within the screen grid. You can place a check in your program to compute the proposed coordinates, given the current location, and take the necessary actions if the current location is not what you expected.

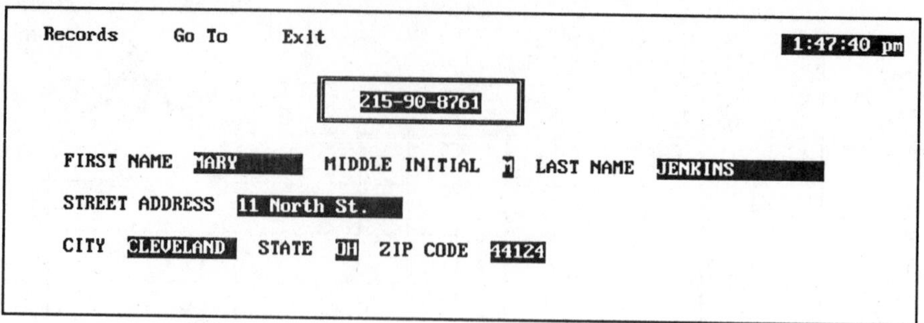

Figure 17-2 Simple data entry screen

or the MODIFY/CREATE FORM from the dot prompt. You will want to take a look at a custom dBASE form since it can be a quick way to generate the basic code for formatting a screen. You can customize this code and execute it from a separate file, or you can make it part of a program that you are writing, using it either in-line with other code or preferably as a separate procedure. Once you see what dBASE can provide for you the next step is studying the options for @SAY..GET in more detail.

Creating a Custom Screen Figure 17-2 provides a look at a simple data entry screen created from the Forms panel in the Control Center. This screen might be used to change address information in employee records. The social security number is highlighted at the top of the screen since this is used as the identifying information to obtain the desired record. It is easy to create this from the Form design screen since you can position the text in a pleasing location and then add field names and boxes. Although you are ultimately choosing the coordinate location for each entry, you are doing it more from a visual perspective than computing field lengths and exact coordinate positions. If the appearance is not pleasing you can select any component and move it to a new location. dBASE will enforce the screen boundaries so you will not have a problem with placing information off the screen.

You can also choose attributes for fields like the pictures and functions discussed in Chapter 7 with the benefit of menu selections. A template was used to create a picture of 999-99-9999 for the social security number. The last name, first name, middle initial, and state code fields use the default picture template but have their picture function modified to restrict entries to alphabetic characters and to convert these entries to upper case.

Composition of the dBASE Form File When you save the form, dBASE creates an .FMT file containing the necessary source code to create the form. Figure 17-3 contains all the code dBASE generated when you saved the Form design screen. The first section of entries contain documentation. The next section contains housekeeping code to initialize the environment. The third section that begins with the comment "*-- @ SAY GETS" contains the commands that format your screen and accepts input in a specific format.

The first command @2,27 TO 4,45 DOUBLE is telling dBASE to draw a double-line box with its upper left corner in row 2 column 27 (actually the third row and the twenty-eighth column) on the screen. The lower right coordinate of the box is 4,45.

Although you will find that there are occasions when you want to both place information on the screen and accept an entry with one command, the dBASE instructions do not include both SAY and GET in one instruction since the text and field templates are placed on the screen separately. The @SAY instructions display information beginning at the coordinates listed. The @ GET instructions expect the user to enter something at the specified location. The picture functions and templates follow the field names and the word PICTURE.

You can use this form file by activating it from the control panel or by referencing it in a program with the command SET FORMAT TO. You would specify the name of the format file to have dBASE use it for tasks where the format is suitable. Screens for APPEND, EDIT, and CHANGE will use this form file to control the display. You can also choose to use the form file with BROWSE to use the field attributes that are part of this file.

Modifying the Format File You can modify the format file and access the modified file with the SET FORMAT TO option. You can incorporate the format file code in your program and make modifications to it from there. The format file (.FMT) contains all the code to create the screen display and accept the operator's input; but it is not a full program, since it does not contain any program logic or actions for processing the application beyond the screen display. You will also need to make some change to the code for handling Memo fields if you

```
*********************************************************************
*-- Name....: CHGNMADD.FMT
*-- Date....: 2-01-89
*-- Version.: dBASE IV, Format 1.0
*-- Notes...: Format files use "" as delimiters!
*********************************************************************

*-- Format file initialization code ---------------------------------

IF SET("TALK")="ON"
   SET TALK OFF
   lc_talk="ON"
ELSE
   lc_talk="OFF"
ENDIF

*-- This form was created in COLOR mode
SET DISPLAY TO COLOR

lc_status=SET("STATUS")
*-- SET STATUS was ON when you went into the Forms Designer.
IF lc_status = "OFF"
   SET STATUS ON
ENDIF


*-- @ SAY GETS Processing. -------------------------------------------

*--  Format Page: 1

@ 2,27 TO 4,45 DOUBLE
@ 3,31 GET ssn PICTURE "999-99-9999"
@ 6,4 SAY "FIRST NAME"
@ 6,16 GET first_name PICTURE "@A! XXXXXXXXXX"
@ 6,28 SAY "MIDDLE INITIAL"
@ 6,44 GET m_initial PICTURE "@A! X"
@ 6,47 SAY "LAST NAME"
@ 6,58 GET last_name PICTURE "@A! XXXXXXXXXXXXXXX"
@ 8,4 SAY "STREET ADDRESS"
@ 8,20 GET address PICTURE "XXXXXXXXXXXXXXX"
@ 10,4 SAY "CITY"
@ 10,10 GET city PICTURE "@A! XXXXXXXXXX"
@ 10,22 SAY "STATE"
@ 10,29 GET state PICTURE "@A! XX"
@ 10,33 SAY "ZIP CODE"
@ 10,43 GET zip_code PICTURE "99999"

*-- Format file exit code -------------------------------------------

*-- SET STATUS was ON when you went into the Forms Designer.
IF lc_status = "OFF"  && Entered form with status off
   SET STATUS OFF     && Turn STATUS "OFF" on the way out
ENDIF

IF lc_talk="ON"
   SET TALK ON
ENDIF

RELEASE lc_talk,lc_fields,lc_status
*-- EOP: CHGNMADD.FMT
```

Figure 17-3 dBASE code in FMT file

elect to create a Memo field window for use within your program. You can look at the example in Chapter 15 that deals with the Employee Skills field.

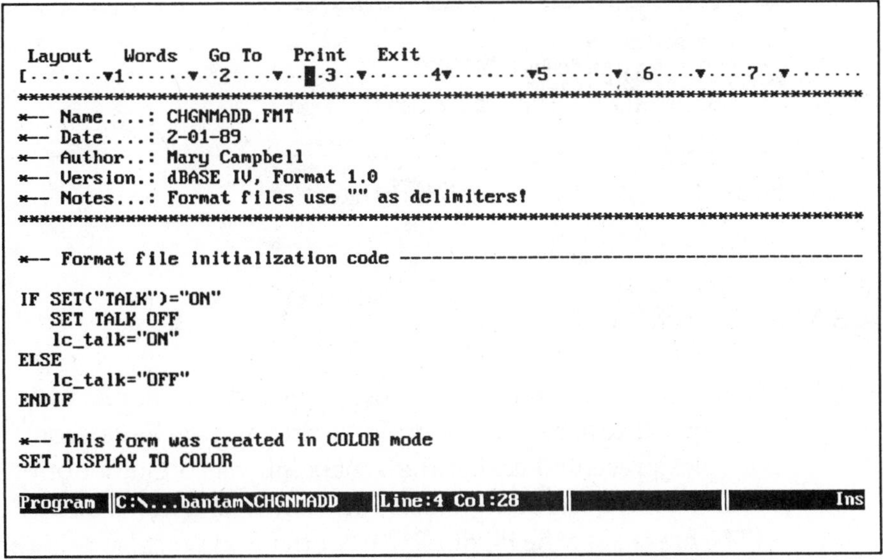

```
Layout   Words   Go To   Print   Exit
[·······▼1······▼··2····▼··█·3··▼······4▼·······▼5······▼··6····▼····7··▼·······
********************************************************************************
*-- Name....: CHGNMADD.FMT
*-- Date....: 2-01-89
*-- Author..: Mary Campbell
*-- Version.: dBASE IV, Format 1.0
*-- Notes...: Format files use "" as delimiters!
********************************************************************************

*-- Format file initialization code --------------------------------------------

IF SET("TALK")="ON"
   SET TALK OFF
   lc_talk="ON"
ELSE
   lc_talk="OFF"
ENDIF

*-- This form was created in COLOR mode
SET DISPLAY TO COLOR

Program  C:\...bantam\CHGNMADD   Line:4 Col:28                Ins
```

Figure 17-4 Minor code modification to add a programmer name

The modifications you make to the code may be minor changes to add an author to the documentation, as shown in Figure 17-4. Note that the format of the original dBASE entries are maintained with this addition. A change history could also be added in this fashion to reflect updates to the screen design over time. You might also want to alter some of the code for setting the color and check for the type of display the user is working with rather than using the setting that dBASE selected based on the machine used to design the original screen.

Any changes that you make to the .FMT will be overwritten if you ever go back to the original design and regenerate the screen. You will want to avoid the MODIFY SCREEN command if you change the .FMT file.

Changes like the ones in Figure 17-5 could also be added to alter the placement of some of the screen information and the location of the field templates. In the original design, state and zip code entries were closer than necessary to the name of the city. The @SAY and @GET statements in Figure 17-5 indicate revised positioning that is easy to accomplish without going back to the Form design. In this instance the column locations were revised by 5 for the state entries and by 10 for the zip code. The revised form will look like Figure 17-6.

```
@ 10,27 SAY "STATE"
@ 10,34 GET state PICTURE "@A! XX"
@ 10,43 SAY "ZIP CODE"
@ 10,53 GET zip_code PICTURE "99999"
```

Figure 17-5 Additional design changes

@ SAY GET in More Detail

The @SAY...GET is one of the most powerful commands in the dBASE language. It can be quite simple to use, as you have seen from the examples presented earlier. Its syntax allows so many options that it can also seem quite complete. If you look at its options one by one you will be amazed at the flexibility they offer and will also find that taken separately each of them are really quite simple. The syntax of @SAY GET is

```
@ <row>, <col>
     [SAY <expression>
          [PICTURE <expC>] [FUNCTION <function list>]]
     [GET <variable>
          [[OPEN]WINDOW <window name>]
          [PICTURE <expc>]
          [FUNCTION <function list>]
          [RANGE [<low>][,<high>]]
          [VALID <condition>[ERROR <expC>]]
          [WHEN <condition>]
```

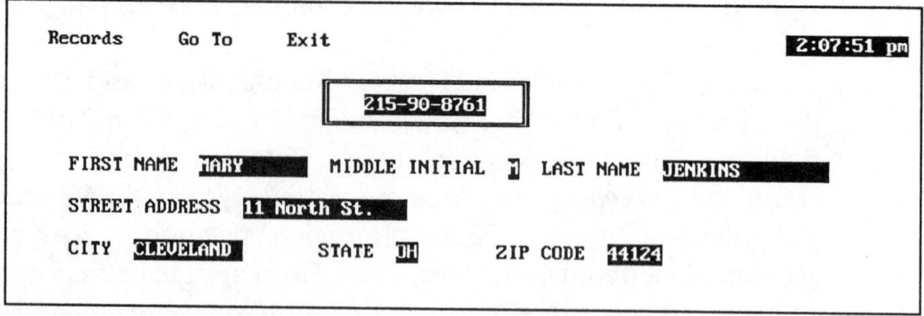

Figure 17-6 Revised form

```
          [DEFAULT <expression>]
          [MESSAGE <expC>]]
     [COLOR [<standard>] [,<enhanced>]]
```

Row and Column Entries As you can see from the syntax, neither SAY nor GET are required entries. When used alone as in @ 7,10 dBASE clears row 7 beginning in column 10. To clear the screen from the specified position to the bottom, you would enter @ 7,10 CLEAR. With SET STATUS and SET SCOREBOARD OFF, you can use all lines on the screen. With SET STATUS ON, line 22 is reserved for status information. Using SET STATUS OFF and SET SCOREBOARD ON reserves line 0 for status information.

Using the Say Option The SAY option allows you to display information on the screen. If you use SET DEVICE TO PRINTER, the command will send information to a printer. This will increase the maximum row number you can indicate to 32,767 and the maximum column to 255, if the printer will support it.

You can specify a PICTURE option to format the data that is displayed. It uses all the symbols that were acceptable in custom forms. Tables 17-1 and 17-2 summarize these symbols for you. You can include a dBASE picture function in the PICTURE expression if you precede it with an @ symbol and leave a space within the expression between the function and the template. For example, you can enter PICTURE "XXXXX" for a five-position character entry, but if you want dBASE to convert this display to upper case you can enter PICTURE "@! XXXXX". You can also use the FUNCTION option to enter a picture function.

Using Function The FUNCTION option allows you to enter a picture function without the need for an @ symbol, although the keyword FUNCTION is required. You can use FUNCTION "!" to convert the display to upper case.

Using the Get Option GET allows you to edit or display data from your database or memory variables. You can issue a series of GET commands to build a full screen for appending or editing records and use READ in conjunction with the GET commands to read a full screen of field values.

Table 17-1 Characters Used In Picture Templates

Character	*Effect*
!	Converts entry to upper case.
#	Restricts input to numeric digits, blanks, and signs.
9	Restricts input to numeric digits and signs.
A	Restricts entries to A through Z.
L	Restricts entry to Y, N, T, or F in either upper or lower case.
N	Restricts entry to letters and digits.
X	Any character.
Y	Restricts entry to Y or N.

Table 17-2 Characters Used in Picture Functions

Character	*Effect*
A	Alphabetic characters only
B	Left align
C	Positive numbers followed by CR
H	Horizontal stretch
I	Center align
J	Right align
L	Leading zeros displayed
M	Multiple choice options
R	Literal characters not stored with data
S	Scroll within display width
T	Trim
V	Vertical stretch
X	Negative numbers followed by DB
Z	Zeros shown as blanks
$	Financial format
^	Exponential format
(	Parentheses used around negative numbers
!	Uppercase conversion
;	Wrap semicolons

❑ **Tip: Only one PICTURE and FUNCTION per command line.**

You can only use PICTURE and FUNCTION once on a command line. Since the SAY and GET portions of your commands are considered separately even if both @SAY and GET are used in one command, you can have one for each part of the combined entry.

The GET portion of the command also supports both PICTURE and FUNCTION. These follow the same rules that you use when adding this information to the SAY portion of this command.

Using Open Window This option is only used with Memo fields. It allows you to define a window for these fields and to add the OPEN WINDOW option to the @ command to display the contents of the Memo field in the window. Figure 17-7 shows a screen that is used to enter SKILLS information for employees. The field SKILLS is a Memo field that would normally appear on the screen as MEMO or memo depending on whether or not it contained data. The WINDOW option allows you to view and enter this field in a window defined to occupy 4,22 to 18,70.

The location of the window must be defined first, as shown in Figure 17-8 in the DEFINE WINDOW command. Once Wnd1 is defined it can be referenced in @ commands. @4,22 GET Skills OPEN WINDOW Wnd1 tells dBASE to open the window for the use of the Skills field.

❑ **Tip: Use READ when creating multipage forms.**

To create multipage forms with @SAY GET commands, you will need to use a READ command at the bottom of each form. You can then reuse the row and column assignments and dBASE will recognize the entries as a new form. Do not put a READ after the last page of the form.

Tip: Don't store literals in a field.

You can display literal values for a field like the -'s in the social security number 213-46-8876 but cannot store them in the database if you use the PICTURE "@R 999-99-9999" This allows you to save two positions in every database record but still provides the display that you want.

Without the OPEN option, CTRL-HOME and CTRL-END must be used to open and close the window, enabling the full-screen editing features.

Using Range The RANGE option allows you to specify a minimum and maximum acceptable entry for character, numeric, and date entries. You must supply the same type of data for both entries if you elect to use a low and a high value. If you want to specify only one, use the comma to mark the place of the other. An entry of RANGE 50,100 establishes a lower bound of 50, indicating that the entry must be more than 50, and an upper bound of 100 indicating the entry is less than 100. If you want a lower bound of 50 enter RANGE 50, and if you want only

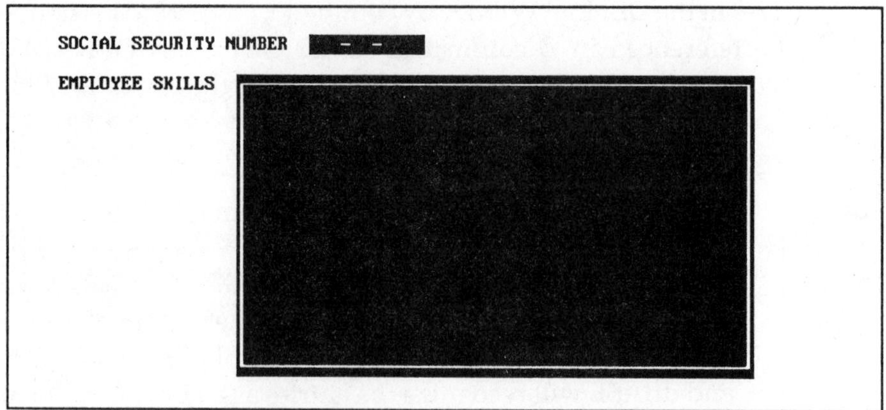

Figure 17-7 Skills entry screen

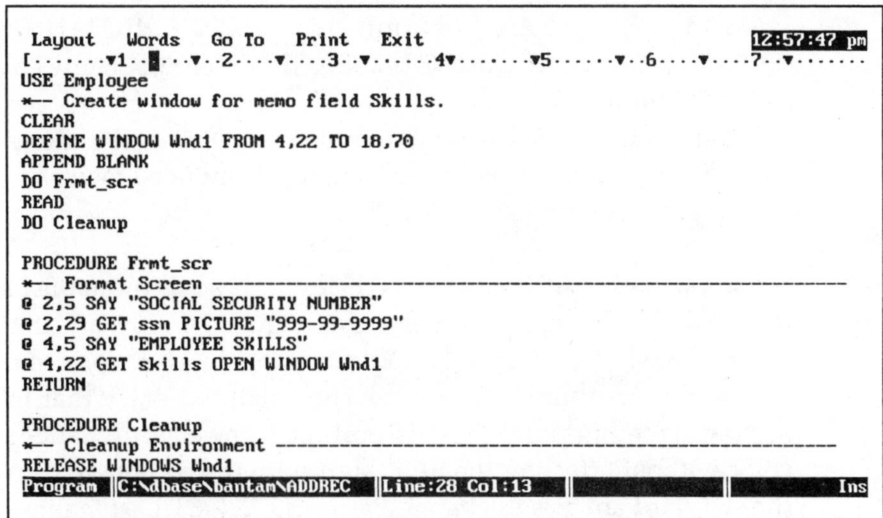
```
 Layout   Words   Go To   Print   Exit                              12:57:47 pm
[·······▼1··█···▼··2····▼····3··▼······4▼········▼5······▼··6····▼····7··▼·······
USE Employee
*-- Create window for memo field Skills.
CLEAR
DEFINE WINDOW Wnd1 FROM 4,22 TO 18,70
APPEND BLANK
DO Frmt_scr
READ
DO Cleanup

PROCEDURE Frmt_scr
*-- Format Screen ---------------------------------------------------------------
@ 2,5 SAY "SOCIAL SECURITY NUMBER"
@ 2,29 GET ssn PICTURE "999-99-9999"
@ 4,5 SAY "EMPLOYEE SKILLS"
@ 4,22 GET skills OPEN WINDOW Wnd1
RETURN

PROCEDURE Cleanup
*-- Cleanup Environment --------------------------------------------------------
RELEASE WINDOWS Wnd1
Program ║C:\dbase\bantam\ADDREC  ║Line:28 Col:13 ║              ║            Ins
```

Figure 17-8 Defining the window

the upper bound enter RANGE ,100. If you use ON READERROR, it will take priority over range checking if there is a conflict.

Using Valid/Error The VALID and ERROR options are used together. You use the VALID option to specify a condition that must be met before data is accepted. The ERROR portion allows you to override the dBASE message "Editing condition not satisfied" with your own message.

Using When The WHEN option supplies a condition. If the condition is true, data can be entered; if false, the cursor will skip the field, preventing entries.

Using Default The DEFAULT option places a preset entry in a field. The entry you supply must match the data type as in {02/15/89} for a date type field or "Dallas" for a character type field.

Using Message This option allows you to display a message for an entry when the cursor is on the entry. For a field of Name, you might use this command:

@SAY 7,15 SAY "Name " GET PICTURE "@!A XXXXXXXXXXXXXXXXXXXX" MESSAGE "Enter First name Last name as in Joe Smith".

When your cursor is on the template for Name, the message will display. Remember to use a semicolon(;) if you need to use more than one line for this entry.

Color Options This option overrides your setting established with the SET COLOR command but these changes only affect this one command. The first entry after COLOR is the standard color and is used for the SAY portion of the entry. The enhanced entry that follows a separating comma is for the GET portion. If you elect to change the GET color without affecting the SAY, start with the comma to signify that the standard entry is unchanged as in @5,15 GET Last_name COLOR ,W/R.

With so many options it is not possible to explore screens that use each of them. The following table provides a few more examples of the possibilities:

Command	Description
@ 2,1 SAY "Home Phone" GET H_Phone; PICTURE "@R (999)999-9999	Displays the phone number with literals but does not store them.
@ 2,1 GET Location WHEN mcnt>10	Allows the entry of Location when the value of mcnt is greater than 10.
@ 2,1 GET Hr_rate RANGE 5,50	Ensures that Hr_rate is greater than 5 and less than 50.
@ 2,1 GET Amount PICTURE ; "@XC$ 999999999"	Displays the amount with a dollar sign and either DB or CR.

?/??/???

The ? commands were introduced in Chapter 10 as a way of viewing fields and variables when working at the dot prompt. You can think of these commands as equating to PRINT. The single question mark produces a line feed before displaying the value of the variable or field in the statement and the ?? command does not. The ??? is a special case used to send characters directly to the printer without using the print driver you have installed.

Although these commands are often used as a quick and dirty way of displaying information they support options like picture template, picture functions, and print style. Each of these can be specified separately for each expression in the statement. The syntax of the command is

```
?/?? [<expression1> [PICTURE <expC>] [FUNCTION <function
     list>] [AT <expN>] [STYLE ,font number>]]
     [,<expression 2>...] [,]
```

The PICTURE option uses templates that accept all of the characters used with the @SAY GET command. You can enter ? mamt PICTURE "99.99" to display 7.00 if mamt contains a 7. The FUNCTION option contains some of the same options found in the picture function options for @SAY GET. You can use mamt in this entry ? mamt PICTURE "9999.99" FUNCTION "$" to display $7.00. The H and V function codes are only available with the ? and ?? commands and allow the field to stretch vertically or horizontally to accommodate data.

The AT option allows you to control the column in which the data displays. ? mamt AT 27 will display the data in column 27.

The STYLE option accepts B for bold, I for italic, U for underline, R for raised, and L for lowered. The latter two provide subscript and superscript positioning. You can also use the numbers 1 through 5 to correspond to your preselected printer fonts to select a specific print style. ? mamt STYLE "B" will print 7 showing the entry in bold.

Tip: Use the correct setting to direct print output.
The @SAY command outputs to the printer with SET DEVICE TO PRINT. The ? command outputs to the printer with SET PRINTER ON.

ACCEPT

The ACCEPT command allows the user to make an entry and stores the entry in the character memory variable that you specify. You can include a prompt message to the user. The syntax is

```
ACCEPT [<prompt>] TO <memvar>
```

A user can type as many as 254 characters for the memory variable ending the entry with ENTER. If ENTER is pressed before an entry is made, the character variable is equal to "" better known as the null or empty string. If SET ESCAPE is ON, pressing ESC in response to the prompt ends the program.

The entry ACCEPT "Enter your last name" TO mlast displays the message and stores your entry in mlast. ACCEPT will create the memory variable if it does not exist. The entry ACCEPT "How many records do you want to add?" TO mcnt stores the number you enter as a character string in mcnt. If you wish to use this number to control a DO WHILE or other iterative construct it will need to be converted to a number first since it is stored as a character.

INPUT

The INPUT command is more flexible than ACCEPT. ACCEPT will only accept character string entries. With INPUT you can enter a number and have it stored in a numeric memory variable. If you use the {} symbols to encase a date entry, the memory variable created will be a date type variable.

The syntax of INPUT is identical to ACCEPT. The only difference is that it accepts data types other than character. INPUT "How many records do you want to add?" TO mcnt with a response of 10 will create a numeric type memory variable and store 10 in it.

WAIT

The WAIT command suspends dBASE processing until a key is pressed. It is a useful command when you display a message to the user and want confirmation that it has been read. The keystroke typed by

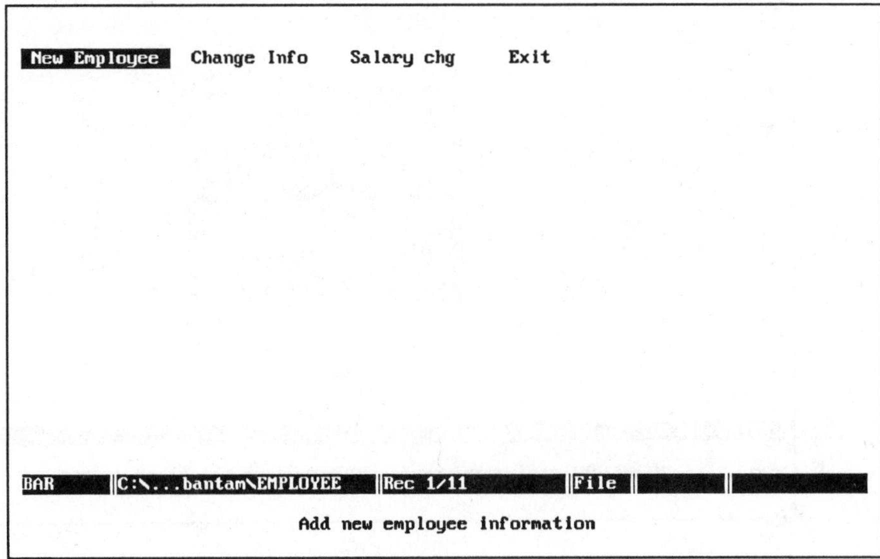

Figure 17-9 Bar menu

the user is retained allowing you to use the command to process a selection or choice.

The syntax of the WAIT command is WAIT [<prompt>] TO <memvar>. dBASE supplies the prompt "Press any key to continue" if you do not supply a prompt message. The entry WAIT "Do you wish to proceed with record deletion Y/N?" TO mchoice will display the message, wait for a keystroke, and store it to mchoice. You can follow this instruction with IF UPPER(mchoice) = "Y" to allow the user to enter either Y, y, N, or n.

Creating Menus

With dBASE III+, your menu had to be created with @SAY or TEXT entries. With dBASE IV you have programming commands that allow you to create the full range of menu possibilities you used with the Applications Generator in Chapter 12. You can create a bar menu across the top of the screen that looks something like Figure 17-9. You can also create pop-up menus at any location on the screen. Figure 17-10 shows

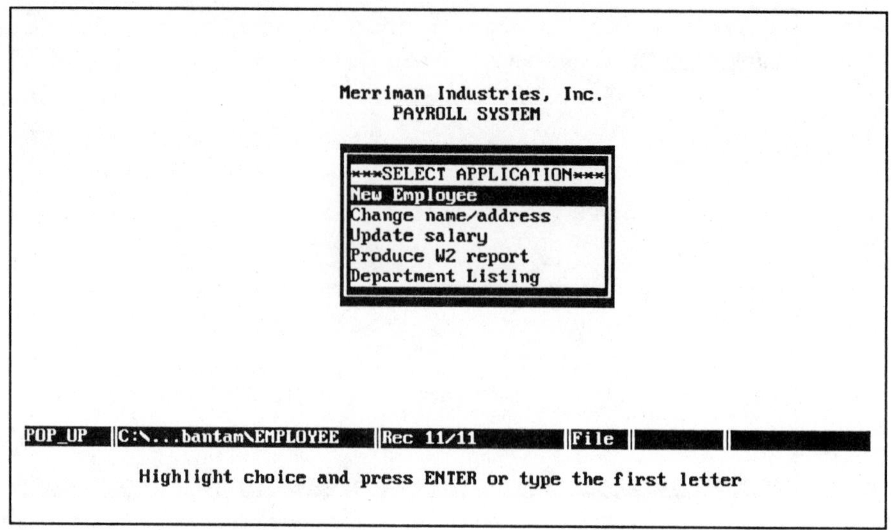

Figure 17-10 Pop-up menu

a pop-up menu. You can also attach pop-up menus to bar menus so they function just like dBASE's pull-down menus.

In this chapter we will look at the commands you need to add menus to your applications. First, a pop-up menu suitable for providing main menu selections will be created. Next, a bar menu for the top of the screen will be used to present information with a different approach. Your system may be a combination approach with pop-ups attached to bar menus or a combination of all three types.

Creating Pop-Up Menus

Creating, activating, and responding to the selection made from a pop-up menu requires multiple steps. The first step is defining the appearance of the pop-up menu. Since this aspect of the task requires numerous steps, it is frequently handled in a separate procedure. At the end of the definition, you will need to take the second step and tell dBASE which routine to execute when the user does make a selection. The code for the selections that can be made is normally stored as another procedure using the DO CASE command structure. The next step is activating the pop-up. This causes the pop-up menu to appear on the screen.

Defining the Pop-Up The definition of a pop-up menu requires that you name the pop-up and specify the upper left corner as the beginning location for the pop-up. You must also define the contents of each of the bars in the pop-up menu, but separate instructions are used for this task.

The first command needed is DEFINE POPUP. The command has two different formats depending on whether you are defining a menu box or a list that contains fields, files, or the database structure. To define a pop-up menu, use this syntax:

```
DEFINE POPUP <popup name> FROM <row1>, <col1> [TO <row2>,
<col2>] [MESSAGE <expC>]
```

If you don't mind computing the size you will need for the pop-up, you can enter DEFINE POPUP pop2 FROM 10,25 TO 18,60 MESSAGE "Type the first letter of your choice or highlight it and press ENTER". If you leave off the TO parameter and enter DEFINE POPUP pop2 FROM 10,25 MESSAGE "Type the first letter of your choice or highlight it and press ENTER", dBASE will calculate the size of the pop-up depending on the menu entries that you define.

The menu bars are defined with the DEFINE BAR command. You will need a DEFINE BAR command for every option that you place in the menu. You will also use this command to create fixed entries like menu titles or dividing lines to separate groups of options.

The typical entry to define a bar in the menu is DEFINE BAR 3 OF Pop2 PROMPT "Enter new order". The Enter new order text will always appear on the third bar of pop2. It can be selected by typing an E or highlighting the bar and pressing ENTER. You can add a message for each option by adding the MESSAGE parameter to the command. When the choice is highlighted, dBASE will display the message in the bottom line of the screen overlaying the message entry from the DEFINE POPUP command. You can add a message to the previous command like this: DEFINE BAR 3 OF Pop2 PROMPT "Enter new order" MESSAGE "Enter a new order including name, address, city, state, and phone number"

Two additional options allow you to use a bar entry as display only or to conditionally allow the display and selection of a bar entry. The SKIP option makes the entry display only. Entering these instructions causes the first two bars to be displayed only:

```
DEFINE BAR 1 OF pop1 PROMPT "APPLICATION OPTIONS" SKIP
DEFINE BAR 3 OF pop1 PROMPT "-------------------" SKIP
```

The first line is the title of the menu and the second divides the selectable options from the title. The cursor will not move to any bar with the SKIP option. The SKIP FOR <condition> option allows you to determine if a bar should display and be selectable based on a condition.

Telling dBASE Where to Find the Instructions for the Menu Bars
After defining each of the bars, you need to tell dBASE which instructions to execute once a selection is made. This is accomplished with the ON SELECTION POPUP command. You can follow the command keywords with the name of the pop-up and a command. For example, you might enter ON SELECTION POPUP Pop2 DO Process_2. When the pop-up Pop2 is active and ENTER or the first letter in a menu selection is pressed, dBASE executes Process_2.

Creating a Routine to Process Menu Selections The routine that processes menu selections must provide a processing option for each alternative in the menu. The BAR() function is frequently used in conjunction with the CASE statement to handle this processing. In essence you would enter the following:

```
DO CASE
     CASE BAR() = 1
          DO Option1
     CASE BAR() = 2
          DO Option2
ENDCASE
```

A CASE BAR() entry is made for each selectable menu option.

```
DO Def_pop1
DO Signscr
ACTIVATE POPUP pop1

PROCEDURE Def_pop1
  DEFINE POPUP pop1 from 8,30 TO 15,55;
    MESSAGE "Highlight choice and press ENTER or type the first letter"
    DEFINE BAR 1 of pop1 PROMPT "***SELECT APPLICATION***" SKIP
    DEFINE BAR 2 of pop1 PROMPT "New Employee"
    DEFINE BAR 3 of pop1 PROMPT "Change name/address"
    DEFINE BAR 4 of pop1 PROMPT "Update salary"
    DEFINE BAR 5 of pop1 PROMPT "Produce W2 report"
    DEFINE BAR 6 of pop1 PROMPT "Department Listing"
    ON SELECTION POPUP pop1 DO Procpop1
  RETURN

PROCEDURE Signscr
  CLEAR
  @ 5,30 SAY "Merriman Industries, Inc."
  @ 6,35 SAY "PAYROLL SYSTEM"
  RETURN

PROCEDURE Procpop1
  DO CASE
    CASE BAR()=2
      ?"New Employee selected"
    *Additional case entries here **********
  ENDCASE
  RETURN
```

Figure 17-11 Active pop-up

Activating a Pop-Up After all the definition work is complete, you can activate a pop-up from anywhere in your program. Entering ACTIVATE POPUP Pop2 will activate the pop-up menu Pop2. The menu remains active until you press ESC, activate another pop-up, or use the DEACTIVATE POPUP command. An appropriate location for the DEACTIVATE command may be at the end of the procedure that processes the bar selections.

Putting All the Instructions Together With a number of specific steps required, you will want to take a look at a section of code that both defines and activates a pop-up menu. Figure 17-11 contains a code that creates a menu Pop1. It places this menu on the screen along with a sign-on type message indicating the company name and the name of the system that is currently active. The sign-on message is created with the @SAY instructions covered earlier in the chapter. The procedure for processing the user's selection only shows one CASE BAR() entry. Additional commands would be added for each bar except the first. Since the first bar is not selectable there is no need for a CASE BAR(1) to process the selection. Figure 17-10, shown earlier, shows the screen with the pop-up menu active.

Creating Bar Menus

Bar menus are normally horizontal menus that stretch across the top line of the dBASE Control Center and design screens like the one in Figure 17-9. They are also more flexible than this structure suggests and can be created vertically, in a random pattern, or a diagonal line. Although these other options would not be required frequently, you may want a radically different layout to catch the users attention in some situations. Regardless of the layout, bar menus are composed of a series of pad entries that are defined separately.

Like the pop-up menus, a number of steps are required to create a bar menu. The first step is naming the menu and providing a prompt message. The second step requires you to define each of the pads that comprise the bar menu. You must also use the ON SELECTION PAD command to tell dBASE which routine will process your selection. The next step is activating the menu. The user's selection is processed as the final step in the menu process.

Defining the Menu The DEFINE MENU command is used to name the bar menu and provide a prompt message. Although it does not produce the menu, it is the essential first step in any application that uses a bar menu. The message that you provide can be as long as 79 characters. The message will display at the bottom of the screen unless there are messages attached to pad entries, since these will override it.

Defining Each Pad The DEFINE PAD command is used to define each of the individual bar entries. The command can be used with a minimum of options to create a horizontal bar beginning in the top line of the screen. The full syntax of the command is

```
DEFINE PAD <pad name> OF <menu name> PROMPT <expC>
     [AT <row>, <col>] [MESSAGE <expC>]
```

The prompt text is the menu option that is highlighted when a particular pad is active. The prompt entries are visible on the screen even when the option is not active. The MESSAGE options allow you to specify a message as long as 79 characters. This message will appear on the bottom line of the screen and will overwrite any message created with the DEFINE MENU command.

If you do not specify an AT option for each pad entry, dBASE places the first entry in the upper right corner, skips a space, and places the next entry on the same line. SET SCOREBOARD must be OFF or it will overlay a bar menu defined in the top line of the screen.

Like the pop-up menu, you need to tell dBASE which routine will process pad selections from the bar menu. This is accomplished with the ON SELECTION PAD command. Unlike the pop-up menu, which use only one ON SELECTION command, you will include an ON SELECTION PAD option for each menu option. These commands will tell dBASE the code to execute when a specific pad is selected. Using ON SELECTION PAD Pad3 without a command following it disables a pad in the menu.

Activating the Menu To activate a bar menu that you have defined, use the ACTIVATE MENU command. The only argument required is the name you used in the DEFINE MENU command. When you no longer want the menu on the screen you can use the DEACTIVATE MENU command. This action is appropriate after the user makes a selection.

Processing Menu Selections When you processed the selection from the pop-up menu only one command ON SELECTION POPUP was needed. With a bar menu you must use an ON SELECTON PAD for each pad that you define. You can use this command with a DO command to execute a procedure or with ACTIVATE POPUP if you want to attach a pull-down menu. If you want to activate a pull-down menu as soon as the bar menu selection is active you would enter ON PAD Rpt ACTIVATE POPUP Pop1 if the pad is named Rpt and the pop-up that you wish to pull down is named Pop1.

Putting All the Instructions Together Figure 17-12 contains the code used to generate the horizontal bar menu shown earlier in Figure 17-9. You will need to add ON SELECTION PAD statement to this code for each of the pads that have been created to tell dBASE which code to execute for each one. After opening the Employee file, the bar menu is defined. DEFINE MENU names the menu providing the name that will be used when you want to activate it. Since the menu options will each display a unique message at the bottom of the screen, there is no need to supply a MESSAGE entry for DEFINE MENU. Each option in this

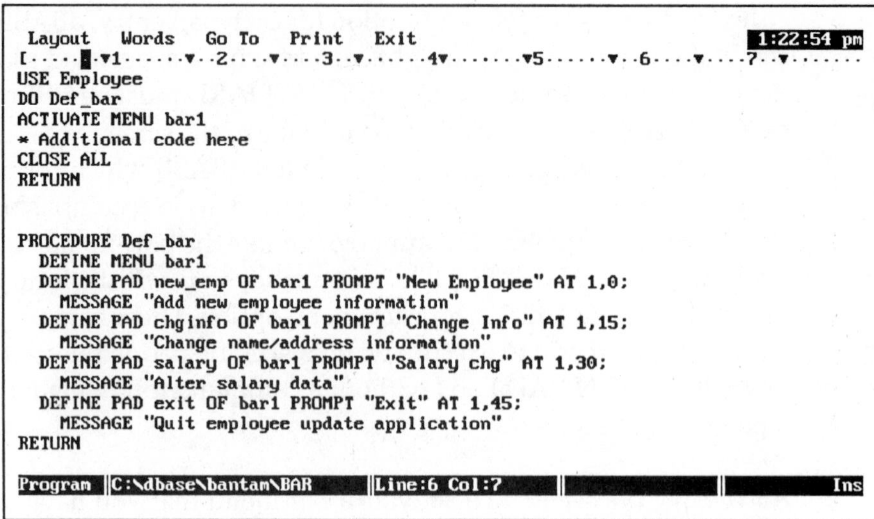

```
 Layout   Words   Go To   Print   Exit                                  1:22:54 pm
[·····▮·▼1······▼··2····▼····3··▼······4▼·······▼5······▼··6····▼····7··▼·······
USE Employee
DO Def_bar
ACTIVATE MENU bar1
* Additional code here
CLOSE ALL
RETURN


PROCEDURE Def_bar
  DEFINE MENU bar1
  DEFINE PAD new_emp OF bar1 PROMPT "New Employee" AT 1,0;
    MESSAGE "Add new employee information"
  DEFINE PAD chginfo OF bar1 PROMPT "Change Info" AT 1,15;
    MESSAGE "Change name/address information"
  DEFINE PAD salary OF bar1 PROMPT "Salary chg" AT 1,30;
    MESSAGE "Alter salary data"
  DEFINE PAD exit OF bar1 PROMPT "Exit" AT 1,45;
    MESSAGE "Quit employee update application"
RETURN

Program ║C:\dbase\bantam\BAR      ║Line:6 Col:7     ║            ║            Ins
```

Figure 17-12 Code for horizontal bar menu

menu is defined with one of the four DEFINE PAD commands. These commands provide a pad name, a prompt, a location, and a message that will display at the bottom of the screen when the pad is active. After the menu is defined an ACTIVATE MENU command makes it active. The additional code that is not supplied would process the selections and deactivate the menu after a selection is made.

Other Menu Options As mentioned earlier, bar menus can take any form including vertical, diagonal, or random patterns. Figure 17-13 shows a menu created with diagonal pad entries. The code used to define this menu is shown in Figure 17-14. The main difference between this menu and the one defined earlier is the AT options for each of the pads. Line 3 shows a pad location of 2,1. With 12 characters required for the prompt, the next pad starts on the following line in position 13.

❑

Tip: Allow for an exit option.

Always allow users an exit from your menu selections in the event that none are suitable. All that is required is creating an Exit pad with an appropriate action.

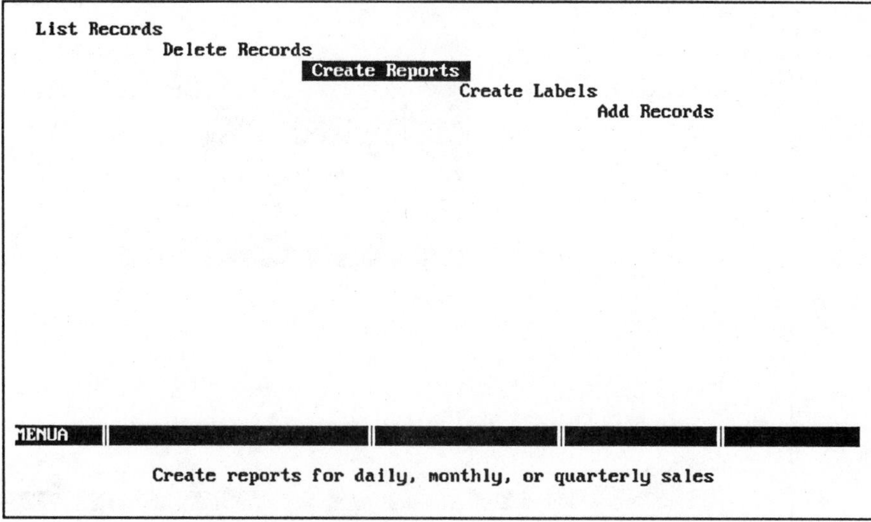

Figure 17-13 Diagonal menu entries

The prompt entry for the second bar is 14 characters placing the third pad on line 4 beginning in column 27. With another 14-character prompt, pad 4 starts in line 5 position 41. Since this prompt is 13 characters the last pad starts in line 6 in column 54.

You can use this approach to create multiple rows of bar entries or any other format. The order in which the pads are defined controls the cursor movement from pad to pad.

```
CLEAR
DEFINE MENU Bara
DEFINE PAD Lst OF Bara PROMPT "List Records" AT 2,1;
        MESSAGE "List records from one or more files"
DEFINE PAD Del OF Bara PROMPT "Delete Records" AT 3,13;
        MESSAGE "Delete current record or specify records to delete"
DEFINE PAD Rpt OF Bara PROMPT "Create Reports" AT 4,27;
        MESSAGE "Create reports for daily, monthly, or quarterly sales"
DEFINE PAD Lbl OF Bara PROMPT "Create Labels" AT 5,41;
        MESSAGE "Create envelopes or labels"
DEFINE PAD Add OF Bara PROMPT "Add Records" AT 6,54;
        MESSAGE "Add new customers or products"

ACTIVATE MENU Bara


```

Figure 17-14 Code for diagonal entries

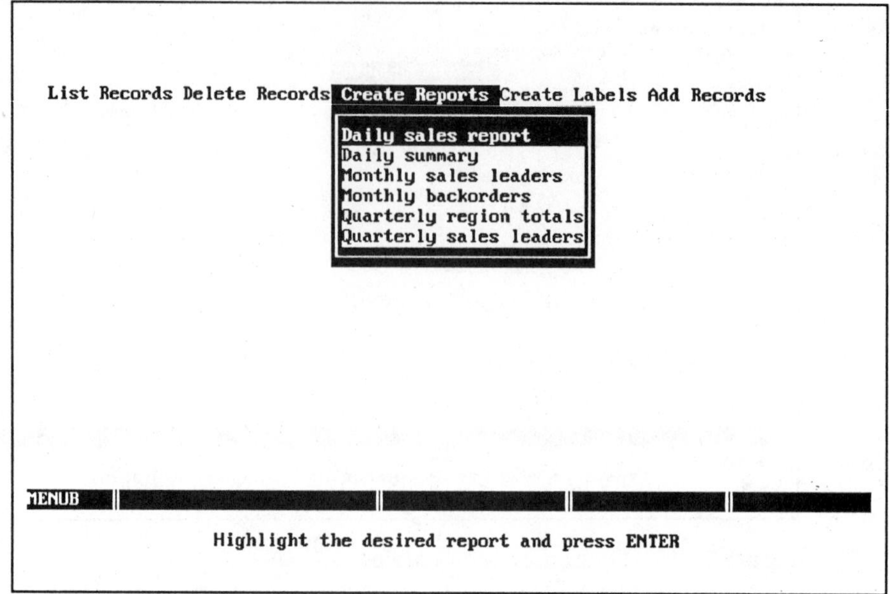

Figure 17-15 Bar menu with active pull-down menu

Figure 17-15 shows a bar menu with an active pull-down menu. You can use the RIGHT and LEFT ARROW keys to move between the selections, but dBASE will not support the use of the HOME and END key. dBASE treats HOME like ESC and ignores the END key. Figure 17-16 shows the code that was used to create the bar menu and the pull-down menu. Although this code only contains the definition for one pull-down attached to the Rpt pad, the same method can used for defining the remaining pull-downs.

As you look at the code in Figure 17-16, the first line clears the screen. Next, the procedure that defines the attached bar is executed. The beginning location of the pop-up is one row below the bar menu and in the same column as the bar menu. Each option in the pull-down is defined with a define bar.

The instruction in line 3 executes the definition of the bar menu. Once this is complete, the ACTIVATE instruction displays the menu. When you select Rpt, the pull-down appears. If you wanted the pull-down to appear as soon as you highlight Rpt, use an ON PAD instruction in the Bara procedure rather than the ON SELECTION PAD.

```
CLEAR
DO Defpopbara
DO Bara
ACTIVATE MENU Bara

*Procedure to define bar menu
PROCEDURE Bara
DEFINE MENU Bara
DEFINE PAD Lst OF Bara PROMPT "List Records" AT 2,1;
        MESSAGE "List records from one or more files"
DEFINE PAD Del OF Bara PROMPT "Delete Records" AT 2,14;
        MESSAGE "Delete current record or specify records to delete"
DEFINE PAD Rpt OF Bara PROMPT "Create Reports" AT 2,29;
        MESSAGE "Create reports for daily, monthly, or quarterly sales"
DEFINE PAD Lbl OF Bara PROMPT "Create Labels" AT 2,44;
        MESSAGE "Create envelopes or labels"
DEFINE PAD Add OF Bara PROMPT "Add Records" AT 2,58;
        MESSAGE "Add new customers or products"
ON SELECTION PAD Rpt OF Bara ACTIVATE POPUP Rpt
RETURN

*Procedure to define popup
PROCEDURE Defpopbara
DEFINE POPUP Rpt FROM 3,29;
        MESSAGE "Highlight the desired report and press ENTER"
DEFINE BAR 1 OF Rpt PROMPT "Daily sales report"
DEFINE BAR 2 OF Rpt PROMPT "Daily summary"
DEFINE BAR 3 OF Rpt PROMPT "Monthly sales leaders"
DEFINE BAR 4 OF Rpt PROMPT "Monthly backorders"
DEFINE BAR 5 OF Rpt PROMPT "Quarterly region totals"
DEFINE BAR 6 OF Rpt PROMPT "Quarterly sales leaders"
RETURN
```

Figure 17-16 Code for bar and pull-down menus

Creating Reports

You have already learned some of the commands that you can use to create reports since they are the same commands that display output on the user's screen during data entry. Your challenge in creating reports will be handling page and group breaks in the report. These may require the addition of several variables to keep track of current values as records are processed. In this section you will have an opportunity to look at the creation of a simple report and to explore some strategies for achieving the correct results painlessly.

Page Definition

You can control the length and appearance of a page of output with the system memory variables and the ON PAGE command. The variable

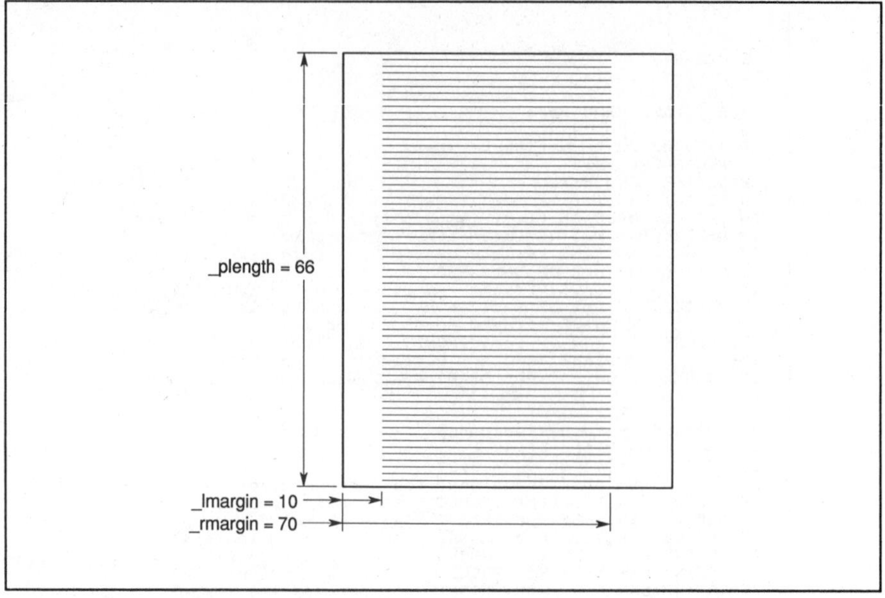

Figure 17-17 Standard page

_plength can be set to the number of lines in a page of your output. In a standard 8 ½ by 11 page like the one in Figure 17-17 there will be 66 lines if your printer is set to print six lines to the inch. You can also set the variable _lmargin for the left margin you want to use. The right margin is set by assigning a value to _rmargin. The offset from the left edge allows you to shift all the output to the left away from the edge of the paper. To create the settings shown in Figure 17-17 you would enter the following lines of code:

```
_plength=66
_lmargin=10
_rmargin=70
_ploffset=0
```

You can use these settings to initialize other memory variables. As an example you may want to stop printing four lines from the end of the page. To establish the variable mlstlne to contain the last line on which print will be placed, you can enter mlstlne=_plength-4. You can use this with the ON PAGE command to control the placement of a footer line.

You might enter ON PAGE AT LINE mlstlne DO Footer if Footer is the name of the procedure that places the footer line of the page.

Other important system variables are _plineno for the line number and _pageno for the page number. If you want the first page printed to have page number 30 at the bottom of the page, you can initialize _pageno to 30 with the instruction _pageno=30. As you print each page, dBASE will automatically increment this number. The same is true for the line number since dBASE initializes the line number when you eject a page and continues to increment it with each line that you print.

Methods for Printing Output

The ? and ?? commands that you looked at earlier are used to create lines of a report. You can use one ? command for each line, specifying the placement of multiple entries on this line with AT parameters after each character string, variable or field as in ?"Last name: " AT 10, Last_name AT 21. This command prints both a constant and a variable field value on the same line. Another option for making this same entry is to use two commands. The first command will print the entry after generating a line feed and the second command will print without a line feed. These two commands generate the same results as the one ? command just reviewed. Your entries would be

```
?"Last name: " AT 10
??Last_name AT 21
```

Another way to generate printed output is with the LIST command. In this case the field lengths control the placement of the data. You will probably want to include the OFF option to prevent the display of the

❑ **Tip: You must control record advancement with DO WHILE.**

When using the DO WHILE construct you must monitor for the end of file condition with EOF(). You also need to advance to each new record with the SKIP command. SCAN can handle both options automatically.

record numbers. Entering LIST OFF Last_name, Ssn, Ytd_fit will display the three fields requested. The ? command will display the data from one record whereas one LIST command will display all the database records. You can use the ? command in an interactive construct like DO WHILE or SCAN. Using SET PRINTER ON will route this output to your printer.

If you want to print a subset of the records the use of an index file will be significantly more efficient when a limited number of records are being printed. If you want to print only the records for zip code 44040, an index for Zip_code will allow you to use this construct:

```
USE Employee TAG Zip_code
SEEK 44040
SCAN WHILE Zip_code = 44040
     ?Last name AT 10, State AT 30, Zip_code AT 35
ENDSCAN
```

The use of SET PRINT ON and SET PRINT OFF will enable printing and disable it when it is no longer needed if you place the appropriate command at the beginning and end of the code. Without indexing you could set a filter for Zip_code = 44040 with SET FILER TO Zip_code = 44040. This method is much less efficient since the unindexed search for the correct records causes dBASE to read every database record.

Creating a Basic Report Program

You will want to create your report with separate procedure for handling page headings, footers, and detail routines. This modular approach makes it much easier to debug your programs and allows you

❑ **Tip: Make the SET PRINTER ON command a comment.**

When you first start testing a program you will want to leave out the SET PRINTER ON command or place a comment indicator in front of it. This allows you to use the screen for the initial testing rather than wasting paper.

```
*Set up environment
DO Environ

*Establish variables
STORE "" TO mstate

*Open data with appropriate index
USE Employee ORDER State
GO TOP
mstate=State
ON PAGE AT LINE 55 DO End_page

*Initial report setup
Do Heading
SCAN WHILE .T.
        IF mstate <> State
                DO End_page
                DO Heading
        ENDIF
        DO D_line
ENDSCAN
*End of detail records
DO End

PROCEDURE End_page
?"End page"
RETURN

PROCEDURE Heading
?"Heading"
RETURN

PROCEDURE D_line
?STATE
mstate=State
RETURN

PROCEDURE End
?"END REPORT"
RETURN

PROCEDURE Environ
SET TALK OFF
SET ECHO OFF
RETURN
```

Figure 17-18 Employee print program

to develop the modules separately. You can begin testing the control logic in your program before you have added the detail code in all the enhancement procedures.

Creating Report Breaks When you create a report you may want to group records with different values or you might want to show subtotal breaks. To do this you must store the value of the grouping field from the current record and compare this value to the next record that you read. You must set up a memory variable to contain this value and update it with each detail record read.

Initial Code Entries Figure 17-18 contains the initial code for a program that prints all the records in the employee file, organizing them by state. Line 2 executes the procedure Environ that establishes set options. Although a second routine is not included to reset these options at the end of the program you would want to add one to your program.

In line 5 the memory variable that stores the last value for state is initialized as a character variable. Lines 8 through 10 open the Employee file using an index that was created with the INDEX ON command.

Line 11 establishes the end of page routine that will be performed when the line count equals 55. Although the routine currently prints "End page" you would probably print the page number in this routine then enter the EJECT PAGE command to advance to the top of the page.

Line 14 performs a routine that prints a heading before any records are printed. The advantage of using a separate procedure is that you can use it again every time you need a top-of-page heading.

Lines 15 through 21 use a SCAN construct that will read every record in the database. Since the State Tag is in effect, the records will be read in order by the value in the State field for each record. The first command within the construct is an IF statement that checks to see if there has been a change in the value of the state entry. Since this is the first record, the variable mstate is still equal to the State entry in the current record and the End_page and Heading procedures will not be executed. Instead the D_line procedure that processes a detail line is executed. In this initial program the D_line procedure lists the State entry and sets the mstate variable equal to the State value in the current record.

dBASE will continue executing the D_line procedure until a record is read that has a different value in the State field. At this time the End_page and Heading routines are executed. You may want to change the program so that End_page routine calls the heading unless an end-of-report flag is set. This requires another memory variable to be used as the end-of-report flag. The flag would be initialized as one value and changed to another when the end of the report was reached by executing the DO End command in line 23. The End_page routine could contain the statement IF mendflag = 1 DO Heading.

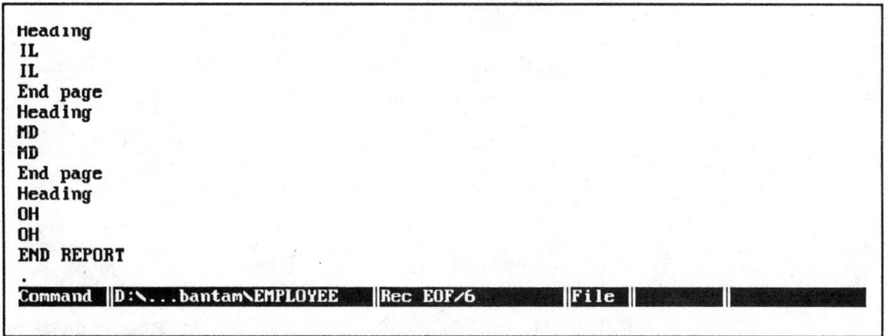
```
Heading
IL
IL
End page
Heading
MD
MD
End page
Heading
OH
OH
END REPORT
.
Command ||D:\...bantam\EMPLOYEE ||Rec EOF/6 ||File ||
```

Figure 17-19 Output from print program

Producing the Output As currently written, the code does not create output that looks much like a report. It does allow you to check the output that will be created by the program before making enhancements. Figure 17-19 shows the output from this program.

The program would execute the Heading routine first then print the first two records for the state code of IL. The End of page routine is executed next followed by the heading and the two records for MD. After another end of page and heading the OH records are printed. The last entry indicates that the End Report is executed. You will notice that End of Page is not executed at the end of the report. This would cause a problem if end of page totals were produced in this routine.

Enhancing the Basic Program

The basic program still requires significant work, but it is obvious at this point that logic change is required for the end of the report. You

```
PROCEDURE Heading
?"Last Name" AT 0, "Social Security Number" AT 20, "State" AT 45,;
        "YTD Federal Tax" AT 55
 RETURN

PROCEDURE D_line
?Last_name AT 0,  Ssn AT 20, State AT 45, Ytd_fit AT 55
mstate=State
RETURN
```

Figure 17-20 Changing the heading and detail line code

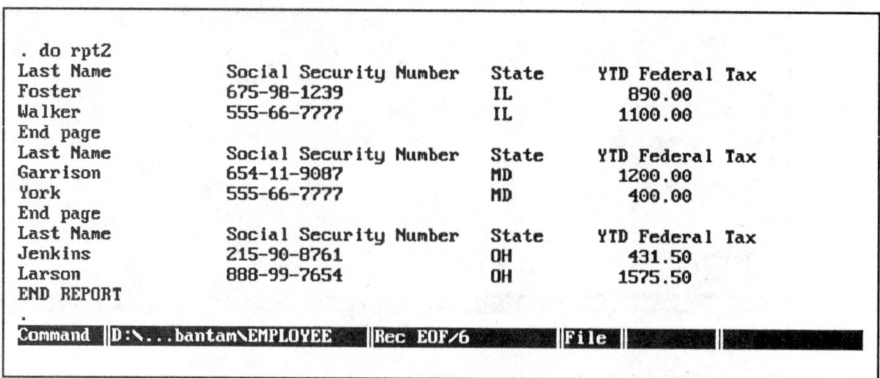

```
. do rpt2
Last Name          Social Security Number   State      YTD Federal Tax
Foster             675-98-1239              IL            890.00
Walker             555-66-7777              IL           1100.00
End page
Last Name          Social Security Number   State      YTD Federal Tax
Garrison           654-11-9087              MD           1200.00
York               555-66-7777              MD            400.00
End page
Last Name          Social Security Number   State      YTD Federal Tax
Jenkins            215-90-8761              OH            431.50
Larson             888-99-7654              OH           1575.50
END REPORT
.
Command  D:\...bantam\EMPLOYEE   Rec EOF/6      File
```

Figure 17-21 **Output from dot prompt entry**

need to complete the procedures one at a time, testing as you go to insure that you maintain the type of output that you are looking for.

Changing the Heading and Detail Line Figure 17-20 shows a change to the Heading and D_line procedures. A description of the field entries is added with the ? command added to the Heading routine. The new command in the D_line routine adds field values for each detail line. If the code for the program is stored as rpt2, entering DO rpt2 at the dot prompt creates the output in Figure 17-21.

Adding a Total at the End of a Page and Other Enhancements Page 2 from the final program is shown in Figure 17-22. Output for each state is placed on a separate page with the page number centered at the bottom and the total for each page placed after the last line of output.

Figure 17-23 contains the code for the revised report. Line 6 through line 9 contain the code for additional variables requiring initialization. Mendp serves as an end-of-page flag; mtotst will be used to accumulate

```
Last Name            Social Security Number   State      YTD Federal Tax
Garrison             654-11-9087              MD            1200.00
York                 555-66-7777              MD             400.00
           Total Federal income tax for employees in MD    1600.00
```

Figure 17-22 **Page 2 of program**

```
*Set up environment
DO Environ

*Establish variables
STORE "" TO mstate
STORE 0 TO mendp
STORE 0 TO mtotst
STORE "" TO moldst
STORE 1 TO _pageno

*Open data with appropriate index
USE Employee ORDER State
GO TOP
mstate=State
ON PAGE AT LINE 55 DO End_page

*Initial report setup
Do Heading
SCAN WHILE .T.
   IF mstate <> State
         DO Total
         DO Blnk_lne
         DO Heading
   ENDIF
   DO D_line
ENDSCAN
*End of detail records
DO End

PROCEDURE Blnk_lne
DO WHILE _plineno < 56 .AND. mendp <> 1
   ?
ENDDO
RETURN

PROCEDURE Heading
?"Last Name" AT 0, "Social Security Number" AT 20, "State" AT 45,;
   "YTD Federal Tax" AT 55
STORE 0 to mendp
RETURN

PROCEDURE D_line
?Last_name AT 0,  Ssn AT 20, State AT 45, Ytd_fit AT 55
mstate=State
moldst=State
mtotst = mtotst + Ytd_fit
RETURN

PROCEDURE TOTAL
?"Total Federal income tax for employees in " AT 11
??moldst AT 53
??mtotst PICTURE "999999.99" AT 55
mtotst=0
RETURN


PROCEDURE End_page
_alignment="CENTER"
_wrap=.T.
?"----"+STR( _pageno,2,0)+"----"
_alignment="LEFT"
_wrap=.F.
EJECT PAGE
STORE 1 to mendp
RETURN

PROCEDURE End
DO Total
```

Figure 17-23 Revised report code *(continued)*

```
69 DO Blnk_lne
70 SET PRINTER OFF
71 SET TALK ON
72 SET ECHO ON
73 RETURN
74
75 PROCEDURE Environ
76 SET TALK OFF
77 SET ECHO OFF
78 SET PRINTER ON
79 RETURN
```

Figure 17-23 Revised report code *(continued)*

state totals; moldst contains the state code from the previous record that will be used in the end-of-state-total line.

A new command has been added in line 22 to perform a Total procedure when the State entry changes. This procedure uses a ? and two ?? commands to create the total line. The PICTURE clause in line 53 formats the total to match existing detail entries.

The Blnk_lne procedure creates blank lines until the ON PAGE option is invoked. The mendp flag stops the execution of the Blnk_lne command after a page is ejected.

As each detail line is processed moldst is equated to the current State entry. The variable mtotst is incremented by the amount of Ytd_fit in the current record.

The End page procedure places the page number at the bottom of the page. To center the entry, _alignment is changed to CENTER and _wrap is changed to .T..

The End procedure reestablishes the settings for PRINTER, TALK, and ECHO. In addition this routine produces a total for the last line and causes an end-of-page condition to place a page number on the last page.

GETTING STARTED

➤ Although you have not as yet seen the full range of programming commands offered by dBASE IV, you have been introduced to a sufficient number of programming instructions to find your way through the other dBASE commands in the command reference in the appendix. You can follow these instructions and enter the code for a working program that uses some of the files you created earlier in this book:

1. At the dot prompt, type **modi comm bgets18** and press ENTER.
2. Enter the lines of code shown in Figure 17-24. Do not enter the line numbers.
3. Press ALT-E and type an **S**.
4. List the EMPLOYEE and WEEK_PAY files and make any necessary changes or additions. Make the entries match the ones in Figures 17-25 and 17-26.
5. Type DO BGETS18 and press ENTER.
6. Compare your output to the results in Figure 17-27.

```
*Initialize environment
DO Environ
*Initialize variables
STORE 0 TO mendp
STORE 0 TO mtot
STORE 1 TO _pageno
*Open files
SELECT 1
USE Week_pay ORDER Ssn
USE Employee IN 2 ORDER Ssn
SET RELATION TO Ssn INTO Employee
ON PAGE AT LINE 58 DO End_page
*Process detail
DO Heading
SCAN WHILE .T.
        DO D_line
ENDSCAN
*End of detail records
DO End
PROCEDURE Heading
?"Last Name" AT 0, "Social Security Number" AT 20, "Hourly Rate" AT 40,;
        "Regular Hours" AT 53, "Regular Pay" AT 68
STORE 0 to mendp
RETURN
PROCEDURE D_line
?Employee->Last_name AT 0, Ssn AT 20, Employee->Hr_rate AT 40, Reg_hours;
        AT 53, Employee->Hr_rate*Reg_hours PICTURE "99999.99" AT 68
mtot = mtot + Employee->Hr_rate*Week_pay->Reg_hours
RETURN
PROCEDURE TOTAL
?"Total regular pay for employees " AT 11
??mtot PICTURE "999999.99" AT 55
RETURN
PROCEDURE End_page
_alignment="CENTER"
```

Figure 17-24 Code for Getting Started exercise *(continued)*

```
_wrap=.T.
?"----"+STR(_pageno,2,0)+"----"
_alignment="LEFT"
_wrap=.F.
EJECT PAGE
STORE 1 to mendp
RETURN

PROCEDURE End
DO Total
SET PRINTER OFF
SET TALK ON
SET ECHO ON
RETURN

PROCEDURE Environ
SET TALK OFF
SET ECHO OFF
SET PRINTER ON
```

Figure 17-24 Code for Getting Started exercise *(continued)*

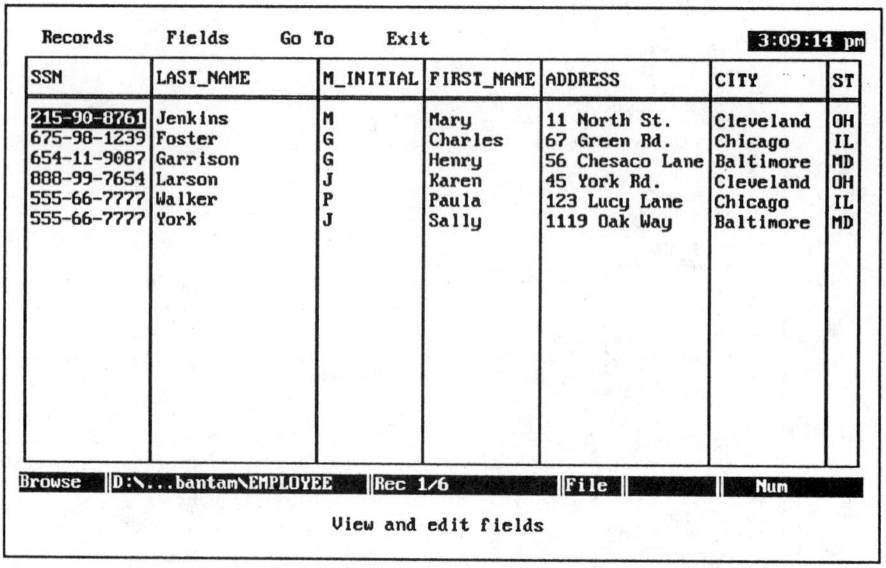

Records Fields Go To Exit 3:09:14 pm

SSN	LAST_NAME	M_INITIAL	FIRST_NAME	ADDRESS	CITY	ST
215-90-8761	Jenkins	M	Mary	11 North St.	Cleveland	OH
675-98-1239	Foster	G	Charles	67 Green Rd.	Chicago	IL
654-11-9087	Garrison	G	Henry	56 Chesaco Lane	Baltimore	MD
888-99-7654	Larson	J	Karen	45 York Rd.	Cleveland	OH
555-66-7777	Walker	P	Paula	123 Lucy Lane	Chicago	IL
555-66-7777	York	J	Sally	1119 Oak Way	Baltimore	MD

Browse D:\...bantam\EMPLOYEE Rec 1/6 File Num

View and edit fields

Figure 17-25 Data in the EMPLOYEE database

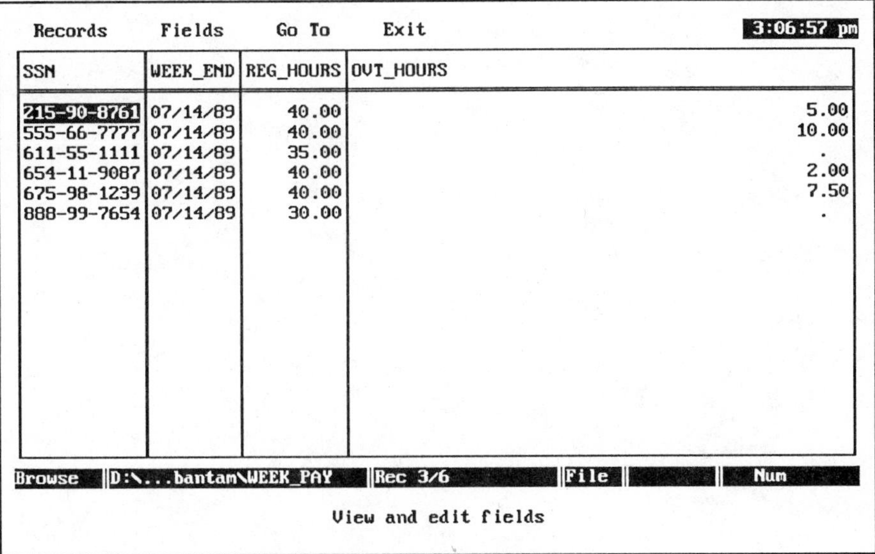

Records Fields Go To Exit 3:06:57 pm

SSN	WEEK_END	REG_HOURS	OUT_HOURS
215-90-8761	07/14/89	40.00	5.00
555-66-7777	07/14/89	40.00	10.00
611-55-1111	07/14/89	35.00	.
654-11-9087	07/14/89	40.00	2.00
675-98-1239	07/14/89	40.00	7.50
888-99-7654	07/14/89	30.00	.

Browse D:\...bantam\WEEK_PAY Rec 3/6 File Num

View and edit fields

Figure 17-26 Data in the WEEK_PAY database

```
Last Name          Social Security NumbHourly Rate  Regular Hours  Regular Pay
                   111-55-1111             0.00     35.00               0.00
Jenkins            215-90-8761             9.75     40.00             390.00
Walker             555-66-7777            12.50     40.00             500.00
Garrison           654-11-9087            12.50     40.00             500.00
Foster             675-98-1239             8.50     40.00             340.00
Larson             888-99-7654            15.75     30.00             472.50
           Total regular pay for employees                 2202.50
```

Figure 17-27 Output from the BGETS18 program

CHAPTER 18

Using Professional Programming Techniques

The last few chapters have provided several ideas for using dBASE IV commands in creating your own programs. The command reference in Appendix C offers even more. Before ending the discussion of programming, it is important to discuss some of the techniques and background activities that are an important part of successful systems. In addition, you have the opportunity to take a quick look at two additional tools that Ashton-Tate offers to assist in professional programming efforts.

Creating Professionally Designed Programs

Throughout the programming chapters a variety of techniques have been introduced that allow you to create better programs. These are summarized briefly in this section and supplemented with a few new ideas to add to your productivity.

Designing Basic Modules

The more programs you create, the more you will realize the repetitiveness of the tasks that you perform. This is especially true in business

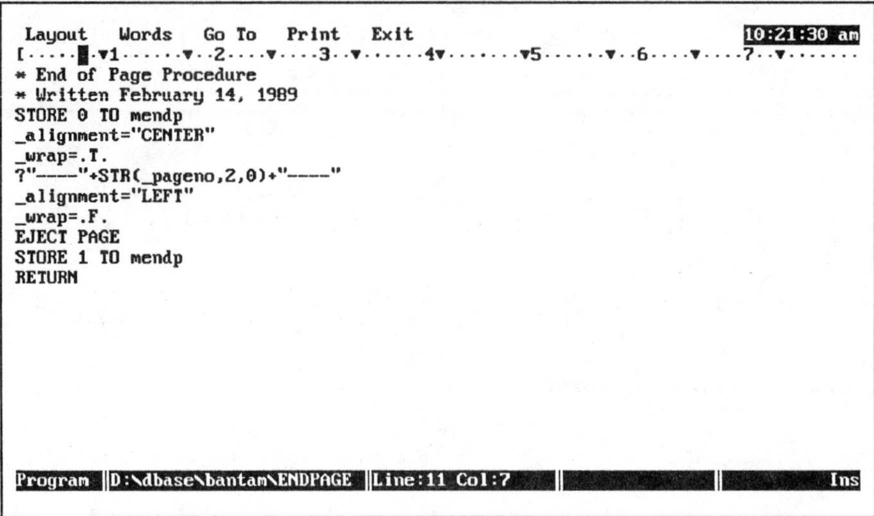

```
 Layout   Words   Go To   Print   Exit                                    10:21:30 am
[·····█·▼1·····▼··2····▼····3··▼······4▼·······▼5······▼··6····▼····7··▼·······
* End of Page Procedure
* Written February 14, 1989
STORE 0 TO mendp
_alignment="CENTER"
_wrap=.T.
?"----"+STR(_pageno,2,0)+"----"
_alignment="LEFT"
_wrap=.F.
EJECT PAGE
STORE 1 TO mendp
RETURN

Program  D:\dbase\bantam\ENDPAGE  Line:11 Col:7                                 Ins
```

Figure 18-1 Generalized program that multiple programs can use

applications since you constantly need to perform tasks like selectively printing records from a file, matching records in a one-to-many relationship, handling end-of-page conditions, and creating subtotal breaks in reports. You can create generalized modules to handle these tasks and make customization changes for a specific application.

The simple end-of-page routine in Figure 18-1 is one example of a generalized routine that can be created, stored as a separate module, and either executed from disk or copied into the program with the Words menu command that copies text files. For a short routine like this that is needed at the end of every page, you can copy the module into your program for efficiency. For a longer routine that is seldom executed, executing the program with a call to the separate module is the preferred approach.

Over time with a little effort you will find that you can develop a library of these routines. You will find yourself constructing programs by copying the necessary building blocks and making minor changes to tailor them to your exact needs.

Passing Data between Modules

You can expand your options for creating modules that work in many situations by using parameters with the modules you create. The

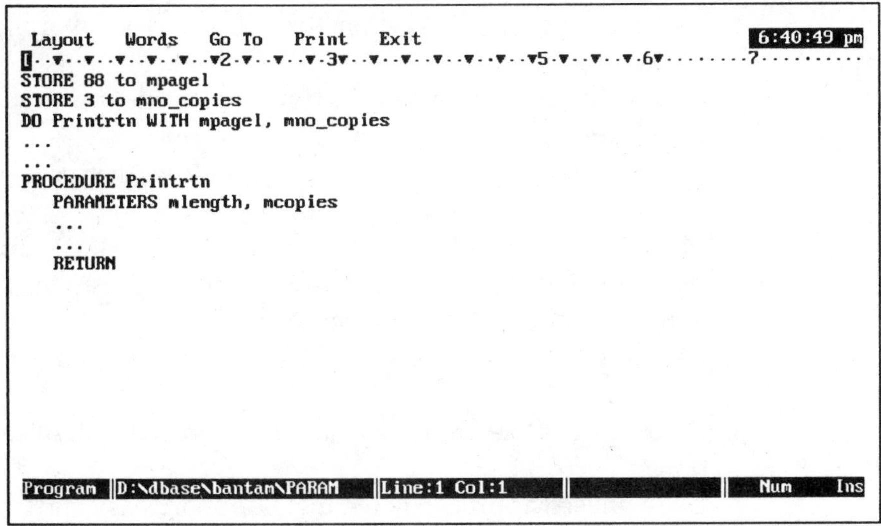
```
 Layout   Words   Go To   Print   Exit                                   6:40:49 pm
STORE 88 to mpagel
STORE 3 to mno_copies
DO Printrtn WITH mpagel, mno_copies
...
...
PROCEDURE Printrtn
   PARAMETERS mlength, mcopies
   ...
   ...
   RETURN

Program  D:\dbase\bantam\PARAM   Line:1 Col:1                          Num    Ins
```

Figure 18-2 Program using parameters

calling program can pass the needed customization option to the program. As an example you might create one print routine and pass a parameter to the routine each time you execute it to indicate the page length or the number of copies you need. With multiple copies, the routine might have the intelligence to write the report to disk and print it from disk several times rather than executing the program again and making multiple passes of the database.

Figure 18-2 provides an example of a routine that expects a parameter to be passed to it. When the routine is executed with DO Printrtn WITH mpagel, mno_copies, the values stored in mpagel and mno_copies are passed to the subroutine and stored in mlength and mcopies. Executing the same routine with other parameter values causes different values to be passed to Printrtn presumably affecting the results of this subroutine.

A Set of Rules to Guide Your Coding

In a number of places throughout the last several chapters, you have been presented with tips and strategies for improving your coding techniques. Although you may choose not to try all of them, here are 10 rules that you can use to improve your coding:

1. Use consistent capitalization for command keywords, fields, filenames, and indexes.
2. Limit abbreviations to quick activities at the dot prompt. Do not abbreviate the commands in your programs.
3. Use modular programming techniques rather than creating long run-on programs that are difficult to understand.
4. Make an investment in creating good documentation for yourself and the users of your applications. You will reap the rewards of these efforts for years to come.
5. Use meaningful names for fields, files, routines, and memory variables.
6. Create generalized routines that can be reused in many applications.
7. Use a phased approach to testing. Use short, easy entries for the first test. Next, use sample data created with the assistance of the application user. As a final step, use erroneous data to check that the system can reject incorrect entries. Save sample test scripts for use any time the application is modified.
8. Use similar structures in all the programs you create. If there are other programmers in the organization, agree upon a common standard. This makes it easier to work on a variety of programs yet feel instantly comfortable with any program.
9. Use comments liberally both on the command line and as separate entries. They will remind you of the purpose of specific code lines and sections long after you have forgotten.
10. Use spacing and indentation to improve the program's appearance and to make the structure instantly visible.

Creating Professional Documentation

If you are new to programming, your final objective is likely to be creating a program that runs correctly. Although that is an important step, additional tasks must be completed. If you have done an adequate job in the design phase of the system, most of your work is already done. All that is required to complete the remaining steps is a bit of cleanup and reformatting to create documentation for both the user and the programmer who may modify the system in the future.

Any one who has survived a major system conversion can vouch for the value of documentation. Unfortunately, for most people the importance of documentation is learned the hard way by having to make do without it. Documentation never seems important until it is time to change the program or a critical employee is lost. If the lost employee is the only one who knew how to coach the correct output from the system, without documentation, it almost seems easier to rewrite it.

Each step in your program seems intuitively obvious when you first create the program. As time passes you may even begin to question "Who wrote this code?" or "Why was this done this way?" Then you remember that you wrote the program and although you begin to consider the code in a more positive light at this point, you will still wish you had taken the time to create some documentation. This documentation that is helpful to you can be called systems documentation. The name comes from before the days of personal computers when almost all programs were created by the Systems and Programming departments in large firms. The technical documentation was retained in the Systems and Programming Group and was called systems documentation as opposed to user documentation. Many people refer to this documentation as program documentation but, as you will see, it is really more than that since it must include more than documentation on the individual programs.

Now that your needs are met if you ever need to modify a program, what about the users who need to run your application? Will system documentation meet their needs? The answer is a definite no since the user is indifferent to what individual lines of code do or which module handles the processing. The end users want an overall understanding of the system, including the output of the system, and clear directions for the tasks they must perform.

Creating Systems Documentation

The objective of system documentation is to provide an overview of the application including information on the system flows and the necessary detail at the program level to make changes as easy as possible. A chart that shows the information flow in the system with the names of the main program modules and the database files can suffice to provide the highest-level overview. The next step is usually to enhance the information presented in diagram form with text that clearly describes the system purpose and important components. The flow diagram of the accounts receivable system in Chapter 12 is an example of this type of chart.

A description of the files required by the system is another important component of the system documentation. As a first step the files description should include a structure listing for each file. You should also include the composition of the file's indexes on this same sheet.

If the fields need further definition or if it is a system where individuals may have different interpretations of field contents, data dictionary entries for each field are a helpful asset. These entries include the field name, a brief description of the field contents, rules for sample entries like acceptable entries or a range of acceptable values, and actual sample entries. Sections within the dictionary can also store the typical template and picture function options that programs use to display the field. These additional entries can assist a programmer who is inexperienced with the system to develop a report in the exact format in which a user expects to see the data, with only minor adjustments required. Figure 18-3 shows an example of a sample data dictionary entry. You can also use the data dictionary to maintain a cross reference for modules that update the values in this field as well as modules that produce reports and labels showing this field. This also helps when you change field characteristics since you want to know which modules are affected by your changes.

The layout of all forms, reports, and labels are important pieces of documentation when system changes are required. The INSET screen-capture program that created the screen shots in this book is a good way to capture screen and label designs. Report design can be captured

❑ **Tip: Save time in building dictionary entries by starting with the database structure.**

You can write the file structure to disk by using the TO FILE option on the DISPLAY STRUCTURE command. You can edit this information from your word processor to add additional entries and page breaks.

DATABASE: Vendors
FIELD: Vend_name
CONTENTS: The name of the firm or individual from whom supplies, equipment, or services are purchased.
LENGTH: 20
DATA TYPE: Character
PICTURE TEMPLATE: XXXXXXXXXXXXXXXXXXXX
PICTURE FUNCTION: ! (capitalizes entire entry)
MODULES WHERE USED: *AP1132 *AP2384 AP8590 AP9111 PA9105 PA9183 YT1901 YT1932 * Indicates modules where the field is added or updated.
REPORTS WHERE DISPLAYED: A1105 A2310 A8514 P9185 Y1923

Figure 18-3 Sample data dictionary entry

in this same way, but multiple screens may be required for one design. Another option is printing a copy of a report, but this does not show the design layout as effectively as the design screen. Yet another option

Modules In The Inventory System	
MODULE	**PURPOSE**
IN1201	Creates order acknowledgments
IN1785	Creates an inventory exception report
IN4531	Prepares a weekly inventory status report
IN4210	Prepares a receiving report
IN3211	Processes sales invoices
IN1321	Creates an error summary report
IN1119	Prepares journal entries

Figure 18-4 Sample module listing sheet

for reports is using some of the special report layout forms available in office supply stores, but filling out these forms is time consuming. Pasting together several screen shots and photocopying them may be quicker than completing the report design forms.

Listing of all programs and procedures is a must. If you use the model-naming standards already mentioned, you can file the listings in order by the model names. It is easy to find the exact module you need at any time. Figure 18-4 shows a simple module listing sheet for the inventory system.

An important part of the documentation is making sure that it is updated in response to changes made to the system. A copy of a report layout or program listing is only valuable if it matches the copy that is currently in use.

Creating User Documentation

The needs of the end user who constantly works with your application are totally different from the needs of the programmer who needs to modify the application at a later date. The user needs documentation that presents information from a functional orientation. The user needs to accomplish certain tasks and wants to understand how the system can help fulfill these needs. The end user is not interested in memory variables, lines of code, or file structures.

The user also needs an overview chart that shows the system input and the deliverables the system produces. The user's documentation should emphasize the business tasks that the system performs. A brief description should accompany this chart and it should include the system purpose and any special equipment that is required to use the system. As an example, the system might need two floppy disks and a minimum of 640K of memory. You want to present this information at the earliest possible point so the user does not begin to run the early parts of the application and then find out the reports cannot be produced because of insufficient memory. If the program is not compatible with memory-resident programs like SideKick or Inset, it is appropriate to supply this information to prevent problems.

You need to provide a schedule for running each of the application components. This allows the user to identify which components should be run daily, weekly, and monthly. Separate instructions should be provided for each of these components. You may even want to provide explicit instructions for starting the computer system and loading the required program. Even if the current user is computer literate, explicit instructions allow a less experienced replacement to operate the application without the need for hand-holding.

Each of the options available within each major functional area needs to be explained. The user needs to know how to select an appropriate menu option as well as the effect that the selection has. After a menu option is selected there may be entries that the user needs to make. A program that can capture a screen image is a helpful asset to capture each of the input screens. You can supply the necessary directions for making entries on a field-by-field basis. A description of the field and its usage, any range limitations, multiple choice entries, or other limitations can be documented. The data dictionary developed as programming documentation can be used if the dual needs of programmers and end users are considered in its design; the one document may serve both purposes.

The end user also benefits from samples of reports and labels. The user wants to see actual samples the application creates rather than the design screens used in the system documentation. Some fields on these documents may require an explanation, including their source or the computations used in the case of a Calculated field. The procedure for creating each of these system outputs should be included. Depending on the complexity of the system, this can include listing the menu selection the user must make, or it can include directions on how to run a program and the menu selections the user makes. The documentation should include any options available to the user. These might include multiple copies or both a summary and a detail version of the report. The run frequency and a distribution list for the individuals scheduled to receive the copies should be shown and may be recorded on a form similar to the one in Figure 18-5. The field shown on the report can be tied to the data dictionary entries by adding an element number next to each field shown in the report. These elements should match the number shown on the data dictionary entry.

Conducting a Post Implementation Review

Another technique that can be borrowed from mainframe programming groups is the post implementation review. This activity is normally conducted several weeks or months after the implementation of a system to assess its performance. It should be conducted by someone other than the system user or programmer although input is obtained from both parties. The information uncovered in a post implementation review can provide valuable insights that permit improvements to be made to future systems and allow corrections to be made to the existing system and its documentation while individuals knowledgeable about the system's design and implementation are still employed by the company. The following are a sampling of the types of questions asked during a follow-up review of an implementation:

- Was the system implemented on schedule?
- What are the major system problems or bugs discovered in the system?
- Did you parallel the old and new system before final implementation?
- Is training adequate to introduce a new person to the system? Is it formal or informal? Will documentation provide adequate information to a new person?
- Are procedures for backup and recovery included with the system documentation?
- Are there sample reports with distribution lists?

REPORT DISTRIBUTION FOR THE	Accounts Receivable System	
REPORT NUMBER	**FREQUENCY**	**DISTRIBUTION**
A1234	Monthly	Jim Smith Karen Jones Bill Horn
A2314	Quarterly	Sam Jones Jim Smith Karen Jones Bill Horn
A3421	Monthly	Sam Jones Jim Smith Karen Jones Bill Horn
A5555	Monthly	Jim Smith (2) Karen Jones (3) Bill Horn (6)

Figure 18-5 Sample run frequency and report distribution listing

- Does the programmer maintain a change log of alterations to the program?
- Are users pleased with the system performance and reports? Is the system information providing timely information or does the reporting cycle need to be more frequent?
- Is the system flexible in meeting the user's business needs?
- Are backup copies of critical files maintained off-site?
- What recommendations could be made to improve the system?

A short report should be prepared as a result of the implementation review. In addition to a synopsis of the findings, the report should contain a list of action steps for the current system as well as recommendations for procedure changes that would benefit future systems development.

Creating RunTime Modules

With RunTime modules you can distribute copies of your programs to run on computers without dBASE. RunTime allows you to create programs that operate as if dBASE was in the users system from the dBASE IV programs that you write. Using the special programs provided in the Developer's Edition of dBASE IV, your programs are interpreted with a utility called BUILD. A second utility called DBLINK can join a number of separate program files into one executable file if you prefer to distribute a single file.

Using RunTime

RunTime is for your use after you have successfully coded and debugged an application. There are a few restrictions that you must keep in mind as you design a potential application for use with RunTime. Neither macro substitution nor menu driven SET commands are supported. RunTime modules cannot perform the dBASE commands listed in Table 18-1.

All of the program files that you want to use with BUILD are in the current directory with the files BUILD.EXE, BUILD.COM, and BUILD.RES in the dBASE directory. Type **BUILD** at the dot prompt.

You can access several options from the BUILD menus. The build menu lets you specify whether you want to compile the program to create object code, link several programs together, specify the output location, or perform BUILD to create a RunTime modules.

The second menu Options shown in Figure 18-6 contains specifications that relate to BUILD. The first options allows you to check for UDFs that use the same name as dBASE functions. These UDFs are not accessed since dBASE functions take priority if there are duplicate names. The default for this option is No.

The Accept only RunTime commands presents a warning message if illegal commands are encountered. The Include file types allows you to determine the file types that are copied to the RunTime application. Additional options allow you to control the disposition of RunTime messages, whether or not RunTime files are copied, and the location of the installed RunTime application.

If you want the BUILD program to segment your application into modules, you must create a text file named BUILD.MOD. This file

Table 18-1 Runtime Restrictions — dBASE Commands Not Supported

ASSIST	SET (Full menu selections)
COMPILE	SET DEBUG
CREATE/MODIFY FILE	SET DOHISTORY
CREATE/MODIFY LABEL	SET ECHO
CREATE/MODIFY QUERY	SET HISTORY
CREATE/MODIFY REPORT	SET INSTRUCT
CREATE/MODIFY SCREEN	SET SQL
CREATE/MODIFY STRUCTURE	SET STEP
CREATE/MODIFY VIEW	SET TRAP
HELP	SUSPEND
HISTORY	Macro (&)

should contain the names of all modules except the main module. The modules are listed one per line and do not contain filename extensions. If you specify Main_rtn as the main module name in the Compile option and list Payroll, Employee, and Tax as three entries in BUILD.MOD, four modules are created at compile time.

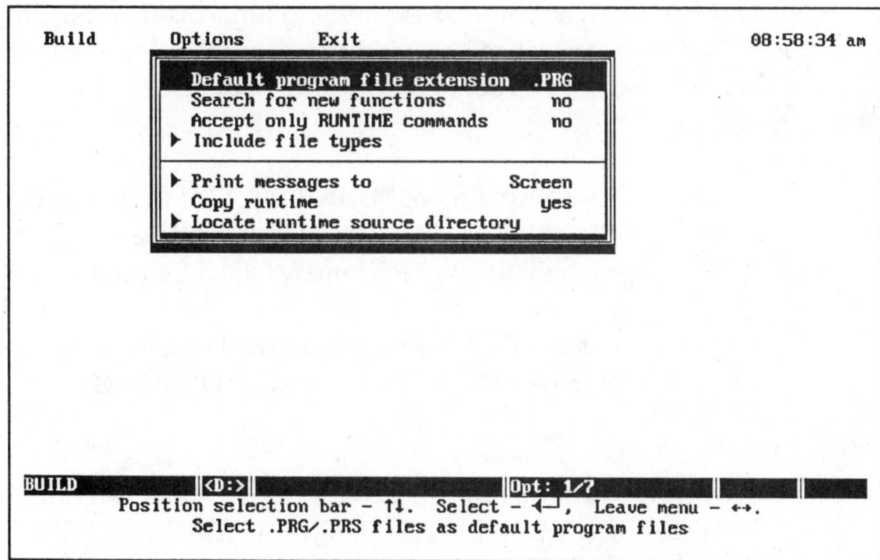

Figure 18-6 Options menu for BUILD

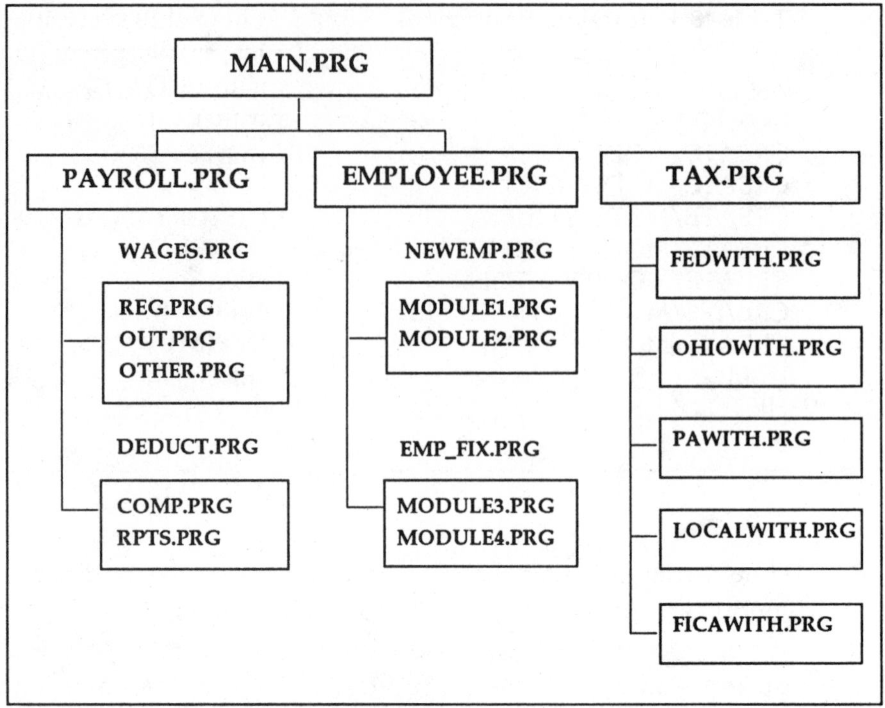

Figure 18-7 Program divided into modules

Looking at a more complex example, assume that Payroll, Employee, and Tax each consist of the modules shown in Figure 18-7. Given Build.mod entries of Main, Payroll, and Tax these modules would be created:

MAIN.DBO — Consisting of MAIN.PRG, EMPLOYEE.PRG, NEWEMP.PRG, MODULE1.PRG, and MODULE2.PRG, EMP_FIX.prg, MODULE3.PRG, and MODULE4.PRG

PAYROLL.DBO — Composed of WAGES.PRG, REG.PRG, OVT.PRG, OTHER.PRG, DEDUCT.PRG, COMP.PRG, and RPTS.PRG.

TAX.DBO — Consisting of FEDWITH.PRG, OHIOWITH.PRG, PAWITH.PRG, LOCALWITH.PRG, and FICAWITH.PRG.

Packaging the Completed Application You will need to supply certain RunTime files with each application that you distribute. These files are: RUNTIME.EXE, RUNTIME1.OVL, RUNTIME2.OVL, RUNTIME3.OVL, RUNTIME4.OVL, and DBASE1.RES. If you want the user to be able to change field access levels with the PROTECT command, also copy RPROTECT1.OVL.

Executing RunTime Applications When the RunTime application is compiled and the appropriate files are copied to the current directory, you can execute the application. Type **RUNTIME FILENAME** where the filename is the name of the RunTime module you wish to execute; if you type **RUNTIME** without a filename, RunTime assumes you want to execute the default file DBRUNCMD.DBO. If you take the latter approach, you must rename your file DBRUNCMD.DBO.

Using Step IVward

With dBASE III+, many users developed applications for their dBASE databases with Clipper, FoxBASE+, or Quicksilver. Performance improvements and features made these languages seem attractive. You may now want to take applications written in these dialects and run them under dBASE IV. The Step IVward product allows you to make this transition.

Step IVward can be executed from the DOS prompt along with your specification for the dialect used in the original program and in most cases can completely translate your application to dBASE IV. It can also use a menu structure that allows you to customize the feature set used in the translation. For a large application you can have Step IVward process all the procedure files and UDFs used in the application with a file-tree processing option. The code from your original application program can be retained as comments in the converted program.

Although Step IVward does an excellent job when translating the various dialects to dBASE IV, you should not plan to run the converted program without printing it and looking at it carefully. A few surprises like a missing space or two or an incorrectly converted syntax may be encountered.

Table 18-2 StepIVward Parameters

Parameter	*Selection*
/S2	Output file
/S3	Programmer
/S4	Copyright
/O1	Suppress file header
/O2	Suppress file footer
/O3	Process files tree
/O4	Prompt before every file
/O5	Use existing code as comments in new program file
/P1	Printer
/T1	Suppress display

Starting Step IVward

If you copy your Step IVward files to the STEP subdirectory, you can activate this subdirectory and type **step filename parameters**. Filename is the name of the file containing the source code in Clipper, Quicksilver, or Foxbase+. You must include the filename extension and follow the filename with /c, /f, or /q. These parameters tell Step IVward what type of file you are providing and are easy to interpret since they use the first letter of the dialect you are translating. The remaining parameters can specify information like the output filename or to control the display during translation. These options are summarized in Table 18-2.

When the translation is finished you want to review the contents of WARNING.TXT. You can use a text editor or the DOS PRINT or TYPE commands to review this file. This file contains all the error and warning messages generated along with program names and line numbers.

Using the Menu System

Another option is entering **step** and selecting options from the menu shown in Figure 18-8. The Setup menu allows you to enter the name of

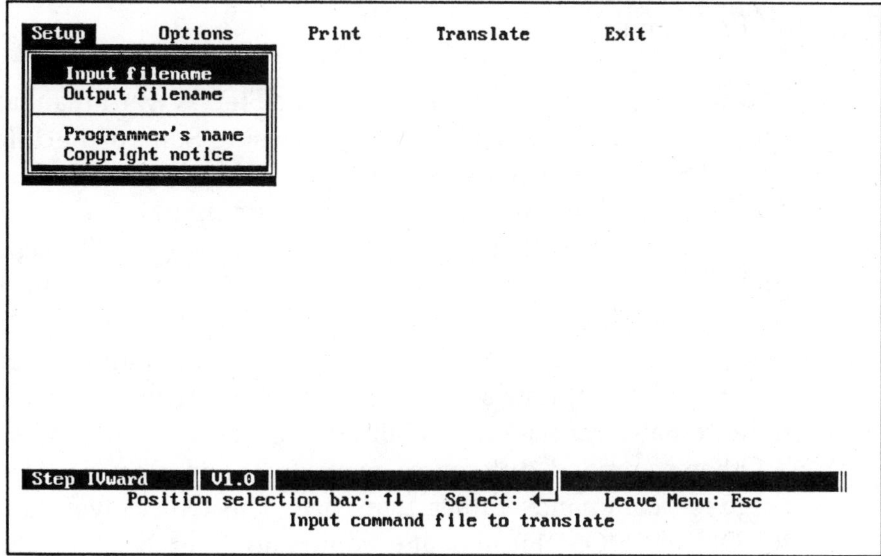

Figure 18-8 Step IVward initial screen

an input and output file as well as the name of the programmer and a copyright notice. The latter two entries are added as comments in the code. The options menu allows you to determine whether comments are added at the beginning and end of the program. If you choose to use a header, the file name, the programmer name, and the copyright notice will appear in this section. The file footer is a conversion comment with a time stamp. The Process files tree and Prompt before each file choice in the Options menu are used together. Setting the Process files tree to Yes causes dBASE to process all the files called by your main program. If you choose to prompt before each file, dBASE displays a message allowing you to decide if you want to translate the file or skip it. The last option allows you to decide if you want to use the original source code lines as comments in the translated file.

The Print menu has a Printer option that you can set OFF or ON. The remaining three selections, Control of printer, Output options, and Destination, activate submenus that provide features similar to the print options from within dBASE.

The Translate menu allows you to select from the Clipper, Foxbase+, or Quicksilver language options. You can also choose to suppress the display of translated information to the screen during translation. The remaining translate option begins the translate process.

Potential Problems

You will want to take a close look at the Step IVward manual in the special section for the dialect that you are using. Some of the differences relate to size restrictions established by the various products and dBASE IV. As an example Clipper supports up to 250 work areas. In the unlikely event that you used that many, you will encounter a problem retrofitting the application to dBASE IV, which supports 10 work areas. Clipper supports as many as 1,028 fields per database whereas dBASE supports 255. Splitting a file into multiple databases may be an appropriate solution anyway but it requires work beyond the automatic translation capabilities.

Other command differences relate to the implementation of the language commands rather than size. The Quicksilver statements *QSON and *QSOFF and any command lines between them are changed to comments in the dBASE IV file. Window support in Quicksilver and dBASE is dramatically different, causing Step IVward to add an array to the translated code. Clipper allows nested macros and @ SAY statements that reference locations off the screen with neither of these features supported in dBASE IV.

The key to a successful translation is a careful review of the translated code followed by adequate testing of the new modules. For most modules you will be pleased with the ease of the conversion and find that your new system runs correctly with few changes.

PART VI

Networking

CHAPTER 19

Migrating From Single-User Applications to a Network Application

Early microcomputer database applications were developed to support single-user applications. If shared data resources were required the user turned to a minicomputer or mainframe solution. Since microcomputers were not in the mainstream of computing solutions in their early years, this did not impose serious restrictions. Now companies both large and small have incorporated microcomputers and their associated database tools as integral parts of their business solutions.

In this chapter you will look at the limitations of stand-alone database solutions. You will also learn about some of the factors you need to consider when deciding to migrate to a network solution. Last, you can see how the change affects the end users of your system with one of the most popular network solutions.

Limitations of Stand-Alone Systems

As microcomputers proliferated in small business, some companies began to develop applications that shared resources with single-user systems. Using a series of single-user systems without a shared-data resource to solve a business need that requires shared data cannot achieve optimal results. A look at two hypothetical situations in an insurance agency operation can show you some of the problems with this method of operation.

Dividing the Work Logically

In situation 1, the agency clients are divided alphabetically. Jane handles all matters for clients whose last names begin with the letters A through F, George maintains the data for clients whose last names begin with G through P, and Mary handles Q through Z. Three different databases are created. Although the databases use the same structure, each database only contains the information for the clients of interest to each employee. Figure 19-1 is a diagram of the data organization and some of the system inputs and outputs.

In one sense there is no problem with this arrangement since it is always clear on which machine to find the client data. Mary adds new client information for Paul Taylor, and George handles an inquiry concerning auto coverage for Sally Harris. Management reports are a problem since daily collections are recorded on three machines. Lapsed policy reports also come from three machines. Not one of the three machines has enough disk capacity to contain the detail records of the other two machines, so it is impractical to consider running the reports against a backup copy stored on one of the machines.

Data backups must be run against all three machines. Since separate client files are maintained on all three machines, the loss of the data on one machine would mean the loss of a third of your database.

Hardware sharing is often impractical on stand-alone systems. Both George and Mary like to use the laser printer attached to Jane's machine for client correspondence, since it produces higher-quality output than the laser printers attached to their machines. Other than at lunch break, they usually use their own printers to avoid interrupting Jane's activities. Since the cost of laser printers is significantly higher than dot matrix printers, it is impractical to purchase two more laser printers.

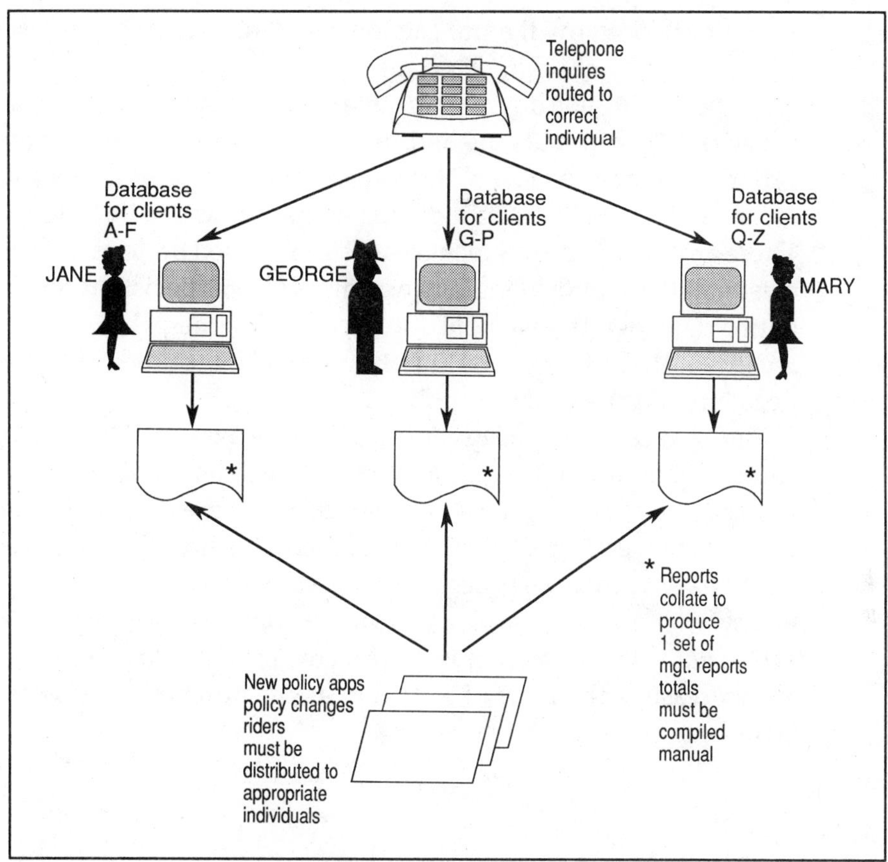

Figure 19-1 Database split alphabetically

Maintaining a Master Database with Separate Transaction Files

In another insurance agency, the situation is different since they have enough space on one system to maintain the entire client file. It is impossible for all of the clerical personnel to schedule sufficient time on this machine to add new clients and to make inquiries about existing clients. For this reason, Jerry handles all inquiries by checking the master file. If the master file does not provide sufficient information, Jerry checks to see if a transaction for the inquiry was entered into one of the other systems but has not as yet updated the master file. Also

Jerry does not know if a transaction is entered but not processed for a client except by checking each machine.

At the end of each day, a program processes the batch of transactions collected on each machine and updates the master file. Although the program processes most of the transactions, the program produces an error report that lists the incorrect transactions it could not process. These errors include payment requests on lapsed policies, adding to an existing policy, and changing an address on a nonexistent policy. If the entire database is available for each clerk when the transaction is recorded, these errors would not occur since the clerk would resolve problems as they occur.

Figure 19-2 shows the organization of the data and the resolution of some problems from the first situation, such as the lack of one set of reports; but new problems have surfaced. There is at least a one-day delay in processing all claims since their validity is not verified until all the transactions are processed. The work load is more balanced since any worker can process any transaction, but an inquiry about a transaction not yet processed must be directed to multiple people. Consider the increase in the level of difficulty as the number of users grows to 10 or 50.

Advantages of a Network Solution

Although there are many more arrangements that can be considered for the insurance agency operation just discussed, it is useful to contrast the two existing arrangements with a network solution.

In this third situation, the client master file is stored on a network file server that manages all of the data, and access is provided by the application program for each user. The laser printer is attached to the file server system and all network output is routed to the file server printer unless otherwise directed. Figure 19-3 provides a diagram of the inflows and outflows for the network system.

Although the machine functioning as the file server in this example has more file storage space than the machines in earlier examples, this is not a requirement. If 20MB of disk space can practically store all of

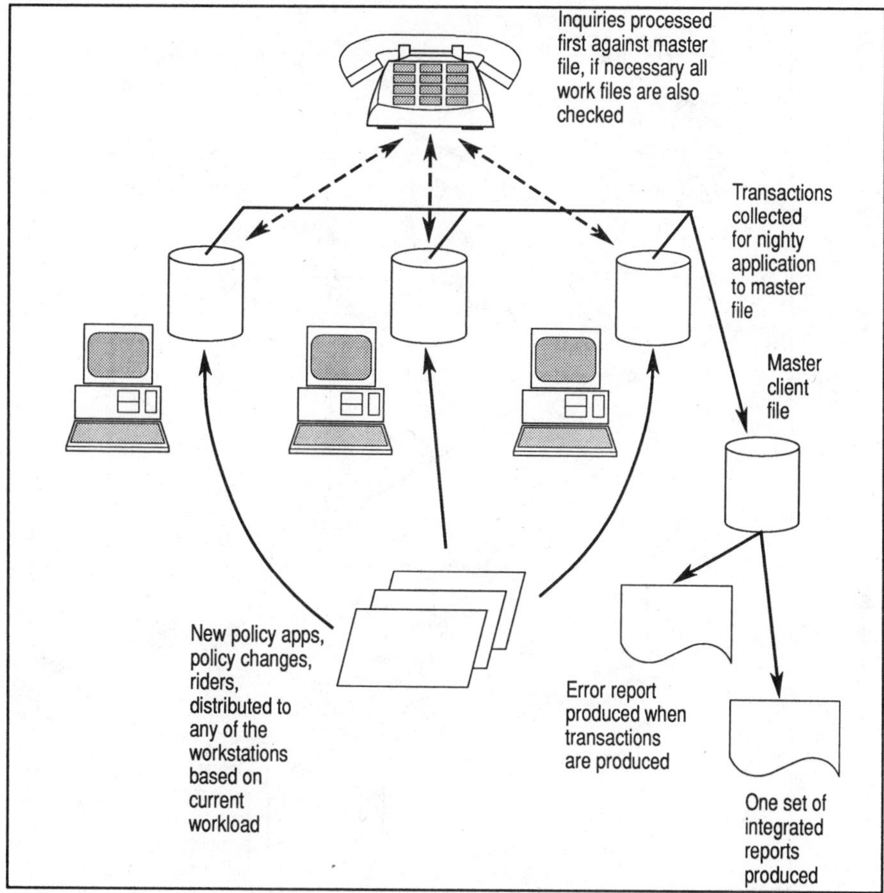

Figure 19-2 Batching transactions

the data your network needs, it is not a requirement that the network has more. Also, note in the network diagram that diskless work stations are permitted. Some of the cost of a larger hard disk may be offset by the ability to buy low-cost work stations without disk drives. This can provide better security since you can restrict access to one system by securing the file server and making it unavailable after hours. You also only have to back up one system and know that you are protecting all of the company's important information.

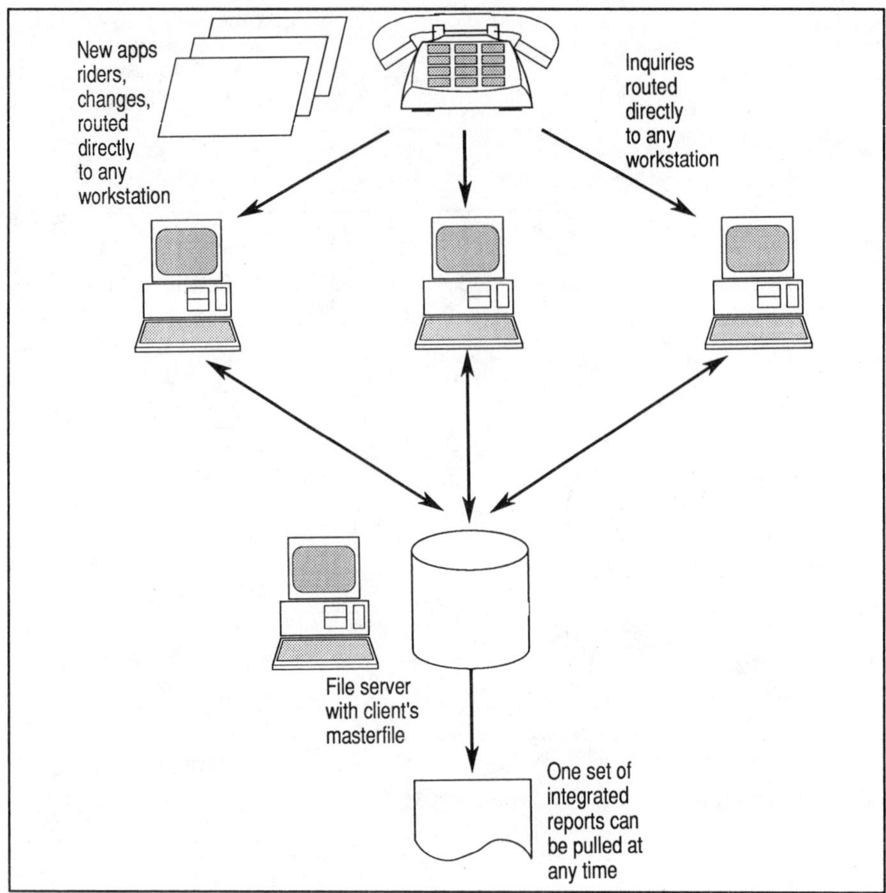

Figure 19-3 Network system

Network Terminology

Networks are really not all that difficult to comprehend. There are some new terms that pertain to both hardware and software options. With so many sophisticated file storage and data transmission concepts, it is not important to understand all the details. At this point you want to understand that network vendors offer a variety of network hardware and software products. You want to know some of your options and their differences. Once you know some of the basics, you will feel comfortable exploring more of thee details in articles in computer magazines, books on networking, and vendor literature.

Network Components

A network is nothing more than a group of computers linked together to share resources. Through these computers, users can also communicate with each other through the network links.

The building blocks of a network are computers or work stations, special network software, network cards inserted in each machine on the network, and some type of cabling to link the machines together. The computers on the network do not need to be identical. At least one of the computers is a file server and uses its hard disk to store network programs and shareable data. Given a variety of computers to work with, you usually want to select the machine with the greatest disk capacity and fastest clock speed as the file server.

The network software is the heart of the system, processing work sheet requests and ensuring the security of the network and the integrity of your data. This software is separate from the operating system that you run;it intercepts operating system requests and directs them to DOS or another operating systems that you use.

A variety of network cards and cabling solutions with multiple options are often offered by the same vendor. The transmission medium is the term used to refer to the cabling option selected and may include options like coaxial cable, fiber-optic, twisted pair, or broadband. You do not need to focus on the transmission medium details since the network throughput, geographic distribution of the work stations, and other factors determine your network selection.

Disk Servers Versus File Servers

The file server approach has replaced the disk server concept with all the leading network vendors. Under the older disk server approach, work stations interfaced directly with the shared disk space on the network. Since disk server technology does not offer data integrity for multiuser database applications, it is not useful when building dBASE IV applications.

Network software is the key to the newer file server approach since this software manages all access to the shared disk space on the network. Each work station sends requests to the network software rather than directly to the disk, maintaining the integrity that is essential to database applications.

Dedicated Versus Nondedicated Servers

One of the decisions you must make before implementing a network is whether to opt for a dedicated or nondedicated file server. Some network solutions require a dedicated file server. Others require a dedicated file server to obtain the performance required to support requests made by the large number of work stations connected to the server. The cost of the dedicated server is offset by the transaction-processing time improvements experienced by every operator logged onto the network. With a large number of users, a small increase in performance can more than offset the cost of the dedicated server. A nondedicated server allows the network server to also perform as another work station. This option is more useful in small networks.

Network Topologies

The term topology refers to the network architecture, or how the workstations are connected to the network. Architecture can describe in very specific terms the offerings of one network. It can also describe in generic terms some of the popular network topologies that have developed. Some network software is developed to fit with one particular topology, and other offerings can work with almost any configuration you have.

Another variable in local area networks (LANs) is the rules that control communications between the server and work stations. These rules are called protocols. Because the same combinations of topologies and protocols are used together so frequently many individuals think of them as inseparable, although they are not.

Each work station that is part of the LAN is a node. The structure that you choose does not determine the transmission medium since each architecture can use various options.

Structure Options The ring design is one of the leading network architectures. Network nodes are connected in circular fashion with this option. IBM's Token Ring network uses data packets with token headers to send data around the ring as shown in Figure 19-4. A network architecture using the star topology has a computer at its center with the various nodes all attached directly to the computer at the center, forming a configuration like the one shown in Figure 19-5.

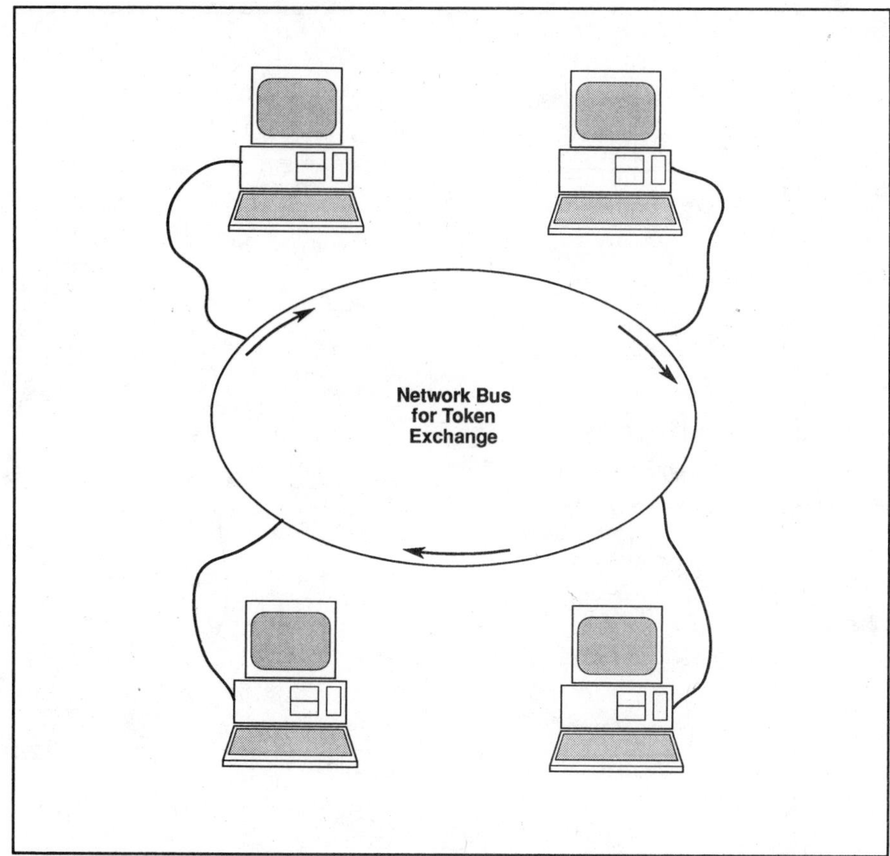

Figure 19-4 IBM Token Ring topology

You can use bridges to connect two networks. The networks may use the same communication method and may need to support the same transmission media and addressing structure. Novell's NetWare product allows you to vary the latter two options, linking a network using the RX-Net addressing structure with RG/62 coaxial cable and a network using the Ethernet addressing structure and RG/58 coaxial cable.

The Ethernet structure was originally developed at Xerox. The file server connects to the nodes along a single bus structure with terminators at each, as shown in Figure 19-6. ARCNET is another topology developed by Datapoint, a computer manufacturer. The file server and

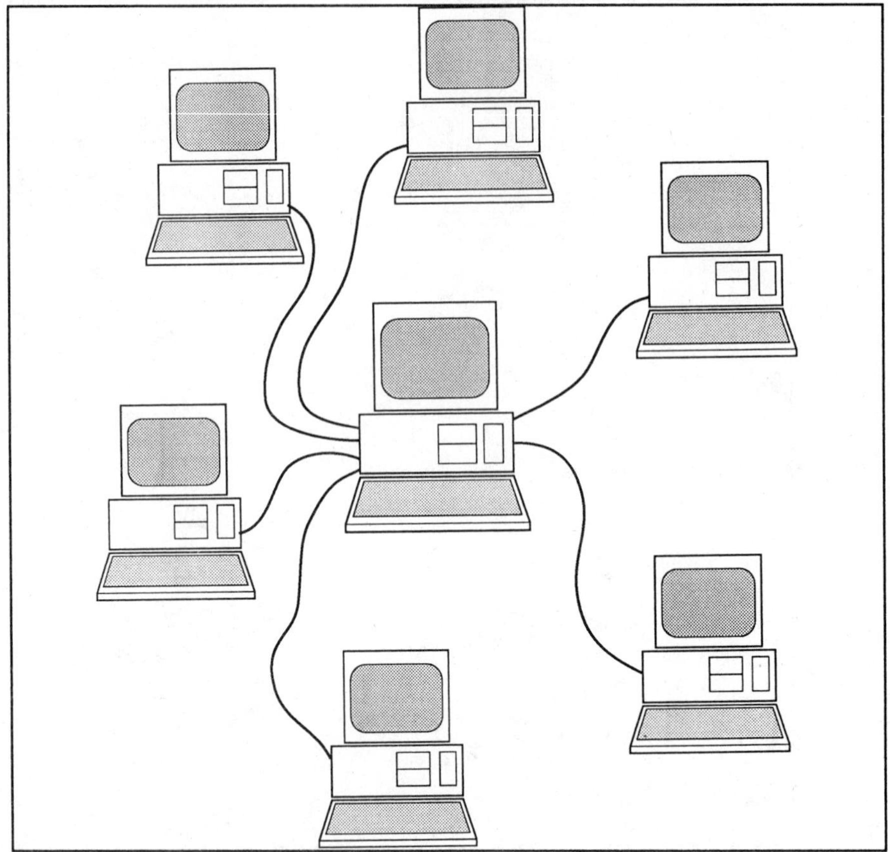

Figure 19-5 Star topology

each of the nodes are connected to a central passive hub as shown in Figure 19-7.

Bridges Bridges are either internal to the file server or external in one of the work stations. Like a dedicated file server, a work station dedicated to serving as a bridge is known as a dedicated bridge. Since network signals become distorted as they travel beyond the cable limitations of the network, networks can use local and remote bridges. Local bridges operate within the cable limitations of the network. Remote bridges connect networks in different locations for limited transmissions with the assistance of a medium like a telephone line.

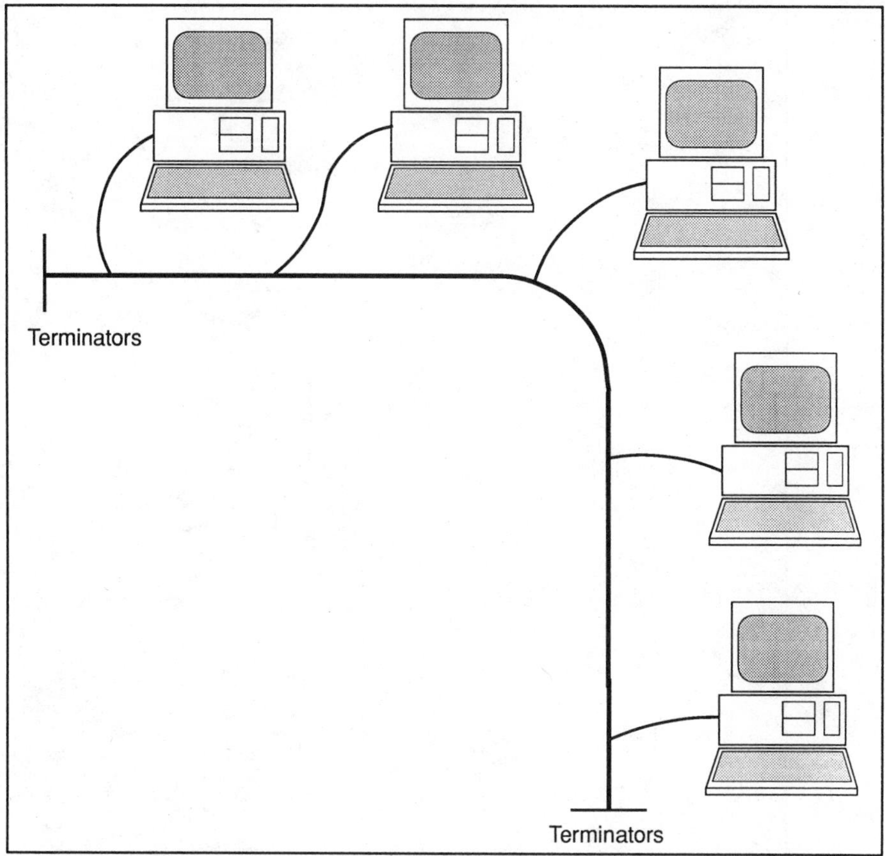

Figure 19-6 Ethernet topology

Network Vendors

There are a variety of network vendors at the manufacturing and retail levels. To run dBASE IV on a network, you want to focus your attention on the IBM Token Ring, 3COM 3+, Novell Netware 286, and Ungermann-Bass Net/One network software offerings. Although dBASE IV can run on other networks, Ashton-Tate provides installation support for the offerings mentioned. A variety of vendors supply the required hardware cards to implement one or more topologies that can meet you needs. You can use the one-stop shopping approach and get guaranteed support regardless of the problem or you can shop around for the cheapest price.

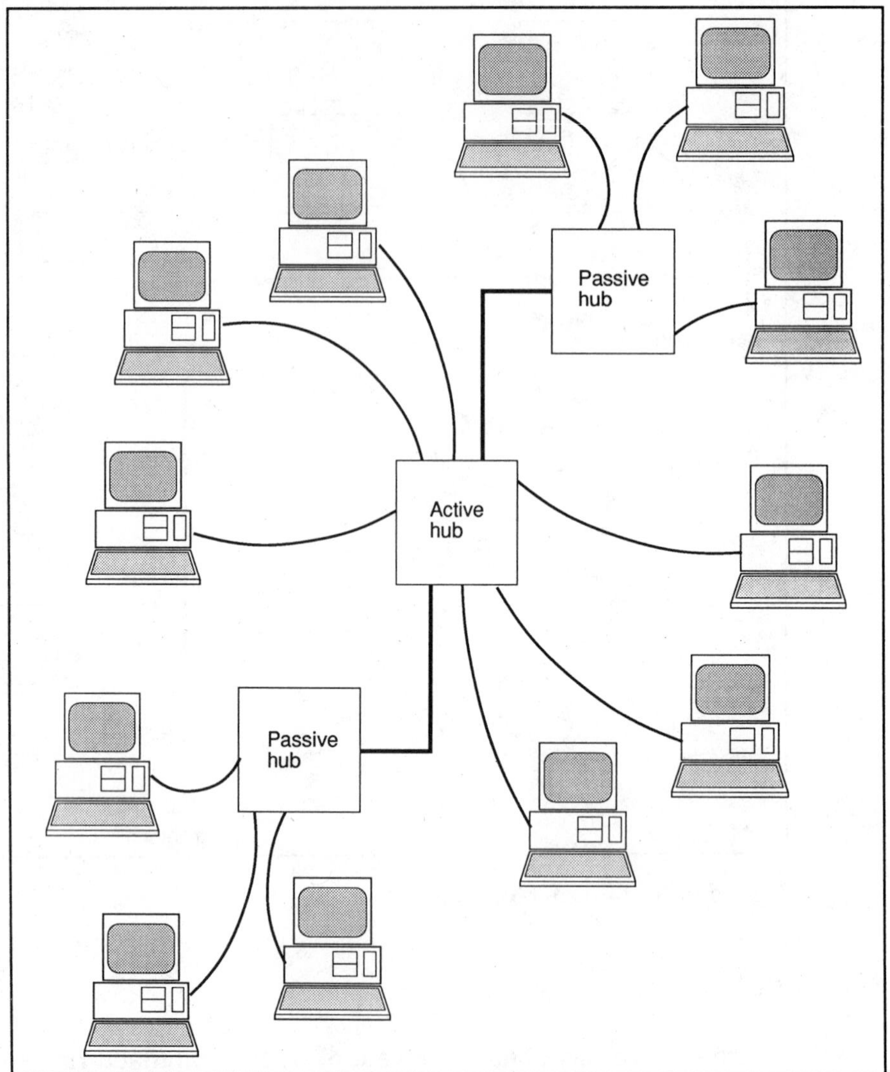

Figure 19-7 ARCNET topology

As you look at the network vendor options, you want to insure that the vendor can provide installation support for hardware, network and systems software and applications, some training for the supervisor, and possibly a brief training session for users. These services cost more than the equipment but offer economical solutions to make the network operational quickly.

Assessing Your Needs and Readiness for a Network

You had an opportunity to analyze user needs for a specific application in earlier chapters. Determining whether or not a local area network is beneficial in your situation requires that you make a similar assessment.

Assessing Improvements a Network Can Provide

The first step is to consider the improvements that you want to implement. List the improvements and mark the ones that a network will help. The beginning of the chapter presented two situations where networks provide several benefits such as avoiding duplicate data, integrating reports, preventing the need to batch transactions to apply against the master, reducing the potential for the use of the wrong disk, securing the data from unauthorized users, and reducing hardware costs by sharing such hardware as high-quality printers, plotters, and individual hard disks.

Current Software Usage

If your initial assessment indicates significant benefits from a network, you want to continue your evaluation. Although dBASE IV is available for networks, what about the other packages that you use, like a word processor or an accounting system? If necessary, you may need to decide if you are willing to switch packages or continue to use the existing packages in single-user mode. Although you can justify a network for dBASE IV applications alone, you want to know all your options during this assessment phase. You can put together a budget for the project that includes all requirements rather than requesting additional funding after implementation.

You must determine the number of users that will use each network application. You can create a chart that lists each program and develop applications to facilitate the data collection process. You also need to estimate how much file space each user will require on the server to determine the disk space requirements for the server.

Creating a Hardware Inventory

You next step is to determine which existing computer systems would become a part of the network. You need to create an inventory containing every system that would become a part of the network. You need to record specifics on each machine including, the primary user's name and phone number, the location, make, model, type of monitor, the amount of memory, and the existing applications on the system. In some cases, IBM compatibles have been compatible in a single-user environment but, due to subtle differences between their ROMs and NETBIOs, they may not be fully compatible when installed on the network. In selecting network cards, it is important to have the specifics on each machine to insure that the required support is available.

You may want to use one of your existing systems as the file server or may choose to purchase another computer or a specialized file server. To help in this determination, list the clock speed and disk space of the machines you are considering for a file server.

You will want to inventory all of the output devices that will be part of the network. You may want to use some of the slower devices such as printers for specific work stations. High-speed devices like laser printers are ideal for print servers on the network. If the manuals for these devices are available, the manuals probably contain the throughput information.

❏ **Tip: An uninterrupted power supply may be required.**

Some network software requires a power supply to supply uninterrupted power to the network if the normal power supply fails. Even if your network software does not require one, you may want to budget the required $800 – $1,200 to purchase one. With the importance of the centralized file server data, you want to have some time to close open files to prevent losing data and to shut the network down.

Geographic Dispersion of the Work Stations

A geographical chart to lay out the network is important. On this chart, you need to show the approximate planned distances between work stations. If you are dealing with a network on multiple floors or in a different building, these factors must be noted. If your building is already wired for network support, you will want to find out the specifics about the transmission media. These are factors that affect the transmission media and topology for the network.

The bridging concept mentioned earlier can help link networks that are physically too far apart for the transmission medium. It can also link two related groups that only need to communicate occasionally.

Making your Selection

If your evaluation indicates that a network offers benefits for your applications, you need to begin to plan the cost. The network solution chosen needs to reflect the company's business plan. A small business that expects to grow rapidly may need a network that offers a low entry cost with the ability to upgrade as the company expands.

You will want to evaluate the options offered by several vendors. You can use some of the information gathered in your evaluation to prepare a request for proposal (RFP) stating both specific application requirements and general needs. After identifying local vendors for several network products, you can provide a copy of your RFP to them to help them offer the best network solution.

If you have never had a network, you probably are only interested in options that provide full support for the installation process and the required fine-tuning that is required.

Changes from a User Perspective with Novell Netware

Although the changes a user experiences are similar for most networks, each network offers different levels of sophistication, quality of user documentation, and other network features. The Novell Advanced NetWare product is used to provide a perspective of expected changes and the training that a network requires. The Novell Advanced NetWare is chosen as the example because of its large installed base of users, its full set of security features, and easy-to-use administrator interface. Novell is also able to offer both hardware and software support.

If you choose Novell for a network solution, Novell also offers an entry-level version. This entry-level system, ELS, is cheaper but can only connect up to 10 nodes. Other than a limitation on network work stations, ELS provides the same access to network utilities and security features as Novell's Advanced NetWare and SFT Advanced NetWare, with only a few exceptions that do not affect the end-user interface.

dBASE-Specific Information

Once the network is installed, the end users need training in several areas to run dBASE applications successfully. The user needs to know how to log in. Once the user logs in, the network becomes transparent. The first area does not differ from a user's needs in a single-user application since the application itself is still the most critical area where expertise is required. In addition to training the user how to use an application, you also want to introduce the user to the types of messages dBASE displays when a record or a file is unavailable. The user should understand the reason behind the message and how to respond when offered the option of retrying access. This is also the time to stress the importance of completing tasks that are started, since the uncompleted task may restrict someone else's access to incomplete information.

The network user needs to understand the security features of dBASE IV that are in effect. If you have been using the dBASE

❑ **Tip: Discourage users from using the dot prompt.**
Working from the dot prompt is riskier than working through an application, since you can access individual files and may wind up with noncurrent data.

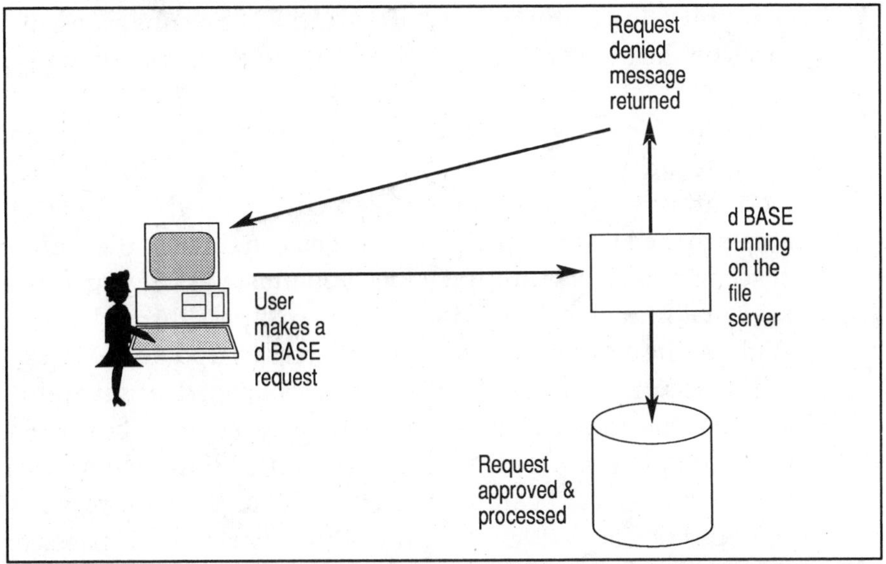

Figure 19-8 Protect determines data access

PROTECT command in a single-user environment, no transition is required. If PROTECT has not been used, the user needs to be taught the effect that PROTECT has on the activities the user performs. Figure 19-8 shows how PROTECT effectively locks a file or fields from access by an unauthorized user.

Depending on their access level the users may or may not have access to all files and fields. They may be able to read some files yet not update them. If they have any difficulty accessing information they feel they have a need to change, they should direct their inquiries to their supervisor or the network administrator. They need to understand the importance of not sharing their dBASE passwords with others.

Vendor-Specific Network Information

Once the network is installed, you want to allow a day or two training time for each network user. Part of this time is spent mastering the new network version of the application. Although you can probably run the existing dBASE applications on the network version of dBASE IV, you may want to add some enhancements. Perhaps you want to use the new dBASE IV menu features to create a full set of menus that drive the application features. Most of the application enhancements should focus on the networking features Novell and dBASE offer.

Security Novell's NetWare security supplements the file- and field-level security that can be implemented with dBASE PROTECT. NetWare offers various levels of file security allowing dBASE to control access to the files and specific fields. You can think of the various levels of security as doors through which you must pass. If you are given the keys that fit each of these doors you can to pass through any of them. Without the correct key you cannot access or update the data.

The security offered by NetWare is managed in several different ways. At the access level there is login or password security. Each user has a unique password. Each person must know that system access with this password can be tracked and that they are responsible for activities performed to discourage their sharing their password with others. At this level, the supervisor can also restrict access to certain times of the day or add an accounting system that limits a user's account. The user cannot successfully log in if the password is incorrect or other conditions necessary for their login are not met.

Depending on organizational rules, a user may be required to change passwords periodically or to use a minimum-length password. Even if it is not required, it is recommended. Making several repeated mistakes may lock your account on the server. This option prevents unauthorized access and requires that you contact the network administrator to correct the problem.

The next level of Novell security features are trustee assignments. Users are assigned these as a group or as an individual. These assignments permit the user read, write, open, create, delete, search, and file modification rights to the files in a directory. Another trustee assignment, parental, allows the user to create, delete, or rename subdirectories. The user only has the trustee assignments the network supervisor establishes, and only if the directory rights established for the individual directory are not more restrictive.

Directory rights take precedence over trustee assignments. Like trustee assignments, they apply to all the files in a directory and let a user perform the same file actions. Directory rights apply to all users.

A user's effective file rights are a combination of the trustee assignments and the directory rights. To have the effective rights to read a file within a specific directory, you need to have the key to read the file provided with trustee assignments, and the directory containing the file must have Read as one of its directory rights. One without the other does not provide effective rights to the action.

File attributes can further limit effective rights. Novell sets file attributes using the menu driven FILER command. If a file has a read-only attribute, the file cannot be modified even with the appropriate trustee assignments and directory rights. Most of the network files are shareable, which allows multiple users to use the same file at once. If a file is nonshareable, it can only be used by one user at a time.

Messages Users need to know how to send messages to other network users. While electronic mail packages can send lengthy messages that the recipient can view when they log in or at another time, you may need to send a short message to a user quickly. This capability is useful when you are trying to gain access to a file or field that another user controls. If your need to make the update is urgent, you may wish to send a message to the other user regarding your needs. Either SESSION or SEND can send a message to a user or a group. Regardless of the method chosen, the message can contain up to 40 characters.

To distribute a message with SESSION follow these steps:

1. Type **SESSION** at the DOS prompt and press ENTER.
2. Select User List from the Available Topics options. Highlight the user name and press ENTER or use F5 to mark several users before pressing ENTER.
3. Choose Send Message from Available Options and press ENTER. Type the message and press ENTER.

Your message appears at the bottom of the user's screen unless the CASTOFF command was executed to prevent messages. The message remains on the screen until the user presses CTRL-ENTER.

You can use the SEND command to distribute a message to a user or a group that is currently logged onto the network. The SEND command is not menu driven so you must know the correct user or group name. The format of the command is **SEND "message" TO USER User1** or **SEND "message" to GROUP Everyone.**

Utilities Just as many users can work with computers for years with only minimal knowledge of DOS commands and utilities, many network users rely on the expertise of others for the few occasions when they need to use a network utility for a task such as canceling a print request.

If you are in charge of planning the training curriculum for new network uses, you should provide each user with a basic toolkit of network utility features and commands for practice in a classroom environment and to master. As a starting point you want to introduce users to the USERLIST command that lists the users on the network. The SYSCON utility Group Information option serves a similar purpose for defined groups. Users are also allowed to look at a list of group members for any group of which they are a member.

Unless the Supervisor has set up the network to not let the user change their password with the login option, a user should know how to modify their NetWare password. In the area of security, a user should know how to use the FILER Utility or the FLAG command to change the file attributes for their own files.

With a package like dBASE, where print requests are handled directly between dBASE and the print spooler for the network, a user only needs to know how to check the print queue and cancel a request. These printer queue features are handled with the PCONSOLE menu-driven utility. This utility can print output files from other programs that cannot print to the network. The COPY and MAP commands are two additional NetWare commands that you want the user to understand.

As a final step, you might introduce the ability to create login scripts that the network performs after the user logs on. Only a small percentage of users are likely to avail themselves of the opportunity to create these files. The percentage of users who elect to create their own login script is approximately the same number that choose to create their own batch files for DOS. Just making users aware of how to create them eliminates some of the mystery and makes users feel more comfortable with this new thing called a network.

CHAPTER 20

dBASE Network Installation and Administrative Tasks

Before you can install dBASE on a network, you must install the network itself. This means that you have to insert network cards in your computers and attach cabling linking them together. You must also install the network software on the file server.

There are several variables in this process that depend on the network software selected, the network cards chosen, and the topology for your network. Because of the many variations and the dealer often includes these tasks in the price of the network, they are not covered here.

If you plan to start from scratch and install the network yourself and then follow it with dBASE installation, you need to allow adequate time. If this is a first-time network installation, several days is not unreasonable. You might be lucky and need less but it is better to plan for the unexpected. The Novell documentation is thorough and well-written if you select this alternative; however, there is quite a bit of it.

If network installation is "old hat" to you, much less time is needed. The total time from start to finish to install the advanced NetWare product on a network of 5 to 10 work stations requires less than half a day, assuming that you are familiar with the process and do not run into difficulties you have never encountered before. In installing the network on System 2 Model 60 and 70 work stations several unexpected problems occurred that were not encountered on similar networks with different computer models. The availability of network support from a dealer or direct Novell support can be invaluable. A question posed to someone who has traveled the exact path before saves countless hours of time and frustration.

This chapter assumes that you have installed the Novell NetWare on your system and are ready to install dBASE. All the steps you need, including administrator functions to set up trustee assignments and logon scripts, are included in this chapter. Since these commands are specific to Novell, the beginning of the chapter is only of use to Novell users. A summary of the requirements for several other popular networks are also included.

The later part of the chapter covers dBASE-specific administrator tasks. You will learn how to implement the security features of the dBASE package to provide adequate protection for the investment you have made in your database environment. You will also learn how to interface with the Novell print spooler and learn other characteristics that change when you use dBASE on a network.

Installing dBASE on a Novell Network

Although there are differences from network to network, many of the basic steps are the same. The specific instructions in the next few sections are for a Novell Advanced NetWare network. This network uses logical drive F on the file server as the network drive. You will see in the following example that you can assign disk-drive letters to physical subdirectories on the file server disk.

Prior to Installing dBASE

Before you are ready to install dBASE on a Novell Advanced network, there are several housekeeping tasks that you must complete if you want to experience correct results. You must decide what actions users can perform on each of the dBASE directories and direct the network where to look for dBASE files. Since dBASE cannot create directories on the Novell network during installation, you must create these directories before beginning.

Trustee assignments allow you to determine the actions that the network will allow a user to perform on the file in a directory. Trustee assignments are made with the Novell NetWare command GRANT or with the Novell network utility SYSCON. In this chapter you will learn how to perform the task with SYSCON. SYSCON can handle other required tasks that you need to perform in this preliminary stage, such as creating groups, creating subdirectories, and creating login scripts to direct where the network looks for files.

Using SYSCON Once Novell NetWare is installed on your file server the SYSCON utility is available. It is easy to use and the tasks you need to perform are well documented in the Novell manuals. To use the SYSCON program, log in as the SUPERVISOR. Then enter SYSCON from the F prompt. Your screen looks like Figure 20-1.

Using SYSCON to Add Groups The first step is adding a group for the dBASE users. Select Group information from the menu. Like most screens in the SYSCON program, you can add a new entry, like a group, by pressing INS. After you complete dBASE's prompt for the new group name by typing the group name and pressing ENTER, SYSCON adds it to the list of existing groups.

Using SYSCON to Add Subdirectories SYSCON can create subdirectories as you add trustee assignments to a group. The DOS command MD can also create subdirectories on the file server but SYSCON is easier since you can create subdirectories as you add trustee assignments. To assign a directory to the group, press ENTER to select the

Tip: Create a group for all dBASE Users.

Creating a group for all dBASE users makes it easier to assign privileges to dBASE users and prevent non-dBASE users from accessing dBASE data or program files. Once you install dBASE you can further limit the options for any of the users by restricting their individual privileges. Individual privileges take priority if they are more restrictive.

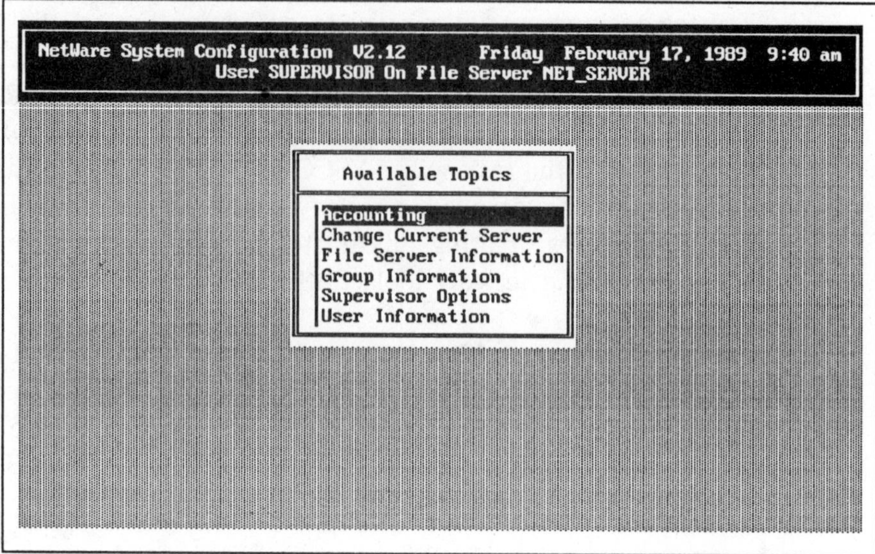

Figure 20-1 Using SYSCON

dBASE group and display a menu box for the group. Select Trustee assignments to display the box in Figure 20-2. Add a subdirectory by pressing INS. dBASE lets you select the network and volume if you have multiple options for either. Press ENTER twice if you only have one of each to select the NET_SERVER/SYS: combination. After you select the network and volume, you can add a directory by pressing ESC and typing the name of the directory. If you are adding a subdirectory beneath an existing directory level, you must separate the directories with a slash (/) instead of a backslash (\).

To install dBASE, you need a DBNETCTL.300, DBASE, and DBASE/SQLHOME directory. You also need a DBASE/SAMPLES directory if you plan to copy the sample files. You will want another directory for your network dBASE files to separate them from the other network files. This chapter uses a DBASE/DB_APPL directory for applications. To add the directories required for dBASE follow these steps:

1. Press ENTER twice, press ESC, type **DBASE**, and press ENTER to create the DBASE subdirectory. Select Yes to confirm that you want to create this subdirectory.

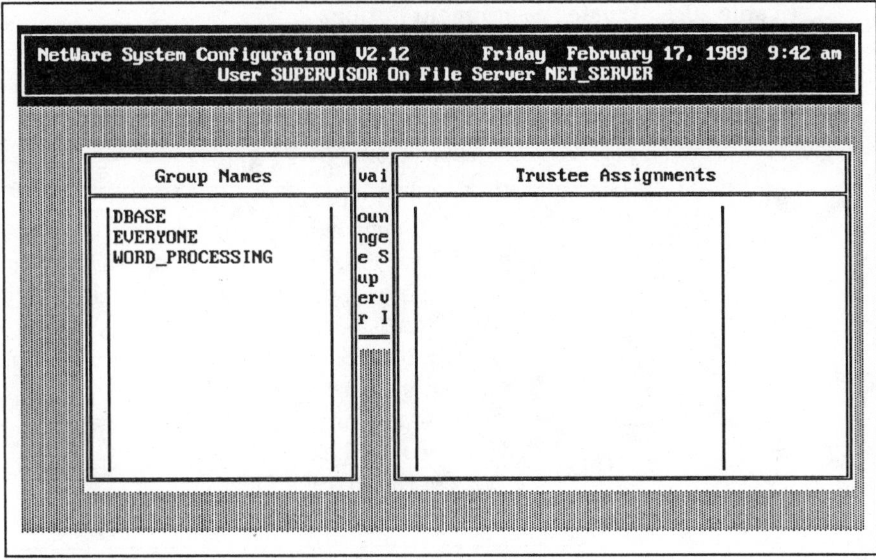

Figure 20-2 Trustee assignments

2. To create the SQLHOME directory in the DBASE subdirectory, press ENTER twice, press ESC, type **DBASE/SQLHOME**, and pressing ENTER. Once you press ENTER, you must select Yes when dBASE prompts you if you want to create the subdirectory.
3. Repeat step 2 for DBASE\SAMPLES and DBASE\DB_APPL.
4. Create DBNETCTL under the root directory by pressing ENTER twice, pressing ESC, typing **DBNETCTL.300**, and pressing ENTER to create the DBASE subdirectory. Select Yes to confirm that you want to create this subdirectory.

Once you create a subdirectory, you can add trustee assignments. The network assigns trustee assignments based on the root directory's trustee assignments for the group.

Adding Trustee Assignments Trustee assignments allow you to set the maximum privileges that a user or group of users has for any of the files in a directory. Further restrictions can be established for the directory, individual files, or users. Before a user's right for a directory is effective, the maximum rights mask for the directory must permit a user to have the specified rights.

Table 20-1 Trustee assignment options

CODE	*RIGHT*
C	Create and open new files.
D	Delete existing files.
M	Modify file attributes.
O	Open existing files.
P	Parental, which includes: Create, rename, erase subdirectories of the directory. Set trustee and directory rights in the directory. Set trustee and directory rights in its subdirectories.
R	Read from open files.
S	Search the directory.
W	Write to open files.

Using a group for making the assignments is much faster than adding assignments for individual users. If you add stricter limitations for users in the group by making individual assignments, these are also in effect.

Trustee assignment options are represented by letters. Table 20-1 lists each of the potential trustee assignments.

Since the menu is still active to add trustee assignments all you need to do is highlight the directory for which you want to add trustee assignments, for the group and press ENTER. SYSCON displays a box listing the current trustee assignments. To add trustee assignments, press INS. Highlight a trustee assignment that you want to add and press ENTER to add a single trustee assignment. To add multiple trustee assignments, highlight each trustee assignment you want to add and press F5. After selecting each trustee you want to add, press ENTER. To remove a trustee assignment, highlight it on the list of current trustee assignments and press DEL. You can return to the list of the directories and the current trustee assignments by pressing ESC.

The completed trustee assignments for the dBASE group are shown in Figure 20-3. All of these trustee assignments are either required or strongly recommended. You can further limit each user's trustee assignments using the User information menu option in the opening

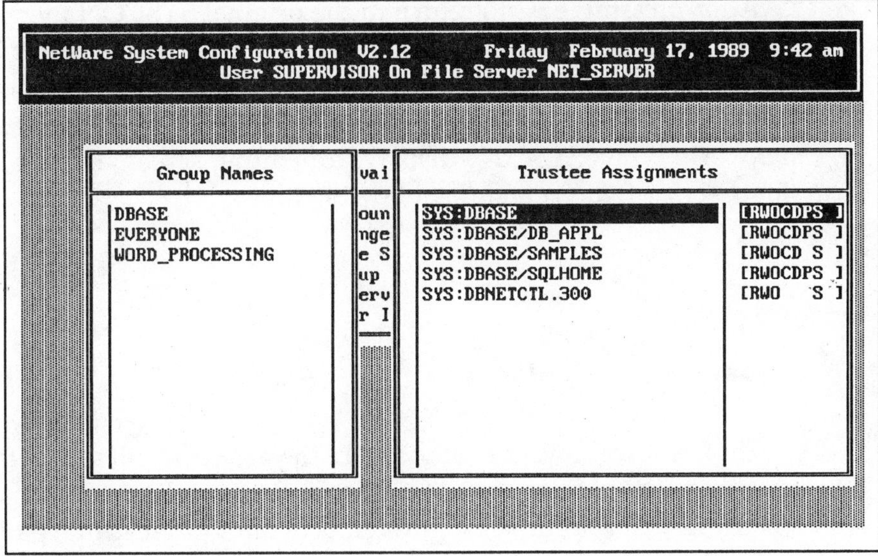

Figure 20-3 Completed trustee assignments for the dBASE group

menu. In the future, you can add trustee assignments for each subdirectory as you create the subdirectory.

Adding Users to a Group Once you press ESC to return to the menu displayed when you selected a group, you can use the Members list menu option to add or remove users from a group. To add a user, press INS and select the users who are not currently in the group, just as you added trustee assignments. You can remove a user by highlighting the user and pressing DEL. You can remove more than one by highlighting each one and pressing F5. After selecting the ones you want to remove, press DEL.

Creating a Login Script Once you add the directories and trustee assignments, you can add network commands that will execute every time a user logs in by placing them in a login script. You can create both system login scripts and individual user login scripts. Only the supervisor or someone with the same authority can create a system login script. Each user or the supervisor can create a user's login script. A system login script executes and displays before an individual user's login script.

After pressing ESC to return to the original SYSCON menu, select Supervisor options and System Login Script. A login script is like the DOS AUTOEXEC.BAT file that executes whenever you boot DOS, except the login script performs or appears every time you log into the network. When SYSCON displays an editing screen and the current login script, if any, enter the following lines:

```
MAP S1:=SYS:PUBLIC
MAP S2:=SYS:DOS
MAP S3:=SYS:DBASE
MAP H:=SYS:DBASE/DB_APPL
```

The first three lines describe where the network will search for files. If your current login script contains the first two lines, do not include them again. If the current login script contains other search paths, you may need to increase the number for the DBASE directory to 4 or 5 by entering MAP S4 or MAP S5. The last line contains a logical disk-drive assignment that assigns drive H to the DBASE\DB_APPL directory. This drive assignment lets you select the directory by typing an H and a colon rather than entering the longer pathname. This feature of Novell networks provides an easy way to set the default directory for dBASE files. Once you enter the login script, press ESC to exit, and select Yes to save the login script. Then press ALT-F10 and select Yes to exit SYSCON.

Checking CONFIG.SYS After making the changes to the network, you need to check that the CONFIG.SYS file for each work station on the network has the statements FILES = 99 and BUFFERS = 15 statements. If CONFIG.SYS does not exist, you need to create one with a text editor or EDLIN and add these lines. If you have a copy without these lines, add them. Change the limits in the FILES and BUFFERS statements if they are lower than 99 and 15. Not including these statements restricts the number of files you can use at one time and may prevent you from completing certain dBASE tasks. If several work stations do not have a CONFIG.SYS file, you can create one copy and copy it to all the work stations that need it.

Installing dBASE

Once you prepare the network for dBASE, you are ready to install dBASE. The installation directions for the Novell network are provided. These instructions differ from the ones provided with the dBASE manuals to ensure better results. These instructions assume that you have not installed dBASE on the network before.

Installing dBASE requires several steps including registering the software, defining the hardware, and copying files to the network. Since the installation program only works from drive A, you must use the ASSIGN command if you need to install dBASE from another drive.

Registering the Software To install dBASE for the higher versions of Novell NetWare, you must register the software on a machine not connected to the network. When you enter INSTALL the program displays a copyright message. After you press ENTER, the program reads drive A. When dBASE finishes writing the information, it prompts for System Disk #1. After you replace the Install disk with System Disk #1, it prompts you for your name, the company name, and the serial number. For each of the three entries type the appropriate information. If you do not want to enter a company name, enter your name again. If you prefer, you can enter the company name for both the name and the company name. For the serial number, remove System Disk #1, type the number that appears on the disk label and replace the disk, making sure to close the disk door. Once you enter the correct information, press CTRL-END to save your entries. When the installation program prompts whether to proceed or exit, select Exit. Replace the System Disk #1 with the Installation disk and select Exit to DOS to return to DOS. The remaining installation steps must be performed on a machine connected to the network.

Specifying the Hardware Once the software is registered, you can select the default hardware. Log into the network and enter the INSTALL program again. When the INSTALL program is reloaded, it displays the hardware configuration box. For the moment, skip the multiuser selection. For the Display mode, select the display selection that most of the network work stations use. Skip the Optimize Color display unless most of the computers using the network display snow as you move the cursor. Since you can create individual CONFIG.DB files for each person on the network, the default settings specified here should contain the most common setting the work stations use to minimize the number of custom files required.

You only need to select the Printer menu option if the network server has it own printers. If the network has its own printers, select the printer name and printer model. For the printer device, select \\SPOOLER so the print output is sent to the file server's print spooler. The file server's print spooler receives print requests from all users and prints them. Since the print spooler holds the data it will print in temporary files on the file server, you do not have to wait until the network prints your output. Press CTRL-END when you select the last printer. Then select the default network server printer. Press CTRL-END to verify the hardware selections you made.

Copying dBASE Files To start copying the dBASE files, select Proceed to continue. When dBASE prompts for the directory for the dBASE files, type an **F** to change C:\DBASE to F:\DBASE and press ENTER. Press ENTER again to use F:\DBASE\SQLHOME as the directory for the SQL files. After the installation program performs other checks, like verifying the availability of 3.8M of disk space, dBASE prompts for you to insert a disk and press a key. Each time dBASE prompts for a new disk, insert the correct disk and press ENTER. dBASE will request the disks in order by the numbers that appear at the top of the disks.

When dBASE prompts for changing the AUTOEXEC.BAT and the CONFIG.SYS files, select Skip both times. Since you are using a network, you want to omit these changes.

After dBASE copies the system disks and prompts about changing the AUTOEXEC.BAT and CONFIG.SYS files, dBASE prompts you if you want to copy nonprogram files. For each of the selections select Proceed or Skip. If you select Proceed, insert the disk for the files you are copying and press ENTER. When you finish copying the files, insert the Installation disk and press ENTER. Select Exit to DOS and press ENTER. Place your dBASE disks in a safe place in case you experience a disk failure at a later time.

Preparing dBASE for a Network After you install dBASE for a single user, you are ready to make the changes required for a multiuser system. First, go to the DBASE directory in the network and delete the DBASE.EXE file. Next, create a DBASE.COM file by inserting the System Disk #1 into drive A and entering INSTALLH. When this program executes it asks for the drive containing the product, drive A, and the hard disk drive, drive F. When the A prompt returns, change to drive F. Enter DBSETUP and select Change hardware options. Change the No for the Multiuser menu option to Yes by pressing the SPACEBAR. After pressing CTRL-END to finalize the hardware settings, insert System Disk #2 in drive A and press a key.

Change the Default Drive Since you will probably want to keep the data files for the users separate from the dBASE program files, you will want to change the default file for dBASE files. Modify the CONFIG.DB file and select the Default option in the Files menu box. When dBASE prompts for a default drive, type the letter assigned to the dBASE application directory. For the DBASE\DB_APPL directory, it is drive H. This is the only change you need to make at this point to operate dBASE on a network. Once you make this change, you can exit DBSETUP.

Making dBASE Files Read-Only To protect the program files that are part of the dBASE package, you want to make them read-only. This prevents a user from deleting the dBASE program files. To make the

Tip: CONFIG.DB files.

An alternative to creating a CONFIG.DB file on the network is creating a CONFIG.DB file for each work station in the drive containing the dBASE files. If each work station has its own CONFIG.DB file, dBASE uses the CONFIG.DB file at the work station. Having a default CONFIG.DB file is a good idea in case a work station lacks a CONFIG.DB file. If the work station will use the network printer, one of the printer selections should be \\SPOOLER.

files read-only, enter **\DOS\ATTRIB +R *.***. This makes all of the files in the current dBASE directory read-only. If you need to modify a file, repeat the command changing the +R to a -R. For example, you would enter **ATTRIB -R CONFIG.DB** if you need to modify the CONFIG.DB file. You can also use the FILER network utility to change the file attributes.

Adding and Removing Users

To use the network version of dBASE, users need access to both dBASE and the network. A separate procedure is required for adding users to the Novell network and dBASE. Once users are added to both, they can use the dBASE programs at the same time as other dBASE users.

Adding Users to a Network and Adding Passwords Adding users to a network lets you define user names and passwords for each user. To add a user to a Novell Advanced network, you must use the SYSCON utility. When you select User information from the opening SYSCON menu, SYSCON displays a list of the available login names. To add a user, press INS. When SYSCON prompts for a user name, enter a user name and press ENTER. SYSCON replaces spaces in the user name with underscores that the user must type to login. Once you add a user, you can add other features such as passwords by selecting a user. To change a feature of the user's account select the feature you want to change. To change the password, highlight Change password and press ENTER. If the user already has a password, SYSCON prompts you for the existing password. Next, SYSCON prompts you for the new password. Once you enter the new password, SYSCON prompts you to enter it again to confirm your first entry. Another selection you make for the new user is the groups the user belongs to. To select the groups a user belongs to, choose Groups belonged to. The network automatically includes the EVERYONE group. To add a group, press INS and select the group you want to add. To remove a group, highlight the group you want to remove and press DEL. Once you finish the group assignments, you can use ESC to return to the previous or an earlier menu.

Adding Users to dBASE The number of users that you can add when you install dBASE on a network depends upon which version of dBASE you use. The Developer's Edition allows up to three users. Each Access Disk in a dBASE IV LAN Pack allows up to five users. To add a user to dBASE you must use the ADDUSER4 program. To use this program, enter **ADDUSER4**. When the program prompts for the drive letter containing the DBNETCTL.300 directory, type an **F**. When the screen for the Access Control Program appears, type a **1** to add a user. Insert the System Disk #1 from a Developer's Edition or the Access Disk from the LAN Pack. The program adds one user from the Developer's Edition or five users from the LAN Pack, up to the limit for each disk. To remove a user, type a **2** and insert the System Disk #1 from a Developer's Edition or the Access Disk from the LAN Pack. The program removes one user for the Developer's Edition or up to five users for the LAN Pack, as long as dBASE has more than one user. To list the number of users currently allowable for dBASE, type a **3**. dBASE displays the maximum number of users that can use dBASE at once. To leave the ADDUSER4 program, type a **4**. Adding a user with the ADDUSER4 program does not create security features. Adding a user increases the number of people who may use dBASE simultaneously.

Using dBASE IV Protection Features for Database Security

You have looked at some of the security that Novell can offer you as part of its NetWare features. You can supplement these options with additional security on a file and field level with dBASE IV protection features.

The dBASE security system is separate from the network security system. Combining the features of the dBASE security system and the Novell NetWare security provides the ultimate in flexible options that allow you to tailor the systems features to your exact needs for groups or individual users. Figure 20-4 is a diagram of how the network and dBASE security combine to select the data a user can read and modify. Both the database administrator and the network supervisor provide keys for the user to access data. These keys can be login names, passwords, access levels, and trustee assignments. The network provides account-level security, password-level security, directory

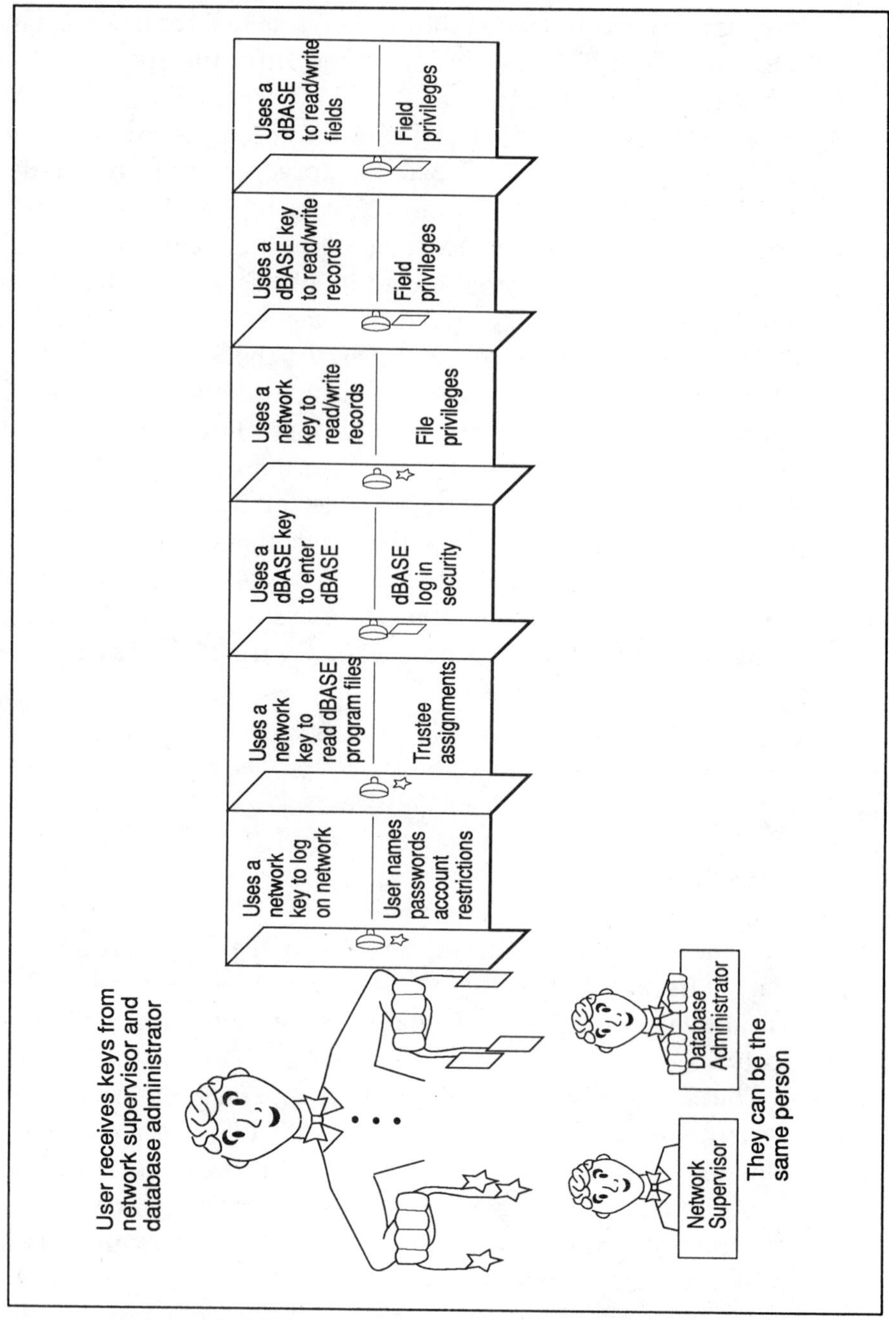

Figure 20-4 Combining security options from Novell and dBASE

security, file security, and internet security if you are bridging multiple networks. dBASE provides login security, file security, and field security.

You can use dBASE's PROTECT on a single-user or a multiuser system. You can use the PROTECT command to require users to log in with valid user names and passwords, encrypt files, and limit which files and fields a user can access. Once you use the PROTECT command, you will always use dBASE's security system.

The security features of Protect are hierarchical. The first level, login user names, passwords, and group names, is the most basic security system. Like other password systems, this security is only worthwhile when the passwords are confidential. After you establish the user names and passwords by developing user profiles, you can add files to groups and set file and field access to control the databases and fields accessed by certain groups of users. Finally, you can encrypt the databases that you have assigned to a group so only the users with the correct passwords can view the data.

Using PROTECT

To add dBASE's security system, you must use the PROTECT command. As a system administrator, you will establish a password that controls your access to PROTECT as well as later assigning different passwords to dBASE users. To use this command select Protect from the Tools menu or enter PROTECT from the dot prompt. dBASE prompts you for a password. This is the password that admits you into dBASE's security system. Enter a password of up to 16 letters and press ENTER. Using all 16 characters creates a password that is difficult for an unauthorized user to stumble upon and offers the maximum protection for encrypted files. It can contain up to 16 letters and numbers. It should not contain personal information that your colleagues might know, such as your pet's name or your middle name. The first time you enter PROTECT, you must enter the password that you will use to enter PROTECT later. Once you enter the password, dBASE prompts for you to reenter the password as confirmation. If the two passwords do not match, press ESC to leave PROTECT and reenter it again. If the two passwords match, dBASE enters the PROTECT screen.

When you enter PROTECT at a later time, dBASE prompts for the password. You must provide the same password you entered the first time to gain access to the security system. Since you cannot display the password once you save the information you enter with the PROTECT command, make sure that you store the password in a secure location such as in a locked drawer for which only you have the key. If you forget the password and do not have a copy of it, you cannot enter the PROTECT menus. Since you cannot change the password, you must store the password where only authorized users can access it.

Access Levels

dBASE's protection system combines three access levels to determine which file and fields a user can read or modify within a group. The first access level is defined when you create a user profile. The other two are defined when you define file and field privileges for a database using the Files menu. Within each group, a user has an access level from 1 to 8. The lower the number the less restrictions placed on the user. For example, you may want to assign a 3 to a user who must modify, delete, and add records and an 8 to a user who only needs to read the data.

The second type of access level is file privilege level. This access level is assigned to a file within a group. This access level contains four privileges. Privileges determine which access levels can read, modify, add, and delete records. The privilege access level sets the highest access number that has the file privilege. For example, if the access number for the Extend privilege (adding records) is 4, the user in the same group with an access level of 3 can add records but the user in the same group with an access level of 8 cannot.

The third type of access level is field access privileges. Each field is defined as FULL, R/O, and NONE for each user access level. FULL allows reading and modifying. R/O allows reading only. NONE omits the field as if it did not exist.

If you are new to database security, all this may seem like a lot to keep organized in your mind as you set down to make the appropriate entries. Without some type of worksheet to lay out file and file access, it is confusing for even experienced pros. Figure 20-5 shows a

File & Field Privileges Form

Filename:_________________ Directory:___________________ Drive:______

List the highest access level that can perform these operations:

- Look at the data: __________
- Modify existing data: __________
- Add new records: __________
- Delete records: __________

Enter a number between 1 and 8

For each access level, specify whether the field can be edited (Full), can be read (R/O), or is unavailable (None).

Access Level	1	2	3	4	5	6	7	8
<u>Fields:</u>								
SSN								
LAST_NAME								
M_INITIAL								
FIRST_NAME								
ADDRESS								
CITY								
STATE								
ZIP_CODE								
HOME_PHONE								
HIRE_DATE								
MARITAL_ST								
NUMB_DEPEN								
HR_RATE								
YTD_WAGES								
YTD_FIT								
HEALTH								
SKILLS								

Figure 20-5 Database security work sheet

worksheet that you may use for the EMPLOYEE file. The first part of the form identifies the file. You need to know the drive, directory, and filename to select the file in the PROTECT menus. The second part of the form identifies the file privileges access level for each of the file privileges. The options correspond to dBASE's READ, UPDATE, EXTEND, and DELETE file privileges. The third part of the form identifies the field privileges for each access level.

The field access levels can be limited by other access file levels and by the operating system or network. For example, if you set a file to be read-only using the network or the operating system, you cannot modify the data regardless of the access levels settings. Another example is that the field privileges can be limited by the file privileges. If a file's update, extend, and delete privileges are lower than a user's access level, the user cannot modify the data even if the field privileges are full. Figure 20-6 shows the steps dBASE evaluates to decide if a user in a group can modify the data in a field.

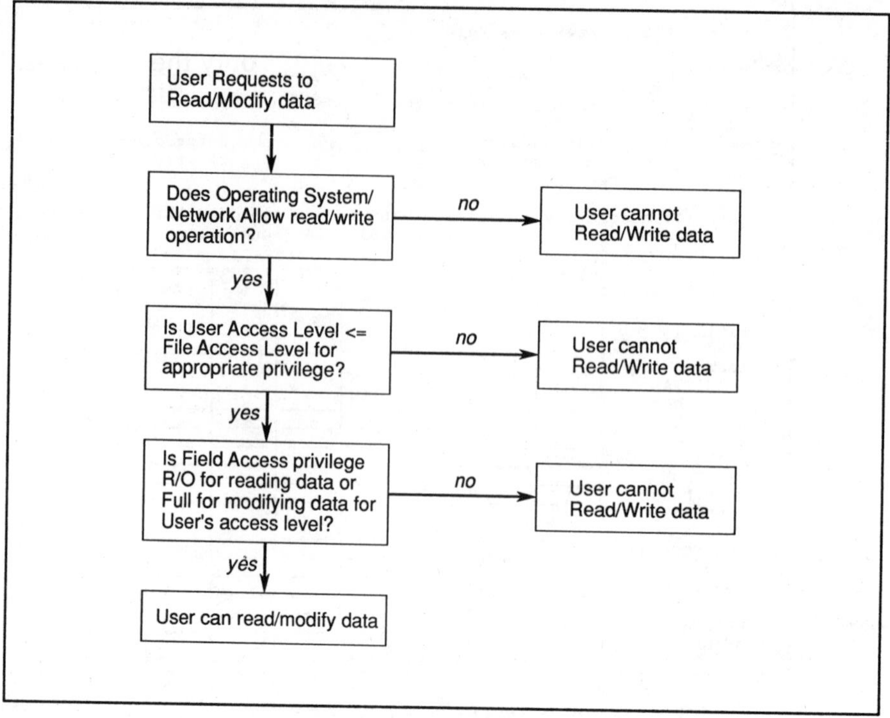

Figure 20-6 dBASE evaluation controlling access

Adding Login Security

Just as you can use login user names and passwords to control access to the network, you can also use user names and passwords to limit dBASE access. You can also divide the files and the users into groups and allow users logged in under a specific group to access only the files belonging to the group. Once you save the information you enter through the PROTECT menus, dBASE prompts for a login name, password, and group name every time you enter dBASE.

Assigning Users to Groups Before you add user profiles, you want to divide the users into groups. A user can belong to multiple groups by creating a user profile for the same user for each group to which the user belongs. A file can only belong to one group. A user can only access files that are assigned to the group the user entered when logging in. The most effective way to organize the users and files is by application.

For example, all of the files for a payroll application may be assigned to the PAYROLL group. In this example, only the users who need to use one of the payroll files have a user profile with a group name of PAYROLL. Since a user can only access data from one group at a time, all of the data files for an application must be in the same group. If a user needs to use files from different groups, the user must log out then log in again.

If you do not assign files to a group, the files can be accessed by any group. You may want to omit assigning files to groups if you only want to use the login feature of dBASE's security system.

Adding User Profiles You must add a user profile for each user who needs to enter dBASE. The login name, password, and group name are required. If you try saving an incomplete user profile, dBASE displays an error message telling you what is missing. All of the entries except Full name are converted to upper case. Using the Users menu shown in Figure 20-7, you must follow these step to add a user profile:

1. Press ENTER or type an **L** to select Login name. Enter up to eight alphanumeric characters and press ENTER.
2. Press ENTER or type a **P** to select Password. Enter up to 16 alphanumeric characters and press ENTER.
3. Press ENTER or type a **G** to select Group name. Enter up to eight characters and press ENTER.
4. Press ENTER or type an **F** to select Full name. Enter up to 24 alphanumeric characters and press ENTER. dBASE does not use this entry. You can use this entry to store any text information.
5. Press ENTER or type an **A** to select Access level. Enter a number between 1 and 8 or use the UP and DOWN ARROW keys to select the access level and press ENTER.
6. Press ENTER or type an **S** to select Store user profile. dBASE saves the user profile information in its memory and clears the

Tip: dBASE Login names.

Login names are easier for the user to remember if they resemble their login names for the network.

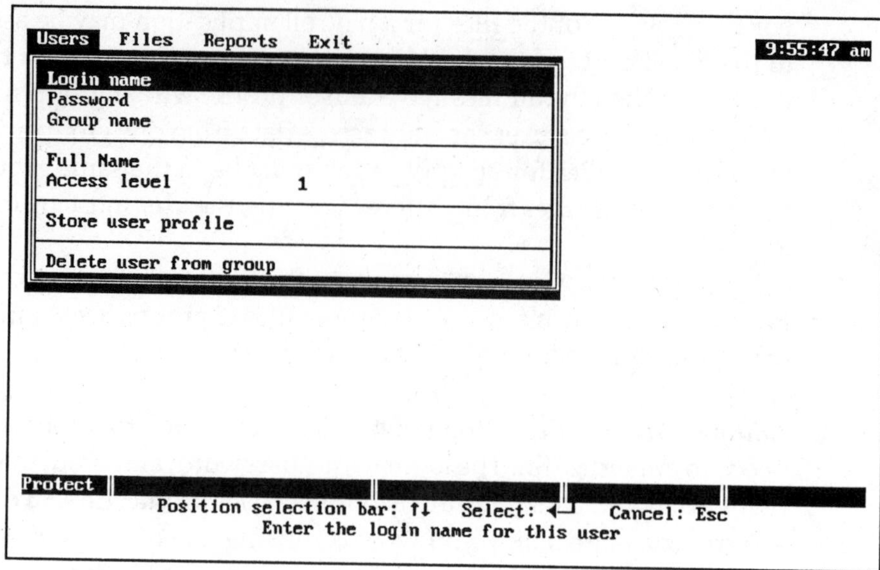

Figure 20-7 User menu to add user profile

screen so you can repeat the process starting at step 1 for each user.

Modifying User Profiles After you create a user profile, you may want to change some of the entries. To change a user profile, enter the login name, password, and group name of the user you want to change. Once you enter the information, dBASE prompts if you want to edit the user's profile. Type a **Y**. dBASE fills in the information for full name and access level. Edit the entries you want to change. You should not change the group name since once you change the group name, you cannot access files associated with the original group. After you finish editing the user profile, type an **S** to select Store user profile.

Deleting User Profiles As you add users to the dBASE security system, you should remove other users who no longer use dBASE. To remove a user profile, enter the login name, password, and group name of the user you want to delete. Once you enter the information, type a D to select Delete user from group.

```
Users  Files  Reports  Exit                                    9:55:58 am
       New file
       Group name
       File access privileges
       Field access privileges
         Access level                   1
         Establish field privileges
       Store file privileges
       Cancel current entry

Protect
         Position selection bar: ↑↓   Select: ←┘   Cancel: Esc
                      Select file name to protect
```

Figure 20-8 File menu

Adding File and Field Access Security

Once you add users and define the groups to which the users belong, you can add further security to individual files and fields by assigning files to groups and adding file and field privileges. Each file can be assigned to only one group. Within each group, access to a particular record or field is controlled by the user's access level, the file access levels, and the field access privilege. dBASE converts the entries to uppercase. Using the Files menu shown in Figure 20-8, you must follow these steps to add file and field privileges:

1. Press ENTER or type an **N** to select New file. dBASE displays a box listing the databases files in current directory. Select one or select the path to the directory then select the database.
2. Press ENTER or type a **G** to select Group name. Enter up to eight alphanumeric characters and press ENTER.
3. Press ENTER or type an **F** to select File access privileges. For each of the options shown in Figure 20-9, highlight the option, press ENTER and type a number between 1 and 8 for the highest access

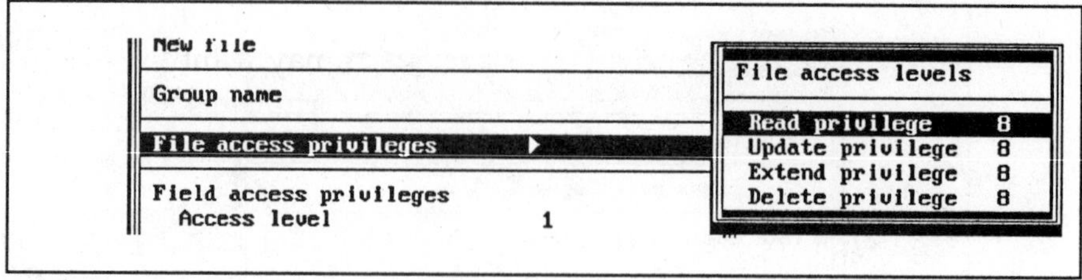

Figure 20-9 File access privileges

level a user can have for the selected file privilege. After selecting the file privileges levels, press the LEFT ARROW to return to the Files menu.

4. Press ENTER or type an **A** to select Access level. Enter a number between 1 and 8 or use the UP and DOWN ARROW keys to select the access level and press ENTER. This is the access level for which you will select the field privileges. If you want to select field privileges for several access levels, you must select an access level and then the field privileges for each access level you want to change.
5. Press ENTER or type an **E** to select Establish field privileges. For each of the fields listed, highlight the field and use the ENTER key to select between FULL, R/O, and NONE. After selecting the field privileges levels, press the LEFT ARROW to return to the Files menu.
6. Repeat steps 4 and 5 for each user access level for which you want to change the field attributes from full.
7. Press ENTER or type an **S** to select Store user profile. dBASE saves the user profile information in its memory and clears the screen so you can repeat the process starting at step 1 for another file.

The PROTECT menus can only store the file and field privileges for up to eight files without using the Save command in the Exit menu. If you try entering file and field privileges for a ninth file, dBASE displays an error message. To save the current PROTECT settings, press ALT-E and type an **S**. When dBASE finishes saving the current PROTECT settings, press ALT-F to return to the Files menu. Once you assign a file to a group, dBASE encrypts the file when you leave the PROTECT menus.

Modifying File and Field Privileges After you assign a file to a group and set the file and field privileges, you may want to change some of the entries. To change the file and field privileges for a file, enter the filename of the file you want to change. Once you enter the filename, dBASE prompts if you want to Overwrite or Cancel. Select Overwrite and reenter the new file name and field privileges. All the menu options use the default settings so you must reenter all the file and field privileges. When you store and save the new file and field privileges, they replace the existing privileges. After you finish editing the file and field privileges, type an **S** to select Store file privileges.

Listing User Profiles and File Privileges

To help keep track of the information you save with the PROTECT command, dBASE can create two reports for you. The first, the user information report, lists the users' login names, passwords, the contents of the full name in the user profiles, and the access levels. The other report, the file information report, lists the access levels for the delete, extend, read, and update file privileges, and the field privileges for each field and each access level. To print or view either report, press the LEFT or RIGHT ARROW key to move to the Reports menu. Highlight the report you want and press ENTER. If you select the file report, you must also select the file that you want to use and enter the group that it belongs to. Then dBASE prompts if you want to send it to the printer. If you select Yes, dBASE prints the report. If you select No, the report appears on the screen. Figure 20-10 shows a user information report, and Figure 20-11 shows a file information report.

Exiting from PROTECT

Once you create the user profiles and the file privileges, you can save them and begin to use dBASE's security features. The Exit menu in PROTECT has three options. The Save option saves all the user profiles and file privileges since you entered PROTECT or saved the user profiles and file privileges last. It also encrypts the database files that you have assigned to a group. The user profiles are stored in a DBSYSTEM.DB file in the DBASE or DBNETCTL.300 directory. The file privileges are stored with the data files. The Abandon operation cancels all of the user profiles and file privileges since you entered PROTECT

```
Users  Files  Reports  Exit                                          10:01:55 am
User name   Password         Group      Fullname                     Level

USER2       PASSWORD         PAYROLL                                  1
TEDDY       In_charge        EMPLOYEE   Mgr - Theordora Smith         1
USER1       password         EMPLOYEE                                 1
T_SMITH     ALFIE            PAYROLL                                  4
W_PICKET    MATH             EMPLOYEE                                 7
C_WRIGHT    CLARINET         ORDERS                                   2
L_GEORGE    ORANGE           INVENTRY                                 7
S_BRADLY    KNIGHT           ORDERS                                   3

Protect                                                              Caps
                      Press any key to continue...
                     Display all users in user file
```

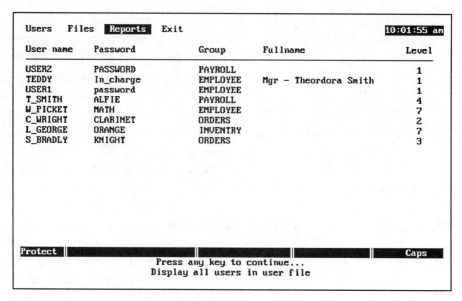

Figure 20-10 User information report

```
Filename     H:\DBASE\DB_APPL\EMPLOYEE.CRP

Group Name   EMPLOYEE
 Read privilege   7
 Update privilege 5
 Extend privilege 3
 Delete privilege 2
                                      Access Levels
Fieldname         1     2     3     4     5     6     7     8
==========      ===== ===== ===== ===== ===== ===== ===== =====
SSN             FULL  FULL  FULL  R/O   R/O   R/O   R/O   R/O
LAST_NAME       FULL  FULL  FULL  FULL  R/O   R/O   R/O   R/O
M_INITIAL       FULL  FULL  FULL  FULL  R/O   R/O   R/O   R/O
FIRST_NAME      FULL  FULL  FULL  FULL  R/O   R/O   R/O   R/O
ADDRESS         FULL  FULL  FULL  FULL  FULL  R/O   R/O   R/O
CITY            FULL  FULL  FULL  FULL  FULL  R/O   R/O   R/O
STATE           FULL  FULL  FULL  FULL  FULL  R/O   R/O   R/O
ZIP_CODE        FULL  FULL  FULL  FULL  FULL  R/O   R/O   R/O
HOME_PHONE      FULL  FULL  FULL  FULL  FULL  R/O   R/O   R/O
HIRE_DATE       FULL  FULL  FULL  R/O   R/O   R/O   R/O   NONE
MARITAL_ST      FULL  FULL  FULL  R/O   R/O   NONE  NONE  NONE
NUMB_DEPEN      FULL  FULL  FULL  R/O   R/O   NONE  NONE  NONE
HR_RATE         FULL  R/O   R/O   NONE  NONE  NONE  NONE  NONE
YTD_WAGES       FULL  FULL  R/O   NONE  NONE  NONE  NONE  NONE
YTD_FIT         FULL  FULL  R/O   NONE  NONE  NONE  NONE  NONE
HEALTH          FULL  FULL  FULL  R/O   R/O   NONE  NONE  NONE
SKILLS          FULL  FULL  FULL  R/O   R/O   R/O   NONE  NONE
```

Figure 20-11 File information report

or saved the user profiles and file privileges last. Unlike most other Abandon menu selections, it does not return to the dot prompt or Control Center. The Exit option saves all the user profiles and file privileges since you entered PROTECT or saved the user profiles and file privileges last. This menu option returns control to the dot prompt or Control Center. You can also leave PROTECT using ESC if you do not want to save any changes you made since you entered PROTECT or saved with the Save menu option.

Data Encryption

Once you add file privileges, dBASE encrypts the databases. These encrypted databases can only be viewed when a user supplies the correct password and has a low enough access level to read and/or modify the data. dBASE encrypts databases by encrypting and copying the database file to a file with the same name and a .CRP extension. dBASE encrypts and copies the memo .DBT file to a file with the same name and a .CPT extension. To use these encrypted files, you must copy them over the .DBF and .DBT files. You can copy the files using the Copy menu option in the Operations menu available from selecting DOS utilities from the Tools menu or using the COPY FILE command. dBASE will reindex the .MDX file the next time you use the REINDEX command. Once you copy the encrypted database and memo files to the .DBF and .DBT extensions, you can delete the original encrypted files with the Delete option in the Operations menu available by selecting DOS utilities from the Tools menu or using the ERASE command. dBASE will not use the file privileges security features until you rename the files since the original database and memo files remain unencrypted.

Occasionally, you may need to unencrypt the database. If you need to change the file privileges for a file, you must unencrypt it first since dBASE cannot assign file and field privileges to an encrypted file. Also, you cannot modify a database structure of an encrypted file.

dBASE automatically encrypts files with file privileges when you save the file privileges. dBASE also encrypts files created with COPY, JOIN, and TOTAL commands if SET ENCRYPTION is ON. SET ENCRYPTION is automatically set ON when you log into a protected system. If you SET ENCRYPTION OFF, new databases you create are not encrypted.

Using dBASE with Protect and Networking Features

Once you use the PROTECT features, you will notice several changes. First, you must log into dBASE, providing a group name, user name, and password. Also, you can only access files not assigned to groups and files assigned to the group you used to log in.

Using dBASE on a network produces additional changes. Accessing data is different since data can be on a network drive or on the workstation's drives. Also, printing is different since you can print your output to a network printer or to a printer connected to the workstation. When you use dBASE in a network, the network has commands that you may want to use.

Logging into dBASE

Once you add dBASE's security features with the PROTECT command, you must log in to use the files. To log into the protected dBASE, enter dBASE just as you normally do. If you are using dBASE on a network, you must log into the network. Once you are on a network drive, enter **DBASE**. Instead of the initial dBASE screen, the screen looks like Figure 20-12. In this screen, you must enter the correct user name and password. If you do not enter the correct information, dBASE lets you try again, aborting dBASE if you cannot log in after your third attempt. Pressing ESC leaves dBASE and returns to the DOS prompt. Once you enter the correct information, dBASE displays the initial screen it displayed before you started dBASE's protection features. If you do not see the initial logon screen, dBASE could not find the DBSYSTEM.DB file. While you can enter dBASE, you cannot access the encrypted files. To access the encrypted files, you must restore the DBSYSTEM.DB file.

When you are in dBASE and you want to log out of dBASE's security system without leaving dBASE, use the LOGOUT command. This command clears the screen and displays the login screen shown in Figure 20-12. From this screen, you or someone else can log into dBASE's security system. If you press ESC to abort the login screen, you will exit dBASE. You can use this command so someone else can use the computer or so you can change to another group to access a different group of files.

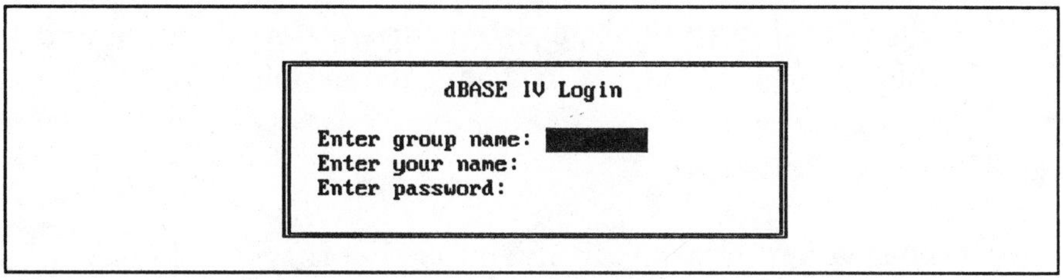

```
dBASE IV Login

Enter group name:
Enter your name:
Enter password:
```

Figure 20-12 Initial screen for network access

Accessing Protected Files

When dBASE is protected, you can only access the files belonging to the group that you logged in as, or files without file and field privileges that therefore remain unencrypted. For files that belong to the group that you logged in as, you must have the appropriate access level for the operation that you want to perform. If you are accessing an unencrypted file or a file that you have a sufficient access level to modify or read, dBASE's security system is transparent after the login screen. If you try accessing a file that you have file and field privileges for but you do not have an appropriate access level, dBASE displays the message Unauthorized access level. dBASE displays the same message if you try reading or modifying a field in a file that you can access but do not have the appropriate file or field privilege.

When you use unencrypted files, their usage is identical to an unprotected dBASE. You can read and modify them just as you have before. They remain unencrypted unless you assign them to a group with the PROTECT command.

Accessing Files on a Network

When you use dBASE on a network, you can store data in more data storage locations. For example, you can use any floppy disk or hard disk at your work station. You can also store data on a network drive. If your work station has its own CONFIG.DB file, you may specify the default drive that dBASE uses for your work station. If your work station does not have its own CONFIG.DB file, you will want use the

SET() function to determine the current default drive and the SET DEFAULT TO command to change the setting.

Printing on a Network

When you print using dBASE on a network, you may have a choice of which printer dBASE prints the output. When you select which printer you want to use, you must tell dBASE which printer to use before printing the output.

Printing to the Network Printer When you print a file using the network printer, the network stores the data that you want to print into a temporary file. The network uses a spooler to control the flow of data from all users' print requests to the printer. For each print job the spooler receives, the spooler prints the temporary files containing the print job in the order that the user requests the job. Many networks, including Novell's Advanced NetWare, offer controls over how the spooler prints the print job. These controls can include a prefacing sheet that includes the name of the user who requested the print job and the time it was requested. Other controls assign users different priority levels so the print jobs with the greatest priority are printed first. To print to the network printer, first use the command from the dot prompt, **SET PRINTER TO \\SPOOLER**. Then, print the output that you want sent to the printer. Unlike printing to your own printer, the network printer will not print your output immediately. Instead the network waits until it receives all of the output that you want to print. Once the network's spooler receives all of the output, it will print it after printing the print jobs it received before receiving yours. However, since the network stores the output data in a file on the network,

❑ **Tip: If dBASE locks the system.**

If dBASE locks the system and you must reboot the system, you may see an error message concerning FAT (file allocation table). Most networks contain a repair utility, such as Novell's VREPAIR utility, that you must use to correct problems such as this.

you do not have to wait until the printer finishes printing. You can immediately work on your next dBASE task.

Printing to the Local Printer Once you set dBASE to print to the network printer, you may want to switch back to the work station's own printer, if it has one. To switch printing from the network printer to the work station's printer, use the **SET PRINTER TO LPT1**. If the printer is not connected to LPT1, replace LPT1 with the device the printer is connected to the computer. Once you perform this command, print requests are directed to the local printer instead of the network's printer spooler.

Using Network Commands for dBASE Applications

While you are working with dBASE in a network environment, the network has some commands that facilitate your networking dBASE tasks. For example, you may want to send a message to another user to tell the user to unlock the record you need. Another network feature you will use is controlling your print jobs in the network's spooler.

Sending Messages When you are using dBASE you may need to ask another user to release a record. If you are the system administrator, you may need to inform users to log out if you are taking the network down or you need users to exit dBASE so you can use PROTECT. Novell's Advanced NetWare and most other network packages usually have a command or program that allows you to send messages to other users. Novell's networks use the SEND command, although other networks use a different command. This command is performed from a network drive. You can perform this command within dBASE using the Tools menu or entering an exclamation point and the command at the dot prompt. You can send a message of up to 40 characters with the

❑ **Tip: Network printing.**

You may want to look at your network features to use multiple print queues for creating multiple priority levels for printing.

Tip: Limiting a user's disk space.

Most network software can limit the amount of disk space a user can add to prevent the network's disks from filling up. For example, using Novell's Advanced or SFT NetWare installation options, you can limit the amount of network hard disk space each user can use.

SEND command to either a single user or an entire network group. For example, if you want to send a message to the user TEDDY to unlock a record, you would enter:

```
SEND "Unlock current record, I need it, SDH" to TEDDY
```

This command sends the message in quotes to the user TEDDY. The message looks like Figure 20-13. For TEDDY to clear the message, Teddy must press CTRL-ENTER. To list user names, you can use the network command USERLIST. When you enter the command, the network displays a list like the one in Figure 20-14. This lists the network user name rather than the user name the person used to enter dBASE. To send a message to users in the dBASE group asking them to exit dBASE, such as when you wanted to use PROTECT, you would type:

```
SEND "Logout Immediately" TO GROUP DBASE
```

This command sends the message in quotes to everyone in the DBASE group who is logged in when the command is entered. Each user must press CTRL-ENTER to remove the message from the screen and resume the user's task.

```
>> From T_SMITH[1]: Unlock current record, I need it, SDH  (CTRL-ENTER to clear)
```

Figure 20-13 Message sent to user

```
User Information for Server NET_SERVER
Connection  User Name         Login Time
----------  ---------------   -------------------
     1    * USER1             2-17-1989 10:41 am
     6      T_SMITH           2-17-1989  9:02 am
```

Figure 20-14 Listing user names

In other instances, you may want to send a message to every computer logged into the network, such as when you are taking a network down. In these instances, you can use the BROADCAST command to send up to 60 characters to every user. This command must be performed from the network console and cannot be performed from within dBASE.

Controlling Print Jobs Each time you print output to the network printer, you are creating a print job that the print spooler prints. Before the spooler prints a job, you can change how the spooler will print the output. Most networks have a print spooler utility that controls how the print spooler prints your print job. Your access to this print spooler may be limited by the network supervisor. If you can access the print spooler utility, you can cancel a print job or change some of the printing characteristics. For example, the Novell Advanced NetWare has a PCONSOLE program that controls the print spooler. If you enter this command from DOS after leaving dBASE, you can change how your output appears. After you enter the PCONSOLE utility, you select Print Queue Information, the printer queue you want to work with, the Current Print Job Entries menu option, and the print job that you want to modify or view. After you select a print job, the screen looks like Figure 20-15. With the PCONSOLE utility, you can only change the print options if you are the user who originated the print job, or if you are the queue supervisor, a privilege granted by the supervisor. As the options in Figure 20-15 show, you can change the number of copies printed or change whether the print spooler places an identification banner before it prints your output. If you return to the listing of the current print jobs by pressing ESC, you can insert or delete print jobs using INS or DEL.

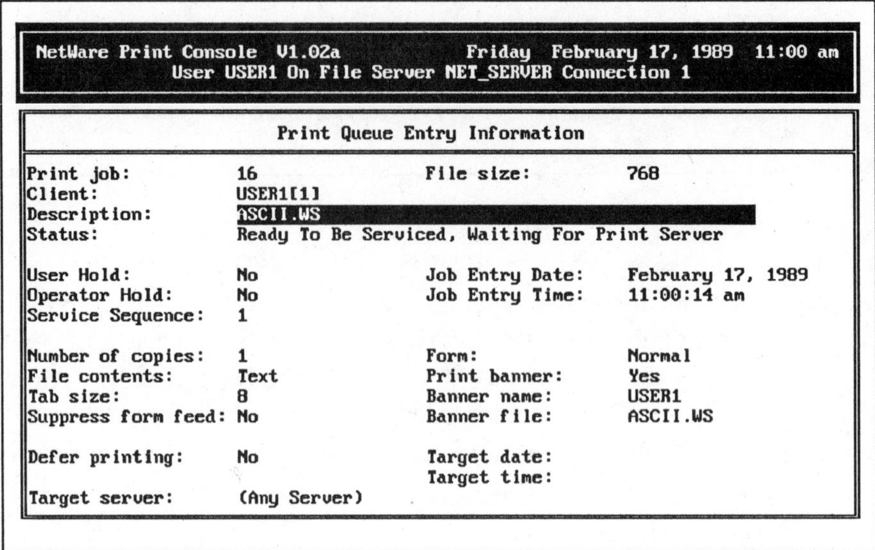
```
NetWare Print Console  V1.02a           Friday  February 17, 1989  11:00 am
       User USER1 On File Server NET_SERVER Connection 1

                    Print Queue Entry Information

Print job:              16                File size:       768
Client:                 USER1[1]
Description:            ASCII.WS
Status:                 Ready To Be Serviced, Waiting For Print Server

User Hold:              No                Job Entry Date:  February 17, 1989
Operator Hold:          No                Job Entry Time:  11:00:14 am
Service Sequence:       1

Number of copies:       1                 Form:            Normal
File contents:          Text              Print banner:    Yes
Tab size:               8                 Banner name:     USER1
Suppress form feed:     No                Banner file:     ASCII.WS

Defer printing:         No                Target date:
                                          Target time:
Target server:          (Any Server)
```

Figure 20-15 Modifying a print job

Installing Other Networks

The dBASE IV installation instructions provided for a Novell network do not work when you are using the network software provided by other vendors. Although the process is similar, you will need to use the commands that are specific to your software. The following sections provide a few specifics about several of the other popular networks.

3Com 3+

There are several preliminary steps that are required to install dBASE IV on a 3COM 3+ network. You must use a 3COM Etherlink or Etherlink Plus card in each work station and run 3COM 3+ Share software 1.2 or greater on the file server.

Your first step is to create a subdirectory for dBASE files. Rather than use the DOS MD command, use 3COM entries. First log in as DBADMN and link to the APPS directory. Run the 3F utility to create a shared subdirectory for dBASE IV by typing SHARE ? and pressing ENTER. Use **DBASE** as a sharename and a path of C:\APPS\DBASE.

Supply a password when requested. When a message indicating access of RWC appears press ENTER. If you want other shared directories for dBASE files you can create them at this time. Exit F and create logical drive assignments for dBASE. You might want to link drive D to the APPS directory with the entry 3F LOGIN USERX; LINK D: \\servname\APPS. If you want to assign a password enter /PASS=password when you use the LINK command.

Check the CONFIG.SYS file on each work station. It requires the following entries:

```
FILES=99
BUFFERS=15
LASTDRIVE=x
```

You can proceed with installation and then protect your dBASE files with the ATTRIB command. You can use the 3F LINK command to establish logical assignments after you start the network.

IBM Token Ring

You can install dBASE IV on an IBM Token Ring network if you are running version 1.2 of the IBM PC LAN program. The special steps involve modifying the AUTOEXEC files on the server and each work station and checking the entries in CONFIG.SYS.

You need to create a directory off the root directory on the file server and name it DBASE. You want to add the NET SHARE command to the AUTOEXEC file on the server and set DBASE equal to C:\DBASE and add the entry /RWC to set the access privileges. The work station AUTOEXEC files all require the NET USE entry to assign drive D to the network name DBASE on the server.

The CONFIG.SYS file should be modified to adjust the number of files that can be open concurrently, the number of file buffers, and the last logical drive. You can make these entries where x is an entry that corresponds to the last logical drive:

```
FILES=99
BUFFERS=15
LASTDRIVE=x
```

After installation is complete you want to protect the dBASE program files. You can change the file attribute to read-only with the DOS command ATTRIB.

When you have completed these steps, installation is next. After installation all you need to do is type PATH=D:\ and press ENTER, then type DBASE and press ENTER.

Ungermann-Bass

You can run dBASE IV on an Ungermann-Bass Net/One PC System. dBASE IV will run on version 15.2 of this network software. The required steps exactly parallel the ones provided for IBM Token Ring networks.

CHAPTER 21

Network Applications

In the chapters covering the Applications Generator and programming, design and programming issues were discussed. Since network applications are likely to have a larger base of end users than an application designed for a single-user system, it is even more important that you follow good design and programming techniques presented in those earlier chapters.

You will also have some special issues to consider when designing network applications. You need to insure that only one user has a record for update and that users are not locked out waiting for the one last record they need to complete a transaction. Also, if an entire series of events must take place for any of them to be valid, you must undo the first group of database activities if it is not possible to complete all of them. These issues and others are not of concern when you are creating a program for a single user. Fortunately, dBASE has many features to assist you built into the package. These features include file and record locking as well as transaction processing and rollback.

In this chapter some of the special dBASE features that allow you to design dBASE network applications are used. You will find these features shown in the context of actual program code in most cases. All of the dBASE commands including network options are also covered in Appendix C. In addition, you will find a complete network application at the end of the chapter. Sections of the code are discussed in separate sections and the entire set of program code is shown at the back of the chapter. Since the application is designed to work with the employee file that you have worked with throughout the book, you can implement it easily.

Design Considerations for Networks

When you create an application for a network, you must be concerned with a number of new issues. For example, a network program must let multiple users access the same data at the same time yet protect the integrity of the data contained in the database. You can allow many users to view a database record but only one user at a time can update it. Otherwise, one user's changes will overlay modifications made by another user.

While programming a network application, you will continue to use the programming skills you developed in Chapters 14 through 18. Network programs, like single-user programs, should be modular and well documented. You also need to test the network application before you use it. Network testing requires all the normal program testing steps with test data ranging from simple to complex and finally erroneous entries. As a final step, the network program must be tested with multiple users working from test scripts. In addition to testing the ability of the program to properly handle situations of contention for the same data, you need to monitor the performance of the network with many users running the application simultaneously.

Restricting Data Access

One of the biggest advantages of network applications is their ability to share data. You can maintain one master file that is accessible by all the work stations rather than the distributed database concept where each work station has one small piece of the database. With security options available through your network software and dBASE, you can decide to limit access to the exact set of information needed by each network user.

Although shareable data offers many advantages, it also has pitfalls that must be guarded against. It is likely that multiple users will work with the same dBASE files in network applications. It is also possible that these users may need to access the same records. This is not a problem if each of the users is reading the data in the record; the problem occurs if multiple users decide to update the record at the same time. When this happens, the changes made by the user who updates the record last override the changes made by the user who updates the record first.

dBASE prevents this data concurrency problem by allowing users to lock files and records explicitly or automatically. An example where record locking is a required feature is the maintenance of the inventory levels for parts. If User A and User B read the record for part number AX1234 at the same time, they see the same number 1000. If User A processes an order for 5 parts, the inventory level in the record for this part is updated to 995. If User B obtains a copy of the record containing the original 1000 for the inventory level and processes an order for 50 parts, the inventory level in the database is updated to 950. This makes the inventory figure for part AX1234 incorrect since the actual inventory level after processing both orders should be 945. The reason the record contains 950 is that User B's change is saved last and overlays the change made by User A. User A does not know that their change was replaced. Even if they looked at the record again, they would assume that the new inventory level reflected their order of 5 units and someone else's order for 45 units.

Locking a record allows a user to have sole updating privileges until the record is unlocked. When another user wants to use a locked record, it is only available on a read-only basis. dBASE displays Read-only in the status line while someone else has locked a record. After the record is unlocked, the second user may obtain a new copy of the record for updating.

Record locking is fine if you need to change a single record but some operations require that the entire file be locked to prevent any access to the file. Once you lock a file, other users cannot update any of the file records until the lock is removed.

Without dBASE's built-in locking features, record and file locking would create a time-consuming housekeeping chore for a programmer. Fortunately, dBASE automatically locks records and files when you use certain commands. While you can still explicitly lock files and records, you can rely on dBASE to lock the records for you most of the time and reserve explicit actions for exception situations. In some cases, opening the file exclusively provides a better alternative than locking the records or files.

Using a File Exclusively When you open a file for exclusive use, you are the only one who can use it. If someone else tries using the file, dBASE does not let them. When you open a file that is not for exclusive use, other users can use the file. Table 21-1 shows all the commands that open files categorizing them by whether they support exclusive or shared use. Once a file is opened exclusively, it remains exclusive until the file is closed.

Some of the commands in Table 21-1 appear in both columns. The USE and SET INDEX TO commands are in both columns since the SET EXCLUSIVE setting determines if the files are exclusively opened or shared. When SET EXCLUSIVE is ON, the files you open with the USE or SET INDEX TO command are opened exclusively. When SET EXCLUSIVE is OFF, files you open with the USE command are shared with other users. You can always override the SET EXCLUSIVE OFF setting by including the word EXCLUSIVE in the USE command that opens the database. The CREATE <f1> TO <f2> command appears in

Table 21-1 dBASE Commands that Open a File

(Type of file indicated in parentheses)

Locked for Exclusive Use	*Shared by All Users*
COPY STRUCTURE TO (.DBF)	APPEND FROM (.DBF)
COPY TO (.DBF)	CREATE <f1> TO <f2> (.DBF)
CREATE (.DBF)	DO <filename> (.PRG)
CREATE <f1> TO <f2> (.DBF)	LABEL FORM (.LBL)
CREATE/MODIFY LABEL (.LBL)	REPORT FORM (.FRM)
CREATE/MODIFY QUERY (.QBE)	RESTORE (.MEM)
CREATE/MODIFY REPORT (.FRM)	SET CATALOG TO (.CAT)
CREATE/MODIFY VIEW (.VUE)	SET FILTER TO FILE (.QBE)
INDEX ON (.NDX, .MDX)	SET FORMAT TO (.FMT)
JOIN (.DBF)	SET INDEX TO (.NDX, .MDX)
MODIFY COMMAND (.PRG, .FMT)	SET PROCEDURE TO (.PRG)
SAVE (.MEM)	SET VIEW TO (.VUE)
SET ALTERNATE TO (.TXT)	UPDATE FROM (.DBF)
SET INDEX TO (.NDX, .MDX)	USE (.DBF, .NDX, .MDX, .DBT)
SORT (.DBF)	
TOTAL (.DBF)	
USE (.DBF, .NDX, .MDX, .DBT)	

the table twice since it opens the first file as an exclusive file and the second file as a shared file.

Certain commands require you to open a file in exclusive mode. If you try to execute one of these commands, dBASE displays an error message telling you that the file must be opened in exclusive mode. Commands in this category are CONVERT, INSERT [BEFORE] [BLANK], MODIFY STRUCTURE, PACK, REINDEX, RESET, and ZAP. To use one of these commands, you must reopen the database you are using as an exclusive file.

The other MODIFY commands only execute if dBASE can exclusively open the appropriate label, query, report, view, or program files. These MODIFY commands do not automatically open the file exclusively for you.

Figure 21-1 shows part of an application that marks records the user selects then packs the database to remove the marked records. The database is initially opened as a shared file when the user selects the records to delete so other users can use the database. When the user is finished and is ready to remove the marked records from the database, the database is reopened exclusively, the records are packed and the database is closed. If dBASE cannot open the file exclusively, the program branches to the error module File_err. If the error number is 108, which is the error number when the File in use by another user, the program informs the user that the records must be packed at another time.

File Locking When you lock a file, you can update the contents of any of the file records. To other users, the file is read-only. When it is not locked, any user can modify data in the file. When you lock a file, you also lock its related files. For example, if you lock a database file, you are also locking the memo field file and the index files.

Some commands automatically lock the database and its related files before executing the command. After dBASE executes the command, it unlocks the database. If dBASE cannot lock the file, it displays an error message. The commands that automatically lock the file are listed in Table 21-2. DELETE, RECALL, and REPLACE perform file locks as long as the scope is not a record number. You can omit locking for all of the commands in Table 21-2 except the APPEND FROM, DELETE <scope>, RECALL <scope>, REPLACE <scope>, and UPDATE commands by using the SET LOCK OFF command. However, the results

```
 Layout  Words  Go To  Print  Exit                                          5:58:55 pm
[··▼··▼··▼··▼··▼··▼2·▼··▼··▼·3▼··▼··▼··▼··▼··▼··▼5·▼··▼··▼·6▼········7·········
ON ERROR DO File_err
SET EXCLUSIVE OFF
USE Employee INDEX Employee ORDER Ssn
DO Del_rec                                   && User selects records to delete
USE Employee INDEX Employee ORDER Ssn EXCLUSIVE
IF RIGHT(DBF(),12)="EMPLOYEE.DBF"            && Able to open file
   PACK
   USE
ENDIF
RETURN

PROCEDURE File_err
IF ERROR()=108                               && Cannot open file exclusively
   ? " The file cannot be opened exclusively at this point."
   ? " Since this is required before you can remove the records that you "
   ? " selected from the database, they remain in the database, although "
   ? " they are still marked for deletion.  "
   ? " Try removing these records from the database at another time. "
ENDIF
RETURN
Program  |H:\dbase\db_appl\B22-1  |Line:1 Col:1  |        |          Ins
```

Figure 21-1 Application code to pack database

Table 21-2 Commands that Lock Files

APPEND FROM
AVERAGE
CALCULATE
COPY
COPY STRUCTURE
COUNT
DELETE <scope>
INDEX ON
JOIN
LABEL FORM
RECALL <scope>
REPLACE <scope>
REPORT FORM
SORT
SUM
TOTAL
UPDATE

of the command may create data integrity problems, unless you include program code to prevent them, because other users can change the data as you use the data for the command. For example, if you are preparing the weekly payroll report, you may want the database locked so other users do not change the data as you are preparing the report. If you SET LOCK OFF, the files the COPY, COPY STRUCTURE, INDEX ON, JOIN, SORT, and TOTAL commands create are opened for exclusive use even if the data that these files use are not locked.

dBASE lets you explicitly lock databases and their related files using the FLOCK function. When you use this function dBASE locks the current file or the file in the work area that you specify. This function also returns a .T. or an .F. value to let you test whether dBASE successfully locked the file. Once you explicitly lock a file, it remains locked until you use the UNLOCK command or you close the database.

Record Locking The same features for locking files are also available for locking records. When a record is locked, you can change the data. When it is not locked, other users can change the data. Like file locking, only one user can lock a particular record.

Some commands automatically lock the record before executing the command. After it executes the command, it unlocks the record. These commands are APPEND [BLANK], DELETE, RECALL, and REPLACE. The last three only lock the record if the scope is a record number. Otherwise, the command tries locking the file. If dBASE cannot lock the record, it displays an error message. When you are editing or browsing through a database, dBASE locks the current record when you press a key that modifies the data. Once you save the data, it unlocks the record. For example, if you are browsing through the WEEK_PAY database and you type **40**, dBASE locks the current record and then enters the 40 into the Browse screen. While the cursor is on the current record, RecLock appears in the status line. When you move to another record, the RecLock indicator disappears and dBASE unlocks the changed record. You can also lock a record by selecting Lock record from the Records menu box in the Browse screen or pressing CTRL-O in the Edit or Browse screen. These record locks disappear when you move to another record.

Most record locks are removed when you execute another command. The REPLACE <field name> WITH <field value> maintains the lock after performing the command until a non-REPLACE command performs; so if you execute multiple REPLACE commands, the record values cannot change due to another user's editing between REPLACE commands.

dBASE lets you explicitly lock records using the RLOCK and LOCK functions. When you use either function, dBASE locks the records that you specify. This function also returns a .T. or an .F. value to let you test whether dBASE was successful in locking the file. Once you have explicitly locked a record, it remains locked until you use the UNLOCK command or you close the database.

Access Levels and Security Design

When you create network applications, you can incorporate some of the security features you created with the PROTECT command. The PROTECT feature that you will most likely incorporate into your programs are the access levels. When you create an application, you can customize the program to change depending upon the user's access level. Figure 21-2 shows an example of one of the uses of the access level in a network program. In the text in the figure, the user can only add records if the user has an access level less than or equal to 5. If the user has an access level greater than 5, commands after the ELSE command display a message before returning to the opening menu. Another use of access levels is changing the data a user sees based upon their access level. Figure 21-3 shows the editing screen for the Employee application for a user with an access level of 4. Some of the fields in the database do not appear and others such as YTD_WAGES only appear but do not allow the user to change their values.

❑ **Tip: Record locking.**

You want to minimize the records that you manually lock. A manual lock remains until it is explicitly UNLOCKed or the database is closed. Keeping a record locked longer than necessary prevents other users from editing the data. Also, you are limited to 50 locked records at a time.

```
Layout   Words   Go To   Print   Exit                                    5:03:29 pm
[··▼··▼··▼··▼··▼··▼2·▼··▼··▼·3▼··▼··▼··▼··▼··▼··▼5·▼··▼··▼·6▼·········7··········
PROCEDURE Add_rec                                && Menu option 1
STORE "Y" TO Mnext_rec                           && Adds records while Mnext_rec=Y
IF ACCESS()<=5                                   && Minimum access level to add data
   USE Employee INDEX Employee.mdx ORDER TAG Ssn
   DO WHILE Mnext_rec="Y"
      APPEND BLANK                               && Locks record at the same time
      DO Rec_edit                                && Data entry screen
      @ 19,20 TO 21,72 DOUBLE
      @ 20,21 SAY "Do you want to add another employee record? (Y/N) "
      @ 20,71 GET Mnext_rec PICTURE "!"&& Determines if user wants to add
      READ                                       && another record.
   ENDDO
   USE
ELSE                                             && Handles Insufficient access
   @ 15,10 SAY "Insufficient access level to add records."
   ? SPACE(10)+"Press any key to continue. "
   WAIT ""
ENDIF
RETURN                                           && End of Add_rec procedure

Program  H:\...db_appl\EMPLOYEE  Line:62 Col:1                      Num    Ins
```

Figure 21-2 Use of access level in a network

```
SSN:        215-90-8761

LAST NAME:  Jenkins          M INITIAL:  J   FIRST NAME: Mary

ADDRESS:    11 North St.

CITY:       Cleveland        STATE:     OH   ZIP CODE:   44124

HOME PHONE: (216)999-9999

HIRE DATE:  12/20/88         MARITAL_ST: M   NUMB_DEPEN:         1


HEALTH:     T

SKILLS:     Typing, Switchboard operator
            Some Spanish


EMPLOYEE  H:\...db_appl\EMPLOYEE  Rec 1/14           File           Num
```

Figure 21-3 Edit screen for the Employee file with an access code of 4

Network SET Commands

When you create a network application, you will use additional settings that you do not include in a single-user application. These network settings are SET EXCLUSIVE, SET LOCK, SET REFRESH TO, and SET REPROCESS TO. The SET EXCLUSIVE command determines whether files opened with the USE and SET INDEX TO commands are opened for exclusive use. When SET EXCLUSIVE is ON, only the user opening the database can use the database. When SET EXCLUSIVE is OFF, other users can read and edit the database a user opens. The SET LOCK command determines whether dBASE locks the file before performing the AVERAGE, CALCULATE, COUNT, LABEL FORM, REPORT FORM, or SUM commands. The SET LOCK command also determines whether dBASE locks the file during the reading portion of the COPY TAG, COPY INDEX, COPY STRUCTURE, INDEX, JOIN, SORT, or TOTAL commands. If SET LOCK is ON, the file is locked when a command performs and unlocked when the command finishes. If SET LOCK is OFF, the file is not locked. The SET REFRESH TO command is used for converted databases to specify when changed data should be updated in Browse and Edit screens. The SET REPROCESS TO command determines the number of attempts dBASE makes to lock a file or record before displaying an error message. It is a number between -1 and 32000 with the numbers between 1 and 32000 representing the number of tries dBASE will make. If SET REPROCESS is set to 0, dBASE continually retries to lock the file or record and displays the message in Figure 21-4 until the file or record lock is successful. If the SET REPROCESS is set to -1, dBASE continually retries to lock the file or record without displaying a message. Indefinitely attempting to lock a file or record prevents you from completing other dBASE tasks with your machine until the file or record lock is successful. By limiting the number of attempts dBASE tries to lock the file or record, you can adjust a program to handle situations where the record or file is not available. For example, in Figure 21-5, the program code tries to open the file for exclusive use before packing the database to remove records marked for deletion. If it cannot lock the file after 10 tries, the program warns the user that the user cannot pack the database at this point. By executing this program, the user knows that the database must be packed at another time.

```
Record in use by USER2
Retrying lock, Press ESC to cancel.
```

Figure 21-4 dBASE message

Network Functions

When you create a network application, you will use functions that you do not include in a single-user application. These network functions are ACCESS, CHANGE, COMPLETED, FLOCK, LKSYS, LOCK, NETWORK, RLOCK, and ROLLBACK.

The ACCESS function returns the current user's access level so that a program can modify the steps it performs based on the user's access level. The COMPLETE function is used with transaction processing to determine whether the transaction is completed with the END TRANSACTION or ROLLBACK command. The FLOCK function locks the

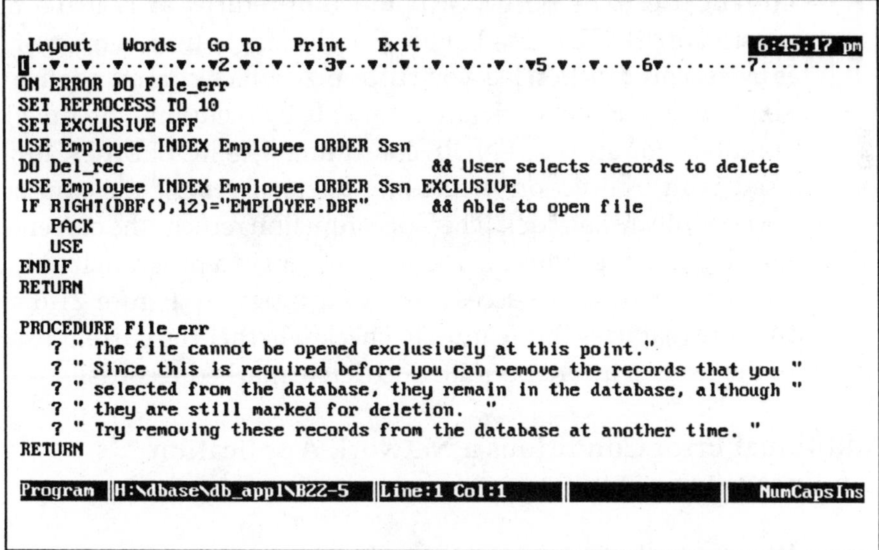

```
Layout   Words   Go To   Print   Exit                                   6:45:17 pm
ON ERROR DO File_err
SET REPROCESS TO 10
SET EXCLUSIVE OFF
USE Employee INDEX Employee ORDER Ssn
DO Del_rec                              && User selects records to delete
USE Employee INDEX Employee ORDER Ssn EXCLUSIVE
IF RIGHT(DBF(),12)="EMPLOYEE.DBF"       && Able to open file
   PACK
   USE
ENDIF
RETURN

PROCEDURE File_err
   ? " The file cannot be opened exclusively at this point."
   ? " Since this is required before you can remove the records that you "
   ? " selected from the database, they remain in the database, although "
   ? " they are still marked for deletion.  "
   ? " Try removing these records from the database at another time. "
RETURN

Program ||H:\dbase\db_appl\B22-5 ||Line:1 Col:1 ||          || NumCapsIns
```

Figure 21-5 Program code that attempts to open the file

❑

Tip: Use the SET REPROCESS command to avoid an infinite loop.

If you are trying to use a file that someone is using exclusively, your program can be locked in an infinite loop if SET REPROCESS is set to 0 or -1. Add conditions to the program to manage what the program should do if it cannot use the file or lock the record or file it wants.

current file and returns a .T. if the file is locked by the current user or an .F. if dBASE is unable to lock the file for the current user. The LKSYS function is used with converted databases and returns the time the record was locked, date the record was locked, or the user who locked the current record. The ISMARKED function is used with transaction processing to determine whether the current database or the database specified has data that is not completely processed by an END TRANSACTION or ROLLBACK command. The LOCK and RLOCK functions lock the current record and return a .T. if the record is locked by the current user or an .F. if dBASE is unable to lock the record for the current user. The NETWORK function returns a .T. if the network version of dBASE is used or an .F. if the single-user version of dBASE is used. This function lets you customize which commands are used in single-user and network environments by including the function as a condition for an IF ... ENDIF constraint. The ROLLBACK function is used with transaction processing to determine if the transaction is successfully rolled back. The USER function returns the current dBASE user login name. You can use this function in a program if only certain users are allowed to access part of a program. Figure 21-6 shows a module that uses this feature to check whether the current user is one of the users who are permitted to delete marked records.

Additional Error Conditions a Network Application Can Encounter

When you design a network application, the program can encounter more errors than a single-user application. For example, the program can halt when a record that the program is trying to process is locked.

```
 Layout   Words   Go To   Print   Exit                                   7:21:25 pm
[··▼··▼··▼··▼··▼··▼2·▼··▼··▼·3▼··▼··▼··▼··▼··▼··▼5·▼··▼··▼·6▼·········7··········
ON ERROR DO File_err
SET REPROCESS TO 10
SET EXCLUSIVE OFF
USE Employee INDEX Employee ORDER Ssn
DO Del_rec                                  && User selects records to delete
IF USER()="TEDDY" .OR. USER()="USER1" .OR. USER()="USER2"
   USE Employee INDEX Employee ORDER Ssn EXCLUSIVE
   IF RIGHT(DBF(),12)="EMPLOYEE.DBF"       && Able to open file
      PACK
      USE
   ENDIF
ELSE
   ? "You are not allowed to delete records."
ENDIF
RETURN

PROCEDURE File_err
IF ERROR()=108 .OR. ERROR()=372            && Cannot open file exclusively
   ? " The file cannot be opened exclusively at this point."
   ? " Since this is required before you can remove the records that you "
Program ║H:\dbase\db_appl\B22-6 ║Line:1 Col:1 ║              ║ NumCapsIns
```

Figure 21-6 Check to determine authority to delete records

A network application must be capable of handling these network-associated problems. Most of these problems are handled by including IF ... ENDIF constraints that check if the problem exists, or using the ON ERROR command to branch when a problem exists. One error condition a network program encounters is file and record locking. When a program locks a file or record, it can use FLOCK and RLOCK to lock the file or test whether the user already has the file or record locked. An example handling this type of problem is shown in Figure 21-7 which uses the FLOCK function in the user-defined functions M_emp and M_week (not shown but identical to the M_emp function) to lock the WEEK_PAY and EMPLOYEE databases before computing the weekly payroll. Another network error that a program must handle is when a file the program wants to use is unavailable. To handle this type of error, the ON ERROR command is more appropriate. Figure 21-8 shows the code for several modules that handle what happens when a file is unavailable.

Converted Files

As each user uses the data in a database, the user needs to know if the data has changed since the program read the information. A program

```
 Layout   Words   Go To   Print   Exit                                        8:24:30 pm
[··▼··▼··▼··▼··▼··▼2·▼··▼··▼·3▼··▼··▼··▼··▼··▼··▼5·▼··▼··▼·6▼········7·········
STORE .T. TO M_continue
USE Employee IN 1 INDEX Employee ORDER Ssn
DO WHILE M_continue .AND. M_emp()="Y"  && Function locks EMPLOYEE
   USE Week_pay IN 2 INDEX Week_pay ORDER Ssn
   DO WHILE M_continue .AND. M_week()="Y" && Function locks Week_pay
      DO WHILE .NOT. EOF() .AND. M_continue
         DO Pay                         && Computes pay.  When it reaches
      ENDDO                             && the end of the file, Pay sets
   ENDDO                                && M_continue to .F. and closes
ENDDO                                   && all databases.
RETURN                                  && End of Wk_payroll procedure

FUNCTION M_EMP                          && Used by Wk_payroll procedure
STORE "Y" TO M_return
IF .NOT. FLOCK()                        && Skips over loop if able to lock
   RUN SEND "Unlock employee records for payroll" TO DBASE
   @ 15,15 SAY "Do you want to try again? (Y/N)" GET M_return PICTURE "!"
   READ                                 && Send is a Novell command
ENDIF
RETURN (M_return)                       && End of M_emp function
Program  H:\dbase\db_appl\B22-7   Line:14 Col:1                    Num    Ins
```

Figure 21-7 FLOCK function

```
 Layout   Words   Go To   Print   Exit                                       12:01:45 pm
[··▼··▼··▼··▼··▼··▼2·▼··▼··▼·3▼··▼··▼··▼··▼··▼··▼5·▼··▼··▼·6▼········7·········
* Main program
ON ERROR DO Err_fix
DO Set_up                               && Initialization and set commands
DO Menu_def                             && Defines menu
DO Make_menu                            && M_continue=.F. when Quit is
DO End_setup                            && Returns SETtings to original
RETURN                                  && End of Main program

PROCEDURE Err_fix                       && Called if error occurs
DO CASE
   CASE ERROR()=108
      ? "Someone else is exclusively using the database file.  "
      ? "Try again later."
   CASE ERROR()=372
      ? "File is locked by "+LKSYS(2)
      ? "Try again later."
   CASE ERROR()=373
      ? "Record is locked by "+LKSYS(2)
      ? "Try modifying this record later."
ENDCASE
Program  H:\dbase\db_appl\B22-8   Line:1 Col:1                     Num    Ins
```

Figure 21-8 Code for unavailable file

```
Number of data records:      8
Date of last update    : 02/23/89
Field  Field Name  Type       Width    Dec    Index
    1  SSN         Character     11               Y
    2  LAST_NAME   Character     15               Y
    3  M_INITIAL   Character      1               N
    4  FIRST_NAME  Character     10               N
    5  ADDRESS     Character     15               N
    6  CITY        Character     10               N
    7  STATE       Character      2               Y
    8  ZIP_CODE    Numeric        5               N
    9  HOME_PHONE  Character     13               N
   10  HIRE_DATE   Date           8               N
   11  MARITAL_ST  Character      1               N
   12  NUMB_DEPEN  Numeric        2               N
   13  HR_RATE     Numeric        6      2        Y
   14  YTD_WAGES   Numeric        9      2        N
   15  YTD_FIT     Numeric        9      2        N
   16  HEALTH      Logical        1               N
   17  SKILLS      Memo          10               N
   18  _DBASELOCK  Character     16               N
** Total **                     145
```

Figure 21-9 Employee file after conversion

can incorporate several functions to check whether the data has changed. These functions use a special field that dBASE adds to the database structure when you CONVERT the file. Once a file is converted, you can use functions that check whether a record changes, who has locked a record or file, and when a user locked a record or file.

To convert a file, you must open the database in exclusive mode. Then, enter **CONVERT** and press ENTER. dBASE copies the database to a file with a .CVT extension. Then it adds a _DBASELOCK field to the database structure. If you look at the database structure for the EMPLOYEE database after converting it, the database structure looks like Figure 21-9. The new _DBASELOCK field has a width of 16. You can use a different field width by adding **TO** and a field width number between 8 and 24 to the end of the CONVERT command. Changing the width changes how much of the user login name the field stores.

While you cannot see the contents of the _DBASELOCK field because it is a hidden field, you want to know the information it contains. The first two positions of the _DBASELOCK field are a counter. Every time the record's data is changed, the count is incremented. The next three positions store the time the record was locked. The sixth through eighth positions store the date the record was locked. The remaining positions store as much of the dBASE user login name as can fit into the field.

Once you have converted the data, you can use other dBASE functions and commands. You can use the SET REFRESH command to update constantly the records in a Browse or Edit screen to show the most recent changes. To use the REFRESH setting, enter **SET REFRESH TO** followed by the number of seconds you want the data in a Browse or Edit screen updated. If you set REFRESH to 0, the Browse or Edit screen is not updated. When you enter the browse or edit screen, dBASE checks the data every interval set by the REFRESH setting to see if the data has changed. If the data changes, dBASE automatically replaces the old data with the new data.

Another feature you can use with a converted database is the CHANGE function. When a program reads data from a record, it reads the count value. The program can check if the record has changed by comparing the original count value with the current count value. When the program replaces values in the record, it increments the count so other users know that the record has changed.

With a converted file, you can find out who has locked the record that you want. The LKSYS function returns the time a record is locked, the date a record is locked, or the user who locked a record. LKSYS(0) returns the time, LKSYS(1) returns the date, and LKSYS(2) returns the user login name stored in the _DBASELOCK field.

Transaction Processing

Transaction processing allows you to perform a set of dBASE commands and return the data to their original state, if it is not possible to complete the related group of activities that you consider to be a transaction. If you think about a transaction for a manual process like the sale of an item of merchandise, you will understand why it is important to complete all aspects of an activity. If a customer brings a piece of merchandise to a cash register, the clerk enters the item number and price. If the item is taxable, the tax is computed and added to the price of the merchandise to compute the total owed. The clerk may manually reduce a number representing the inventory of this item on hand or the cash register may handle the computation. To allow the customer to leave the store without computing the tax, paying for the item, or recording the sale would not represent a fully completed transaction. Also, if a customer decides not to purchase the item after the clerk has recorded the sale, the activities completed by the clerk must be voided from the system to be in sync with the business activity fully completed.

The same transaction processing concept is important for computer systems. You want to insure that a transaction is completed fully or fully backed out of the system. Transaction processing provides an all-or-none capability. For example, if you are processing the weekly payroll and you want to update the year-to-date amounts in the employee master database, you want to update the year-to-date amounts for all of the employees or none of the employees. If you can only process half of them, it is difficult to start the updating process in the middle of the database at a later time. In this example, you are better off undoing the updates that you have completed and performing the updates at a later time. Transaction processing can be used in either single- or multiuser environments, but it is primarily used in multiuser environments since multiuser environments present a greater potential for some of the data to be unavailable. dBASE's rollback features allow you to eliminate the effect of partially completed transactions from the database.

When you use transaction processing, dBASE stores changes to database files in a transaction log file. If the situation requires it, the data can be restored to their original values. The transaction log file uses the user's dBASE login name as a filename to store the transactions and adds a .LOG extension. The names assigned to transaction files requires that only one user use a specific login name. If two people log in using the same user name, dBASE stores their transaction logs in the same file, which prevents either user from successfully returning the data to the original values, if the rollback feature is needed. You can also test the transaction to check that the transaction is successfully completed, the transaction is successfully rolled back, or the database is in the middle of a transaction.

Starting and Stopping a Transaction Creating an application that uses transaction processing is identical to creating an application that does not use transaction processing. The main difference is that an application that uses transaction processing includes a BEGIN TRANSACTION command where you want dBASE to begin creating a transaction log file of the new and old data values and an END TRANSACTION command where you want dBASE to stop adding to the transaction log file. The BEGIN TRANSACTION command belongs

```
[]··▼··▼··▼··▼··▼··▼2·▼··▼··▼·3▼··▼··▼··▼··▼··▼··▼5·▼··▼··▼·6▼········7·········
BEGIN TRANSACTION                           && Updates retail prices for 10 % increase
USE Inventry INDEX Inventry ORDER Part_numb
REPLACE ALL Rtl_price WITH Rtl_price*1.1
END TRANSACTION
RETURN
```

Figure 21-10 Begin and end transaction

at the point in the program that you want to be able to return to. The END TRANSACTION command is placed at the point in the program that represents the end of the transaction. If this instruction is reached, the program does not need to rollback activities already completed as part of the transaction. The END TRANSACTION command commits all of the changes that you have made since the BEGIN TRANSACTION command as permanent updates to the database.

For example, using the updating year-to-date fields in a weekly payroll application example discussed previously, the program includes the BEGIN TRANSACTION before you start changing the year-to-date fields for the first record, and the END TRANSACTION belongs after you finish changing the last year-to-date fields for the last record. Figure 21-10 shows a module that uses the BEGIN and END TRANSACTION commands to group a set of commands together. The program replaces the retail cost for each of the inventory items with the retail price increased by ten percent. When you perform this application, dBASE creates a transaction log file that contains the old retail prices and new retail prices for each of the inventory item. Once dBASE performs the END TRANSACTION command, it deletes the transaction log file. The END TRANSACTION command also removes the locks set during the transaction.

Recovering An Interrupted Transaction Once you add the BEGIN and END TRANSACTION commands to an application, you can determine what conditions force the program to return the data to the original values. This is called recovering a transaction. To recover a transaction, use the ROLLBACK command. This command is used from the dot prompt if there is a system interruption, such as a power failure. A program uses this command when the application contains a condition that specifies when the transaction should be rolled back.

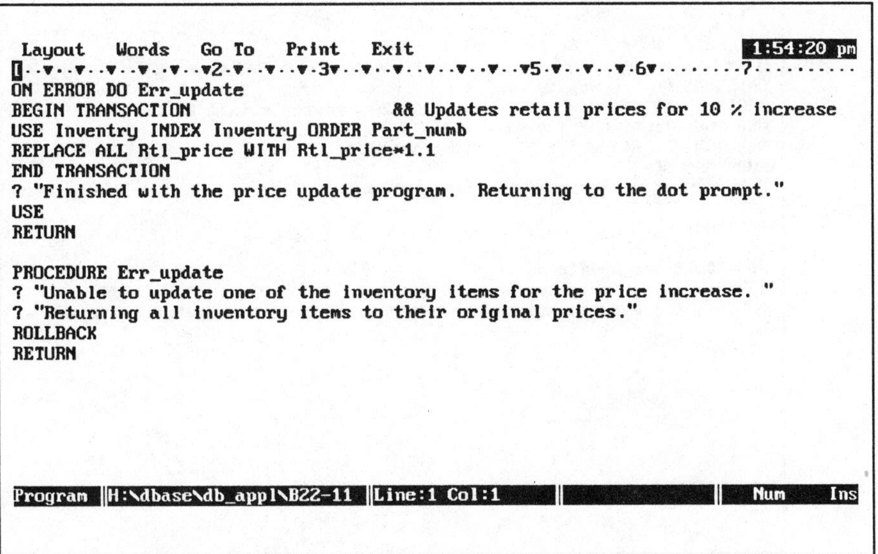

```
 Layout   Words   Go To   Print   Exit                                    1:54:20 pm
[]··▼··▼··▼··▼··▼··▼2·▼··▼··▼·3▼··▼··▼··▼··▼··▼··▼5·▼··▼··▼·6▼········7·········
ON ERROR DO Err_update
BEGIN TRANSACTION                          && Updates retail prices for 10 % increase
USE Inventry INDEX Inventry ORDER Part_numb
REPLACE ALL Rtl_price WITH Rtl_price*1.1
END TRANSACTION
? "Finished with the price update program.  Returning to the dot prompt."
USE
RETURN

PROCEDURE Err_update
? "Unable to update one of the inventory items for the price increase. "
? "Returning all inventory items to their original prices."
ROLLBACK
RETURN

Program  ||H:\dbase\db_appl\B22-11  ||Line:1 Col:1  ||          ||     Num     Ins
```

Figure 21-11 Module that uses transaction processing

Figure 21-11 shows the module that uses transaction processing. If dBASE cannot lock the current record, the entire transaction is recovered. When you roll back a transaction, dBASE rolls back the transaction then executes the next command after the END TRANSACTION command. For example, if the transaction in Figure 21-11 (shown earlier) is rolled back, the next command performed is ? "Finished with the price update program. Returning to the dot prompt."

If your network has a system failure, multiple users will need to recover the current transaction. For each user, the user logs in and issues the ROLLBACK command from the dot prompt.

An alternative to rolling back a transaction, especially when the amount of data to be rolled back is substantial, is retrying it. Figure 21-12 shows two modules — one uses transaction processing and the other performs if the transaction processing encounters a record lock error. If the initial program encounters a record-lock error, the ERR_UPDATE module shows the user who has locked the record the program wants to use. This lets the user identify the user who has locked the record and send them a message to unlock it. Once the other user has unlocked the record, the first user can press a key and the Err_update procedure returns to the main program and retries replacing the old retail price with the new retail price.

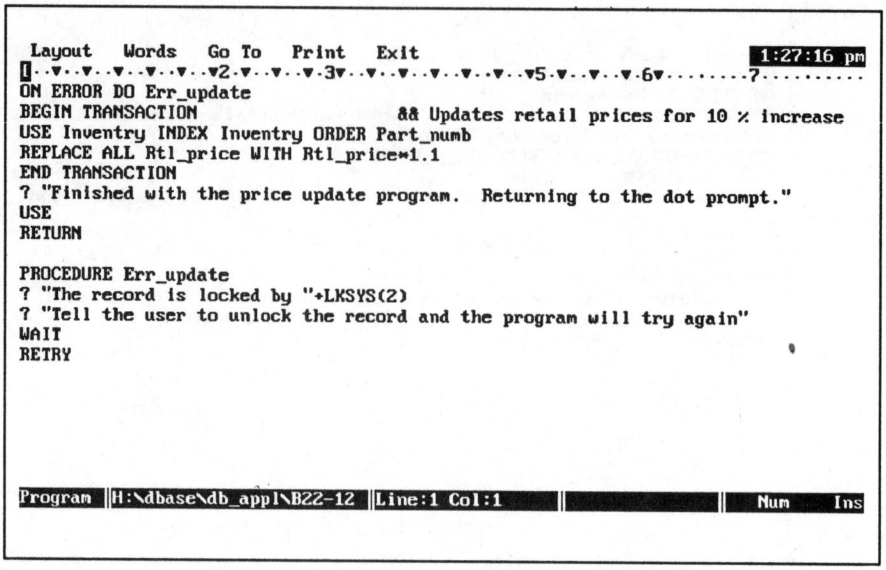

```
 Layout   Words   Go To   Print   Exit                                  1:27:16 pm
[·▼··▼··▼··▼··▼··▼2·▼··▼··▼·3▼··▼··▼··▼··▼··▼··▼5·▼··▼··▼·6▼········7·········
ON ERROR DO Err_update
BEGIN TRANSACTION                     && Updates retail prices for 10 % increase
USE Inventry INDEX Inventry ORDER Part_numb
REPLACE ALL Rtl_price WITH Rtl_price*1.1
END TRANSACTION
? "Finished with the price update program.  Returning to the dot prompt."
USE
RETURN

PROCEDURE Err_update
? "The record is locked by "+LKSYS(2)
? "Tell the user to unlock the record and the program will try again"
WAIT
RETRY




Program ║H:\dbase\db_appl\B22-12 ║Line:1 Col:1 ║           ║        Num    Ins
```

Figure 21-12 Two program modules

Testing the Transaction You can use dBASE functions to test a transaction. You can test if a transaction is successfully completed, a transaction is successfully rolled back, or the database is in the middle of a transaction. The COMPLETED function returns a .T. if a transaction is successfully completed with an END TRANSACTION or ROLLBACK command, or an .F. otherwise. The ROLLBACK function returns a .T. if a transaction is successfully rolled back, or an .F. otherwise. Figure 21-13 shows a module that uses the ROLLBACK and COMPLETED functions to determine whether the transaction is completed, rolled back, or incomplete. The ISMARKED function returns a .T. if a database in the specified work area is involved in a transaction. You can use this function in an error condition when you have an ON ERROR command that is intended to operate for several situations. Figure 21-14 shows a module that performs when the main program encounters an error. The module in the figure modifies the action depending upon whether the calling module is in the middle of a transaction. The ISMARKED function can also prevent a user from accessing a database that another user has locked. Figure 21-15 shows two modules that multiple users can use. If a user is performing the transaction in the first module,

```
 Layout   Words   Go To   Print   Exit                                     1:58:40 pm
[··▼··▼··▼··▼··▼··▼2·▼··▼··▼·3▼··▼··▼··▼··▼··▼··▼5·▼··▼··▼·6▼········7·········
ON ERROR DO Err_update
BEGIN TRANSACTION                     && Updates retail prices for 10 % increase
USE Inventry INDEX Inventry ORDER Part_numb
REPLACE ALL Rtl_price WITH Rtl_price*1.1
END TRANSACTION
IF COMPLETE()
   ? "Transaction successfully completed or rolled back."
ENDIF
? "Finished with the price update program.  Returning to the dot prompt."
USE
RETURN

PROCEDURE Err_update
? "Unable to update one of the inventory items for the price increase. "
? "Returning all inventory items to their original prices."
ROLLBACK
IF .NOT. ROLLBACK()
   ? "Unable to roll back transaction.  Use backup of database."
ENDIF
RETURN
Program  H:\dbase\db_appl\B22-13  Line:1 Col:1                         Num    Ins
```

Figure 21-13 ROLLBACK and COMPLETED functions

```
 Layout   Words   Go To   Print   Exit                                     2:13:58 pm
[··▼··▼··▼··▼··▼··▼2·▼··▼··▼·3▼··▼··▼··▼··▼··▼··▼5·▼··▼··▼·6▼········7·········
ON ERROR DO Err_fix
BEGIN TRANSACTION                     && Updates retail prices for 10 % increase
USE Inventry INDEX Inventry ORDER Part_numb
IF RIGHT(DBF(),12)="INVENTRY.DBF"
   REPLACE ALL Rtl_price WITH Rtl_price*1.1
ENDIF
END TRANSACTION
USE
RETURN

PROCEDURE Err_fix
IF ISMARKED()                         && Error occurred during Replace command
   ? "Unable to update one of the inventory items for the price increase. "
   ? "Returning all inventory items to their original prices."
   ROLLBACK
ELSE
   ? "Unable to open Inventry database."
   ? "Try program at another time."
ENDIF
RETURN
Program  H:\dbase\db_appl\B22-14  Line:1 Col:1                       NumCapsIns
```

Figure 21-14 Error routine

```
 Layout   Words   Go To   Print   Exit                                          2:16:05 pm
[]··▼··▼··▼··▼··▼··▼2·▼··▼··▼·3▼··▼··▼··▼··▼··▼··▼5·▼··▼··▼·6▼········7··········
ON ERROR DO Err_update
IF ISMARKED()
   ? "Someone else is using database in a transaction."
   ? "Perform this program at another time to prevent transaction"
   ? "log file conflicts."
   RETURN
ENDIF
BEGIN TRANSACTION                         && Updates retail prices for 10 % increase
USE Inventry INDEX Inventry ORDER Part_numb
REPLACE ALL Rtl_price WITH Rtl_price*1.1
END TRANSACTION
? "Finished with the price update program.  Returning to the dot prompt."
USE
RETURN

PROCEDURE Err_update
? "Unable to update one of the inventory items for the price increase. "
? "Returning all inventory items to their original prices."
ROLLBACK
RETURN
Program  ||H:\dbase\db_appl\B22-15  ||Line:1 Col:1  ||            ||  NumCapsIns
```

Figure 21-15 Two multiple-user modules

another user will want to wait until the first user's transaction is completed to perform the second module.

Other Networking Commands

In a network application, you will need to use other commands than have been discussed in this chapter. When you use DISPLAY STATUS or LIST STATUS in a network, dBASE returns additional information than when you use the command in a single-user network. Figure 21-16 shows the beginning of the LIST STATUS command output. The lock list shows which records are locked by any dBASE users. In a network version of dBASE, you may want to use the DISPLAY USERS or LIST USERS command to list the other users logged into dBASE. Unlike the USERS and LKSYS functions, the DISPLAY or LIST USERS returns the network login names rather than the dBASE login names. You can use this information if you want to send a message to another user and are unsure of the user's login name. When you use this command dBASE adds a greater than sign to indicate your login user name.

```
Currently Selected Database:
Select area:  1, Database in Use: H:\DBASE\DB_APPL\INVENTRY.DBF    Alias: INVENTR
Y
Production   MDX file:  H:\DBASE\DB_APPL\INVENTRY.MDX
          Index TAG:       PART_NUMB  Key: PART_NUMB
          Lock list:       25,      15,      4,      10,      18
                             3  locked
```

Figure 21-16 LIST STATUS output

Finally, you may want to incorporate the LOGOUT command into a network application as an option when the user quits the application. Figure 21-17 shows a module that executes when a user selects Quit from the opening menu. The user can select whether to quit dBASE or to log out, such as when someone else wants to use dBASE or the user wants to use dBASE but with a different group login name.

Sample Application Program

The sample network application that you will examine in this section is a program that handles the major tasks that a company performs on an employee database like the one you have created with the Getting Started sections of the earlier chapters. The initial menu is shown in Figure 21-18. An employee database program must be able to add records as employees are hired, edit records as the employee's information changes, create reports to inform management how the human resources and payroll systems are functioning, delete employee

```
[··▼··▼··▼··▼··▼··▼2·▼··▼··▼·3▼··▼··▼··▼··▼··▼··▼5·▼··▼··▼·6▼·········7·········
* EMPLOYEE.PRG
DO Set_up                                   && Initializes settings
DO WHILE .T.                                && Exits program with QUIT command
   DO Menu_def                              && Defines menu
   ACTIVATE POPUP Openmenu                  && Uses menu
   LOGOUT
ENDDO
```

Figure 21-17 Incorporating logout into a program

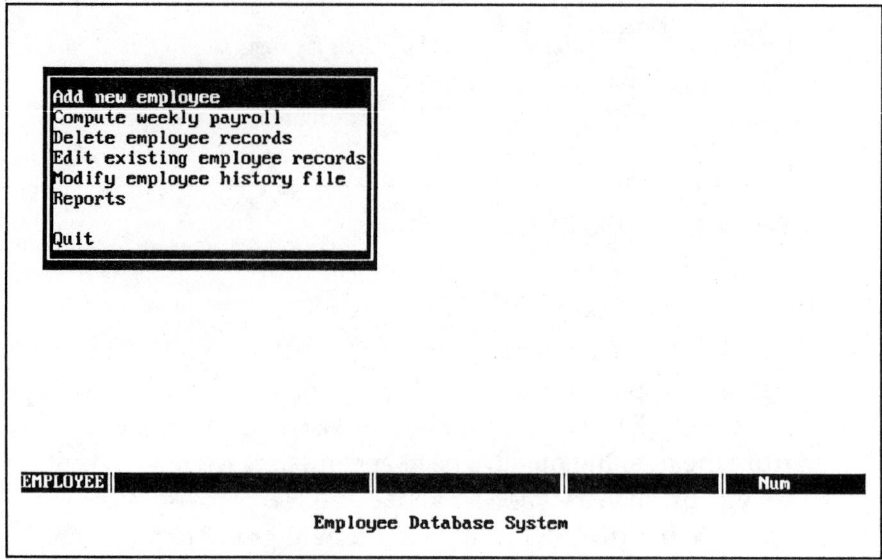

Figure 21-18 Initial menu

records for employees who have left the company, and exit from the application. This application also includes an option to modify the employee history file. In the remainder of the chapter, the text discusses the program and the network features the program uses. Some of the code is shown with the text that discusses it and a full listing is included at the end of the chapter. The program code includes dummy modules for the Compute weekly payroll, Delete employee records, and Reports menu items.

Tip: Creating your own network applications.

When you create a network application, develop the application for a single-user environment first. It helps you find the nonnetwork bugs of the program and minimizes the effect of the program to other users. Once the program works for the single-user environment, modify it for the multiuser environment. The changeover takes less time than you might think since you only have to focus on network-related problems.

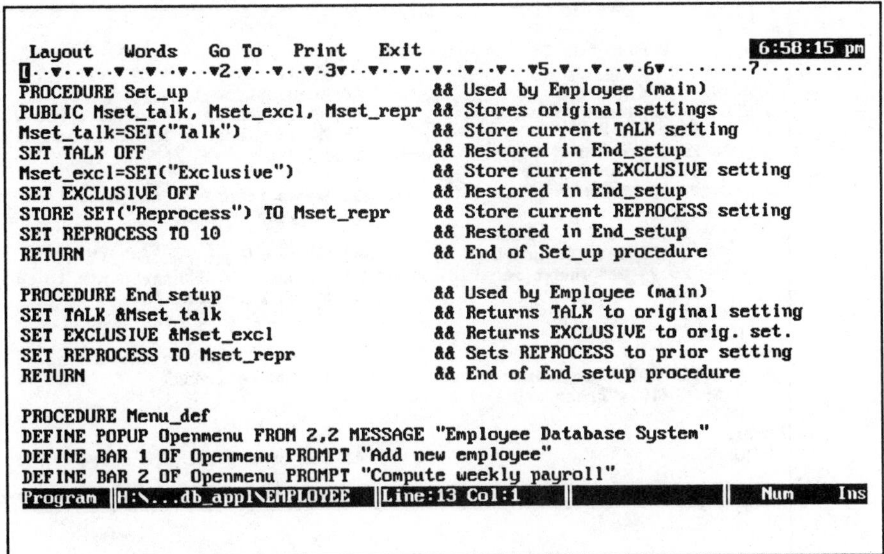

Layout Words Go To Print Exit 6:58:15 pm
PROCEDURE Set_up && Used by Employee (main)
PUBLIC Mset_talk, Mset_excl, Mset_repr && Stores original settings
Mset_talk=SET("Talk") && Store current TALK setting
SET TALK OFF && Restored in End_setup
Mset_excl=SET("Exclusive") && Store current EXCLUSIVE setting
SET EXCLUSIVE OFF && Restored in End_setup
STORE SET("Reprocess") TO Mset_repr && Store current REPROCESS setting
SET REPROCESS TO 10 && Restored in End_setup
RETURN && End of Set_up procedure
PROCEDURE End_setup && Used by Employee (main)
SET TALK &Mset_talk && Returns TALK to original setting
SET EXCLUSIVE &Mset_excl && Returns EXCLUSIVE to orig. set.
SET REPROCESS TO Mset_repr && Sets REPROCESS to prior setting
RETURN && End of End_setup procedure
PROCEDURE Menu_def
DEFINE POPUP Openmenu FROM 2,2 MESSAGE "Employee Database System"
DEFINE BAR 1 OF Openmenu PROMPT "Add new employee"
DEFINE BAR 2 OF Openmenu PROMPT "Compute weekly payroll"
Program H:\...db_appl\EMPLOYEE Line:13 Col:1 Num Ins

Figure 21-19 Program code to change settings

Changing Settings

When you create network application programs, you should not rely upon each machine starting with the same default settings. For a network application to run identically for everyone, you must use the SET commands to establish the settings that you need. Also, you want to return the settings to their original entries so other applications can continue to operate properly. Figure 21-19 shows the part of the EMPLOYEE.PRG program that sets the TALK, EXCLUSIVE, and REPROCESS settings to the entries that the program expects. Since different modules establish the settings and return the settings to their original values, the variables that store the initial setting values must be public. The SET EXCLUSIVE setting prevents users from exclusively opening the EMPLOYEE database. It allows multiple users to use the database at once. The SET REPROCESS sets the number of attempts dBASE makes to lock a file or record. Without this setting, the program can try indefinitely to lock a record. Figure 21-19 shows the module that restores the settings to their original values. While these modules only affect three settings, you will probably want to include additional settings in your own network applications. For example, your applica-

```
 Layout   Words   Go To   Print   Exit                                                5:03:29 pm
[··▼··▼··▼··▼··▼··▼2·▼··▼··▼·3▼··▼··▼··▼··▼··▼··▼5·▼··▼··▼·6▼········7·········
PROCEDURE Add_rec                              && Menu option 1
STORE "Y" TO Mnext_rec                         && Adds records while Mnext_rec=Y
IF ACCESS()<=5                                 && Minimum access level to add data
   USE Employee INDEX Employee.mdx ORDER TAG Ssn
   DO WHILE Mnext_rec="Y"
      APPEND BLANK                             && Locks record at the same time
      DO Rec_edit                              && Data entry screen
      @ 19,20 TO 21,72 DOUBLE
      @ 20,21 SAY "Do you want to add another employee record? (Y/N) "
      @ 20,71 GET Mnext_rec PICTURE "!"&& Determines if user wants to add
      READ                                     && another record.
   ENDDO
   USE
ELSE                                           && Handles Insufficient access
   @ 15,10 SAY "Insufficient access level to add records."
   ? SPACE(10)+"Press any key to continue. "
   WAIT ""
ENDIF
RETURN                                         && End of Add_rec procedure

Program  H:\...db_appl\EMPLOYEE  Line:62 Col:1                        Num    Ins
```

Figure 21-20 Add_rec module

tion may need to include the SET ECHO, SET CONFIRM, and SET LOCK commands.

Locking Records

Most of the time you do not need to lock records explicitly. The network program locks records three places, each using a different method. In the Add_rec module for adding records, the APPEND BLANK command in Figure 21-20 automatically locks the record when it adds a blank record that the Rec_edit module modifies. The Edit_rec module for editing existing records explicitly locks the record with the RLOCK function in the Rec_edit module shown in Figure 21-21. In the Rec_edit module, the RLOCK function tests whether the module can lock the current record. It does not matter that the code also performs this step for adding records since the RLOCK function returns a .T. if the record is locked for the current user. It waits until this point so a user does not tie up the system if the user does not immediately finish editing data. In the Modi_hist module, the records are locked for the correct and incorrect social security numbers if they exist with the RLOCK command. The RLOCK command also locks other records with the incor-

```
Layout   Words   Go To   Print   Exit                                   3:50:50 pm
...▼..[..▼..▼..▼..▼2.▼..▼..▼.3▼..▼..▼..▼..▼..▼..▼5.▼..▼..▼.6▼........7..........
      IF RLOCK()
         DO Repl_field                      && Places new data in fields.
      ELSE                                  && User cannot change edited data
         @ 16,10 CLEAR TO 20,75             && because another user has locked
         @ 16,10 TO 20,75 DOUBLE            && the necessary record.
         @ 17,11 SAY "Record is locked by user: "+LKSYS(2)
         @ 18,11 SAY "Reenter the data a another time."
         @ 19,11 SAY "Press any key to continue."
         WAIT ""
      ENDIF
      M_nochange=.F.                        && Prevents DO WHILE loop from
   ELSE                                     && executing again
      @ 16,10 CLEAR TO 20,75
      @ 16,10 TO 20,75 DOUBLE
      @ 17,11 SAY "Record has changed, updating screen to show ;
new record data."
      @ 18,11 SAY "Re-edit the data."
      @ 19,11 SAY "Press any key to continue."
      WAIT ""
      GOTO RECNO()                          && updates count used to check
Program  |H:\...db_appl\EMPLOYEE  |Line:290 Col:7 |              |  Num    Ins
```

Figure 21-21 Rec_edit module

rect social security number as the program finds it in the transaction. In this module and the Rec_edit module, the modules use the results of the RLOCK function to determine the next step to perform.

None of the records in the program is specifically unlocked. All the records become unlocked when the database is closed.

Using Access Levels to Control Security

You can combine the security features that you add with the PROTECT command to a program. For adding records and modifying the employee history file, the code for the menu item sets a minimum access level, as Figure 21-20 shows for the Adding records menu item. Also, in the Rec_edit module that customizes the editing screen for new and old records, the code only displays and prompts for field information if the user has a low enough access level, since the lower the access, the more privileges the user has. The access levels for each of the fields is shown in Figure 21-22. Figure 21-23 shows the code for the NUMB_DEPEN and HR_RATE fields. For each field, if the R/O privilege level for the field is greater than or equal to the user's access level, the field description and contents appears. If the FULL privilege

Delete privilege 2

Fieldname	Access Levels 1	2	3	4	5	6	7	8
SSN	FULL	FULL	FULL	R/O	R/O	R/O	R/O	R/O
LAST_NAME	FULL	FULL	FULL	FULL	R/O	R/O	R/O	R/O
M_INITIAL	FULL	FULL	FULL	FULL	R/O	R/O	R/O	R/O
FIRST_NAME	FULL	FULL	FULL	FULL	R/O	R/O	R/O	R/O
ADDRESS	FULL	FULL	FULL	FULL	FULL	R/O	R/O	R/O
CITY	FULL	FULL	FULL	FULL	FULL	R/O	R/O	R/O
STATE	FULL	FULL	FULL	FULL	FULL	R/O	R/O	R/O
ZIP_CODE	FULL	FULL	FULL	FULL	FULL	R/O	R/O	R/O
HOME_PHONE	FULL	FULL	FULL	FULL	FULL	R/O	R/O	R/O
HIRE_DATE	FULL	FULL	FULL	R/O	R/O	R/O	R/O	NONE
MARITAL_ST	FULL	FULL	FULL	R/O	R/O	NONE	NONE	NONE
NUMB_DEPEN	FULL	FULL	FULL	R/O	R/O	NONE	NONE	NONE
HR_RATE	FULL	R/O	R/O	NONE	NONE	NONE	NONE	NONE
YTD_WAGES	FULL	FULL	R/O	NONE	NONE	NONE	NONE	NONE
YTD_FIT	FULL	FULL	R/O	NONE	NONE	NONE	NONE	NONE
HEALTH	FULL	FULL	FULL	R/O	R/O	NONE	NONE	NONE
SKILLS	FULL	FULL	FULL	R/O	R/O	R/O	NONE	NONE

Figure 21-22 Record access levels

```
Layout   Words   Go To   Print   Exit                                    3:53:29 pm
···[··▼··▼··▼··▼··▼2·▼··▼··▼·3▼··▼··▼··▼··▼··▼··▼5·▼··▼··▼·6▼·········7··········
   IF ACCESS()<=5                          && Numb_depen field - R/O access
      @ 11,46 SAY "NUMB_DEPEN:"            && level is 5, FULL is 3
      IF ACCESS()<=3
         @ 11,58 GET M_depen PICTURE "99"
      ELSE
         @ 11,58 SAY M_depen
      ENDIF
   ENDIF

   IF ACCESS()<=3                          && Hr_rate field - R/O access level
      @ 13,0 SAY "HOURLY RATE:"            && is 3, FULL is 1
      IF ACCESS()<=1
         @ 13,12 GET Mhr_rate PICTURE "999.99" RANGE 3.35,50
      ELSE
         @ 13,12 SAY Mhr_rate
      ENDIF
   ENDIF

   IF ACCESS()<=3                          && Ytd_wages field - R/O access
      @ 12,30 TO 15,53 DOUBLE              && level is 3, FULL is 2
Program ║H:\...db_appl\EMPLOYEE ║Line:229 Col:4 ║              ║   Num    Ins
```

Figure 21-23 Numb_depend and Hr_rate field

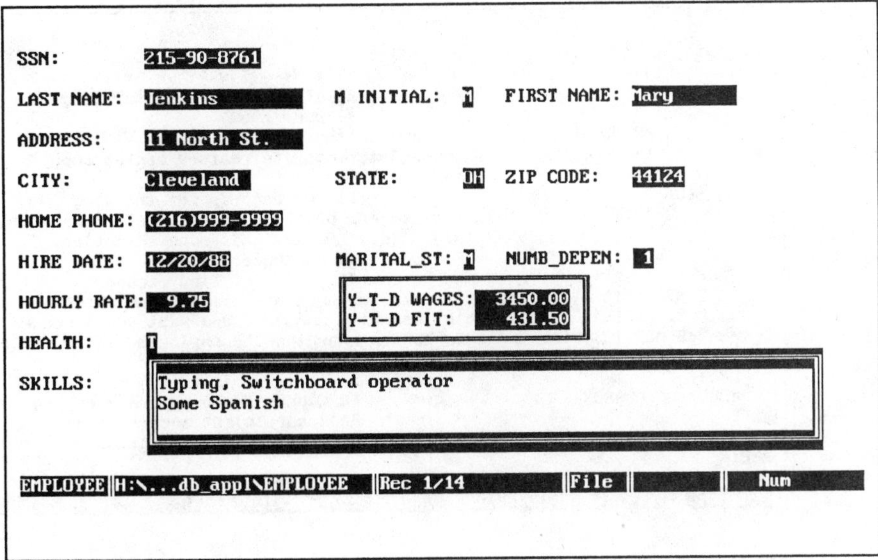

SSN: 215-90-8761
LAST NAME: Jenkins
M INITIAL: T
FIRST NAME: Mary
ADDRESS: 11 North St.
CITY: Cleveland
STATE: OH
ZIP CODE: 44124
HOME PHONE: (216)999-9999
HIRE DATE: 12/20/88
MARITAL_ST: T
NUMB_DEPEN: 1
HOURLY RATE: 9.75
Y-T-D WAGES: 3450.00
Y-T-D FIT: 431.50
HEALTH: T
SKILLS:
Typing, Switchboard operator
Some Spanish
EMPLOYEE
H:\...db_appl\EMPLOYEE
Rec 1/14
File
Num

Figure 21-24 User access level 1 screen

level for the field is greater than or equal to the user's access level, the field's text appears and the program prompts for a new value. Figure 21-24 shows the screen for a user with an access level of 1. This screen contains all of the information for the record. This is a different screen from the one in Figure 21-3. While the code is the same, it adapts for each user to match the user's access code.

Network Functions

In the employee database application, the modules use various functions that would not be included in a single-user application. As mentioned with combining access levels and security design, the application uses the ACCESS function to determine whether the user can perform the task defined by the menu item, and for editing and adding data, which selects the data the user can see and edit. The LKSYS function in the Rec_edit module tells the user who has locked the record the user wants to edit. Since record locking is not an issue for adding

```
Layout   Words   Go To   Print   Exit                                      5:09:04 pm
···▼··▼··[··▼··▼··▼2·▼··▼··▼·3▼··▼··▼··▼··▼··▼··▼5·▼··▼··▼·6▼········7··········
           IF .NOT. ROLLBACK()                  && If a problem exists, lets
              ? ""                              && user know.
              ? "Unable to return data to the original values.  "
              ? "Contact database administrator to restore backup copy."
           ENDIF
        ELSE                                    && Two records for the same
           @ 17,0 SAY "You must delete one of these records before updating "
           ? "the employee history file.  Leaving this menu selection. "
        ENDIF                                   && employee.
     ELSE                                       && Could not find record
        ? SPACE(13)+"No records in the employee master database match the new"
        ? SPACE(13)+"or old social security number.  You must add a record for"
        ? SPACE(13)+"the employee before changing the employee history file.  "
        ? ""
     ENDIF
     CLOSE DATABASES                            && Closes Employee and Week_pay
  ELSE                                          && Insufficient access level
     @ 13,5 SAY "Insufficient access level for this menu selection"
  ENDIF
  WAIT                                          && keeps last displayed message
Program  ||H:\...db_appl\EMPLOYEE  ||Line:427 Col:10  ||                 ||  Num    Ins
```

Figure 21-25 ROLLBACK function

records that locks the record when the module adds a blank record, it is only an issue for editing records. The RLOCK function locks records in the Rec_edit and Modi_hist modules. It also serves as a test to determine which steps the modules perform if it can or cannot lock the record. The ROLLBACK function shown in Figure 21-25 is used with the transaction processing in Modi_hist to determine if the transaction is successfully rolled back.

Handling Error Conditions

Most of the potential errors the employee database can encounter are handled in the application using IF ... ENDIF constraints and network functions as conditions. Figure 21-25 shows the code for the Modi_hist module if the ROLLBACK command is successful. The application also uses this error handling for record locking in Modi_hist and Rec_edit.

Converted Files

The EMPLOYEE database is a converted file. This application uses several of the features a converted file provides. The file must be converted before the application is used. This program uses the CHANGE function to determine if the values the program read from the current record before the user edited the data are the same as the data in the record before the program updated the old contents with the edited values. If the record data has not changed, the program proceeds to replace the old data with the new data. If the current record data has changed since the program read the data for the user to edit it, the module repeats and lets the user edit the data from the current record after updating the screen to show the current data. The application also uses the LKSYS function of Rec_edit to tell the user who has locked the record that is causing the user's edited data to be rejected.

Transaction Processing in Modi_hist

The Modi_hist module uses transaction processing to perform an all-or-nothing replacement of the incorrect social security number with the correct social security number. The BEGIN TRANSACTION command precedes when the program replaces the old social security number with the correct social security number in the employee master database. The END TRANSACTION command follows the ENDSCAN command after the module has completely replaced all occurrences of the incorrect social security number with the correct social security number. If the module is unable to lock a record before it replaces the social security number, it rolls back all of the data and returns the original social security numbers for the EMPLOYEE and WEEK_PAY databases. If something prevents the transaction from rolling back, the next command after the END TRANSACTION command displays a warning message for the user.

```
* EMPLOYEE.PRG
* Employee database program for network
* Procedure order: main (Employee), Set_up, End_setup, Menu_def, Menu_pick
* Add_rec, Wk_payroll, Del_rec, Edit_rec, Rec_edit, Init_var, Repl_field,
* Chng_memo, Modi_hist, Same_recs, Rpt_menu
DO Set_up                           && Initialization and set commands
CLEAR                               && Clears screen of prior contents
DO Menu_def                         && Defines menu
ACTIVATE POPUP Openmenu             && Starts menu
DO End_setup                        && Returns SETtings to original
RETURN                              && End of Employee.prg

PROCEDURE Set_up                    && Used by Employee (main)
PUBLIC Mset_talk, Mset_excl, Mset_repr  && Stores original settings
Mset_talk=SET("Talk")               && Store current TALK setting
SET TALK OFF                        && Restored in End_setup
Mset_excl=SET("Exclusive")          && Store current EXCLUSIVE setting
SET EXCLUSIVE OFF                   && Restored in End_setup
STORE SET("Reprocess") TO Mset_repr && Store current REPROCESS setting
SET REPROCESS TO 10                 && Restored in End_setup
RETURN                              && End of Set_up procedure

PROCEDURE End_setup                 && Used by Employee (main)
SET TALK &Mset_talk                 && Returns TALK to original setting
SET EXCLUSIVE &Mset_excl            && Returns EXCLUSIVE to orig. set.
SET REPROCESS TO Mset_repr          && Sets REPROCESS to prior setting
RETURN                              && End of End_setup procedure

PROCEDURE Menu_def
DEFINE POPUP Openmenu FROM 2,2 MESSAGE "Employee Database System"
DEFINE BAR 1 OF Openmenu PROMPT "Add new employee"
DEFINE BAR 2 OF Openmenu PROMPT "Compute weekly payroll"
DEFINE BAR 3 OF Openmenu PROMPT "Delete employee records"
DEFINE BAR 4 OF Openmenu PROMPT "Edit existing employee records"
DEFINE BAR 5 OF Openmenu PROMPT "Modify employee history file"
DEFINE BAR 6 OF Openmenu PROMPT "Reports"
DEFINE BAR 7 OF Openmenu PROMPT " " SKIP
DEFINE BAR 8 OF Openmenu PROMPT "Quit"
ON SELECTION POPUP Openmenu DO Menu_pick
RETURN                              && End of Menu_def procedure

PROCEDURE Menu_pick
DO CASE
 CASE BAR() = 1                     && Adds records
     DO Add_rec
 CASE BAR() = 2                     && Computes weekly payroll
     DO Wk_payroll
 CASE BAR() = 3                     && Deletes employee records
     DO Del_rec
 CASE BAR() = 4                     && Edits records
     DO Edit_rec
 CASE BAR() = 5                     && Modifies employee history file
     DO Modi_hist
 CASE BAR() = 6                     && Reports
     DO Rpt_menu
*    CASE BAR() = 7                 && Unavailable - for spacing
 CASE BAR() = 8                     && Quits
     DEACTIVATE POPUP
ENDCASE
CLEAR                               && Clears screen before next menu
RETURN                              && End of Menu_pick procedure

PROCEDURE Add_rec                   && Menu option 1
STORE "Y" TO Mnext_rec              && Adds records while Mnext_rec=Y
IF ACCESS()<=5                      && Minimum access level to add data
 USE Employee INDEX Employee.mdx ORDER Ssn
 DO WHILE Mnext_rec="Y"
    APPEND BLANK                    && Locks record at the same time
    DO Rec_edit                     && Data entry screen
    @ 19,20 TO 21,72 DOUBLE
```

```
    @ 20,21 SAY "Do you want to add another employee record? (Y/N) "
    @ 20,71 GET Mnext_rec PICTURE "!"&& Determines if user wants to add
    READ                              && another record.
 ENDDO
 USE
ELSE                                  && Handles Insufficient access
 @ 15,10 SAY "Insufficient access level to add records."
 ? SPACE(10)+"Press any key to continue. "
 WAIT ""
ENDIF
RETURN                                && End of Add_rec procedure

PROCEDURE Wk_payroll                  && Menu option 2
* Commands for this procedure are here
RETURN                                && End of Wk_payroll procedure

PROCEDURE Del_rec                     && Menu option 3
* Commands for this procedure are here
RETURN                                && End of Del_rec procedure

PROCEDURE Edit_rec                    && Menu option 4
STORE "   -  -    " TO Mssn
STORE "Y" TO Mnext_rec
USE Employee INDEX Employee.mdx ORDER Ssn
DO WHILE Mnext_rec="Y"
 @ 19,20 TO 21,76 DOUBLE
 @ 20,21 SAY "Enter the employee's social security number:"
 @ 20,65 GET Mssn PICTURE "999-99-9999"
 READ
 FIND &Mssn
 IF FOUND()
    DO Rec_edit
 ELSE
    @ 17,20 TO 19,76 DOUBLE
    @ 18,21 SAY "Could not find record. Press a key to continue."
    WAIT ""
 ENDIF
 @ 19,20 TO 21,76 DOUBLE
 @ 20,21 SAY "Do you want to edit another employee's record? (Y/N)   "
 @ 20,75 GET Mnext_rec PICTURE "!"
 READ
ENDDO
USE
RETURN                                && End of Edit_rec procedure

PROCEDURE Rec_edit                    && Used by Add_rec and Edit_rec
* Data screen for editing and appending records,
* customized for access level

* This loop is performed once for appending records.
* For editing records, it is performed once if the record data has not
* changed since the data was read.  If the record's data changes, this
* loop repeats if another user changes the data that the current users is
* editing.
* The database has been CONVERTed to include the _DBASELOCK field
PUBLIC Mssn_edit, Mlast_name, Maddress, Mm_initial, Mmarital, Mfirst
PUBLIC Mcity, Mstate, Mzip_code, M_depen, Mhr_rate, Mytd_wages, Mytd_fit
PUBLIC Mphone, Mhire_date, Mhealth
STORE "            " TO Mfilename     && Used for Skills memo field
DEFINE WINDOW W_skills FROM 16,12 TO 20,75
CLEAR
STORE .T. TO M_nochange               && Changes to .F. when data is
DO WHILE M_nochange                   && successfully appended or edited
 DO Init_var                          && Initializes memory variables
* The following code displays the memory variable and text for each field,
* changing the display depending upon the user's access code.
* This is the code for each field:
*   IF ACCESS()<=(access level field can be read)
*      @ (screen position) SAY (field name)
*      IF ACCESS()<=(Access level field can be edited)
```

Employee.txt *(continued)*

```
*           @ (screen position) GET (field name)
*        ELSE
*           @ (screen position) SAY (field name)
*        ENDIF
*     ENDIF
* First IF ... ENDIF loop is absent if read access level is 8

 @ 1,0 SAY "SSN:"                        && Ssn field - R/O access level
    IF ACCESS()<=3                       && is 8, FULL is 3
    @ 1,12 GET Mssn_edit PICTURE "999-99-9999"
 ELSE
    @ 1,12 SAY Mssn_edit
 ENDIF

 @ 3,0 SAY "LAST NAME:"                  && Last_name field - R/O access
 IF ACCESS()<=4                          && level is 8, FULL is 4
    @ 3,12 GET Mlast_name PICTURE "XXXXXXXXXXXXXXX"
 ELSE
    @ 3,12 SAY Mlast_name
 ENDIF

 @ 3,30 SAY "M INITIAL:"                 && M_initial field - R/O access
 IF ACCESS()<=4                          && level is 8, FULL is 4
    @ 3,42 GET Mm_initial PICTURE "X"
 ELSE
    @ 3,42 SAY Mm_initial
 ENDIF

 @ 3,46 SAY "FIRST NAME:"                && First_name field - R/O access
 IF ACCESS()<=4                          && level is 8, FULL is 4
    @ 3,58 GET Mfirst PICTURE "XXXXXXXXXX"
 ELSE
    @ 3,58 SAY Mfirst
 ENDIF

 @ 5,0 SAY "ADDRESS:"                    && Address field - R/O access level
 IF ACCESS()<=5                          && is 8, FULL is 5
    @ 5,12 GET Maddress PICTURE "XXXXXXXXXXXXXXX"
 ELSE
    @ 5,12 SAY Maddress
 ENDIF

 @ 7,0 SAY "CITY:"                       && City field - R/O access level
 IF ACCESS()<=5                          && is 8, FULL is 5
    @ 7,12 GET Mcity PICTURE "XXXXXXXXXX"
 ELSE
    @ 7,12 SAY Mcity
 ENDIF

 @ 7,30 SAY "STATE:"                     && State field - R/O access level
 IF ACCESS()<=5                          && is 8, FULL is 5
    @ 7,42 GET Mstate PICTURE "XX"
 ELSE
    @ 7,42 SAY Mstate
 ENDIF

 @ 7,46 SAY "ZIP CODE:"                  && Zip_code field - R/O access
 IF ACCESS()<=5                          && level is 8, FULL is 5
    @ 7,58 GET Mzip_code PICTURE "99999"
 ELSE
    @ 7,58 SAY Mzip_code
 ENDIF

 @ 9,0 SAY "HOME PHONE:"                 && Home_phone field - R/O access
 IF ACCESS()<=5                          && level is 8, FULL is 5
    @ 9,12 GET Mphone PICTURE "(999)999-9999"
 ELSE
    @ 9,12 SAY Mphone
 ENDIF
```

Employee.txt *(continued)*

```
IF ACCESS()<=7                          && Hire_date field - R/O access
   @ 11,0 SAY "HIRE DATE:"              && level is 7, FULL is 3
   IF ACCESS()<=3
      @ 11,12 GET Mhire_date DEFAULT date()
   ELSE
      @ 11,12 SAY Mhire_date
   ENDIF
ENDIF

IF ACCESS()<=5                          && Marital_st field - R/O access
   @ 11,30 SAY "MARITAL_ST:"            && level is 5, FULL is 3
   IF ACCESS()<=3
      @ 11,42 GET Mmarital PICTURE "X"
   ELSE
      @ 11,42 SAY Mmarital
   ENDIF
ENDIF

IF ACCESS()<=5                          && Numb_depen field - R/O access
   @ 11,46 SAY "NUMB_DEPEN:"            && level is 5, FULL is 3
   IF ACCESS()<=3
      @ 11,58 GET M_depen PICTURE "99"
   ELSE
      @ 11,58 SAY M_depen
   ENDIF
ENDIF

IF ACCESS()<=3                          && Hr_rate field - R/O access level
   @ 13,0 SAY "HOURLY RATE:"            && is 3, FULL is 1
   IF ACCESS()<=1
      @ 13,12 GET Mhr_rate PICTURE "999.99" RANGE 3.35,50
   ELSE
      @ 13,12 SAY Mhr_rate
   ENDIF
ENDIF

IF ACCESS()<=3                          && Ytd_wages field - R/O access
   @ 12,30 TO 15,53 DOUBLE              && level is 3, FULL is 2
   @ 13,31 SAY "Y-T-D WAGES:"
   IF ACCESS()<=2
      @ 13,43 GET Mytd_wages PICTURE "999999.99"
   ELSE
      @ 13,43 SAY Mytd_wages
   ENDIF
ENDIF

IF ACCESS()<=3                          && Ytd_fit field - R/O access level
   @ 14,31 SAY "Y-T-D FIT:"             && is 3, FULL is 2
   IF ACCESS()<=2
      @ 14,43 GET Mytd_fit PICTURE "999999.99"
   ELSE
      @ 14,43 SAY Mytd_fit
   ENDIF
ENDIF

IF ACCESS()<=5                          && Health field - R/O access level
   @ 15,0 SAY "HEALTH:"                 && is 5, FULL is 3
   IF ACCESS()<=3
      @ 15,12 GET Mhealth PICTURE "L"
   ELSE
      @ 15,12 SAY Mhealth
   ENDIF
ENDIF

IF ACCESS()<=6                          && Skills field - R/O access level
   @ 17,0 SAY "SKILLS:"                 && is 6, FULL is 3
   ACTIVATE WINDOW W_skills             && Editing Skills is done after
   ? MLINE(Skills,1)                    && replacing the data in other
   ? MLINE(Skills,2)                    && fields since the record is
   ? MLINE(Skills,3)                    && locked when you replace the
```

Employee.txt *(continued)*

```
     ACTIVATE SCREEN                       && data.
  ENDIF

  * Only reads if access is less than or equal to 5,
  * higher access levels only have read privileges
  IF ACCESS()<=5
  READ
 ENDIF
  IF .NOT. CHANGE()
     IF RLOCK()
        DO Repl_field                      && Places new data in fields.
     ELSE                                  && User cannot change edited data
        @ 16,10 CLEAR TO 20,75             && because another user has locked
        @ 16,10 TO 20,75 DOUBLE            && the necessary record.
        @ 17,11 SAY "Record is locked by user: "+LKSYS(2)
        @ 18,11 SAY "Reenter the data a another time."
        @ 19,11 SAY "Press any key to continue."
        WAIT ""
     ENDIF
     M nochange=.F.                        && Prevents DO WHILE loop from
  ELSE                                     && executing again
     @ 16,10 CLEAR TO 20,75
     @ 16,10 TO 20,75 DOUBLE
     @ 17,11 SAY "Record has changed, updating screen to show ;
 new record data."
     @ 18,11 SAY "Reedit the data."
     @ 19,11 SAY "Press any key to continue."
     WAIT ""
     GOTO RECNO()                          && updates count used to check
  ENDIF                                    && if record data changes
 ENDDO
 RELEASE WINDOWS W_skills
 RETURN                                    && End of Rec_edit procedure

 PROCEDURE Init_var                        && Used by Rec_edit
 IF BAR()=4                                   && BAR()=4 when Edit is selected
  STORE Ssn TO Mssn_edit                         && For editing records
  STORE Last_name TO Mlast_name            && initializes memory values
  STORE M_initial TO Mm_initial            && to current record values
  STORE First_name TO Mfirst
  STORE Address TO Maddress
  STORE City TO Mcity
  STORE State TO Mstate
  STORE Zip_code TO Mzip_code
  STORE Home_phone TO Mphone
  STORE Hire_date TO Mhire_date
  STORE Marital_St TO Mmarital
  STORE Numb_Depen TO M_depen
  STORE Hr_Rate TO Mhr_Rate
  STORE Ytd_wages TO Mytd_wages
  STORE Ytd_fit TO Mytd_fit
  STORE Health TO Mhealth
 ELSE                                      && For appending records
  STORE "   -  -    " TO Mssn_edit         && initializes to blank values
  STORE "               " TO Mlast_name, Maddress
  STORE " " TO Mm_initial, Mmarital
  STORE "          " TO Mfirst, Mcity
  STORE "  " TO Mstate
  STORE 0 TO Mzip_code, M_depen, Mhr_rate, Mytd_wages, Mytd_fit
  STORE "             " TO Mphone
  STORE DATE() TO Mhire_date
  STORE .T. TO Mhealth
 ENDIF
 RETURN

 PROCEDURE Repl_field
 IF ACCESS()<=5
  REPLACE Address WITH Maddress, City WITH Mcity
  REPLACE State WITH Mstate, Zip_code WITH Mzip_code
  REPLACE Home_phone WITH Mphone
```

Employee.txt *(continued)*

```
ENDIF
IF ACCESS()<=4
 REPLACE Last_name WITH Mlast_name, M_initial WITH Mm_initial
 REPLACE First_name WITH Mfirst
ENDIF
IF ACCESS()<=2
 REPLACE Ytd_wages WITH Mytd_wages, Ytd_fit WITH Mytd_fit
ENDIF
IF ACCESS()<=1
 REPLACE Hr_Rate WITH Mhr_Rate
ENDIF
IF ACCESS()<=3                       && Last because of DO Chng_memo
 REPLACE Ssn WITH Mssn_edit, Hire_date WITH Mhire_date
 REPLACE Marital_St WITH Mmarital, Numb_Depen WITH M_depen
 REPLACE Health WITH Mhealth
 DO Chng_memo
ENDIF
RETURN                               && End of Repl_field procedure

PROCEDURE Chng_memo                  && Used by Repl_field
STORE " " TO M_confirm               && Used for Y/N replies
@ 16,10 TO 18,55 DOUBLE              && This procedure saves Skills data
@ 17,11 SAY "Do you want to edit the skills data? (Y/N) "
@ 17,54 GET M_confirm PICTURE "!"    && to a file (name determined by
READ                                 && record number in case two users
IF M_confirm="Y"                     && are modifying Skills data at
 STORE "M_S"+LTRIM(STR(RECNO()))+".txt" TO Mfilename  && once), lets
 COPY MEMO Skills TO &Mfilename      && the user modify the file and
 MODI COMM &Mfilename                && replaces the memo field with the
 APPEND MEMO Skills FROM &Mfilename OVERWRITE   && file's contents.  It
 ERASE &Mfilename                    && is necessary since you cannot
ENDIF                                && store memo field data in a
RETURN                               && memory variable. (End-Chgn_memo)

PROCEDURE Modi_hist                  && Menu option 5
STORE "   -  -    " TO Mssn_old, Mssn_new
STORE 0 TO Mrec_old, Mrec_new
IF ACCESS()<=3
 @ 12,10 TO 15,70 DOUBLE
 @ 13,12 SAY "Enter incorrect social security number: "
 @ 13,52 GET Mssn_old PICTURE "999-99-9999"
 @ 14,12 SAY "Enter correct social security number: "
 @ 14,52 GET Mssn_new PICTURE "999-99-9999"
 READ
 USE Employee INDEX Employee.mdx ORDER Ssn
 FIND &Mssn_old
 IF FOUND() .AND. RLOCK()
      STORE RECNO() TO Mrec_old
 ENDIF
 FIND &Mssn_new
 IF FOUND() .AND. RLOCK()
      STORE RECNO() TO Mrec_new
 ENDIF
 IF Mrec_new<>0 .OR. Mrec_old<>0
    CLEAR
    IF Same_recs(Mrec_old,Mrec_new)<>"Y"&& Checks if employee database
       BEGIN TRANSACTION             && has records under new & old SSN.
       IF Mrec_old>0                 && Finds old SSN & replaces with
          GOTO Mrec_old              && new SSN
          REPLACE Ssn WITH Mssn_new
       ENDIF
       SELECT 2
       USE WEEK_PAY INDEX WEEK_PAY ORDER SSN
       SCAN                          && Keeps going until end of file.
          FIND &Mssn_old             && If it found a record in Week_pay
          IF FOUND()                 && locks record & replaces the old
             IF RLOCK()              && Record stays locked in case of
                REPLACE Ssn WITH Mssn_new  && SSN with the new SSN.
                ? "New SSN replaced old SSN for record:"+STR(RECNO())
             ELSE                    && ROLLBACK.  With no user input
```

Employee.txt *(continued)*

```
                ? ""                 && after BEGIN TRANSACTION, the
                ? "Unable to lock record to replace SSN. " && user input
                ? "Returning data to their original values. " && after
                WAIT                 && records are locked for a short
                ROLLBACK             && time.  ROLLBACK occurs when the
             ENDIF                   && program cannot lock a record
          ENDIF                      && with the old SSN.
       ENDSCAN
       END TRANSACTION
       IF .NOT. ROLLBACK()           && If a problem exists, lets
          ? ""                       && user know.
          ? "Unable to return data to the original values.  "
          ? "Contact database administrator to restore backup copy."
       ENDIF
       SELECT 1
    ELSE                             && Two records for the same
       @ 17,0 SAY "You must delete one of these records before updating "
       ? "the employee history file.  Leaving this menu selection. "
    ENDIF                            && employee.
 ELSE                                && Could not find record
    ? SPACE(13)+"No records in the employee master database match the new"
    ? SPACE(13)+"or old social security number.  You must add a record for"
    ? SPACE(13)+"the employee before changing the employee history file.  "
    ? ""
 ENDIF
 CLOSE DATABASES                     && Closes Employee and Week_pay
ELSE                                 && Insufficient access level
 @ 13,5 SAY "Insufficient access level for this menu selection"
ENDIF
WAIT                                 && keeps last displayed message
RETURN                               && End of Modi_hist procedure

FUNCTION Same_recs                   && Used by Modi_hist.  Displays
PARAMETERS Mrec_old, Mrec_new        && new and/or old SSN records.
STORE " " TO M_confirm               && Returns a Y if same
IF Mrec_old>0                        && Displays old SSN record
 GOTO Mrec_old
 ? "Old social security number: "+Ssn
 ? "Name: "+First_name+" "+M_initial+". "+Last_name
 ? "Address: "+Address
 ? SPACE(9)+City+", "+State+" "+str(Zip_code,5)
 ? "Home phone: "+Home_phone
ENDIF
IF Mrec_old>0 .AND. Mrec_new>0       && Draws dashed line if an old and
 ? ""                                && new SSN record exist
 ? REPLICATE("=",80)
 ? ""
ENDIF
IF Mrec_new>0                        && Displays new SSN record
 GOTO Mrec_new
 ? "New social security number: "+Ssn
 ? "Name: "+First_name+" "+M_initial+". "+Last_name
 ? "Address: "+Address
 ? SPACE(9)+City+", "+State+" "+str(Zip_code,5)
 ? "Home phone: "+Home_phone
ENDIF
? ""
IF Mrec_old>0 .AND. Mrec_new>0       && If a old and a new SSN record
 @ ROW()+1,0 SAY "Are these the same records? (Y/N)" && exists, prompts
 @ ROW(),34 GET M_confirm PICTURE "!"&& if they are the same.  If yes,
 READ                                && Modi_hist tells user to resolve
ENDIF                                && conflict before changing history
RETURN(M_confirm)                    && End of Same_recs procedure

PROCEDURE Rpt_menu                   && Menu option 1
* Commands for this procedure are here
RETURN                               && End of Rpt_menu procedure
```

Employee.txt

CHAPTER 22

dBASE IV SQL Concepts

SQL (Structured Query Language) is a database language initially developed to support mainframe and minicomputer applications. With the release of dBASE IV 1.1, Ashton-Tate will be offering a high-end relational database-server product, SQL Server, developed jointly with Microsoft. The SQL Server is designed to bring many of the advantages of mini and mainframe computers to networks of personal computers. Among the advantages are high performance, concurrency protection, and high security.

SQL Server will support a superset of the ANSI standard SQL commands and will offer compatibility with IBM's SAA (System Application Architecture) , designed to provide identical user interfaces across computer environments. SQL Server is designed to support work group computing applications with high-performance processing, advanced data integrity and security, and distributed database support. The dBASE IV language includes SQL extensions to allow you to work with SQL's relational databases.

Although you will need to wait for the availability of dBASE IV 1.1 for the availability of SQL Server, you will find the SQL language commands a part of the existing version of dBASE. You can explore the advantages of the SQL language now and create SQL applications without the server architecture. Your familiarity with SQL commands will give you a head start when the SQL Server version of dBASE is made available. You do not need to have OS/2 on your machine to use the SQL language although it will be required for the machine on which

SQL Server is installed. You do not even need a network to use SQL in either the interactive mode or embedded in programs. In the current version 1.0 of dBASE IV, the SQL commands that you enter are transparently converted into dBASE code before being executed. With this interim method of executing SQL commands you will notice some performance degradation, which will be eliminated with the introduction of version 1.1.

Your first step will be to understand the new concepts inherent in the use of SQL. You will need to follow some rules regarding the combination of SQL commands and dBASE commands and functions. You will also need to master the syntax of the SQL language.

In this chapter, you will be introduced to SQL concepts. You will also have an opportunity to try some of the SQL commands to gain a familiarity with the syntax of SQL requests.

SQL Concepts

In the current version of dBASE IV, you will find that your SQL requests are translated by dBASE and processed against SQL tables that are stored as DBF files. Although the same file storage techniques that are used for dBASE are currently used, the basic concepts of SQL are quite different from dBASE.

The concepts of a database and the basic unit of data storage have different meanings than they do in dBASE. SQL operates on data as logical sets called tables. The code required to accomplish some tasks is much more concise in SQL than dBASE. Also, there are many built-in features to support network activities.

Data Storage

In dBASE, data is stored in records composed of a number of fields. All records of a given type are organized together in a dBASE database. In SQL, things are different. Instead of all the related pieces of information about an entity being stored in a database, they are stored in a table. An SQL database is composed of a group of related tables. Within a table each element of information is stored in a column of the table with an entire row containing elements for each type of information captured for an entity.

SQL System Catalogs

Although catalogs can play an important organizational role in your dBASE applications they are not mandatory unless you are working from the Control Center. You can write programs and create reports without ever grouping the related files together in a catalog.

SQL catalogs play a different role. They are the center of the SQL system keeping track of all tables, indexes, and views. When you create a database in SQL, a series of catalog tables are automatically established to monitor information relative to the database. These tables are stored in a separate directory that dBASE creates using the same name that you supply for the database. Table 22-1 provides a list of these tables and the type of information they contain.

You should not access these catalog tables directly through dBASE. Maintaining the information placed in these tables is important to the integrity of your SQL database tables.

Table 22-1 Catalog tables

Table	*Contents*
Sysauth	User privileges for views and tables.
Syscolau	User update privileges for each column in a table or view.
Syscols	Describes each column in every table or view.
Sysdbs	Master catalog table maintaining information on each table.
Sysidxs	Describes every index created for the tables in a database.
Syskeys	Describes each column defined as an index key.
Syssyns	Describes synonyms in the current database.
Systabls	Describes database tables and views.
Systimes	Used in multiuser system to ensure that user copies of tables reflect the current catalog status.
Sysvdeps	Describes the tables or views from which a view is defined.
Sysviews	Describes each view.

Network Support

Support is available for SQL in both single and multiuser versions of dBASE IV. SQL will automatically implement protection for data tables when you execute a request that updates, inserts, or deletes data in the table.

Concise Code

The SQL language consists of 30 commands. Each command is powerful and most have many options extending their functionality much further than you would expect with this number of commands. As an example, you can perform an SQL query that selects data from multiple tables if the entries match a set of criteria with only one SELECT command possessing a FROM and WHERE clause. In dBASE you would need two USE commands, at least one SELECT command, a SET RELATION, a SEEK command, potentially a STORE command, and an IF command as well as a SCAN command. You would also need to specify the INDEX option with the USE commands. The task is a common one, yet it is markedly quicker to enter in SQL with one simple command; this makes the task seem easy.

SQL's Relationship to dBASE IV

dBASE and SQL have separate modes because of the differences between a Record pointer and Set access method for data. This does not mean that the use of either totally precludes the other. SQL may be the ideal vehicle with which to create and execute queries against multiple files because of the streamlined code with which these requests can be handled. On the other hand, dBASE provides an unsurpassed set of tools with which to design screens, reports, and labels.

You will want to look carefully at the restrictions that are placed on the use of dBASE commands and functions from within SQL mode. You will want to take a close look at your options before using SQL in either interactive or embedded mode.

Terminology Differences

Since SQL and dBASE were developed independently there are both differences and an overlap in the terminology used. Terms like tables that refer to the data storage structure are new. Other terms like objects, which dBASE uses to refer to reports, forms, databases and screens, are still used but with SQL objects are considered to be tables, views, and indexes.

Some commands are also shared by the two languages. When you are creating a SQL dBASE program, only the SQL version of these commands can be used.

When you are dealing with commands or terms that are shared by the two languages it helps eliminate misunderstanding when communicating with others to specify either SQL or dBASE as an adjective prefacing the command or term. For example, if you are referring to objects in the context of SQL you need to use the term SQL objects. If you are referencing the SQL SELECT command, stating it in this way eliminates any confusion that might otherwise occur.

Interactive SQL

You can use SQL in an interactive mode just as you use dBASE from the dot prompt. The first step is moving to the dot prompt and typing **SET SQL ON** and pressing ENTER. dBASE returns the prompt SQL. as shown in Figure 22-1. Although you will learn more about syntax differences in the two languages in the next section, it is important to note that many of the same features that work when entering dBASE code at the dot prompt will also support your efforts when making SQL entries.

Figure 22-1 SQL prompt

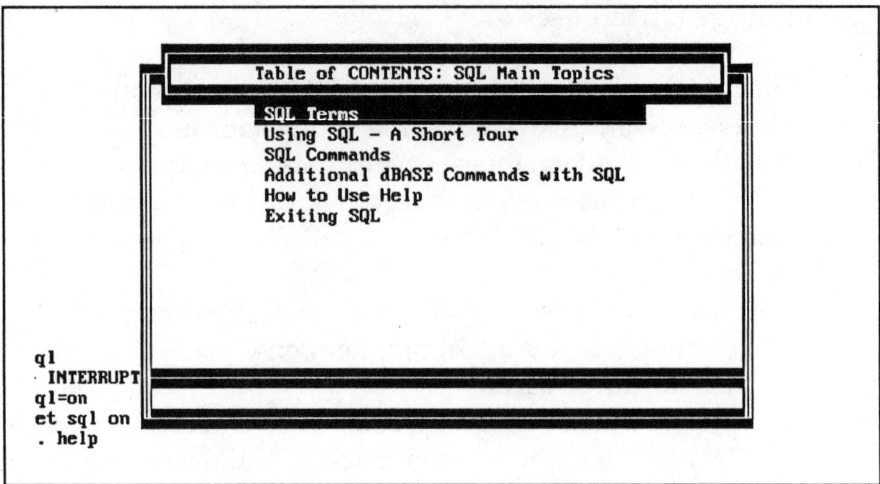

Figure 22-2 SQL Help display

Using the Edit Window You can activate the edit window for the entry of long command lines by pressing CTRL-HOME. The use of CTRL-END also works to save your entry.

You will find the edit window a much more convenient way to work with entries that contain a long list of fields. Since SQL interprets the entry of a semicolon as the end of a command, the use of a window allows you to continue commands on multiple lines.

Accessing History You can access history information in the same way that you do with dBASE. Pressing the UP ARROW key displays the previous command and permits you to edit a command and reexecute it by pressing ENTER.

The default is to retain the last 20 commands. You can use SET HISTORY TO to increase this default setting.

Accessing Help Once you activate SQL mode, the Help display changes even though you activate it in the same way. Figure 22-2 shows the main Help screen for SQL mode.

If you are new to SQL you might find it useful to review the options on SQL concepts and commands. When you make a syntax error in entering a command you will be able to select Help from the box that appears and have immediate access to context-sensitive help. You can also enter the word **HELP** followed by the name of an SQL command like SELECT as in **HELP SELECT** to have SQL provide syntax information for the command.

Embedded SQL

You can store SQL commands in programs but you must tell dBASE that the program contains SQL statements, since dBASE and SQL use different methods for manipulating data. You need to use .PRS as the filename extension in files that contain SQL statements. If you use SQL commands you cannot use dBASE commands to open or access database files. Likewise you cannot use SQL commands in dBASE files that are performing these activities.

Just as at the SQL prompt, the semicolon indicates the end of a command. You cannot use the semicolon to indicate a continuation to a new line.

You can continue to use dBASE memory variables in your programs to pass data between procedures. You can also use them to store temporary results. SQL commands can use memory variables in expressions that are part of WHERE clauses or with IN or LIKE.

User-defined functions are not supported in a dBASE/SQL program. You also cannot define UDFs that contain SQL statements.

Using the SQL Language

The SQL language is an English-like language that is similar to the dBASE language. It is keyword-oriented and often has a series of clauses that refine the specifications provided by a command. The language is more concise than dBASE due to the many tasks automatically handled by SQL. In some cases the work of five or six dBASE commands can be accomplished with one SQL statement.

Syntax

SQL commands follow the same basic syntax descriptions as dBASE commands. Throughout the chapter all command keywords will be shown in upper case. Required entries are shown between a pair of matching angle brackets <>. Matching braces [] enclose optional entries. Just as in dBASE commands a slash (/) separates a series of options for an entry where one of the options will be selected.

Unlike dBASE commands, SQL commands can be continued on multiple lines with no need for a continuation character at the end of a line. A semicolon is required at the end of the last line of a SQL command to indicate the end of the command.

Limitations

dBASE and SQL use different methods for accessing stored data. You must follow the rules for the dBASE commands that are acceptable in a program containing embedded dBASE code. Table 22-2 is a list of dBASE commands that can be used from SQL mode.

Some of the dBASE functions can be used from within an SQL command. Others can be used in SQL mode but not within an SQL statement. Table 22-3 shows the functions that can be used in SQL mode. Functions shown in boldface can be used within an SQL statement.

Categories of SQL Commands

The SQL commands in dBASE can be grouped by the type of task they perform. The following classifications are used for commands:

Creation/Startup of Database
Creation/Modification of Objects
Database Security
Deletion of Objects
Embedded SQL (only allowed in a program)
Query and Data Update
Utilities

Although all commands will not be covered in this chapter, a representative group of commands have been selected to introduce all the features needed to create and manipulate databases and tables.

Table 22-2 dBASE Commands Acceptable in SQL Mode

!
?,??, or ???
&&
*
@...CLEAR...
@...DOUBLE/PANEL/NONE...
@...FILL TO...
@...SAY...GET
ACCEPT
ACTIVATE MENU
ACTIVATE POPUP
ACTIVATE SCREEN
ACTIVATE WINDOW
BEGIN...END TRANSACTION
CALL CANCEL
CLEAR GETS
CLEAR MENUS
CLEAR POPUPS
CLEAR TYPEHEAD
CLEAR WINDOWS
CLOSE ALTERNATE
CLOSE FORMAT
CLOSE PROCEDURE
COMPILE
COPY FILE
DEACTIVATE MENU
DEACTIVATE POPUP
DEACTIVATE WINDOW
DEBUG
DECLARE DEFINE BAR
DEFINE BOX
DEFINE MENU
DEFINE PAD
DEFINE POPUP
DEFINE WINDOW
DELETE FILE
DIR/DIRECTORY
DISPLAY FILES
DISPLAY HISTORY
DISPLAY STATUS
DISPLAY USERS
DO
DO CASE...CASE...
OTHERWISE...ENDCASE
DOWHILE
EJECT
ERASE
EXIT
FUNCTION
HELP
IF...ELSE...ENDIF
INPUT
LIST FILES
LIST HISTORY
LIST MEMORY
LIST STATUS
LIST USERS
LOAD
LOGOUT
LOOP
MODIFY COMMAND/FILE
MOVE GETS
MOVE WINDOW
NOTE
ON ERROR/ESCAPE/KEY
ON PAD
ON PAGE
ON READERROR
ON SELECTION PAD
ON SELECTION POPUP
PARAMETERS
PLAY MACRO
PRINTJOB...ENDPRINTJOB
PRIVATE
PROCEDURE
PROTECT
PUBLIC
QUIT
READ [SAVE]
RELEASE
RELEASE MENUS
RELEASE MODULE
RELEASE POPUPS
RELEASE WINDOWS

(continued)

Table 22-2 dBASE Commands Acceptable in SQL Mode *(continued)*

RENAME
RESTORE FROM
RESTORE MACROS
RESTORE MENU
RESTORE WINDOW
RESUME
RETRY
RETURN
RUN
SAVE MACROS
SAVE TO
SAVE WINDOW
SET
SET ALTERNATE ON/OFF
SET ALTERNATE TO
SET AUTOSAVE ON/OFF
SET BELL ON/OFF
SET BELL TO
SET BORDER
SET CENTURY ON/OFF
SET CLOCK ON/OFF
SET CLOCK TO
SET COLOR OF
SET COLOR ON/OFF
SET COLOR TO
SET CONFIEM ON/OFF
SET CONSOLE ON/OFF
SET CURRENCY LEFT/RIGHT
SET CURRENCY TO
SET DATE
SET DEBUG ON/OFF
SET DECIMALS TO
SET DEFAULT TO
SET DELETED ON/OFF
SET DELIMITERS ON/OFF
SET DELIMITERS TO
SET DEVELOPMENT ON/OFF
SET DEVICE TO
SET DISPLAY TO
SET DOHISTORY ON/OFF
SET ECHO ON/OFF
SET ENCRYTION ON/OFF
SET ESCAPE ON/OFF
SET EXACT ON/OFF
SET EXCLUSIVE ON/OFF
SET FIXED ON/OFF
SET FORMAT TO
SET FUNCTION
SET HEADING ON/OFF
SET HELP ON/OFF
SET HISTORY ON/OFF
SET HISTORY TO
SET HOURS TO
SET INTENSITY ON/OFF
SET LOCK ON/OFF
SET MARGIN TO
SET MARK TO
SET MENUS ON/OFF
SET POINT TO
SET PRECISION TO
SET PRINTER ON/OFF
SET PRINTER TO
SET PROCEDURE TO
SET REFRESH TO
SET REPROCESS TO
SET SAFETY ON/OFF
SET SCOREBOARD ON/OFF
SET SEPARATOR TO
SET SPACE ON/OFF
SET SQL ON/OFF
SET STATUS ON/OFF
SET STEP ON/OFF
SET TALK ON/OFF
SET TRAP ON/OFF
SET TYPEHEAD TO
SHOW MENU
SHOW POPUP
STORE
SUSPEND
TEST...ENDTEXT
TYPE
WAIT

Table 22-3 dBASE Functions Acceptable in SQL Mode

&

ABS()

ACOS()

ASC()

ASIN()

AT()

ATAN()

ATN2()

BAR()

CALL()

CDOW()

CEILING()

CHR()

CMONTH()

COL()

COMPLETED()

COS()

CTOD()

DATE()

DAY()

DIFFERENCE()

DISKSPACE()

DMY()

DOW()

DTOC()

DTOR()

DTOS()

ERROR()

EXP()

FILE()

FIXED()

FKLABEL()

FKMAX()

FLOAT()

FLOOR()

GETENV()

IIF()

INKEY()

INT()

ISALPHA()

ISCOLOR()

ISLOWER()

ISUPPER()

LASTKEY()

LEFT()

LEN()

LIKE()

LINENO()

LOG()

LOG10()

LOWER()

LTRIM()

MAX()

MDY()

MEMORY()

MENU()

MESSAGE()MIN()

MOD()

MONTH()

NETWORK()

OS()

PAD()

PCOL()

PI()

POPUP()

PRINTSTATUS()

PROGRAM()

PROMPT()

PROW()

RAND()

READKEY()

REPLICATE()

RIGHT()

ROLLBACK()

ROUND()

ROW()

RTOD()

RTRIM()

SET()

SIGN()

SIN()

SOUNDEX()

SPACE()

SQRT()

(continued)

Table 22-3 dBASE Functions Acceptable in SQL Mode *(continued)*

STR()	**TYPE()**
STUFF()	**UPPER()**
SUBSTR()	**USER()**
SUM()	**VAL()**
TAN()	VARREAD()
TIME()	VERSION()
TRANSFORM()	**YEAR()**
TRIM()	

Boldface entries can be used in SQL statements.

Creating a Database

Creating a database in SQL creates a subdirectory with the database name that you supply. This subdirectory is placed under the current directory and contains catalog tables. You can provide a valid DOS name containing as many as eight characters or, if you prefer, you can provide an explicit DOS path. If the name you specify already exists, the SQL catalog files will be added to the directory.

The catalog tables contain information on SQL statistics and object definitions that you create for tables, synonyms, indexes, and views. dBASE updates catalog entries when you create a new index, and run DBDEFINE. Additions and changes to the data within dBASE tables does not show up in the catalog. To maintain optimum performance, the catalog tables need to have their statistics updated periodically. This can be done by running RUNSTATS for the various tables in a database. If you specify a table name after RUNSTATS, only the catalog entries for the table indicated will be updated.

The CREATE DATABASE command cannot be embedded in a program. It is designed to be used interactively. Figure 22-3 shows the entry of the appropriate command at the SQL dot prompt.

You can list the current SQL database with the SHOW DATABASE command. You can activate a database with the START DATABASE

```
SQL. CREATE DATABASE SALESAPP;
Database SALESAPP created
SQL.
```

Figure 22-3 Creating an SQL database

<database name> command. Once a database is active, only the tables in this database can be accessed. The DROP DATABASE <database name> command deletes the database and all its objects. It cannot be executed on an active database. When executed on an inactive database it will purge all database objects including tables, indexes, and database catalog files from the database if you confirm the action.

Creating an SQL Table

SQL tables take the place of dBASE databases. You can use the CREATE TABLE command to establish a table name and supply column names and types. The syntax of the command is

```
CREATE TABLE <table name>
     (<column name> <datatype>
     [,<column name> <datatype>...]);
```

The table name can be from one to eight characters and must conform to the rules for valid filenames since dBASE is actually creating a dBASE.DBF file for the table. It will create an MDX file with the same name. The column names can be from 1 to 10 characters conforming to the rules for valid dBASE field names.

Data types like Logical, Date, Smallint, and Integer have defined widths inherent in the selection of the data type. For Decimal, Numeric, Float, and Char fields you must define the desired column width; the first three types also require the entry of the number of decimal digits. Table 22-4 contains a list of all the SQL data types.

The CREATE TABLE command does not allow you to make entries in the table. It does update the database catalog tables to indicate the presence of the new table. Figure 22-4 shows the entries made to the

Table 22-4 Datatypes Used in SQL Tables

Datatype	*Description*
CHAR	Contains a character string of from 1 to 254 characters depending on the width specified.
DATE	Contains a date with the format specified by the entries in the SET DATE and SET CENTURY commands.
DECIMAL	Contains a number with a fixed decimal point. Specified as DECIMAL(x,y) where x is the total number of digits including the sign. The entry y is the number of decimal digits. Tne entry x can range from 1 to 19 and y can range from 0 to 18. DECIMAL(5,2) can contain a number as large as 999.99.
FLOAT	Contains a signed floating-point number. Specified as FLOAT(x,y) with c and y having the representation as in DECIMAL entries. The limitation for y is the same as in DECIMAL and for x the range is 1 to 20.
INTEGER	Contains an integer with from 1 to 11 digits including the sign.
LOGICAL	Contains true or false values .T. or .F..
NUMERIC	Contains a signed fixed decimal number. Specified as NUMERIC(x,y) where x indicates the total number of digits including both the sign and the decimal point. x can range from 1 to 20 any from 0 to 18. NUMERIC(5,2) can contain a number as large as 99.99 or -9.99.
SMALLINT	Contains an integer from 1 to 6 digits including sign.

Orders table for Order_no, Cust_no, Item and Quantity. Figure 22-5 shows the addition of a second table, Stock, to the Salesapp database.

Adding and Changing Data You can add data to any of the tables that you create with the INSERT INTO command. The syntax of this command is

```
Layout   Words   Go To   Print   Exit                                   10:46:52 am
........[1......▼..2....▼..█.3..▼......4▼.......▼5......▼..6....▼....7..▼......]
CREATE TABLE Orders
        (Order_no SMALLINT,
        Cust_no CHAR(6),
        Item CHAR(6),
        Quantity SMALLINT);
```

Figure 22-4 Creating the Orders table

```
INSERT INTO <table name>
      [(<column list>)]
      VALUES (value list));
```

If you specify values in the same order as the table column, you do not need to list the columns. You will need to enclose character data in quotation marks (") and dates within braces ({}) as you specify the values for the columns. Figure 22-6 shows the entry of several commands that insert data into an existing table. Note the use of quotation marks for character entries. If you are making your entries interactively, you can use the UP ARROW key and edit the values to enter the subsequent records.

After the data is entered you can use the SELECT command to display the table rows. SELECT * FROM Stock displays the rows in the table Stock. SELECT * FROM Orders displays the rows in Orders shown in Figure 22-7. You can also use a number of other options with SELECT, including a WHERE clause that allows you to select the rows that you wish to display. Clauses in SQL can be thought of as dBASE expressions, as in WHERE Vendor = "ABC" or WHERE Amt_due > 120. Figure 22-8 shows the rows in Orders where Quantity is greater than 10.

The SELECT command is one clear example of the overlap in dBASE and SQL commands. Since they have totally different effects in dBASE and SQL, it is obvious why dBASE needs to know whether or not to expect SQL statements in a program.

To change the values in existing rows of a table, use the UPDATE command. The syntax of the command is

```
UPDATE <table name>
      SET <column name> = <expression> [,<column name> =
      <expression>....] {WHERE <clause>];
```

```
 Layout   Words   Go To   Print   Exit                                       12:22:39 pm
........[1.......▼..2....▼....3..▼.......4▼........▼5.......▼..6....▼....7..▼......]
CREATE TABLE Stock
        Item_no CHAR(6)
        Item_desc CHAR (20)
        Price NUMERIC(8,2)
        Qty_hand SMALLINT
        Vendor_cde CHAR;
```

Figure 22-5 Stock table creation

You might enter

```
UPDATE Stock SET Price = Price * 1.1 WHERE Vendor_cde =
"AX1103";
```

This will update the price for the Rolltop desk to 604.95 and update the Coat rack price to 165.00. The updated entries are shown in Figure 22-9.

Deleting Data You can delete rows from an SQL table with the DELETE command. The syntax of the command is

```
DELETE FROM <table name>
       [WHERE <clause>];
```

You might enter the command DELETE FROM Stock WHERE Vendor_cde = "AX1103";

```
SQL. INSERT INTO Orders VALUES(891022,"N65489","KY1249",3);
         1 row(s) inserted
SQL. INSERT INTO Orders VALUES(891023,"B11298","TR1782",50);
         1 row(s) inserted
SQL. INSERT INTO Orders VALUES(891024,"Y65754","RE3421",10);
         1 row(s) inserted
SQL. INSERT INTO Orders VALUES(891025,"L11123","ST3501",200);
         1 row(s) inserted
SQL. INSERT INTO Orders VALUES(891026,"H77186","LA1235",7);
         1 row(s) inserted
SQL. INSERT INTO Orders VALUES(891027,"T45321","MY8976",14);
         1 row(s) inserted
```

Figure 22-6 Inserting rows in Order

```
SQL. SELECT * FROM Ord;
 ORDER_NO CUST_NO ITEM    QUANTITY
   891021 A65438  BY6549         6
   891022 N65489  KY1249         3
   891023 B11298  TR1782        50
   891024 Y65754  RE3421        10
   891025 L11123  ST3501       200
   891026 H77186  LA1235         7
   891027 T45321  MY8976        14

SQL.
SQL      C:\...bantam\salesapp\          DB:SALESAPP            Ins
              Type a dBASE IV command and press the ENTER key (←┘)
```

Figure 22-7 Displaying the Orders rows

Modifying the Table You can add new columns to a table. After adding the new column, you can use the UPDATE command to add new data. The ALTER TABLE command will allow you to enter one or more new columns to a table. Just as when you initially define a table you must supply the column names and the data types for each column that you add. The syntax of the command is

```
ALTER TABLE <table name> ADD (<column name> <data type>
     [,<column name> <data type>...]);
```

The ALTER TABLE command is used to add a date column to the ORDERS file. The entry ALTER TABLE Orders ADD(Order_date date); the UPDATE command to complete the date entries. To add the date 3/15/89 to all the records UPDATE Orders SET Order_date = {03/15/89};. When you use an Update command without a WHERE statement every row in the database is affected. SQL prompts you with a warning in case this is not what you want, as shown in Figure 22-10.

```
SQL. SELECT * FROM Orders WHERE Quantity >10;
 ORDER_NO CUST_NO ITEM    QUANTITY ORDER_DATE
   891023 B11298  TR1782        50 03/15/89
   891025 L11123  ST3501       200 03/15/89
   891027 T45321  MY8976        14 03/15/89
```

Figure 22-8 Orders rows where Quantity is greater than 10

```
SQL. UPDATE Stock SET Price = Price * 1.1 WHERE Vendor_cde = "AX1103";
        2 row(s) updated
SQL. select * from stock;
 ITEM_NO ITEM_DESC              PRICE QTY_HAND VENDOR_CDE
 BY6549  Rolltop desk          604.95        5 AX1103
 KY1249  Computer table        198.00       12 LT7865
 TR1782  Swivel chair          225.00      100 LT9901
 RE3421  Credenza              525.00       10 RK8765
 ST3501  Bookcase              325.00      120 YT6754
 LA1235  Printer stand         250.00       20 LT9901
 MY8976  Coat rack             165.00       25 AX1103

SQL.
SQL      C:\...bantam\salesapp\          DB:SALESAPP          Ins
          Type a dBASE IV command and press the ENTER key (◄─┘)
```

Figure 22-9 Updating Stock Price entries

SQL Views

SQL supports a special type of table called a view. A view can be thought of as a virtual table since it is created in memory and is not actually a file on disk. You can use a view to combine rows and columns from one or more tables. If you create a view for a single table you will be using it to selectively view the data from the table, selecting some or all of the columns based on the column names you wish to work with. You may also want to select rows from the table based on a set of criteria that you enter.

You can use the CREATE VIEW command to define a view. The syntax of the command is

❑ **Tip: Try the WHERE clause with a SELECT statement before deleting records.**

A mistake in entering a WHERE clause for DELETE can have disastrous results. You can check out the number of records that will be deleted by first executing a SELECT with the same clause.

```
SQL. update Orders SET Order_date={03/15/89};
Warning - No WHERE clause specified in UPDATE statement
Press ESC to abandon operation, any other key to continue...
        7 row(s) updated
SQL.
SQL      ||C:\...bantam\salesapp\ ||              ||DB:SALESAPP ||          Ins
              Type a dBASE IV command and press the ENTER key (◄─┘)
```

Figure 22-10 Warning when ALTER is used with a WHERE clause

```
CREATE VIEW <view name> [(<view column list>)]
     AS <SELECT statement>
     [WITH CHECK OPTION]
```

You will notice from the syntax that you can optionally list the column names that will be used in the view. If you do not include column names, the view will use the same names as the tables from which the columns are selected. The SELECT statement determines the rows and columns that will be selected. CREATE VIEW By_ord AS SELECT Order_no, Cust_no, Quantity FROM Orders WHERE Quantity > 10; performs the same selection as the earlier SELECT statement except that it doesn't display the date immediately. You must enter a SELECT statement as shown in Figure 22-11. This method may seem longer, but it allows you to repeat the query anytime by referencing By_ord where your query, not your data, is stored.

```
SQL. CREATE VIEW Big_ord AS SELECT Order_no, Cust_no, Quantity FROM Orders WHERE
 Quantity >10;
View BIG_ORD created
SQL. SELECT * FROM Big_ord;
 ORDER_NO CUST_NO QUANTITY
   891023 B11298        50
   891025 L11123       200
   891027 T45321        14
```

Figure 22-11 Selecting view entries

The optional clause WITH CHECK OPTION is used with updatable views. If you include it, inserted rows will be checked against the view definition.

Creating Indexes

Indexes provide access to your data in a variety of sequences without duplicating any of the data. An index keeps track of the order in which you will need to see the rows in a table to provide the sequence that you need. If you need to see the rows in a table in social security number sequence, you will build an index using the column that contains the social security number. If you sometimes need the same records in salary sequence, another index will be useful to ensure efficient response time.

Since SQL indexes are defined as tags within a dBASE MDX file you have a limit of 47 indexes for each table. The indexes you build will require disk space and update time when records are added or changed. You will want to create all the indexes you need but you should not plan on indexing all the columns just in case you might need them, since that would waste space and time.

To create an index, use the CREATE INDEX command. Its syntax is

```
CREATE [UNIQUE] INDEX <index name> ON <table name> (<column
     name> [ASC/DESC] [,<column name> [ASC/DESC]...);
```

If you enter multiple columns, the contents of each will be used in building the index keys. The combined length of the column entries for a single index is limited to 100.

A simple index entry might be CREATE INDEX Quan ON Orders (Quantity);. Ascending is the default order if you omit the option.

When the keyword UNIQUE is added to the statement, specified index entries in the rows need to be unique. Since dBASE has to check entries for a new row against all the existing rows, you should limit your use of unique indexes, as they will slow performance. You can use this feature to prevent the duplicate assignment of customer numbers, invoice numbers, or Customer IDs.

Creating Queries

The SELECT command is one of the most flexible commands in the SQL language. You have already seen a brief example of this command, but it offers much more. With it you can retrieve data, update data, or delete data. You will use the SELECT command to build queries that access one or more database tables.

The syntax of the select command seems complicated because there are so many options. You can build simple queries with a simple entry that consists of SELECT <columns> FROM <tables>;. Even when you create more complex queries you will not be using all the options at one time. The full syntax of SELECT is

```
SELECT <clause>
     [INTO <clause>]
     FROM <clause>
     [WHERE <clause>]
     [GROUP BY <clause>]
     [HAVING <clause>]
     [UNION subselect]...
     [ORDER BY <clause>/FOR UPDATE OF <clause>]
     [SAVE TO TEMP <clause>][KEEP];
```

In its simplest form you can use SELECT to query the Orders table with the entry **SELECT Order_no, Quantity FROM Orders WHERE Quantity >10;**. Just like the virtual table created with views, the output of SELECT is not stored. It is referred to as a result table. You can save the result table for use in the current session with the SAVE TO TEMP option. If you use the KEEP option you can save the result table as a DBF file.

The FROM specification allows you to control the tables used in the selection. The WHERE option permits you to enter specifications for the rows that match a set of criteria. The GROUP BY option permits the order of data along with the provision for using aggregate functions to compute results for the members of a group. Figure 22-12 shows the use of SELECT to compute the average price of items ordered from the various vendors. HAVING allows you to exclude groups of rows. SELECT defines columns and calculations that are included in the result table. UNION combines result tables. ORDER BY sorts the rows

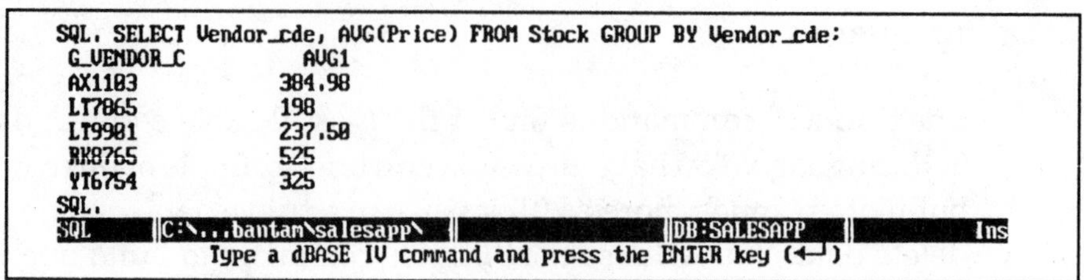
```
SQL. SELECT Vendor_cde, AVG(Price) FROM Stock GROUP BY Vendor_cde;
 G_VENDOR_C          AVG1
 AX1103              304.98
 LT7865              198
 LT9901              237.50
 RK8765              525
 YT6754              325
SQL.
SQL     C:\...bantam\salesapp\          DB:SALESAPP          Ins
        Type a dBASE IV command and press the ENTER key (←┘)
```

Figure 22-12 Using SELECT and GROUP BY

in a result table according to the values in a particular column. The other options, FOR UPDATE OF, specifies which columns can be updated.

Creating Joins

You have looked at a query created to look selectively at the data in a table. With the same ease, you can use a SQL SELECT statement to select information from multiple tables. This operation is referred to as a join.

SQL does not require a complicated series of commands to join the data in the tables. A simple SELECT statement that is easily modifiable to produce different results is sufficient. The first part of the SELECT statement indicates the columns that you want from the tables. If column names occur in multiple tables, you preface them with the name of the table to distinguish which column is of interest. For example, to use the Ssn column from the employee file where Ssn is in multiple tables, enter Employee.Ssn as in SELECT Employee.Ssn, Salary, Pay.Dept. The second part of the SELECT statement is a FROM clause that lists the table names containing the data, as in FROM Employee, Pay. The last part is an optional WHERE clause that allows

❑ **Tip: SET PAUSE ON to view result tables a screen at a time.**

The entries in a result table with scroll off the screen unless you press CTRL-S to stop the scrolling or SET PAUSE ON.

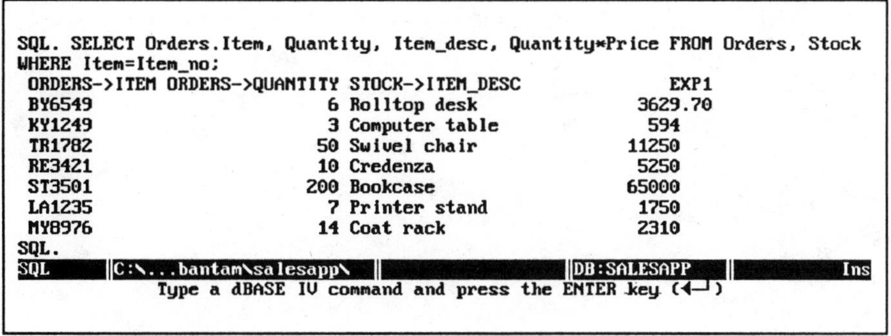
SQL. SELECT Orders.Item, Quantity, Item_desc, Quantity*Price FROM Orders, Stock
WHERE Item=Item_no;
ORDERS->ITEM ORDERS->QUANTITY STOCK->ITEM_DESC EXP1
BY6549 6 Rolltop desk 3629.70
KY1249 3 Computer table 594
TR1782 50 Swivel chair 11250
RE3421 10 Credenza 5250
ST3501 200 Bookcase 65000
LA1235 7 Printer stand 1750
MY8976 14 Coat rack 2310
SQL.
SQL C:\...bantam\salesapp\ DB:SALESAPP Ins
Type a dBASE IV command and press the ENTER key (◄┘)

Figure 22-13 Joining data from Stock and Orders

you to determine which rows from the table you want to see. You might enter WHERE Employee.Ssn = Pay.Ssn to display only those rows where there are matches in the two tables. SQL uses the term equijoin to refer to a join that uses the equal operator. If one of the equijoin columns is eliminated from the display it is called a natural equijoin. SQL contains a built-in query optimizer that works with the statistical information in the catalog tables to determine the most efficient way to create the result table produced by the join.

You can create joins that reference the data in the Orders and Stock tables. Entering SELECT Orders Item Quantity, Item_desc, Quantity * Price FROM Orders, Stock WHERE Item = Item_no;, produces the result in Figure 22-13.

SQL offers many more sophisticated features including subqueries. Subqueries allow you to nest SELECT statements within WHERE clauses to combine one query with another. Although you will find that SQL offers much more, the examples in this chapter serve to get you started with this new command language. By the time you have mastered these basics, version 1.1 of dBASE will be available and provide full SQL Server features.

PART VII

Appendix

APPENDIX A

Upgrading from dBASE III+ to dBASE IV

dBASE IV continues to offer support for existing dBASE III+ files and associated indexes but adds an exciting complement of new features. In the sections that follow you will find some of the highlights of the expanded capacity and functionality of dBASE IV. No one user will ever need all the expansions that have been added but it is good to know that so many possibilities exist. After browsing through the list that follows you will want to take a look at Chapter 15 for a more in-depth presentation of the new package functions. Appendix B contains additional information on the new and enhanced commands that you can use at the dot prompt or in dBASE programs.

Commands

- A COMPILE command has been added to generate object code.
- A full-screen window is available for dot prompt entry of commands exceeding 254 characters.
- The ??? command has been added to send printer control codes to the printer.
- AT, FUNCTION, PICTURE, and STYLE support has been added for ?? and ??

- APPEND MEMO adds text to memo fields from an external file.
- CALL can pass up to seven optional parameters.
- Character expressions can be used as filenames in commands.
- Commands to support bar menus, pull-down menus, and pop-up menus have been added.
- Date values are identified with curly braces, as in {02/22/89}.
- Enhanced statistical capabilities use the new CALCULATE command and summary operators.
- COPY commands have been expanded for indexes, tags, memo fields, and arrays.
- Functionality for the @SAY...GET command has been increased.
- Many DISPLAY command options have been expanded to include printer support.
- ON PAGE allows you to establish page break routines.
- ON READERROR responds to invalid date entry, RANGE conditions, and VALID conditions.
- Rapid change of color attributes is available with @..FILL TO..COLOR.
- Selection of characters can be used to draw boxes.
- SET commands have been expanded and enhanced.
- SORT TO supports ascending and descending options.
- Support for appending database records from other file structure with APPEND FROM has been added.
- The DO command supports an optional parameter list.
- The LIST command contains a TO FILE option.
- The MODIFY COMMAND statement will delete the old DBO file that contains the code for your dBASE program.
- The SCAN programming construct has been added to process records meeting a condition.
- The SKIP command can move the record pointer in work areas other than the one selected.
- UNLOCK can release records in work areas other than the current one.

Data Integrity

- Automatic rollback with CANCEL to eliminate the effect of partially completed transactions is now available.

- Autosave feature supports automatic and immediate updating.
- Full transaction processing support allows you to either complete a group of commands or eliminate their effect completely if all are not completed.
- Transaction rollback capability is available.

Database Design

- Creation of MDX indexes during design
- New data type suitable for scientific calculations — Float
- Support for both NDX and the new MDX file structure

Development/Programming

- A new applications generator to create code for new and advanced programmers
- A stand-alone BUILD utility in the Developer's Edition to create distribution disks after compiling, linking, and copying applications
- Support for transaction processing that allows you to rollback command actions with CANCEL and to insure that a series of commands is either completed in their entirity or their effect is completely eliminated
- Commands to support bar menus, pull-down menus, and pop-up menu
- Expanded memory variable support
- Extended edit capability in editor
- Full-featured debugger with multiple windows and breakpoint capabilities
- Inclusion of features to support the creation of run-time modules in the Developer's Edition
- Increased functionality for the @SAY...GET command
- Optimization tools for system performance included in DBSETUP
- Procedure lists maintained for each program object file and available to any called command file
- Procedures can be a maximum of 64K of object code
- Program file editor increased to 32,000 lines

- PROTECT features now internal
- Stand-alone DBLINK program added to the Developer's Edition with the ability to join up to 256 object files
- Support for arrays of memory variables
- Support for keyboard macros
- Support for menus in the Applications Generator
- Support for storing a library of macros in a file
- Support for up to 20 windows at once
- Support for user-defined functions
- Inclusion of a template language in the Developer's Edition to customize design objects or applications
- The SCAN programming construct added to process records meeting a condition
- Total procedures in a program increased from 32 to 963
- Use of procedures within any program file

DOS

- dBASE supports the DOS Read-only attribute.
- DOS commands can be accessed with Control Center menu options.

Error Handling

- Dot-prompt error handling has been improved and provides direct access to Help features.
- Error messages have been expanded.

Forms

- Automatic layout provides a quick way to create a custom form.
- Colors can be assigned to form design elements.
- Forms design supports expanded picture functions and template characters.
- Memo fields can be placed in a window on a form.
- Text, fields, and boxes can be copied in forms design.

- You can add conditions in forms design that enable the editing of a specific field.

Functions

- A number of existing functions have been enhanced, including DELETED, EOF, and SEEK.
- Financial functions have been added to dBASE IV.
- Many new dBASE functions have been added.
- New functions have been added to support Memo fields, including MEMLINES and MLINE. MEMLINES returns the number of lines in a Memo field with the current value for the memo width. MLINE extracts a specific line of text from a Memo field.
- Support for user-defined functions has been added.
- The LOOKUP function can return a field value from an unselected database.
- Trigonometric functions and other math functions have been added.

Help

- A nested table of contents has been added to Help.
- A print option allows you to print the current Help screen for reference.
- Help System has been expanded.
- Syntax examples have been added to Help for all commands.
- There is a separate Help system for SQL.

Increased Limits

- A report cannot exceed 32,767 pages.
- System memory variables for settings like margins or page length have been added.
- An unlimited number of reports can be created for each database.
- As many as 15 labels across can be requested.
- As many as 28 function keys can be programmed.

- As many as 32,767 copies of a report can be requested.
- As many as five fonts can be used for each print driver.
- CALL can pass up to seven optional parameters.
- Character field length can now be up to 254 characters.
- Command lines up to 1,024 are supported.
- Database record size is now 4,000 bytes.
- dBASE databases can contain up to 255 fields per record.
- Configuration options have been expanded.
- Support for other file formats has been expanded.
- In dBASE IV/SQL the maximum tables in a join is limited only by memory.
- In dBASE IV/SQL there can be 10 cursors and as many as 47 indexes per table.
- The number of memory variables allowed has been increased.
- Maximum number of counts for reprocess is 32,000.
- Maximum number of locks for fields and records combined is 50.
- Maximum number of open database files has been increased to 10.
- Maximum number of open index files per database is now 10.
- Maximum number of open files increased from 15 to 99.
- Up to 10 work areas can be used.
- Number of database records increased to one billion.
- Reports can access data in as many as nine databases.
- Procedures can be a maximum of 64K of object code.
- Queries can join up to eight files.
- Recursive calls are limited by the size of the virtual stack and memory.
- Relationships between multiple files can be established simultaneously.
- Simultaneous sort levels cannot exceed 16.
- Support for international currencies and dates has been added.
- Support for optional installable print drivers has been added.
- The default number of memory variables is now 500, although it can be increased to 15,000.
- The line length for word-wrap editor lines is 1,024 except for reports that have a maximum line length of 255.
- The maximum number of lines in a label is 255.
- The maximum width for a label is 255 characters.
- The number of nested group bands in a report cannot exceed 44.
- The number of rows in a custom form can be as large as 32,767.

- The size limit for a procedure is 65,520 bytes of code.
- The word wrap editor now supports 32,000 lines.
- Total number of bytes in a database file increased to two billion.
- Total procedures in a program increased from 32 to 963.
- Up to 16 binary files can be loaded at once.
- Up to 2,000 GET commands can be included in a format file.
- Up to 35 macros can be created at one time.
- Up to four print drivers can be configured with install or DBSETUP.
- Up to 47 indexes can be stored in an MDX file.

Labels

- dBASE expressions are no longer required for building label lines.
- Labels support the addition of calculated fields and special fields such as the current date.
- The layout surface for labels provides the same options and menu structure as other dBASE IV layouts.

Networking

- Automatic record locking
- Automatic refreshing data changed by another user in Browse or Edit
- Support for many popular networks

Queries

- Query forms make it easy to join files, select fields, and filter records.
- The query work surface has been completely redesigned.
- Update queries permit you to change records to match your specifications.

Reports

- Report designs are completely controlled by bands that determine where design elements are placed.
- Text style options are menu selectable and allow you to use features like italics or boldface.
- The report design is completely new.
- The report design uses a "WYSIWYG" interface.
- Three automatic report layouts provide instant access to column, form, and mail merge design reports.
- You can choose from either layout or word-wrap editing modes in report design.

User Interface

- "WYSIWYG" design screens are available for labels, reports, and forms.
- A Query-By-Example (QBE) interface makes view and query-building easy.
- Ability to move between Browse and Edit screen easily has been added.
- Access to DOS commands from the Control Center menus is now available.
- All files in the current catalog display in the Control Center screen for easy access.
- Pull-down menus now exist for all features including Append and Set.
- The editor available for program entry now supports memo fields and includes search features.

APPENDIX B

Cursor Movement Keys

For the Control Center, menus in full-edit and design screens, and selection boxes, dBASE IV displays are listed in Table B-1.

Table B-1 Menu Selection Keys

UP ARROW	Highlights the option above the current one. If the first one is highlighted, highlights the last option.
RIGHT ARROW	Highlights the menu box to the right. If the menu box farthest to the right is highlighted, highlights the leftmost menu box.
DOWN ARROW	Highlights the option below the current one. If the last one is highlighted, highlights the first option.
LEFT ARROW	Highlights the menu box to the left. If the menu box farthest to the left is highlighted, highlights the rightmost menu box.
END	Highlights the last menu option in a menu box or last item in a list of choices.
HOME	Highlights the first menu option in a menu box or first item in a list of choices.
PGDN	Highlights the next section of choices.
PGUP	Highlights the previous section of choices.

(continued)

Table B-1 Menu Selection Keys *(continued)*

ESC	Aborts current menu option or item selection. Pressing this repeatedly can remove Control Center, menu box, or selection box.
ENTER	Selects highlighted menu option or item selection. For some menu options with multiple columns, also highlights the next column. If the menu item has a sideways triangle, selecting it displays the next submenu.
CTRL-END	Finalizes entries for some menu options.
TAB	Highlights the next column for some menu options.
SHIFT-TAB	Highlights the previous column for some menu options.
letter	Highlights menu options in a menu box or an item in a selection box that starts with the letter. If the letter is typed in a menu box and only one menu item starts with the letter, it also selects the menu option. This also works for user-defined pop-up menus.
ALT-letter	Highlights menu box starting with the letter.
F10	Activates menus.

Table B-2 Edit and Browse Screen Keys

RIGHT ARROW or CTRL-D	Moves the cursor right one character.
LEFT ARROW or CTRL-S	Moves the cursor left one character.
UP ARROW or CTRL-E	Moves the cursor up one field (Edit) or record (Browse).
DOWN ARROW or CTRL-X	Moves the cursor down one field (Edit) or record (Browse).
PGDN or CTRL-C	Moves the cursor to the next screen.
PGUP or CTRL-R	Moves the cursor to the next screen.
CTRL-RIGHT ARROW or CTRL-F	Moves the cursor to the beginning of the next word or field.
CTRL-LEFT ARROW or CTRL-A	Moves the cursor to the beginning of the previous word or field.
CTRL-PGUP or CTRL-R	Moves the cursor to the first record staying in the current field.

(continued)

Table B-2 Edit and Browse Screen Keys *(continued)*

CTRL-PGDN or CTRL-C	Moves the cursor to the last record staying in the current field.
HOME or CTRL-Z	Moves the cursor to the beginning of the field (Edit) or to the first field in the record (Browse).
END or CTRL-B	Moves the cursor to the end of the field (Edit) or to the last field in the record (Browse).
CTRL-HOME	Opens the entry screen for the highlighted Memo field.
CTRL-END or CTRL-W	Saves and closes the edit, browse, or memo entry field screen.
CTRL-ENTER	Saves the entries — does not exit.
ESC or CTRL-Q	Abandons the changes and exits.
DEL or CTRL-G	Deletes the characters at cursor.
ENTER or TAB	Move the cursor to the next field.
SHIFT-TAB	Moves the cursor to the previous field.
INS or CTRL-V	Switches between insert (characters add to the current entry) and typeover (characters replace the current entry).
CTRL-T	Deletes the current entry until the end of the field or the next space.
CTRL-Y	Deletes the current entry until the end of the field.

Table B-3 Design Screen Keys

RIGHT ARROW or CTRL-D	Moves the cursor right one position.
LEFT ARROW or CTRL-S	Moves the cursor left one position.
UP ARROW or CTRL-E	Moves the cursor up one position. In Query design screens moves to the previous file skeleton.
DOWN ARROW or CTRL-X	Moves the cursor down one position. In Query design screens moves to the next file skeleton.
PGDN or CTRL-C	Moves the cursor to the previous next screen.
PGUP or CTRL-R	Moves the cursor to the next screen.
CTRL-RIGHT ARROW or CTRL-F	Moves the cursor to the beginning of the previous word or field.

(continued)

Table B-3 Design Screen Keys *(continued)*

CTRL-PGUP or CTRL-R	Moves the cusor to the beginning of the design screen. In a report design screen, moves to the beginning of the Detail Band if the cursor is in the Detail Band.
CTRL-PGDN or CTRL-C	Moves the cursor to the end of the design screen. In a report design screen, moves to the end of the Detail Band if the cursor is in the Detail Band.
HOME or CTRL-Z	Moves the cursor to the beginning of the line (forms and reports) or skeleton (queries).
END or CTRL-B	Moves the cursor to the next position after the last field template or text in a line.
CTRL-END or CTRL-W	Saves the design and exits.
CTRL-ENTER	Saves the design and remains in design screen.
DEL or CTRL-G	Deletes character at cursor.
BACKSPACE	Deletes character left of cursor.
ENTER	In Insert mode, inserts a new line in the design and moves design contents to the right of the cursor to the new line. In Typeover mode, moves the cursor to the next line.
TAB	Moves the cursor to the next tab stop. In Query design screens moves to the next field.
SHIFT-TAB	Moves the cursor to the previous tab stop. In Query design screens moves to the previous field.
ESC or CTRL-Q	Abandons changes and exits.
INS or CTRL-V	Switches between Insert (characters are added to the current entry) and Typeover (characters replace the current entry) mode.
CTRL-T	Deletes characters or field templates until the next space or blank position.
CTRL-Y	Deletes the line or all of the characters in the entry.

APPENDIX C

dBASE IV Command Reference

This appendix includes all of the dBASE IV commands. While the description for each command is not comprehensive, the command descriptions cover the major points of syntax and usage and provide examples for each command. When a command includes an item in square brackets ([ ]), the item is optional. Items not in square brackets are required. Variable and field names start with a letter and contain one to ten letters, numbers, and underscores. Filenames are one to eight characters that include letters, numbers, and underscores. Avoid filenames that are the same as dBASE IV commands and the letters A through J, which dBASE uses for aliases. If a catalog is open and SET CATALOG is ON, when you create a file, dBASE automatically adds it to the current catalog.

?/??

Syntax

```
?/?? [<expression1>[PICTURE <expC>][FUNCTION <function
list>] [AT <expN>][STYLE <font number>]][,<expression2>
...][, ...]
```

Usage

This command displays the values of expressions to the screen or printer. The PICTURE, FUNCTION, AT, and STYLE options customize the expressions' appearance and location. This command is for simple queries from the dot prompt and for screen layouts in programs. The ? advances to the next line before displaying or printing the expressions and the ?? displays or prints the expressions at the current row and column position.

Examples

```
? TRIM(First_name)+" "+TRIM(Last_name)+"'s social security ;
 number is "+Ssn
```

Returns the string Charlie Foster's social security number is 675-98-1239 if Charlie Foster's record in the EMPLOYEE database is current.

```
? Ssn, First_name, M_initial, Last_name
```

Returns the social security number, first name, middle initial, and last name for the current record in the EMPLOYEE database.

```
?? Ytd_wages
```

Returns the year-to-date wages on the current line.

???

Syntax

```
??? <expC>
```

Usage

This command sends a character expression containing printable and nonprintable codes to the printer. This command is for activating printing features by printing the codes that activate the printing features. ASCII characters and control-character specifiers must be inside curly braces.

Examples

```
??? "{Esc}818D"
```

Sets the printer to print eight lines per inch.

```
??? "{27}{38}{108}{54}{68}"
```

Sets the printer to print six lines per inch.

@

Syntax

```
@ <row>, <col> [SAY <expression> [PICTURE <expC>][FUNCTION
<function list>]][GET <expression> [[OPEN] WINDOW <window
name>[PICTURE <expC>][FUNCTION <function list>][RANGE
[<low>][,<high>]][VALID <condition> [ERROR <expC>]][WHEN
<condition>][DEFAULT <expression>][MESSAGE <expC>]][COLOR
[<standard>][,<enhanced>]]
```

Usage

This command is for data input and output to the screen or printer. This command positions the input or output on the screen, and the other features change what the command accepts as valid input and its appearance. The SAY keyword is for output and the GET keyword is for input. The data from a GET statement is not recorded until the READ command. The COLOR keyword determines the colors of the input or output.

Examples

```
@ 5,5 SAY "Employee of the month is "+First_name+" "+;
Last_name FUNCTION "!" COLOR B/W
```

Returns EMPLOYEE OF THE MONTH IS MARY JENKINS in blue letters on a white background when the first record of the EMPLOYEE database is current.

```
@ 3,5 SAY "Enter the employee's social security number:"
@ 3,50 GET Mssn PICTURE "999-99-9999"
```

or

```
@ 3,5 SAY "Enter the employee's social security number:";
GET Mssn PICTURE "999-99-9999"
```

Displays Enter the employee's social security number: and prompts for an entry. The PICTURE option for the GET option automatically places the hyphens correctly and accepts only numbers for input. The first two statements perform the same step as the last command. dBASE does not store the data for the social security number until dBASE performs the READ command.

@ ... *CLEAR*

Syntax

```
@ <row1>, <col1> CLEAR [TO <row2>, <col2>]
```

Usage

This command clears part of the screen or window display. The first row and column position is where dBASE starts clearing the screen. If the command uses the TO option, dBASE clears the screen to the second row and column position instead of the default of the lower right corner of the screen. This command is for partially removing screen output. The CLEAR command removes the entire screen output.

Example

```
@ 5,0 CLEAR TO 10,79
```

Clears rows 5 through 10.

@ ... FILL

Syntax

```
@ <row1>, <col1> FILL TO <row1>, <col2> [COLOR <color at-
tribute>]
```

Usage

This command sets the color for a portion of the screen or window display. The first row and column position is the upper left corner. The second row and column position is the lower right corner of the rectangle that dBASE fills with the specified colors. The COLOR option specifies the text and background colors for the rectangle using the color code for the SET COLOR option. If the COLOR option is absent, dBASE fills the rectangle with the default background color, which makes it equivalent to the @ CLEAR command. The SET COLOR command sets the screen colors for the entire screen.

Example

```
@ 5,0 FILL TO 10,79 COLOR G/N
```

Sets the colors for rows 5 through 10 to green letters on a black background.

ACCEPT

Syntax

```
ACCEPT [<prompt>] TO <memvar>
```

Usage

This command inputs data into a character memory variable. When this command is performed, dBASE prompts for the user to input data. When the user presses ENTER, dBASE stores the user's input in the memory variable as character data. This command does not provide any checking features and stores as much as 254 characters in the memory variable.

Example

```
ACCEPT "Do you want to add another record? (Y/N) " TO Mcheck
```

Displays Do you want to add another record? (Y/N) and prompts for an entry. dBASE stores the user's input in the memory variable Mcheck.

ACTIVATE MENU

Syntax

```
ACTIVATE MENU <menu name> [PAD <pad name>]
```

Usage

This command activates a defined bar menu. When the menu is active and the user selects a menu pad, dBASE performs the command at the end of the appropriate ON SELECTION PAD or ON PAD command. If PAD and a pad name are included, dBASE highlights the named pad rather than the first one defined.

Example

```
DEFINE MENU Next_menu
DEFINE PAD Payroll OF Next_menu PROMPT "Compute weekly payroll"
DEFINE PAD Leave OF Next_menu PROMPT "Quit"
ON SELECTION PAD Payroll OF Next_menu DO Pay
ON SELECTION PAD Leave OF Next_menu RETURN
ACTIVATE MENU Next_menu
```

Defines and activates Next_menu. The Compute weekly payroll bar is highlighted since the ACTIVATE MENU command does not use the PAD option. The next step the program performs depends upon which menu bar the user selects.

ACTIVATE POPUP

Syntax

```
ACTIVATE POPUP <pop-up name>
```

Usage

This command activates a defined pop-up menu. Using a pop-up menu lets the user select from one of many options by typing the first letter of the menu item. Unlike bar menus that have the ON SELECTION PAD and ON PAD commands, the action performed when a user selects a pop-up menu item is usually another program containing dBASE commands such as DO CASE and IF.

Example

```
DEFINE POPUP Open_menu FROM 2,2
DEFINE BAR 1 OF Open_menu PROMPT "PAYROLL APPLICATIONS" SKIP
DEFINE BAR 2 OF Open_menu PROMPT "Compute weekly payroll"
DEFINE BAR 3 OF Open_menu PROMPT "Quit"
```

```
ON SELECTION POPUP Open_menu DO Menu_pick
ACTIVATE MENU Open_menu
```

Defines and activates OPEN_MENU. dBASE highlights the first bar-defined item without the SKIP option. When the user selects a menu bar, dBASE performs the MENU_PICK program or procedure.

ACTIVATE SCREEN

Syntax

```
ACTIVATE SCREEN
```

Usage

This command transfers the direction of screen input and output from a window to the entire screen. This command lets a program use the full screen while leaving windows and pop-up menus on the screen.

Example

```
DEFINE WINDOW Temp FROM 0,0 TO 4,79 DOUBLE
ACTIVATE WINDOW Temp
ACTIVATE SCREEN
```

Returns the cursor from the Temp window to the full screen. The Temp window and its contents remain on the screen.

ACTIVATE WINDOW

Syntax

```
ACTIVATE WINDOW <window name list> /ALL
```

Usage

This command transfers the direction of screen input and output from the entire screen to a defined window. This command is for using a smaller window for input and output. The contents on the full screen are visible but are inaccessible.

Example

```
DEFINE WINDOW Temp FROM 0,0 TO 4,79 DOUBLE
ACTIVATE WINDOW Temp
```

Changes all screen input and output from the full screen to the defined window. The other contents on the screen remain.

APPEND

Syntax

```
APPEND [BLANK]
```

Usage

This command adds records in the full-screen editing screen or adds a blank record to fill in later. Without the BLANK option, dBASE enters the editing screen using the default edit screen unless the SET FORMAT TO command specifies a format file. Pressing F2 changes the screen to the Browse screen. This command moves the record pointer to the end of the file.

Example

```
SET FORMAT TO Enteremp
APPEND
```

Moves the record pointer to the end of the file and enters the edit screen using the ENTEREMP format screen.

APPEND FROM

Syntax

```
APPEND FROM <filename>/? [[TYPE] <file type>] [FOR <condi-
tion>]
```

Usage

This command adds data from a non-dBASE file or another dBASE database into the current database. If the source file the command uses is a dBASE file, dBASE appends fields found in both databases. Using the ? option instead a filename lists the files in the current catalog or directory. When a file is selected, dBASE uses the selected file for the command. dBASE includes records marked for deletion in the source file if SET DELETED is OFF. dBASE ignores marked records if SET DELETED is ON. The TYPE option and file type is for appending from a non-dBASE file. dBASE expects the data type order in the source file to match the data type in the current database. The FOR option selects which records dBASE adds.

Example

```
APPEND FROM Week_pay FOR Week_end>{07/14/89}
```

Appends records from the WEEK_PAY database with a WEEK_END date greater than or equal to July 14, 1989 to the current database.

APPEND FROM ARRAY

Syntax

```
APPEND FROM ARRAY <array name> [FOR <condition>]
```

Usage

This command copies data from a memory variable array to the current database. Each row in the array becomes a record in the database; each column in the array becomes a field in the current database. The data type stored in each column in the array must match the field data type in the database structure. If the array has more columns than database fields, dBASE ignores the excess columns. If the database contains more fields than array columns, the excess fields are empty in the added records. The FOR option lets you select which array rows become database records. This command transfers data in an array to the current database.

Example

```
APPEND FROM ARRAY Temp_field
```

Appends rows in the Temp_field array as database records in the current database. Each column in the Temp_field array becomes a field in the current database.

APPEND MEMO

Syntax

```
APPEND MEMO <memo field name> FROM <filename> [OVERWRITE]
```

Usage

This command copies data from an external file to a Memo field. The data can replace or concatenate to the existing Memo field.

Example

```
APPEND MEMO Skills FROM Tempmemo OVERWRITE
```

Replaces current record's SKILLS Memo field with the data in the Tempmemo file. If the OVERWRITE option is omitted, dBASE adds the Tempmemo file data to the end of the Memo field data.

ASSIST

Syntax

```
ASSIST
```

Usage

This command activates dBASE's Control Center. If a catalog is not current when dBASE performs this command, the last catalog used becomes active. This command switches from the dot prompt to the Control Center. dBASE adds any open files to the current catalog when it switches to the Control Center.

Example

```
ASSIST
```

The dot prompt screen disappears and the Control Center appears. The current or last catalog used becomes active again.

AVERAGE

Syntax

```
AVERAGE [<expN list>] [<scope>] [FOR <condition>] [WHILE
<condition>] [TO <memvar list>/TO ARRAY <array name>]
```

Usage

This command computes the arithmetic mean of numeric expressions. The numeric expression lists which Numeric and Floating fields the command averages. If a fields list is absent, dBASE averages all of the fields. The scope, FOR, and WHILE options limit the records averaged. The last option stores the results in memory variables or a one-dimension array.

Examples

```
AVERAGE Hr_rate, Ytd_wages
```

Returns 11.33 for the HR_RATE field and 8598.33 for the YTD_WAGES field if the EMPLOYEE database is open and SET TALK is ON.

```
AVERAGE FOR RECNO()<3 TO Mavg_zip, Mavg_depen, Mavg_rate, ;
Mavg_wages, Mavg_fit
```

Returns and stores 32147.83, 2, 11.33, 8598.33, 932.83 as the values of Mavg_zip, Mavg_depen, Mavg_rate, Mavg_wages, and Mavg_fit respectively.

BEGIN/END TRANSACTION

Syntax

```
BEGIN TRANSACTION [<path name>]
<transaction commands>
END TRANSACTION
```

Usage

These commands store the data values before and after dBASE performs the commands between the BEGIN TRANSACTION and END TRANSACTION commands and stores them in a transaction log file. If necessary, dBASE can restore the original data values with the ROLLBACK command if dBASE has not performed the END TRANSACTION command. These commands perform a task and have an all-or-nothing result. All files open during a transaction must remain open until after the END TRANSACTION command. The same is true for locked files and records. This command is primarily for network applications, although single-user applications can also use transaction processing. dBASE deletes the transaction log file when it performs the END TRANSACTION command.

Example

```
BEGIN TRANSACTION [<path name>]
REPLACE ALL Hr_rate WITH Hr_rate*1.1
END TRANSACTION
```

The BEGIN TRANSACTION command opens a log file and stores the old and new hourly rates as the REPLACE command increases the hourly rates by 10%. When the END TRANSACTION command performs, dBASE deletes the transaction log file.

BROWSE

Syntax

```
BROWSE [NOINIT] [NOFOLLOW] [NOAPPEND] [NOMENU] [NOEDIT]
[NODELETE] [NOCLEAR] [COMPRESS] [FORMAT] [LOCK <expN>]
[WIDTH <expN>] [FREEZE <field name>][WINDOW <window name>]
[FIELDS <field name 1> [/R] [/<column width>] / <calculated
field name 1> = <expression 1> [,<field name 2> [/R]
[/<column width>] / <calculated field name 2> = <expression
2>]...]
```

Usage

This command is for full-screen editing and appending records in a table format. The options limit which Browse screen features are available. Pressing F2 switches to the edit screen. You cannot edit Calculated fields and Read-only fields. Most of the command options mimic Browse menu options.

Examples

```
BROWSE NOAPPEND NOMENU NOEDIT NODELETE
```

Displays records for viewing but prevents the user from adding, editing, and deleting records. The command also prevents the user from using the menu options. To leave the Browse screen, the user presses ESC.

```
BROWSE LOCK 2
```

Displays the records in the Browse screen with full privileges and locks the first two fields to the left side of the screen.

CALCULATE

Syntax

```
CALCULATE [scope] <option list> [FOR <condition>] [WHILE
<condition>] [TO <memvar list> /TO ARRAY <array name>]
```

Where <option list> can be any one of the following functions:

```
AVG(<expN>), CNT(), MAX(<exp>), MIN(<exp>),
NPV(<rate>,<flows>,<initial>), STD(<expN>), SUM(<expN>),
VAR(<expN>)
```

Usage

This command calculates statistical data for the current database. The scope, FOR, and WHILE options limit which records dBASE includes in the CALCULATE command. The option's expression specifies the fields included in the CALCULATE command. If SET TALK is ON, the results appear on the screen. If SET HEADING is ON, the results include the field name and the name of the function.

Examples

```
CALCULATE AVG(Hr_rate), MAX(Hr_rate), MIN(Hr_rate) TO ;
M_average, M_maximum, M_minimum
```

Computes and displays the average, maximum, and minimum of hourly rate and stores them to the memory variables M_average, M_maximum, and M_minimum respectively.

```
CALCULATE STD(Hr_rate), MAX(Numb_depen)
```

Computes and displays the standard deviation for the hourly rate and the maximum number of dependents.

CALL

Syntax

```
CALL <module name> [WITH <expression list>]
```

Usage

This command calls a binary file program previously loaded with the LOAD command. dBASE treats binary programs as modules just like procedures and programs. The WITH contains character expressions or memory variable names, including arrays, which dBASE passes to the binary module as parameters.

Example

```
LOAD Formmake
CALL Formmake WITH DTOC(DATE())
```

Loads and performs the Formmake binary module and passes the current date as a character string to the Formmake module.

CANCEL

Syntax

```
CANCEL
```

Usage

This command terminates the command file and closes all open command files. All other files remain open. This command is for handling errors in a program and a tool for debugging a program.

Example

```
ON ERROR DO Err_notice
<program commands>
RETURN
PROCEDURE Err_notice
? "Error number is: "+TRIM(STR(ERROR()))
? "Error message is: "+MESSAGE()
CANCEL
```

When the program reaches an error, it displays the error number and the error message. Then it closes all open command files.

CHANGE

Syntax

```
CHANGE [NOINIT] [NOFOLLOW] [NOAPPEND] [NOMENU] [NOEDIT]
[NODELETE] [NOCLEAR] [<record number>] [FIELDS <field
list>] [<scope>] [FOR <condition>] [WHILE <condition>]
```

Usage

This command is equivalent to the EDIT command. The command's options are identical to the EDIT command's options.

Example

```
CHANGE FOR Hire_date>={01/01/88}
```

Enters the Edit screen and lets the user edit records with hiring dates on or after January 1, 1988.

CLEAR

Syntax

```
CLEAR [ALL/FIELDS/GETS/MEMORY/MENUS/POPUPS/TYPEAHEAD/WIN-
DOWS]
```

Usage

This command clears the screen and releases various elements a program or dot prompt commands use from memory. The command's options can close databases, their related files, and format files; remove the fields list created with the SET FIELDS command; clear @ GET commands issued since the last CLEAR ALL, CLEAR GETS, or READ command; remove memory variables, bar menus, pop-up menus, and windows; and clear the typeahead buffer. This command uses one or no options. When dBASE clears the screen in a program, it positions the cursor in the upper left corner. When dBASE clears the screen from the dot prompt, it positions the cursor in the lower left corner.

Examples

```
CLEAR
```

Clears the screen and positions the cursor to the upper left corner if dBASE executes this command in a program, or the lower left corner if dBASE executes this command from the dot prompt.

```
CLEAR ALL
```

This command clears the typeahead buffer; closes the database, its related files, any open format files, and the current catalog; and releases user-defined memory variables, bar menus, pop-up menus, and windows. It also selects the first work area.

CLOSE

Syntax

```
CLOSE ALL/ALTERNATE/DATABASES/FORMAT/INDEX/PROCEDURE
```

Usage

This command closes the files specified by the command option.

Example

```
CLOSE FORMAT
```

Closes the open format files. Next time a user edits a database, dBASE uses the default edit screen.

COMPILE

Syntax

```
COMPILE <filename>[RUNTIME]
```

Usage

This command creates an executable object code file with a .DBO extension from a source file. Source files include program (.PRG), SQL program (.PRS), screen format (.FMT), report (.FRG), label (.LBG), view query (.QBE), and update query (.UPD) files. dBASE automatically compiles source files when it performs a DO, REPORT FORM, or LABEL FORM command if the source file is not compiled. The RUNTIME option prints an error report listing commands in the source code that RunTime prohibits. When dBASE compiles a source file, it verifies the syntax of the dBASE commands. Compiling a program does not find all errors.

Example

```
COMPILE Enteremp.fmt
```

Compiles the screen format source file in Enteremp.FMT and creates Enteremp.DBO.

CONTINUE

Syntax

```
CONTINUE
```

Usage

This command finds for the next record in the active database that meets the criteria of the last LOCATE command.

Example

```
LOCATE City="Chicago"
CONTINUE
```

The first command finds Charlie Foster's record. The second command finds Paula Walker's record.

CONVERT

Syntax

```
CONVERT [TO <expN>]
```

Usage

This command adds a hidden _DBASELOCK field to the current database that several dBASE functions use. The original database is copied to a file with a .CVT extension. The field contains information about when a record changes, who locked a record or file, and when a user locked a record or file.

Example

```
CONVERT TO 24
```

Converts the active database to a converted file with the _DBASELOCK field having a width of 24.

COPY

Syntax

```
COPY TO <filename> [[TYPE] <file type>] [FIELDS <field
list>] [<scope>] [FOR <condition>] [WHILE <condition>]
```

Usage

This command copies data from the current database to a new dBASE database or non-dBASE file. This command only copies Memo fields if the new file is a dBASE database. The scope, FOR, and WHILE options limit which records dBASE copies. dBASE copies records marked for deletion if SET DELETED is OFF and ignores marked records if SET DELETED is ON. The TYPE option tells dBASE the format of the destination file. If a relation is established and the SET FIELDS command or the FIELDS option in the COPY command includes fields from the noncurrent database, dBASE copies the fields from the noncurrent database to the new file.

Example

```
USE Employee
COPY TO Hire_new FIELDS Ssn, Last_name, First_name, ;
Hire_date FOR Hire_date>={01/01/88}
```

Copies the SSN, LAST_NAME, FIRST_NAME, and HIRE_DATE fields from the records in the EMPLOYEE database that have a Hire_date on or after January 1, 1988 to a dBASE database file called HIRE_NEW.

COPY FILE

Syntax

```
COPY FILE <filename> TO <filename>
```

Usage

This command copies one file to another file. Both filenames must include the filename extension. dBASE assumes the default drive and directory for the files, unless other information is provided. Since this command cannot use the wildcard characters, it only copies files one at a time. To copy a database, its Memo field and production index file, use the Save database structure in the Layout menu in the MODIFY STRUCTURE command to copy all of the files at once.

Example

```
COPY FILE Employee.dbf TO Employ.dbf
```

Copies the EMPLOYEE.DBF file in the default directory to the EMPLOY.DBF file in the default directory.

COPY INDEXES

Syntax

```
COPY INDEXES <.ndx file list> [TO <.mdx filename>]
```

Usage

This command creates an index tag in the .MDX index file that contains the index information in .NDX index files. If the command omits the .MDX filename, the command adds the new index tag to the production .MDX file, creating it if necessary. This command is for changing from dBASE III .NDX index files to dBASE IV .MDX index files.

Example

```
COPY INDEXES City TO Employee
```

Creates a CITY index tag in the EMPLOYEE.MDX file containing the index information in the CITY.NDX index file.

COPY MEMO

Syntax

```
COPY MEMO <memo field name> TO <filename> [ADDITIVE]
```

Usage

This command copies the contents of the current Memo field to a file. This command exports Memo field data. If a filename omits a file extension, dBASE adds a .TXT extension. The ADDITIVE option adds the Memo field data to the end of the file rather than replacing the existing file with the Memo field data.

Example

```
COPY MEMO Skills TO Jenkins
```

Copies the data in Mary Jenkins' SKILLS Memo field data to the file JENKINS.TXT.

COPY STRUCTURE

Syntax

```
COPY STRUCTURE TO <filename> [FIELDS <field list>]
```

Usage

This command copies the structure of the current database to a new database but does not copy any records. If the command includes the FIELDS option, dBASE only copies the fields provided in the fields list. This command is for creating temporary files in a program or creating a database with a similar structure.

Example

```
COPY STRUCTURE TO Employ FIELDS Ssn, First_name,
M_initial, Last_name
```

Creates a new database called EMPLOY containing the SSN, FIRST_NAME, M_INITIAL, and LAST_NAME fields but the EMPLOY database does not contain any records.

COPY STRUCTURE EXTENDED

Syntax

```
COPY TO <filename> STRUCTURE EXTENDED
```

Usage

This command creates a new database with records containing the database structure information of the current file. The new database file contains the FIELD_NAME, FIELD_TYPE, FIELD_LEN, FIELD_DEC, and FIELD_IDX fields. This command is for modifying a database structure within a program. The resulting database can generate a database with the CREATE FROM command.

Example

```
USE Employee
COPY TO Emp_stru STRUCTURE EXTENDED
```

Creates a database called EMP_STRU containing records with the field names, types, widths, decimal digits, and index field flags data for the fields in the EMPLOYEE database.

COPY TAG

Syntax

```
COPY TAG <tag name> [OF .mdx filename] TO <.ndx filename>
```

Usage

This command creates a .NDX index file containing the index information of an index tag in a .MDX index file. If the .MDX filename is omitted, dBASE uses the production .MDX file. This command is for converting dBASE IV .MDX index files to dBASE III .NDX index files.

Example

```
COPY TAG Ssn OF Employee TO Ssn
```

Creates a SSN.NDX index file with the information in the Ssn index tag in the EMPLOYEE.MDX index file.

COPY TO ARRAY

Syntax

```
COPY TO ARRAY <array name> [FIELDS <fields list>] [<scope>]
[FOR <condition>] [WHILE <condition>]
```

Usage

This command copies data from the current database to a memory variable array. This command stores each record in a row in the array and each field in a different column of the array. This command does not copy Memo field values. If the array contains more columns or rows than dBASE needs to store the data, dBASE ignores the excess columns or rows. If the database contains more fields or records than array columns or rows, dBASE ignores the fields and records that cannot fit into the array. The scope, FOR, and WHILE option limits that record the command copies to the array. This command is for storing data in an array that a program can manipulate.

Example

```
DECLARE Temp_recs[5,16]
USE EMPLOYEE
COPY TO ARRAY Temp_recs
```

Copies the data in the first 5 records of EMPLOYEE to the array TEMP_RECS. Since the number of columns is less than the number of fields, command copies the first 16 fields' data for each of the 5 records.

COUNT

Syntax

```
COUNT [TO <memvar>] [<scope>] [FOR <condition>] [WHILE <con-
dition>]
```

Usage

This command counts the number records in the active database that meet the conditions specified by the scope, FOR, or WHILE options. If SET TALK is ON, dBASE displays the results on the screen. The TO memvar option stores the result in a memory variable.

Example

```
COUNT FOR State="OH"
```

Counts the number of employees in the EMPLOYEE database with OH in the STATE field and displays the result of two.

CREATE or MODIFY STRUCTURE

Syntax

```
CREATE <filename> /MODIFY STRUCTURE
```

Usage

This command creates a new database structure or modifies an existing structure by accessing the database file design screen. The menus in this screen can also create indexes, sort a file, delete marked records, and import data. While creating or modifying a database structure, you must provide field names, field types, widths, decimal places, and field index flags. Since dBASE uses the field names to keep track of the fields, use different MODIFY STRUCTURE commands to modify field names, to modify field types or widths, or to add or delete fields.

Examples

```
CREATE New_file
```

Creates a database called NEW_FILE using the structure you enter in the database design screen. The database does not contain any records until you add them.

```
MODIFY STRUCTURE
```

Modifies the current database structure. When you save your modifications, dBASE copies the database's records to fit the new database structure.

CREATE FROM

Syntax

```
CREATE <filename> FROM <structure extended file>
```

Usage

This command creates a database using the field descriptions contained in the records in the database created with the COPY STRUCTURE EXTENDED command. This command is used in a program with the COPY STRUCTURE EXTENDED command to copy a database structure to a structure-extended database and modify the structure. Once the program finishes modifying the structure-extended database, the program uses the CREATE FROM command to create a database with the modified structure-extended database.

Example

```
USE Employee
COPY TO Emp_temp STRUCTURE EXTENDED
USE Emp_temp
APPEND BLANK
REPLACE Field_name WITH "Job_Code", Field_type WITH "N"
REPLACE Field_len WITH 4, Field_dec WITH 0
CREATE Emp_new FROM Emp_temp
```

The second command creates a structure-extended database storing the field descriptions of the EMPLOYEE database. The fourth, fifth, and sixth commands add a record to the structure-extended database. The last command creates a new database with the structure-extended file. The record added to the structure-extended database has become a new field in the EMP_NEW database.

CREATE VIEW FROM ENVIRONMENT

Syntax

```
CREATE VIEW <.vue filename> FROM ENVIRONMENT
```

Usage

This command creates a view (.VUE) file compatible with dBASE III+. These view files do not contain all of the features available in the dBASE IV view query files. The .VUE file stores the open databases and index files for each work area, the relations between the databases, the current work area number, the active field list, open format files, and filters in effect. The SET VIEW TO command activates a view created with this command.

Example

```
USE Employee INDEX Employee
SET FILTER TO Health=.T.
CREATE VIEW Emp_view FROM ENVIRONMENT
```

Stores the EMPLOYEE.DBF filename, the EMPLOYEE.NDX filename, and the HEALTH=.T. condition to a dBASE III+ view called EMP_VIEW.VUE.

CREATE/MODIFY APPLICATION

Syntax

```
CREATE/MODIFY APPLICATION <filename> /?
```

Usage

This command creates or modifies an Applications Generator design file (.APP). The Applications Generator can create horizontal bar menus, pop-up menus, files list, structure list, values list, and batch processes. The Applications Generator can combine databases, indexes, queries, forms, reports, and labels. The CREATE APPLICATION and MODIFY APPLICATION commands are synonymous. The presence or absence of an application design file determines whether the command creates or modifies an application design file.

Example

```
CREATE APPLICATION Empl_app
```

Enters the Applications Generator. If the EMPL_APP.APP file exists, this command modifies the existing design. If the EMPL_APP.APP file does not exist, this command creates a EMPL_APP.APP file to be designed in the Applications Generator.

CREATE/MODIFY LABEL

Syntax

```
CREATE/MODIFY LABEL <filename> /?
```

Usage

This command creates or modifies a label design. The CREATE LABEL and MODIFY LABEL commands are synonymous. The presence or absence of a label design file determines whether a design file is created or modified. When the file is saved, dBASE converts the label design into source code file (.LBG) that creates the labels.

Example

```
MODIFY LABEL Empl_lbl
```

Enters the label design screen. If the EMPL_LBL.LBL file exists, the EMPL_LBL label design appears. If the EMPL_LBL.LBL file does not exist, this command creates a EMPL_LBL.LBL design file.

CREATE/MODIFY QUERY/VIEW

Syntax

```
CREATE/MODIFY QUERY <filename> /?
```

or

```
CREATE/MODIFY VIEW <filename> /?
```

Usage

This command creates or modifies a view query or update query design using the full-screen Query design screen. The CREATE and MODIFY versions of the command are synonymous. The presence or absence of a query design file determines whether this command creates or modifies a design file. The query file has .UPD extension if the query design contains an update operator in the file skeleton and a .QBE otherwise. You can override the file extension by providing another one.

Example

```
CREATE VIEW Health
```

Enters the Query design screen. If the HEALTH.QBE or HEALTH.UPD file exists, the existing design appears in the Query design screen. If a HEALTH query file does not exist, it displays an empty Query design screen containing the file and view skeleton for the active database.

CREATE/MODIFY REPORT

Syntax

```
CREATE/MODIFY REPORT <filename> /?
```

Usage

This command creates or modifies a report design using the full-screen Report design screen. The CREATE and MODIFY versions of the command are equivalent. The presence or absence of the report design file determines whether the command creates or modifies a report design. The report design has a .FRM extension unless another one is provided. When you save the report design, dBASE generates a source code file (.FRG) that dBASE uses with the REPORT FORM command to generate a report with the data.

Example

```
CREATE REPORT Employee
```

Enters the Report design screen. If the EMPLOYEE.FRM file exists, the EMPLOYEE report design appears in the Report design screen. If a EMPLOYEE.FRM report file does not exist, it displays an empty Report design screen to create a new report.

CREATE/MODIFY SCREEN

Syntax

```
CREATE/MODIFY SCREEN <filename> /?
```

Usage

This command creates or modifies a screen design dBASE uses for the EDIT or APPEND command. The CREATE and MODIFY versions of the command are equivalent. The presence or absence of the screen design file determines whether the command creates or modifies a screen design. The screen design has a .SCR extension unless another one is provided. When you save the screen design, dBASE generates a source code file (.FMT) that dBASE uses for the EDIT or APPEND command to look and edit the data.

Example

```
MODIFY SCREEN Employee
```

Enters the Form design screen. If the EMPLOYEE.SCR file exists, the EMPLOYEE screen design appears. If an EMPLOYEE.SCR screen design file does not exist, dBASE displays an empty Form design screen to create a new format screen.

DEACTIVATE MENU

Syntax

```
DEACTIVATE MENU
```

Usage

This command removes the active bar menu from the screen and displays the screen's contents underneath the menu. This command is the command for the ON SELECTION command or a command in a procedure called by the ON SELECTION command. The menu remains in dBASE's memory so it can be reactivated at any time. After dBASE performs this command, dBASE performs the next command after the command that activated the menu.

Example

```
DEFINE MENU Inv
DEFINE PAD Inv_report OF Inv PROMPT "Print inventory report"
DEFINE PAD Inv_return OF Inv PROMPT "Return to prior menu"
ON SELECTION PAD Inv_report OF Inv DO Inv_repo
ON SELECTION PAD Inv_return OF Inv DEACTIVATE MENU
ACTIVATE MENU Inv
RETURN
```

Creates a bar menu with two menu items, Print inventory report and Return to prior menu. When dBASE activates the menu and the user selects Return to prior menu, dBASE deactivates the menu then returns to the calling program since RETURN follows the ACTIVATE MENU command.

DEACTIVATE POPUP

Syntax

```
DEACTIVATE POPUP
```

Usage

This command removes the active pop-up menu from the screen and displays the screen's contents underneath the menu. This command normally appears in a procedure called by selecting one of the pop-up menu items. The menu remains in dBASE's memory so you can reactivate the menu at any time. After dBASE performs this command, dBASE performs the next command after the command that activated the menu.

Example

```
DEFINE POPUP Open_menu FROM 2,2
DEFINE BAR 1 OF Open_menu PROMPT "Compute weekly payroll"
```

```
DEFINE BAR 2 OF Open_menu PROMPT "Quit"
ON SELECTION POPUP Open_menu DO Menu_pick
ACTIVATE POPUP Open_menu
RETURN
PROCEDURE Menu_pick
DO CASE
   CASE BAR() = 1
      DO Wk_payroll
   CASE BAR() = 2
      DEACTIVATE POPUP
ENDCASE
RETURN
```

Creates a pop-up menu with two menu items, Compute weekly payroll and Quit. When dBASE activates the menu and the user selects Quit, dBASE deactivates the menu and then returns to the calling program since RETURN follows the ACTIVATE POPUP command.

DEACTIVATE WINDOW

Syntax

```
DEACTIVATE WINDOW <window name list> /ALL
```

Usage

This command removes the listed windows from the screen and displays the screen's contents underneath the windows. Deactivating the active window reactivates the previously activated window. The ALL option deactivates all windows. When all windows are deactivated, dBASE uses the full screen mode. The windows remain in dBASE's memory so the windows can be reactivated at any time.

Example

```
USE EMPLOYEE
DEFINE WINDOW W_skills FROM 0,0 to 4,79 DOUBLE
```

```
ACTIVATE WINDOW W_skills
? MLINE(Skills,1)
? MLINE(Skills,2)
? MLINE(Skills,3)
DEACTIVATE WINDOW W_skills
```

Creates a window and displays the first three lines of the SKILLS Memo field for the current record. Then dBASE deactivates the window so the program uses the full screen for screen displays.

DEBUG

Syntax

```
DEBUG <filename> / <procedure name> [WITH <parameter list>]
```

Usage

This command executes a program using dBASE IV's program debugger. You can use dBASE's program debugger to execute programs a step at a time, a specified number of steps, or until a condition is reached. Other debugger options let you display variable values and program trace values. The debugger shows a step-by-step approach to how dBASE performs a program. This command is for removing errors in a program. From the debugger screen, the F1 key lists the potential actions the debugger can perform and F9 switches the display of the debugger screens on and off. The WITH option passes the same parameters that the DO command can pass to a program or procedure.

Examples

```
DEBUG Employee
```

Executes the program or procedure EMPLOYEE through the debugger. The debugger's screen appears. To execute the program, press ENTER for dBASE to perform the next step.

```
DEBUG Employee WITH M_recs_add
```

Executes the program or procedure EMPLOYEE using the debugger passing the M_recs_add parameter to the program or procedure. The debuggers screen appears. To execute the program, press ENTER for dBASE to perform the next step.

DECLARE

Syntax

```
DECLARE <array name 1> [{<number of rows>,}{<number of
columns>}] {,<array name 2> [{<number of rows>,}{<number of
columns>}]...}
```

The curly braces represent optional items. The square brackets are required.

Usage

This command defines and creates an array. If an array is PUBLIC, it does not need to be declared. An array can be one dimensional by including a single number in the square brackets or two dimensional by including two numbers in the square brackets separated by commas. The data types of the array elements do not have to be uniform and are set when data is stored to them. Once dBASE declares an array, dBASE treats it like a memory variable. Array elements initially equal a logical .F. until another value is stored to them.

Examples

```
DECLARE M_codes[25]
```

Creates a one-dimensional array that contains 25 elements.

```
DECLARE M_records[10,17]
```

Creates a two-dimensional array that contains 170 elements (17 X 10). The array has 10 rows and 17 columns. An array like this can store data from the EMPLOYEE database using the COPY TO ARRAY command.

DEFINE BAR

Syntax

```
DEFINE BAR <line number> OF <pop-up name> PROMPT <expC>
[MESSAGE <expC>] [SKIP [FOR <condition>]]
```

Usage

This command defines a menu item in a pop-up menu. Each menu item must have its own DEFINE BAR command. This option is not used for pop-up menus using the PROMPT FIELD, PROMPT FILES, or PROMPT STRUCTURE options in the DEFINE POPUP command. The line number for the bar is unique. If two DEFINE BAR commands define the same bar, the first DEFINE BAR command is ignored after dBASE performs the second DEFINE BAR command. The MESSAGE option displays the message in place of previously defined messages when the user highlights the bar. The SKIP option makes the bar read-only. The FOR option makes a bar available when the FOR's option condition is true. A pop-up menu can use read-only menu bars to display text in a menu that a user cannot select.

Example

```
DEFINE POPUP Open_menu FROM 2,2
DEFINE BAR 1 OF Open_menu PROMPT "PAYROLL APPLICATIONS" SKIP
DEFINE BAR 2 OF Open_menu PROMPT "Compute weekly payroll"
DEFINE BAR 3 OF Open_menu PROMPT "Quit"
ON SELECTION POPUP Open_menu DO Menu_pick
ACTIVATE POPUP Open_menu
```

Creates pop-up menu with three menu items, PAYROLL APPLICATIONS, Compute weekly payroll, and Quit. The first menu option is for display only.

DEFINE BOX

Syntax

```
DEFINE BOX FROM <print column> TO <print column> HEIGHT
<expN> [AT LINE <print line>] [SINGLE/DOUBLE/<border defini-
tion string>]
```

Usage

This command prints a box around printed text. It is performed before the program or procedure prints the text that appears in the box. The height must be at least the number of lines of text that the box will enclose plus two lines for the border. If the command omits the AT LINE option, the box appears on the current line but does not advance the printer row position to the next line. The last option selects the box's border. The box only prints if the _box system memory variable equals .T..

Example

```
DEFINE BOX FROM 5 TO 35 HEIGHT 3 AT LINE 5 SINGLE
@ 6, 7 SAY "Invoice Number:" + INVOICE
```

Draws a box starting on row 5 and column 5 to row 7 and column 35 with the text Invoice Number: and an invoice number inside the box.

DEFINE MENU

Syntax

```
DEFINE MENU <menu name> [MESSAGE <expC>]
```

Usage

This command defines a bar menu's name and message. The DEFINE PAD command defines the menu items in the bar menu.

Example

```
DEFINE MENU Pay MESSAGE "PAYROLL APPLICATIONS"
DEFINE PAD Payroll OF Pay PROMPT "Compute weekly payroll"
DEFINE PAD Leave OF Pay PROMPT "Quit"
```

Creates bar menu with two menu items, Compute weekly payroll and Quit. The DEFINE MENU command defines the menu bar name and the message for the bar menu items.

DEFINE PAD

Syntax

```
DEFINE PAD <pad name> OF <menu name> PROMPT <expC> [AT
<row>,<col>] [MESSAGE <expC>]
```

Usage

This command defines a menu item, called a pad, in a bar menu. Each menu pad must have its own DEFINE PAD command. The pad names must follow the rules for field names. The AT option positions the pad on the screen. Using the AT option, you can create vertical as well as horizontal menus. If the DEFINE PAD command omits this option, the menu pad appears three spaces after the previous one. If the menu items do not fit in the default position, dBASE returns the Coordinates of the screen error message. Unlike pop-up menus, you cannot select a bar menu item by typing the first letter of a menu item. To move between menu items, use the LEFT ARROW and RIGHT ARROW keys. Since the order of the DEFINE PAD commands determine which menu item dBASE moves to when the user presses the LEFT ARROW or RIGHT ARROW, the DEFINE PAD commands should be in the order that they appear on screen. If the scoreboard indicators are appearing on top of the menu pads, SET SCOREBOARD to OFF. The MESSAGE option displays the message in place of previously defined messages when the user highlights the pad.

Example

```
DEFINE MENU Pay MESSAGE "PAYROLL APPLICATIONS"
DEFINE PAD Payroll OF Pay PROMPT "Compute weekly payroll"
DEFINE PAD Leave OF Pay PROMPT "Quit"
```

Creates bar menu with two menu items, Compute weekly payroll and Quit. The DEFINE PAD command defines each menu pad. The ON SELECTION PAD and ON PAD commands determine the action taken when the user selects one of these menu items.

DEFINE POPUP

Syntax

```
DEFINE POPUP <pop-up name> FROM <row1>,<col1> [TO
<row2>,<col2>] [PROMPT FIELD <field name>/PROMPT FILES
[LIKE <skeleton>]/PROMPT STRUCTURE] [MESSAGE <expC>]
```

Usage

This command defines a pop-up menu's name, starting position, size, contents, and message. The FROM option defines the pop-up menu's starting position. The TO option defines the pop-up menu's ending position. If the command skips this option, dBASE automatically sets the lower right corner of the menu box based on the menu's contents, limiting the size to fit the screen's boundaries. If the pop-up menu it too short to list all of the menu bars defined for the menu, the user can scroll through the selections when the menu is activated. If the pop-up menu it too narrow for the menu bar text, the pop-up menu text is truncated. The PROMPT FIELD followed by a field name creates a pop-up menu listing the field values for the specified non-Memo field. The PROMPT FILES creates a pop-up menu listing the catalog files matching a file skeleton or all of the catalog files if the LIKE option is omitted. The PROMPT STRUCTURE creates a pop-up menu listing the field names of the active database file or the fields in the SET FIELDS list if SET FIELDS is ON. The PROMPT FIELD option, PROMPT FILES option, PROMPT STRUCTURE option, and adding menu items are mutually exclusive. The MESSAGE option appears in place of previously defined messages when the pop-up menu is activated.

Examples

```
DEFINE POPUP Files_list FROM 1,40 PROMPT FILES LIKE *.DBF
ON SELECTION POPUP Files_list DO File_open
ACTIVATE Files_list
RETURN
PROCEDURE File_open
USE PROMPT()
DEACTIVATE POPUP
RETURN
```

Creates a selection box listing the database files in the current catalog, if one is active, or the current directory. When the user selects a file, the FILE_OPEN procedure opens it for them.

```
DEFINE POPUP Open_menu FROM 2,2
DEFINE BAR 1 OF Open_menu PROMPT "Compute weekly payroll"
DEFINE BAR 2 OF Open_menu PROMPT "Quit"
ON SELECTION POPUP Open_menu DO Menu_pick
ACTIVATE POPUP Open_menu
RETURN
PROCEDURE Menu_pick
```

```
<procedure commands>
RETURN
```

Creates a pop-up menu with two menu items, Compute weekly payroll and Quit. The DEFINE POPUP command lets dBASE determine the size of the pop-up menu.

DEFINE WINDOW

Syntax

```
DEFINE WINDOW <window name> FROM <row1>,<col1> TO
<row2>,<col2> [DOUBLE/PANEL/NONE/<border definition
string>][COLOR[<standard>] [,<enhanced>] [,<frame>]]
```

Usage

This command defines a window. You can define the window's name, position, border, and color. If the command skips the border definition option, dBASE uses the settings of the SET BORDER command or the default of a single-line box. You can store up to 20 windows in memory at once.

Example

```
DEFINE WINDOW Temp FROM 0,0 TO 4,79 DOUBLE
```

Defines window Temp as a double-line box from the upper left corner to the right edge of the fifth row.

DELETE

Syntax

```
DELETE [<scope>] [FOR <condition>] [WHILE <condition>]
```

Usage

This command marks one or more records for deletion. The scope, FOR, and WHILE options limit which records dBASE marks. This command does not remove the records from the database. The RECALL command can unmark the records marked for deletion at any time before dBASE removes them from the database with the PACK command. Pressing CTRL-U in the Browse or Edit screen also marks or unmarks the current record for deletion.

Examples

```
DELETE 5
```

Deletes the fifth record.

```
DELETE
```

Deletes the current record.

```
DELETE FOR State="OH"
```

Deletes records that have STATE field values equal to OH.

DELETE TAG

Syntax

```
DELETE TAG <tag name 1> [OF <.mdx filename>]/<.ndx filename
1>  [,<tag name 2> [OF <.mdx filename>]/<.ndx filename
2>...]
```

Usage

This command removes index tags from a .MDX file or closes an .NDX index file. If the command includes a tag name but not an .MDX index filename, dBASE uses the production .MDX index file. The index file must be open when dBASE executes this command, although another index can control the database order at the time. If the DELETE TAG command deletes the last index tag in a .MDX file, the command deletes the .MDX file and removes the reference to the .MDX file in the database. For .NDX index files, the DELETE TAG selectively closes index files without closing all of the open .NDX index files.

Examples

```
USE Employee INDEX Employee.mdx, Lastname.ndx ORDER TAG Ssn
DELETE TAG Last_name OF Employee
```

Removes the Last_name tag in the EMPLOYEE.MDX file.

```
DELETE TAG Lastname
```

Closes the LASTNAME.NDX file.

DIR

Syntax

```
DIRECTORY/DIR [[ON] <drive>:] [[LIKE] [<path>]<skeleton>]
```

Usage

This command provides directory information on files. If a drive and path are not specified, dBASE uses the default directory for this command. If a file skeleton is not provided, dBASE lists the database files, the number of records, the date of the last update, bytes each file uses, number of files displayed, and the number of bytes remaining on the disk. If a file skeleton is provided, the output is similar to the DOS DIR command. The file skeleton can include the question mark and asterisk wildcard characters to represent one or more characters.

Examples

```
DIR
```

dBASE lists the database file like this:

```
Database Files      # Records     Last Update      Size
WEEK_PAY.DBF               12     02/23/89          842
EMPLOYEE.DBF               13     02/23/89          522
INVENTRY.DBF               26     02/24/89          910

   7262 bytes in      5 files

38346752 bytes remaining on drive
```

```
DIR a:*.prg
```

dBASE IV lists the program files on drive A.

DO

Syntax

```
DO <program filename>/<procedure name> [WITH <parameter
list>]
```

Usage

This command executes a program or procedure. The WITH option lets you pass parameters to the program or procedure. If the program or procedure is not compiled, dBASE compiles it. If the date and time for the source and compiled file differ, dBASE recompiles the program or procedure if SET DEVELOPMENT is ON. When dBASE performs the DO command from within a program, dBASE looks for the named procedure within the current .DBO file, the procedure file set by the SET PROCEDURE command, other open .DBO files, .DBO files with the program or procedure's name, a .PRG file with the program or procedure's name, or a .PRS file with the program or procedure's name. When dBASE performs the DO command from the dot prompt, it looks for the program name in a file with a .DBO, .PRG, or .PRS file extension.

Examples

```
DO Employee
```

Executes the program or procedure EMPLOYEE. If the file containing the program or procedure has not been compiled or was edited since last compiled and SET DEVELOPMENT is ON, dBASE compiles the program or procedure before executing it.

```
DO Employee WITH M_recs_add
```

Executes the program or procedure EMPLOYEE passing the M_recs_add parameter to the program or procedure. If the file containing the EMPLOYEE program or procedure was not compiled or edited since last compiled and SET DEVELOPMENT is ON, dBASE recompiles it.

DO CASE

Syntax

```
DO CASE
   CASE <condition>
      <commands>
   [CASE <condition>
      <commands>]
   . . .
   [OTHERWISE
      <commands>]
ENDCASE
```

Usage

This command selects one group of commands out of several alternatives based upon conditions. dBASE evaluates each of the conditions after the CASE command to a true CASE or a false CASE. The conditions for the CASE commands can include different fields, memory variables, and other condition criteria. Once dBASE evaluates a true CASE, it executes the subsequent statements until it encounters a CASE, OTHERWISE, or ENDCASE command. Once dBASE performs the commands associated with one of the cases, it performs the next statement after the ENDCASE command. If all of the conditions evaluate to false values, dBASE does not perform any of the commands in the DO CASE ... ENDCASE constraint. If the DO CASE ... ENDCASE constraint includes an OTHERWISE command, dBASE performs the commands between OTHERWISE and ENDCASE if dBASE cannot find a true CASE.

Example

```
DO CASE
   CASE State="OH"
      DO Ohio_state
   CASE Hr_rate>5
      DO Hour_pay
   OTHERWISE
      DO Remaining
ENDCASE
```

This DO CASE ... ENDCASE constraint evaluates the value of the STATE field. If it equals OH, it performs the OHIO_STATE procedure or program, then it performs the next command after ENDCASE. If the first case is false, the DO CASE ... ENDCASE constraint evaluates the codition if the HR_RATE field is greater than 5. If the hourly rate is greater than 5, it performs the HOUR_PAY procedure or program, then it performs the next command after ENDCASE. If both cases are false, the DO CASE ... ENDCASE constraint performs the REMAINING procedure or program, then it performs the next command after ENDCASE.

DO WHILE

Syntax

```
DO WHILE <condition>
   <commands>
   [LOOP]
   [EXIT]
ENDDO
```

Usage

This command performs a group of commands while a condition is true. This lets a program omit a group of commands or repeat a group of commands until the condition evaluates as false. When dBASE performs the DO WHILE command, it evaluates the condition. If the condition is true, it performs the commands until it reaches the LOOP, EXIT, or ENDDO command. The LOOP and ENDDO commands switch control to the DO WHILE command to evaluate the condition again and perform the commands in the loop again if necessary. The LOOP command, however, skips over the commands between the LOOP command and the ENDDO command. The EXIT command tells dBASE to skip the rest of the DO WHILE ... ENDDO constraint and perform the next command after the ENDDO command. You can nest these constraints, although one DO WHILE ... ENDDO constraint must be totally inside the other DO WHILE ... ENDDO or other programming constraint. If the condition includes macro substitutions, dBASE evaluates these values the first time it performs the DO WHILE command.

Example

```
DO WHILE .NOT. EOF()
   ? First_name+" "+Last_name+" was hired on "+DTOC(DATE())
   SKIP
ENDDO
```

This DO WHILE ... ENDDO constraint performs the loop for each record in the active database until dBASE reaches the end of the file.

EDIT

Syntax

```
EDIT [NOINIT] [NOFOLLOW] [NOAPPEND] [NOMENU] [NOEDIT]
   [NODELETE] [NOCLEAR] [<record name>] [FIELDS
   <field list>] [<scope>] [FOR <condition>] [WHILE
   <condition>]
```

Usage

This command is for full-screen editing and appending records displaying one record at a time. The NOINIT, NOFOLLOW, NOAPPEND, NOMENU, NOEDIT, NODELETE, and NOCLEAR options limit the menu options available in the Edit screen. The record name, scope, FOR, and WHILE options limit which records this command edits. The FIELDS option limits which fields appear in the Edit screen. Pressing F2 switches to the Browse screen. dBASE uses the default edit screen unless the SET FORMAT TO command has selected a different screen design.

Examples

```
EDIT NOAPPEND NOMENU NOEDIT NODELETE
```

Displays records for viewing but prevents the user from adding, editing, and deleting records, and using the menu. To leave the edit screen, the user presses ESC.

```
EDIT FIELDS Ssn, Last_name, M_initial, First_name
```

Displays the SSN, LAST_NAME, M_INITIAL, and FIRST_NAME fields for the current record in the edit screen with full privileges for editing, adding, and deleting records and using the menu.

EJECT

Syntax

```
EJECT
```

Usage

This command advances the paper in the printer to the next page. If dBASE is not printing the output, this command has no effect. This command also sets the values of PROW() and PCOL() to zero. The paper in the printer must be initially aligned correctly for this command to function properly. This command does not change the _pageno and _plineno system variables.

Example

```
EJECT
```

Advances the paper in the printer to the next page.

EJECT PAGE

Syntax

```
EJECT PAGE
```

Usage

This command advances the printer to the next page or activates a defined page handler. Unlike the EJECT command, the EJECT PAGE command changes the _pageno and _plineno system variables. If the ON PAGE command defines a page handler, the EJECT PAGE command sends line feeds until the _plineno equals the line number specified by the AT option in the ON PAGE command. You can use the EJECT PAGE command in combination with the ON PAGE command to have the page handler print a footer, eject the page, and print a header. If the _plineno already is greater than the AT option in the ON PAGE command, dBASE advances to the next page, adds 1 to the _pageno system variable, and sets the _plineno system variable to 0. The EJECT PAGE command performs these tasks if the ON PAGE command has not enabled a page handler.

Example

```
ON PAGE AT LINE 55 DO Page_break
...
EJECT PAGE
...
ON PAGE
RETURN
PROCEDURE Page_break
EJECT PAGE
? DTOC(DATE()) AT 10, TIME() AT 60
RETURN
```

The first EJECT PAGE command advances the printer to line 60. Then dBASE performs the Page_break procedure. The EJECT PAGE command in the Page_break procedure advances to the next page, increments the _pageno system variable by 1, and sets the _plineno system variable to 0.

ERASE

Syntax

```
ERASE <filename> /?
```

or

```
DELETE FILE <filename> /?
```

Usage

This command removes a file from the disk. If the file is not on the default directory, you must include a path. You also must include the file extension. You cannot delete an open file. Since this command does not accept the wildcard characters, it can only erase files one at a time. To delete a database, use separate commands to erase the database file, the Memo field file, and the index files.

Example

```
ERASE Employ.dbf
```

Deletes the EMPLOY database file in the default directory.

EXPORT

Syntax

```
EXPORT TO <filename> [TYPE] PFS/DBASEII/FW2/RPD [FIELD
<field list>] [<scope>] [FOR <condition>] [WHILE <condi-
tion>]
```

Usage

This command copies data from the current database to a new file that PFS:FILE, dBASE II, Framework, or RapidFile can use. If the current database is indexed, the command exports records in the indexed order. The scope, FOR, and WHILE options limit which records the command copies. The FIELDS option lists which non-Memo fields the command exported. This command exports records marked for deletion if SET DELETED is OFF and does not export them if SET DELETED is ON. If a relation is established and the SET FIELDS command includes fields from the noncurrent database, or some of the fields from the noncurrent database are included in the fields list, dBASE exports the fields from the noncurrent database to the new file.

Example

```
USE EMPLOYEE
EXPORT TO Hire_new FIELDS Ssn, Last_name, First_name, ;
Hire_date FOR Hire_date>={01/01/88} DBASEII
```

Copies the SSN, LAST_NAME, FIRST_NAME, and HIRE_DATE fields from the records in the EMPLOYEE database with a HIRE_DATE on or after January 1, 1988 to a dBASE II database file called HIRE_NEW.DB2.

FIND

Syntax

```
FIND <literal key>
```

Usage

This command finds the first record with an index key that matches the literal key. Since this uses the index rather than checking each record, this command finds the desired record quicker that the LOCATE command. The literal key is the value of the index key that you want to find. If it is a character expression, it does not need quotes unless the character string begins with spaces. To find the record with an index key equal to a memory variable, precede the memory variable with the & macro substitution function. If dBASE finds a record with the literal key matching the index key, it positions the record pointer on the first matching record. If SET NEAR is OFF and dBASE cannot find a record with the literal key matching the index key, it positions the record pointer at the end of the file and returns a message of Find not successful. If SET NEAR is ON and dBASE cannot find a record with the literal key matching the index key, it positions the record pointer on the record that would be after a matching record if the database contained a matching record. The FIND command only finds records marked for deletion if SET DELETED is OFF. Also, the FIND command does not find records not included in a SET FILTER command. If SET

EXACT is OFF, the FIND command can find a matching record if only the beginning characters are provided.

Examples

```
USE Employee INDEX Employee ORDER Last_name
FIND "Larson"
```

Positions the record pointer on record 4 of the EMPLOYEE database.

```
STORE "Foster" TO M_name
FIND &M_name
```

Positions the record pointer on record 2 of the EMPLOYEE database.

FUNCTION

Syntax

```
FUNCTION <procedure name>
```

Usage

This command declares the beginning of a user-defined function. The code for a user-defined function begins with this command and ends with a RETURN command. A user-defined function must be compiled before the program or procedure that calls it executes. Therefore, the user-defined function must be explicitly compiled or in a program or procedure file that dBASE compiles before calling the function.

Example

```
FUNCTION Same_recs
PARAMETERS Mrec_old, Mrec_new
(function commands)
RETURN(M_confirm)
```

These commands define a user-defined function called Same_recs. When a procedure or program calls this function, it passes the function two parameters. The first one is called Mrec_old by the function and the second parameter is called Mrec_new. The function returns the value of M_confirm that the user-defined function defines.

GO/GOTO

Syntax

```
GO/GOTO BOTTOM/TOP [IN <alias>]
```

or

```
GO/GOTO [RECORD] <record number> [IN <alias>]
```

or

```
<record number>
```

Usage

This command moves the record pointer to a specific record in the database. If the database is indexed, the TOP and BOTTOM options refer to the first and last records according to the indexed order. If the database is unindexed, the TOP and BOTTOM options refer to the first and last records according to the physical order. If the command specifies a record number, this command goes to the specified record number regardless of whether the database is indexed. When this command uses a record number, it can move the record pointer to a record that is excluded from listings due to a SET FILTER command, or the SET DELETED ON command if the record is marked for deletion.

Examples

```
GOTO BOTTOM
```

Moves to the last physical record if the database is unindexed or to the last record according to the index key value if the database is indexed.

```
GO 7
```

Moves to record 7.

HELP

Syntax

```
HELP [<dBASE IV keyword>]
```

Usage

This command activates the menu-driven help screens. If the command supplies a keyword, dBASE displays the help screen for the keyword. The keyword can be a dBASE command, function, or help screen name. If the command omits a keyword, dBASE displays the Help Table of Contents, just as if you pressed F1. F3 and F4 move you back and forth through multipage help screens and through more general and more specific tables of contents. To exit help, press ESC.

Examples

```
HELP
```

Displays the Help Table of Contents for you to select the topic that you want help with.

```
HELP IF
```

Displays the Help screen for the IF command.

IF

Syntax

```
IF <condition>
   <commands>
[ELSE
   <commands>]
ENDIF
```

Usage

This command selects whether dBASE performs a group of commands, depending upon a condition. The condition after the IF command is a logical expression that dBASE evaluates as true or false. If the condition is true, dBASE performs subsequent commands until dBASE finds an ELSE or ENDIF command. If the condition is false and the IF ... ENDIF constraint has an ELSE command, dBASE performs the commands after the ELSE command until it finds an ENDIF command. If the condition is false, and the IF ... ENDIF constraint does not contain an ELSE command, dBASE skips over the IF ... ENDIF constraint. Once dBASE finishes evaluating an IF ... ENDIF constraint, it continues performing the program or procedure starting with the command after the ENDIF command. The IF ... ENDIF constraint can include other programming constraints such as DO WHILE ... ENDDO and other IF ... ENDIF constraints if the beginning and end of the other programming constraints are within the set of commands between the IF and the ELSE, or ENDIF command if no ELSE command, or between the ELSE and ENDIF commands.

Example

```
IF State="OH"
   DO Ohio_state
ELSE
   IF Hr_rate>5
      DO Hour_pay
```

```
    ENDIF
  ENDIF
```

This IF ... ENDIF constraint performs the OHIO_STATE program or procedure if the value of the STATE field is OH. If the value of STATE does not equal OH, the second IF ... ENDIF constraint performs the HOUR_PAY procedure or program if the HR_RATE field is greater than 5. If the STATE field does not equal OH and the hourly rate is equal or less than 5, dBASE skips over the commands in the IF ... ENDIF constraint.

IMPORT

Syntax

```
IMPORT FROM <filename> [TYPE] PFS/DBASEII/FW2/RPD/WK1
```

Usage

This command creates dBASE IV files from PFS:FILE, dBASE II, Framework, or RapidFile data files. The file extension is only necessary if the imported file does not use the default extension for the type of data file. The PFS, DBASEII, FW2, RPD, or WK1 option tells dBASE IV the type of data file it is importing. A dBASE II file should be renamed to have a .DB2 extension to prevent confusion with the dBASE IV files. When you import a file, dBASE creates a dBASE IV database with the same name as the original data file with a .DBF file extension. The filename must include the path if it is not in the default directory. If dBASE is importing a PFS file, the PFS file can only have 255 items per form and 254 characters per data item. When dBASE imports a PFS file, dBASE creates a database file with a .DBF extension, a format source file with a .FMT extension, and a format-compiled file with a .FMO extension.

Example

```
IMPORT FROM Emp_data.DB2 DBASEII
```

Imports a dBASE II file called EMP_DATA.DB2. The new database is called EMP_DATA.DBF.

INDEX

Syntax

```
INDEX ON <key expression> TO <.ndx filename>/TAG <tag name>
[OF <.mdx filename>] [UNIQUE] [DESCENDING]
```

Usage

This command creates an .NDX index file or an index tag for an .MDX file from the data in the active database and makes it the controlling index. dBASE uses the index file or tag to list the records in the order specified by the key expression. Indexing a database does not change the physical order of the records. The key expression must contain the same type of data. To combine different types of data, convert the data-using functions to a single data type. dBASE assumes the default drive and a default .MDX or .NDX file extension unless the command provides different information. If the command includes a tag name but not the .MDX index file, dBASE uses the production .MDX index file, creating it if necessary. The TAG name must follow the same rules for field names. The UNIQUE option only includes the first occurrence of a key expression value in an .NDX index file. This option remains if the database is reindexed. The DESCENDING option builds an .MDX index file in descending ASCII order. dBASE includes records hidden with the SET DELETED ON and SET FILTER TO commands. Once an index is created and is open, dBASE automatically updates the index file for changes made to the index expression's value.

Examples

```
USE Employee INDEX Employee.mdx
INDEX ON City+STR(Zip_code,5) TO Location
```

Creates a LOCATION.NDX file that indexes the employee records according to their city and zip code. Since the zip code is a numeric data type, the index expression converts it to character data.

```
INDEX ON Marital_st TAG Filestatus OF TAXES
```

Indexes the database according to the MARITAL_ST field and adds a FILESTATUS index tag to the TAXES.MDX index file, creating it if necessary.

INPUT

Syntax

```
INPUT [<prompt>] TO <memvar>
```

Usage

This command is for entering a dBASE expression within a program and storing the expression in a memory variable. When dBASE performs this command, dBASE waits for a response. When the user presses ENTER, dBASE stores the user's input in the memory variable, creating it if necessary. If the user presses ENTER without entering a response, dBASE performs this command again. The entry determines the data type of the memory variable, unlike the ACCEPT command, which assumes that the entry is character data. This command does not provide any data validation features and stores as much as 254 characters in the memory variable. The prompt is a memory variable or a literal character expression enclosed in single quotes (' '), double quotes (" "), or square brackets([ ]). If the user inputs a date, the user must enclose the date in curly braces ({ }). A program can include this command to prompt the user for a condition the program uses in a programming constraint, such as the IF ... ENDIF constraint.

Example

```
INPUT "Enter the date you want in curly braces: "
```

TO M_date Displays Enter the date you want in curly braces and prompts for an entry. dBASE stores the user's entry in the memory variable M_date. The data type is a date if the user entered the date in curly braces.

INSERT

Syntax

```
INSERT [BEFORE] [BLANK]
```

Usage

This command adds a record at the current record location. The BLANK option inserts a blank record but does not enter the Edit screen. Without the BLANK option, dBASE enters the Edit screen. This command renumbers the existing records that are after the inserted record. dBASE uses the default edit screen unless a SET FORMAT TO has selected a format file. The BEFORE option adds the record before the current record instead of adding it after the current record. For example, if the current record number is 5 and dBASE performs the INSERT BEFORE command, the new record is record 5 and the old record is now record 6. If dBASE performs INSERT instead, the old record remains record 5, the new record is record 6, and the old record 6 is now record 7.

Example

```
GOTO 3
INSERT BLANK
```

Moves to the third record and inserts a blank record. The last command does not enter the default edit screen.

JOIN

Syntax

```
JOIN WITH <alias> TO <filename> FOR <condition> [FIELDS <field
list>]
```

Usage

This command creates a new database by merging two databases. This command can join two related databases. The first database must be current. The command supplies the alias for the work area containing the second database. dBASE assumes that the files are in default directory and uses the default extension unless the command provides path or extension information. The FOR option determines how dBASE joins the records from the two databases. When dBASE performs the JOIN command, dBASE starts at the beginning of the first file. Then, for each record in the second file, dBASE evaluates whether the condition for the FOR option is true. If the condition is true, dBASE creates a record in the new database containing the fields from both databases. If multiple records in the second database evaluate to a true condition, dBASE creates a new record for each record in the second database that has a true condition for the record in the first database. The FIELDS option specifies which non-Memo fields the command copies from each databases. Fields in the fields list from the second database must start with the alias name, a hyphen, and a greater than sign. If the SET FIELDS command lists which fields to display, the FIELDS option is unnecessary. The new database only contains one copy of duplicate fields. dBASE ignores records marked for deletion if SET DELETED is ON.

Example

```
USE Employee
USE Week_pay IN 2
JOIN WITH B TO New_week FOR Ssn=B->Ssn FIELDS Ssn, Last_name;
First_name, B->Week_end, B->Reg_hours, B->Ovt_hours
```

This command creates a database called NEW_WEEK and adds records for all cases where the social security number in the EMPLOYEE database match the social security number in the WEEK_PAY database. For each record in the new database, the record contains the SSN, LAST_NAME, and FIRST_NAME fields from the EMPLOYEE database and the WEEK_END, REG_HRS and OVT_HOURS fields from the WEEK_PAY database. For each employee, the NEW_WEEK database has a new record for every week they worked, because when dBASE joins the records for an employee, the record in the EMPLOYEE database matches with each record in the WEEK_PAY database for the employee.

LABEL FORM

Syntax

```
LABEL FORM <label filename> /?  [<scope>] [FOR <condition>]
[WHILE <condition>] [SAMPLE] [TO PRINTER/TO FILE <filename>]
```

Usage

This command uses the label design created with the CREATE LABEL or MODIFY LABEL command and generates labels for the records in the current database. Entering a question mark for the filename lists the label design files in the current catalog or directory to select. The scope, FOR, and WHILE options restrict which records the command uses. The SAMPLE option determines whether dBASE generates sample labels before generating the labels for the records in the database file. The TO PRINTER and TO FILE options send the labels to the printer or a file. As dBASE generates the labels, they appear on the screen.

Example

```
USE EMPLOYEE
LABEL FORM Empl_lbl FOR Hire_date>={01/01/88} TO PRINTER
```

Generates and prints labels for employees in the EMPLOYEE database whose hire date is on or after January 1, 1988.

LIST/DISPLAY

Syntax

```
LIST/DISPLAY [[FIELDS] <expression list>] [OFF] [<scope>]
[FOR <condition>] [WHILE <condition>] [TO PRINTER/TO FILE
<filename>]
```

Usage

This command displays the records in the active database in unformatted columns. The DISPLAY command stops after each screen and prompts for the user to press a key before showing the next screen. The LIST command does not have automatic pauses. The FIELDS option lists which fields the command displays. Memo field data only appears if the command uses the FIELDS option and the Memo field name is in the fields list. If the FIELDS option is absent, the Memo field data appears as memo or MEMO depending on whether the field contains any data. The OFF option removes the record numbers that dBASE otherwise displays. The scope, FOR, and WHILE options control which records dBASE lists. If the scope, FOR, and WHILE options are absent, DISPLAY shows only the current record and LIST shows the entire database. The TO PRINTER and TO FILE options send the output to the printer or to a file. This command ignores records marked for deletion or not included in a filter activated with the SET FILTER TO commands. dBASE adds headings for each column if SET HEADING is ON. The capitalization of the headings matches the capitalization of the LIST or DISPLAY command and its options.

Examples

```
LIST FIELDS Ssn, First_name, M_initial, Last_name TO PRINTER
```

Prints the SSN, FIRST_NAME, M_INITIAL and LAST_NAME fields of all of the records in the current database (EMPLOYEE). The headings are in upper and lowercase.

```
DISPLAY NEXT 3
```

Displays the next three records. The headings are in upper case.

LIST/DISPLAY FILES

Syntax

```
LIST/DISPLAY FILES [LIKE <skeleton>] [TO PRINTER/TO FILE
<filename>]
```

Usage

This command displays directory information such as the DIR/DIRECTORY command with options to send the output to the printer or to a file. The DISPLAY command stops after every screen and prompts for the user to press a key to continue before showing the next screen. The LIST command does not have the automatic pauses. If a drive and path are not specified, dBASE uses the default directory for this command. If a file skeleton is not provided, dBASE lists the database files, the number of records, the date of the last update, bytes each file uses, number of files displayed, and the number of bytes remaining on the disk. The file skeleton can include the question mark and asterisk wildcard characters to represent one or multiple characters. The TO PRINTER and TO FILE options send the output to the printer or to a file.

Examples

```
LIST FILES TO PRINTER
```

dBASE prints the database files like this:

```
Database Files     # Records    Last Update     Size
WEEK_PAY.DBF              12    02/23/89         842
EMPLOYEE.DBF              13    02/23/89         522
INVENTRY.DBF              26    02/24/89         910

   7262 bytes in     5 files

38346752 bytes remaining on drive

DISPLAY FILES a:*.prg
```

dBASE IV displays the .PRG files on drive A one screen at a time.

LIST/DISPLAY HISTORY

Syntax

```
LIST/DISPLAY HISTORY [LAST <expN>] [TO PRINTER/TO FILE
<filename>]
```

Usage

This command displays the commands that dBASE has performed and stored in the history buffer with the option Send the output to the printer or to a file. The DISPLAY command stops after every screen and prompts for the user to press a key to continue before showing the next screen. The LIST command does not have automatic pauses. The number of commands in the command history is 20 or the value set with the SET HISTORY command. The LAST option determines how many commands dBASE lists. The TO PRINTER and TO FILE options send the output to the printer or to a file with a .TXT file extension. This command can convert dot prompt commands into a program.

Example

```
LIST LAST 5 TO FILE New_prog.prg
```

Stores the last five commands performed into a file called NEW_PROG.PRG. To perform the commands in this file, type DO New_prog.

LIST/DISPLAY MEMORY

Syntax

```
LIST/DISPLAY MEMORY [TO PRINTER/TO FILE <filename>]
```

Usage

This command displays information about how dBASE uses the computer's memory. The DISPLAY command stops after every screen and prompts for the user to press a key before showing the next screen. The LIST command does not automatically pause. The TO PRINTER and TO FILE options send the information to the printer or to a file. This command lists the number, names, data types, public or private status, and contents of the user-defined and system memory variables; MEMVAR and RTSYM memory usage; the names, definitions, and amount of memory used by all active windows, pop-ups, menus, and pads; and the amount of memory still available.

Example

```
LIST MEMORY TO PRINTER
```

Prints the data about how dBASE is using the computer's memory.

LIST/DISPLAY STATUS

Syntax

```
LIST/DISPLAY STATUS [TO PRINTER/TO FILE <filename>]
```

Usage

This command displays information about the current dBASE session. The DISPLAY command stops after every screen's display and prompts for the user to press a key to continue before showing the next screen. The LIST command does not have automatic pauses. The TO PRINTER and TO FILE options send the output to the printer or to a file. This command lists the current work area; the database names, drives, paths, aliases, indexes, read-only status, filters, relations, format files, locked records (network only), and open memo filenames for all active work areas; file search path; default disk drive; print destination; loaded modules; left margin setting, open procedure files, reprocess count, refresh count, number of files open, values for most SET commands; and function key assignments.

Example

```
DISPLAY STATUS
```

Shows information about the current dBASE session and prompts the user to press a key after every screen of information.

LIST/DISPLAY STRUCTURE

Syntax

```
LIST/DISPLAY STRUCTURE [IN <alias>] [TO PRINTER/TO FILE
<filename>]
```

Usage

This command displays the database structure of the specified database. The IN alias option selects which active database the command uses by selecting the work area. If this option is absent, the command uses the active database. The DISPLAY command fills a screen and prompts for the user to press a key to continue before showing the next screen. The LIST command does not pause automatically. The TO PRINTER and TO FILE options send the database structure listing to the printer or to a file. This command lists the filename, the number of records, the date of last update, and the field name, data type, width, decimal places, and field index flag for each field.

Example

```
USE Employee
DISPLAY STRUCTURE IN 2 TO FILE Emp_stru.txt
```

Lists the structure of the EMPLOYEE database and stores the information in the file EMP_STRU.TXT.

LIST/DISPLAY USERS

Syntax

```
LIST/DISPLAY USERS
```

Usage

This network command lists the work stations logged into dBASE. This command is for finding out who is using dBASE. This command returns the work station or network login names. Your login name has a greater than sign next to it. The DISPLAY command stops after every screen and prompts for the user to press a key to continue before showing the next screen. The LIST command does not pause automatically.

Example

```
DISPLAY USERS
```

Returns a listing of the current dBASE users like this:

```
 Computer Name
>SMITH
 WILLIAMS
```

LOAD

Syntax

```
LOAD <binary filename>
```

Usage

This command loads a binary file program that the CALL command or function can execute. dBASE treats binary programs as modules just like procedures in a program.

Example

```
LOAD Formmake
```

Loads the Formmake binary module so a later CALL command or function can execute it.

LOCATE

Syntax

```
LOCATE [FOR] <condition> [<scope>] [WHILE <condition>]
```

Usage

This command finds the first record that matches a specified condition. This command is for finding a record based on a condition that does not match an index expression. This command sequentially checks each record and compares it to the condition. If the condition is true, the LOCATE command positions the record pointer on the current record and stops searching. The LOCATE command starts searching from the beginning of the database unless the LOCATE command includes the NEXT or REST scope options, which start at the current record pointer position. The NEXT scope details the number of records the command searches and the REST scope uses the remaining portion of the database in the LOCATE command. If the database is indexed, LOCATE searches the records by their indexed order. The FOR, scope, and WHILE options limit which records are searched. To find the next occurrence of the condition, use the CONTINUE command. The LOCATE and CONTINUE commands are specific to each work area, which lets each work area have its own conditions for locating records. If dBASE cannot find a match between the condition and the data, dBASE moves the pointer to the end of the file and returns the message End of LOCATE scope. dBASE does not include records hidden with SET FILTER TO or a SET DELETED ON command.

Example

```
LOCATE FOR SUBSTR(Home_phone,2,3)="301"
```

Finds the first record with an area code of 301. The area code is the second, third, and fourth position of the HOME_PHONE field.

LOGOUT

Syntax

```
LOGOUT
```

Usage

This dBASE security command logs out the current user and displays the login screen. This command is for establishing dBASE security features with PROTECT command. When dBASE performs the LOGOUT command, dBASE closes open files during the current dBASE session. This prevents someone from accessing files without permission. If you use ESC to leave the login screen or unsuccessfully login three times, dBASE terminates the current dBASE session.

Example

```
LOGOUT
```

Logs out the current user, closes open files, and displays a login screen.

MODIFY COMMAND/FILE

Syntax

```
MODIFY COMMAND/FILE <filename> [WINDOW <window name>]
```

Usage

This command activates dBASE IV's full-screen text editor and modifies or creates the specified file. This command is for creating and editing ASCII text files that can store various types of data including dBASE programs. If you use the MODIFY COMMAND command, dBASE expects a .PRG file extension. If you use the MODIFY FILE command, dBASE expects no file extension. With both commands, you can override the default by providing a file extension. dBASE also expects that the file is in the default drive and directory, unless another drive and directory are provided. If a window is active when dBASE performs the command, dBASE places the full-screen text editor in the active window. The WINDOW option activates the editor in a defined window to modify the file while displaying the remaining screen contents. When you edit a file with the MODIFY COMMAND or MODIFY FILE command, dBASE saves the old version of the file with a .BAK file extension.

Examples

```
MODIFY COMMAND Employee
```

Opens EMPLOYEE.PRG or creates it if it does not exist and displays the file in dBASE's full-screen text editor.

```
LIST STATUS TO FILE Status.txt
MODIFY FILE Status.txt
```

The first command creates a file containing the LIST STATUS command information. The second command enters the full-screen text editor and loads the file containing the status information.

MOVE WINDOW

Syntax

```
MOVE WINDOW <window name> TO <row>,<column>/BY <delta
row>,<delta column>
```

Usage

This command moves a previously defined and activated window. To move a window to a specific location, use the TO option and provide the coordinates for the upper left corner of the window moved. This command can also move a window incrementally, using the BY option and providing the number of rows down and columns to the left you want the window moved. To move the window incrementally up or to the left, use negative numbers for the delta row and column. To move a moved window to its original position, use another MOVE WINDOW command.

Example

```
DEFINE WINDOW Temp FROM 5,10 TO 9,40 DOUBLE
ACTIVATE WINDOW Temp
<commands>
MOVE WINDOW Temp TO 10,20
```

The MOVE WINDOW command moves the Temp window defined and activated in the first two commands to 10, 20 to 9, 50. The last command could also be MOVE WINDOW Temp BY 5,10

NOTE//&&*

Syntax

```
NOTE/* <text>
```

and

```
[<command>]&&<text>
```

Usage

This command adds comments to a program or procedure file. These commands can document a program or procedure. A comment line can contain any characters, numbers, or symbols except the semicolon. The NOTE or asterisk marks the beginning of a line containing a comment. The double ampersands mark the beginning of a portion of a line containing a comment.

Examples

```
* Main procedure
DO Set_up
```

The text in the first line is a comment. It does not affect the program's performance.

```
REPLACE ALL Hr_rate WITH Hr_rate*1.1  && Gives a 10% raise.
```

The text to the right of the double ampersands is a comment and does not affect the program's performance.

ON ERROR/ESCAPE/KEY

Syntax

```
ON ERROR <command>/ESCAPE <command>/KEY [LABEL <key label
name>] [<command>]
```

Usage

This command directs dBASE to perform another command when dBASE encounters an error, the user presses the ESC key, or the user presses a specified key. These commands normally appear in the initial procedure. The ON ERROR command executes when dBASE encounters a dBASE error, such as a syntax error, rather than a DOS error, such as the printer not working. The LABEL option for the ON KEY command associates a task with a specific key. The keynames for this command match the keynames for macros except the DOWN ARROW is DNARROW. If the ON KEY command omits the LABEL option, the command at the end of the ON KEY command executes when the user presses any key. When SET ESCAPE is OFF, the ON ESCAPE command has no effect. If the command at the end of the ON ERROR/ESCAPE/KEY command is a program or user-defined function, it must be compiled before dBASE executes it. Using ON ERROR, ON ESCAPE, or ON KEY without a command after it resets the actions dBASE performs to the default. Since dBASE remembers the ON ERROR/ESCAPE/KEY commands after completing a program, a program should reset any ON ERROR/ESCAPE/KEY commands before it ends the program.

Examples

```
ON KEY LABEL F10 QUIT
```

This command terminates the current dBASE session when the user presses F10.

```
ON ERROR DO Err_found
<other commands>
ON ERROR
RETURN
PROCEDURE Err_found
? "Error message is: "+MESSAGE()
CANCEL
```

The ON ERROR command tells dBASE to perform the Err_found procedure if dBASE encounters an error. If an error occurs, dBASE displays the message Error message is: and the dBASE error message. Then it returns to the dot prompt.

ON PAD

Syntax

```
ON PAD <pad name> OF <menu name> [ACTIVATE POPUP <pop-up
name>]
```

Usage

This command associates a pop-up menu with a pad in a bar menu. Once a pad is associated with a pop-up menu, the pop-up menu appears whenever a user highlights the pad. The user can select a pop-up menu bar using the UP and DOWN ARROW once the user has pressed the LEFT ARROW and RIGHT ARROW keys to highlight the pad in the bar menu. This command creates the attached pop-up menus associated with bar menus that dBASE uses in the Control Center. This command belongs after defining the menu and pads but before activating the menu. The pop-up menus activated by the bar menu pads are defined after the ON PAD commands. If the pad in a bar menu does not activate a pop-up menu, use the ON SELECTION PAD command instead. The ACTIVATE POPUP option for this command is only omitted to disable the prompt.

Example

```
DEFINE MENU Inv
DEFINE PAD Inv_report OF Inv PROMPT "Print inventory report"
DEFINE PAD Inv_return OF Inv PROMPT "Return to prior menu"
ON PAD Inv_report OF Inv ACTIVATE POPUP Inv_repo
ON SELECTION PAD Inv_return OF Inv DEACTIVATE MENU
DEFINE POPUP Inv_repo FROM 1,1
DEFINE BAR 1 OF Inv_repo PROMPT "Current valuation"
DEFINE BAR 2 OF Inv_repo PROMPT "Year-end valuation"
ON SELECTION POPUP Inv_repo DO Make_repo
ACTIVATE MENU Inv
RETURN
```

Creates bar menu with two menu items, Print inventory report and Return to prior menu. When dBASE activates the menu and Print inventory report is highlighted, dBASE displays the INV_REPO pop-up menu with its two bars. When a user selects one of these bars, dBASE performs the MAKE_REPO procedure. Until the user selects a pop-up menu bar, the other bar menu pads are still available.

ON PAGE

Syntax

```
ON PAGE [AT LINE <expN> <command>]
```

Usage

This command creates a page handler by performing a command when the device to which dBASE is sending output reaches a specified line number. dBASE stores the current line number in the _plineno system variable and updates it for output commands. This command usually appears in the beginning of the program with the AT LINE option to define the page handler and at the end without the AT LINE option to reset the page handler. This command can add headers and footers to reports since dBASE performs the command at the end of the ON PAGE command, when dBASE reaches what is near the bottom of the page. If the command at the end of the ON PAGE command is a program or user-defined function, it must be compiled before dBASE executes it. The number for the AT LINE option is the page length less number of lines used by the footer and bottom margin.

Example

```
ON PAGE AT 55 DO Page_break
DO HEADER
DO WHILE .NOT. EOF()
   ? TRIM(First_name)+" "+M_initial+". "+TRIM(Last_name)
   SKIP
ENDDO
DO FOOTER
ON PAGE
RETURN
PROCEDURE Page_break
DO FOOTER
EJECT PAGE
DO HEADER
RETURN
```

The ON PAGE command in the first line sets dBASE to perform the PAGE_BREAK procedure every time the _plineno system variable equals 55. As the main program prints the names for each of the records, dBASE compares the _plineno system variable to 55. When _plineno equals 55, dBASE performs the PAGE_BREAK procedure, then returns to the main program.

ON READERROR

Syntax

```
ON READERROR [<command>]
```

Usage

This command tells dBASE to perform another command when dBASE encounters an error during full-screen operations. The ON READERROR command traps errors resulting from invalid dates, data out of range, or an unmet VALID condition in a @ GET command. The command the ON READERROR command performs has the same limits of commands it can use as user-defined functions. If the command at the end of the ON READERROR command is a procedure or user-defined function, it must be compiled before dBASE executes it. Using ON READERROR without a command after it disables the action selected by a previous READERROR command. A program should reset any the ON READERROR commands before it exits the program.

Example

```
ON READERROR DO Get_err
@ 5,5 SAY "Enter New Salary:" GET M_salary RANGE 10000,60000
READ
RETURN
PROCEDURE Get_err
@ 18,10 "Invalid salary, try again. "
RETRY
```

The ON READERROR command directs dBASE to perform the GET_ERR procedure if dBASE encounters an full-screen error such as entering a salary that is too low or too high. If an error occurs, dBASE displays the message Invalid salary, try again, and dBASE accepts the users next entry.

ON SELECTION PAD

Syntax

```
ON SELECTION PAD <pad name> OF <menu name> [<command>]
```

Usage

This command assigns an action to a pad in a bar menu. Once this command assigns an action to a bar menu pad, the action is performed whenever the pad is selected. Often the bar menu pad action is to perform a program or procedure. After dBASE performs the command for the bar menu pad, dBASE returns to the bar menu. This command belongs after defining the menu and pads but before activating the menu. The ON SELECTION PAD and ON PAD commands are mutually exclusive.

Example

```
DEFINE MENU Inv
DEFINE PAD Inv_report OF Inv PROMPT "Print inventory report"
DEFINE PAD Inv_return OF Inv PROMPT "Return to prior menu"
ON SELECTION PAD Inv_report OF Inv DO Make_repo
ON SELECTION PAD Inv_return OF Inv DEACTIVATE MENU
ACTIVATE MENU Inv
RETURN
```

Creates bar menu with two menu items, Print inventory report and Return to prior menu. When dBASE activates the menu and the user selects Print inventory report, dBASE performs the Make_repo program or procedure and then returns to the bar menu. If Return to prior menu is selected, dBASE deactivates the menu and then returns to the calling program.

ON SELECTION POPUP

Syntax

```
ON SELECTION POPUP <pop-up name>/ALL [<command>]
```

Usage

This command defines the command performed when a user selects a pop-up menu bar. When a user selects a menu bar, dBASE temporarily disables the pop-up menu while it performs the command at the end of the ON SELECTION POPUP command. After dBASE performs the command for the ON SELECTION POPUP command, dBASE returns to the pop-up menu. The command at the end of the ON SELECTION POPUP is often a DO procedure that includes the DO CASE ... ENDDO programming constraint, using the BAR function as the condition for each CASE. This command belongs after defining the menu and bars but before activating the menu.

Example

```
DEFINE POPUP Open_menu FROM 2,2
DEFINE BAR 1 OF Open_menu PROMPT "PAYROLL APPLICATIONS" SKIP
DEFINE BAR 2 OF Open_menu PROMPT "Compute weekly payroll"
DEFINE BAR 3 OF Open_menu PROMPT "Quit"
ON SELECTION POPUP Open_menu DO Menu_pick
ACTIVATE POPUP Open_menu
```

Creates a pop-up menu with three menu items, PAYROLL APPLICATIONS, Compute weekly payroll, and Quit. The first menu option is for display only. When either of the two bottom menu options are selected, dBASE temporarily disables the pop-up menu while it performs the Menu_pick procedure, which is the command at the end of the ON SELECTION POPUP command.

PACK

Syntax

```
PACK
```

Usage

This command removes records marked for deletion in the active database and rebuilds all open index files. The disk space the database no longer needs becomes available when dBASE closes the file.

Example

```
DELETE
PACK
```

The first command deletes the current record and the second command removes it from the database.

PARAMETERS

Syntax

```
PARAMETERS <parameter list>
```

Usage

This command defines the variables a program has passed and provides their local variable names. This command is the first executable command in a program or procedure that uses parameters. The parameter list must match the number and the order of the variables passed by the calling program or procedure. dBASE can pass up to 50 parameters to a program. An array counts as a single variable. A memory variable passed as a parameter to another program or procedure can be changed in the program or procedure and the changed value remains when control returns to the calling procedure. The calling program passes the variables with the DO WITH or DEBUG WITH command.

Example

```
DO Employee WITH M_recs_add
<program commands>
```

```
RETURN
PROCEDURE Employee
PARAMETERS M_add_rec
<procedure commands>
RETURN
```

The DO command executes the procedure EMPLOYEE and passes the M_recs_add variable to the procedure. In the EMPLOYEE procedure, the procedure calls the parameter it is passed M_add_rec.

PLAY MACRO

Syntax

```
PLAY MACRO <macro name>
```

Usage

This command executes a macro from the current macro library. The macro name is either the assigned key or a longer name if the macro has been renamed. You can also play a macro by pressing ALT-F10 and typing the macro's assigned key or pressing ALT-F1 through ALT-F9. Before dBASE can play a macro, the RESTORE MACROS FROM command must load a macro library or the macro must be created. A program can use this command. However, if the program contains multiple sequential PLAY MACRO commands, dBASE performs the last macro first and performs the macros in the opposite order that the program plays them. Also, dBASE does not perform a macro in a program until another command stimulates input, such as APPEND, EDIT, and BROWSE.

Example

```
RESTORE MACROS Mac_lib
PLAY MACRO Run_progs
```

The first command loads the macros stored in MAC_LIB.KEY. The second command performs the RUN_PROGS macro contained in the MAC_LIB macro library.

PRINTJOB/ENDPRINTJOB

Syntax

```
PRINTJOB
<commands>
ENDPRINTJOB
```

Usage

These commands control a printing task. The commands begin and end the section of program code that prints output to the printer or to a file. The PRINTJOB command prints the codes in the _pscodes system variable, ejects the page if _peject equals BEFORE or BOTH, and sets the _pcolno system variable to 0. The ENDPRINTJOB command prints the codes in the _pecodes system variable, ejects the page if _peject equals BOTH or AFTER, and branches to the PRINTJOB command if _pcopies is greater than the number of copies printed. Unlike other programming constraints, a program cannot nest the PRINTJOB and ENDPRINTJOB commands.

Example

```
_pcopies=5
_peject="AFTER"
PRINTJOB
REPORT FORM EMP_REPO TO PRINTER
ENDPRINTJOB
```

The first command sets the number of copies to 5. The third command starts the printjob. The fourth command prints a report. The fifth command ejects a page and loops back to the PRINTJOB command until the program makes five copies.

PRIVATE

Syntax

```
PRIVATE ALL [LIKE/EXCEPT <skeleton>]
```

or

```
PRIVATE <memvar list>
```

Usage

This command defines memory variables used in a program or procedure as different variables than the memory variables with the same name in a calling program or in a program that declared them PUBLIC. After you return to the calling program, the private variables disappear from dBASE's memory.

Example

```
PUBLIC M_lname, M_fname, M_ssn
<other commands>
DO Add_recs
<other commands>
RETURN
PROCEDURE Add_recs
PRIVATE M_lname, M_fname, M_ssn
<other commands>
RETURN
```

The first command makes the M_LNAME, M_FNAME, and M_SSN variables public for all programs and procedures. When the ADD_RECS procedure is called, the PRIVATE command creates three new variables called M_LNAME, M_FNAME, and M_SSN that are different from the public M_LNAME, M_FNAME, and M_SSN variables. After dBASE finishes the ADD_RECS procedure, dBASE clears the local M_LNAME, M_FNAME, and M_SSN variables.

PROCEDURE

Syntax

```
PROCEDURE <procedure name>
```

Usage

This command declares the beginning of a procedure. The code for a procedure begins with this command and ends with a RETURN command. The DO command calls a procedure. Procedure names can be up to eight nonspace characters. dBASE allows longer names, such as for identification purposes, but the first eight characters must be unique. A procedure can be in a program or procedure file.

Example

```
<program commands>
DO Same_recs
<program commands>
RETURN
PROCEDURE Same_recs
<procedure commands>
RETURN
```

When dBASE performs this program, it performs the first set of program commands, then it branches to the SAME_RECS procedure. After dBASE performs the SAME_RECS procedure, dBASE returns to the main program and performs the second set of program commands before returning to the Control Center or the dot prompt.

PROTECT

Syntax

```
PROTECT
```

Usage

This command creates and maintains dBASE's security system. dBASE's security system is primarily for networks where multiple users can access the data. Once this command saves the security features, dBASE's security system is always present. dBASE's security system provides login security, file and field access security, and data encryption. The command options are menu driven. You only have to add the security features that you want. You do not have to use all of dBASE's security system. When you use the PROTECT command, dBASE prompts for the administrator password. If it is the first time, dBASE prompts for it again for confirmation. You must use this password every time to access the PROTECT command features. Since dBASE does not display the administrator password, you must keep a written copy in a safe space.

Example

```
PROTECT
```

This command activates dBASE's security system. dBASE prompts for the administrator password. If it is the first time you are using PROTECT, you must enter the password again for confirmation before dBASE displays the PROTECT command's menus. If you enter the correct password, dBASE displays the PROTECT command's menus. Without the correct password, dBASE does not enter the PROTECT command menus.

PUBLIC

Syntax

```
PUBLIC <memory variable list> /[ARRAY <array element list>]
```

Usage

This command makes the named memory variables available to any program. dBASE only removes public memory variables from memory with the CLEAR ALL or CLEAR MEMORY command. Memory variables in a calling program are automatically available to the programs and procedures they call. The PUBLIC command makes memory variables available to programs and procedures not called by the program that declares the public memory variables. dBASE initializes public memory variables to a logical true (.T.).

Example

```
DO Init_value
STORE "Y" TO M_confirm
<other commands>
DO Add_recs
<other commands>
RETURN
PROCEDURE Init_value
PUBLIC M_lname, M_fname, M_ssn
STORE "                    " TO M_lname, M_fname, M_ssn
RETURN
PROCEDURE Add_recs
<other commands>
RETURN
```

The first command calls the INIT_VALUE procedure that makes the M_LNAME, M_FNAME, and M_SSN variables public for all programs and procedures. Since this procedure does not call other programs, the memory variables declared are not available unless explicitly stated. When the program calls the ADD_RECS procedure, the ADD_REC procedure can use the M_LNAME, M_FNAME, and M_SSN memory variables. The M_CONFIRM variable is automatically available to the ADD_RECS procedure since the calling procedure uses it.

QUIT

Syntax

```
QUIT
```

Usage

This command closes open files, terminates the current dBASE session, and returns to DOS. It removes dBASE from your computer's memory so you can use other software.

Example

```
USE EMPLOYEE
QUIT
```

The first command opens a file. The second command closes the file and terminates the current dBASE session. If you turn off the machine, you risk losing data in the open file.

READ

Syntax

```
READ [SAVE]
```

Usage

This command stores the data for all of the @ GET commands since the last CLEAR, CLEAR ALL, CLEAR GETS, or READ command. Until dBASE performs the READ command, dBASE does not save the data entered in a screen designed with the @ GET command. When a screen uses @ GETs and a READ command, all of the full-screen editing keys for the EDIT and APPEND commands are available. Once you press ENTER on the last entry on the screen or press PGDN, dBASE stores the entered information to the variables in the @ GET commands and performs the next command after the READ command. If a program creates a multipage editing screen, the program must include a READ command for each page. The SAVE option prevents the READ command from clearing the GET's input. This option is for keeping the entered information on the screen after the READ command.

Example

```
@ 3,5 SAY "Enter the social security number: " GET M_ssn ;
PICTURE "999-99-9999"
@ 3,5 SAY "Enter the last name: " GET M_lname PICTURE ;
"!!!!!!!!!!!!!!"
READ
```

Displays Enter the employee's social security number: and prompts for an entry. Displays Enter the employee's last name: and prompts for an entry. dBASE does not store the social security number and last name entries until dBASE performs the READ command.

RECALL

Syntax

```
RECALL [<scope>] [FOR <condition>] [WHILE <condition>]
```

Usage

This command unmarks one or more records marked for deletion. The scope, FOR, and WHILE options select which records the command unmarks. This command can unmark the records marked for deletion at any time before the PACK command removes them from the database. The RECALL command has no effect on records not marked for deletion.

Examples

```
RECALL 5
```

Removes the deletion mark from the fifth record.

```
RECALL ALL
```

Unmarks all records in the database that have been marked for deletion.

REINDEX

Syntax

```
REINDEX
```

Usage

This command rebuilds the open .NDX index files and the tags in the open .MDX files. If an index is created while the SET UNIQUE is ON or with the UNIQUE INDEX command option, the unique characteristic remains with the index regardless of the SET UNIQUE setting when dBASE reindexes the database. Since dBASE only reindexes the open indexes, the REINDEX command does not rebuild closed index files.

Example

```
USE Employee INDEX Employee.mdx, Lastname.ndx, City.ndx ORDER Ssn
REINDEX
```

The first command opens the EMPLOYEE database, the production index and the LASTNAME.NDX and CITY.NDX index files. The second command reindexes all of the tags in the EMPLOYEE production index file and the LASTNAME.NDX and CITY.NDX index file.

RELEASE

Syntax

```
RELEASE <memvar list>
```

or

```
RELEASE ALL [LIKE/EXCEPT <skeleton>]
```

or

```
RELEASE MODULE [<module name list>]/MENUS [<menu name
list>]/POPUPS [<pop-up name list>]/WINDOWS [<window name list>]
```

Usage

This command removes memory variables, modules, menus, and windows from memory. This command is for clearing part of the computer's memory so an application can put other dBASE items into memory. The command's option determines what the command removes from memory. The ALL option releases all user-defined memory variables if entered from the dot prompt and all private user-defined memory variables if performed in a program. The ALL LIKE and ALL EXCEPT select which memory variables the command releases by the memory variable name pattern. The pattern, or skeleton, can include the question mark and asterisk to represent one or more characters. The MODULE, MENUS, POPUPS, and WINDOWS options remove the specified binary modules, bar menus, pop-up menus, and windows from memory. If a list is not provided, the option applies to all modules, deactivated bar menus, pop-up menus, and windows.

Examples

```
RELEASE M_ssn
```

Releases the M_ssn memory variable from memory.

```
RELEASE ALL LIKE M_*
```

Releases all user-defined memory variables that begin with an M and an underscore. If this is executed from within a program, dBASE does not release the public memory variables that start with an M and an underscore.

```
RELEASE POPUPS
```

Releases all pop-up menus from dBASE's memory.

RENAME

Syntax

```
RENAME <old filename> TO <new filename>
```

Usage

This command renames a file to another filename. Both filenames must include the filename extension. If the path is not the default drive and directory, the command must include the path. Since this command does not accept the wildcard characters, it renames files one at a time. To rename a database, use separate commands to rename the index file and the Memo field file.

Example

```
RENAME Employee.dbf TO Employ.dbf
```

Copies the EMPLOYEE database file in the default directory to the EMPLOY database in the default directory.

REPLACE

Syntax

```
REPLACE <field> WITH <exp> [ADDITIVE] [,<field> WITH <exp>
[ADDITIVE]] [<scope>] [FOR <condition>]
  [WHILE <condition>]
```

Usage

This command replaces data in the current database. The expression must be the same data type as the field it is replacing. The scope, FOR, and WHILE options select which records the command replaces. If the command does not use one of these options, the REPLACE command only applies to the current record. The ADDITIVE option adds the expression to the end of a Memo field instead of replacing it. When the REPLACE command changes the index expression in an indexed database, dBASE moves the record to its new location. As a result, some records can be overlooked or included twice. The solution is to SET ORDER to 0, which disables the index ordering without closing index files. If the REPLACE command replaces the data for two or more fields, the data types of the fields must be the same. To replace multiple data types, use separate REPLACE commands.

Examples

```
REPLACE Hr_rate WITH Hr_rate*1.1 FOR Hire_date>{01/01/88}
```

Increases the hourly rate by 10% for all employees hired after January 1, 1988.

```
REPLACE Skills WITH "Can fix most small office appliances ;
such as pencil sharpeners and typewriters." ADDITIVE
```

Adds "Fixes most small office appliances such as pencil sharpeners and typewriters" to the end of the SKILLS Memo field for the current record.

REPORT FORM

Syntax

```
REPORT FORM <report form filename> /? [PLAIN] [HEADING
<expC>] [NOEJECT] [SUMMARY] [<scope>] [FOR <condition>]
[WHILE <condition>] [TO PRINTER/TO FILE <filename>]
```

Usage

This command takes the report design created with the CREATE or MODIFY REPORT command and generates the reports using the records in the current database. Entering a question mark instead of a filename lists the report design files in the current catalog or directory to select. The PLAIN option only puts headers and footers on the first page. The HEADING option adds an additional heading. The PLAIN and HEADING options are mutually exclusive. The NOEJECT option suppresses the initial page eject. The SUMMARY option excludes the Detail Band from the report. The scope, FOR, and WHILE options select which records dBASE uses in the report. The TO PRINTER and TO FILE options direct the report to the printer or to a file. As dBASE generates the report, the report appears on the screen.

Example

```
USE EMPLOYEE
REPORT FORM Emp_repo TO FILE Emp_repo
```

Generates the EMP_REPO report and stores it in the EMP_REPO.PRT file. The report uses all of the records in the EMPLOYEE database.

RESET

Syntax

```
RESET [IN <alias>]
```

Usage

This command removes the integrity tag that dBASE adds to a file when a program uses a file in transaction processing. This command is for after an unsuccessful ROLLBACK command and the file has been corrected manually. Once the integrity tag is reset, a program can use the file in another transaction. The IN option selects which database is reset. If a program uses this command, it usually combines the RESET command with messages describing the problem the transaction encountered.

Example

```
BEGIN TRANSACTION
<transaction processing commands>
END TRANSACTION
IF .NOT. COMPLETE()
   RESET
ENDIF
```

If the transaction is incomplete, dBASE resets the integrity tag.

RESTORE

Syntax

```
RESTORE FROM <filename> [ADDITIVE]
```

Usage

This command retrieves and activates memory variables, including arrays, from a memory file. dBASE assumes the file has a .MEM extension and is in the default drive and directory unless the command provides different information. dBASE releases the previously defined user-defined memory variables unless the command uses the ADDITIVE option. The restored variables are public if dBASE performs this command from the dot prompt and private if dBASE performs this command in a program, unless the program has a PUBLIC command to make them public before restoring them and the RESTORE command uses the ADDITIVE option.

Example

```
STORE .T. TO M_confirm
RESTORE FROM Newvalue
```

Releases the M_confirm memory variable and loads the memory variables in NEWVALUE.MEM into memory. If the command included the ADDITIVE option, dBASE would retain the M_confirm memory variable.

RESTORE MACROS

Syntax

```
RESTORE MACROS FROM <macro file>
```

Usage

This command loads a macro library. After dBASE loads the macros, dBASE can play the macros. dBASE assumes the file has a .KEY extension and is in the default drive and directory unless the command provides different information. Before dBASE loads a macro library, it releases any macros currently in memory. Once dBASE loads a macro library, dBASE does not save changes made to a macro unless dBASE performs the SAVE MACROS command.

Example

```
RESTORE MACROS Mac_lib
```

This command loads the macros stored in MAC_LIB.KEY. After dBASE loads the macros, the PLAY MACROS command can play them.

RESTORE WINDOW

Syntax

```
RESTORE WINDOW <window name list>/ALL FROM <filename>
```

Usage

This command loads window definitions saved with the SAVE WINDOW command into memory. After dBASE loads the windows, the ACTIVATE WINDOW command can activate the windows. dBASE assumes the file has a .WIN extension and is in the default drive and directory unless the command provides different information. Using the window name list instead of the ALL option selects which windows from a window definition file the command restores instead of loading all of the window definitions from the file.

Example

```
RESTORE WINDOW ALL FROM Wind_def
```

This command loads all window definitions stored in WIND_DEF.WIN. After dBASE loads the windows, the ACTIVATE WINDOW command can activate them.

RESUME

Syntax

```
RESUME
```

Usage

This command restarts program execution when the SUSPEND command discontinues execution. The RESUME and SUSPEND commands temporarily halt programs to remove errors. The SUSPEND command makes the dot prompt available to test the values of variables. A program should use the CLEAR command after the SUSPEND command to clear the screen so the dot prompt commands entered while the RESUME command suspends the program do not affect the program's screen output.

Example

```
RESUME
```

Starts executing a program that the SUSPEND command halted.

RETRY

Syntax

```
RETRY
```

Usage

This command returns control to a calling procedure and retries the command that called the procedure. This command normally ends the procedure called by the ON ERROR command to retry the command that caused the error.

Example

```
ON ERROR DO Err_update
USE Employee INDEX Employee ORDER Ssn
SCAN
   ? "Number of hours worked is: "+STR(Ytd_wages/Hr_rate)
ENDSCAN
USE
RETURN
PROCEDURE Err_update
ACCEPT "Hourly rate is incorrect. What is the correct ;
```

```
hourly rate? " TO M_rate
REPLACE Hr_rate WITH M_rate
RETRY
```

The program displays the number of hours each employee worked. If the hourly rate is 0, dBASE performs the ERR_UPDATE procedure that asks for a new hourly rate. After the ERR_UPDATE procedure replaces the old hourly rate with the new hourly rate, dBASE retries the command in the SCAN ... ENDSCAN constraint.

RETURN

Syntax

```
RETURN [<expression>/TO MASTER/TO <procedure name>]
```

Usage

This command returns control to a calling program or procedure, the dot prompt, or the Control Center. When dBASE returns to a calling program or procedure, it performs the command after the DO command that called the program or procedure, or evaluates the command that called the user-defined function. Every program, procedure, or user-defined function must end with a RETURN, RETRY, or CANCEL command. The RETURN command releases the private memory variables and the value an ERROR function may have. RETURN without any options returns control to the specific program or procedure that called it. A user-defined function uses the expression option to define the value the user-defined function returns. The TO MASTER option returns control to the initially executed program and performs the command after the command that eventually called the program or procedure with the RETURN TO MASTER command. The TO procedure name returns control to the named program or procedure and performs the command after the command that eventually called the program or procedure with the RETURN TO command.

Example

```
ON ERROR DO Err_found
<program commands>
DO Add_recs
<program commands>
RETURN
PROCEDURE Add_recs
<procedure commands>
RETURN
PROCEDURE Err_found
<procedure commands>
RETURN TO MASTER
```

The abbreviated program and procedures use the RETURN command in three different ways. In the initial program, the RETURN command returns control to the dot prompt. In the ADD_RECS procedure, the RETURN command returns control to the main program and performs the command after the DO Add_recs command. The RETURN TO MASTER command in the ERR_FOUND procedure returns control to the main program. If an error occurs during the ADD_RECS procedure, the RETURN in the ERR_FOUND procedure returns control to the main program after the DO Add_recs command. If an error occurs during the main program, the RETURN TO MASTER in the ERR_FOUND procedure returns control to the command after the command that caused dBASE to branch to the ERR_FOUND procedure.

ROLLBACK

Syntax

```
ROLLBACK [<database filename>]
```

Usage

This command restores the database and index files as they existed when dBASE performed the BEGIN TRANSACTION command then closes the files. This command has no effect after an END TRANSACTION command.

Example

```
ON ERROR ROLLBACK
<program commands>
BEGIN TRANSACTION
<transaction processing commands>
END TRANSACTION
<program commands>
RETURN
```

This program performs some commands using transaction processing and some commands without transaction processing. If an error occurs before or after the transaction, the ROLLBACK command has no effect. If an error occurs during the transaction, dBASE rolls back the transaction so all data has original values and performs the next command after END TRANSACTION.

RUN/!

Syntax

```
RUN/! <DOS command>
```

Usage

This command runs a DOS command or a program that DOS can execute. Since dBASE does not remove itself from the computer's memory, the computer has a limited amount of memory to run DOS commands and programs. If the computer does not have enough memory, the message Insufficient memory appears. Avoid commands like ASSIGN and PRINT, which remain in memory. The DOS command can include macro substitution and variables. dBASE evaluates the variables in the command before performing the command. The DOS command uses the current drive rather than the default drive. If you perform a command such as DIR and the default drive is different from the current drive, the DOS DIR command provides different results than the dBASE DIR command.

Examples

```
RUN DIR | SORT > Dir_file
```

Using the DOS DIR and SORT commands creates a file called DIR_FILE that contains the files on the current drive in alphabetical order.

```
STORE "A:" TO Drive
!FORMAT &Drive
```

Uses the DOS FORMAT command to format, prepare a blank disk to store data, the disk in drive A.

SAVE

Syntax

```
SAVE TO <filename> [ALL LIKE/EXCEPT <skeleton>]
```

Usage

This command saves some or all of the current memory variables, including arrays, to a memory file. dBASE saves the file on the default drive and directory, and uses a .MEM extension unless the command provides other information. The ALL LIKE and ALL EXCEPT select which memory variables the command saves. After dBASE saves the memory variables, the RESTORE command can restore them.

Example

```
STORE .T. TO M_confirm
STORE DATE() TO M_date
SAVE TO Newvalue
```

The SAVE command creates a file called NEWVALUE.MEM containing the M_CONFIRM variable with a .T. value and the M_DATE variable with the current date as the variable.

SAVE MACROS

Syntax

```
SAVE MACROS TO <macro file>
```

Usage

This command saves the current macros to a macro library. After dBASE saves the macros, the RESTORE MACROS command can load the macros into memory. dBASE saves the file on the default drive and directory, and uses a .KEY extension unless the command provides different information. Saving the macros does not remove them from dBASE's memory.

Example

```
SAVE MACROS TO Mac_lib
```

This command saves the current macros in a macros library called MAC_LIB.KEY.

SAVE WINDOW

Syntax

```
SAVE WINDOW <window name list>/ALL TO <filename>
```

Usage

This command saves window definitions to a file. dBASE saves the file to the default drive and directory using a .WIN extension, unless the command provides different information. The window name list option saves the listed definitions and the ALL option saves all window definitions.

Example

```
SAVE WINDOW Memo_wind, Edit_wind TO Wind_def
```

This command saves the MEMO_WIND and EDIT_WIND window definitions to the WIND_DEF.WIN file.

SCAN

Syntax

```
SCAN [<scope>] [FOR <condition>] [WHILE <condition>]
   [<commands>]
      [LOOP]
      [EXIT]
ENDSCAN
```

Usage

This command is an alternative to the DO WHILE ... ENDDO programming constraint. Unlike the DO WHILE command, the SCAN command automatically moves the record pointer to the first record in the database that matches the scope, FOR, and WHILE conditions, and implicitly includes .AND. EOF() as a condition. Also, the ENDSCAN and LOOP commands automatically advance the record pointer to the next record that matches the scope, FOR, and WHILE conditions. The SCAN ... ENDSCAN constraint is for performing a group of commands using individual records. Like the DO WHILE ... ENDDO constraint, when dBASE finds a record that matches the scope, FOR, and WHILE conditions, dBASE performs the commands in the SCAN ... ENDSCAN constraint until it reaches the LOOP, EXIT, or ENDSCAN command. The LOOP command skips the commands between the LOOP command and the ENDSCAN command. The EXIT command ends the SCAN ... ENDSCAN constraint and performs the next command after the ENDSCAN command. You can nest a SCAN ... ENDSCAN constraint in another programming constraint or put another programming constraint in a SCAN ... ENDSCAN constraint, although each constraint must be totally inside or outside the other programming constraint.

Example

```
SCAN
    ? First_name+" "+Last_name+" was hired on "+DTOC(DATE())
ENDSCAN
```

This SCAN ... ENDSCAN constraint performs the same commands as the example for the DO WHILE ... ENDDO constraint. It requires less commands since the SCAN command automatically tests for the end of the file, and the ENDSCAN command advances the record pointer to the next record.

SEEK

Syntax

```
SEEK <exp>
```

Usage

This command finds the first record with an index key that matches the expression's value. Like the FIND command, the SEEK command uses the index rather than checking each record, which finds the desired record quicker that the LOCATE command. The expression is a dBASE expression dBASE evaluates to determine the value of the index key that you want to find. The SEEK command expression normally contains memory variables. If dBASE finds the desired record, it positions the record pointer on the first matching record. If SET NEAR is OFF and the search is unsuccessful, it positions the record pointer at the end of the file and returns a message of Find not successful. If SET NEAR is ON and the search is unsuccessful, it positions the record pointer on the record that would be after a matching record if the database contained a matching record. The SEEK command ignores records marked for deletion if SET DELETED is ON and records not included in a SET FILTER command. If SET EXACT is OFF, the SEEK command can find a matching record if only the beginning characters are provided.

Examples

```
USE Employee INDEX Employee ORDER TAG Last_name
STORE "Larson" TO M_lastname
SEEK M_lastname
```

Positions the record pointer on record 4 of the EMPLOYEE database.

SELECT

Syntax

```
SELECT <work area name/alias>
```

Usage

This command makes another work area current. The work area name or alias can be a number from 1 to 10, a letter from A to J, the alias name, usually the database name, or a variable in parentheses, unless it is part of an expression that evaluates to one of the work area values. Each work area can contain only one database. The tenth work area contains the open catalog, if one is used. Selecting a different work area makes the database open in the selected work area of the current database. Each work area uses a separate record pointer.

Examples

```
SELECT 8
```

Makes the eighth work area current. If the eighth work area has an active database, the database becomes current.

```
USE Employee IN 3
SELECT Employee
```

Makes the third work area and the EMPLOYEE database current.

SHOW MENU

Syntax

```
SHOW MENU <menu name> [PAD <pad name>]
```

Usage

This command displays the named bar menu and highlights a particular pad. This command does not activate the menu and the menu options are inaccessible. This command is for program development to check a menu's appearance.

Example

```
DEFINE MENU Pay
DEFINE PAD Payroll OF Pay PROMPT "Compute weekly payroll"
DEFINE PAD Leave OF Pay PROMPT "Quit"
SHOW MENU Pay PAD Payroll
```

The first three commands create a bar menu with two menu items, Compute weekly payroll and Quit. The SHOW MENU command displays the menu and highlights the first pad.

SHOW POPUP

Syntax

```
SHOW POPUP <pop-up name>
```

Usage

This command displays the named pop-up menu. Since this command does not activate the menu, the menu options are unavailable for selection. This command is for program development to view the menu's appearance.

Example

```
DEFINE POPUP Files_list FROM 1,40 PROMPT FILES LIKE *.DBF
SHOW POPUP Files_list
```

The first command defines a pop-up menu that lists the database files. The second command displays the pop-up menu box on the screen without activating it.

SKIP

Syntax

```
SKIP [<expN>] [IN <alias>]
```

Usage

This command moves the record pointer in a database. In an unindexed file, this command follows the record number order. In an indexed file, this command follows the index record order. The SKIP command ignores records hidden by a SET FILTER TO or a SET DELETED ON command. A positive numeric expression moves the record pointer forward in the database and a negative numeric expression moves the record pointer backwards. The IN option moves the record pointer in a noncurrent work area. If the SKIP command moves to the end of the file, the record number is one greater than the number of records in the database. If this command moves to the beginning of the file, the record number is 1 or the record number of the first record according to the index record order.

Examples

```
SKIP 5
```

Advances the current record pointer forward five records.

```
SKIP -3 IN 2
```

Moves the record pointer in the second work area backwards three records.

SORT

Syntax

```
SORT TO <filename> ON <field1> [/A] [/C] [/D] [,<field2>
[/A] [/C] [/D]...] [ASCENDING]/[DESCENDING] [<scope>] [FOR
<condition>] [WHILE <condition>]
```

Usage

This command creates a new database containing the records in the current database in a sorted order. This command rearranges the physical order of the records in the new database. Since dBASE rearranges the physical order of the records, the SORT command takes longer than the INDEX command. dBASE sorts the records by their field's ASCII values instead of a dBASE expression value such as the INDEX command uses. The sort criteria can use up to 10 character, date, numeric, and floating fields. dBASE saves the new database in the default drive and drive using .DBF file extension unless the command provides other information. The /A and /D options designate whether dBASE sorts the records in ascending or descending order for a particular field's value. The /C option determines whether dBASE ignores the differences between upper and lower case. The ASCENDING and DESCENDING options set the sort order for fields that do not include an /A or /D option. The scope, FOR, and WHILE options select which records the command copies to the new database. Unlike the INDEX command, dBASE does not continually update the record order of a sorted database. In the SORT command, the fields appear in the order of the their importance.

Example

```
USE Employee
SORT ON Ssn TO New_emp FOR Hire_date>={01/01/88}
```

The second command creates a database called NEW_EMP.DBF that contains the records in the EMPLOYEE database for the employees hired on or after January 1, 1988 in ascending order according to their social security numbers.

STORE

Syntax

```
STORE <expression> TO <memvar list> / <array element list>
```

An alternative syntax for STORE is:

```
<memvar> / <array element> = <expression>
```

Usage

This command creates memory variables, if necessary, and assigns values to memory variables and arrays. The DECLARE command must previously define arrays. A memory variable can contain any type of data and up to 254 characters.

Examples

```
STORE 0 TO M_counter, M_rec_add, M_runtotal
```

Creates and initializes the M_COUNTER, M_REC_ADD, and M_RUNTOTAL memory variables to 0.

```
STORE 0 TO M_temp
STORE "Y" TO M_temp
```

The first command creates M_TEMP and initializes its value to 0. The second command changes its value to the letter Y.

```
M_due_date=DATE()+30
```

Creates the M_DUE_DATE memory variable and initializes its value to thirty days after today's date.

SUM

Syntax

```
SUM [<expN list>] [TO <memvar list>/TO ARRAY <array name>]
[<SCOPE>] [FOR <condition>] [WHILE <condition>]
```

Usage

This command computes the total of numeric expressions. The numeric expression list can contain various numeric expressions such as Numeric and Floating field names. If it is omitted, the command sums all Numeric and Floating fields in the current database. The TO option lets you store the floating number type results in memory variables or a one-dimension array. The scope, FOR, and WHILE options limit the records totaled.

Examples

```
USE Employee
DECLARE M_total[2]
SUM Hr_rate, Ytd_wages TO ARRAY M_total
```

Returns and stores 68 and 51590 as the values of M_TOTAL[1] and M_TOTAL[2].

```
SUM FOR Hire_date>={01/01/88} TO Msum_zip, Msum_depen, ;
Msum_rate, Msum_wages, Msum_fit
```

Returns and stores 96273, 3, 27.25, 15340, and 1721.50 as the values of MSUM_ZIP, MSUM_DEPEN, MSUM_RATE, MSUM_WAGES, and MSUM_FIT respectively.

SUSPEND

Syntax

```
SUSPEND
```

Usage

This command interrupts a program and returns control to the dot prompt. dBASE retains all of the memory variables in memory when the SUSPEND command halts a program. This command is for correcting errors. When the command temporarily halts the program, the memory variable values can be checked. The RESUME command continues the program's execution where it left off. To permanently halt a program, use the CANCEL command. While a program is suspended, you cannot modify an open program or procedure file.

Example

```
STORE 0 TO M_counter, M_rec_add, M_runtotal
<program commands>
SUSPEND
<program commands>
RETURN
```

When dBASE performs this program, it halts when it reaches the SUSPEND command. While the dot prompt has control, you can confirm the values for the M_counter, M_rec_add, and M_runtotal fields. The program finishes executing by using the RESUME command.

TEXT

Syntax

```
TEXT
<text characters>
ENDTEXT
```

Usage

The TEXT and ENDTEXT commands display the text between the commands exactly as it appears in the program. dBASE does not evaluate the text between the two commands. This command is for displaying or printing blocks of text without any formatting.

Example

```
TEXT
The next phases of the program ask you for the records that
you want to include in the report. Since you are entering
dBASE expressions, remember to enter dates in curly braces
({ }) and precede macro substitutions with an ampersand (&).
ENDTEXT
```

The TEXT and ENDTEXT commands place the paragraph between the two commands exactly as it appears in the program.

TOTAL

Syntax

```
TOTAL ON <key field> TO <filename> [FIELDS <field list>]
[<scope>] [FOR <condition>] [WHILE <condition>]
```

Usage

This command creates a new database containing the key fields and the total for the Numeric fields for each value of the key field. The TOTAL command is different from the SUM command since it groups records in the current database according to a key field, sums the Numeric and Floating fields for the group, and places the key field value and the total of the Numeric fields for the group as a record in the new database. The FIELDS option selects which Numeric and Floating fields the command sums. The scope, FOR, and WHILE options select which records the command uses. The new database has the same field definitions for the key field and the fields the command totals. The database must be indexed or sorted so the records are in the same order as the key field.

Example

```
USE Salary INDEX Salary ORDER Ssn
TOTAL ON Ssn TO Emp_w2 FIELDS Gross_pay, Net_pay, Fica, ;
State_tax
```

The first command opens a database that has the weekly pay records for the salaried employees. This database contains each week's gross pay, net pay, fica, and state tax. To create the W-2 for each employee, the TOTAL command totals the GROSS_PAY, NET_PAY, FICA, and STATE_TAX fields for each social security number. The Emp_w2 database contains the SSN, GROSS_PAY, NET_PAY, FICA, and STATE_TAX fields using the same field definitions the SALARY database uses. In the EMP_W2 database, the database has one record for each employee with the year's total gross pay, net pay, F.I.C.A. withheld, and state tax withheld.

TYPE

Syntax

```
TYPE <filename> [TO PRINTER/TO FILE <filename>] [NUMBER]
```

Usage

This command displays or prints an ASCII text file. Using this command on a non-ASCII text file, such as a word processing file, distorts the file's appearance when dBASE displays or prints the special characters in the non-ASCII file. This command is for displaying and printing programs and output created with other commands. The filename must include the extension. The TO PRINTER and TO FILE options direct the output to the printer or to a file as well as appearing on the screen. The NUMBER option adds line numbers to the beginning of each line, which is especially useful for printing programs.

Example

```
TYPE Employee.prg TO PRINTER NUMBER
```

This command prints EMPLOYEE.PRG and places line numbers at the beginning of each line.

UNLOCK

Syntax

```
UNLOCK [ALL/IN <alias>]
```

Usage

This command releases file and record locks. The ALL option releases all file and record locks in all work areas. The IN option releases all file and record locks in the specified work area. Without either option, this command releases all file and record locks in the current work area. dBASE determines whether this command unlocks a file or a record by which dBASE locked last. Since most dBASE commands that automatically lock records automatically unlock records, this command is primarily for unlocking explicitly locked records. This command has no effect during transaction processing. Just as locking a file or record locks the related files or records, unlocking a file or record unlocks the related files or records.

Example

```
UNLOCK
```

This command unlocks file and record locks in the current work area.

UPDATE

Syntax

```
UPDATE ON <key field> FROM <alias> REPLACE <field name 1>
WITH <expression 1> [,<field name 2> WITH <expression
2>...] [RANDOM]
```

Usage

This command updates data in the current database with data from another database. This requires that the two databases have a common field. The key field is the common field that the two fields share. The FROM option indicates the work area that contains the open database where the replacement values originate. The REPLACE ... WITH option is identical to the REPLACE command. To refer to a field in the noncurrent database precede the field name with the alias, a hyphen, and a greater than sign. While normally both databases must be indexed or sorted in ascending order on the key field for the command to work, the replacement value database can be in a different order if the RANDOM option is used.

Example

```
USE Week_pay INDEX Week_pay ORDER Ssn
SET FILTER TO Week_end={07/14/89}
SELECT 2
USE Employee INDEX Employee ORDER Ssn
UPDATE ON Ssn FROM Week_pay REPLACE Ytd_wages WITH Ytd_wages;
(Week_pay->Reg_hours+Week_pay->Ovt_hrs*1.5)*Hr_pay))
```

For each employee in the EMPLOYEE database, dBASE replaces the YTD_WAGES field with the prior YTD_WAGES plus the current week's wages.

USE

Syntax

```
USE [<database filename>/?] [IN <work area number>] [[INDEX <.ndx
or .mdx file list>] [ORDER [TAG] <.ndx filename> / <.mdx tag>
[OF <.mdx filename>]] [ALIAS <alias>] [EXCLUSIVE] [NOUPDATE]]
```

Usage

This command opens a database, its Memo field file (if it has one), and any named index files. This command can set the index order, the work area, and, in networks, open the file exclusively. The NOUPDATE option makes the file read-only. Without any options, this command closes the open database. dBASE assumes the default file extensions for the database (.DBF), Memo field file (.DBT), and index files (.NDX and .MDX), and the files are in the default drive and directory unless different information is specified. This command moves the record pointer to record 1 or the first record according to the index record order.

Example

```
USE Employee IN 2 INDEX Employee.mdx, City.ndx, Lastname.ndx ORDER
TAG Ssn
```

This command opens EMPLOYEE.DBF, EMPLOYEE.MDX, CITY.NDX, and LASTNAME.NDX in work area 2 and sets the current index order to the SSN tag in the production (EMPLOYEE.MDX) index file.

WAIT

Syntax

```
WAIT [<prompt>] [TO <memvar>]
```

Usage

This command suspends program execution until the user presses a key. If the command provides a prompt, the command displays the prompt instead of displaying Press any key to continue. The TO option stores the character pressed to a memory variable. If the user presses ENTER, dBASE stores ASCII value 0.

Example

```
WAIT "Invalid data. Press a key to continue"
```

This command displays the text between the quotes as a prompt. When the user presses a key, dBASE performs the next command after the WAIT command.

ZAP

Syntax

```
ZAP
```

Usage

This command removes all records from the active database and reindexes the database to reflect the records' removal. The room occupied by the data that dBASE no longer needs is available to the operating system to store new data.

Example

```
ZAP
```

Once this command is performed, the records that were in the database are no longer retrievable.

APPENDIX D

dBASE IV Functions

Function	***Category***
ABS(<expN>)	Math
ACCESS()	Network
ALIAS([expN>])	Math
ASC(<expC>)	Identification
ASIN(<expN>)	Conversion
ATAN(<expN>)	Math
ATN2(expN1>,<expN2>)	Math
AT(<expC>,<expC>/<memofield name>)	Character
BAR()	Identification
BOF([<alias>])	Testing
CALL(<expC>,<expC>/<memvar name>)	Special
CDOW(<expD>)	Date
CEILING(<expN>)	Math
CHANGE()	Network
CHR(<expN>)	Conversion
CMONTH(<expD>)	Date
COL()	Testing
COMPLETED()	Network
COS(<expN>)	Math
CTOD(<expC>)/{expC}	Date
DATE()	Date
DAY(<expD>)	Date
DBF([<alias>])	Identification
DELETED([<alias>])	Testing
DIFFERENCE(<expC>,<expC>)	Testing
DISKSPACE()	Testing

Function	*Category*
DMY(<expD>)	Date
DOW(<expD>)	Date
DTOC(<expD>)	Date
DTOR(<expN>)	Math
DTOS(<expD>)	Date
EOF([<alias>])	Testing
ERROR()	Testing
EXP(<expN>)	Math
FIELD(<expN>[,<alias>])	Identification
FILE(<expC>)	Testing
FIXED(<expN>)	Math
FKLABEL(<expN>)	Identification
FKMAX()	Identification
FLOAT(<expN>)	Math
FLOCK([alias])	Network
FLOOR(<expN>)	Math
FOUND([<alias>])	Testing
FV(<payment>,<rate>,<periods>)	Financial
GETENV(<expC>)	Identification
IIF(<condition>,<exp1>,<exp2>)	Testing
INKEY([n])	Input
INT(<expN>)	Math
ISALPHA(<expC>)	Testing
ISCOLOR()	Testing
ISLOWER(<expC>)	Testing
ISMARKED([<alias>])	Network
ISUPPER(<expC>)	Testing
KEY([<.mdx filename>,]<expN>[,<alias>])	Identification
LASTKEY()	Input
LEFT(<expC>/<memofield name>,<expN>)	Character
LEN(<expC>/<memofield name>)	Testing
LIKE(<pattern>,<expC>)	Testing
LINE NO()	Testing
LKSYS(n)	Network
LOCK([<expC list>,<alais>]/[<alias>])	Network
LOG10(<expN>)	Math
LOG(<expN>)	Math
LOOKUP(<return field>,<look-for exp>, <look-in field>)	Testing
LOWER(<expC>)	Character
LTRIM(<expC>)	Character
LUPDATE([<alias>])	Testing

Function	*Category*
MAX(<expN1>/<expD1>, <expN2>/<expD2>)	Math
MDX(<expN>[,<alias>])	Identification
MDY(<expD>)	Date
MEMLINES(<memo field name>)	Testing
MEMORY([0])	Testing
MENU()	Identification
MESSAGE()	Testing
MIN(<expN1>/<expD1>, <expN2>/<expD2>)	Math
MLINE(<memo field name>,<expN>)	Character
MOD(expN1>,<expN2>)	Math
MONTH(<expD>)	Date
NDX(<expN>[,<alias>])	Identification
NETWORK()	Network
ORDER([<alias>])	Identification
OS()	Identification
PAD()	Identification
PAYMENT(<principal>,<rate>,<periods>)	Financial
PCOL()	Testing
PI()	Math
POPUP()	Identification
PRINTSTATUS()	Testing
PROGRAM()	Identification
PROMPT()	Identification
PROW()	Testing
PV(<payment>,<rate>,<periods>)	Financial
RAND([<expN>])	Math
READKEY()	Input
RECCOUNT([<alias>])	Testing
RECNO([<alias>])	Testing
RECSIZE([<alias>])	Testing
REPLICATE(<expC>,<expN>)	Character
RIGHT(<expC>/<variable>,<expN>)	Character
RLOCK([<expC list>,<alias>]/[<alias>])	Network
ROLLBACK()	Network
ROUND(<expN1>,<expN2>)	Math
ROW()	Testing
RTOD(<expN>)	Math
RTRIM(<expC>)	Character
SEEK(<exp>[,<alias>])	Testing
SELECT()	Identification

Function	*Category*
SET(<expC>)	Testing
SIGN(<expN>)	Math
SIN(<expN>)	Math
SOUNDEX(<expC>)	Character
SPACE(<expN>)	Character
SQRT(<expN>)	Math
STR(<expN> [,<length>][<decimal>])	Conversion
STUFF(<expC1>,<expN1>,<expN2>, <expC2>)	Character
SUBSTR(<expC>/<memo field name>, <starting position> [,<number of characters>])	Character
TAG([<.mdx filename>,]<expN>[,<alias>])	Identification
TAN(<expN>)	Math
TIME()	Date
TRANSFORM(<exp>,<expC>)	Character
TRIM(<expC>)	Character
TYPE(<expC>)	Testing
UPPER(<expC>)	Character
USER()	Network
VAL(<expC>)	Conversion
VARREAD()	Identification
VERSION()	Identification
YEAR(<expD>)	Date

APPENDIX E

SQL Command Reference

Thirty commands make up the dBASE IV/SQL command set. In addition to following the rules shown for the syntax of each command you will want to avoid using dBASE command and function keywords as the names of SQL tables, views, memory variables, columns, synonyms, or indexes. Commands that allow the use of a SELECT statement within the command will display subselect as part of the command syntax.

ALTER TABLE

Syntax

```
ALTER TABLE <table name>
     ADD (<column name> <data type>
     [,<column name> <data type>...]);
```

Usage

You can use this command to add columns to an existing SQL table. Depending on the data type of the column you are adding, you may be able to specify the column name and type or you may have to enter the length and the number of decimal places. You must continue to maintain the maximum table width of 4,000 bytes and 255 columns even after the additions. This command can be used either interactively or embedded as long as you are the creator of the table or have alter privileges for it.

Example

```
ALTER TABLE Inventory
     ADD (Supplier CHAR(20));
```

This entry would add a new column to the Inventory table. The column would allow entries of as many as 20 characters but would be initialized as blanks.

CLOSE

Syntax

```
CLOSE <cursor name>;
```

Usage

In SQL, cursors are used rather than record pointers. They maintain a place within the table but can only be advanced in one direction. The CLOSE command is one of four cursor commands. It closes the cursor and releases the values stored in variables for the entries in the current row of the table. The CLOSE command is only used for open cursors. This command is only valid in embedded SQL mode. It can be used either interactively or embedded.

Example

```
DECLARE Cr_Supp FOR SELECT Supplier, Address, City, State
     Phone FROM Supplies
     WHERE Active;
OPEN Cr_Supp;
..
```

```
..
CLOSE Cr_Supp;
```

The sequence of the three cursor instructions indicates the sequence in which the instructions would be used.

CREATE DATABASE

Syntax

```
CREATE DATABASE [<path>] <database>;
```

Usage

This command creates an SQL database that can hold many tables and files. The execution of this command establishes catalog tables to maintain all the information on dBASE files. This command can only be used interactively.

Example

```
CREATE DATABASE Account;
CREATE DATABASE C:\DBASE\BANTAM\Account;
```

The first command creates a new subdirectory beneath the current directory and the second establishes a directory for the new database with the exact name entered.

CREATE INDEX

Syntax

```
CREATE [UNIQUE]INDEX <index name>
     ON <table name>
     (<column name> [ASC/DESC]
     [,column name> [ASC/DESC]...]);
```

Usage

This command can be used to create up to 47 indexes for each SQL table. This allows you to create an index for all the ways that you want to be able to retrieve the data in the various rows of the table. SQL indexes are maintained in dBASE .MDX files. This command can be used embedded or in interactive mode.

The UNIQUE option causes SQL to maintain entries only for unique entries in the column being used to build the index. SQL tables with UNIQUE indexes are available from within dBASE in read-only mode.

Example

```
CREATE INDEX Ssn ON Employee (Ssn ASC);
```

This creates an index in ascending order on the entries in the Ssn column of the Employee table.

```
CREATE UNIQUE INDEX Cust_no ON Orders (Cust_no ASC);
```

This command only creates index entries for the unique entries in the Cust_no column.

CREATE SYNONYM

Syntax

```
CREATE SYNONYM <synonym name> FOR <table name>;
```

Usage

Synonyms are alternate names that you can create for tables and views. Once assigned you can use these names in SQL commands in place of the actual table or view names. You can use this command in embedded or interactive mode.

Example

```
CREATE SYNONYM Pay FOR Acct_pay
```

Once this SQL command is processed, you can use PAy to indicate the table name with any command. You can use this command interactively or embedded.

CREATE TABLE

Syntax

```
CREATE TABLE <table name>
(<column name> <data type> [,<column name> <data type>..]);
```

Usage

This command is used to create a new table within the SQL database. It allows you to provide the names, data types and sizes of the columns. You can select from the following data types, which are explained in more detail in Chapter 22: SMALLINT, INTEGER, DECIMAL, NUMERIC, FLOAT, CHAR, DATE, and LOGICAL. Note that Memo fields are conspicuously absent.

When you create an SQL table, a DBF file is created with this name. You can use this command embedded or interactively.

Example

```
CREATE TABLE Employee
     (SsnChar       (11),
     F_nameChar     (15),
     L_nameChar     (15),
     SalaryNumeric (8,2),
     Hire_date      Date);
```

In this example an Employee table with five columns would be created.

CREATE VIEW

Syntax

```
CREATE VIEW <View name> [(<column name>, <column name>...)]
      AS <subselect>
      WITH CHECK OPTION;
```

Usage

This command creates a special virtual table in memory from selected rows and columns of the database. Depending on how you define the SELECT statement used as part of the sSyntax, you may be able to update the view. This command can be used interactively or embedded.

Example

```
CREATE VIEW Dallas AS SELECT Ssn, L_name, Salary FROM
      Employee WHERE Location = "Dallas";
```

This command will create a virtual table from entries in the table Employee where the LOcation in the column entry for an employee is Dallas.

DBCHECK

Syntax

```
DBCHECK [<table name>];
```

Usage

You can use DBCHECK to verify that the entries in the SQL catalog tables for a table correspond to the structure of the .DBF and .MDX files. You will want to run this command interactively and DROP the tables for which errors display.

Examples

```
DBCHECK Employee;
```

This causes dBASE to check the SQL catalog table entries for Employee against the structure for the files Employee.dbf and Employee.mdx.

```
DBCHECK;
```

This causes SQL to check the catalog entries for all the tables against their associated .DBF and .MDX files. If there is not a match an error will be returned and you can run DBDEFINE against the DBF file to correct the entries in the SQL catalog tables.

DBDEFINE

Syntax

```
DBDEFINE [<.dbf file>];
```

Usage

This command creates SQL catalog table entries for one or more .DBF and .MDX files. This command can be used in embedded or interactive mode.

Example

```
DBDEFINE Employee;
```

This will cause dBASE to update the SQL catalog table entries for Employee.dbf and Employee.mdx.

```
DBDEFINE;
```

This causes dBASE to update the SQL catalog tables for all .DBF and .MDX files in the current directory.

DECLARE CURSOR

Syntax

```
DECLARE ,cursor name> CURSOR FOR <SELECT statement>
    [FOR UPDATE OF ,column list>/ORDER BY <clause>];
```

Usage

SQL cursors are similar to dBASE record pointers since they allow you to point to a row in a table. You can use the cursor to allow you to process a single row at a time. Although the SELECT statement is specified with the DECLARE command it will not be executed until an OPEN command is processed. FETCH is used to move the pointer forward. The UPDATE option allows you to update the data in table rows. DECLARE CURSOR is never used interactively.

Example

```
DECLARE This_one CURSOR FOR SELECT Ssn, L_name, F_name,
    Salary FROM Employee WHERE Current;
```

This command can be used to work with information in the Employee file.

DELETE

Syntax

```
DELETE FROM <table name> [<alias>] [WHERE <clause>];
```

or

```
DELETE FROM <table name> WHERE CURRENT OF <cursor name>;
```

Usage

The DELETE command allows you to remove rows from a table. The two different forms of the command allow you to specify a WHERE clause to control row removal or to control the removal by the rows a cursor points to. The first form of DELETE can be used embedded or interactively whereas the second command can only be used in embedded mode.

Example

```
DELETE FROM Employee WHERE Term_date < {"01/01/83"};
```

This command will eliminate all table rows with a termination date that is less than January 1, 1983.

```
DELETE FROM Employee WHERE CURRENT OF Pay;
```

This deletes the row currently referenced by the cursor. Naturally the cursor Pay must already be declared and opened.

DROP DATABASE

Syntax

```
DROP DATABASE <database name>;
```

Usage

This command allows you to delete a database. The command deletes all the .DBF and .MDX files in the database directory. It also adjusts entries in the SQL catalog tables. Although the directory is emptied, it is not deleted. This command cannot be embedded.

Example

```
DROP DATABASE Account;
```

This command would delete all the database and index files in the directory Account.

DROP INDEX

Syntax

```
DROP INDEX <index name>;
```

Usage

This command removes an index created with the CREATE INDEX command. It does not delete the .MDX file. This command can be used in interactive or embedded mode.

Example

```
DROP INDEX Ssn;
```

This would remove the index for the social security number.

DROP SYNONYM

Syntax

```
DROP SYNONYM <synonym name>;
```

Usage

This command deletes a synonym you defined for a table or a view. This command can be used in interactive or embedded mode.

Example

```
DROP SYNONYM Pay;
```

This command would eliminate the synonym for the table Acct_pay although it would not affect the table.

DROP TABLE

Syntax

```
DROP TABLE <table name>;
```

Usage

This command deletes a database table. The .DBF file associated with the table is deleted and cannot be restored without reentering all the data. All indexes, synonyms, and views of the dropped table are also eliminated. This command can be used interactively or embedded.

Example

```
DROP TABLE Employee;
```

This command would delete the employee table and all its data. Index files would be deleted and any synonyms created for Employee would be deleted as well.

DROP VIEW

Syntax

```
DROP VIEW <view name>;
```

Usage

This command allows you to delete an SQL view. All synonyms and views based on the deleted view are also eliminated. This command can be used in embedded or interactive mode.

Example

```
DROP VIEW New_emp;
```

This entry would delete the view named New_emp although dBASE is actually only deleting the view definition since view data is stored in a virtual table and does not affect the real table entries.

FETCH

Syntax

FETCH <cursor name> INTO <variable list>;

Usage

This command transfers values from the next table row into memory variables. The cursor must be declared and opened before you can use this command. To return the cursor to the first row in the table, you can use the CLOSE command followed by OPEN. The variable Sqlcode indicates the status of the FETCH operation. Zero indicates a successful fetch and -1 indicates an error condition. A value of 100 indicates that FETCH used the last row in the FETCH statement. Sqlcnt indicates the number of rows in an SQL table. For an empty table, Sqlcnt is 0 and Sqlcode is 100. You cannot use this command interactively.

Example

```
FETCH Pay INTO mssn, ml_name, mf_name, msalary;
```

This command fetches the entries in four column of the next table row and places them in memory variables.

GRANT

Syntax

```
GRANT ALL [PRIVILEGES/<privilege list> ON [TABLE] <table
     list> TO PUBLIC/ <user list>
     [WITH GRANT OPTION];
```

Usage

When Protect features are used after a user is logged in and SQL is activated, their privileges are controlled by GRANT and REVOKE. The privileges that can be assigned with GRANT are ALTER, DELETE, INDEX, INSERT, SELECT, and UPDATE. The TO PUBLIC option can be used to grant the rights listed to everyone. Once PUBLIC privileges are assigned, the WITH GRANT OPTION cannot be used after PUBLIC rights are assigned. You will want to use this command interactively.

Example

```
GRANT ALL ON Employee TO MaryJ;
GRANT SELECT ON Employee TO RobH;
```

The first command grants all privileges to MaryJ. The second command only grants select privileges to RobH.

INSERT

Syntax

```
INSERT INTO <table name> [<column list>] VALUES (<value
     list>);
INSERT INTO <table name> [<column list>] <subselect>;
```

Usage

The INSERT command allows you to add rows to an SQL table. Either form of the INSERT command will work interactively or embedded.

Example

```
INSERT INTO Employee VALUES ("213-89-7654", "Smith", "Mary",
     CTOD("05/17/89", 35000);
```

This command would enter values in a row assuming that the Employee file consisted of entries for the social security number, last name, first name, date of hire, and salary.

LOAD DATA

Syntax

```
LOAD DATA FROM [path] <filename> INTO TABLE <table name>
     [[TYPE] SDF/DIF/WKS/SYLK/FW2/RPD/DBASEII/DELIMITED
     [WITH BLANK/WITH <delimiter>];
```

Usage

The LOAD DATA command imports data into existing SQL tables from non-SQL files. The same formats supported with the dBASE APPEND FROM command are supported. If the file you are importing from is not in the current directory, you can use the path option. The default for DELIMITED is commas. The DELIMITED WITH BLANK option allows you to import data separated by a single space. You can also use DELIMITED WITH and specify your own delimiter. You will want to use the LOAD DATA command interactively.

Example

```
LOAD DATA FROM C:\DBASE\BANTAM\Budget.wks INTO TABLE
     Accts TYPE WKS;
```

This command loads data into the table Accts from the spreadsheet file Budget.wks assuming that the format of the spreadsheet entries and the Accts table match. Each row in the spreadsheet will become a row in the SQL table.

OPEN

Syntax

```
OPEN <cursor name>;
```

Usage

This command opens the cursor that has been previously declared. It executes the SELECT statement associated with the DECLARE statement for the cursor. This command is only used in embedded SQL mode.

Example

```
DECLARE Pay CURSOR FOR SELECT * FROM Employee WHERE
     Salary > 25000;
     .
     .
     OPEN CURSOR Pay;
```

This code declares the cursor Pay and opens it.

REVOKE

Syntax

```
REVOKE ALL [PRIVILEGES]/<privileges list> ON [TABLE] <table
     list> FROM PUBLIC/<user list>
```

Usage

This command revokes privileges granted with the GRANT command. The same privilege list that is acceptable with GRANT can be used with this command. You will want to use this command interactively.

Example

```
REVOKE UPDATE ON Employee FROM RobH;
REVOKE ALL ON Payroll FROM PUBLIC;
```

The first command revokes update privileges from RobH for the Employee table. The second command revokes all PUBLIC privileges for the Payroll table.

ROLLBACK

Syntax

```
ROLLBACK [WORK];
```

Usage

This command restores a table or view to its status prior to beginning execution of the commands between a begin and end transaction. The WORK keyword provides compatibility with IBM's DB2 implementation of SQL.

Example

```
ON ERROR DO Err_rtn
BEGIN TRANSACTION
     ..
     ..;
END TRANSACTION
PROCEDURE Err_rtn
```

```
..
..
ROLLBACK;
```

The ROLLBACK instruction will only undo activities that took place between the BEGIN TRANSACTION and END TRANSACTION statements if the Err_rtn is executed. It is used in embedded mode.

RUNSTATS

Syntax

```
RUNSTATS [ <table name>];
```

Usage

This command updates the statistics for databases in the SQL catalog tables. Using the command without a table name will update statistics for all the tables in the current database.

Example

```
RUNSTATS Employee;
```

This updates statistics for the Employee table in the current database.

SELECT

Syntax

```
SELECT <clause> [INTO <clause>] FROM <clause>
[WHERE <clause>] [GROUP BY <clause>] [HAVING <clause>]
[UNION <subselect>] [ORDER BY <clause>/FOR UPDATE OF
<clause>] {SAVE TO TEMP <clause>];
```

Usage

The SELECT command is one of the most versatile commands in SQL. It selects rows and columns from tables or views to produce a results table matching your specifications. It can be used interactively or embedded within a program.

The INTO option is only used in embedded mode in special cases where a single-row table is desired. If no rows are returned, the memory variables specified as part of the INTO clause are not created. The FROM clause is required and identifies the names of the tables and view that will supply the data. The WHERE clause is optional and will allow you to restrict the rows that are used in the result table. Standard logical operators can be used in addition to the ! which reverses comparison logic. The GROUP BY clause is optional and causes the rows in the result table to be grouped by the values in a particular column. The UNION clause is also optional and is used to combine the results of two or more tables. The ORDER BY clause is optional and controls the order of rows in the results table. The FOR UPDATE OF clause is optional and is used with cursor definitions to specify columns that are updatable. The SAVE TO TEMP option is an extension to SQL that saves the results table as a temporary table during the remainder of your SQL session.

Example

```
SELECT * FROM Employee;
```

This command selects all rows and columns from the Employee table.

```
SELECT Ssn, Last_name, Salary FROM Employee;
```

This command selects three columns from all rows of the Employee table.

```
SELECT Ssn, Last_name, Salary FROM Employee WHERE Salary <
10000;
```

This command selects entries from the same three columns as the last select statement except that only rows with a number less than 10000 in the Salary column are included.

SHOW DATABASE

Syntax

```
SHOW DATABASE
```

Usage

This command lists the name of each database, the date it was created, and its DOS path or directory. On password protected systems the name of the user who created the database is also shown. This command would be used interactively.

Example

```
SHOW DATABASE;
```

This will list all the databases.

START DATABASE

Syntax

```
START DATABASE <database name>;
```

Usage

Unless a default database is specified in the Config.db file with the statement SQLDATABASE =, the START DATABASE command must be used before executing any SQL commands. It can be used in interactive or embedded mode.

Example

```
START DATABASE Accounts;
```

This command opens the database Accounts. It can be used interactively or embedded.

STOP DATABASE

Syntax

```
STOP DATABASE;
```

Usage

This command is used to close a database. You cannot drop an open database so you would use the STOP DATABASE command before trying to delete an open database. It can be used interactively or embedded.

Example

```
START DATABASE Accounts;
..
..
STOP DATABASE;
```

The STOP DATABASE command in this example would close the Accounts database.

UNLOAD DATA

Syntax

```
UNLOAD DATA TO [path] <filename> FROM TABLE <table name>
     [[TYPE] SDF/DIF/WKS/SYLK/FW2/RPD/DBASEII/DELIMITED
     [WITH BLANK/WITH <delimiter>]];
```

Usage

This command exports data from an SQL table to a non-SQL file. You will want to use this command interactively.

Example

```
UNLOAD DATA TO C:\DBASE\BANTAM\Budget FROM TABLE Employee
     FROM TABLE Acct TYPE WKS;
```

This command creates a WKS work sheet with the data from the Employee table. Each worksheet row will contain the entries in one table row.

UPDATE

Syntax

```
UPDATE <table name>/<view name> SET <column name> =
     expression> [,<column name> = <expression>...] [WHERE
     <search condition>];
UPDATE <table name> SET <column name> =
     expression> [,<column name> = <expression>...] WHERE
     CURRENT OF <cursor name>;
```

Usage

This command changes column values for specified table rows or rows in updatable views. The first form of the command can be used in either interactive or embedded mode; the second is only used with a cursor in embedded mode.

Example

```
UPDATE Employee SET Salary = Salary * 1.04 WHERE Last_rev
    > 2;
```

This command will update the salary if the entry in the Last_review for any row is greater than 2.

Index